D1287598

encyclopedia year book

1970

Cover photos NASA

ISBN 0-7172-0801-X
Library of Congress Catalog Card Number: 48-171

Copyright © 1970 by  Grolier INCORPORATED

Copyright © 1970 by Grolier Limited

Editor in Chief	Helen Hynson Merrick
Executive Editor	James E. Churchill, Jr.
Art Director	Frank H. Senyk

Vice-President and Editorial Director Grolier Incorporated	Wallace S. Murray
Editorial Consultant	Lowell A. Martin
Consultant on Canada	J. Cromwell Young

Staff

Production Editor	Helen Riehl Hitchcock
Production Assistant	Harriet L. Spiegel
Style Editors	J. M. A. Raikes, Chief
	Eleanor C. Wood
Researcher	Fern L. Mamberg
Photo Researcher	Anita I. Lindholm
Indexer	Kathleen Leerburger
Executive Assistant	Ellen Wiley Todd
Staff Assistants	Ruth E. Northlane
	Janet H. Ramlow
	Gloria James
	Helen P. Herzberg

Manufacturing

Director	Edward C. McKenna
Assistant Director	Raymond H. Labott

contributors

HELMUT A. ABT is an astronomer at the Kitt Peak National Observatory, Tucson, Ariz.
ASTRONOMY

FRANK BALDWIN is assistant professor at the East Asian Institute, Columbia University. KOREA

CLIVE BARNES, dance and theater critic of *The New York Times,* writes a column for *Holiday* magazine. SEX IN THE PERFORMING ARTS

JACK STRALEY BATTELL was executive editor of *Chess Review* in 1969. GAMES: CHESS

WILLIAM M. BEANEY joined the faculty of the University of Colorado in Denver in 1969 as professor of law. CRIME

JOHN BELINDO served as executive director of the National Congress of American Indians in 1969. INDIANS, AMERICAN

CHARLES W. BELL is a member of the Rome bureau of United Press International.
GREECE; ITALY

ANNA S. BENJAMIN, editor of *Archaeology* magazine, is professor of classics at Douglass College, Rutgers University. ARCHEOLOGY

GEORGE A. W. BOEHM, free-lance science writer, is a member of the National Association of Science Writers. PHYSICAL SCIENCES

BOB BROEG is sports editor of the *St. Louis Post-Dispatch.* SPORTS: HIGHLIGHTS; ICE HOCKEY

STEPHENS BROENING is a correspondent in the Paris bureau of The Associated Press.
EUROPE; FRANCE; NORTH ATLANTIC TREATY ORGANIZATION; GEORGES POMPIDOU

LEON CARNOVSKY is a professor in the Graduate Library School of the University of Chicago.
LIBRARIES

JAMES CHACE became managing editor of *Foreign Affairs* in December 1969.
ALBANIA; BULGARIA; HUNGARY; POLAND; RUMANIA

DWIGHT CHAPIN is a sportswriter for the *Los Angeles Times.* SPORTS: SWIMMING; TRACK

H. PETER CHASE, M.D., a specialist in the field of nutrition, is assistant professor of pediatrics at the University of Colorado. NUTRITION

MARQUIS W. CHILDS has been a leading Washington correspondent for many years. In 1969 he became contributing editor of the *St. Louis Post-Dispatch.* SPIRO T. AGNEW; RICHARD M. NIXON

JAMES E. CHURCHILL, JR., is executive editor of the *Encyclopedia Year Book.*
DIARY OF EVENTS 1969

HAROLD (SPIKE) CLAASSEN retired as assistant general sports editor of The Associated Press in 1969. SPORTS: BOXING; GOLF

BOB COLLINS is sports editor of *The Indianapolis Star.* SPORTS: AUTOMOBILE RACING

DEREK DAVIES is editor of the *Far Eastern Economic Review,* published in Hong Kong.
HONG KONG; MALAYSIA; PHILIPPINE REPUBLIC; SINGAPORE

KEN DAVIS, formerly chief of the Madrid bureau of The Associated Press, was transferred to the news service's London bureau in late 1969.
PRINCE JUAN CARLOS; PORTUGAL; SPAIN

PETER A. DESBARATS, associate editor of the Canadian magazine *Saturday Night,* frequently comments on the Canadian scene for the Canadian Broadcasting Company in Montreal.
CANADA; PIERRE TRUDEAU

JACOB DESCHIN serves as photography editor of *The New York Times:* PHOTOGRAPHY

LAWRENCE DeVINE is drama editor and film critic for the *Detroit Free Press.* MOTION PICTURES

ROBERT W. DIETSCH, business-economics editor of the Scripps-Howard Newspapers, contributes to *The New Republic* and *Saturday Review.*
WELFARE

MARTIN DISKIN is assistant professor of anthropology at the Massachusetts Institute of Technology. ANTHROPOLOGY

RICK DU BROW writes the "Television in Review" column for United Press International.
TELEVISION

JOHN DUFFY is editor of *Shipping Digest.* (On Jan. 5, 1969, James E. Duffy, former marine editor of *The World-Telegram and Sun,* died in New York City. In the 1969 *Encyclopedia Year Book* the editors erroneously reported that John Duffy had died.) SHIPS AND SHIPPING

DEAN EAGLE is sports editor of *The Courier-Journal,* published in Louisville, Ky.
SPORTS: HORSE RACING

WILLIAM J. EATON is a Washington correspondent for the *Chicago Daily News*.
DEFENSE; FOREIGN AID

MOULTON H. FARNHAM, author of *Sailing for Beginners,* is editor of *Boating* magazine.
SPORTS: ROWING; YACHTING

JACK FOISIE lives in Bangkok, Thailand, where he serves as Southeast Asia correspondent for the *Los Angeles Times*.
CAMBODIA; LAOS

RICHARD FREEDMAN, assistant professor of English at Simmons College, Boston, Mass., reviews the world of books for such publications as *Life, The New Republic, The Nation* and *Book World*.
LITERATURE, NORTH AMERICAN

ERIK J. FRIIS is editor of *The American-Scandinavian Review*.
DENMARK; FINLAND; NORWAY; SWEDEN

W. DAVID GARDNER has written articles on medicine for *The Nation* and *The New Republic* as well as major medical journals. In 1969 he became a writer for Fairchild Publications.
MEDICINE AND HEALTH

LILLIAN N. GERHARDT is executive editor of *School Library Journal Book Review* and R. R. Bowker Co. Juvenile Projects.
LITERATURE, JUVENILE

FRANK GIFFORD, former popular football star of the New York Giants, is a sportscaster for CBS-TV.
SPORTS: FOOTBALL

CHARLES H. GOREN is a world-famous bridge expert.
GAMES: BRIDGE

FRED P. GRAHAM is U.S. Supreme Court correspondent of *The New York Times*.
WARREN E. BURGER; LAW

PHILIP GREER has been New York financial correspondent of *The Washington Post* since 1966. He also comments on financial developments for the Westinghouse Broadcasting Company.
ECONOMY

JAMES J. HAGGERTY, editor of *Aerospace Year Book,* has written 11 books on aerospace subjects.
MISSILES AND ROCKETS; SPACE

JOSEPH W. HALL, JR., is a member of the U.S. Senate staff of The Associated Press.
DISTRICT OF COLUMBIA; PEACE CORPS; POSTAL SERVICES; VETERANS

PAUL HANEY was a member of the public-affairs staff of the National Aeronautics and Space Administration from 1958 until early 1969 and served as a public-affairs adviser to the nation's astronauts.
APOLLO 11. . . . MAN'S FIRST STEP ON THE MOON

CLIFFORD M. HARDIN became U.S. secretary of agriculture in 1969.
AGRICULTURE

VERN HAUGLAND is aviation editor of The Associated Press.
AVIATION

FRED M. HECHINGER, education editor of *The New York Times* from 1959, was appointed a member of the editorial board of the *Times* in August 1969.
EDUCATION

WALTER HERBERT, Fellow of the Royal Society of Arts, is a self-employed consultant on Canadian cultural matters.
CANADA: ARTS AND LETTERS

DORIS HERING, associate editor and principal critic of *Dance Magazine,* is president of the National Association for Regional Ballet.
DANCE

RONALD HILTON is a founder and the executive director of the California Institute of International Studies. A professor at Stanford University since 1949, he also founded and edited *Hispanic American Reports 1948–64*.
LATIN AMERICA; ORGANIZATION OF AMERICAN STATES

PAUL HOFMANN is chief of *The New York Times* bureau in Vienna, Austria. He was transferred to Vienna in August 1969 after the Czechoslovak Government ordered the *Times'* bureau in Prague closed.
CZECHOSLOVAKIA

JACK HOPE is senior editor of *Natural History* magazine.
PARKS

ARNOLD L. HORELICK joined the RAND Corporation in 1959 as a senior staff member of the social science department. Previously he was a political-affairs analyst for the Foreign Broadcast Information Service in Washington.
UNION OF SOVIET SOCIALIST REPUBLICS

FREDERIC HUNTER is African correspondent of *The Christian Science Monitor,* stationed in Nairobi, Kenya.
AFRICA, SUB-SAHARA

CHET HUNTLEY, of the famous NBC-TV's *Huntley-Brinkley Report,* is considered the dean of U.S. radio-television news commentators.
A SUMMARY OF THE YEAR

MARY E. JESSUPS is news editor of *Civil Engineering* magazine, published by the American Society of Civil Engineers.
ENGINEERING, CIVIL

CHARLES S. JULES is librarian of Triangle Broadcasting.
RADIO

STEPHEN W. KANN is editor and publisher of *Industrial World* magazine.
INDUSTRY

LESTER D. LANGLEY is associate professor at Central Washington State College.
CARIBBEAN ISLANDS

RUBEN LEVIN is editor and manager of *Labor,* a weekly newspaper published by the Labor Cooperative Educational and Publishing Society. He has been on the staff of 15 daily newspapers. **LABOR**

JOHN H. LICHTBLAU is executive director of the Petroleum Industry Research Foundation, Inc. **FUELS**

DAVID LIDMAN, stamp editor of *The New York Times,* is a former editor of *The American Philatelist.* **HOBBIES: STAMP COLLECTING**

WILLIAM LIVINGSTONE serves as managing editor of *Stereo Review.* **RECORDINGS**

F. ROY LOCKHEIMER has been covering Japan for the American Universities Field Staff since 1966. **JAPAN**

SIGURDUR A. MAGNUSSON edits *Samvinnan,* a bimonthly cultural and political magazine published in Reykjavik, Iceland. **ICELAND**

DAVID M. MASON spent 1969 in South Vietnam as chief correspondent for The Associated Press. **VIETNAM**

JOHN ALLAN MAY, a member of the Economic Research Council of Great Britain, is chief of the London bureau of *The Christian Science Monitor.* **BELGIUM; IRELAND; LUXEMBOURG; NETHERLANDS; UNITED KINGDOM**

HORST MENDERSHAUSEN, author of *Two Postwar Recoveries of the German Economy,* is a senior staff member of the social science department of the RAND Corporation. **GERMANY; GUSTAV HEINEMANN**

ARTHUR MILLER is senior editor of *The Asia Letter,* an authoritative newsletter on Asian affairs published in Hong Kong. **AFGHANISTAN; BURMA; CEYLON; PAKISTAN; YAHYA KHAN**

MILT MILLER is editor of *Soccer News.* **SPORTS: SOCCER**

BRUCE W. MUNN has been chief United Nations correspondent of United Press International since 1949. **DISARMAMENT; UNITED NATIONS**

EDMUND S. MUSKIE has represented the state of Maine in the U.S. Senate since 1959. As chairman of the subcommittee on air and water pollution, the Senator takes a special interest in the quality of man's environment. **HUMAN ECOLOGY**

EDWARD NEILAN, chief of the China and Southeast Asia bureau of Copley News Service, is stationed in Hong Kong. **CHINA; INDONESIA; TAIWAN; THAILAND**

THOMAS D. NICHOLSON became director of the American Museum of Natural History on July 1, 1969. **AMERICAN MUSEUM OF NATURAL HISTORY**

JAMES P. O'DONNELL, a journalist living in Berlin, specializes in the field of ethology. **ZOOLOGY: ETHOLOGY**

JAMES V. O'GARA is editor of *Advertising Age* magazine. **ADVERTISING**

JOHN PERREAULT lectures at the School of Visual Arts in New York City and serves as art critic for *The Village Voice* and as New York art critic for the Paris newspaper *Le Monde.* **PAINTING**

HENRY POPKIN, New York drama critic of *The Times* of London, is professor of English at the State University of New York at Buffalo. **THEATER**

SHIRLEY POVICH is sports editor of *The Washington Post.* **SPORTS: BASEBALL**

JOHN QUIRT is presently a free-lance, economic writer living in Paris. **COST OF LIVING**

ALAN RICH is music critic of *New York* magazine and wrote *Music: Mirror of the Arts,* published in 1969. **MUSIC, CLASSICAL**

JAMES RIDGEWAY, editor of *Hard Times* magazine and a contributing editor of *The New Republic,* wrote *Closed Corporation.* **INSURANCE, AUTOMOBILE**

BENJAMIN RIVLIN is chairman and professor of political science at Brooklyn College of the City University of New York. **AFRICA, NORTH**

JOHN R. ROBERSON is a senior editor of *Holiday* magazine. **TRAVEL**

EDWARD C. ROCHETTE is editor of *The Numismatist.* **HOBBIES: COIN COLLECTING**

RICHARD L. ROE is vice-president and editorial director of the psychology-book division of *Psychology Today* and CRM Books. **PSYCHIATRY AND PSYCHOLOGY**

LOUIS RUKEYSER is economic editor of the American Broadcasting Company. Twice honored by the Overseas Press Club, he has served as chief of the New Delhi, India, bureau of *The Baltimore Sun* and as chief London correspondent of ABC. **CONGLOMERATES . . . . WAVE OF THE FUTURE?**

DENNISON RUSINOW has been reporting for the American University Field Staff from Belgrade since 1963. **YUGOSLAVIA**

EUGENE L. SCOTT is captain of the International Lawn Tennis Club. **SPORTS: TENNIS**

EILEEN SHANAHAN is a financial reporter in the Washington bureau of *The New York Times*.
TAXATION

ROBERT W. SHAW is executive assistant, consultation division, Multiple Access, General Computer Corporation Ltd., Ottawa.
GEOGRAPHICAL DATA BANK, COMPUTERIZED

CURTIS J. SITOMER lives in Los Angeles where he acts as staff correspondent for *The Christian Science Monitor*. In 1969 he collaborated with Lt. Edward R. Murphy, executive officer of the USS *Pueblo*, on a series for the *Monitor*, "Last Man across the Bridge."
INTELLIGENCE, MILITARY

MARC SLONIM contributes the column "European Notebook" to *The New York Times Book Review*. Dr. Slonim is professor emeritus of the Sarah Lawrence College literature faculty.
LITERATURE, INTERNATIONAL

NORA ANN SMYTH is an associate editor of *Lands and Peoples*, a geographical reference set.
AUSTRIA; PUERTO RICO; SOUTH AFRICA; SWITZERLAND

WILLIAM SPENCER was awarded a grant in 1969 to study social change in North Africa. Professor of Middle East history at Florida State University, he wrote *Lands and Peoples of Algeria* (1969).
MIDDLE EAST

HARRY A. STARK is editor of Wards Automotive Reports, published in Detroit.
AUTOMOBILES

FRED B. STAUFFER was transportation editor of the former *New York Herald Tribune*.
RAILROADS

CLAIRE A. STEIN is executive secretary of the National Sculpture Society.
SCULPTURE

ROBERT O. SWAIN is president of the International Road Federation.
HIGHWAYS

WILLIAM H. TAFT is professor of journalism at the University of Missouri.
PUBLISHING

J. F. terHORST, author of a twice-weekly syndicated column for the North American Newspaper Alliance, has been chief of the Washington bureau of *The Detroit News* since 1961.
UNITED STATES

JENNY TESAR is an associate editor of *The Book of Popular Science* and *Encyclopedia Science Supplement*.
OCEANOGRAPHY

JACK C. THOMPSON is professor of meteorology at San Jose (Calif.) State College.
METEOROLOGY

W. H. TIMMONS, member of the Latin American Studies Association, teaches history at the University of Texas at El Paso.
MEXICO

JAMES B. TREFETHEN is director of publications for the Wildlife Management Institute.
CONSERVATION

JACK TWYMAN, former all-star player for the Cincinnati Royals basketball team, acts as commentator on ABC's *NBA Game of the Week*.
SPORTS: BASKETBALL

WILLIAM H. VAN PRECHT is a consultant to the Hobby Industry Association of America.
HOBBIES

WOLF VON ECKARDT, who wrote *A Place to Live—The Crisis of the Cities* (1968), is architecture critic of *The Washington Post*.
ARCHITECTURE; CITIES

C. H. WADDINGTON is professor of genetics at the University of Edinburgh, Scotland, and Visiting Einstein Professor at the State University of New York at Buffalo.
BIOLOGICAL SCIENCES

HILEY H. WARD, first vice-president of the Religious Newswriters Association, is religion editor of the *Detroit Free Press*. He has written seven books, including *Space-Age Sunday* and *God and Marx Today*.
RELIGION

GORDON L. WEIL directs the public-information division of the Twentieth Century Fund. He wrote *A Foreign Policy for Europe*, published in 1969.
TRADE

WAYNE WILCOX, professor and chairman of the Department of Political Science at Columbia University, spent part of 1969 doing research in India and Pakistan.
INDIA

FRANCIS M. WILHOIT is professor of political science at Drake University, Des Moines, Iowa.
NATIONALISM

HARRISON WILLIAMS, JR., junior U.S. senator from New Jersey, is chairman of the Senate Subcommittee on Labor.
MINE SAFETY

JOHN S. WILSON reviews popular music for *The New York Times*.
MUSIC, POPULAR

J. TUZO WILSON, coauthor of *Physics and Geology*, is professor of geophysics at the University of Toronto.
GEOLOGY

R. NORRIS WILSON is executive vice-president of the United States Committee for Refugees.
WORLD REFUGEES

R. M. YOUNGER, former director of the Australian News and Information Bureau in New York City, wrote *Australia and the Australians*.
AUSTRALIA; NEW ZEALAND

ILLUSTRATION

Creative Chartists   Blaise Zito Associates

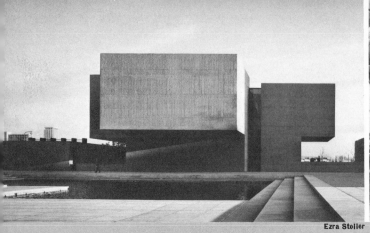

Ezra Stoller   Pictorial Parade

TABLE OF CONTENTS

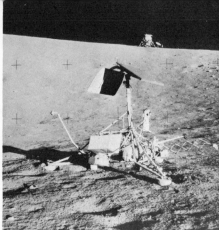

"The New York Times" Wide World NASA

UPI

Caron-Gamma-PIX

Pages 68-496 Alphabetical Section
(partial listing)

Pages 497-512 Index

NBC

a summary of the year

by Chet Huntley

Did the trial balance for the final year of the decade reveal us as living on a somewhat more secure and tranquil planet? Old conflicts endured, new ones threatened; but the year permitted us to magnify a few joys by offering hope.

In Southeast Asia and in the Middle East, wars dragged on toward some indefinite conclusion. In Vietnam, the United States policy of "Vietnamization" produced a 35 per cent drop in the number of American war dead as compared with 1968, but there was no assurance of how far the policy might go and what might be its end result.

In both the Soviet Union and Red China there was too much talk of impending war against the other, and the year ended with the disquieting report that the Chinese were building hundreds of thousands of bomb shelters.

The Brezhnev doctrine of Soviet interference in the affairs of any communist nation that might pursue revisionism too far was vigorously applied in Czechoslovakia. Yet Moscow paid a price for it as the other East European communist nations adopted correct but cool relations with their big neighbor.

The year 1969 brought some swift changes. A new administration slowly settled into the leadership of the United States. The De Gaulle era came to a sudden and dramatic end. Willy Brandt and his Social Democrats came to power in West Germany, and served soft warning that they could no longer defer to France in all matters. Premier Sato won reelection in Japan and turned his nation slightly in the direction of Japanese big-power status in the Pacific. President Marcos was reelected in the Philippines in a process that made a mockery out of democracy and all but bankrupted his nation.

In July, two Americans set foot on the moon...expanding man's credulity.

The United States fought economic inflation with little success. Studies and reports from groups of distinguished Americans admonished their fellows again to remove from themselves the last trace of racism and to undertake at once the long and costly task of remaking the U.S. cities so that they would be livable and satisfying environments. Americans were urged to care. Yet at year's end the major problems of the United States still remained.

Politically the year included an alleged articulate outcry from "the silent majority." It was an outcry from those who appeared to resent what they believed to be the undue attention paid to the young, the poor, the violent, the hungry, the unemployed, the blacks and the educated.

American and Soviet delegations met in Helsinki to explore the possibilities of reaching agreements that might yield security to each yet permit some reduction of the frightful expenditures on super-weapons.

A Soviet proposal for a European security conference was offered. German Chancellor Brandt invited the Polish Government to the conference table and the Poles accepted. The East Germans opened communications with the Bonn Government.

NATO, the Council of Europe, the United Nations and virtually every government of the Western world resolved to begin at once protecting the environment of the planet to guarantee the future of life on earth.

NASA

NASA

diary of events
1969

3 The first session of the 91st Congress of the United States convenes. Sen. Edward M. Kennedy (D-Mass.) is elected Senate majority whip; the House of Representatives votes to seat Adam Clayton Powell, Jr. (D-N.Y.) and to fine him $25,000 for alleged misuse of House funds.

Noon, Jan. 20: Chief Justice Earl Warren (1) administers presidential oath of office to Richard Nixon, as Mrs. Nixon holds the Bible. Outgoing President Lyndon B. Johnson and Vice-President Hubert H. Humphrey (r), the man Nixon defeated for the presidency, look on.

4 U.S. President-elect Richard M. Nixon announces that he will ask Ellsworth Bunker to remain ambassador to South Vietnam "for a period of time."

5 President-elect Nixon nominates Henry Cabot Lodge to replace W. Averell Harriman as chief U.S. negotiator at the Paris peace talks on Vietnam.

Pictorial Parade

JANUARY
headline highlights

S M T W T F S S M T W T F S S M T W T F S
1 2 3 4 5 6 7 8 9 10 11 12 13 14 15 16 17 18
19 20 21 22 23 24 25 26 27 28 29 30 31

7 The French Government confirms its ban on the sale and shipment of all military equipment to Israel.

10 The Swedish Government announces that it will grant full diplomatic recognition to North Vietnam—the first Western European country to do so.

14 Oklahoma Sen. Fred R. Harris is named chairman of the Democratic National Committee.

15 In Lebanon, Rashid Karami forms a Cabinet ending a nine-day government crisis. The Government of Premier Abdullah Yaffi had resigned in the wake of Israel's attack on the Beirut airport on Dec. 28.

16 Spokesmen for the U.S. and North Vietnamese delegates to the Paris peace talks announce agreement on expanded peace talks to end the Vietnam war. In accordance with the agreement, delegates from the United States, South Vietnam, North Vietnam and the National Liberation Front will be seated at a circular table without nameplates, flags or markings. The question of seating had been a major obstacle to expanded talks from Oct. 31, 1968, when U.S. President Lyndon B. Johnson ordered the bombing of North Vietnam stopped.

17 President Johnson signs bill doubling the president's yearly salary, to $200,000.

18 Soviet spacecraft Soyuz 5 (launched on Jan. 15) lands safely in Kazakhstan, following the landing of Soyuz 4 (launched on Jan. 14) there the day before. These initial space flights of 1969 marked the first time that manned spaceships docked in space successfully. Aboard Soyuz 4 was Lt. Col. Vladimir A. Shatalov; and aboard Soyuz 5, Lt. Col. Boris V. Volynov, Aleksei S. Yeliseyev and Lt. Col. Yevgeni V. Khrunov. On Jan. 16, cosmonauts Khrunov and Yeliseyev had joined Shatalov in Soyuz 4.

19 In Czechoslovakia, Jan Palach, 21-year-old student who set himself on fire in protest against the Soviet occupation of Czechoslovakia, dies in a Prague hospital.

20 Richard Milhous Nixon is inaugurated as 37th president of the United States; Spiro Theodore Agnew is sworn in as the nation's 39th vice-president.

23 President Nixon appoints Arthur F. Burns counselor to the president.

24 The Spanish Government enforces a "state of exception" (semimartial law) because of recent student disorders. Five articles of the constitution, including freedom of expression, are suspended, and full censorship of the press is restored.

25 The first plenary session of the Vietnam peace talks is held in Paris.

27 Fourteen men, including nine Jews, are hanged by the Iraqi Government on charges of spying for Israel.

Henry Cabot Lodge, former U.S. ambassador to South Vietnam and West Germany, is Richard Nixon's choice to head the U.S. delegation to the Vietnam peace talks.

UPI

15

1 Peru and the Soviet Union agree to establish diplomatic relations.

4 Liao Ho-shu, China's acting chargé d'affaires to the Netherlands, arrives in Washington, becoming the highest-ranking Communist Chinese official to defect to the United States to date.

5 Italian workers stage a general strike—the third in three months—for higher government pensions.

6 Juan Velasco Alvarado, president of Peru's ruling military junta, announces that the Government will seize all remaining assets of the International Petroleum Company (IPC), a subsidiary of Standard Oil of New Jersey.

10 Mitchell Sharp, Canada's secretary of state for external affairs,

Crude oil, escaping from a leaking undersea well in the Pacific Ocean off California, spreads a noxious scum on Santa Barbara beaches.

UPI

Wide World

FEBRUARY

headline
highlights

S M T W T F S S M T W T F S S M T W T F S
1 2 3 4 5 6 7 8 9 10 11 12 13 14 15
16 17 18 19 20 21 22 23 24 25 26 27 28

reveals that the Canadian Embassy in Stockholm will approach the Communist Chinese Mission there about the possibility of establishing diplomatic relations between Ottawa and Peking.

Thailand's United Thai People's Party of Premier Thanom Kittikachorn wins in popular elections to the House of Representatives.

12 President Nixon nominates James Farmer, former director of the Congress of Racial Equality (CORE), as assistant secretary of health, education, and welfare.

14 Members of the International Longshoremen's Association (ILA) in New York City approve a new 3-year contract ending a 57-day New York City dock strike. (About 43,000 other ILA dock workers remain on strike in 20 ports along the East and Gulf coasts.)

A Peruvian Navy gunboat attacks two American fishing vessels off the coast of Peru.

17 Aquanaut Berry L. Cannon dies while working at a depth of 600 feet on the continental shelf of the Pacific Ocean during the first day of the planned 60-day Sealab 3 project.

18 The Communist Chinese Government cancels meetings with representatives of the U.S. Government, scheduled to open in Warsaw on Feb. 20.

A U.S. military spokesman in Saigon reports that although no major fighting occurred in Vietnam during a 24-hour truce period, observing the lunar New Year (Feb. 16–17), the enemy initiated 196 incidents. Eight Americans, 4 South Vietnamese and 151 enemy soldiers were killed.

Four Arab terrorists attack an Israeli El Al airliner at Zurich, Switzerland, airport, injuring six persons.

24 Israeli planes attack two Arab commando bases in Syria which are reported to be bases for Al Fatah, the largest Arab commando organization.

25 New Zealand Prime Minister Keith Holyoake declares that his country and Australia will maintain military forces in Malaysia and Singapore after Great Britain withdraws its forces from the area in 1971.

26 Rep. Rogers C. B. Morton (Md.) is named to succeed Raymond C. Bliss as chairman of the Republican National Committee.

During the fourth day of mounting enemy attacks in Vietnam, heavy fighting breaks out at two major military installations within 20 miles of Saigon.

27 Great Britain increases its bank rate from 7 to 8 per cent.

28 U.S. Secretary of the Interior Walter J. Hickel urges Congress to pass legislation protecting offshore waters from pollution. (Late in January, a Union Oil Company well blew out off the coast of Santa Barbara, Calif., resulting in widespread pollution and death of waterfowl.)

On Feb. 12 the New York City dock strike enters its 55th day.

UPI

ISRAEL AND PAKISTAN GET NEW GOVERNMENTS ●U.S. SENATE RATIFIES NONPROLIFERATION TREATY ●GENERAL EISENHOWER DIES AT 78

1 East Berlin border guards close main *Autobahn* access route to West Berlin for about two hours.

In Criminal District Court in New Orleans, La., Clay L. Shaw is acquitted of charges of conspiring to assassinate President John F. Kennedy.

2 President Nixon returns to Washington after eight-day European tour.

The Soviet Government announces that a Chinese military unit crossed the Soviet-Chinese border and fired on Soviet border guards. Although there were casualties, the specific number was not revealed.

The French-British supersonic transport *Concorde* makes its initial test flight successfully.

5 Gustav Heinemann, West Germany's minister of justice, is elected president of the Federal Republic.

6 U.S. military-command spokesman in Saigon reports that 453 U.S. soldiers were killed in Vietnam during the week ending Mar. 1.

Washington National Cathedral, Mar. 31: 191 chiefs of state and heads of government from 85 nations join the Eisenhower and Nixon families at funeral services for Gen. Dwight D. Eisenhower. The former President died on Mar. 28 at Walter Reed Hospital after a long illness.

UPI

MARCH

headline
highlights

S M T W T F S S M T W T F S S M T W T F S
1 2 3 4 5 6 7 8 9 10 11 12 13 14 15
16 17 18 19 20 21 22 23 24 25 26 27 28 29 30 31

The total was the highest weekly U.S. casualty figure since May 1968.

9 Lt. Gen. Abdel Moneim Riad, chief of staff of Egypt's armed forces, is killed during a heavy Israeli-Egyptian artillery exchange across the Suez Canal.

10 In Memphis, Tenn., James Earl Ray pleads guilty (to avoid a probable death sentence) to murdering Dr. Martin Luther King, Jr., on Apr. 4, 1968, and is sentenced by Judge W. Preston Battle to 99 years in the state prison in Nashville.

11 French workers hold 24-hour general strike.

12 President Nixon nominates Gen. Andrew J. Goodpaster as Supreme Allied Commander in Europe.

13 Apollo 9 lands safely in the Atlantic Ocean, about 360 miles northwest of San Juan, Puerto Rico. During the 10-day Apollo 9 flight, Air Force Col. James A. McDivitt and civilian Russell L. Schweikart flew the lunar module (LM), the vehicle designed to land man on the moon, independently for 6½ hours.

By a vote of 83–15, the U.S. Senate ratifies the treaty to prevent the spread of nuclear weapons.

At 70, Mrs. Golda Meir becomes the fourth prime minister of Israel.

"Israel Sun," PIX

14 President Nixon presents to the nation and Congress his plan for a Sentinel antiballistic-missile system.

15 Uruguay President Jorge Pacheco Areco ends nine-month period of censorship and civil-rights restrictions.

17 Mrs. Golda Meir is sworn in as Israel's fourth prime minister; she succeeds Levi Eshkol, who died on Feb. 26.

21 The Spanish Government announces that the state of exception (semimartial law) in effect in Spain since Jan. 24 will cease on Mar. 25.

25 Pakistan President Mohammad Ayub Khan resigns; a state of martial law is declared, and Gen. A. M. Yahya Khan, commander in chief of the Army, is named chief martial-law administrator.

26 Prime Minister Pierre Elliott Trudeau returns to Ottawa after making the first official visit of any head of government to the United States as a guest of the Nixon administration. The Prime Minister tells the House of Commons that he and President Nixon "fortified the channels of communications so necessary to the effective conduct" of U.S.-Canadian relations.

28 Pope Paul VI names 33 new members to the college of cardinals.

31 Great Britain and Anguilla announce the signing of an agreement by which the administration of the Caribbean island will be conducted by representatives of Queen Elizabeth "in full consultation and cooperation with representatives of the people of Anguilla." (On Mar. 19, armed British paratroopers invaded the island to avert Anguilla's attempt to establish itself as an independent republic.)

DE GAULLE RESIGNS ● NORTH KOREA DOWNS U. S. JET ● HUSAK SUCCEEDS DUBCEK ● STUDENTS DEMONSTRATE AT CORNELL AND AT HARVARD

In final television appearance prior to national referendum (Apr. 25), Charles de Gaulle asks the French electorate for a "show of confidence" that will enable him to serve out his presidential term and complete his "30-year chapter" in French history.

1 The United Nations Security Council condemns Israel for the Mar. 26 air attack on Jordan. The attack, on the town of Salt, killed 18 civilians.

President Nixon confers separately with 12 world leaders who are in Washington for the funeral of Gen. Dwight D. Eisenhower. (The former President died on Mar. 28 at Walter Reed Hospital.)

2 Admitting that he had accepted private funds for political purposes, Lt. Gen. Joseph A. Ankrah resigns as Ghana's head of state. Brig. Akwasi A. Afrifa succeeds Ankrah.

3 Illinois Gov. Richard B. Ogilvie mobilizes Illinois National Guardsmen as street violence erupts in Negro districts of Chicago on the eve of the first anniversary of the murder of Dr. King.

The U.S. Federal Reserve Board raises its discount rate from 5½ to 6 per cent as "a further move against inflation."

Paul Pougnet from Rapho Guillumette

APRIL

headline highlights

S M T W T F S S M T W T F S S M T W T F S
1 2 3 4 5 6 7 8 9 10 11 12 13 14 15 16 17 18 19
20 21 22 23 24 25 26 27 28 29 30

Prime Minister Trudeau declares that the Canadian Government will "take early steps to bring about" a planned reduction in the number of Canadian troops assigned to the North Atlantic Treaty Organization.

9 About three hundred students seize main administration building of Harvard University in Cambridge, Mass.

14 The ninth congress of the Chinese Communist Party unanimously adopts a new charter naming Defense Minister Lin Piao as the eventual successor to Chairman Mao Tse-tung.

17 In Los Angeles, Calif., a jury of seven men and five women convicts Sirhan Bishara Sirhan of murder in the first degree for the slaying of Sen. Robert F. Kennedy on June 5, 1968.

The Czechoslovak Central Committee names Gustav Husak to replace Alexander Dubcek as first secretary of the Czechoslovak Communist Party. As a further step to curb liberalization, the ruling Presidium is reduced from 21 to 11 members.

Gustav Husak, 56.

Pictorial Parade

19 Mrs. Virginia Knauer is sworn in as President Nixon's adviser for consumer affairs.

Roman Catholic civil-rights demonstrators clash with the ruling Protestant majority in Londonderry, Northern Ireland.

20 Armed Negro students at Cornell University, Ithaca, N.Y., end occupation of student-union building.

21 President Nixon nominates Rep. Donald Rumsfeld (R-Ill.) as director of the Office of Economic Opportunity.

A U.S. Navy task force of 23 warships starts through the Sea of Japan. On Apr. 14, North Korean MiG's had shot down an unarmed U.S. Navy reconnaissance plane over the sea; the plane's crew of 31 men were presumed dead.

22 In a report on the Middle East, UN Secretary-General U Thant avers that there is "a virtual state of active war" between Israel and the United Arab Republic.

24 Lebanon Premier Rashid Karami resigns in the midst of criticism of his Government's policy of restricting guerrillas from using Lebanon as a base to launch attacks on Israel.

27 Following the death of Bolivia's President René Barrientos Ortuño in a helicopter crash, Vice-President Luis Adolfo Siles Salinas is sworn in as president.

28 After a French Government bill calling for constitutional reform is defeated by the electorate in a referendum, Charles de Gaulle resigns as president; Alain Poher, the Senate president, is installed as interim president until elections can be scheduled "in a few weeks."

29 Georges Pompidou announces his candidacy for the French presidency and immediately receives the endorsement of the Gaullist party.

1 Maj. James D. Chichester-Clark is chosen as Northern Ireland's fifth prime minister.

Yemen President Abdul Rahman al-Iryani reports that the six-year civil war between Royalists and Republicans has ended. (Fighting ceased in December 1968.)

6 U.S. Navy Secretary John H. Chafee declares that "no disciplinary action" will be taken against any member of the crew of the *Pueblo*, the U.S. intelligence ship captured by North Korea in January 1968.

11 Flying to Mexico City, Gov. Nelson A. Rockefeller (R-N.Y.) starts out on the first of four fact-finding missions to Latin America requested by President Nixon.

13 Charles Evers, Negro civil-rights leader, is nominated as the

Newly nominated mayor of Fayette, Miss., Negro leader Charles Evers.

MAY

**headline
highlights**

S M T W T F S S M T W T F S S M T W T F S
1 2 3 4 5 6 7 8 9 10 11 12 13 14 15 16 17
18 19 20 21 22 23 24 25 26 27 28 29 30 31

Democratic candidate for mayor of Fayette, Miss. (The nomination is tantamount to election, since Evers will be unopposed in the June election.)

British Prime Minister Wilson dismisses James Callaghan from the position of Home Secretary in the inner Cabinet.

14 In his first full-length report to the nation on the Vietnam war, President Nixon proposes a phased, mutual withdrawal of U.S. and North Vietnamese troops from South Vietnam over a 12-month period.

Prime Minister Abdul Rahman suspends Malaysia's constitution and assumes complete governmental power as racial strife between the Chinese and Malay ethnic communities in the capital city, Kuala Lumpur, continues.

Canada's House of Commons approves a new criminal-code bill.

Abe Fortas resigns as an associate justice of the U.S. Supreme Court. In announcing his resignation, Fortas admits that he had arranged in 1965 to receive a fee of $20,000 a year for "continuing services" to the Louis E. Wolfson Foundation. (Wolfson is serving a one-year prison sentence for selling unregistered securities.)

17 Venera 6, an unmanned Soviet spacecraft, floats through the atmosphere of the planet Venus and transmits information back to earth for 51 minutes. (On May 16, Venera 5 had penetrated the Venusian atmosphere and transmitted information back to earth for 53 minutes.)

21 Warren Earl Burger, 61-year-old judge of the U.S. Court of Appeals for the District of Columbia, is nominated by President Nixon to succeed Earl Warren as chief justice of the Supreme Court.

23 Viktor Kopytin—a correspondent for the Soviet Union's official press agency, Tass—is expelled from the United States. Earlier, Anatole Shub, Moscow correspondent for *The Washington Post*, was ordered to leave the Soviet Union.

25 A group of military officers overthrows Sudan's coalition Government; former Chief Justice Abubakr Awadallah is named premier and foreign minister.

26 Following the successful eight-day, moon-orbiting flight of Apollo 10, the National Aeronautics and Space Administration (NASA) gives go-ahead for a man landing on the moon, scheduled for July.

27 Samuel W. Yorty (D) is reelected mayor of Los Angeles.

30 Striking workers in Argentina shut down most heavy industry; transportation stops in six provincial cities. (As the date of the strike neared, a limited state of siege throughout the nation had been ordered.)

At least four persons are killed and 150 persons are injured as striking refinery workers riot on the Caribbean island of Curaçao.

Northern Ireland's new Prime Minister, James D. Chichester-Clark.

"London Daily Express," Pictorial Parade

EL SALVADOR AND HONDURAS TAKE UP ARMS● POMPIDOU IS ELECTED FRENCH PRESIDENT●U. S. BEGINS WITHDRAWING VIETNAM TROOPS

2 During maneuvers in the South China Sea, the *Melbourne,* an Australian aircraft carrier, and the *Frank E. Evans,* a U.S. Navy destroyer, collide, splitting the *Evans* in two. Seventy-three members of the crew of the *Evans* are reported as unaccounted for.

4 The state of siege that was imposed throughout Argentina on May 28 is lifted by President Ongania.

8 After meeting with South Vietnam President Nguyen Van Thieu on Midway Island, President Nixon announces that 25,000 American troops will be withdrawn from South Vietnam before the end of August.

10 Pope Paul VI becomes the first Roman Catholic pontiff since the sixteenth century to visit Protestant stronghold Geneva, Switzerland.

15 Former Premier Georges Pompidou is elected president of the French Republic.

Moscow, June 17: Delegates from 75 countries attend concluding session of the 13-day international Communist Party conference.

Tass from Sovfoto

JUNE

headline highlights

S M T W T F S S M T W T F S S M T W T F S
1 2 3 4 5 6 7 8 9 10 11 12 13 14 15 16 17 18 19 20 21
22 23 24 25 26 27 28 29 30

16 In a 7-1 decision, the U.S. Supreme Court rules that the House of Representatives violated the Federal Constitution when it barred Rep. Adam Clayton Powell, Jr. (D-N.Y.) from taking his seat in the 90th Congress.

17 A 13-day conference of Communist Party leaders from 75 countries ends in Moscow. The conference failed to agree on a common policy toward Communist China, which was not represented at the meetings.

20 President Pompidou appoints National Assembly President Jacques Chaban-Delmas premier of France.

On the eve of Governor Rockefeller's scheduled visit to Uruguay, terrorists in Montevideo set fire to a General Motors building, resulting in damage estimated at $1,000,000.

Spain and the United States sign an agreement permitting U.S. military bases to remain on Spanish soil until Sept. 26, 1970.

22 Southern Yemen President Qahtan al-Shaabi resigns; a five-man presidential council assumes control of the Government.

24 Faced with renewed strikes and general unrest by workers and students, Uruguay President Jorge Pacheco Areco orders a limited state of siege.

25 Taiwan President Chiang Kai-shek names Chiang Ching-kuo, the President's elder son, deputy premier.

26 Chile President Eduardo Frei Montalva announces that the Government and the Anaconda Company have agreed on a plan for the "negotiated and progressive" nationalization of the company's major copper mines in Chile.

27 El Salvador and Honduras formally break diplomatic relations. (Earlier, riots had broken out after the El Salvador and Honduras national soccer teams competed in regional play-offs for the World Soccer Cup. Honduras had defeated El Salvador in Honduras, and El Salvador was victorious over Honduras in El Salvador.)

President Nixon and Prime Minister Trudeau participate in ceremonies commemorating the tenth anniversary of the opening of the St. Lawrence Seaway.

In Charleston, S.C., the three-month-old strike by Negro hospital workers at the Medical College Hospital ends; the strike by workers at the Charleston County Hospital remains unsettled. (On June 21, the Rev. Ralph D. Abernathy, president of the Southern Christian Leadership Conference, was arrested on charges of inciting to riot after he had led demonstrations in support of the strikes.)

The Spanish Government suspends ferry service between the Spanish mainland and Gibraltar.

28 Dr. Roger O. Egeberg of California is selected by President Nixon as assistant secretary for health and scientific affairs in the Department of Health, Education, and Welfare.

As June ends, Dr. Roger O. Egeberg, dean of the University of Southern California's School of Medicine, is named the top health officer in the U. S. Government.

UPI

MAN WALKS ON THE MOON ● SPAIN'S FRANCO DESIGNATES SUCCESSOR ● TED KENNEDY ADMITS GUILT IN LEAVING SCENE OF AUTO ACCIDENT

1 In a sixty-minute bilingual ceremony at Caernarvon Castle, Prince Charles is formally invested as Prince of Wales and Earl of Chester by his mother, Queen Elizabeth II.

Israel moves its national police headquarters from Tel Aviv to East Jerusalem, the former Jordanian section of the city.

5 Tom Mboya, Kenya's minister of economic planning and development, is assassinated in Nairobi.

7 Canada's House of Commons passes legislation by which French, side by side with English, will become an official language of Canada.

11 A United States Court of Appeals overrules the convictions of Dr. Benjamin Spock and three other men who were convicted in 1968 of conspiring to counsel young men to avoid the draft.

Apollo 11 astronaut Col. Edwin E. Aldrin, Jr., descends the steps of the lunar module—the second man to walk on the moon.

NASA

JULY

**headline
highlights**

S M T W T F S S M T W T F S S M T W T F S
1 2 3 4 5 6 7 8 9 10 11 12 13 14 15 16 17 18 19
20 21 22 23 24 25 26 27 28 29 30 31

13 Luna 15, an unmanned Soviet spacecraft, is "launched to the moon from the orbit of an artificial earth satellite."

Portugal Premier Marcelo Caetano concludes five-day state visit to Brazil; the two nations agree to increase their commercial and cultural exchanges.

18 El Salvador and Honduras accept a four-point peace program, drafted by the Organization of American States, to end their five-day undeclared war.

The 113-day strike by Negro workers at the Charleston (S.C.) County Hospital ends.

19 India's Government nationalizes 14 of the country's largest banks.

20 Neil A. Armstrong, 38-year-old civilian commander of the Apollo 11, and Col. Edwin E. Aldrin, Jr., walk on the moon.

Israeli and Egyptian forces engage in a four-hour-long, ground-and-air battle along the Suez Canal. For the first time since the June 1967 war, Israel reports air losses (Five Egyptian jets are shot down.)

21 The U.S. State Department announces that from July 23, U.S. citizens traveling abroad will be permitted to bring back to the United States $100 worth of Chinese manufactured goods.

For the first time since 1950, scholars, students, scientists, physicians and newsmen will be allowed to travel to China.

22 Generalissimo Francisco Franco designates Prince Juan Carlos of Bourbon as the future king of Spain.

24 Completing the Apollo 11 flight, astronauts Neil A. Armstrong, Col. Edwin E. Aldrin, Jr., and Lt. Col. Michael Collins are welcomed aboard the carrier USS *Hornet* by President Nixon. The splashdown, at 12:50 P.M. Eastern daylight time, was about 950 miles southwest of Hawaii.

25 Sen. Edward M. Kennedy (D-Mass.) pleads guilty to charges of leaving the scene of an accident and receives a suspended sentence of two months in jail. Later, on nationwide television, the Senator gives his account of the July 19 auto accident in which Mary Jo Kopechne, 28-year-old former secretary to the late Sen. Robert F. Kennedy, lost her life.

28 The U.S. Treasury reports a budget surplus of $3,100,000,000 for the 1969 fiscal year.

West Germany and Yugoslavia sign two cultural-exchange agreements.

29 In Alabama, four Negroes are elected to the five-man Greene County Commission.

30 President Nixon visits South Vietnam for 5½ hours.

Anatoly V. Kuznetsov, 39-year-old Russian writer, defects to the West.

Edward M. Kennedy returns on July 31 to his duties as Massachusetts' senior senator, and Democratic majority whip, after tragic auto accident near Edgartown, Mass.

UPI

2 In Kampala, Uganda, for three days, Pope Paul VI meets with representatives of the Nigerian Federal Government and of Biafra in an attempt to find a solution to their two-year-old war.

President Nixon arrives in Bucharest, Rumania, the first U.S. president in 24 years to visit a communist nation.

3 President Nixon confers with Prime Minister Wilson near London, and then returns to Washington concluding world tour.

4 Hanoi radio announces the release of three U.S. servicemen who had been held captive by North Vietnam.

The U.S. House of Representatives passes a bill extending the 10 per cent income surtax for six months (through Dec. 31, 1969).

6 In Saigon, a U.S. Army release states that "eight former members of the U.S. Army 5th Special Forces Group (Airborne) are being held pending investigation of charges growing out of the fatal shooting of a Vietnamese national."

PIX

Party chief Nicolae Ceausescu (r) and some Bucharest citizens clad in regional costumes greet President Nixon as he arrives in Rumania.

Premier Mariano Rumor and a minority cabinet of Christian Democrats are sworn in by Italy's President Giuseppe Saragat. (Rumor's Center-Left coalition cabinet had resigned on July 5.)

8 The French Government devalues the franc by 11.1 per cent. In a nationwide television speech, President Nixon proposes a new welfare system, calling for a minimum standard of Federal aid for every needy family with children.

Concluding two days of talks at the White House, President Nixon and West German Chancellor Kiesinger agree to establish a communication "hot line" between Washington and Bonn.

12 Jordan's King Hussein names former Premier Bahjat al-Talhouni to head a new cabinet.

16 British troops restore order in Belfast, Northern Ireland, after four days of clashes between Roman Catholics and Protestants. During the strife, 8 persons were killed, 532 civilians and 226 policemen were wounded.

19 The British Government assumes full responsibility for security in Northern Ireland.

20 Following Aug. 16 elections, V. V. Giri, supported by Prime Minister Indira Gandhi, is declared president of India.

21 On the first anniversary of the Soviet occupation of Czechoslovakia, anti-Soviet demonstrators clash with police and soldiers; the Czechoslovak Army orders reinforcements into the center of Prague.

U.S. Defense Secretary Melvin Laird announces that the strength of U.S. armed forces will be cut by 100,000 men.

22 Israeli police arrest an Australian Christian and charge him with setting the fire (Aug. 21) that severely damaged the Mosque of Al Aksa, a sacred Muslim shrine, in the Old City of Jerusalem.

23 President Thieu selects Gen. Tran Thien Khiem, deputy premier and interior minister, to succeed Tran Van Huong as premier of South Vietnam.

25 In Baghdad, Iraq, 15 Iraqis, including 2 Jews, are executed on charges of spying for Israel and the United States.

26 The UN Security Council unanimously condemns Israel for a "premeditated air attack" on Lebanese villages on Aug. 11.

29 A North Korean spokesman declares that three men shot down in a U.S. OH-23 helicopter over North Korea on Aug. 17 are alive.

Over southern Italy, two young Arabs hijack a Trans World Airlines jet; the plane, with 113 persons aboard, is taken to Damascus, Syria.

31 After Brazil's President Artur da Costa e Silva suffers a stroke, the ministers of the Army, Navy and Air Force assume control of the Government.

President Milton Obote (seated) and other members of the Government listen as Pope Paul VI addresses the Uganda Parliament.

Gamma—PIX

GERMAN ELECTIONS RESULT IN GOVERNMENT CRISIS ● HO CHI MINH DIES ● U. S. ENVOY TO BRAZIL IS RELEASED AFTER BEING KIDNAPED

1 Following a coup, ousting King Idris I, a revolutionary council takes control of the Government of Libya.

In Cairo, U.A.R. President Gamal Abdel Nasser, King Hussein of Jordan, and Syria President Nureddin al-Attassi meet to coordinate Arab activities against Israel.

2 A dusk-to-dawn curfew is imposed as racial violence continues in Hartford, Conn., for a second night.

4 In Vietnam, the Vietcong declares a three-day cease-fire in honor of North Vietnam's President Ho Chi Minh, who died of a heart attack on Sept. 3.

7 C. Burke Elbrick, U.S. ambassador to Brazil, is released after being kidnaped and held by terrorists for three days. To obtain the

Peking Airport, Sept. 11: Chinese Premier Chou En-lai and Soviet Premier Kosygin discuss the Sino-Soviet border dispute.

Pictorial Parade

SEPTEMBER
headline
highlights

S M T W T F S S M T W T F S S M T W T F S
1 2 3 4 5 6 7 8 9 10 11 12 13 14 15 16 17 18 19 20
21 22 23 24 25 26 27 28 29 30

Ambassador's release, the Brazilian Government freed 15 political prisoners.

10 A forty-kiloton nuclear device is exploded underground on the western side of the Rocky Mountains in Colorado.

11 En route home from Ho Chi Minh's funeral in Hanoi, Soviet Premier Kosygin stops off in Peking for talks with Premier Chou En-lai. According to Tass, the Soviet news agency, the two leaders "frankly made known their positions and had a conversation useful for both sides." It was the first top-level Sino-Soviet meeting since February 1965.

14 For the fourth time in five days, Israeli jets strike at Egyptian positions along the Gulf of Suez.

16 The White House announces that an additional 35,000 troops will be withdrawn from Vietnam by Dec. 15.

At the opening session of the 24th General Assembly of the United Nations, Miss Angie Brooks of Liberia is elected Assembly president.

19 President Nixon announces that draft calls for the remaining months of 1969 will be reduced by 50,000.

22 U.S. Secretary of State William P. Rogers and Soviet Foreign Minister Andrei A. Gromyko discuss the Middle East and other international issues for 2½ hours.

23 Although Ton Duc Thang is selected by the National Assembly as North Vietnam's new president, the 81-year-old former Vice-President is not named to the influential position of head of the Communist Party.

24 Sen. Hugh Scott (Penn.) is elected to succeed the late Sen. Everett McKinley Dirksen as Senate minority leader. Sen. Robert P. Griffin (Mich.) is chosen as new Republican whip.

26 In Bolivia, a military junta overthrows President Luis Adolfo Siles Salinas "to avoid the danger of anarchy, capitulation and disorder." Gen. Alfredo Ovando Candia, commander of the armed forces, assumes the presidency.

28 Alexander Dubcek, former first secretary of the Czechoslovak Communist Party, is expelled from the ruling Presidium; 29 liberals are removed from the party's Central Committee.

Following renewed violence in Northern Ireland, 600 additional British troops are sent to Ulster.

The Christian Democratic Union of West German Chancellor Kurt Georg Kiesinger fails to win a majority in national elections.

29 The U.S. Army drops charges against six Special Forces (Green Berets) soldiers who were arrested in July in connection with the alleged murder of a Vietnamese agent. "In the interest of national security," the Central Intelligence Agency refused to provide witnesses in the case.

Angie Brooks, 41-year-old assistant secretary of state of Liberia, is second woman to become UN General Assembly president.

UPI

3 The Government of Greece modifies its strict martial law regarding press censorship, arbitrary arrest, and trial by military court.

4 Communist China confirms a U.S. Atomic Energy Commission report that it made its first underground nuclear test (Sept. 23) and exploded another hydrogen bomb (Sept. 29).

6 The U.S. Bureau of Labor Statistics reports that for the first time since October 1967, the U.S. unemployment rate rose to 4 per cent (in September).

7 Peking announces that China and the U.S.S.R. will open negotiations on their border dispute.

For the first time as West German chancellor, Willy Brandt enters the Bundestag. Two of Brandt's predecessors, Ludwig Erhard and Kurt Georg Kiesinger, observe occasion from front-row center.

Bureau, Gamma—PIX

32

The armed forces name Gen. Emilio Garrastazu Medici as Brazil's new president.

In Montreal, Canada, policemen and firemen stage a one-day strike for higher wages.

10 President Nixon announces that Lt. Gen. Lewis B. Hershey will be relieved as director of the Selective Service System on Feb. 16, 1970. The 76-year-old General, who will become a presidential adviser on manpower mobilization, held the post for 28 years.

13 The Soviet Union launches its third manned Soyuz spacecraft in as many days.

14 Sweden's Minister of Education Olof Palme, who was elected on Oct. 1 to succeed retiring Tage Erlander as leader of the Social Democratic Party, is sworn in as premier.

15 In protest against the Vietnam war, a moratorium is observed by hundreds of thousands of people throughout the United States.

Somalia President Abdirashid Ali Shermarke is assassinated.

Prime Minister Trudeau announces that Canada and the Vatican have agreed to establish diplomatic relations. Dr. John E. Robbins, former president of Brandon University, Manitoba, is appointed Canada's first ambassador.

17 Bolivia's military Government seizes and nationalizes the Bolivia Gulf Company, a subsidiary of the Gulf Oil Corporation.

Dr. Arthur F. Burns is named by President Nixon to succeed William McChesney Martin as chairman of the Federal Reserve Board.

20 The 1969 Nobel Peace Prize is awarded to the International Labor Organization.

21 Social Democratic Party leader Willy Brandt is sworn in as West Germany's fourth chancellor.

24 The West German mark is revalued upward, to 27.3224 U.S. cents.

25 The White House announces that preliminary strategic-arms-limitation talks between the United States and the Soviet Union will begin in Helsinki, Finland, on Nov. 17.

Three hundred Arab militants invade Lebanon from Syria, as clashes between Lebanese Government forces and Al Fatah and other guerrillas continue for the second day. (The conflict concerns Lebanon's policy of refusing to allow anti-Israeli commando bases to be set up near the Israeli border.)

26 In Portugal's first parliamentary elections to be significantly contested in 43 years, the opposition fails to win a single seat to the National Assembly.

28 In national elections in Israel, Premier Golda Meir's Labor Party is victorious.

29 The U.S. Supreme Court unanimously rules that all school districts must end segregation "at once."

Gen. Emilio G. Medici, 63-year-old commander of Brazil's Third Army and former chief of the National Intelligence Service, is chosen by the nation's armed forces to become president of Brazil.

Pictorial Parade

1 Lance Cpl. Raffaele Minichiello, a 20-year-old U.S. marine, is arrested in Rome, Italy, after hijacking a Trans World Airlines jet from Fresno, Calif., to Rome.

The National Commission on the Causes and Prevention of Violence issues a report recommending that Federal, state and local budgets for law enforcement be doubled.

2 The Lebanese Government and Palestinian guerrilla leaders agree to a cease-fire effective at midnight.

3 Although refusing to set a deadline or a definite pace, President Nixon, in a nationally televised address, pledges to bring home all U.S. combat ground forces in Vietnam in an orderly manner.

4 Rep. William T. Cahill (R) and Linwood Holton (R) are elected governors of New Jersey and Virginia respectively. Running on the Liberal Party ticket and as an independent, John V. Lindsay is reelected mayor of New York City. Carl B. Stokes, a Negro Democrat, is reelected mayor of Cleveland, Ohio.

11 By a vote of 56 to 48, with 21 abstentions, the UN General Assembly refuses to admit Communist China as a member.

The owners of the *Torrey Canyon*, the oil tanker that went aground off Cornwall, England, in the spring of 1967, agree to pay $7,200,-

Washington, D.C., Nov. 15: An estimated 300,000 persons parade down Pennsylvania Avenue demanding U.S. withdrawal from Vietnam.

Paul Conklin, PIX

000 to the governments of Great Britain and France for damages.

Several thousand persons hold rally at the Washington Monument supporting President Nixon's Vietnam policy.

Ferdinand E. Marcos is reelected president of the Philippine Republic.

13 India's Prime Minister Indira Gandhi receives vote of "full confidence" from a majority of Congress Party members in Parliament. On Nov. 12, a group of old-guard party members had expelled Mrs. Gandhi from the governing party.

The FBI charges three men and a woman with setting off a series of bombs in several private-business and Government buildings in New York City.

In an address criticizing television news, Vice-President Agnew asks the American people to "let the networks know that they want their news straight and objective."

15 Demanding U.S. withdrawal from Vietnam, a crowd, estimated at over 300,000 persons, parades on Washington's Pennsylvania Avenue and attends a rally at the Washington Monument.

17 The United States and Soviet Union open preliminary Strategic Arms Limitation Talks (SALT) in Helsinki, Finland.

20 The White House announces that Henry Cabot Lodge will resign on Dec. 8 as chief U.S. delegate to the Paris peace talks.

21 With a vote of 45 to 55, the U.S. Senate rejects the nomination of Clement F. Haynsworth, Jr., to the Supreme Court.

After three days of meetings in Washington, Japanese Premier Eisaku Sato and President Nixon issue communiqué outlining conditions for the return of Okinawa to Japan in 1972.

24 Comdr. Charles Conrad, Jr., Comdr. Richard F. Gordon, Jr., and Comdr. Alan L. Bean land safely in the Pacific Ocean after successfully completing the 10-day Apollo 12 mission. On Nov. 19, Conrad and Bean each took two moon walks.

The U.S. Army announces that First Lt. William L. Calley, Jr., will be brought before a general court-martial on charges of murdering at least 109 persons, including children, in the village of Songmy, South Vietnam, in March 1968.

25 President Nixon pledges that the United States will never use germ warfare and that chemical-warfare weapons will be used only for defensive purposes.

Seven months after resigning because of widespread rioting in Lebanon, Rashid Karami succeeds in forming a Government.

28 West Germany signs the treaty to prevent the spread of nuclear weapons. On Nov. 24, the United States and the Soviet Union had become the 23rd and 24th nations to sign the documents ratifying the treaty.

New York City Mayor John V. Lindsay describes his reelection victory as a "message to Albany and Washington that they can no longer starve our cities."

Wide World

U. S. CONGRESS ADJOURNS AFTER PASSING TAX REFORM ● SATO'S PARTY IS REELECTED IN JAPAN ● ARAB CONFERENCE ENDS IN DISPUTE

1   In accordance with a bill signed by President Nixon on Nov. 26, the first U.S. draft lottery in a generation is held in Washington.

4   In a predawn raid by police on an apartment near the headquarters of the Black Panther Party in Chicago, two Panther leaders are killed and four are injured by police. According to the police, two of whom were injured, the Panthers fired on them as they entered the apartment.

5   Warren E. Burger, chief justice of the U.S. Supreme Court, names ten Federal judges to oversee the financial and out-of-court activities of all Federal judges except those on the Supreme Court.

10   William A. Boyle claims victory in elections for the presidency of the United Mine Workers of America.
Dahomey President Emile-Derlin Zinsou is ousted in a coup led by Army officers.

11   In Warsaw, U.S. Ambassador Walter J. Stoessel and Chinese Chargé d'Affaires Lei Yang discuss the possibility of the United States and China resuming formal ambassadorial talks.

Five Israeli-commissioned gunboats, which left Cherbourg, France, on Christmas Eve despite an embargo, arrive in Israel as 1969 ends.

"Israel Sun"—PIX

DECEMBER

**headline
highlights**

S M T W T F S S M T W T F S S M T W T F S
1 2 3 4 5 6 7 8 9 10 11 12 13 14 15 16 17 18 19 20
21 22 23 24 25 26 27 28 29 30 31

Israeli jet fighters and Syrian MiG's clash near Damascus.

Harvard University suspends some 75 black students who occupied the dean's office, the faculty club and a major construction site, demanding more black construction workers on campus.

12 Greece withdraws from the Council of Europe.

15 President Nixon announces that an additional 50,000 U.S. troops will be withdrawn from Vietnam by Apr. 15, 1970.

Czechoslovakia President Ludvik Svoboda names former party chief Alexander Dubcek ambassador to Turkey.

16 Brig. Gen. Omar Torrijos is restored as commander of Panama's armed forces. On Dec. 15, Torrijos' two top aides announced that he had been removed as Panama's strong man.

The Philippine Republic and Malaysia resume diplomatic relations suspended since 1968 because of a dispute over Sabah.

17 Newark, N.J., Mayor Hugh J. Addonizio and 14 other persons, including 9 current or former municipal officials, are indicted by a Federal grand jury on charges including income-tax evasion, extortion and conspiracy. On Dec. 16, 55 persons were indicted in Newark on Federal charges of operating an interstate lottery.

The 24th session of the UN General Assembly adjourns.

In Czechoslovakia, 11 liberals, including Dubcek's former deputy, Josef Smrkovsky, resign from Parliament.

19 Uganda President Milton Obote is shot and wounded as he leaves his party's convention in Kampala.

23 In Rabat, Morocco, a conference of Arab leaders to coordinate policy against Israel ends in dispute. Saudi Arabia and Kuwait refuse to increase their financial support of the Arab armies.

The first session of the 91st U.S. Congress adjourns.

27 Japan's Liberal-Democratic Party, headed by Premier Sato, wins a majority in elections to the 486-seat House of Representatives.

29 In Manila, the Philippines, a small bomb is tossed at the limousine of Vice-President Spiro Agnew. The U.S. Vice-President is on a 23-day, 11-nation tour.

30 President Nixon signs the tax-reform bill and the mine health and safety bill into law.

A district court in Jerusalem commits Denis Michael Rohan, a 28-year-old Australian, to a mental institution for an indefinite period. Rohan had been on trial since Oct. 6 for setting fire in August to the Mosque of Al Aksa in Jerusalem.

31 Five unarmed gunboats, built in Cherbourg, France, for Israel but under an arms embargo, arrive at the port of Haifa, Israel. The French Government suspends two high defense officials pending an inquiry into how the gunboats escaped from France.

Commander of Panama's armed forces, Brig. Gen. Omar Torrijos.

UPI

All photos this article, NASA

Lunar soil is disturbed for the first time by a living
agency: an earthly astronaut's footstep.

Apollo 11....
Man's first step on the moon

by Paul Haney, Journalist,
Former Voice of Apollo

Astronaut Aldrin starts toward lunar ship after setting up seismic detector, to register moonquakes.

"Houston. . . . . .Tranquility Base here. The *Eagle* has landed."

Apollo 11 commander Neil Armstrong used those simple, direct words to advise an anxious earth that man indeed had landed for the first time on another celestial body. The day was July 20, 1969. The time was 4:17 P.M. EDT.

In earth time, it had been 2,978 days since President John F. Kennedy established the manned-lunar-landing project as a national goal to be achieved "in this decade." But the manned lunar landing actually took centuries to accomplish, for man had always been dreaming about it. In the same vein, it was truly a planet-earth triumph, far more than just a great score for the United States of America. As Armstrong put it the instant he set foot on the lunar surface: "That's one small step for a man, one giant leap for mankind."

The manned lunar landing was in fact the most significant transportation feat since fish crawled out of the sea and managed to survive on land. And the world marked it appropriately. About a billion of the earth's four billion people listened to the drama as it happened "live" on television and radio. Another two billion knew of it within hours of the actual happening. It was one of those events that people would recall years afterward in terms of what they were doing on that particular day.

Evolving man has forever celebrated his transportation progress. Think of the stir the invention of the wheel must have caused! Then ships. Harnessing of animals. Balloons. The railroad. Airplanes. Cars. Space flight.

And with the emergence of each new transportation triumph, an individual or two are swept to immortality. Like Columbus. The brothers Wright. And now three new names could be added: Armstrong, Edwin Aldrin, Jr., and Michael Collins.

Heroes for the ages (left to right): Neil A. Armstrong, Apollo 11 commander and first man on the moon; Michael Collins, command-module pilot; and Edwin E. Aldrin, Jr., lunar-module pilot.

Each astronaut was born in 1930. Each stands about 5 feet 11 inches and weighs about 165 pounds. Each shares a love of flying. Armstrong in fact had a pilot's license before he had a driver's license.

A civilian employee of the National Aeronautics and Space Administration, Armstrong had had several brushes with death while flying. A steel cable had clipped off a wing of a Navy jet he was piloting in combat over Korea. He made a difficult dead-stick landing with the X-15 rocket plane. His Gemini 8 spacecraft tumbled out of control for over an hour in man's first real space emergency. And he ejected from a lunar-landing training vehicle when it went out of control 200 feet off the ground. Perhaps these incidents help to explain why this Wapakoneta, Ohio, native normally talks with some hesitation, just this side of a stutter. Prior to the lunar flight, his voice and manner seemed to become even more hesitant.

If similar pressures weighed down on Aldrin and Collins, they did not show so clearly. Both career Air Force officers, they had been graduated from the Military Academy at West Point. Aldrin grew up in Montclair, N. J. Collins, an "Army brat," was born in Rome, Italy, and grew up all over the world.

Mechanical preparations leading to Apollo 11 went precisely according to a well-rehearsed countdown. By coincidence, Apollo would reach lunar maturity

"Houston, Tranquility Base here. The Eagle has landed."

on the 21st manned U.S. mission in space. Three crews had already ridden the 363-foot Apollo-Saturn 5 stack. Two crews had "man-rated" the lunar module in space. Two crews had orbited the moon. One crew had skimmed within 47,000 feet of what Aldrin called "the magnificent desolation" of the lunar surface.

The "11" crew would make the 240,000-mile traverse from earth to moon in a 13-by-12-foot, conic-shaped command-service ship called *Columbia.*

The service module, housing a 20,500-pound-thrust engine to "brake" the spacecraft into lunar orbit and push it back to earth when necessary, rode attached to the bottom of the command module. Docked in orbit to *Columbia's* nose was *Eagle,* the spidery-looking lunar ship. Armstrong and Aldrin would make the descent and return from the lunar surface in *Eagle* while Collins orbited alone 69 miles above the moon in *Columbia.* The technique is called lunar-orbit rendezvous, similar in many ways to the techniques used by seafarers for centuries: Anchor the main ship in deep water offshore and use a small boat to go to and from the beach.

Let's pick up the action as it unfolded in lunar orbit about 1:50 P.M. EDT on July 20. *Eagle* and *Columbia* have just parted. *"Eagle* has wings," Armstrong reports happily.

"You've got a fine-looking flying machine there, *Eagle,* despite the fact you're upside down," jokes Collins as he inspects the lunar ship. "Somebody's upside down," Armstrong shoots back. Obviously it makes no difference to them at this point.

Two hours pass and *Eagle* starts PDI, space jargon for powered descent initiation, a 12-minute burn that will place them helicopter fashion on the lunar surface. A 10,000-pound-thrust engine, the first rocket engine that can be throttled, slows *Eagle.* Armstrong and Aldrin begin the burn looking straight down, stomachs toward the moon, feet pointed in the direction of flight. A minute later, the craft rolls them heads up.

Seven minutes tick by. They are quiet, tense minutes. *Eagle* is 500 feet from the surface. The pilots call it "low gate"—the last major planned abort point, although the equipment will tolerate an abort right down to the moment of landing. But "11" is "go" for touchdown.

Armstrong is on the semiautomatic mode, one hand on the throttle, ready to override the computer steering if the craft isn't doing what he wants it to do. Aldrin is scanning the instruments in a set pattern, talking almost constantly, calling out readings to Armstrong and anxious earthlings a quarter million miles away.

In the last critical minutes, *Eagle* sounds a computer-program alarm. This means trouble. Millions of hearts start beating faster.

But it's a false alarm. In Houston a flight controller wisely and quickly diagnoses the trouble as an overworked computer. It happens 3 times in 90 seconds. "Press on," Houston tells the crew.

Then Aldrin is talking: "......350, down at 4. 330, 3¹/₂ down. We're pegged on horizontal velocity. .....Got the shadow out there.....Lights on. Down 2¹/₂. Picking up some dust. 30 feet and 2¹/₂ down. Faint shadow....Drifting right. Contact light. Okay, engines stop. ACA out of detent. Engine arm, off...."

"We copy you down, *Eagle,*" Houston says. And Armstrong assures Houston that the *Eagle* has landed. With unabashed emotion, astronaut Charles Duke, acting as Houston capsule communicator during this period, tells *Eagle:* "You've got a bunch of guys about to turn blue. We're breathing again. Thanks a lot."

Wearing a life-support suit and backpack, Aldrin carefully descends to the surface of an airless orb with a gravity only about a sixth that of earth's.

Extravehicular suit consists of: 1. visor; 2. backpack-control box; 3. oxygen-purge-system switch; 4. penlight pocket; 5. connector cover; 6. communication, ventilation and liquid-cooling tubes; 7. extravehicular glove; 8. utility pocket; 9. lunar overshoe; 10. urine-transfer connector, biomedical injection, dosimeter-access flap and donning-lanyard pocket; 11. thermal meteoroid garment; 12. lunar-module restraint ring; 13. oxygen-purge-system tube; 14. backpack; 15. sunglasses pocket; 16. oxygen-purge-system; 17. backpack-support straps.

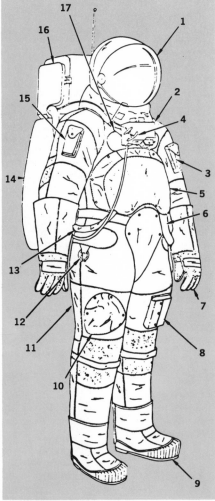

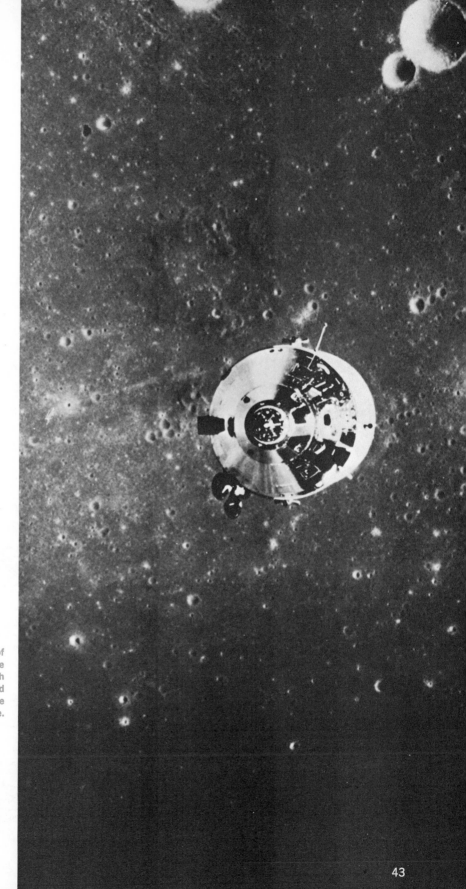

Against a background of "pockmarked" moon, the command module, with Collins left alone aboard it, recedes from the separated lunar module.

Safely home, the astronauts wait in a life raft for helicopter pickup while a pararescueman closes the ship's hatch.

From mobile quarantine quarters, on the U.S. carrier "Hornet," the spacemen chat happily with President Richard M. Nixon.

HORNET + 3

But there's little time for small talk. Armstrong explains how he took control in the final phase to avoid a boulder-filled field which would have been the computed touchdown point. *Eagle* had only 30 seconds of descent fuel left at engine shutdown.

During the descent Armstrong's heartbeat, monitored in Houston, tells the drama in far more human terms than Neil could in his hesitant, flat Midwestern voice. His heartbeat soars to nearly 160 beats per minute—50 beats a minute higher than when the Saturn 5 hurled him into space.

On the lunar surface, everything is checking out nicely. Armstrong decides to begin the moon walk several hours earlier than planned. But first, some dinner and a little rest. Then the two start donning their cumbersome, oxygen-filled backpacks. It's like two football players trying to dress for a game in a phone booth.

At 10:51 P.M., Armstrong steps out on *Eagle's* "front porch." Home viewers gasp as a shadowy white-suited figure makes its way down a ladder in full view of a television camera that transmits the pictures back to earth. At the base of the ladder, Armstrong tests the surface with his toe, much as a swimmer might check the water temperature.

"The LM [lunar module] footpads are only depressed in the surface about one or two inches, although the surface appears to be very, very fine-grained as you get close to it. It's almost like a powder. It's very fine. I'm going to step off the LM now," Armstrong says.

And off he steps. "The lighting is great," he reports, as he picks up his first of nearly 48 pounds of rock samples. "It has a stark beauty all its own," Armstrong says, "like much of the high desert of the United States."

Minutes later, Aldrin goes down the ladder. And the two move through a routine with stopwatch precision. Collecting samples. Checking the mobility of his suit, Aldrin does a kangaroo hop across the television screens of the entire world. They implant a U.S. flag, leave behind medals of dead Russian cosmonauts as well as fallen fellow astronauts. They deposit a moonquake sensor, so sensitive it records their very footsteps, and a mirror array to measure laser reflections from earth.

Things are going well on the southern edge of the Sea of Tranquility, so well that the men are asked to pause for a moment to talk directly with President Richard Nixon in the White House. In the exchange, Armstrong's voice betrays more emotion than it will at any other point in the mission.

After 2¼ hours on the surface, the two return to *Eagle* for a sleepless "sleep period."

Nearly 22 hours after it landed, *Eagle* lifts off from the moon with its priceless cargo of lunar vagabonds and extraterrestrial samples. *Columbia* is there for the rendezvous. *Eagle* is discarded to the vastness of space. And the three speed happily homeward, first to 18 days of quarantine to make sure that no moon germs have made the return trip.

Then came the tremendous national and international tributes, including New York, Chicago and Los Angeles festivities all lumped into one gigantic 19-hour day. The crush and tumult accompanying them might well have been recorded by that lunar seismometer. The tumult was understandable.

For this story will be told and retold a thousand years from now, on planets millions of miles from earth, in the words of a plaque on the Apollo 11 lunar-module descent stage at Tranquility Base:

Here Men from the Planet Earth
First Set Foot upon the Moon
July 1969 A.D.
We Came in Peace for All Mankind.

For other missions, see Space, page 392.

encyclopedia year book
feature:

World
Refugees

by R. Norris Wilson

Executive
Vice-President,
United States
Committee
for Refugees

U.S. Committee for Refugees

Camp outside Beirut, Lebanon, is only home the
young refugee has ever known. Huts (background)
are of rusty tin and broken packing cases.

For most people in such countries as the United States, the word "refugee"
calls up the masses of homeless, dislocated persons left in the wake of World
War II, or the Palestinian Arabs uprooted by the creation of the new state of
Israel in 1948, or perhaps scurrying Vietnamese villagers seen on television
news.

The shocking fact is that the estimated refugee population of the world today
is greater than at any other time since the end of World War II. Since 1964 alone
the total has grown from 7,910,000 to almost 17,500,000, in more than 80 nations. The total includes refugees in Asia (where South Vietnam accounts for
about 1,200,000), the Middle East (some 2,000,000 Arabs) and Africa (in Ni-
geria/Biafra alone, 3,500,000).

What is a refugee? The answer may seem obvious, yet the term has had to be
defined as precisely as possible for legal reasons. Various laws, some of them
national and others going back to the days of League of Nations mandates, had
to be enacted in regard to refugees. Such matters as immigration quotas, pass-

U.S. Committee for Refugees

A future with more uncertainty than most people must bear hangs over a Chinese family in Hong Kong, refugees from the Communists.

port regulations or lack of a passport, identification of people without a country (that is, stateless) and so on were—and are—involved.

Legally therefore, a refugee is a person who has left his home and cannot, or will not, return because (1) he has been persecuted—or fears persecution—on the grounds of his religion, nationality, social class or political beliefs; or (2) as a result of a natural disaster, for example, an earthquake; or (3) his home has been overrun in the course of war. As the thousands left homeless by the war in Korea in the early 1950's and, since then, by the wars in Vietnam and Nigeria/Biafra have remained mostly within their national boundaries, they are not considered international refugees. Their plight is just as grave nevertheless.

Whatever has made a person a refugee, he needs one or, more likely, most of the following: legal protection, recognized status by the country to which he has moved, help with passports or other documents, and to become a part of and a productive member of his new community with a feeling that he and his family have a future there. This, of course, is in addition to such fundamentals as adequate food, shelter and clothing, and schools for the children.

Besides the United Nations and the United States Government, there are many private organizations that have responded to the needs of refugees out of humanitarian concern.

In November 1969 a National Conference on World Refugee problems was held in Washington, D.C. Representatives of more than 60 private American organizations, serving refugees all over the world, met to tackle the growing and increasingly complicated problems of refugees in more than 80 nations. Addressing the conference, President Nixon stated, "The challenge of refugees is a world problem and it is in that form that it must be faced. No matter where refugees have originated or for what reason, the United States will seek solutions in a world context. For only by considering all refugees in this context can we avoid the acrimony and suspicion and refueling of animosity that our nation seeks to avoid. The refugee problem is properly the responsibility of every nation and a charge on the conscience of every individual, and I ask that in your proceedings you so consider it. All of us must do more and we must do more together."

In the political, social, racial and sometimes tribal conflicts of our time, the refugee is the innocent bystander caught in the cross fire "of a world he never made." In 1959, during the United Nations World Refugee Year, the countries taking part raised special funds for the purpose of clearing the remaining refugee camps from Europe, the aftermath for the most part of World War II. The effort was largely successful though there is a smaller but continuing problem of refugees in Europe for other reasons, such as the political situation in Czechoslovakia.

However, the scene of the major refugee flights has shifted from Europe to Africa and Asia. The African problems are mainly the result of the independence won by most African states in the last ten years or so. Practically all of these states have kept the old, arbitrary colonial boundaries, which cut across ancient tribal units. To the majority of sub-Saharan Africans, their first and overwhelming loyalty is still to their tribe. Consequently, since independence, some 5,000,000 Africans have fled to escape domination and possible persecution by a tribe other than their own.

Most of the problems in Asia have their roots in the rise to power of the communist regime in China. Hong Kong has some 2,000,000 refugees from China. About 55,000 Tibetans, driven from their homeland by the Chinese Communists, have found asylum in India. There are also several small groups of Tibetan refugees in Switzerland, where the terrain and the climate are more like the Tibetans' homeland in the Himalayas.

Through the office of its High Commissioner for Refugees (with headquarters in Geneva, Switzerland), the United Nations has responsibility for some 2,500,-000 refugees, mostly in Africa. The United States has extensive programs in Africa and Asia. The private, voluntary agencies in the United States work in close cooperation with governmental and intergovernmental programs. All the agencies cooperate to bring emergency relief, that is, health and welfare services, to the refugees as they migrate into asylum countries. The overall aim is to help the refugee reestablish himself and achieve self-sufficiency in his new homeland.

In the United States, service and assistance programs by governmental and private organizations continue as refugees arrive from Cuba, Hong Kong and central Europe. Ironically, the programs have become so efficient and humane as to be unobtrusive; the general public is hardly aware that the United States is still receiving refugees as it has since World War II.

The unfortunate fact is that, for many reasons, both the problems of refugees around the world and their solutions are "hidden." As most people have no idea that almost 17,500,000 refugees exist, so are they equally unaware that the presence of the refugees and their problems are both cause and effect of world tensions.

In addition to the UN High Commission for Refugees in Geneva, information about refugees in general or on specific refugee problems may be obtained from: United Nations High Commissioner for Refugees (UN mandated refugees), c/o United Nations Plaza, Box 20, Grand Central Station, New York, New York 10017; United Nations Relief and Works Agency (Palestine refugees), New York Office, United Nations Plaza, New York, New York 10017; Office of Refugee and Migration Affairs (ORM), United States Department of State, Washington, D.C. 20520; United States Committee for Refugees (all refugees), 20 West 40th Street, New York, New York 10018.

Human Ecology

by Senator Edmund S. Muskie of Maine

© The New York Times

UPI

Senators Edmund Muskie and Alan Cranston (Cal.) inspect foul mess resulting from leaking oil well off Santa Barbara, Cal.

Cleveland physician John J. Poland tests sample of polluted river; he blames it for growing number of ills.

In 1969, an era came to a close. It was an era of exploration, outreach and headlong advance. Interrupted by two world wars, slowed by a constant tug between peace and war, and fueled by the eager consumption of technology and material accomplishment, man had forced his way out of his environment and landed on the moon.

No matter how far afield our explorations take us, however, we must always return to this earth.

In some future time, we may find another environment in which we can live without artificial assistance. But for the foreseeable future we have but one home and one natural environment. If we do not begin to repair the damage we have caused as we have flexed our technological muscle, we will soon be ecological orphans—faced with an environment that cannot support simple human existence, much less the exploration of outer space.

So as we embark on a new era, it would be the greatest of human failures if we neglected to make some elementary decisions as to what our focus for this era must be.

Our responsibility on earth—for our own survival—is to maintain that which is not defiled, enhance that which is degraded and restore that which has been destroyed. While we may dream of the frontiers of space, we must act on the frontier of recovery.

If we set goals for the 1970's, this must be one of them. If we are to embark on a romantic adventure, this must be it. There is no time to lose.

The environmental crisis is unlike any other we have ever faced. There is no one moment at which the critical point is reached. In fact, there is no such thing as a critical point.

Mankind may simply reach the day when there is not enough air, water and land to support life on this earth. We may reach a day when the task of restoration is too great. And we may reach a day when the task of replacement is impossible. We are in the midst of the environmental crisis, not approaching it.

Whatever our past performance, we can change course. We can make a commitment to a livable environment just as we made a commitment to put a man on the moon—if it is important enough to us.

John Jacqua

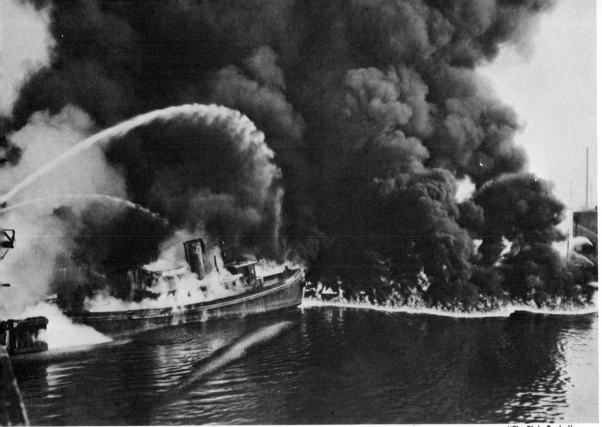

"The Plain Dealer"

So filthy is Cleveland's Cuyahoga River that it caught
fire in summer of 1969; tug was trapped in the flames.

We can say that by 1976:

1. We will develop the technology to control all sources of air pollution and insist that adequate controls be in effect;

2. We will require tertiary treatment for all discharges into our streams and rivers, and we will invest the funds to accomplish this purpose; and,

3. We will recover resources instead of destroy them.

Such commitments are critical if the United States is to avoid an environmental debacle during the next two decades; and they are no less valid for much of the rest of the earth.

Additional legislation is necessary to control sources of pollution not now subject to abatement—including aircraft, heavy construction equipment, large vessels, and other moving sources. Present programs must be funded adequately as authorized.

Federal facilities and Federal licensees, such as nuclear-power plants, should not escape environmental standards.

The Congress should review carefully the development of advanced emission controls for motor vehicles, and stimulate development of alternatives to internal-combustion engines.

The states and communities must give greater consideration to the problems of pollution in planning highways and in other land-use decisions. In some cases, changing the location of highways will reduce the unacceptable amount of air pollution in a given area. In other instances, where the specific transportation needs and the problem of air pollution cannot be reconciled, a community or state should develop alternative forms of transportation.

UPI

To get rid of auto junk heaps, machine has been devised that chews car into chunks that can be turned into usable steel.

Untreated black smoke that power plant is giving off may be as hazardous to health of human beings as cigarette smoking.

UPI

53

UPI

Threat to life is shown starkly by duck so saturated with crude oil, from Santa Barbara leak, that it can hardly move.

During the next decade many metropolitan areas may be forced to consider banning the individual use of the automobile. Even if we are successful in reducing emissions from internal-combustion engines, there will still be too many motor vehicles, too few highways and too limited space in central-city areas. The city will be strangled by congestion and the people by air pollution.

When this kind of metropolitan action is taken, different forms of individual transportation will have to be developed, such as one- and two-passenger automobiles, moving sidewalks and sophisticated forms of intra-city mass transportation.

Another area that should be a focus of pollution-control efforts is industrial-site selection. For example, the location of a steel plant in a congested, polluted, water-starved area, and the location of a Federal office building in a residential neighborhood are environmental hazards that we have tended to ignore in the past.

These needs and others will require a significant change in public attitude. But sooner or later all of us must reach the conclusion that individual convenience, preference and self-interest must take a back seat to the preservation of a livable environment.

These considerations and decisions will not be as dramatic as our space program, but they are the kind of adventures and technological quests that are essential if we are to make our environment wholesome for living things.

They are also the kind of adventures without which none other will ever be possible.

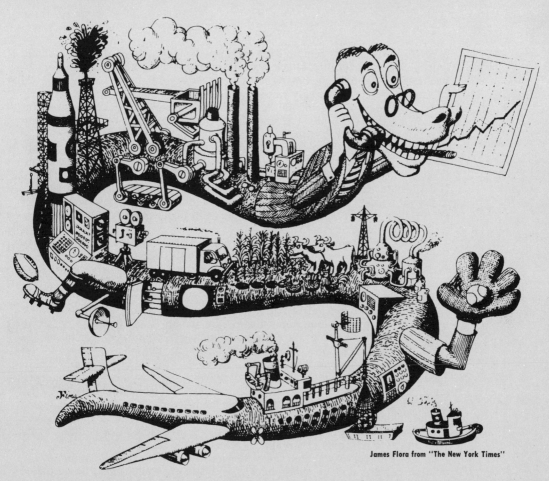

James Flora from "The New York Times"

Conglomerates...
Wave of the Future?

by Louis Rukeyser, Economic Editor, American Broadcasting Company

The story of the American economy in 1969 could have been written by Lewis Carroll as a sequel to *Alice in Wonderland*. It was surely a world of looking-glass reversals: traditionally "bad" news (a slowdown in economic growth) was eagerly anticipated by the Government as "good" news (in the fight against inflation). Wall Street, which Marxists habitually denounce as a haven of "warmongers," surged ahead on every whisper of peace in Vietnam. And a new administration run by Republicans, supposedly the party of businessmen, launched the most violent attack in years on an important segment of American business—the giant conglomerates.

"Conglomerate" is an ugly word that means the same thing in business as it does in geology: a mass of unrelated pebbles cemented together into one fat rock. The fellow who does the cementing runs the conglomerate—and the beauty of it is that he is usually able to do it with other people's money.

Business conglomerates come about when companies take over completely unrelated companies: when a fish company, for example, joins with an electronics firm. Such strange marriages had become so increasingly popular in the United States that there were more in 1968 involving very large companies—those with assets of $250,000,000 or more—than in the preceding twenty years put together. When this trend accelerated even faster in early 1969, it became a key target of government concern.

The urge to merge has been as recurrent among American corporations as among American teen-agers, and in both cases that urge has been subject to the strictures of the established community. Antimonopoly legislation has long made life uncomfortable for companies essaying either or both of the traditional varieties of corporate merger: the "horizontal" merger, in which a company takes over a competitor; and the "vertical" merger, in which a company takes over either a customer or a supplier. So, unable to move in either of these directions, shrewd corporate raiders hit on what could be described as the "zigzag" merger: the formation of a conglomerate.

There were several compelling attractions. One was the belief (challenged in 1969) that the Government has no legal power to oppose this kind of merger. Another was the lure of "instant diversification": in which a company, by acquiring a going concern in another field, immediately lessens its dependence on the fickle consumer's demand for any one particular kind of product. And a third was the array of flashy financial gimmicks available for would-be Davids who sought to take over corporate Goliaths in other fields.

One of the most successful such "Davids"—indeed a classic example of the modern conglomerateur—was James Joseph Ling of Ling-Temco-Vought, Inc. Using just $3,000 as the stone in his slingshot, Jimmy Ling felled a succession of corporate Goliaths...until he himself became so huge that in 1969 the Government turned on *him*.

The LTV saga began in Dallas in the mid-1940's when Ling, a high-school dropout and a Navy veteran, put that $3,000 into a small electrical firm. Then started a pyramiding success story that makes even the biblical comparison seem inadequate; it was as if Horatio Alger, Jr., had been crossed with a third-generation computer. By 1961, LTV was a full-fledged conglomerate, which means that it was adding on completely unrelated businesses, starting with the faltering Chance Vought aircraft company. Ling got this one with the help of some highly risky short-term bank loans, and already the original $3,000 was producing some $350,000,000 in annual sales.

LTV kept on growing, in every direction: into cable and wire in 1965; into sporting goods, meat and chemicals in 1966; into airlines, car rentals and life insurance in 1967. The money came from the unlikeliest sources: from the Rothschilds of London, from the bankers of Switzerland...and even from the companies themselves. When LTV took over Greatamerica Corporation in 1967, for example, the new acquisition coughed up $140,000,000 to help in the next take-over—of Jones & Laughlin Steel. And this, as it turned out, was the red flag that brought the Government charging into the conglomerate arena. It sought to block the Jones & Laughlin take-over and generally cast a suspicious eye at this new-style business bonanza.

Osrin from Cleveland "Plain Dealer"

"Who're you callin' a conglomerate?!"

Dazzling record (figures in millions) is reported at Ling-Temco-Vought, Inc., stockholders meeting. However, its mergers have multiplied so rapidly that the Justice Department brought suit in 1969.

Before the year was three months old, half a dozen government agencies had begun investigations of the conglomerate phenomenon, and the Nixon administration was plainly concerned that the trend had gotten out of hand. Two primary dangers were seen. The familiar one was that these, like other mergers, might lessen free competition and endanger smaller companies. The newer danger was that the fancy means devised for financing the take-overs might be a sort of trick with mirrors to tempt unwary investors.

The net effect of all this unwanted attention was to accelerate a decline in the value of common stock in the leading conglomerates, some of which were sliced to less than a third of their all-time highs. (This slide actually had begun more than a year earlier when Litton Industries, one of the earliest and most successful of the postwar conglomerates, reported that for the first time in its history it was about to record a decline in profits. Many investors were stunned by this intimation that even the conglomerates were run by mortals.)

But if the conglomerateurs felt like crying the corporate version of *"et tu, Brute!"* at this assault by a Republican administration, they had scant sympathy in Washington. Richard M. Nixon had said little of substance about antitrust law during his presidential campaign other than a vague promise of "clear" merger guidelines. And his antitrust chief at the Justice Department, a former Chicago lawyer named Richard W. McLaren, was certainly nothing if not clear in his attitude toward conglomerate mergers. "Actually, I've been expressing a standard Republican attitude," McLaren said. "When the economy is dominated by 200 large companies—a very real threat now—individual initiative and free enterprise are circumscribed. The 'in' thing of late has been merger and

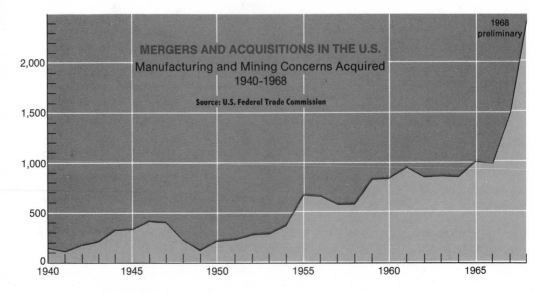

MERGERS AND ACQUISITIONS IN THE U.S.
Manufacturing and Mining Concerns Acquired
1940-1968

Source: U.S. Federal Trade Commission

1968
preliminary

2,000
1,500
1,000
500
0

1940   1945   1950   1955   1960   1965

acquisition. Maybe, if we can make it an 'out' thing, the law won't have to over-react."

The attack on the conglomerates in 1969 was as many-sided as the corporations themselves. McLaren's boss, Attorney General John N. Mitchell, served notice that the Justice Department was likely to take legal action to block any future merger between two corporate giants—specifically including all 200 of the largest manufacturing firms. The Federal Trade Commission demanded special advance notice of any major planned merger, contending that such mergers often weakened local management, reduced jobs, discouraged inventiveness and hurt small firms. The New York Stock Exchange refused to list certain debt securities of two companies, and warned that it might act further against companies that used an abundance of borrowings to buy out other firms. And, in the year's closing months, Congress studied several plans to discourage conglomerate mergers, including an administration-backed plan to deny many companies a tax deduction for interest on bonds offered in exchange for stock of other firms.

Ironically, this let's-all-jump-on-the-conglomerates mood struck America at a time when other nations were smiling on corporate mergers. Merger fever in Britain proceeded generally with the blessing of the nominally socialist Government, which found that it needed bigger firms to compete successfully for world business. The same mood was discernible in West Germany and France. And in Japan, now the United States' second-biggest trading partner (and the one with which the United States runs the largest annual deficit), the conglomerate is a proud national specialty. Three conglomerates—Mitsubishi, Mitsui and Sumitomo—alone account for from 30 to 100 per cent of all production in each of 20 major industries. And the Japanese, like their would-be American counterparts, see no other rational means of dealing with worldwide industrial competition.

The year-long shake-out of the U.S. conglomerates delayed, at least temporarily, the rush toward multi-industry corporations (more than a dozen major mergers were canceled). The 1970's were clearly going to put the burden of proof on the conglomerates—so much a phenomenon of the 1960's—to demonstrate that they were indeed the corporate wave of the future.

"Newsweek" photo by Bernard Gotfryd

encyclopedia year book feature:

Sex in the Performing Arts

by Clive Barnes,
Theater Critic, *The New York Times*

Herbert Migdoll

Though famous writers contributed the sketches, "Oh! Calcutta!" achieved a long run mostly on the basis of nudity.

Robert Joffrey's psychedelic ballet "Astarte" is an encounter between the love goddess and a young man on a "trip."

Friedman-Abeles

The sexual revolution and the permissive society may be neither so revolutionary nor so permissive as certain sociologically inclined journalists assure us. However, in the past 20 years—particularly in the past 5 years and even more particularly in the past 2 years, for such is the current acceleration rate of social change—Western society has started at least to reexamine its sexual mores and sexual taboos.

The reasons for this need hardly detain us: the developing emancipation of women, the introduction of the contraceptive pill, the fruits of mass education, the emerging sophistication of the affluent society—many suggestions could be put forward. The facts are undeniable.

We are now in an age of sexual frankness, something that should not be confused with sexuality itself. The Victorians were among the least sexually frank people in recorded history, yet a strong streak of occasionally repressed sexuality ran straight, and sometimes not so straight, through their society.

The results of this new sexual frankness can easily be illustrated by our developing attitude toward obscenity. It has been a long but surprisingly fast journey from the days when *Ulysses* could be impounded at the U.S. customs, through to the times of Lady Chatterley's acquittal in London and then on to the remarkable day when Portnoy, with both his mother and his complaint in attendance, can become a best seller throughout the English-speaking world. Who could possibly have thought it?

In terms of permissiveness there has always been a lag between the world of books and the performing arts. Books suggest a certain scholarly privacy far removed from the market places of the performing arts. But in the theater and in the movies we have now reached a point where perhaps the only linguistic obscenities and taboos left are those suggesting racial insults.

The rapidity with which the concept of verbal obscenity has changed during this century is admirably illustrated by the story of Eliza Doolittle. When Shaw, in 1912, wanted to startle his audience in *Pygmalion,* he had Eliza use the then taboo word "bloody." Even in 1938, when the film version was made by Gabriel Pascal, the word still retained its power to shock. However, by 1956, when Alan Jay Lerner wanted to create a similar effect of shock in *My Fair Lady* he used the word "arse." Now in 1970 I cannot imagine what word would be needed—the imagination boggles.

One of the most notable developments in the recent theater and cinema has been the permissive attitude toward nudity and the simulation of sexual acts. This is something quite new that has overtaken the performing arts at a fever rate.

Nudity has been known in the cinema for years, even before World War II. However, as time went on the nudity became franker and franker, until genitalia could be shown and various sexual activities were shown in a manner more and more explicit. In America the Swedish film *I am Curious (Yellow)* and its remarkable box-office success revealed a new level of acceptability and commercial possibility. Nudity was not only possible but exploitable; nudity and sex were here to stay in the performing arts. The public not only did not censure them but, to a gratifying extent for the entrepreneurs, it welcomed them.

The theater moved fast in emulation of its cinematic cousin. In March 1967, Robert Anderson offered four playlets on Broadway under the omnibus title *You Know I Can't Hear You When the Water's Running.* The first playlet was was called *The Shock of Recognition.* It involved a playwright requesting, for the purposes of realism, an actor to appear stark naked on stage. The premise of the joke was that the audience would instantly find such a request ludicrous. Within little more than a year nudity was all but a commonplace on-Broadway, off-Broadway, off-off-Broadway. *Hair,* with its nude be-in scene, was one sign

THEY THINK THEY'RE SHOCKING ME. | BUT I'M NOT SHOCKED. | SICKENED, YES. | DEGRADED, YES. | AND BORED. |

of the times during the 1967-68 season. The following year came *Oh, Calcutta!* and it was apparent that for the time being, and at least in New York, anything went. The show itself was of minimal interest. It had gathered, under the distinguished auspices of Kenneth Tynan, drama critic and resident guru of Britain's National Theater, and the distinguished direction of Jacques Levy, some of the world's most distinguished writers telling some less than distinguished dirty jokes. Most of the participants in these dirty jokes were totally nude. The strange, almost the sad thing, was that it did not prove, as far as one can tell, at all erotic.

Sexual frankness has developed vastly in both screen and cinema. A spade is now called a spade, words are used on screen and stage that the underprivileged critic cannot even quote in his family newspaper. The first big laugh of the family comedy *Forty Carats* arrives with the mention of a common expletive for excrement, and relationships, homosexual and at times even heterosexual, are spelled out in a way that would have been shattering just a decade ago.

Is this bad? I think not. I am personally—and on these matters we all have to examine our personal mores—in favor of pornography, on the grounds that it is a comparatively harmless sexual outlet, and as such is of overwhelming social value for the sexually underprivileged. But is this art?

Franco Zeffirelli's "Romeo and Juliet" was sexually frank but also had a feeling of tenderness and vulnerability.

UPI

62

VERY VERY BORED.

IF ANYTHING MORE BORED THAN IN REAL LIFE.

OH, BOY! A FIST FIGHT!

Jules Feiffer

Nudity and permissiveness do, I think, perform an artistic function. For example, as Franco Zeffirelli demonstrated in his film, a nude Romeo and Juliet have a certain tenderness, vulnerability, even frank likelihood that earlier Shakespearian lovers, wrapped up in layers of unrevealing flannel, may have lacked. Yes, nudity can have a place in the theater. And obscene language also. What is worse than the asterisk school of writing, where commonly used words (and the words commonly used seem continually on the increase) are replaced by tame yet sneaking euphemisms?

It is a matter of personal values, but I welcome the new freedom. Yet I welcome it with two fears. The first is a matter of taste. If you go to *Oh, Calcutta!,* or even *Hair,* you go in full awareness of what you are going to see. But if you go to *Forty Carats* you go, I think, with different premises. There is a word used there that my own newspaper would, quite rightly, not permit me to use in print (out of print I admit I use it in front of my children) and this may offend. Such unexpected offense is an invasion of privacy, and this I think should be taken into account.

In the English-speaking world the performing arts are controlled by the tastes of a comparatively few men living in New York and London. Chicago doesn't matter, Manchester doesn't matter. The people controlling Anglo-American taste (and I assure you in this matter that New York and London are like the twin cities of Buda and Pest, even though the river separating them is wider, and I would hesitate to suggest which one is Buda and which one is Pest) do not necessarily represent the views of anyone except those in their own cultural oligarchy. This may matter less than it seems. Art should be unfettered. But once unfettered we should recognize its power to give offense to tastes different from those of its practitioners, entrepreneurs and publicists.

The other danger is that of confusing pornography with art. I happen to be in favor of both, but I draw a strict line between the two. We are developing a theater in New York—particularly a homosexual theater—that has very little to do with art, and everything to do with a rather sensational form of pornography. A similar situation exists in film.

At the moment a number of virtually pornographic shows, shows primarily intended as vehicles for sexual exploitation, are inviting critical reviews—in the certain knowledge that even a bad critical notice simply by description will advertise their wares—and this is perhaps less than fair. It is better for people going to see good pornography not to go under the hypocritical illusion that they might be going to see bad art.

How long will sexual freedom prevail in the performing arts? The arts tend to be a mirror of society—less perhaps than some people hope, more perhaps than some people fear—and just as long as we have a permissive society we will have permissive arts. But freedom, particularly freedom coupled with personal and corporate morality, will never be all bad.

Culver Pictures, Inc.

The Beatles established trends in music and fashion.

Sept. 1960: Premier Khrushchev delivers anti-UN speech.

"Paris Match," Pictorial Parade

"Paris Match," Pictorial Parade

Pope John XXIII closes first session of Vatican II.

John Glenn was first American to orbit the earth.

"Paris Match," Pictorial Parade

UPI

Lyndon Johnson often spent 18 hours a day at White House desk.

MILESTONES
OF THE 1960'S

UPI

' Aug. 1963: Dr. King leads first March on Washington.

JFK, Jr., salutes his fallen father.

Pictorial Parade

"Paris Match," Pictorial Parade

June 1967: Israeli soldiers recapture Wailing Wall.

Bonnie Freer, Pictorial Parade

April 1968: Students take over Columbia University.

Nov. 1968: Richard M. Nixon is elected U.S. president.

Wide World

A Vietnamese mother and family escape aerial attacks.

UPI

events of the year

Charles de Gaulle goes
into retirement.

"Paris Match," Pictorial Parade

ACCIDENTS AND DISASTERS

According to the National Safety Council, 86,300 persons lost their lives in accidents in the United States during the first nine months of 1969. In this same period, auto accidents took the lives of 41,160 Americans. □ A study, released by the University of Denver Law School as 1970 opened, reported that the physically handicapped are among the world's safest drivers. □ In May, President Nixon named John H. Reed as chairman of the National Transportation Safety Board; and in October, the President established a Task Force on Highway Safety. □ List of the major accidents and disasters of 1969 follows.

January	3-4	Iran: Blizzards and additional tremors hamper rescue efforts after an earthquake strikes Khorasan Province; about 50 persons are killed, 300 injured and 2,000 left homeless.
	5	England: An Ariana Afghan Airways jetliner, bound for London from Kabul, crashes into a house near Gatwick Airport, south of London; 50 persons die.
	14	Pacific Ocean: During a training cruise, in the Pacific Ocean southwest of Hawaii, explosions and fire sweep the flight deck of the nuclear-powered U.S. carrier *Enterprise;* 27 crewmen are dead, 15 jet aircraft destroyed.
	18	United States: A United Air Lines Boeing 727 jetliner explodes and plunges into Santa Monica Bay shortly after taking off from Los Angeles International Airport; all 38 persons aboard are killed.
	18-26	United States: Torrential rains strike southern California, resulting in 91 dead, 9,000 homeless, $35,000,000 property damage.
	23	United States: Southern Mississippi is struck by a series of tornadoes; 29 persons die.
	31	South Korea: During a snowstorm, two passenger trains collide at Chonan, sixty miles south of Seoul; at least 35 persons are killed, 77 seriously injured.
February	3	Pakistan: A train hits a bus at a railroad crossing near Raihind, resulting in 29 dead and 11 injured.
	6	Philippine Republic: A ferry capsizes in Illana Bay of Lanao del Norte; at least 48 persons die.
	18	United States: On a return "gamblers flight" from Hawthorne, Nev., to Burbank, Calif., a DC-3 airliner with 35 persons aboard disappears over the High Sierra and the Nevada desert; no trace of the plane is found.
	24	Taiwan: After reporting engine trouble, a Chinese Nationalist twin-engine propjet crashes 24 miles north of Kaohsiung; 36 persons die.
March	8	Indonesia: An earthquake strikes the west coast of Celebes Island; at least 600 persons are missing, presumed dead.
	16	Venezuela: A Venezuelan DC-9 loses altitude and falls in the suburb of La Coruba, near Maracaibo; 155 persons are killed, including all 84 persons aboard the plane.
	17	Brazil: Following days of torrential rains, severe floods sweep Mundau Valley in the northeastern state of Alagoas; the unofficial toll is 400 dead, some 5,000 homeless.
	20	United Arab Republic: A U.A.R. Airlines Ilyushin-18 crashes while landing at Aswan Airport; 96 persons die, including 89 pilgrims returning from Mecca.
	21	Brazil: A crowded, electrically powered train and a locomotive collide in the suburbs of São Paulo; some 40 persons are killed, over 300 injured.
	28	Turkey: At about 4 A.M. an earthquake strikes near Alasehir; at least 53 persons are killed, 350 injured.
	31	Mexico: A gas explosion traps an estimated 183 miners in a desert coal mine in Coahuila State.
April	3	Poland: A Soviet-built Polish Airlines plane crashes 37 miles south of Cracow; 53 are killed.
	6	United States: On the Mississippi River, beneath the Greater New Orleans Bridge, a China Lines, Ltd., freighter and a barge, towed by two tugs, collide; 25 seamen are killed.
	13	Kuwait: A small boat, crowded with 50 Iranians trying to enter Kuwait illegally, capsizes and sinks 5 miles off the coast; only 15 known survivors.
	14	Pakistan: A 90-mile-an-hour cyclone lashes East capital city of Dacca; at least 540 persons die, more than 1,000 are injured.
	16	Congo (Kinshasa): A Congolese Air Force transport plane crashes into the Congo River near the capital; 45 persons are killed.
	21	Pakistan: An Indian Airlines Corporation plane, bound for Calcutta from Assam, northeast India, crashes near Khulna, East Pakistan; 40 passengers and 4 crew members are reported killed.
May	17	India: Ferry capsizes in the Ganges River near Calcutta; at least 40 persons drown.
	24	India: A cyclone strikes coastal area of the southern region of Andhra; 618 known deaths.
June	2	South China Sea: During maneuvers about 650 nautical miles southwest of Manila, the U.S. destroyer *Frank E. Evans* and the Australian aircraft carrier *Melbourne* collide; 74 Americans are killed.
	4	Mexico: On a 6,000-foot mountain near Monterrey, a Mexican Airways jetliner crashes and burns in bad weather; all 79 persons aboard—including tennis star Rafael Osuna and Carlos Madrazo, leader of Mexico's ruling Institutional Revolutionary Party—are killed.
	5	Philippine Republic: A bus falls into a ravine, killing at least 40 persons.
	15	Spain: During opening ceremonies, a crowded restaurant, in a mountain housing development northwest of Madrid, collapses; at least 57 persons die, 142 are injured.
	21	India: An express train derails near Benares, resulting in 62 deaths, 141 injured.
		Mozambique: A barge, crossing the Zambezi River north of Beira, capsizes; 108 Portuguese soldiers drown.
July	12	Nepal: A Royal Nepal Airlines DC-3 crashes after takeoff from Katmandu; 35 persons, most of them Indian pilgrims, die.

UPI

The U.S. nuclear aircraft carrier's stern shows the scars of the fire that occurred while she was on a bombing-practice mission, on Jan. 14. To control fire, she was turned into the wind so flames would blow off her stern.

	14	India: In India's second train disaster within a month, a freight train rams a crowded passenger train at Jaipur, a town 180 miles southwest of Calcutta; at least 85 persons die, 130 are injured.
	26	Algeria: A chartered Algerian airliner crashes in the desert 200 miles south of Algiers; 35 persons die.
August 17-25		United States: Hurricane Camille devastates large areas of Mississippi, Louisiana, Tennessee, Virginia and West Virginia, resulting in 292 deaths and property damage estimated at $1,000,000,000.
	31	Peru: A bus plunges into a ravine east of Lima; 37 persons are reported killed.
September	9	United States: A small flying-school plane smashes into the tail section of an Allegheny Airlines DC-9 jetliner about 25 miles southeast of Indianapolis, Ind.; 83 persons die.
	12	Philippine Republic: Approaching Manila International Airport, a Philippine Air Lines jetliner rams into a hillside; 45 of the 47 persons aboard die.
	20	Mexico: On a nonstop flight from Chicago, a Mexicana Airlines jet crashes while landing in Mexico City; 27 persons lose their lives.
		South Vietnam: A civilian airliner and a U.S. Phantom jet collide near Danang air base; 64 persons killed.
	21	South Korea: Official toll resulting from South Korea's worst floods in 10 years is 327 persons dead, 78 missing and 407 injured.
October	5	Algeria: Severe floods strike western section of the nation; 68 persons die, 218 are injured, over 100,000 are left homeless.
		Taiwan: Government releases official count of casualties during typhoon Flossie's 4 days of rain; 75 dead, 31,000 homeless.
	8	Tunisia: Weeks of floods leave more than 500 persons dead and 50,000 homes destroyed.
November	5	United States: In heavy seas some 300 miles off the coast of New Jersey, a transatlantic oil tanker splits in two; 36 men drown.
	7	South Africa: A dynamite explosion in the Buffelsfontein gold mine, 100 miles southwest of Johannesburg, kills 64 men and injures 14.
	20	Nigeria: A Nigerian VC-10 jet crashes and burns in a thick forest near Iju; all 87 persons aboard die.
December	2	Canada: Fire sweeps a 75-year-old wooden nursing home in the town of Notre Dame du Lac, Quebec, near the Maine border; police estimate that 54 persons perish.
	3	Venezuela: Shortly after takeoff from Caracas, an Air France jetliner, bound for Paris from Santiago, Chile, plummets into the Caribbean; all 62 persons aboard are killed.
	8	Greece: During a storm an Olympic Airways DC-6B airliner crashes near Athens; all 90 persons aboard are killed.

ADVERTISING

On the whole, advertising fared well in most countries in 1968–69. Dollar-volume gains generally ranged between 5 per cent and 10 per cent.

The United States was the leading country, with $18,300,000,000 invested in advertising in 1968. West Germany increased its advertising expenditure from $1,800,000,000 in 1967 to $2,100,000,000 in 1968. Great Britain, in third place, put $1,700,000,000 into advertising, up from $1,500,000,000. Japan advanced from $1,200,000,000 to $1,400,000,000, and Canada moved up from $853,700,000 to $902,-100,000. In many countries, including West Germany, Greece, Sweden, New Zealand, advertising benefited from improved economic situations. On the other hand, a tighter economic squeeze in Great Britain brought a slump in consumer spending; and the devaluation of the French franc was a matter of concern for French advertising men. Meanwhile it was predicted that U.S. companies would spend $5,000,000,000 on advertising in overseas markets in 1970. This would represent a 400 per cent increase since 1965.

Moves to ban cigarette advertising—already effective in Italy and on British television—spread to Ireland and to Canada, where the Canadian Broadcasting Corp. barred tobacco advertising beginning on Jan. 1, 1970. In the United States, governmental foes of cigarettes continued their efforts to curb such advertising, particularly on television and radio. The 5 biggest cigarette advertisers planned to remove

A "black hand" offers help to a "white hand." The advertisement was typical of the increasing use in 1969 of black models in all the advertising media.

John F. Murray Advertising Agency, Inc.

more than $200,000,000 from broadcast commercials and divert their advertising funds to other media. One network of 12 radio and television stations, Westinghouse's Group W, voluntarily banned cigarette advertising. *The New York Times* announced it would not accept cigarette advertising beginning Jan. 1, 1970, unless it contained a "hazardous" warning and listed the tar and nicotine contents of the brands. The major cigarette companies promptly dropped the newspaper rather than meet the requirements.

National advertising volume for 9 media in the United States was expected to advance to a record $10,300,000,000 in 1969, up from about $9,400,000,000 in 1968. The biggest media expected these totals: direct mail $2,900,000,000, network television $1,700,-000,000, spot television $1,300,000,000, and magazines $1,240,000,000. Advertising-agency billings continued to escalate, from $8,300,-000,000 in 1967 to $8,900,000,000 in 1968. The biggest agencies were the J. Walter Thompson Co., with billings of $638,000,000; McCann-Erickson $478,500,000; and Young & Rubicam $472,600,000. Outside the United States, agencies billed $4,800,000,000 in 1968, up from $3,700,000,000. The largest of these agencies were Dentsu, in Japan, with $376,-800,000; Lintas, in England, $155,900,000; and the London Press Exchange $141,400,000. Later in the year, a portion of the London Press Exchange, with billings of $85,000,000, was acquired by the Leo Burnett Co., Chicago, which became the fifth largest agency in the world with combined billings of $350,000,000. Another major development was the decision of the world's biggest agency, J. Walter Thompson Co., to go public. Mary Wells Lawrence, president of Wells Rich Greene, became the highest-paid woman executive in America, with a salary of $225,000.

The 125 biggest national advertisers in the United States put $4,800,000,000 into all kinds of promotion in 1968, a record. At the top of the list were Procter & Gamble, with an investment of $270,000,000, followed by General Motors at $214,000,000, and General Foods with $154,000,000. The Hershey Foods Corp., maker of the famous Hershey chocolate bar, decided, after 60 years of ignoring consumer advertising in the United States, to name an advertising agency. Ogilvy & Mather, New York, got the account. The biggest account change of 1969 was Lorillard, which moved $16,000,000 in cigarette billings to Benton & Bowles, New York.

JAMES V. O'GARA
Editor, *Advertising Age*

On the outskirts of Kabul the site of a new reservoir is surveyed. It will be part of a much-needed housing development financed by both the Government and private sources.

United Nations

AFGHANISTAN

Early in the 1960's, Afghanistan set its sights on embracing democracy through a constitutional monarchy and on entering more fully into the twentieth century through rapid economic development. While important steps had been taken by the end of the 1960's, the goals had yet to be fully realized.

The greatest progress was found in the political sphere. One of the most significant developments of 1969 came in September when an estimated 2,500,000 Afghans went to the polls to elect a 216-seat Wolesi Jirga (lower house of Parliament). Nearly 2,000 candidates stood for the elections, the second such exercise in parliamentary democracy (the first was in 1965) under the Constitution of 1964. But an essential element of democratic elections was missing: political parties. Although many of the candidates represented one or the other of four major "movements"—national, social, people's and progressive—there were no formal parties. The responsibility for this lay with Mohammad Zahir Shah, the Afghan ruler, who holds real

AFGHANISTAN

Area: 250,000 sq. mi.
Population: 16,500,000
Capital: Kabul (pop., 450,000)
Government: Mohammad Zahir Shah, king—1933; Noor Ahmad Etemadi, premier—1967
Gross National Product: $1,340,000,000
Monetary unit: afghani (45 afghani=U.S. $1.00)
Chief products: grains, cotton, oilseeds, fruits, lapis lazuli, carpets and rugs, leather goods
Foreign trade: exports, $65,000,000; imports, $140,000,000
Communications: 9,800 telephones
Transportation: roads, 1,240 mi.; no railroads
Education: 2 universities
Armed forces: about 80,000

power through the Army. He had failed to approve a Political Parties Bill, passed in 1968 by the Wolesi Jirga, in time to affect the elections. As most observers believe that the King would like to be remembered as the man who brought parliamentary democracy to Afghanistan, his failure to approve the bill, an essential move for a true parliamentary democracy, was somewhat inexplicable.

Following the election and the opening of a new Parliament on Oct. 14, the King called on Premier Noor Ahmad Etemadi to form a new Government. Etemadi had been prime minister since October 1967 when his predecessor, Mohammad Hashim Maiwandwal, resigned due to ill health. In the new cabinet, approved by the King on Dec. 2, the Prime Minister retained the post of foreign minister.

Economically the year saw few major developments. International lending institutions continued to provide economic assistance. The International Development Association (IDA) granted a $5,000,000 loan to help provide urgently needed highway maintenance. A grant of $1,700,000 to complement the IDA credit was provided by the UN Development Program. Exports and imports for the year showed little change. Exports, mainly fruits and nuts, cotton, karakul and carpets, totaled an estimated $65,-000,000, about the same as the year before. Imports—foodstuffs, textiles, machinery and used clothing (the last, $2,000,000)—remained at the 1968 level of about $140,000,000.

In international relations, Afghanistan had a quiet year. The highlight was the sending of a strong delegation, headed by the Premier and the Minister of Information and Culture, to the Islamic Summit Conference in Rabat, Morocco.

ARTHUR C. MILLER
Senior Editor, *The Asia Letter*

AFRICA, NORTH

The outstanding development of 1969 in North Africa was the Sept. 1 *coup d'état* in the oil-rich kingdom of Libya. A group of young officers led by 27-year-old Capt. Mohammad al-Qadafi, a Sandhurst-trained officer, toppled the 79-year-old, traditional, conservative and ailing King Mohammad Idris al-Senussi, while he was abroad, and established a republic headed by a Revolutionary Command Council. In the lightning coup that startled the world, both the Chief of Staff and the Director of Security were arrested, and the heir apparent, Prince Hassan al-Rida, quickly announced his abdication and support for the new regime.

The Revolutionary Command Council abolished all legislative institutions of the monarchy and announced that it was creating a "revolutionary and undoctrinal socialist state" which would transform Libya into a "progressive nation fighting against colonialism and racialism." On Sept. 8, Libya's first republican Government

Army officer Mohammad al-Qadafi makes Libya a republic after leading coup that ousted King Idris.

"Paris Match," Pictorial Parade

was formed, consisting of seven civilians and two army officers as ministers. Heading the Government as prime minister was 35-year-old Dr. Mahmoud Soliman al-Maghreby, an American-educated lawyer, who had been in prison until three weeks before the coup. Dr. Maghreby stated his Government's policy to be "freedom, socialism and Arab unity" and cooperation with other Arab countries "in the struggle against Israel." Overshadowing the Government in importance was the Revolutionary Council, whose chairman, Lt. Col. (formerly Capt.) Qadafi, was serving simultaneously as commander of the Libyan armed forces and as Libya's "strong man."

In mid-December, Qadafi headed Libya's delegation to the Arab summit conference in Rabat, Morocco. Following this conference, Qadafi played host to meetings in Tripoli with President Gamal Abdel Nasser, of the United Arab Republic, and Premier Gaafar al-Nimeiry, of Sudan. The three revolutionary leaders agreed to forge closer ties among their contiguous countries to coordinate action against Israel in the military, political and economic fields.

Upon assuming power, the Revolutionary Command Council announced that the new regime would not interfere with foreign-owned property and oil interests and that existing treaties would be honored. However, it indicated that it would not renew treaties governing foreign (British and U.S.) air bases in Libya. In November, the Government nationalized all foreign banks; and in December, agreements were reached with the United States and Great Britain respectively on the closing down of the American Wheelus Air Base by June 30, 1970, and the British bases at Tobruk and El Adem by Mar. 31, 1970. The agreement on Wheelus Field between the United States and Libya was originally to expire on Dec. 23, 1971, while the British had an indefinite defense agreement with Libya signed in 1953.

Shortly after the Libyan coup, an equally significant basic change in orientation and governmental power took place in Tunisia, albeit without a military coup. Beginning in September, the strongly socialist direction of the country's economic-development plan was arrested when its chief architect, Ahmed Ben Salah, was removed as head of the powerful superagency, the Ministry of Planning and Economic Affairs. Since 1961, Ben Salah, enjoying the full confidence of President Bourguiba and responsible only to him, had vigorously applied his development plan involving a policy of austerity, forced savings, nationalization of industry and farm collectivization. Later, President Bourguiba added the Ministry of Education to

UPI

At official dinner of Arab summit meeting held in Rabat, Morocco, in December, King Faisal of Saudi Arabia, King Hassan II (host), U.A.R. President Gamal Nasser, and King Hussein of Jordan (l to r) sit together.

Ben Salah's portfolio, thus making him the most powerful figure in the country after the President himself and the most logical heir apparent to Bourguiba's mantle. As a result of his stringent policies, Ben Salah became increasingly unpopular throughout the country. The situation came to a head in September when Ben Salah's efforts toward total collectivization of the country's agriculture led to widespread popular resentment and opposition as well as some serious rioting throughout most of Tunisia's rural areas. In addition, indications were confirmed of considerable mismanagement in the many cooperatives Ben Salah had instituted. The removal of Ben Salah was accompanied by governmental assurance that no one would be forced to join a cooperative and that the entire system of cooperatives already in existence would be reviewed.

It was also accompanied by a major shift in political power and governmental structure within the Bourguiba regime. Bahi Ladgham, who for years had simultaneously occupied the position of secretary of state to the presidency and secretary-general of the Destour Socialist Party, was given full responsibility for the Government, in essence being made prime minister save in title, and wielding much of the au-

thority previously exercised by President Bourguiba. Ben Salah remained in the Government as minister of education but only until the national elections, held on Nov. 2. President Bourguiba, the sole candidate, was reelected to his third five-year term and immediately formed a new Cabinet, in which Ladgham was made prime minister in fact, while Ben Salah was dropped as minister of education. Ben Salah's eclipse was completed with his removal from the ruling party, his exclusion from the National Assembly, and his denunciation by President Bourguiba for having been obsessed with power and vanity, and leading Tunisia to the brink of ruin.

As the year ended, the new Government of Bahi Ladgham was faced with the challenge of restoring the confidence of the people, overcoming economic stagnation, meeting the needs of the poorest section of the population, and evolving a workable development plan acceptable to the people. Added to the burdens of the Ladgham Government was a disaster caused by weeks of constant rain and floods that wrecked bridges, damaged railways, destroyed towns, left 300,000 people homeless, killed 542, and essentially brought the entire country's economy to a standstill.

"Paris Match," Pictorial Parade

Visit of Algerian President Boumedienne (r) to Moroccan King Hassan produces solidarity-cooperation pact.

In Algeria the year was marked by continued efforts at consolidation of authority by the incumbent Boumedienne regime. In March and July, two political trials, respectively involving 56 and 180 persons accused of plotting against the security of the state, were held. On the positive side, the regime took steps to resurrect the Algerian labor organization the UGTA (General Union of Algerian Workers) and to define its relationship to the country's single party, the FLN. In May, the UGTA was permitted to hold its third congress (earlier ones were held in 1963 and 1965) after careful preparation by the FLN (National Liberation Front). In the opinion of the authorities, the establishment of harmonious relations between the UGTA and FLN was deemed desirable at this moment in Algeria's history as the country embarked on a program of accelerated industrialization. In May, the Government introduced a sweeping reform of the Wilaya (province) administration. A charter for the Wilayas was adopted specifying the role of the Wilayas as links between local and national communities. Headed by an appointed Wali (governor), each Wilaya also has an elected popular assembly, though with only deliberative, consultative powers. On May 25, elections to the assemblies were held from a single list of candidates, numbering twice the number of seats to be filled, which was nominated by the FLN.

Algeria manifested its greater involvement in African affairs by playing host between July 21 and Aug. 1 to the first Pan-African Cultural Festival sponsored by the Organization of African Unity and attended by some four thousand artists.

In Morocco, the Government remained securely in the hands of King Hassan II, despite student unrest in February and continued criticism from the weakened opposition parties. Thus demands from the Istiqlal and UNFP parties to have the "state of emergency," in effect since 1965, lifted, before the local elections scheduled for October, were not heeded. Most political parties did not participate actively in the election, and "independent" candidates favorable to the regime were elected to 80 per cent of the seats. In February, King Hassan brought back Reda Guedira to the Cabinet as minister of state for planning. He had been a key figure in the Government until his withdrawal from the political scene in 1964. In October, the King replaced Dr. Mohammad Benhima as prime minister with Dr. Ahmed Laraki.

The major preoccupation of the Government during the year was with external relations. Following protracted negotiations, Morocco: (1) on Mar. 31, signed a treaty of association with the European Common Market (the same treaty was signed by Tunisia on Mar. 28); (2) on May 13, completed arrangements with Spain for the return of the enclave of Ifni to Moroccan sovereignty. In January, signaling the end of strained relations between Morocco and neighboring Algeria, President Boumedienne of Algeria paid his first official visit to Morocco, which culminated in a Treaty of Solidarity and Cooperation between Morocco and Algeria. King Hassan brought Morocco into greater involvement in Arab and Islamic affairs when, in September, he was the host of the first Islamic summit conference in Rabat, called as a consequence of the fire in Al Aksa Mosque in Jerusalem. In December he similarly played host to the Arab summit meeting devoted to the problem of Palestine and Israel.

BENJAMIN RIVLIN, Chairman and Professor
Department of Political Science
Brooklyn College/The City University of New York

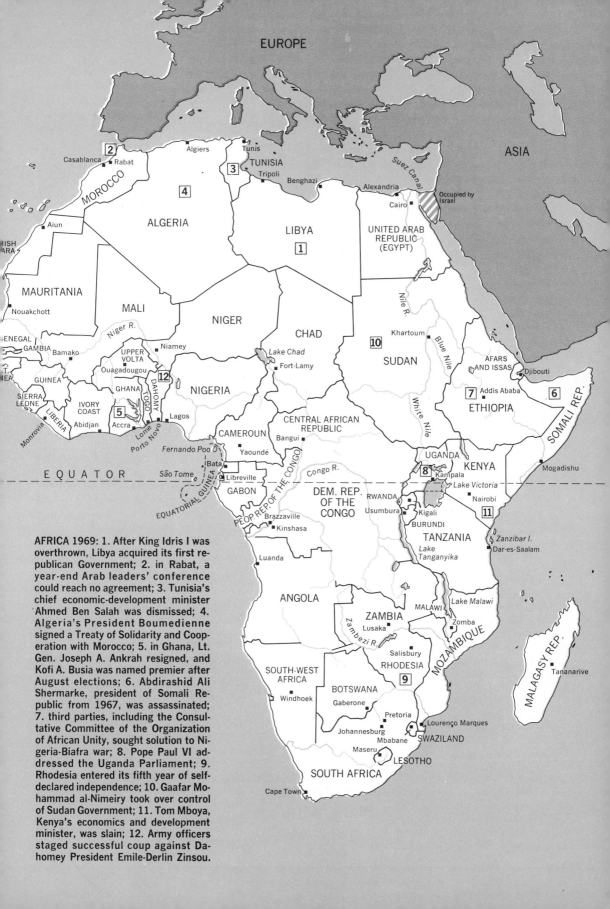

EUROPE

ASIA

Algiers

Tunis

Casablanca Rabat ☐2

☐3 TUNISIA
Tripoli

MOROCCO

☐4

Benghazi

LIBYA Alexandria

Suez Canal

Occupied by Israel

Cairo

Aiun

ALGERIA

☐1

UNITED ARAB REPUBLIC (EGYPT)

NISH ARA

MAURITANIA

Nouakchott

MALI

NIGER

CHAD

Nile R.

SUDAN

Khartoum

☐10

Blue Nile

AFARS AND ISSAS Djibouti

Niger R.

Niamey

Lake Chad

Fort-Lamy

ENEGAL
GAMBIA Bamako

UPPER VOLTA
Ouagadougou ☐12

☐7 Addis Ababa

White Nile

GUINEA
SIERRA LEONE

GHANA

NIGERIA

ETHIOPIA

☐6

SOMALI REP.

IVORY COAST
Abidjan

☐5 Accra
Lome
Porto Novo

DAHOMEY
TOGO

Lagos

LIBERIA
Monrovia

CAMEROUN

Yaoundé

CENTRAL AFRICAN REPUBLIC

Bangui

UGANDA

KENYA

EQUATOR

Fernando Poo
São Tome

Bata

Libreville

Congo R.

☐8 Kampala

Lake Victoria

Mogadishu

EQUATORIAL GUINEA

GABON

PEOP. REP. OF THE CONGO

DEM. REP. OF THE CONGO

RWANDA

Nairobi

☐11

Brazzaville

Kinshasa

Usumbura

Kigali

BURUNDI

Zanzibar I.
Dar-es-Saalam

Luanda

TANZANIA

Lake Tanganyika

ANGOLA

ZAMBIA

MALAWI

Lake Malawi

Lusaka

Zambezi R.

Zomba

MOZAMBIQUE

Salisbury

MALAGASY REP.

Tananarive

SOUTH-WEST AFRICA

RHODESIA

☐9

Windhoek

BOTSWANA

Gaberone

Pretoria

Lourenço Marques

Johannesburg

SWAZILAND

Mbabane

Maseru

LESOTHO

SOUTH AFRICA

Cape Town

AFRICA 1969: 1. After King Idris I was overthrown, Libya acquired its first republican Government; 2. in Rabat, a year-end Arab leaders' conference could reach no agreement; 3. Tunisia's chief economic-development minister Ahmed Ben Salah was dismissed; 4. Algeria's President Boumedienne signed a Treaty of Solidarity and Cooperation with Morocco; 5. in Ghana, Lt. Gen. Joseph A. Ankrah resigned, and Kofi A. Busia was named premier after August elections; 6. Abdirashid Ali Shermarke, president of Somali Republic from 1967, was assassinated; 7. third parties, including the Consultative Committee of the Organization of African Unity, sought solution to Nigeria-Biafra war; 8. Pope Paul VI addressed the Uganda Parliament; 9. Rhodesia entered its fifth year of self-declared independence; 10. Gaafar Mohammad al-Nimeiry took over control of Sudan Government; 11. Tom Mboya, Kenya's economics and development minister, was slain; 12. Army officers staged successful coup against Dahomey President Emile-Derlin Zinsou.

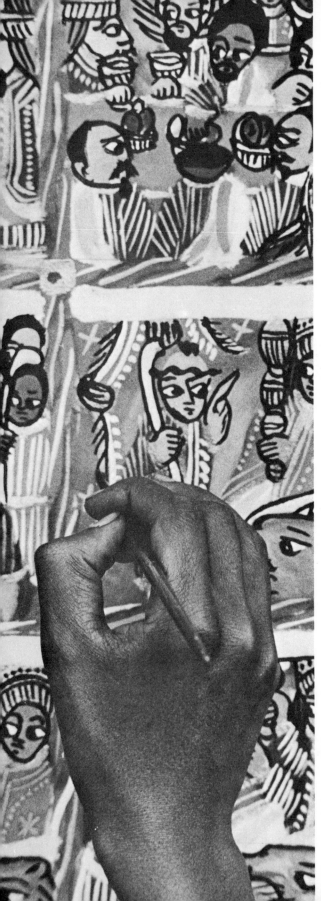

africa, sub-sahara

Black Africa ended its "decade of independence" wrestling with the same problems that plagued it when independence first swept across the continent.

Those problems included the conflict between tribal and national loyalties, the lack of political stability and true economic independence, the confrontation with white-ruled southern Africa, the widespread existence of political opportunism and corruption, the necessity of improving education, economic organization and political understanding, and the need to narrow gaps between the elite and the masses, between urban and rural populations. Some countries made sound attacks on these problems; others continued—sometimes wittingly, sometimes not—to confuse words with deeds.

In general, the events of 1969 underlined the depth of the problems. Some surfaced in disturbing forms such as tribalism in Kenya; others, like the Nigerian civil war, continued to elude solution.

The year was not without a hopeful event, however. Some observers believed that in the long run it might prove to be the most significant African political occurrence of the year.

Ghana. That event was the orderly return to civilian rule in Ghana. There the military/police-controlled National Liberation Council (NLC) handed the reins of government back to civilians after the August elections.

The NLC had ruled Ghana since the February 1966 overthrow of President Kwame Nkrumah. The transfer followed the drafting of a new constitution by an 18-member commission, its approval by a 149-member Constituent Assembly and the resumption of national political life, including the formation of new political parties, and a 4-month electoral campaign.

The Progress Party captured 105 of the 140 National Assembly seats in the Aug. 29 general election. Its leader, Oxford-trained sociologist Dr. Kofi A. Busia, was named prime minister.

The election outcome reflected ethnic cleavage. It tended to restrict the Ewes, of the Volta region in southeastern Ghana, to representation

In the act of creation: the story of Solomon and the Queen of Sheba is told in small sections on a long canvas by a painter at a school in Addis Ababa.

Marc and Evelyne Bernheim from Rapho Guillumette Pictures

by members of Ewe Komla Gbedemah's National Alliance of Liberals. Some quarters interpreted these results as indicative of tribal problems ahead. Others felt they reflected local issues or factors peculiar to this election such as allegations of corruption against Gbedemah and his association with the ousted Nkrumah.

As one of its final actions the Constituent Assembly endorsed the idea of a three-year presidential commission consisting of the NLC's three top leaders: Brigadier A. A. Afrifa, Police Chief J. W. K. Harlley and General A. K. Ocran. Some observers regarded the action as NLC-inspired and predicted that political power would remain in military/police hands despite the civilian facade. Others less skeptically viewed it as a sensible transition move which tended to involve top military/police leaders in making the new civilian government a success.

In any case the importance of Ghana's return to civilian rule was that (1) it proved an orderly transfer could be made and (2) provided a model for making it.

If events in Ghana suggested a path toward order, those in several other areas underlined the tendencies toward fragmentation and conflict.

Nigeria. At year's end the Nigerian civil war was dragging on toward its thirtieth month. The quick end, which came on Jan. 12, 1970, was not then in sight.

Modern African art flourishes. The figure above, being copied from a prized original, is for export from Ivory Coast. Below: The Virgin Mary pounds yams in a carving for Ibadan University chapel doors, Nigeria.

Photos, Marc and Evelyne Bernheim from Rapho Guillumette Pictures

Photos UPI

In Biafra (top) a priest (in white) must make a terrible decision: who are to be sent home after treatment at a hospital—which, because food and supplies are short, means the sick past help. Emperor Haile Selassie of Ethiopia addresses meeting (above) of the Organization of African Unity at its headquarters in Addis Ababa.

Militarily, neither side seemed able to dominate the other. Nigerian forces seized the Biafran provisional capital, Umuahia, in April; Biafran forces recaptured Owerri several days later. Thereafter the fighting bogged down. The federals were hampered by long supply lines, lack of trained manpower, flagging morale and some fears among Nigerian leaders that crushing Biafra militarily would exacerbate the tribal tensions from which the war partly sprang.

Reduced to a landlocked enclave of about 6,000 square miles, Biafra was clearly in no position to win the war militarily, despite unofficial arms support from France. Nonetheless, secessionist soldiers and Swedish-piloted aircraft continued harassing raids against federal-held territory, seriously cutting federal oil production.

Third parties continued their efforts to arrange a settlement. Optimism over negotiations rose in January 1969 at the London Commonwealth Conference; in April when the Organization of African Unity's Consultative Committee met with representatives of the belligerents in Monrovia, Liberia; in August both during Pope

NATION	POPULATION (latest est., in millions)	CAPITAL	AREA (Approx., in sq. mi.)	HEAD OF STATE AND/OR GOVERNMENT, DATE INSTALLED (as of January 1, 1970)
Algeria	13.3	Algiers	846,124	Houri Boumedienne, pres. and prem., 1965
Botswana	0.6	Gaberones	222,000	Sir Seretse Khama, pres., 1966
Burundi	3.5	Usumbura	10,747	Michel Micombero, pres., 1966
Cameroun	5.7	Yaoundé	193,681	Ahmadou Ahidjo, pres., 1960
Central African Rep.	1.5	Bangui	240,000	Jean Bedel Bokassa, pres. and prem., 1966
Chad	3.5	Fort-Lamy	485,750	François Tombalbaye, pres., 1960
Congo, Dem. Rep. of the	17.1	Kinshasa	904,754	Joseph Mobutu, pres., 1965
Congo, People's Rep.	0.9	Brazzaville	134,749	Marien Ngouabi, pres., 1968
Dahomey	2.7	Porto-Novo	45,560	Paul Emile de Souza, head, military junta, 1969
Equatorial Guinea	0.3	Santa Isabel	10,900	Francisco Macias Nguema, pres., 1968
Ethiopia	24.4	Addis Ababa	395,000	Haile Selassie, emperor, 1930
Gabon	0.5	Libreville	103,089	Albert Bongo, pres., 1967
Gambia	0.4	Bathurst	4,000	Sir Dauda Jawara, p. min., 1965
Ghana	8.6	Accra	92,100	Dr. Kofi A. Busia, prem., 1969
Guinea	3.9	Conakry	95,350	Ahmed Sékou Touré, pres., 1958
Ivory Coast	4.2	Abidjan	127,800	F. Houphouet-Boigny, pres., 1960
Kenya	10.2	Nairobi	224,960	Jomo Kenyatta, pres., 1964
Lesotho	0.9	Maseru	11,716	Moshoeshoe II, king, 1966 Leabua Jonathan, p. min., 1966
Liberia	1.2	Monrovia	43,000	William Tubman, pres., 1943
Libya	1.9	Tripoli	680,000	Mohammad al-Qadafi, head of Revolutionary Command Council, 1969 Mahmoud Soliman al-Maghreby, p. min., 1969
Malagasy Rep.	6.7	Tananarive	229,602	Philibert Tsiranana, pres., 1960
Malawi	4.3	Zomba	47,949	H. Kamuzu Banda, pres., 1966
Mali	4.9	Bamako	465,000	Yoro Diakite, head of state, 1968
Mauritania	1.1	Nouakchott	419,000	Moktar O. Daddah, pres. and prem., 1958
Mauritius	0.8	Port Louis	720	Sir Seewoosagur Ramgoolam, p. min., 1968
Morocco	15.0	Rabat	174,580	Hassan II, king, 1961 Ahmed Laraki, p. min., 1969
Niger	3.7	Niamey	489,000	Hamani Diori, pres. and prem., 1960
Nigeria	53.7	Lagos	357,000	Yakubu Gowon, chief of state, 1966
Rhodesia	4.8	Salisbury	150,820	Ian D. Smith, p. min., 1964
Rwanda	3.5	Kigali	10,000	Gregoire Kayibanda, pres. and prem., 1961
Senegal	3.9	Dakar	75,750	Léopold Senghor, pres., 1960
Sierra Leone	2.5	Freetown	27,968	Siaka Stevens, p. min., 1968
Somalia	2.8	Mogadishu	246,135	Mohammad Siyad Barreh, pres. Supreme Revolutionary Council, 1969
South Africa, Rep. of	19.6	Pretoria Cape Town	472,359	J. J. Fouche, pres., 1968 Balthazar J. Vorster, p. min., 1966
Sudan	15.2	Khartoum	967,500	Gaafar Mohammad al-Nimeiry, pres. Revolutionary Council, 1969
Swaziland	0.4	Mbabane	6,705	Sobhuza II, king, 1921 Makhosini Dlamini, p. min., 1968
Tanzania	12.9	Dar es Salaam	363,000	Julius Nyerere, pres., 1964
Togo	1.8	Lomé	22,000	Etienne Eyadema, pres., 1967
Tunisia	4.8	Tunis	48,300	Habib Bourguiba, pres., 1957 Bahia Ladgham, p. min., 1969
Uganda	8.3	Kampala	94,000	Milton Obote, pres., 1966
United Arab Republic	32.5	Cairo	386,198	Gamal Abdel Nasser, pres., 1952
Upper Volta	5.3	Ouagadougou	105,900	Sangoulé Lamizana, pres., 1966
Zambia	4.2	Lusaka	290,000	Kenneth Kaunda, pres., 1964

Paul's visit to Kampala, Uganda, and when Ibo leader Dr. Nnambi Azikiwe made the first contacts with the Nigerian Government; and late in the year due to a spate of hopeful rumors. The negotiating stance of neither side changed substantially, however.

As the war dragged on, starvation, malnutrition and disease continued to claim the lives of thousands of innocent victims. The International Red Cross suspended flights into Biafra after one of its planes was downed in early June. Despite prolonged efforts it failed to reach an agreement with the warring parties over resumption of mercy flights. Joint Church Aid and Caritas International continued night flights of relief food to Uli airport; these operations served to cover flights of arms into Biafran territory.

Chad. Northeast of Nigeria in the vast, parched, little-populated former French colony of Chad, the Government of President François Tombalbaye came under increasing attack from Frolina-movement guerrillas. While dismissing the attacks as mere banditry, the Government still relied heavily on French military aid, estimated at more than two thousand men.

Although inept government administration was generally regarded as the basic cause of unrest, ethnic and cultural aspects were also present. They set Muslim, Arabized peoples of the northern desert against the animist or Christianized blacks of the south. At the same time, rebellions springing from ethnic and cultural differences continued in southern Sudan and in Ethiopia's Red Sea province of Eritrea.

Despite popular fears of a "little Vietnam," the French Government defended its involvement in Chad as necessary under the terms of defense agreements. Some commentators also stressed France's desire for a base in the heart of Africa from which to protect French commercial and mineral interests, particularly the uranium deposits in neighboring Central African Republic. A number of observers were also struck by the anomaly of France's abetting secession in Nigeria and suppressing it in Chad.

Rhodesia. As the breakaway colony entered its fifth year of self-declared independence in November, it was clear that Britain's policy of economic sanctions had failed, at least in the short run.

Instead of breaking Rhodesia economically, the sanctions appeared to have stimulated economic diversification and ingenuity. They had also produced political cohesion among the ruling minority. In June the white-dominated electorate passed a referendum on a republican constitution, later adopted by Parliament, that pushed Rhodesia nearer South African-style apartheid. It amended the former Declaration of Rights and virtually divided the total land area equally between whites and blacks, despite a 20 to 1 black-white ratio in the population. More significantly, the constitution linked eventual African "parity" with white political representation to a rise in African income-tax remittances, a device that forestalls the possibility of black majority rule indefinitely.

Though accurate economic information was difficult to get or assess, it appeared that Rhodesia's 1969 exports would show the first increase since 1965. Industrial and mining output as well as agricultural production (up 20 per cent over 1968) were expected to set records. Retail sales rose as did tourism and even African employment.

Despite these statistics, Britain maintained that sanctions would eventually prevail. Some British economists argued, for instance, that Rhodesia's real growth rate was not nearly high enough to prevent eventual stagnation. Time alone would prove the validity of this view. However, the Government's invoking of emergency powers to thwart a mid-November strike by white railway workers, and the December trial of two whites accused of contravening Rhodesia's Official Secrets Act suggested that the battle for economic viability had not been won by the end of 1969.

Portuguese Africa. Another external threat to southern African governments was that of guerrilla infiltrations from the north. In fact, though liberation movements made little headway in 1969, Portuguese authorities claimed gains (both in fighting and in defections) against guerrillas in Angola and Mozambique. The assassination of Eduardo Mondlane in early February deprived the Mozambique Liberation Front (Frelimo) of its unifying figure; its leadership was seriously disrupted in early November.

Visiting Portugal's African territories in April, Premier Marcelo Caetano spoke of extending the administrative autonomy of local governments and African involvement in politics and administration. He implied that these policies, combined with increased military effectiveness, would solve Portugal's guerrilla problems. Other Portuguese Government spokesmen admitted, however, that these principles could not be expected to yield solutions until the 1980's.

The year saw threats to the stability of East Africa, hitherto a region of relative calm.

Kenya. The assassination on July 5 of Economic Planning and Development Minister Tom Mboya shattered the apparent tranquility of Kenya. Deep-rooted Luo-Kikuyu tribal animosities flared. Luos stoned the car of President Jomo Kenyatta, a Kikuyu, at funeral services for Mboya, a Luo. Tribal tensions grew when a Kikuyu was convicted of the assassination

The murder of Tom Mboya, Kenya's gifted economic minister, brings anguish to women of his tribe, the Luo.

UPI

and shortly thereafter when many Kikuyus, some voluntarily, some under duress, subscribed to tribal oaths. Through his inaction, President Kenyatta appeared to condone the oaths.

Following the second stoning of his car, this time in the Luo stronghold of Kisumu, the President detained leaders of the opposition Kenya People's Union and banned the party on charges of conspiring to subvert the republic. This move gave the ruling Kenya African National Union a clear field in the general elections held in December. It also limited the scope of discussion during the electoral campaign since all candidates subscribed to the development philosophy outlined in the party's manifesto. Meanwhile, tribal enmity continued to bubble just beneath the surface of Kenyan life.

Somalia. The assassination of President Abdirashid Ali Shermarke on Oct. 15 led to a military coup on Oct. 21, although the two events were unrelated. The coup ended what many observers had regarded as a promising start in Somalia toward a firmly rooted democratic government.

Somalia had been the only newly independent African state to effect a change of government through the ballot. While its National Assembly elections in late March had returned the ruling Somali Youth League to power with a reduced majority, all but one representative later joined the league, a situation that led to military charges of clique rule.

Zambia. While the elections of December 1968 returned President Kenneth Kaunda to firm power, they also underlined Lozi tribal dissatisfaction with his rule. Before this problem could be resolved, anti-white demonstrations broke out following a controversial ruling by the all-white High Court. Tribal friction also surfaced within the ruling United National Independence Party's inner circles over the role of politicians of the Bemba tribe.

At year's end President Kaunda appeared to have won control of the situation by moving to reorganize the party machinery, by conciliating the Lozi and by diverting public attention through successful moves to nationalize Zambian copper production. Nevertheless, the divisive tribal frictions remained, if muted.

The International Picture. Coordinating meaningful efforts above the national level still eluded Africa's newly independent countries. Though it had had some successes, the Organization of African Unity failed to act effectively in the Nigerian crisis. In addition, its members were split on the question of how to confront white-ruled southern Africa.

UPI

To curtail outbreak of robberies in Kenya, President Kenyatta, at May Day rally, says police will be armed.

Although numerous regional cooperation schemes have been proposed, few have been carried out. The two-year-old East African Community continued its promising start. Distrust among the partner states—Kenya, Tanzania and Uganda—was still strong, however. By the end of 1969, it had yet to tackle such hard problems as industry allocation and the formation of a regional market (to replace national markets).

On the world scene the African nations themselves remained unable to generate action needed to solve the continent's problems. The sizable African bloc in the United Nations influenced little action there though it guided the passage of numerous resolutions. In addition, Africa commanded little interest among the superpowers, a fact underlined by the failure of the Nixon administration to enunciate an African policy during its first year in office.

See South Africa, Republic of.

FREDERIC HUNTER
African Correspondent,
The Christian Science Monitor

The White House

AGNEW, SPIRO T.

On the morning after Spiro Theodore Agnew was nominated vice-president at the Republican convention in Miami, *The Miami Herald,* in on-the-street interviews, asked a dozen or more passersby the question: "What is Spiro Agnew?" Almost no one knew the answer. One woman said she thought it was a hair spray. A Baltimore city official and subsequently elected governor of Maryland against a Democratic candidate, a man who stressed law and order with racist overtones, Agnew had never before been in the national spotlight. He had been tapped by Nixon in the belief that as a Southerner he would underwrite the Southern strategy in the Nixon-Agnew campaign. The total of 87 electoral votes supplied by 8 Southern and border states gave the Republican ticket a winning total of 301.

Agnew began modestly enough. His humor was often self-deprecatory. He accounted himself a loyal lieutenant of the President, who knew his place and intended to keep it. As the months passed, however, he grew more and more bold. The climax in the headlines came with his attack on network television and the unfair treatment he said had been accorded the President. Agnew followed this up with an attack on *The New York Times* and *The Washington Post,* which had both been critical of administration policy. An audience in Montgomery, Ala., warmly applauded this attack.

The question widely raised was whether Agnew voiced sentiments that the President himself did not care to express but left to his loyal lieutenant, or whether the Vice-President was on his own. The White House repeatedly said that Agnew spoke for himself without direction or guidance from on high. Nevertheless, the suspicion persisted that he was the President's "other voice." Of the loyalty between them there could be no question. At the end of the year, Nixon sent his Vice-President on an Asian tour where beyond doubt he spoke for the Nixon administration.

MARQUIS W. CHILDS
Contributing Editor
St. Louis Post-Dispatch

Grant Heilman

The feedlot, which serves 100,000 cattle, at Monfort, near Greeley, Col., is probably the largest in the United States. In the great farming states, vast acreages rather than family-size farms are the rule.

AGRICULTURE

The year 1969 brought significant developments in U.S. agriculture. Crop yields set a new record, and farm output continued at or slightly above the all-time high of 1968. Although net farm income in 1969 was estimated at about $1,000,000,000 more than the $14,800,000,000 level of 1968, farmers were still caught in a cost-price squeeze. The rise in 1969 was far from adequate.

Other agricultural highlights of 1969 include: efforts to develop new commodity programs adapted to the needs of the 1970's; proposals for the most comprehensive and far-reaching attack on malnutrition ever presented in the United States; activities aimed at expanding U.S. agricultural exports; and increased attention to rural development.

New Farm Programs. The existing farm programs provided by the Food and Agriculture Act of 1965 expire after the 1970 crops. New legislation is needed to take effect in 1971. For years the most persistent characteristic of American agriculture has been the ability of farmers to produce in excess of market demand, both foreign and domestic. The objective of farm legislation is to provide programs that will regulate production and result in satisfactory farm income without inhibiting the growth of markets or placing needless obstacles in the way of efficient farm operation.

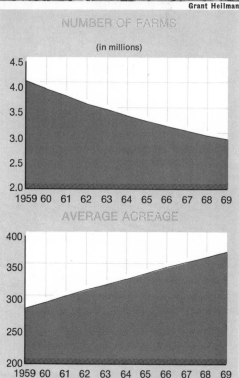

Following meetings with members of Congress, regional conferences attended by farm and rural leaders from 32 states, and numerous consultations with representatives of farm organizations and the land-grant colleges, the administration recommended a series of farm-program approaches to the Congress. The proposals were designed to maintain and improve farm income, to restore more decision-making to the individual farmer, and to keep the marketplace free so that U.S. farm commodities will be able to compete more effectively, especially in foreign markets.

Malnutrition in the U.S. There is a double paradox in U.S. malnutrition: first, that it exists in the midst of plenty; second, that it is caused by lack of knowledge as well as lack of money.

"The moment is at hand to put an end to hunger in America itself for all time." With these words, President Nixon proposed in 1969 the largest, most comprehensive effort to eliminate poverty-based hunger and malnutrition ever advanced by any administration. It would involve complementary programs of realistic family assistance and expanded food-aid and nutrition education.

At the end of fiscal year 1969, 6,700,000 low-income people were receiving food stamps or donated foods, compared with 5,600,000 a year earlier. An expansion of the Food Stamp Program was proposed that would enable low-income families to purchase enough food for a nutritionally adequate diet. Stamps would be provided at no cost to those in the lowest income brackets and at not more than 30 per cent of income for others.

More than 20,000,000 children participated in the National School Lunch Program. About 300,000 children received nutritional breakfasts under the School Breakfast Program. Supplementary food donations aimed at correcting nutritional deficiencies in expectant and new mothers, infants and young children were being provided to more than 40,000 persons in 21 states and the District of Columbia at the end of the fiscal year.

During the year 1969 about 5,000 nutrition aides, recruited from low-income groups, were working with poor families in about 650 counties and cities helping them with food buying, budgeting and food preparation and educating them in nutrition. This program will be expanded as rapidly as feasible.

To make the administration and coordination of USDA food programs more effective, a Food and Nutrition Service was established as a separate Department agency in August 1969. In December, President Nixon convened a White House Conference on Food, Nutrition, and Health to help promote a positive, viable national nutrition policy.

U.S. Agricultural Exports. One of U.S. agriculture's pressing problems has been a downtrend in agricultural exports, especially during 1968 and early 1969. Although a heavy world wheat surplus and a prolonged U.S. dock strike contributed to the decline, a more fundamental problem has been the world trend toward increased nationalism and trade protectionlsm. This has been true particularly within the European Economic Community, the largest foreign market for American farm products. In an attempt to promote an atmosphere of freer trade, the administration held continuing discussions with the EEC and major importing nations, including Japan. An Export Marketing Service was established in the U.S. Department of Agriculture to improve the efficiency with which the department works with private enterprise in developing export markets.

Rural Development. Another area of vital concern in 1969 centered on efforts to help rural America participate more fully in national growth and development. Since 1950 the U.S. population has grown by 50,000,000 people—and the total increase has been in urban areas. Many current urban problems stem from this situation. By the year 2000, another 100,000,000 Americans may be added. Will they be concentrated in already-crowded urban and metropolitan areas, or will there be a healthy dispersal of population into smaller cities, county-seat towns and villages of rural America? This is one of the most serious problems America faces today. One of the administration's major aims therefore is to help local people make rural America a more attractive place to live, economically, culturally and socially. A reorganization of the USDA Rural Development Program was begun.

With strong local leadership and government assistance in community planning, encouragement to industry to locate in rural areas, and the establishment of modern facilities and services, the administration hopes to create a climate of opportunity in rural America. This climate should counteract recent trends and result in significant population growth in nonmetropolitan areas. In addition, the proposed Family Assistance Program should reach into rural areas much more effectively than existing welfare programs. It is estimated that some 400,000 low-income families living in farming areas might be eligible for assistance under the President's proposals.

In pursuit of other major objectives in 1969, the administration sought to protect the quality and safety of U.S. food. Significant strides were made toward achieving the ultimate goal of a single, uniform standard of wholesomeness and truthful labeling for all meat and poultry supplies.

CLIFFORD M. HARDIN
U.S. Secretary of Agriculture

ALABAMA

On July 29, in an election ordered by the U.S. Supreme Court (because the names of 6 black candidates had been omitted from the general-election ballot in November 1968), Negroes won control of Greene County, where they outnumber whites by 10,000 to 3,000. □ Near Selma a new warehouse and office building were completed to serve as headquarters of the Southwest Alabama Farmers Cooperative Association. Covering 10 counties, it is one of the oldest and largest of black co-ops in the rural South.

ALASKA

Expansion of the state's oil industry (the Arctic field may prove to be one of the world's largest) aroused the fears of two groups: the state's 55,000 aborigines (Eskimos, Aleuts and Indians) and conservationists. In an effort to forestall the possibility of being deprived of their lands, the natives filed claims that covered almost the whole state. Though various proposals were put forward, the issue remained unsettled through 1969. Besides the threat to the wilderness of plans for an 800-mile pipeline system and a 53-mile supplementary road (permission for the road was granted in August by Secretary of the Interior Hickel), conservationists were also alarmed by plans for powerful underground nuclear tests at Amchitka Island (in the Aleutian chain), a wildlife refuge. □ George Sharrock was named director of the Federal Field Committee for Development Planning in Alaska.

ALBANIA

Albania's close alliance with Communist China went unimpaired in 1969. After eight years of what Tirana quite rightly calls "their special relationship," China and Albania have if anything broadened their mutual commitments. At the end of 1968, new loans to Albania were arranged by Premier Chou En-lai. The Albanian Chamber of Commerce, breaking a policy of secretiveness, disclosed that Chinese-Albanian trade had risen between 1961 and 1966 with a great deal of aid earmarked "for realizing economic plans, including long-term plans."

In an ironic defense of Rumania's position vis-à-vis the Soviet Union, Albania denounced Moscow's new doctrine of "limited sovereignty." The doctrine, used by the Soviets to justify the 1968 invasion of Czechoslovakia, was denounced by the Albanian Premier as "imperialist and fascist as that of Mussolini, expressed in the 1926 treaty between the [prewar Albanian] feudal regime and Mussolini's

fascist regime." The Prime Minister noted that "on Apr. 7, 1939, Mussolini acted precisely according to this concept in occupying Albania, and the Moscow clique applied the same fascist concept in occupying Czechoslovakia on Aug. 21, 1968." Nevertheless, while criticizing Moscow for its behavior toward Czechoslovakia, Tirana expressed no particular affection for either the former Czechoslovak party chief Alexander Dubcek, who was termed "capitulationist and revisionist," or the old-line, pro-Moscow faction of former party leader Antonin Novotny.

In economic matters, Albania showed record improvement. By the end of 1969, it had become one of the few countries to abolish personal income taxes. Describing the economy as booming, Tirana announced that its entire population of 2,100,000 would have no more income taxes to pay. At the same time, farm debts were forgiven and prices of basic commodities and equipment were slashed. With industrial development advancing and agriculture fully collectivized, Albania's gross national product stood at about $550,000,000. The per capita consumption of goods increased between 1951 and 1969 by 2.5 times, while the real wages of workers rose 1.7 times, and those of the peasantry doubled. As usual, in announcing the new measures, the party resolution contrasted Albanian tax relief with conditions in "the countries where the modern revisionists are in power [with their] uninterrupted rises in prices, taxes and unemployment, bringing about greater exploitation and misery of the working masses."

JAMES CHACE
Managing Editor, *Foreign Affairs*

ALBANIA

Area: 10,629 sq. mi.
Population: 2,100,000
Capital: Tirana (pop., 170,000)
Government: Enver Hoxha, Communist Party secretary—1946; Mehmet Shehu, premier—1954
Gross national product: $550,000,000
Monetary unit: lek (4 leks = U.S. $1.00)
Chief products: grains, timber, copper, livestock, oil, textiles
Foreign trade: exports, $60,000,000; imports, $98,000,000
Communications: 10,150 telephones, 104,873 radios, 2,000 TV sets, 19 daily newspapers
Transportation: roads, 1,922 mi.; 1,900 passenger cars; railroads, 94 mi.
Education: 465,557 elementary and secondary students, 1 university
Armed forces: 38,000

See map on page 185

FROM U.S.	COUNTRIES	TO U.S.
Robert G. Neumann	AFGHANISTAN	Abdullah Malikyar
	ALGERIA[a]	
John D. Lodge	ARGENTINA	Rafael M. Vazquez[b]
Walter L. Rice	AUSTRALIA	Keith Waller
John P. Humes	AUSTRIA	Karl Gruber
Eileen R. Donovan	BARBADOS	Valerie T. McComie
John S. D. Eisenhower	BELGIUM	Walter Loridan
E. V. Siracusa	BOLIVIA	Julio Sanjines-Goytia
(vacant)	BOTSWANA	Chief Lenchwe II
C. B. Elbrick	BRAZIL	Celso Diniz[b]
John M. McSweeney	BULGARIA	Luben Guerassimov
Arthur W. Hummel, Jr.	BURMA	U Hla Maung
Thomas P. Melady	BURUNDI	Terence Nsanze
Lloyd M. Rives[b]	CAMBODIA	Thay Sok[b]
Lewis Hoffacker	CAMEROUN	Joseph Owono
Adolph W. Schmidt	CANADA	Marcel Cadieux
Geoffrey W. Lewis	CENTRAL AFR. REP.	Michel Gallin-Douathe
R. Strausz-Hupe	CEYLON	Oliver Weerasinghe
T. A. Todman	CHAD	Lazare Massibe
Edward M. Korry	CHILE	Domingo Santa Maria
Walter P. McConaughy	CHINA (TAIWAN)	Chow Shu-kai
Jack H. Vaughn	COLOMBIA	Douglas Botero Boshell
Sheldon B. Vance	CONGO, DEM. REP. OF THE	Justin-Marie Bomboko
Clarence A. Boonstra	COSTA RICA	Luis Demetrio Tinoco
David H. Popper	CYPRUS	Zenon Rossides
Malcolm Toon	CZECHOSLOVAKIA	Ivan Rohal-Ilkiv
M. J. Looram, Jr.	DAHOMEY	Maxime-Leopold Zollner
G. Dudley, Jr.	DENMARK	Torben Ronne
Francis E. Meloy, Jr.	DOMINICAN REP.	Mario Read-Vittini
Edson O. Sessions	ECUADOR	C. Mantilla-Ortega
William G. Bowdler	EL SALVADOR	Julio Rivera
Lewis Hoffacker	EQUATORIAL GUINEA	(vacant)
William O. Hall	ETHIOPIA	Minasse Haile
Val Peterson	FINLAND	Olavi Munkki
R. Sargent Shriver	FRANCE	Charles Lucet
Richard Funkhouser	GABON	Leonard Antoine Badinga
L. Dean Brown	GAMBIA	(vacant)
Kenneth Rush	GERMANY (W.)	Rolf Pauls
Thomas W. McElhiney	GHANA	Ebenezer M. Debrah
Walter H. Annenberg	GREAT BRITAIN	John Freeman
Henry J. Tasca	GREECE	Basil G. Vitsaxis
Nathaniel Davis	GUATEMALA	F. Linares Aranda
(vacant)	GUINEA	Fadiala Keita
Spencer King	GUYANA	John Carter
Clinton E. Knox	HAITI	Arthur Bonhomme
Hewson A. Ryan	HONDURAS	A. Alvarez Martinez
Alfred Puhan	HUNGARY	Janos Nagy
Luther I. Replogle	ICELAND	Magnus V. Magnusson
Kenneth B. Keating	INDIA	Nawab A. Y. Jung
Francis J. Galbraith	INDONESIA	Soedjatmoko
Douglas MacArthur 2d	IRAN	Aslan Afshar
	IRAQ[a]	
John D. J. Moore	IRELAND	Sean O hEideain[b]
Walworth Barbour	ISRAEL	Yitzhak Rabin
Graham A. Martin	ITALY	Egidio Ortona
John Root	IVORY COAST	Timothee Ahoua
Vincent de Roulet	JAMAICA	Egerton R. Richardson
Armin H. Meyer	JAPAN	Takeso Shimoda
Harrison M. Symmes	JORDAN	Abdul Hamid Sharaf
Robinson McIlvaine	KENYA	L. O. Kibinge
William J. Porter	KOREA (S.)	Dong Jo Kim
John P. Walsh	KUWAIT	Talat Al-Ghoussein
G. McMurtrie Godley	LAOS	Khamking Souvanlasy
Dwight J. Porter	LEBANON	Najati Kabbani
(vacant)	LESOTHO	M. T. Mashologu
S. Z. Westerfield, Jr.	LIBERIA	S. Edward Peal
Joseph Palmer 2d	LIBYA	Fathi Abidia
Kingdon Gould, Jr.	LUXEMBOURG	Jean Wagner
Anthony D. Marshall	MALAGASY REP.	Rene G. Ralison[b]
Marshall P. Jones	MALAWI	Nyemba W. Mbekeani
J. W. Lydman	MALAYSIA	Tan Sri Ong Yoke Lin
R. Strausz-Hupe	MALDIVE IS.	Abdul Sattar
G. Edward Clark	MALI	Seydou Traore
J. C. Pritzlaff, Jr.	MALTA	Arvid Pardo
	MAURITANIA[a]	
(vacant)	MAURITIUS	Pierre G. G. Balancy
Robert H. McBride	MEXICO	Hugo B. Margain
(vacant)	MOROCCO	Ahmed Osman
Carol C. Laise	NEPAL	Kul S. Sharma
J. W. Middendorf 2d	NETHERLANDS	R. B. van Lynden
Kenneth Franzheim	NEW ZEALAND	Frank Corner
Kennedy M. Crockett	NICARAGUA	G. Sevilla-Sacasa
Samuel C. Adams, Jr.	NIGER	Adamou Mayaki
William C. Trueheart	NIGERIA	Joe Iyalla
Philip K. Crowe	NORWAY	Arne Gunneng
Joseph S. Farland	PAKISTAN	Agha Hilaly
Robert M. Sayre	PANAMA	Roberto R. Aleman
J. R. Ylitalo	PARAGUAY	Roque J. Avila
Taylor G. Belcher	PERU	Fernando Berckemeyer
Henry A. Byroade	PHILIPPINES	E. V. Lagdameo
Walter J. Stoessel, Jr.	POLAND	Jerzy Michalowski
Ridgway B. Knight	PORTUGAL	Vasco Vieira Garin
L. C. Meeker	RUMANIA	Corneliu Bogdan
Leo G. Cyr	RWANDA	F. Nkundabagenzi
Hermann F. Eilts	SAUDI ARABIA	Ibrahim Al-Sowayel
L. Dean Brown	SENEGAL	Cheikh Ibrahima Fall
Robert G. Miner	SIERRA LEONE	John J. Akar
Charles T. Cross	SINGAPORE	E. S. Monteiro
F. L. Hadsel	SOMALI REP.	Yusuf O. Azhari
William M. Rountree	SOUTH AFRICA	H. L. T. Taswell
William Eagleton[b]	SOUTHERN YEMEN	(vacant)
Robert C. Hill	SPAIN	Marquis de Merry del Val
(vacant)	SUDAN[a]	
J. H. Holland	SWAZILAND	S. T. M. Sukati
S. C. Davis	SWEDEN	Hubert de Besche
	SWITZERLAND	Felix Schnyder
	SYRIAN ARAB REP.[a]	
Claude G. Ross	TANZANIA	G. M. Rutabanzibwa
Leonard Unger	THAILAND	Sunthorn Hongladarom
Albert W. Sherer	TOGO	Alexandre Ohin
J. F. Symington, Jr.	TRINADAD AND TOBAGO	Ellis Clarke
John A. Calhoun	TUNISIA	Slaheddine El-Goulli
W. J. Handley	TURKEY	Melih Esenbel
H. E. Stebbins	UGANDA	E. Otema Allimadi
Jacob D. Beam	U.S.S.R.	Anatoly F. Dobrynin
	UNITED ARAB REP.[a]	
William Schaufele, Jr.	UPPER VOLTA	Paul Rouamba
Charles W. Adair, Jr.	URUGUAY	Hector Luisi
(vacant)	VENEZUELA	J. Sosa-Rodriguez
Ellsworth Bunker	VIETNAM (S.)	Bui Diem
	YEMEN[a]	
William Leonhart	YUGOSLAVIA	Bogdan Crnobrnja
Oliver L. Troxel, Jr.	ZAMBIA	Rupiah B. Banda

[a] Broke diplomatic relations in 1967 because of Middle East war.
[b] chargé d'affaires

AMERICAN MUSEUM OF NATURAL HISTORY, THE

The American Museum of Natural History in New York City celebrated its centennial throughout 1969 with a series of events and exhibitions that demonstrated the universality of the museum's interests.

The American Museum of Natural History, which has traditionally concerned itself with the discovery and interpretation of information about the myriad forms of life, turned its attention in 1969 to man's own relationship with his environment. In a widely discussed exhibition, which was opened on May 16, it asked the question "Can Man Survive?" The exhibition demonstrated the delicate balance between the natural ecology and those dangers presented by the increasing imposition of an unthinking human technology. One result of the exhibition has been a renewed public discussion of the degree to which the human species is threatened by a polluted and overpopulated environment.

The museum's charter was signed on April 9, 1869, and the Centennial Day was celebrated exactly 100 years later. At an academic convocation of delegates from many other museums and institutions of science and learning, the centennial address was delivered by Mr. Russell E. Train, undersecretary of the Department of the Interior. Other addresses were given by Mr. Gardner D. Stout, president of the museum; Dr. Bobb Schaeffer, dean of the Scientific Council of the museum; and Dr. James A. Oliver, then director of the museum. (Dr. Thomas D. Nicholson became director on July 1.)

That evening a dinner for 700 guests was held in the Hall of Ocean Life and Biology of Fishes. It was followed by an awards ceremony in which The American Museum of Natural History Gold Medal was presented to eight distinguished persons. Three were the Apollo 9 astronauts: Mr. Russell L. Schweickart, Col. David R. Scott and Col. James A. McDivitt.

The five scientists who received the Gold Medal were Dr. Theodosius Dobzhansky, the eminent geneticist and philosopher who is with Rockefeller University; Dr. Libbie Henrietta Hyman of The American Museum of Natural History, biologist, world renowned for her definitive treatise *The Invertebrates,* who died on Aug. 3, 1969; Dr. Ernst Mayr, famous for his classic work in systematics and evolution and is the director of the Museum of Comparative Zoology at Harvard University; Dr. Margaret Mead, the famous anthropologist; and Dr. George Gaylord Simpson, regarded as the leading theoretician of evolutionary biology.

The first hall to be completed during the centennial year was the John Lindsley Hall of Earth History, which was opened on Jan. 16. The magnitude of the earth and the dynamic processes that have formed and continue to shape it are impressively displayed in this hall. The Hall of Ocean Life and Biology of Fishes was opened Feb. 26. The hall received considerable popular attention well in advance of its opening, with the disclosure that a 94-foot model of a blue whale, hung in suspension from the ceiling, would be its focal point. On the first Sunday after the hall opened, a record crowd of 35,000 people visited the museum.

In February a new laboratory and residence were dedicated at the museum's Lerner Marine Laboratory at Bimini, Bahamas. Another centennial highlight, later in the year, was the installation of a magnificent Zeiss Model VI projector in The American Museum–Hayden Planetarium.

THOMAS D. NICHOLSON
Director
The American Museum of Natural History

American Museum of Natural History

A model of a 94-foot blue whale seems to float benignly over the guests at the centennial banquet, held in the museum's new Hall of Ocean Life.

ANTHROPOLOGY

Anthropology, the study of man, came into being as a distinct discipline only when several other fields had matured sufficiently to shed light on the questions of the origins and structure of humans and human groups. Over the years, certain kinds of anthropological investigation have become highly specialized and technical, each requiring specific training in allied fields. Each of these approaches—physical anthropology, linguistics, archeology, and cultural or social anthropology—is considered to be a subfield of anthropology. Each subfield has been enriched and changed through contact with the others as well as through work done in related fields in the social and physical sciences. This short article will mention some of the highlights of this process.

Physical anthropology concerns itself with the history of the human species and its predecessors as well as the distribution and nature of contemporary human populations. One major trend in physical anthropology is the use of methods of population genetics: taking as the unit of study the breeding population and the application of broad statistical measurements. With the recent insights of molecular biology—the functioning of RNA and DNA in the transmission of genetic information—physical anthropologists are able to compare genetic traits not only that result in overt differences such as skin color but also to compare blood factors, such as hemoglobins, red-cell antigens and serum factors, as well as enzymes of the red cell. Given this refinement in unit of study and in techniques for collecting information, it is not surprising that the idea of "race" is now found to be too loose for accurate scientific work. Aside from the psychological and social implications of the term, "race" is much harder to define than breeding population or species.

Linguistics, the study of the history and structure of human languages, has undergone significant changes largely due to the advances made in recent years in the field of transformational grammar. Briefly, this point of view holds that a description of the surface form of sentences is not sufficient to explain all of their grammatical properties. Thus, this theory holds, there is an underlying level of deep structure. This view has implications for understanding language as a universal system and also for theories of language acquisition. If deep structures of all languages are similar, then it seems likely that all humans have an identical capacity for language and that all languages are equally complex. What a given person learns as he acquires normal competence in a language is the ability to "generate" an infinite number of grammatical sentences in that language from a series of rules learned as a child.

This view of language contrasts sharply with the taxonomic (classifying) view of language that holds that one learns a language by categorizing what he hears and sorting out the acceptable, rejecting ungrammatical sentences and remembering grammatical ones for future use.

Work continues on historical aspects of language and language change. Lexicostatistics, or glottochronology, a way of dating the separation between two languages that diverged from a common stock, has benefited from a refinement of the underlying mathematics and the comparative use of carbon-14 dates obtained from archeological sources.

Archeology, which describes ways of life in the past by analysis of their physical remains, has changed a great deal in recent years. While archeologists maintain their interest in artifacts, the units of observation and analysis are not the artifacts themselves but rather the contexts in which these artifacts appear. Thus the things that people once used take on additional meaning if they are seen as part of patterns of settlement, ways of cultivating the earth, existing within given modes of political organization, kin structures, and religious practices. By using categories derived from other parts of social theory, especially from cultural anthropology, much more information becomes available about the past. From ecology comes the sensitivity to the landscape that man always uses and changes as part of his evolution. Subtle differences in the physical environment help archeologists formulate ideas about settlement patterns, or the ability of a given environment to support a group of people, the possibilities for changes in the way of earning a living (e.g., the change from hunting and gathering to agriculture), even such things as trade between settlements that specialize in certain kinds of production.

Other research techniques in archeology have been refined in recent years as well. The radiocarbon method of dating certain artifacts has improved, and other methods, such as potassium-argon, have been developed. Dating objects by the use of the tree rings in the wood used to make them, called dendrochronology, has become more accurate. Archeologists are using written sources to aid in their excavation, and these sources can sometimes be used to verify the results of excavation.

Because of improved techniques and ideas, archeological information has been used to develop theories about the origins and growth of cultures and civilizations. Archeologists are able to learn a great deal from analyses of physical remains about population density, techniques of cultivation such as irrigation and other patterns of land use, house and settlement types, ancient art and science, religion, politics and even kinship. To an extent much greater than ever before, archeology is becoming the cultural anthropology of ancient peoples.

The part of anthropology that deals with the study of living groups, called cultural anthropology, or social anthropology, has changed in subject matter, technique and emphasis. Small tribal groupings used to be the most intensively studied, but now many anthropologists are studying rural people who live in contact with national governments and economic systems, and even people living in cities are being studied by anthropologists. This is for two reasons. First, tribal peoples are less isolated than before and less able to live within their tribal boundaries and tribal political, religious and economic ways as before. Also, the bulk of the world's people are rural members of nations, a category now called peasants by most anthropologists. These people are neither tribal nor fully incorporated into modern life. They produce things, mainly food that people who live in the cities need, and they are becoming an important political force in some places such as Vietnam.

Anthropologists study these people in much the same manner as they study any other: they live with them and to some extent participate in their lives, work and play. However, in studying peasants there is often an opportunity to study their history, which may be quite extensive. For example, a scholar of the Indian peasantry can read about the history of India and can consult ancient written sources that explain classical Indian religion. Then he can compare the practices of the people he is living with with the texts he has read. Also, the anthropologist must know other details of the nation in which these people live, such as the political system, education, taxation. Sometimes even foreign policy may be important.

Other aspects of cultural anthropology show the increasing influence of linguistic study. The effort to understand native ways of seeing the world by learning how they classify things, events and kinsmen reflects the use of linguistic mathematical models, analogies with a taxonomic view of language and even attention to generative models. While most of these efforts are formal in nature—they seek to develop general methods—the structuralist approach, using data from many different sources,

attempts to show the kinds of models people use that underly all their activities.

In addition to the above changes indicated in the various fields of anthropology, the impact of computers has been felt wherever high-speed computation is needed. Anthropology will continue to profit from general developments in science and technology and will continue to teach us all something about mankind.

MARTIN DISKIN
Department of Humanities
Massachusetts Institute of Technology

ARCHEOLOGY

Large-scale efforts to salvage archeological sites in danger of disappearing engaged numerous archeologists in 1969. In Pakistan, Mohenjo-Daro, site of the Indus civilization, one of the oldest urban cultures known (2500–1700 B.C.), was threatened by a rising water table caused by a change in the course of the Indus River. The project of raising funds to save Mohenjo-Daro was put before UNESCO. In Turkey, the remote Keban area, which will be covered in 1972 by waters backing up from the Keban Dam, was surveyed by teams from various countries. The sites discovered range from Chalcolithic (before 4000 B.C.) to Islamic times. In February in the United States, water covered the site of Marmes, Washington. An expensive effort to hold the waters back with a cofferdam had failed, and the Lower Monumental Dam resulted in a lake. Excavated from 1953, Marmes held evidence of one of the earliest human Americans, Marmes Man, often dated as far back as 13,000 years ago. A dramatic reminder of the success of the salvage program to save the antiquities of Lower Nubia (Egypt), covered in 1968 by the Nile as a result of the Aswan High Dam, was the arrival in New York of the ancient Temple of Dendur. It was a gift of the U.A.R. Government to the United States. The blocks are in storage at the Metropolitan Museum of Art, awaiting their new $1,800,000, glass-walled home, to be ready in 1971.

On May 25, Dr. Thor Heyerdahl sailed from Safi, Morocco, in a 12-ton papyrus boat, the *Ra*, built to the same specifications as ancient Egyptian boats that were studied from frescoes. He aimed to prove that ancient Egyptian culture could have been carried to South and Central America. He seemed close to achieving it when, only six hundred miles from Barbados, he and his crew had to abandon the *Ra* (July 18), in danger of sinking. Dr. Heyerdahl blamed inexperience in sailing a papyrus vessel,

Marble figure of a priestess is from the Temple of Aphrodite rediscovered at Cnidus (Turkey), famous in antiquity for its statue of the goddess by Praxiteles.

a problem not faced by the ancient sailors, for much of the trouble.

Speculation about early man continued with a report in August from Dr. Mary Leakey of the discovery in Olduvai Gorge (Tanzania) of the most complete skeleton yet of *Homo habilis,* a manlike creature of 2,000,000 years ago.

Doctors Elwyn Simons and David Pilbeam, of Yale University, reported finding two fossilized jawbones—one in the British Museum, London, the other in the Calcutta Museum, India— proving that a human species lived between 8,000,000 and 15,000,000 years ago. Near Santander, Spain, in the Morin Cave, Dr. Leslie Freeman, of the University of Chicago, discovered the body of a Stone Age man (perhaps of 30,000 B.C.) in an extraordinary state of preservation. Clay had filled the cavities of the decaying body, permitting the appearance of Paleolithic man to be studied for the first time. The search for early man in the Western Hemisphere continued with the restudy of a controversial skull found in 1933 at Laguna Beach, Calif. Dr. Rainer Berger, of UCLA, using carbon-14 tests, now dates the skull to 17,150 years ago.

In England, among the sites associated with Arthurian legend, Glastonbury, Somerset, is being scientifically excavated under Philip Rahtz of the University of Birmingham. Occupied since Neolithic times (c. 2800 B.C.), the site produced little to connect it with "Arthur."

In the Mediterranean and Middle East, 1969 was a year of gathering and synthesizing evidence from known sites. In Italy the study of the terracotta sculpture reliefs from Acqua Rossa (excavated by the Swedish Institute in Rome) and from Poggio Civitate (excavations by Bryn Mawr College) reaffirmed the high quality, originality and varied repertoire of Etruscan sculpture. In Greece, Professor Spyro Marinatos opened up complete rooms, furnished as they were at the moment of disaster, in buildings of several stories at Akrotiri, on Thera (Santorini), both destroyed and preserved by volcanic action. At Franchthi Cave in the Peloponnesus, near Porto Cheli, Dr. Thomas Jacobsen of Indiana University continued research in the substantial stratigraphic evidence of the Mesolithic period. It is the first site in southern Greece to show a sequence of occupation from late Pleistocene times through the Neolithic period.

In Turkey more of the civilizations of ancient Anatolia were uncovered, at the key sites of Altintepe, Acemhoyuk, Elmali, Bogazköy, Lake Van. The site of Aphrodisias, excavated under the direction of Dr. Kenen Erim, of New York University, continued to produce extensive evidence of the Bronze Age and the Archaic period—as yet poorly known from this area. From the Classical period at Aphrodisias, when the city was famous for its sculpture, there were new finds from a sculptor's workshop and of extensive inscriptions.

The vigor of archeological activity in the Soviet Union can be judged from a press release that in mid-1968 alone, fifty archeological expeditions were being sent to western Siberia, the Ukraine, Byelorussia, the northern Caucasus and the Volga Basin. Their work continued into 1969. The Paleolithic settlements of Sungir, about 120 miles east of Moscow, yielded excellent skeletal material. Knowledge of Kushan history and culture was given renewed impetus by material from the sites of Dalversin-tepe and Khalchayan, excavated under Professor Galina Pugachenkova of the Uzbekistan Institute of the History of Art. In the Far East the caves along the Suchan River valley have produced abundant evidence of early man and his ecology. (The short Suchan River flows southeast of Vladivostok.)

In the New World, among the oldest and most intriguing problems is the meaning of the Mayan script (glyphs), the only early writing in the Americas that was more than rudimentary. A plan to amass all the available writings and study the glyphs systematically was under way, under the direction of Ian Graham, a British archeologist at the Peabody Museum, Harvard University. In the United States, preserving the heritage of past cultures is difficult in view of real-estate and construction operations. One of the most complete systems for the preservation and collection of archeological material is now in full operation in Arkansas, under the direction of Dr. Charles R. McGimsey III of the University of Arkansas, Fayetteville. Archeological remains are being

UPI

Sandstone slabs carved with strange forms were among objects found on site in Tasmania, Australia, that hints at human occupation going back 32,000 years.

given special care through the system of Federal and state parks. In 1969 the pre-Spanish Indian rock pictures near Gila Bend, Ariz., became a part of Arizona's new state-park system, evidence of the increasing trend of the states to preserve their cultural heritage.

ANNA SHAW BENJAMIN
Professor of Classics, Douglass College, Rutgers
Editor, *Archaeology*

More buildings of ancient Rome are unearthed in digging for a subway beneath the pavement of the Piazza Esedra. As Rome's officials give great weight to archeological concerns, the subway may be halted or rerouted.

UPI

architecture

With the death of Walter Gropius at 86 on July 5, 1969, and of Ludwig Mies van der Rohe at 83 on Aug. 17, the great pioneers of twentieth-century architecture were gone. Frank Lloyd Wright had died in 1959, and Le Corbusier in 1965. Whether Mies' pure and cubic steel-and-glass architecture will survive him for long remains an open question. The trend toward more sculptural and even neobaroque forms, which Le Corbusier started and to which Gropius and his group, The Architects' Collaborative, or TAC, made increasing concession, speaks against it.

But style aside, in the year of his death the philosophy of Gropius seemed to exert a more pervasive influence on U.S. architecture than at any time during his life. The Bauhaus school in Germany, which Gropius had founded in 1919 and which Mies directed from 1930 to 1933 (when he closed it rather than make concessions to the nazi Government), had, of course, revolutionized both art education and design methods. But Gropius' two fundamental tenets had been largely ignored in the United States until recent years. One principle considers architecture not the individual creation of isolated monuments but rather a social art that must be responsive and responsible to total human needs and the ecological unity of the environment. The other insists on teamwork to break away from limited, specialized and individual solutions and to assure "thinking in relationships."

Most of the 16 building designs singled out for the 1969 Honor Awards of the American Institute of Architects reflected this social concern. In contrast to what the late architecture critic S. Giedion had called the "playboy architecture" of previous years, the award winners indicated that U.S. architecture seems to have become more sober and mature. Examples are: Hugh Newell Jacobsen's Bolton Square, a moderately priced town-house complex in Baltimore; Neill Smith's student dormitories at Sacramento; Vincent Kling's subterranean cafeteria for employees of the Monsanto Company in St. Louis; and I. M. Pei's Everson Museum of Art in Syracuse. A restored theater in Chicago and an art-center wing in Des Moines, Iowa, were also cited.

The new mood was also strongly evident at the AIA's annual convention in Chicago. For the first time, it was held jointly with the Royal Architectural Institute of Canada. After hearing Daniel P. Moynihan, President Nixon's urban-affairs adviser, tell them that "we have entered a time of trouble and we are young no more," the architects passed numerous resolutions. They demanded that housing at home be given at least the same priority as expeditionary ventures in Asia and to the moon; that blacks be given equal employment opportunity in architecture and the building industry; that more Federal funds be allocated to public transportation and the industrialization of housing construction; and that a joint Canadian-U.S. pro-

Ezra Stoller

The American Institute of Architects

Designed by I. M. Pei, the Everson Museum of Art, in Syracuse, N.Y., is a freestanding sculptural form from the outside. The interior is a series of neutral spaces, a quiet background for exhibits.

gram be launched to halt the pollution of the Great Lakes and develop this region with planned communities and new recreation parks.

After long discussions, AIA members even voted to reach into their own pockets to help ameliorate the urban crisis. In response to a student demand, presented by Taylor Culver, the first Negro to head the AIA Association of Student Chapters, they committed $15,000,000, the equivalent of 10 per cent of their annual business income, to aid nonaccredited, black architecture schools and establish neighborhood design centers in the ghettos.

Newly formed "design concept teams," composed, much as Gropius envisioned them, of architects, sociologists, ecologists, historians and other disciplines in addition to engineers, were meanwhile attempting in Baltimore, Chicago and other cities to make freeways in the city something more than ugly concrete ribbons that displace homes, remove land from the city tax rolls, cut up neighborhoods and destroy recrea-

Neill Smith's student dormitories in Sacramento, Calif., answer a need for low-income student housing.

Morley Baer

The American Institute of Architects

Baltimore's Bolton Square, with a large inner "meadow," re-creates a neighborhood style of a century ago.

tion parks. Such interdisciplinary teams also began to be formed to "think relationships" about the rehabilitation of old neighborhoods and design of new ones and to extend the planning of mere buildings or airports to a comprehensive consideration of their impact on the life of nature and man. The new term is "environmental design," and the publication of *Design with Nature,* a book by the landscape architect-ecologist Ian McHarg of the University of Pennsylvania, provides both a theoretical and practical guide for such teamwork.

But what some thought "playboy architecture" was also still rampant. Among the most controversial was the design by William Pereira & Associates of a 55-story, pyramidical skyscraper, topped by a 240-foot spire, for the Transamerica Corporation in San Francisco. Advertised as "the tallest building west of Chicago," the structure would be an offense to San Francisco's skyline, critics protested, not only because of its spire-inflated height but also because of its needlessly bizarre needle shape. In New York City the fight to preserve the neoclassic Grand Central Terminal and keep yet another office skyscraper out of the already overcongested area continued. Yielding to widespread outrage over his proposal to top the landmark with a huge slab, Marcel Breuer proposed to replace the old building with a new one which would, however, retain the much admired old concourse inside. In Dallas the developer of Griffin Square announced that he

would build "the world's tallest concrete building," a 913-foot-high cylinder designed by Pratt, Box & Henderson. It will house a hotel as well as offices and be crowned by the now almost obligatory rotating restaurant.

A more promising architectural innovation, a "floating city" conceived by Buckminster Fuller, was proposed for Baltimore Harbor. To be built like an ocean liner and in shipyards, the structure will consist of high-rise buildings and town houses for 5,000 people plus community facilities at a cost of about $8,000 a person. The town houses are to be stacked atop each other and stepped back. They would open onto 18-foot-wide "streets in the air," much

Reinforced-plastic greenhouses, with steel supports, enclose almost four acres of tall trees and other plants in the Nagashima Tropical Garden, near Nagoya, Japan.

Photo, Lawrence S. Williams Inc.; Vincent G. Kling & Assocs., Architects

In St. Louis, the Monsanto Company's cafeteria makes pleasant use of a courtyard formed by new buildings.

like promenade decks on a ship. The resulting pyramid is open in the center to accommodate a public square. One of the advantages of housing people on the water is that they can live close to the downtown center without disrupting the existing urban fabric.

The year's most ingenious new work of architecture was probably the new office building for the Czechoslovak Parliament on Prague's Wenceslaus Square. A design competition specified that the historic Parliament had to be preserved; that 307,000 square feet of office space was needed; and that the building could not be higher than the nearby National Museum. The winner, a Prague civil-engineering firm, solved the problem by placing a two-story frame, supported by 72-foot-high columns, somewhat like a square halo, over the old building. Similarly ingenious is the new Nagashima Tropical Garden near Nagoya, Japan. A modern version of Joseph Paxton's famous Crystal Palace, it encloses 150,000 square feet of plants and tall trees in a delightfully varied complex of greenhouses of corrugated and translucent sheets of reinforced plastic supported by a lithe steel structure. The architects were anonymous members of the Takenaka Komuten construction company.

WOLF VON ECKARDT
Architecture Critic, *The Washington Post*

Takenaka Komuten Co., Ltd.

ARIZONA

The state continued to produce more than half of U.S. copper as two big mines came "on stream," others increased their yield, and several mills introduced a new process—electro-winning (or solvent extraction)—that requires neither smelters nor refineries. ☐ To time irrigation the use of water-need forecasts from a computer was spreading; farmers get the forecasts by telephone. ☐ In the state budget, construction-fund requests by the three state universities were cut from $53,200,000 to $12,200,000. ☐ The state's redistricting law, passed in 1968, was found invalid; and its wiretap law was declared unconstitutional.

ARKANSAS

The legislature rejected Gov. Winthrop Rocke-feller's $100,000,000 tax program—to promote an "era of excellence"—in March. ☐ In southeastern Arkansas, in June, the Mobile Academy of the Performing Arts, a project of the National Guild of Community Music Schools, began operations with the purpose of encouraging active participation by rural schoolchildren in the performing arts and exposing them to live performances. ☐ On July 11 a U.S. grand jury indicted 15 former prison officials and guards, charged with brutal acts against inmates of the state penitentiary and two county penal farms. It was the second time such charges were filed against officials since disclosure of prison conditions began in 1966.

ASTRONOMY

As the universe yields ever more of its secrets, news terms and new concepts are coming into wide use in astronomy and, in a sense, are a measure of its advances.

Lunar Mascons. When a spacecraft, such as the Lunar Orbiter 5, moves around the moon, it does not do so in a regular ellipse, but dips inward slightly when it passes over certain places on the moon. Evidently at these places there are mass concentrations (abbreviated "mascons") below the surface. The mascons are below maria—the flat plains that were once thought to be seas. Either these areas have denser material than the surrounding regions or their surfaces have been hit by large bodies such as asteroids.

Pulsars. These mysterious objects give off bursts of radio noise at very precise periodic intervals. In some cases X rays and light rays are given off. The intervals range from 0.03 seconds for the shortest to 3.74 seconds for the longest. A pulsar has been found in the Crab nebula that has a rate of 30 times a second. The nebula is the remnant of a supernova, the gaseous cloud left after the gigantic explosion of a star. Quite possibly the pulsar is the remains of the star. But what can vary in such short periods? Double stars and pulsating (expanding and contracting) stars seem to be ruled out. The only likely explanation is that of rotating neutron stars: objects that are roughly ten miles in diameter and compressed to the point where all the material has been changed to neutrons. Such objects would rotate in a second or less; and as flares occurred on their surfaces, their magnetic fields would direct the resulting radiation outward in a beam, like a rotating beacon in a lighthouse, to sweep periodically across the earth.

These pulsars evidently are not close to the earth: one shows absorption from interstellar gas clouds indicating that it is at least 13,000 light-years away. The periods of pulsars seem to increase slowly, doubling in several thousand years. So they are unsuitable for general relativity experiments.

Mass of Pluto. The outermost planet, Pluto, was discovered in 1930 as the result of an intensive search after irregularities were discovered in the motion of Uranus. After Pluto was found, an analysis of the motion of Neptune indicated that Pluto had nearly as much material (mass) as the earth. In 1965 a measurement of the diameter of Pluto indicated that it is half that of the earth, and so must be much more dense than the earth. Now a new analysis of the motion of Neptune shows that Pluto has only 18 per cent of the earth's mass and therefore a normal density; it is slightly larger than Mars.

Molecules in Space. Astronomers have known for decades that elements such as calcium, sodium, titanium and iron occur in minute quantities in the space between stars. Simple molecules such as CN (cyanogen) and CH were discovered later. In 1969, radio astronomers discovered interstellar hydroxyl (OH) radicals, ammonia (NH_3), water (H_2O) and formaldehyde (H_2CO), and other complex molecules may also be discovered. The ammonia molecules will be disrupted by ultraviolet starlight in roughly a century, so new molecules are being formed constantly.

Planets around Barnard's Star. The second nearest star to the solar system is called Barnard's star. Thousands of photographs of this star, taken by Dr. Peter van de Kamp of Swarthmore's Sproul Observatory, show that it has a motion evidently caused by an invisible companion. A more recent analysis shows that there are actually two companions, each with a mass

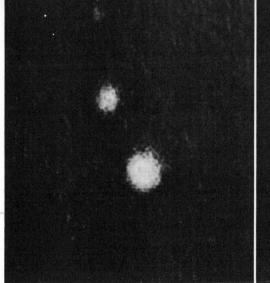

Lick Observatory

The larger bright object on the left above is a pulsar, which has a precise flashing sequence. In the photo at right, of the same section of sky, the pulsar is turned off.

The Crab nebula, like other nebulas, is a gaseous cloud left from the explosion of a star. The pulsar that has been found in the Crab nebula may be the remains of the exploded star.

Mount Wilson and Palomar Observatories

similar to that of Jupiter. Such objects cannot be stars because they do not have enough gravitation to sustain internal nuclear reactions; they must be planets. Several other stars have similar invisible planets as companions.

Gravitational Waves. If one object moves relative to another, its pull of gravity will vary. However, in 1916 Einstein predicted that the change would appear as gravity waves. For most objects the energy of these waves is much too small to measure, but for astronomical-sized objects the energy may be detectable. Recent attempts to detect gravity waves may, for the first time, have been successful. University of Maryland physicist Joseph Weber set up detectors in Maryland and Illinois with a telephone link to tell when both were activated (one could be affected by an earthquake or other disturbance). On 17 occasions, far more than chance would predict, such waves were detected. It is not known yet where the waves originate, presumably among some nearby stars.

Orbiting Astronomical Observatory. The first in a series of satellites devoted to stellar astronomical research was successfully launched in December 1968 and has been operating since. It sends measurements of stellar brightnesses in the ultraviolet range (University of Wisconsin experiment) and television pictures in ultraviolet light (Smithsonian Astrophysical Observatory experiment). To date, several Orbiting Solar Observatories have been launched and are also very productive.

Solar Neutrinos. While hydrogen is being converted to helium in a series of nuclear reactions in the core of the sun, large quantities of neutrinos are released. Unlike other particles from these reactions, the neutrinos are not absorbed by the solar material but stream out unretarded.

Miyamoto, University of Hawaii

The dome of the University of Hawaii's observatory, highest in the world, rises near the top of Mauna Kea, the great peak on Hawaii, the state's largest island.

Kitt Peak's new 158-inch telescope (cutaway drawing) rides in a horseshoe bearing that holds the declination axes. Dome included, building is 180 feet high.

Solar neutrinos can cause transmutations of atoms on the earth, but so can cosmic rays. However, by making tests a mile underground, where cosmic rays do not penetrate, the effects of neutrinos should be detectable. Dr. Raymond Davis, of Brookhaven National Laboratory, has been making such tests in a mine in South Dakota, counting about one neutrino per day. Such tests are direct measurements of the nuclear-reaction rates in the sun.

Meteors Striking the Earth. The earth is bombarded daily with several million minute specks of dust and rock swept up as it moves through space. Such particles are of little concern to terrestrial life because most of the particles burn up in the earth's atmosphere before reaching the surface. On the atmosphereless surface of the moon there is no such protection. How much material hits the earth's atmosphere daily, and has this changed with time? Measurements by Australian physicist J. W. Morgan show that in rocks 400,000,000 years old the earth received about 8,000 tons of rock daily, which is about the present rate as measured by metallic material found in Antarctic ice.

HELMUT A. ABT
Kitt Peak National Observatory

Skidmore, Owings & Merrill, Architects/Engineers

AUSTRALIA

For Australia, 1969 was a landmark year in which intensive national soul-searching coincided with sustained prosperity and an unprecedented economic growth that lifted the gross national product by at least 7 per cent. More than 170,000 new settlers arrived from abroad, and with production expanding rapidly the nation ended the 1960's on a rising note.

Throughout the year Australians grappled with the question of national defense in a rapidly changing world. In February the Government announced that it would maintain forward defense in Malaysia and Singapore, and thus continue to have a role in regional security after Britain's withdrawal from most of the area in 1971. The Government emphasized the importance of its alliances with the United States (ANZUS and SEATO) as cornerstones of defense and foreign policy. Nevertheless, uncertainty about future U.S. policy in Southeast Asia precluded any major reshaping of Australia's role there.

The encroachment of Soviet naval power into the Indian Ocean aroused concern, and the Government activated long-discussed plans for a naval base at Cockburn Sound, Western Australia. Meanwhile the establishment of a U.S. defense-space-research installation at Pine Gap and approval of a joint defense-communications-space facility at Woomera (both in central Australia) were widely discussed and taken to indicate a deepening involvement in U.S. strategic plans.

The Government withheld decision on the nuclear-nonproliferation treaty while it continued to study the treaty's implications in terms of Australia's security and national development. In the field of mutual assistance Australia's bilateral aid (which was wholly in the form of grants) to various countries was maintained at about A$150,000,000 (US$166,000,-000).

Politics attracted more headlines than usual. On a national level, a host of carry-over issues were sharpened as political campaigning reached a crescendo late in October. A record 499 candidates contested the 125 seats in the House of Representatives in the triennial general elections. The government parties stressed defense measures and a record of economic stability, while the Opposition saw the issues as health, education and social welfare. Amid the many crosscurrents, party lines were breached by those concerned primarily with Federal-state relationships, Federal aid to schools, and the Vietnam involvement.

Prime Minister John Grey Gorton was caught in the political crossfire. The Democratic Labor Party, on which the Government relied for electoral backing and Senate support, demanded a "harder" defense policy. Gorton, holding to support of President Nixon's Vietnam policy and promising to increase defense outlays on a graduated scale, carried the Liberal-Country party coalition to victory, holding 66 seats against the 59 won by a rejuvenated Australian Labor Party. However, the sharp reduction in the coalition's 36-seat majority—almost all of it suffered by the Liberals—opened the way for a direct challenge to Gorton's leadership. The Prime Minister set about

UPI

On May 5, Prime Minister John Gorton, with his wife, arrives in Washington for talks with President Nixon.

AUSTRALIA

Area: 2,974,581 sq. mi.
Population: 12,200,000
Capital: Canberra (pop., 93,000)
Government: Sir Paul Hasluck, governor-general
—1969; John G. Gorton, prime minister—
1968
Gross national product: $26,800,000,000
Monetary unit: Australian dollar ($A 1 = $US
1.11)
Chief products: meats, dairy products, grains,
wool, ores, sugar cane
Foreign trade: exports, $3,402,000,000; im-
ports, $3,858,000,000
Communications: 3,178,278 telephones, 2,846,-
400 TV sets, 17 daily newspapers
Transportation: roads, 564,000 mi.; 4,222,894
passenger cars; railroads, 25,059
Education: 2,588,339 elementary and secondary
students, 14 universities
Armed forces: 87,150

See map on page 481

"identifying and rectifying" aspects of policy that were causing disquiet. To defeat the attempt to unseat him, he rallied support within the Liberal Party successfully. Nevertheless, his style of leadership kept him under fire.

Country Party leader John McEwen won concessions for his party, and the coalition (in office since 1949) remained intact. However, political commentators spoke freely of the likelihood that friction would continue within the Liberal Party and between the coalition partners on policy issues.

Meanwhile the unexpectedly strong showing of the Australian Labor Party, under the energetic leadership of Edward Gough Whitlam, led to speculation that with factionalism no longer in evidence, the party's years of wandering in the political wilderness might be nearing an end. Labor's policy makers had adopted new goals. The modified platform stressed the need for a coordinated plan embracing urban development, decentralization, and conservation, with the Federal Government taking greater responsibility for them. The party also advocated comprehensive national health and social-security plans that would cover all contributors irrespective of their means. Further, the party urged faster withdrawal from Vietnam and declared that Australian armed forces should not be stationed in other countries. It proposed replacement of the draft system with a wholly volunteer army.

The nation's economic upsurge sprang from all sources. Lifted by an excellent season, agricultural output rose by about 18 per cent, to close to A$4,000,000,000 (US$4,480,000,000). Major investment, particularly in large-scale mining projects in the north, was a spur. In the cities, commercial-building and housing construction continued at a record pace. Manufacturing and transportation facilities expanded. Total investment reached A$2,000,000,000 (US$2,240,000,000). Factory output expanded as a result of new plant and fuller use of industrial capacity. Few companies failed to report enhanced earnings, and most paid higher dividends. Consumer credit expanded to A$1,500,000,000 (US$1,675,000,000). New-car registrations were at record levels—close to 500,000 for the year. There was some inflation: prices generally rose about 3 per cent. But wages, overtime earnings and other personal income showed a marked increase.

At close to A$4,000,000,000 (US$4,480,000,000), export earnings were up sharply, with minerals moving ahead of wool for the first time as the most important single contributor. Apart from minerals, the gain was mainly the result of improved sales abroad of meat and other pastoral products, grains (including wheat, barley and oats), sugar and a wide range of manufactured items. Tourism added significantly to income. Capital continued to flow strongly from abroad and gave substantial support to Australia's balance of payments. At the end of 1969, as the oil fields offshore from Victoria came into production, the end of Australia's dependence on overseas petroleum supplies seemed in sight.

Successive discoveries of major mineral deposits touched off intense activity on the stock exchanges. More than 12,000 mineral claims were staked in the state of Western Australia alone. New nickel stocks, as well as stocks in established mining enterprises, soared. Swept along by the mining boom, general stocks reached an all-time peak in February. After a 14 per cent drift, prices moved back smartly in the last three months of 1969 to close at about the year's opening level.

In the Federal budget introduced in August, receipts for 1969-70 were estimated at A$7,788,000,000 (US$8,720,000,000), a 13.5 per cent increase; expenditures, up 7.25 per cent, were estimated at A$7,820,000,000 (US$8,758,000,000). Work was initiated on a five-year water-resources program. Meanwhile, surveys disclosed significant supplies of underground water in some dry regions. Construction of a nuclear-power station at Jervis Bay (New South Wales) was approved. Federal grants for education were increased. Universities and colleges were promised A$420,000,000 (US$470,000,000) over three years, with A$490,000,000 (US$548,000,000) from state-government sources. Considerably increased funds were allotted to the Australian Council for the Arts to support cultural activities. These included the establishment of a second national orchestra, an opera school, and a film and TV training school. The council was encouraged to extend its work in rural areas.

To spur long-term job training for the Aborigines, the Government supported a plan to repay employers one third of the wages involved, and to pay allowances to young Aborigines taking jobs away from their families.

State governments faced severe budgetary problems arising from expanded commitments and limited revenue sources. As their demands for Federal funds rose so did resistance in Canberra. The crisis was heightened by a High Court ruling denying the states the right to levy a "receipts" (or turnover) tax on sales.

Newspaper articles focused attention on pollution problems, and there was greater public concern over the assault on the environment. Conservationists protested mining and oil-search proposals along the Great Barrier Reef and other coastal areas.

In the United Nations, Australia supported the idea of creating an international body to institute a code for the exploration and exploitation of the resources of the seabeds beyond national jurisdiction. Stress was given to the need for agreement on basic conditions and on essential standards to guide any regulatory authority.

A statement by the Chief Justice of the High Court, Sir Garfield Barwick, was widely quoted; lawyers should be among the innovators of society, and lawmakers should be ready to change laws before they are challenged by civil disobedience. "Unless the law moves with the times, society is in for trouble," he said.

In April, Lord Casey of Berwick, Australian-born governor-general, retired. He was succeeded by Sir Paul Hasluck, who had been minister for external affairs since 1964.

On the island of Bougainville, friction developed at the start of a great copper-mining project. Villagers protested that their rights were not being adequately protected in the acquisition of land for a new township. After a clash with police, the issue was settled amicably when Prime Minister Gorton offered concessions to those whose land was being acquired. In May, on the island of New Britain, 10,000 Tolai tribespeople protested a change in the Gazelle Peninsula Local Government Council. From a totally indigenous organization it was changed to a multiracial one.

R. M. YOUNGER
Author, *Australia and the Australians*

Ore piles up at mill at Kambalda, site of Australia's first nickel mine, on shore of a salt lake in Western Australia.

Australian News and Information Bureau

Keystone

On state visit, Queen Elizabeth and Prince Philip enjoy performance of Vienna's Spanish Riding School.

AUSTRIA

On Jan. 18, 1969, Franz Cardinal König of Vienna announced some of the decisions reached by a Synod of Austrian Catholics. The 180 clergymen and 160 laymen had resolved upon major moves to democratize the Church in Austria. For instance, it was decided that the Vienna diocese should be split into three divisions, each one to be headed by a vicar, the vicar to be chosen by the local synods.

Queen Elizabeth II made an official visit to Austria in May. Her visit included a two-day tour of the provinces. Just a few days before her arrival, Otto Mitterer, minister of commerce and industry, strongly criticized British restrictions on the amount of money that could be taken out of the country by British citizens

AUSTRIA

Area: 32,376 sq. mi.
Population: 7,400,000
Capital: Vienna (pop., 1,660,000)
Government: Franz Jonas, president—1965; Josef Klaus, chancellor—1964
Gross national product: $11,300,000,000
Monetary unit: schilling (25.9 schillings = U.S. $1.00)
Chief products: Grains, dairy products, graphite, iron ore, petroleum
Foreign trade: exports, $1,989,000,000; imports, $2,497,000,000
Communications: 1,163,194 telephones, 2,170,138 radios, 1,112,000 TV sets, 32 daily newspapers
Transportation: roads, 20,802 mi.; 964,929 passenger cars, railroads, 3,673 mi.
Education: 1,000,024 elementary and secondary students, 4 universities
Armed forces: 50,000

See map on page 185

going on holiday. He claimed that the restrictions had caused a 33 per cent drop in Austrian tourism in the previous 18 months.

In August the Canadian Embassy in Vienna was set on fire by a gasoline bomb thrown by a Colman Losonczy. In a letter to the Interior Ministry, Losonczy said that he had done it to protest the tyrannical and degrading treatment he had received in Canada. Losonczy was a Czech who first became a Hungarian citizen and then emigrated to Canada where he had become a naturalized citizen. In 1967 he had left Canada for Austria where his request for citizenship was turned down.

On Oct. 15, the Austrian Government announced that political asylum had been granted to Zdenek Hejzlar, the first secretary of the Czech Legation in Vienna. Hejzlar had served as director of the Czech radio before the Soviet invasion of 1968. In June the Government had announced a plan to end the overcrowding of the refugee camps maintained in Austria. The number of people entering the camps had risen by 250 per cent in the first five months of 1969. The camps will no longer accept "economic" refugees, mostly Yugoslavs and most of whom enter Austria legally. Henceforth, only those seeking political refuge will be eligible to enter the camps.

Austria's economy boomed in 1969, but the boom brought with it the specter of inflation. The revaluation of the German mark put additional pressure on the Austrian economy, though the Austrians indicated that they would not revalue the schilling. The Central Bank raised the discount rate from 3¾ to 4¾ per cent in September to slow the gold outflow. In October the funds of a short-term credit network to which Austria and 13 other nations belong were increased. The network is designed to help the various countries during periods of short-term currency outflows.

In the spring the city of Vienna announced plans for the development of an 11-mile-long island in the Danube River to provide a recreation area for the city. The island will include lakes, sports areas, camping sites, and beaches. The project also includes a canal which will provide flood control for Vienna's low-lying districts.

In 1969, Austria broke the four-year-old French rule of the skiing world. The Austrian team took the World Cup at Vail, Colo., on Mar. 8. The men's World Cup was won by Austria's Karl Schranz, the women's Cup by Austria's Gertrud Gabl.

NORA ANN SMYTH
Associate Editor
Lands and Peoples

AUTOMOBILES

The U.S. automobile industry achieved record new-vehicle sales in the 1969 model year, or during the 12 months ending on Sept. 30, 1969. However, inflationary pressures, economic uncertainty, and the possibility of UAW strikes prefacing contract expirations with the Big Three auto makers in 1970 made predictions for a similar volume in the 1970 model year anything but certain.

Retail sales by dealers totaled 11,500,000 units, including 9,600,000 domestic and imported cars and 1,900,000 trucks. This was better than the 10,700,000 in the 1968 model year, composed of 9,000,000 cars and 1,700,000 trucks. It also topped the record 10,800,000.

On a calendar-year basis, domestic-import new-car sales crowded the 1968 record of 9,600,000, but truck sales soared well above the 1968 mark of 1,805,000. Included in the car count were more than 1,000,000 import makes, rising above the 1968 record of 985,767 to post their fourth consecutive peak effort—this despite a crippling dock strike in the eastern United States early in the year.

Actually it appeared that the imports in 1969 had reached the peak of their popularity with a 10 per cent market share. But you would never guess it from the American car scene. In quick succession, from April through December, Ford introduced its compact Maverick; Chevrolet ended production of its rear-engine Corvair after a ten-year run; American Motors introduced its compact Hornet; and Ford ended production of its Falcon. However, such moves were but a prelude to the introduction in 1970 of true subcompacts by American Motors, Chevrolet and Ford, and in 1971 by Chrysler Corp. The American producers were launching an all-out drive at the "below $2,000" import market in earnest.

Despite a history of poor earnings, the subcompacts were needed by the American producers. They were being squeezed out of nearly 1,000,000 sales annually by the import brands, and also had to contend with the profit-eating surtax enacted in 1968 to help curb inflation. In addition, constantly rising wage and material costs were certain to jump again when the new contracts with the UAW were signed in 1970.

From January through September of 1969, General Motors' profit margin (net profits as per cent of sales) dropped to 6.8 per cent from 7.1 per cent a year earlier, with Ford Motor Co. showing a decline to 3.8 per cent from 4.5 per cent, and Chrysler Corp. to 1.8 per cent from 3.4 per cent, a dismal performance that brought on a retrenchment in expenditures. Reduced earnings were foreseen as a key bargaining tool in the 1970 contract negotiations with the union.

If there was a rallying cry it was sounded by American Motors, the struggling auto maker eking out a $4,927,896 profit in its fight for survival in the fiscal year ending Sept. 30, 1969. Indicating that it was still very much alive, the company announced plans to introduce a new car every six months for the next three years.

As the major styling changes for 1970 were applied to the hot-selling Intermediate cars, they had to share the headlines. Among sports cars, Thunderbird, Camaro and Firebird received all-new styling, and Dodge introduced its Challenger, and Chevrolet its Monte Carlo. This swelled the industry's bill to approximately

On the Monte Carlo sports coupe, "sculptured" surfaces stress the longest hood ever to appear on a Chevrolet.

General Motors Corp.

Ford Motor Co.

American Motors Corp.

American compact cars were pushed again to meet the competition of imported cars "below $2,000." Compacts included Ford's Maverick (top photo) and American Motors' Hornet, the latter available also as a four-door sedan.

$1,500,000,000 for bringing its 1970 products to market.

Itemized, the bill included the industry's first 500-cubic-inch auto engine by Cadillac; a 455 "cube" V-8 that Pontiac, Oldsmobile and Buick shared; introduction of high-rise front-seat backs, which had the effect of building in the headrests required by law; and of course the all-new Intermediates which were expected to upend the regular-size cars in sales in 1970 for the first time in history.

The Intermediates became twin-purpose cars serving the family buyer and the hot-perform-

ance bug, and their names were changed to fit the new image. "Skylark" replaced the "Special" at Buick just as Montego had replaced the Comet name at Mercury a year earlier.

On a more commonsense level, close watchers could see signs in the 1970 models that the industry was beginning to back off from its runaway many-models-and-options proliferation kick. It was a trend certain to grow.

The essence of the automobile industry in 1969 was orderly confusion, and change. Uncertain economic trends made the future, even on a quarterly basis, difficult to predict. New safety regulations and proposals were steadily pouring forth from a Washington mill that had already made mandatory front-seat headrests; padded instrument panels; seat belts and shoulder harnesses; collapsible steering columns; and starting with the 1970 models, three-way anti-theft steering-column locks.

Strikes took their toll. A major setback was a series of strikes from April through July, at seven General Motors plants, resulting in a decision to extend Corvette, Camaro and Firebird 1969 model output past the Aug. 1 deadline into December. Coincidentally, on the same day that GM announced its 1970 car-price increases, Ford Motor Co. announced that its President, lured to Ford from General Motors just 19 months previously, had been summarily fired on Sept. 2.

The excitement did not end there. No sooner had glass-belted, bias-ply tires been put on virtually all makes of 1970 cars in September than a controversy developed over their performance. Evoking no controversy were air bags, proposed in Washington for the 1972 cars. Buried in the steering wheel or instrument panel, the air bags would inflate instantaneously if a vehicle were hit, cushioning the front-seat passengers.

Jolting observers was one of the stiffest auto-price hikes in years, the 1970 models going up $125 at General Motors, $103 at Ford, $107 at Chrysler and $81 on the average at American Motors. GM set the pattern, but Ford's move in rolling back its auto warranty was one its competitors refused to follow.

Ford kept its foot in the door, however. For $15, Ford buyers could extend their warranty coverage to the five-year or 50,000-mile powertrain warranty GM and Chrysler kept as standard. Joining the parade, Volkswagen boosted its American prices $40 in October with threats of another possible increase in early 1970.

Federal Trade Commission hearings in September focused on auto pricing, labeling, advertising and warranties. Earlier in 1969 General Motors had blasted a FTC report on auto warranties and service as distorted and misleading. In effect, the auto makers were taking a firmer stand with their critics. But they could not escape the attention accorded recall campaigns. In March, GM recalled a whopping 4,900,000 vehicles for either a part replacement or for inspection service. Ford Motor Co. in May recalled 382,000 vehicles to check for possibly defective hood latches. Other recalls involved foreign-make cars in the United States and overseas, creating a furor especially in Japan, where disclosure is not compulsory as in the United States.

Ford Motor Co.

Steering-column ignition lock: removing the ignition key locks the wheel in place, and car cannot be moved.

One solution was to build greater serviceability into the cars. Instrument panels with quick-change features appeared on some GM models. Easier serviceability was featured on Ford's new Maverick. Auto makers said that these were only the first steps in the area, steps that echoed the acute shortage of trained auto mechanics.

These developments came as a Senate subcommittee held hearings in October on the soaring costs of auto repairs. Testimony blamed "delicate cars." Shock-absorbing bumpers were proposed. Soaring costs in replacements parts were cited as a principal clause of rising auto-insurance rates. In a bold step, the nation's fifth largest auto insurer announced a 50 per cent boost in insurance rates for overpowered muscle cars because of their alleged higher accident factor.

It was proposed that cars be designed and manufactured that are safer, less vulnerable to damage and less costly to repair. Being challenged was the auto industry's practice of planned obsolescence in passenger-car design.

With Americans spending an estimated $29,-000,000,000 each year to repair and to maintain their 100,000,000 vehicles, or almost as much as the $20,000,000,000 they spend to buy them, automobiles were certain to remain controversial—at a time of record sales volume —for some time to come.

HARRY A. STARK
Editor, *Wards Automotive Reports*

AVIATION

Air congestion, air fares and hijacking were major issues in 1969 as the air-transport industry sought to cope with increasing traffic demands and even more steeply rising costs. At the same time, the industry was preparing for the introduction in 1970 of larger and faster equipment.

The U.S. Civil Aeronautics Board approved a 3.8 per cent domestic-fare increase in February, as an interim measure to tide the U.S. airlines over an immediate financial crisis. In October the industry introduced new CAB-approved fares, up 6.35 per cent for the 11 trunk airlines and 7 per cent higher for the 9 local-service airlines. The estimated resultant total increase in annual revenue was close to $500,000,000.

In the transatlantic market the airlines tried a direct approach to fiscal woes by introducing an assortment of fare cuts designed to stimulate travel. Alitalia touched off what had the appearance of a rate war by offering new low excursion fares between Italy and the United States. Pan American World Airways and Trans World Airlines matched Alitalia's lower fares, and then in succession Swissair, Lufthansa, SAS, BOAC and others expanded the area of rate cutting to other parts of Europe. This occurred outside the normal fare agreements of the International Air Transport Association. That organization held an emergency conference in Lausanne, Switzerland, to attempt to reach new agreements that would apply when the heavy volume of tourist traffic began in the spring.

Other rate issues notwithstanding, the CAB found that one of its thorniest problems was the special discounts granted in recent years to young people: the so-called student-standby and youth-reservation fares. In January a CAB examiner ruled that such fares, although reasonable as to cost level, were unjustly discriminatory and should be canceled. On review the board concluded that the fares were indeed discriminatory, but not unjustly or offensively so. The board found the evidence insufficient on whether the youth fares were reasonable and remanded the proceeding for further hearings on this point. Meanwhile the youth fares remained in effect, although at the higher level provided for by the fare increases of October.

The dilemma of airplane hijacking remained unsolved, but in mid-October, Eastern Air Lines, a prime target of Cuba-bound hijackers, became the first airline to install weapons-screening devices at strategic points, such as boarding gates, at various terminals. The metal-object detectors, employed in concert with a hijacker behavioral profile developed by the Federal Aviation Administration, pinpointed individuals who should be checked more thoroughly before being allowed to board a plane. From January 1969 through Oct. 9, there had been 46 successful hijackings to Cuba: 28 involving U.S. airlines, and 18 belonging to non-U.S. lines. In addition, other planes had been hijacked to countries other than Cuba.

Increasing traffic congestion prompted the FAA to impose landing quotas, effective June 1, at the five most crowded terminal areas: Washington National Airport, Chicago's

The USAF's huge Lockheed C-5 Galaxy has a payload of up to 265,000 pounds; its cargo hold is 19 feet wide, 13.5 feet high and 144.6 feet long. Cargo enters through a visor nose, opening upward to expose hold fully.

Pictorial Parade

UPI

At Everett, Washington, the 231-foot Boeing 747 rolls out for its maiden flight. The enormous airliner seats from 362 to 490 passengers in spacious comfort (r).

Pictorial Parade

O'Hare, and the three airports serving the New York sector. The airlines went along reluctantly with what they described as "one of the strangest exercises in aviation history—an exercise which, if allowed to continue indefinitely, could close the door on the potential business for which the airlines have been gearing at such vast expense."

On Sept. 9, near Indianapolis, a collision between a jet airliner and a private plane, killing all 83 persons aboard, set off a new wave of concern over air safety. There was public airing of the continuing shortcomings of airways and airport systems. Traffic controllers complained bitterly about inadequate equipment and excessive demands on their resources. The Congress considered a number of ways to finance needed airport and airways development.

At a conference on world airports in London, Knut Hammarskjöld, director general of IATA, reported that world scheduled passenger air traffic had increased 7 times since 1954, a growth rate rivaled by few other industries. North Atlantic traffic has increased 10 times since 1953, at an average rate of 17 per cent a year, and transpacific traffic has increased at an even more rapid rate since 1964, 21 per cent a year. World traffic is expected to double by 1975 and increase 5 times by 1980. The estimated 1969 traffic volume on IATA airlines was more than 300,000,000 passengers carried some 350,000,000,000 passenger-kilometers. At the start of 1969 the international airlines of the free world had some 676,000 employees, including 40,000 pilots, 14,000 other flight-deck personnel and 50,000 cabin attendants.

Visitors to Bourget Airport, Paris, pass through a model of an airbus, which will be built by France and Germany together, designed to provide short-run shuttle service between European capitals.

Pictorial Parade

In the United States the airlines took delivery during 1969 of some 337 jets, costing more than $2,000,000,000, among the 628 they had on order. Dominant in the delivery list were Boeing jets, more than 200 of them. Products of British Aircraft Corp. and of Japan's Nihon Co. also were among the purchases of U.S. airlines. The Air Transport Association said that by 1974 the major U.S. airlines would have to spend $10,300,000,000 for flight equipment and $2,200,000,000 for associated ground equipment. The impact of the superjets on airline buying was felt in the fact that the total capital expenditures going to ground support rose from 5.5 per cent in 1968 to 18.4 per cent in 1969, and were expected to climb to 18.1 per cent in 1970.

The era of the wide-bodied aircraft, supposed to dawn in 1969, was deferred until 1970 in part because of delays in delivery of the Pratt & Whitney engines for the first superjet to enter airline service, the Boeing 747. The giant plane made its bow to the public on a flight from Seattle to Paris, for the air show there in June, and on its return flight stopped over at Washington's Dulles International Airport. Twice the size and 10 per cent faster than the popular 707 jet, the 747 has seating capacities ranging from 362 to 490. Even more awesome in appearance than the 747, if possible, was the Lockheed C-5, the tremendous Air Force cargo plane that made its formal debut at the National Aviation Exposition at Dulles in August.

Britain's Rolls-Royce achieved one of the marketing coups of commercial-aviation history by winning—over the intense competition of 2 major U.S. firms: General Electric and Pratt & Whitney—the contract to provide the engines for the Lockheed L-1011 TriStar airbus. The value of the contract was expected to total some $2,000,000,000 over a 10-year period. Involved in the arrangement was an order from a new British firm, Air Holdings, Ltd., for 30 L-1011's at $15,000,000 each, with options for 20 more. Air Holdings was licensed to sell the planes to airlines elsewhere than in the United States.

Both the Soviet TU-144 and the British-French Concorde supersonic transports flew many times in proving flights and were expected to enter service in the early 1970's. Late in the year, President Richard M. Nixon ordered a go-ahead on the U.S. SST program, which had been undergoing exhaustive re-evaluation. The 280-passenger, 1,800-mile-an-hour Boeing SST, with General Electric engines—which are larger and faster than those of Boeing's competitors abroad—was not expected to go into commercial operation for quite a few years, probably about 1978.

In the U.S. airline industry there was a great deal of merger talk, involving in one way or another virtually all of the major carriers, but there was little action. In the matter of route expansion, however, the CAB was extremely active. Some of the biggest plums were routes from Los Angeles to Hong Kong, by way of Honolulu, to TWA; from eastern and midwestern U.S. cities to New Zealand and Australia, to American Airlines; and from Miami to London for National Airlines.

VERN HAUGLAND
Aviation Editor, The Associated Press

BELGIUM

The Kingdom of Belgium took fresh steps to deal with an old problem and first steps to deal with a relatively new one in 1969.

The old problem was the split in the country between Flemish-speakers and French-speakers, Flamands and Walloons. The new was a sudden burst of wage-price inflation.

The linguistic division spread to the armed forces in the early part of the year. It was claimed that in the Army some 60 per cent of the rank and file were Flemish while two thirds of the generals were Walloons.

Deputy Prime Minister Joseph-Jean Merlot was involved in a car crash, and died on Jan. 21. He had been a key figure in the Government between the two groups. Flemish-speakers held 15 positions out of 29, the Walloons 14. Merlot was a Walloon-speaker. He was replaced by French-speaking socialist André Cools.

Further clashes occurred at Louvain University in March, and finally a cabinet crisis erupted in May. The eventual result, later in the year, was to set up a 28-man Working Party to draw up acceptable terms for a final settlement of "the language war."

Economically, Belgium in mid-1969 seemed headed for a new boom. Production was up 10.6 per cent over the previous summer. Belgian exports had risen 21 per cent, imports 19. But prices were rising much faster than usual, as were wages (at an annual rate of 4 per cent and 8 per cent respectively).

The proposal to introduce the value-added tax, as required by the rules of the European Economic Community (of which Belgium is a founder member), was resisted on the grounds of inflationary pressure. Its introduction was postponed until Jan. 1, 1971. (See Netherlands, The.)

Belgium's main discount rate was raised to one of its highest levels. Starting at 3.75 per cent at the beginning of 1968, the rate reached 7 per cent in July and 7.5 per cent in September after Belgium also drew $46,500,000 from the International Monetary Fund.

President Nixon visited Brussels on Feb. 23-24. He had talks with King Baudouin, Prime Minister Gaston Eyskens and Foreign Minister Pierre Harmel, and also addressed the Council of the North Atlantic Treaty Organization.

Col. John Eisenhower, son of the late U.S. President, was appointed American ambassador to Belgium, succeeding Ridgway Knight.

JOHN ALLAN MAY
Chief, London Bureau
The Christian Science Monitor

BELGIUM

Area: 11,750 sq. mi.
Population: 9,700,000
Capital: Brussels (pop., 1,080,000)
Government: Baudouin I, king—1951; Gaston Eyskens, prime minister—1968
Gross National Product: $20,300,000,000
Monetary unit: Belgian franc (50.2 BF = U.S. $1.00)
Chief Products: textiles, metals, chemicals, cut gem diamonds
Foreign trade: (incl. Luxembourg), exports, $8,150,000,000; imports, $8,195,000,000
Communications: 1,753,698 telephones, 1,900,000 TV sets, 44 daily newspapers
Transportation: roads, 7,302 mi.; 1,503,117 passenger cars; railroads, 2,688 mi.; navigable waterways, 952 mi.
Education: 575,012 elementary and secondary students, 59,172 university students
Armed forces: 102,400

See map on page 185

BIOLOGICAL SCIENCES:
Genetic Engineering

Strictly speaking, genetic engineering should mean manipulating the genes, which determine the hereditary potentialities of the fertilized egg. However, the term is commonly used also to cover various procedures that aim at controlling the early stages of the egg's development as a whole. The word "engineering" implies that this control is to produce useful results. Actually, of course, many of the same procedures are followed less for immediately useful results than as methods of fundamental science whose aim is to deepen our understanding of how the processes work.

In considering the work to be described, both these points of view must be kept in mind. In many ways the second is even more important than the first. Recently much publicity has been given to the possibilities of carrying out far-reaching and drastic experiments on the human genetic system. Although some of these methods will be described here, it is worth emphasizing that they are very unlikely to be used unless the majority of people in a society call for them. Man has known for centuries of a somewhat slow but eventually effective method of genetic engineering, namely, selective breeding. By this means he has produced such drastically modified individuals as the different races of dogs.

There is no *biological* reason why similar procedures should not prove equally effective with human beings. In practice, social forces have prevented it. Many of the farfetched types of genetic engineering discussed in the

Friedman-Abeles

A cell's chromosome pattern is analyzed by comparing it with diagrams of normal chromosomes (sheet on tray).

public press would not only meet similar repudiation but are still less likely to occur because they are not yet technically perfected. It is one thing to say that one can change the number of chromosomes in a frog's egg, or keep a rabbit embryo alive for one or two days outside the mother—and actually I was the first person to perform both of these feats, some thirty years ago. But it is a totally different thing to say that these methods could be used on human eggs to produce viable, healthy human babies. The possibilities may be there in theory, but it would probably take millions of dollars and two or three hundred man-years of skilled research to elaborate the technique to the point where it could actually be used in man, supposing that society agreed to it.

The most radical type of genetic engineering would be to manufacture new hereditary material designed to produce a given effect, and then to insert it into the hereditary constitution of an animal or plant. The manufacture of new DNA molecules with a preselected sequence of nucleotide bases would be a major step to understanding the biochemistry of this substance, and a good deal of work is going in this direction. However, the second two parts of the whole project are much more remote as practical possibilities. We have, as yet, almost no understanding of the precise relationship between a certain sequence of nucleotide bases in DNA and the functional effect of the protein produced by this gene. It looks as though it would be a very, very long time before we get near to understanding the problem.

Then there is the final stage of incorporating such a gene, if it could be produced, into the hereditary material. This is perhaps not quite so far away. We know that under some circumstances certain viruses can carry genes from one species of bacteria into another. In a higher organism, such as man, the DNA of the genes is combined with protein, whereas in bacteria the gene DNA is not protected in this way. So far no one has produced satisfactory evidence that viruses can transfer DNA-protein genes in the same way as they can pure DNA genes.

If any way is discovered for making the process work, then the next stage of the difficulty might be tackled: seeing that the virus picks up the right gene and transfers it into the right place in the recipient cell. It is just possible to contemplate the possibility of using some method of this sort to exchange a defective gene in some organism, not for a newly synthesized one but one selected from those already existing in healthy animals. The first glimmerings of success might come relatively soon. Yet to make the process work reliably enough to be useful even in such crude enterprises as animal or plant breeding would probably need at least one or two decades after the first demonstration of the mere possibility.

To refine it so that it worked reliably enough for human use would probably take the same amount of time again.

There are much greater possibilities of altering hereditary constitutions by transferring not single genes but rather whole chromosomes, which contain a few hundred or thousand genes. This is a trick that has been used for many years in the breeding of plants. Here it is relatively easy to make hybrids, and a vast production of infertile seeds or worthless plants can be afforded for the sake of getting one with a good combination of hereditary characters. An important method for transferring disease resistance from a wild species of plant has been to transfer single chromosomes from the wild species in the hope that one of these chromosomes carries the factors for disease resistance. In animal breeding this has not been possible until recently. Now techniques for achieving the result are in sight, although not yet developed. Suppose a grazing animal suitable for central Africa were wanted and it was suspected that some combination of chromosomes from the cow and a species of antelope would produce a suitable beast. To begin, cell cultures of cow and antelope cells would be set up. If cultures of the two types were then mixed and treated with certain inactivated viruses, the cells would tend to fuse together in pairs or greater numbers. It should not be impossible to pick out cells resulting from the fusion of a cow and an antelope cell, and to form cultures from them. In these cultures of double-size cells many abnormalities could be expected in the process of division, and these would give rise to a whole range of cell types with various combinations of cow and antelope chromosomes. From these mixed cells, the next step would involve getting complete *animals* with mixed sets of chromosomes. To do this the most hopeful technique would be to transplant nuclei from the mixed cells into a cow or an antelope egg whose own nucleus had been removed or killed. One might in this way finish up with some quite novel "genetically engineered" hybrids, putting such as "purple cows" in the shade.

This sequence of processes cannot yet be carried out in animals like cattle or antelopes. All the necessary steps, however, have been done in some animal or other. The most difficult is probably the nuclear transplantation into the egg, which has been satisfactorily achieved as yet only in amphibia and one or two insects. It seems most likely that only ten years or so of not very large-scale research and development would be enough to make the whole idea a practical one for animal-breeding purposes.

The reader may well say: but could we not use the same process to make most sinister hybrids between man and his anthropoid-ape cousins? The answer is that from a purely biological point of view this need not be technically much more difficult than making a cow-antelope hybrid. But it is not the kind of thing that could be done in a hurry, in secret, on a scale large enough to produce more than one or two abhorrent freaks, before the good sense of society stepped in and stopped it.

It is perhaps worth noting that there is another technique for making a rather different kind of hybrid between strains of mammals. Several embryologists studying mammalian development have recently found it possible to fuse together very young embryos of different strains of mice at a time, for instance, when the eggs have divided into only four or eight cells. From these fused eggs they have been able to rear normal, healthy adults, which are built up of cells coming from the two different strains. Such an animal is known as a "mosaic

Isolated for the first time in 1969, a single gene appears as a thread (center) in an electron-microscope photograph, magnifying the gene 79,300 times.

UPI

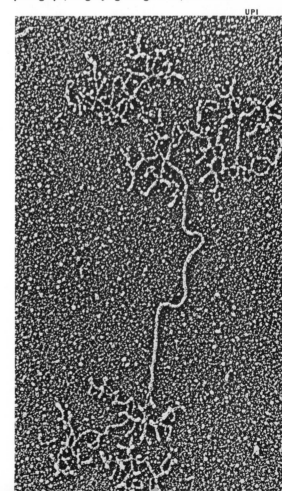

hybrid" because its body is a mosaic of one type of cell mixed in with the other type. For complex reasons, there is a deficiency of females among these animals, but otherwise they have appeared quite healthy and surprisingly, perhaps disappointingly, normal. Perhaps this is because in the experiments made so far the fusion was between strains that differed only in genes controlling such easily recognizable, but superficial, characters as coat color, type of hair, and so on. One is bound to ask what would happen if one fused together strains that differed markedly in some aspect of their behavior and brain functioning? This is a new type of genetic engineering that will bear watching.

All these possibilities of genuine genetic engineering are still quite a long distance in the future. In the immediate future, we shall continue to work largely on treatment of the harmful effects of deficient hereditary potentialities rather than on the radical methods of removing the inferior genes and replacing them with good ones. The techniques of genetic engineering in the broad sense will be helpful even in the less radical approach. In the first place, as we acquire a fuller understanding of the nature of genes and of the kind of deficiencies caused by abnormal and ineffective genes, so our methods of treatment will be able to get nearer the root of the hereditary diseases rather than merely their symptoms.

The ultimate hope is that even if the defective DNA of the genes could not be repaired, at least the defective RNA, which is the next step in the process of gene activity, could be replaced. This is again a theoretical possibility, which does not look very much easier to achieve than repair of the DNA itself. It seems more likely that in the immediate future the main point of our therapeutic attack will be on the nature and effectiveness of the proteins, which are the third step in the chain set going by the genes.

One further procedure that might be considered genetic engineering seems likely to play a considerable role quite soon. This is the development of techniques for spotting defective embryos at an early stage in their development, when it may be possible either to treat them more effectively than later on, or even bring about their abortion at such an early stage that the objections to this procedure would be minimized. In the main these techniques depend on being able to take small samples of cells from an early developing embryo and check these for the presence of hereditary defects. Quite active work is proceeding on several such techniques. If successful they would save a

great deal of unhappiness due to the birth of defective children.

C. H. Waddington
Professor of Genetics, University of Edinburgh
Visiting Einstein Professor, SUNY, Buffalo

BRANDT, WILLY

Promising that he would be a "chancellor of internal reforms," Willy Brandt was sworn in as the fourth chancellor of West Germany on Oct. 21, 1969. Brandt, who had been vice-chancellor and foreign minister from Dec. 1, 1966, was the first Socialist to head a German Government since 1930.

Brandt's rise to the leadership of West Germany was not achieved without a struggle. In national elections on Sept. 28, the Christian Democratic Union of Chancellor Kurt Kiesinger won 46.1 per cent of the vote, while Brandt's Social Democratic Party won 42.7 per cent. Brandt (who had tried to win the chancellorship in 1961 and 1965) immediately began negotiating with the nation's third major party, the Free Democrats, in the hope that a coalition government could be formed with himself at its head. On Oct. 21, at 11:20 A.M., 91 years after Bismarck had banned the Socialists from imperial Germany, the lower house of Parliament (the Bundestag) elected Brandt chancellor by a margin of three votes. A streamlined coalition Cabinet, with Free Democratic leader Walter Scheel as foreign minister, was presented the next day.

In his first speech on policy to the Bundestag, the new Chancellor declared that his Government would offer to negotiate agreements with the Soviet Union, East Germany and other Eastern European nations that would "acknowledge the territorial integrity of the respective partners." He also promised major domestic reforms.

Born in Lübeck on Dec. 18, 1913, and politically alert at a very young age, Brandt was called "the only Socialist" to attend Johanneum High School in that city. When Hitler came to power, Brandt fled to Scandinavia, where he earned his living as a journalist. After covering the Nuremberg trials for various Scandinavian newspapers, the future chancellor resumed German citizenship in 1948.

Brandt first came to international attention in 1956 when, as president of the West Berlin Parliament, he controlled a mob that was heading for the Soviet sector of Berlin to protest the Soviet Union's invasion of Hungary. Upon the death of Otto Suhr a year later, Brandt was elected mayor of West Berlin, a post he retained until 1966.

BULGARIA

Of all the countries of communist Eastern Europe, only Bulgaria feels a genuine desire for alignment with the U.S.S.R. Though Poland under Gomulka remains closely tied to Moscow, and East Germany under Ulbricht urged the Russian invasion of Czechoslovakia, most of their people show little pro-Russian sentiment. In the past, both nations have been restive under the hard-line Communist who rule them. Bulgaria, however, has steadily hewed to the Russian line, apparently without any resistance inside the party itself. In Moscow at the end of 1968, Bulgarian party chief Todor Zhivkov stressed the danger of Western ideological penetration. He held that the class struggle had not disappeared under communism, and that this justified the never-ending battle against bourgeois values. Warning against manifestations of nationalism, anti-Sovietism and liberalism, Zhivkov stated very firmly that Bulgaria would never catch the virus of Czech freedom.

The Government was still tinkering with the Bulgarian economy. Shunning the kind of economic reforms put through in Czechoslovakia, Hungary and Poland, which in recent years emphasized decentralization, Bulgaria concentrated its reforms, following Lenin's principle of "democratic centralism," on "greater centralism." To implement what is, in fact, traditional Soviet-inspired management of the economy, the party created a new Committee for Economic Coordination within the Cabinet. The state plan for 1969 called for a 10 per cent increase in Bulgaria's gross national product. Total industrial production was scheduled to rise by 11.6 per cent. Per capita real income was to increase by 5.7 per cent. All in all, the Government presented an optimistic but not incautious budget showing a modest surplus.

The ties between the Soviet and Bulgarian economies were recognized officially when the Bulgarian party leader visited Moscow in the fall of 1969. In Moscow, Zhivkov announced that over the next five years, the two countries would link not only their economies more closely but also achieve a functional synthesis in some areas of industrial production. Coordination of the division of labor, long a Soviet aim within the East European economic bloc COMECON, is the result desired. By relegating small industries to Bulgaria, the U.S.S.R. also guaranteed to Sofia that it would become Bulgaria's largest buyer. Since overall planning in COMECON has never worked out quite to Soviet specifications, the Russian leaders decided to concentrate on two-sided economic pacts.

JAMES CHACE
Managing Editor, *Foreign Affairs*

BULGARIA

Area: 42,796 sq. mi.
Population: 8,400,000
Capital: Sofia (pop., 860,000)
Government: Todor Zhivkov, Communist Party secretary—1954, and premier—1962
Gross national product: $8,000,000,000
Monetary unit: lev (1.16 leva = U.S. $1.00)
Chief products: coal, crude steel, iron ore, wheat, maize, oil
Foreign trade: exports, $1,611,000,000; imports, $1,759,000,000
Communications: 338,446 telephones, 1,468,930 radios, 287,880 TV sets, 12 daily newspapers
Transportation: roads, 18,124 mi.; railroads, 3,589 mi.
Education: 1,796,958 elementary and secondary students, 1 university
Armed forces: 154,000

See map on page 185

BURGER, WARREN EARL·

On the evening of May 21, 1969, when Richard Nixon presented Warren Earl Burger before television cameras as his surprise nominee to be chief justice of the United States, the nation saw a man who looked as if he might have been born to the office. Tall, suitably portly, white-haired, serious, Warren Burger could have been sent by Central Casting to play the role of Chief Justice.

On closer scrutiny, however, it appeared that while the new Chief Justice admirably fit the image of the job, Warren Earl Burger was the opposite of Earl Warren, his predecessor, in many ways other than the accident of names.

President Nixon had been elected on a pledge to turn the liberal Supreme Court around on crime, and he made it clear that he had picked a "law and order" judge to direct the job. The unpredictability of some newly appointed justices is legend, but early analyses of Warren Burger's background and record made a persuasive case that he would probably tend to be the type of chief justice that the President wished to see in the Court's center seat.

Pundits lost no time in declaring that the Burger appointment reflected President Nixon's studied association with the values of middle-brow, middle-aged, middle-class America. The nominee's background justified that view, but his record as a judge on the United States Court of Appeals for the District of Columbia reflected a stronger, more individualistic set of values.

Following his swearing-in on June 23, U.S. Chief Justice Warren Burger adjusts his robes with the help of his wife.

Warren Burger was born on Sept. 17, 1907, in St. Paul, Minn., of middle-class, Presbyterian parents. Hard work and a knack for learning earned him a good record at the University of Minnesota and a law degree from the St. Paul College of Law, a night law school. Law practice in St. Paul led him into Republican politics, where he caught the eye of Herbert Brownell. When Brownell became attorney general in the Eisenhower administration, Burger became an assistant attorney general. In 1956, President Eisenhower named him to the Court of Appeals.

On the Court of Appeals, Burger soon began to show an independence, a willingness to stand against the prevailing wisdom that marked him as a man separate and apart from his moderate-Republican background. Although there was scattered grumbling across the land about the liberal trend of the Warren Court on crime, in sophisticated judicial circles few voices were heard in the early 1960's to criticize the Supreme Court's course. Warren Burger was different. He began to deliver speeches and to publish dissents and law-review articles, warning that the emphasis on defendants' rights was making the law too brittle to deal with crime. He also deplored some judges' tendency "to require not merely a fair trial, but a perfect trial."

Burger felt that the Supreme Court's case-by-case system of establishing police procedures warped the law and froze unwise and rigid rules into the Constitution. Instead, he urged the Supreme Court to use its rule-making power to lay down rules for the Federal system that could serve as a proving ground for state procedures. He became one of the few leading judges to question the Supreme Court's technique of excluding illegally obtained evidence as a way to police the police. Such evidence should be admitted and the erring policemen should be punished, he said.

Burger was above all a practical man. He thought that the criminal-justice system should concentrate on swifter justice and better rehabilitation; that psychiatric jargon in criminal-insanity cases should give way to commonsense testimony by mental doctors; that fiercely combative courtroom tactics should be replaced with less contentious procedures aimed primarily at finding the truth. Throughout all his beliefs ran the strong Burger independence, the willingness to swim upstream in pursuit of what he believed to be right. (See Supreme Court decisions under Law.)

Thus Warren Burger took his seat in October of 1969 with a record of views that were strong, clear and often at odds with those of his predecessor. Yet his opposition to existing law was at some points pegged to alternatives that some observers considered implausible or impractical, and it remained to be seen if he could put his views into practice now that he had become chief justice.

FRED P. GRAHAM
Supreme Court Correspondent
The New York Times

BURMA

Rarely has any openly declared campaign to overthrow an existing government captured as wide attention as the one launched in 1969 by former Prime Minister U Nu. Although U Nu's campaign was most open in the speeches the 62-year-old leader made around the world away from home, it clearly stirred vibrations in Burma. U Nu had left home in April, after the Burmese head of state, Gen. Ne Win, had turned down U Nu's proposal to return Burma to parliamentary democracy. U Nu then set off on a campaign to rally moral support and financial help for the overthrow of Ne Win, by force if necessary. In August he spoke in Britain, and in September in the United States and at the UN. Finally, in October, he sought and was granted political asylum in Thailand. From there, it was presumed, U Nu would continue his drive to oust Ne Win.

In a clearly related political move, Foreign Affairs and National Planning Minister U Thi Han resigned from his post in June. He declared that he resigned because he did not want his "personal feelings toward former politicians and ex-army officers to interfere with [his] official responsibilities." The Foreign Minister's post was taken over by Col. Maung Lwin, the former minister for social welfare.

Local insurgencies continued to simmer in five areas of the northeast and east. Most of them were revolts by noncommunist hill tribes supplied with arms and equipment by Communist China. The United States, at the same time, continued to deliver weapons to the military forces loyal to Ne Win.

On Mar. 20 the Chinese Communist Party acknowledged that Thakin Than Tun, chairman of the Burmese Communist Party, had been assassinated in September 1968. A Burmese Communist Party statement charged that the assassin was an agent of Gen. Ne Win.

Burma's economy, though perhaps not deteriorating, remained stagnant. The Government indicated indirectly that it was thinking of some economic liberalization, though in fact the program of nationalization continued. In February, 24 shipping agencies were taken over by the Government. On July 24 the Government announced nationalization of the entire jade industry, including prospecting, mining and sales.

The only significant change in attitude was a decision by the Ne Win administration to open Burma's doors to tourism. The Union of Burma Airways began flying a Boeing 727 in August, and an offer of "easy visas" for all tourists was widely advertised. Obviously, need for foreign exchange was behind the move. In

---

BURMA

Area: 263,589 sq. mi.
Population: 27,000,000
Capital: Rangoon (pop., 1,617,000)
Government: Ne Win, chairman of the council of ministers—1962
Gross National Product: $2,200,000,000
Monetary unit: kyat (4.8 kyat=U.S. $1.00)
Chief products: hardwood, teak, rice, sugar cane, petroleum
Foreign trade: exports, $111,000,000; imports, $112,000,000
Communications: 20,783 telephones, 7 daily newspapers
Transportation: roads, 9,582 mi.; railroads, 1,856 mi.
Education: 3,377,496 elementary and secondary students, 2 universities
Armed forces: 142,500

see map on page 481

---

part, that need was heightened during 1969 because of the world surplus of rice and a consequent drop in Burma's rice exports. (Rice accounts for more than 50 per cent of Burma's exports and is its major source of foreign exchange.)

In international relations, Burma maintained its strict neutrality. The Japanese Government agreed early in the year to extend a 10,800,-000,000-yen ($30,000,000) credit to help finance a number of industrial projects. In late March, Prime Minister Indira Gandhi of India paid a three-day visit to the country.

ARTHUR C. MILLER
Senior Editor
The Asia Letter

CALIFORNIA

For nine days in January, torrential rains fell on California, especially in the south, in the worst deluge there since 1938, resulting in 91 deaths and property damage amounting to perhaps $200,000,000. President Nixon declared the whole state a disaster area. ☐ On Jan. 28 an oil well blew 6 miles offshore from Santa Barbara. Seepage continued for almost a month despite frantic efforts to plug the leaks and the use of chemicals to repel the viscous fluid. A slick extending over 400 square miles accumulated, and some 16 miles of beaches were fouled. The state planned to bring suit against the Federal Government and several oil companies for $1,060,000,000 for damage incurred. ☐ In a surprise victory, Samuel W. Yorty was reelected mayor of Los Angeles, defeating City Councilman Thomas Bradley, a Negro. ☐ In August, San Diego began a year-long celebration of its 200th anniversary.

Marking the resumption of Cambodia-U.S. diplomatic relations, the American flag again flies in Pnom Penh.

CAMBODIA

In 1969, wily Prince Norodom Sihanouk, chief of state of Cambodia, continued his maneuvering to keep his nation from becoming engulfed in the wars in South Vietnam and Laos. Despite his best efforts, some fighting related to these conflicts flared occasionally in his border provinces.

The most significant development was his decision, in which President Nixon concurred, to resume diplomatic relations with the United States. U.S. charge d'affaires Lloyd Rives, an Indochina expert, arrived in August at Pnom Penh to reestablish the thread severed in 1965 when American warplanes began bombing and shelling, perhaps at first accidentally, the fringes of Cambodian territory in pursuit of the Vietcong.

Sen. Mike Mansfield, U.S. Democratic majority leader, who has been a Sihanouk admirer for years, visited Pnom Penh in late August. He came away convinced that ambassadorial-level diplomacy, and possibly a request for American military and economic aid, would follow Rives' settling-in period. Thus the United States would have another ally besides Thailand adjacent to the fighting. This had not developed by the end of 1969.

The Prince's wariness seemed to substantiate the belief that improvement in Cambodian-American relations was not so much an embrace of the anticommunists. Rather, it was more of his same zigzagging to keep his keystone Southeast Asian nation independent and his socialist-leaning economy viable without becoming wed to any great power.

It was an admirable stance but even Sihanouk's admirers wondered how much longer he could walk the tightrope.

While periodically outraged over American and South Vietnam violation of his borders, Sihanouk was having more trouble with the North Vietnamese (whom he calls Viet Minh) and the Vietcong. He admitted at midyear, after long denying their presence on Cambodian soil, that there were 40,000 Viet Minh and Vietcong in more or less permanent "sanctuary" in his eastern provinces. They sortie across the border into Vietnam to fight, and then retire to rest and refit.

Concerned that Hanoi intends to keep its troops in Cambodia after a Vietnam war settlement, Sihanouk sent Premier Lon Nol to talk with Communist China's Prime Minister Chou En-lai. The aim was to get Peking's assurances that it would prevail on its "brothers" in North Vietnam to leave Cambodia alone.

The Prince has internal troubles as well. In most of his remote provinces there are subversive groups in varying stages of defiance. He identifies these "disloyal Khmers" (Cambodians) by colors: communist reds, rightist blues, and white Khmer, whom he claims are trained by his hostile neighbor Thailand.

Sihanouk's scorn of foreign aid that has "strings attached" has left him with little means for economic improvement. Even the French did not give their former colony enthusiastic support, although they continued to be on friendly political terms, until he devalued the Cambodian riel to bring it in line with the franc more realistically.

Politically the Prince continued as the supreme ruler, although he lost Lon Nol in November because of illness which sent the Premier to France.

JACK FOISIE
Correspondent, Southeast Asia
The Los Angeles Times

CAMBODIA

Area: 66,800 sq. mi.
Population: 6,700,000
Capital: Pnom Penh (pop., 400,000)
Government: Prince Norodom Sihanouk, chief of state—1960
Gross national product: $1,000,000,000
Monetary unit: riel (54 riels = U.S. $1.00)
Chief products: rice, rubber, maize, pepper
Foreign trade: exports, $83,000,000; imports, $96,000,000
Communications: 5,900 telephones, 25,000 TV sets
Transportation: roads, 3,221 mi.
Education: 1,105,000 pupils
Armed forces: 38,500

See map on page 481

canada

The last year of the 1960's was for Canada a violent summing-up of a turbulent decade and a step toward a more stable future.

It was a year of unprecedented violence in Montreal, the largest city in Canada and the focal point of discontent for French-speaking Canadians, who represent about one quarter of the total national population of 21,300,000. Economically, Montreal is the only major Canadian city with a French-speaking majority, yet its economic life still remains largely in the hands of English-speaking businessmen. Discontent with this state of affairs kept the city in turmoil in 1969. Police Director Jean Paul Gilbert warned that bombs were becoming "the commonplace expression of feelings and ideas" in Montreal's divided society.

The breakdown of law and order reached a climax on Oct. 7 when Montreal's policemen and firemen staged an illegal 16-hour strike to enforce wage demands. During daylight hours the city managed surprisingly well. In the afternoon a number of banks and other businesses closed their doors as armed robberies were reported. Evening brought a few hours of ominous calm and then—chaos.

A radical group of taxi drivers, calling itself Le Mouvement de la Libération du Taxi, decided to attack the headquarters of a charter limousine service to settle a long-standing feud over passenger-pickup rights at Montreal International Airport. The demonstration erupted into a shoot-out between them that claimed the life of a young Quebec Provincial Police trooper.

By this time the Provincial Police had been ordered into the city along with 750 French-speaking soldiers of the Royal 22nd Regiment. But most of them arrived too late. Shortly before midnight, demonstrators surged into the downtown area where they smashed more than $2,000,000 worth of plate glass and looted almost every store along St. Catherine Street, the city's "department-store row." A few of the looters were captured after midnight by Montreal policemen who had been ordered back to work by an emergency session of Quebec's National Assembly.

Montreal remained under outside police and Army supervision for several days. In November the city council passed a controversial by-law enabling it to ban any public gathering or demonstration that it deemed a threat to public order. The first demonstration to be banned under this bylaw was the Vietnam Moratorium protest.

The city was troubled throughout the year by sporadic bombings by fanatic "separatists" who want to turn the Province of Quebec, where most French Canadians live, into an in-

As turmoil continues in Montreal on Oct. 10, police speed their motorcycles along the sidewalks, forcing walkers to take refuge in doorways, in effort to forestall a threatened march on City Hall.

UPI

Slowly getting back to work, stock exchange in Montreal substitutes chalk and blackboard for electronic boards shattered by bomb explosion on Feb. 13.

UPI

dependent, French-speaking nation. Apart from the arrest of a 25-year-old student, who received a life sentence after pleading guilty to 129 charges arising from the bombings, police were unsuccessful in their efforts to stop the attacks. There were no fatalities in 1969, but 27 people were injured in February when a bomb exploded in the Montreal and Canadian stock exchanges. English-language universities also were hit.

In September a dispute over languages at the elementary-school level brought 1,500 young French Canadians into the streets of suburban St. Léonard where they smashed windows and looted small businesses, most of them owned by Italian immigrants. Fifty people were arrested and more than 100 were injured. Total costs of damage to property were relatively slight.

CANADA

Area: 3,851,809 sq. mi.
Population: 21,300,000
Capital: Ottawa (pop., 300,000)
Government: Roland Michener, governor-general—1967; Pierre Elliott Trudeau, prime minister—1968
Gross national product: $67,368,000,000
Monetary unit: Canadian dollar (CD$1.08 = U.S. $1.00)
Chief products: wheat, wood, fishing, furs, nickel, zinc, aluminum, crude steel, gasoline
Foreign trade: exports, $12,556,000,000; imports, $11,431,000,000
Communications: 8,385,476 telephones, 7,271,000 TV sets, 118 daily newspapers
Transportation: roads, 445,767 mi.; 5,499,527 passenger cars; railroads, 58,530 mi.
Education: 5,281,463 elementary and secondary students, 261,207 students of higher education
Armed forces: 98,000

At the political level, partisans of an independent Quebec started to nominate candidates of their Parti Québecois for a provincial election, expected in 1970. The party's showing in this election, its first, will determine whether separatism is to remain a dominant issue in the 1970's. Public-opinion polls in the 1960's usually revealed support of 10 to 13 per cent for the separatists among French-speaking Quebecers, with most of the separatists among the young and the intelligentsia.

Despite the leadership of a former Quebec cabinet minister, René Lévesque, the separatists in 1969 met firmer opposition from the older parties, which believe in maintaining Quebec within the Canadian Confederation. Quebec's Union Nationale government brought in legislation to give French Canadians more control of education and municipal government in the Montreal area. Measures were taken to encourage a wider use of French in business and among immigrants, who have shown a preference in the past for learning English.

Across Canada, the Federal Government's Official Languages Act came into effect Sept. 7. This gives French the same status as English in government services in Ottawa and in designated "bilingual districts" across the country.

Canada's "dual personality" created external problems during the 1960's. Relations with France were frigid after President de Gaulle's famous *Québec Libre* balcony speech at Montreal's City Hall in 1967. Canada also broke off relations with the small African nation of Gabon after it gave Quebec equality with Canada at an international conference on education. Both these situations returned to normal in 1969. A new and more friendly era in Franco-Canadian relations was confirmed in December when Canada's External Affairs

Tanks and soldiers' helmets are camouflaged during Canadian Army maneuvers. Total number of armed forces, including the units serving in Europe with NATO, is being reduced.

Canadian Forces, Dept. of National Defence, Canada

Minister Mitchell Sharp had a cordial meeting in Brussels with Foreign Minister Maurice Schumann of France. Their talk seemed to mark the end of divisive Gaullist diplomacy in Canada.

The improvement in relations between Paris and Ottawa was a minor event compared with Canada's 1969 decision to reduce its NATO forces in Europe. A review of the NATO commitment had been part of Prime Minister Trudeau's election campaign the previous year. In May, Defense Minister Léo Cadieux informed NATO that Canada's decision to reduce its forces by 1972 was irrevocable. Despite protests from Britain that Canada was not doing its share, and more subtle disapproval by Washington, Cadieux announced in September that Canadian forces in Europe would be reduced from 9,800 to 5,000 men by the fall of 1970. This is part of a previously announced reduction in Canada's total armed forces, from 98,000 to 82,000 men in the next 3 years.

Another example of adventurous Canadian diplomacy was the opening of talks in 1969 in Stockholm with representatives of mainland China. Despite publicly expressed "concern" by the United States, Canada moved slowly during the year toward official recognition of Communist China, although it continued to abstain during the annual vote on the admission of Peking to the United Nations.

Both the NATO revision and the new China policy reflected the personal views of Prime Minister Trudeau. Before he joined the Liberals, one of Canada's two "old" parties, he was an active member of the socialist New Democratic Party and an outspoken critic of former Prime Minister Pearson's decision to permit U.S. nuclear warheads on Canadian territory. Trudeau also visited China during the early

years of the Mao regime. On his return, he coauthored a sympathetic book about his visit.

Another source of friction with the United States was the detonation of a 1.2-megaton thermonuclear device on Oct. 2 beneath the Aleutian island of Amchitka. As demonstrators

Only rubble is left of home for aged at Notre Dame du Lac, Quebec, after fire in which over 50 persons died.

UPI

UPI

Order of Canada recipients Cardinal Leger and Lorne Greene chat with Governor-General and Mrs. Michener.

marched in front of U.S. consulates across Canada, Ottawa told Washington that it would hold the United States responsible for any damage caused by this and subsequent Aleutian tests.

The nuclear test was the second time in as many months that Canadians became aware of an American presence to the north—an unexpected direction. When the Humble Oil tanker *Manhattan* made history on Sept. 15 as the first commercial ship to sail through the Northwest Passage, it reminded Canadians of their tenuous claim to Arctic sovereignty. The possibility of pollution of Canadian Arctic waters was one of the main questions raised by Prime Minister Trudeau in November during his first meeting with United Nations Secretary-General U Thant.

Two small nations absorbed a disproportionate amount of Canadian attention in 1969. There was a mild flurry of criticism in October when Ottawa announced an exchange of ambassadors with the Vatican. The move had been expected since January when Prime Minister Trudeau was received in Rome by the Pope, but there were objections nonetheless from some Protestant leaders. Dr. John E. Robbins, former president of Brandon University, was appointed ambassador.

More serious was the widespread dissatisfaction with the Government's cautious Nigerian policy. For reasons difficult to define, the Nigerian-Biafran conflict was a much larger issue in Canada than in any other developed nation.

Canada's church-sponsored program of Biafran relief was the beleaguered state's most important single source of food and medical assistance. Despite public pressure, the Canadian Government insisted that its desire to help Biafrans should not conflict with its respect for the sovereignty of Nigeria, a fellow Commonwealth nation. Canada's firmness on this policy probably reflected, to a limited extent, Prime Minister Trudeau's impatience with separatist tendencies within his own nation.

Student protest was a feature of North American life in 1969, and Montreal was the scene of its most destructive manifestation. In February a simmering dispute between six black students and a biology professor accused of racism escalated into a student occupation, by whites and blacks, of the computer center at downtown Sir George Williams University. The students managed to wreak $2,000,000 worth of damage before police evicted them from the smoke-filled building. Ninety-seven students were arrested; most of their cases were still before the courts as the year ended.

The "computer party" at Sir George Williams University was the most serious of a wave of student sit-ins, strikes and demonstrations in the first half of 1969. By fall there were signs of a conservative reaction. Moderate student leaders began to emerge on many campuses. One result in the last months of 1969 was the decline and dissolution of the Canadian Union of Students, the largest student association.

Province of Quebec

Quebec Premier Jean-Jacques Bertrand points to dedication of dam named for the late Premier Daniel Johnson.

Youthful activists came under fire again in November when a parliamentary committee investigated the Company of Young Canadians, a domestic "peace corps." The inquiry started after the administration of Montreal's Mayor Jean Drapeau accused members of the Company of provoking civil disorder and advocating violence. It revealed that the Company in Quebec included convicted separatist-terrorists and that some Company funds were being used to finance separatist activities. The Government was able to resist demands for the aboli-tion of the Company, but it promised closer government supervision in future.

The Canadian economy in 1969 progressed reasonably well through an obstacle course of strikes, poor export markets for wheat, and inflation. After peaking in the last quarter of 1968, the economy slowed down in 1969. Most experts predicted a further deceleration in the year 1970, from a 9 per cent increase in gross national product in 1969 to an increase of no more than 5.5 per cent in the next twelve months.

UPI

President Nixon and Prime Minister Trudeau shake hands during ceremonies marking the tenth anniversary of the opening of the St. Lawrence Seaway.

Skins await pickup after annual seal hunt in the Gulf of St. Lawrence. Clubbing of baby seals was protested so strongly that in October, Canada restricted future hunts to seals well beyond "whitecoat" pup stage.

Concerned about an increase of more than 4 per cent in consumer prices in 1969, the Federal Government created a Prices and Incomes Commission to institute a policy of voluntary restraint. By the end of the year, Canadian unions had rejected the commission's initial proposals. In August, Prime Minister Trudeau announced a freeze on Federal spending for 1970-71 and a program to reduce the Federal payroll by 25,000 jobs from its 1968 peak of 236,736 civil servants.

"We'd be on the road to financial disaster if nothing were done to bring spending under control," he said.

Many of the spending cuts were felt immediately in such "controllable" areas as regional economic development, medical research, low-income housing, and aid to Indians and Eskimos.

The Government's program was stabbed in September by its own Economic Council, a high-powered advisory body which warned that a forecast 35 per cent increase in Canadian living standards by 1975 would not be achieved if the Government exercised "overkill" in its fight against inflation. Said the council, opening up a rabid debate among Canadian economists: "Further fiscal and monetary restraints conceivably could result simply in higher rates

of unemployment and economic slack with no more than marginal effects on current rates of unemployment and rates of increase in prices and costs."

For the fourth consecutive year, world wheat production in 1969 exceeded 10,000,000,000 bushels. Continuing bumper crops in Canada and tougher markets abroad gave the prairies a record backlog of 848,284,000 bushels by the end of July. It was revealed in October that Russia, with good crops of its own and a shortage of storage facilities, had yet to take 133,-000,000 of 337,500,000 bushels contracted for in 1966 under a three-year deal. The position of wheat as a dominant factor in Canadian exports was insecure, and there was an increased effort to investigate other sources of income, farm and otherwise, for wheatgrowers. However, in December, Otto E. Lang, minister without portfolio, announced that the U.S.S.R. had agreed to accept delivery of 75,000,000 bushels of wheat, including 13,000,000 bushels of flour to be shipped directly to Cuba, by Dec. 31, 1970.

In Saskatchewan, Premier Ross Thatcher attempted to use wheat for barter on the international market, offering a preference to manufacturers who would accept wheat in payment for transformers worth $300,000 required by

UPI

A huge grain cargo ship is loaded from one of Vancouver's several giant grain elevators. The British Columbian city, the world's number one wheat port, is playing a major role in Canada's developing Pacific trade.

the state-owned Saskatchewan Power Corporation. Ottawa said it did not like the idea because it would disrupt Canada's normal markets.

The unsatisfactory wheat situation continued to give Prime Minister Trudeau political trouble in the western provinces. When the bachelor Prime Minister toured Saskatchewan in July, he was greeted with placards saying: "Hustle Wheat Not Women." The Prime Minister also ran into trouble later in the year in British Columbia when he allegedly punched or shoved a young antiwar demonstrator who was preventing him from making a speech. A charge against the Prime Minister was subsequently thrown out of court.

Ottawa announced in October that it intended to lower the age at which citizens can vote from 21 to 18.

Ottawa promised new antipollution measures, and said that industries or municipalities causing pollution would have to bear the cost of prevention. A survey of 19 major Canadian cities revealed that only 8 treated all of their sewage. Following the lead of the United States, Canada banned cyclamates in 1969; Ontario banned the use of DDT without a permit, and other provinces were expected to adopt similar measures.

At the eastern end of the nation, Premier "Joey" Smallwood of Newfoundland resigned at the age of 68, announced a leadership convention to choose a successor, entered it at the last minute and won hands down. One of the most famous passenger trains in North America, the narrow-gage "Newfie Bullet," made its last run. Canadians were reminded in 1969 that Newfoundland had been part of Canada for a mere twenty years, and still was not too sure about it.

In September a ten-stick dynamite bomb wrecked the home of Montreal's Mayor Jean Drapeau. No one was injured.

Ottawa announced new legislation to outlaw all electronic eavesdropping and wiretapping equipment except when used by the police under strict control. Justice Minister John Turner warned that "the open society has become the bugged society."

Influenced by the success of Expo 67 in Montreal, the Federal Government and three provinces will give Canada the largest participation of any country at Expo 70 in Osaka, Japan. The Canadian Pavilion will be matched by pavilions from the provinces of Quebec, Ontario and British Columbia.

PETER DESBARATS
Associate Editor, *Saturday Night*

Kryn Taconis

Pipeline is laid in wild country to bring gas from the Edson and Brazeau fields west of Edmonton, Alberta.

CANADA: Provinces and Territories

ALBERTA

In a by-election on Feb. 10 a Conservative, Bill Yurko, unexpectedly won the seat of former Premier E. C. Manning (Social Credit). ☐ On Feb. 18 the cabinet approved a loan of $32,-000,000. It was the first time in 33 years that the Social Credit government had borrowed to cover a budget deficit. ☐ The 235-mile, $96-000,000 Alberta Resources Railway was completed on May 28. It links the rich resources of the Peace River area, in the north, with Pacific markets. ☐ On July 1 the province joined the national medical-care plan; and a 5 per cent increase in provincial personal income taxes went into effect.

BRITISH COLUMBIA

Work was started, to be completed in 1970, on dredging Vancouver Harbor to a depth of 50 feet to accommodate 80,000-deadweight-ton bulk carriers. ☐ Hovercraft service began on Feb. 23 across the sheltered Strait of Georgia, between the city of Vancouver (on the mainland) and Nanaimo (on Vancouver Island). The $420,000 vessel, which carries up to 35 passengers, makes the 34-mile run in about 45 minutes. ☐ On May 22, Premier W. A. C. Bennett laid the cornerstone, at Houston, of what will be the largest enclosed sawmill in Canada.

It is the initial stage of a $100,000,000 integrated forest-products development. ☐ The 170-foot-high High Arrow Dam on the Columbia River was dedicated on June 9, for flood control of a 14,000-square-mile drainage area. ☐ On Aug. 27, Premier Bennett led his Social Credit Party to its sixth successive victory.

MANITOBA

In general elections on June 25, Edward Schreyer, New Democratic Party, won a surprise victory over Premier Walter Weir, Progressive Conservative; and the Liberal opposition was reduced to five members. Schreyer, who calls himself a Social Democrat, thus formed the first New Democratic Party in Canada outside of Saskatchewan and emerged as a political figure of national stature. Low prices for surplus wheat appeared to be a factor in his triumph.

NEW BRUNSWICK

Long called the "land of covered bridges," New Brunswick launched plans to preserve some of the remaining 142 wooden structures, which are to be restored as closely as possible to their original state. ☐ Progress continued on Saint John's $300,000,000 urban-renewal program. It includes an 18-story City Hall complex, a cross-city throughway to the new harbor bridge (the city's first western gateway), a new campus

Camera Press-PIX

"Village" floating on Shuswap Lake, amid British Columbia's great forests, is the temporary home of loggers.

for the city's branch of the University of New Brunswick, expansion of hospitals and recreation areas, and 200 new public-housing units in the East End area. □ Numerous tax increases went into effect on Apr. 1, placing New Brunswick's taxes among the highest of any Canadian province.

NEWFOUNDLAND

During 1969, work was proceeding so smoothly on the hydroelectric project at Churchill Falls, Labrador, that completion was expected before the target date, 1976. The huge caverns being dug out will house the world's largest underground hydro power plant. Its 11 gigantic generators will occupy a chamber as long as three football fields. The $950,000,000 development was the biggest single civil-engineering project currently being built in North America.

NORTHWEST TERRITORIES

The territorial Council chose a flag: the territorial coat of arms superimposed on a white midsection with blue borders at each end. □ Construction started on a new modern town at Frobisher Bay (the administrative center for the eastern Arctic), at the southeastern end of Baffin Island. Completion was scheduled for July 1971, including an apartment block, a series of row houses, a hotel, and business, recreational and shopping buildings. The de-

velopment, to cost $15,000,000 to $20,000,000, is a joint venture of private firms and the Canadian Government. All new accommodations are to be open to both Eskimos and whites (Frobisher Bay is the largest Eskimo settlement in Canada).

NOVA SCOTIA

On Apr. 1, Nova Scotia joined the national medical-care plan. □ Higher taxes on gasoline, liquor and tobacco went into effect on Apr. 4, when the sales tax also was increased from 5 to 7 per cent. □ On May 8 it was announced that the world's first commercial plant to produce high-purity fish protein would be built at Canso. The $500,000 project will have an initial output of 30 tons of pure protein a day, requiring 200 tons of fresh fish. □ In August, Nova Scotia was host to the Olympic-style Canada Games. Some 2,600 athletes took part from all 12 provinces and territories.

ONTARIO

On Feb. 1, Ontario's first prepaid drug-insurance plan went into effect; and the province entered the national medical-care program on Oct. 1. □ Legislation announced in April provides that after Jan. 1, 1970, all Ontario ores must be processed and treated in Canada. □ A law passed later provides for payment to victims for injuries inflicted during a criminal attack. □

Orillia began celebrations marking the 100th anniversary of the birth of Stephen Leacock, the great humorist (born in England on Dec. 30, 1869). He made Orillia famous in *Sunshine Sketches of a Little Town*.

PRINCE EDWARD ISLAND

A deficit budget and an increase in the sales tax, from 5 to 7 per cent, effective at once, were announced on Apr. 15. □ In June a fourth ferry went into service on Northumberland Strait, between Cape Tormentine, N.B., and Borden, P.E.I. The new vessel, purchased from Sweden, carries up to 100 automobiles and 1,000 passengers.

QUEBEC

At the opening of the legislature on Feb. 25, Lt. Gov. Hugues Lapointe read an "inaugural speech" instead of a "speech from the throne," implying more self-determination for Quebec. □ On May 12 a contract, involving $5,000,-000,000, was signed by which Quebec will buy nearly all the electricity generated at Churchill Falls, Labrador, for 40 years from completion (scheduled for 1976), to be renewed automatically for 25 years. □ Also in May, Ottawa and Quebec agreed on the creation of a national park in the Gaspé area, the first national park in Quebec. □ On June 22, Premier Jean-Jacques Bertrand (who favored cooperation with Prime Minister Trudeau on a new Federal constitution) triumphed in the convention of the National Union Party, thereby retaining his party's leadership and the premiership.

SASKATCHEWAN

On Mar. 12 a bill was approved in principle by which a new Department of Indians and Métis will be established; $1,000,000 was set aside for it in the 1969–70 budget. □ An official flag was adopted on Mar. 31: a green upper half (representing the northern parklands), a yellow lower half (representing the southern wheat fields), a prairie lily at the left, and the provincial emblem (a lion and three sheaves of wheat) in the upper right corner. □ Some $25,000,000 to $30,000,000 was spent during 1969 on aerial search, ground exploration and drilling in northern Saskatchewan in one of the most intense mineral searches Canada has ever seen. It followed on the discovery late in 1968 of uranium deposits at Wollaston Lake.

YUKON TERRITORY

In April a new Municipal Affairs Department was established. □ In view of the huge deposits of oil being discovered in neighboring Alaska, the search for oil in the Yukon was intensified.

Kryn Taconis

At salt mine near Windsor, Ontario, the salt is brought up by way of the shaft towering over the railroad siding. Province is exceptionally rich in minerals.

CANADA: Arts and Letters

The 1969 cultural year in Canada came in like a lion and went out like a lamb, and in the process Canadians received an impressive lesson on the relation between cultural activities and the national economy. At the year's beginning there was eager enthusiasm for bigger and better and costlier cultural activities. By April the wave had become a ripple, in reaction to "inflation" warnings from the Bank of Canada and the Federal Government. By midsummer a tough crackdown by Ottawa on the country's inflationary spiral put the damper on many plans and programs, a notable example being the chopping of $350,000 from the promotion budget of the brand-new National Arts Centre. In spite of all this, however, it was a rich and rewarding year for Canadians interested in theater, music, art and all the other forms of the fine and lively arts.

The opening of Canada's National Arts Centre, in Ottawa, was the cultural highlight of 1969 and a historic occasion. The multimillion-dollar complex of buildings, designed to provide the last word in enjoyment for patrons and facilities for performers, had been a controversial matter throughout the several years it was being built. Political, professional and artistic battles raged over its location, its appearance, its functions and its cost. Totally financed by the Federal Government, the center was a citizen project from the start. As the cost climbed from an initial estimate of $9,000,000 to an eventual $46,400,000, almost everyone in Canada got into the act. Whatever his opinion, hardly anyone was indifferent.

But all was forgiven on May 31, 1969, when Prime Minister Trudeau, before a glittering audience of distinguished Canadians and foreign celebrities, declared the opulent, avantgarde buildings open and ready to provide the best in the performing arts for the people of Canada and their guests. The following two weeks were devoted to an Opening Festival of Canadian talents, which saw the opera house-concert hall, the theater and the intimate experimental studio filled to capacity for performances by the National Ballet Company, the Montreal and Toronto symphony orchestras, Le Théâtre du Nouveau Monde, the Vancouver Playhouse Theatre Company, chamber ensembles, experimental groups and eminent soloists. The fortnight was truly a Canadian cultural binge, and its coverage by many Canadian and foreign journalists and critics stimulated unprecedented public interest.

Once the launching festival, with its colorful formality and understandable nationalistic pomp, was over, the center got down to the business of offering entertainment of a variety and scale to make the whole operation a paying proposition. Whether this is a realistic ambition remains to be seen; but certainly the center's management has shown a determination to offer almost everything that is notably popular as well as things that are classically superb. The first season catered to low, middle and high brows, with a bill of fare that included Van Cliburn, Maureen Forrester, Harry Belafonte, Gordon Lightfoot, Duke Ellington and Marlene Dietrich; the New York Philharmonic, the Canadian Opera Company and Les Grands Ballets Canadiens; The Bathtub Ring, Modern Rock Quartette, *Pop Electronique* (a music-and-light show) and Kensington Market; *Anne of Green Gables, The Ecstasy of Rita Joe* and *Johnny Belinda*.

It was a satisfactory year for professional theater throughout Canada. The well-established operations—the Stratford Festival, Winnipeg's Theater Centre, Montreal's Nouveau Monde, Vancouver's Playhouse-Holiday Theatre—enjoyed good seasons at home and on tour. There were no artistic or financial disasters. The Stratford Festival's seventeenth season, May to October, directed jointly by Jean Gascon and John Hirsch, presented a rich variety of experimental and classical theater: *Hamlet, Measure for Measure, Tartuffe, The Alchemist* and *Hadrian VII*. Featured actors included Hume Cronyn, Powys Thomas and William Hutt, but youth was the keynote of the overall acting personnel. The Festival Company is now associated with the National Arts Centre to form the Stratford National Theatre of Canada. In this capacity it toured Canada and the United States during 1969 and presented a winter season in Ottawa. The French-language component of Canada's National Theatre—Le Théâtre du Capricorne—made its debut on Sept. 30 with an impressive production of the very difficult *La Visite de la Vieille Dame*. In the Maritime Provinces the three resident companies—Halifax's Neptune Theatre, Fredericton's Theatre New Brunswick and Charlottetown's Confederation Theatre—all became touring groups in 1969, assuring the Atlantic area for the first time of a year-round variety of professional entertainment. University theaters in all parts of the country enjoyed a particularly successful year. The Canada Council's generous encouragement continued to be an important factor in the development of professional theater: one noteworthy example being a grant of $290,000 to the National Theatre School, in Montreal, which accepts students from all parts of Canada on a merit basis and trains them for professional careers.

John Evans, Ottawa

Press News Ltd., Canada

National Film Board of Canada

128   CANADA: ARTS AND LETTERS

Crombie McNeill Photographers, Ottawa

Canada's National Arts Centre is both a superb setting for the performing arts and a dazzling experience in itself. Among its features are 22-foot-high, sculptured aluminum doors (opposite), which move at a fingertip; a 65-foot-long glass mobile (above); and the opera house's state box (below, with Premier Trudeau at far right). The hexagon in upper left of the poster is center's design theme.

National Centre
Arts national
Centre des Arts

John Evans, Ottawa

Carlos, National Arts Centre

In October, the Stratford National Theatre announced that Galt MacDermot, composer of the New York rock-music success *Hair,* would write the music for its 1970 production of Richard Sheridan's *School for Scandal.* In addition, the company will present *The Merchant of Venice* during a ten-week, winter-spring tour of Chicago, Montreal and Ottawa.

According to the Canada Council's twelfth annual report, released in October, the council donated almost $9,000,000 to the arts during fiscal year 1969, an increase of $2,000,000 over fiscal 1968. In the field of music, council grants totaled $2,000,000, and a National Concert Bureau was created. Its purpose is to act as a personal manager for outstanding young Canadian artists.

Canada's musical life, which has always been vigorous and well supported, flourished during 1969, with several items of unusual interest making the headlines. The Toronto Symphony Orchestra, with its director Seiji Ozawa, made a successful whirlwind tour of Japan; and the National Youth Orchestra—employing talented young performers from all parts of Canada—received enthusiastic criticisms in every city visited during an extensive European tour. The long-awaited National Arts Centre Orchestra made its debut in October under its newly appointed director Mario Bernardi. The Festival Singers of Canada, a Toronto-based group that in 1968 became North America's first fully professional chamber choir, received a grant of $43,000 from the Canada Council. Personal recognition in the musical field included the appointment of Dr. David Ouchterlony as principal of the Royal Conservatory Music School, and the election of Gilles Lefebvre as international president of Jeunesses Musicales. The Canadian Opera Company came of age in 1969, celebrating its 21st year with intense activity. The fully professional company played 28 performances of 5 productions for its Toronto audience and toured 15,000 miles to provide 80 performances in Canada and the United States. Highlight was its October presentations of *Rigoletto* in Italian and *Fledermaus* in English at the new opera house of the National Arts Centre.

For many years Canadians have had a special interest, and eminence, in documentary film making, stimulated by the pervasive influence of two Federal government agencies: the National Film Board and the Canadian Broadcasting Corporation. In 1969, film activities were newsworthy. The appointment of Michael Spencer as executive director of the Canadian Film Development Corporation set in motion a new Federal government effort—with a $5,-000,000 revolving loan fund—to encourage the production of commercial theatrical films. A virtual explosion of interest in Canadian universities in the subject of film making led to the establishment, in June, of the National Centre for Advanced Study of Films. The new activity will be sponsored by the nongovernment Canadian Film Institute, which has been a leader in film study and archives for many years. The CFI also launched a new bilingual magazine, *Film Canadiana,* with a generous grant from the Canada Council. In July it was announced that the Public Archives of Canada would establish a National Film Collection, a move that had been advocated by Canadian film buffs for many years.

Canada's three professional ballet companies enjoyed a robust year, although the effects of the official "reduced-spending" policy had them worried. The Royal Winnipeg company traveled 25,000 miles in North America to provide 100 performances in 90 cities, while Montreal's Grands Ballets Canadiens enjoyed a successful European jaunt. The National Ballet Company, of Toronto, was honored to provide the premiere entertainment at the opening of the National Arts Centre.

The visual arts, still suffering a letdown from the fabulous happenings of Centennial Year, attracted considerable public attention with more and more avant-garde exhibitions, but nothing of exceptional interest was shown, despite Canada Council grants of $623,000 to 13 public art galleries. The mural paintings, wall hangings, curtains and sculptures unveiled at the opening of the National Arts Centre received the major comment—and acclaim.

Publishing continued to enjoy profitable activity—more publishers, more authors, more bookstores, more magazines—but on the whole it was not a vintage year for Canadian literature. Several cultural titles were well up on the best-sellers list, including books about the Canadian painters Lawren Harris, Tom Thomson and Emily Carr; a catalogue of the Hart House collection of Canadian paintings; and a new history of music in Canada. Most surprising, and most enlightening, was a special issue of the American magazine *Cultural Affairs* devoted entirely to happenings in Canada.

On the whole it was a satisfying and rewarding year in the Canadian cultural field, but the slowdown that occurred in the final quarter, as a result of inflationary worries, left many cultural planners and entrepreneurs wondering how serious the deceleration would prove to be.

WALTER HERBERT
Fellow of the Royal Society of Arts
Consultant on Canadian Cultural Matters

Gamma, PIX

Smiles rather than frowns greet a British paratrooper on Anguilla during the brief Operation Sheepskin.

CARIBBEAN ISLANDS

Of all the Caribbean islands, Cuba remains dominant in political and economic discussions. In 1969, Fidel Castro entered his second decade of power, and most North Americans have apparently reconciled themselves to the fact of a communist state ninety miles from the United States. In Washington, D.C., official policy, inherited from the Kennedy-Johnson years, is to maintain Cuba's expulsion from the inter-American system (Organization of American States) and to punish Castro's Government economically by diplomatic pressure against other Latin-American and European nations that trade with Cuba.

Whether Castro's economic woes in 1969 stemmed directly from U.S. policy is uncertain, although it is clear that American actions compel the Soviet Union, for political reasons, to continue its expensive ($1,000,000 per day) subsidy of a communist regime in Havana. Indeed, Cuba's economic situation in 1969 was unpromising. Castro himself admitted that the government slogan for the year, "the year of decisive effort," had not been pursued energetically by the Cuban people. The annual May Day festivities were canceled in order to send city residents into the sugarcane fields.

Aside from an occasional hijacking of a commercial plane—there were 43 "skyjackings" from Jan. 1 to Sept. 30—the major considerations are Castro's threat to the hemisphere through subversion, a fear that has subsided somewhat with the capture and death of Ernesto Che Guevara in Bolivia in 1967, and the political and economic strains within Cuba, a fact that leads some commentators to predict the imminent downfall of the dictator. The refugee flights from Havana, which disgorge 160 of the alienated each day in Miami, offer some evidence of a deep cleavage within Cuban society. It is now possible, although difficult, to travel to Cuba, and several observers have written accounts of the island's troubles in the second decade of the revolution. Politically, there is a polarization between two extremes, the loyal and dedicated *fidelistas,* and the disenchanted. In between are the great majority of Cubans. These dislike the long lines at the markets and the shortages of durable goods, but admit that Castro's Government has made advances in public services, especially education, and has greatly improved the lot of rural dwellers.

In neighboring Haiti, François (Papa Doc) Duvalier, also in his second decade of power, has become, with the 1961 assassination of Rafael Trujillo in the Dominican Republic, Castro's chief adversary. Cuban radio broadcasts continually extol the blessings of communism to Haitian receivers, for Castro is convinced that Haiti is ripe for revolution. A subservient legislature has proclaimed Duvalier "President for Life." Thus there is no provision for orderly succession if the ailing Duvalier suddenly passes from the scene. Currently he enforces his political will with the 30,000 to 50,000 Volunteers of National Security (Tonton Macoutes). Social and economic conditions are incredibly backward: 4,700,000 people, 95 per cent of them black, occupy a territory the size of Maryland, and 80 per cent are illiterate. Despite the aggravating social situation, the Kennedy administration cut Haiti's aid in 1963 because of the unsavory politics of the regime. American-financed businesses have become wary of Haiti's financial future; a few have already pulled out. But Duvalier believes that the Nixon administration will restore the aid; and he made sure that Nelson Rockefeller's July visit to Port-au-Prince remained an orderly affair.

By some kind of chain reaction, the political turbulence that one normally associates with Cuba or Hispaniola may be passing, at least in part, to the smaller islands of the Lesser Antilles. On Curaçao in the Netherlands Antilles, serious rioting broke out on May 30 in the capital, Willemstad, during a labor dispute between employees and management of Wescar, which contracts for Shell Oil Company. As the Wescar officials were reaching an agreement with their workers, several hundred oil and dock laborers, who were marching in a sympathy strike for the Wescar employees, broke ranks and began rioting. The trouble grew out of an incident between the marchers and the police. The heaviest damage occurred on the waterfront and in the city's business district. Dutch-owned industries were apparently singled out for destruction. The government, led by Premier Ciro de Kroon, has favored low wages for workers in order to attract foreign investment. Officials in the labor union issued ultimata on May 31 and June 2 threatening a general strike unless De Kroon resigned. New elections were scheduled, and the government promised the use of radio and television facilities to the unions in order to air their protests.

Compared with the Curaçao troubles, the Anguillan crisis might be classified as tragicomedy. Anguilla is a case study in the agony of the "little members" of a fading British Empire. In the West Indies, Britain has followed a policy of gradualism in preparing its former colonies for independent status, a practice often unacceptable to nationalistic elements. For three months in 1967, Anguilla was a member of the newly formed Associated State of St. Kitts-Nevis-Anguilla. The Anguillans disliked this tripartite arrangement, and Anthony Lee, a British Commonwealth official, arrived in January 1968 to serve as administrator for one year and help settle the dispute. But a *de facto* government, headed by Ronald Webster, remained unshakable in its convictions, and announced that Anguilla would become completely independent in January 1969.

Anguilla, with its 32 square miles and 6,000 inhabitants, who have neither telephones nor paved roads, is obviously not another "Rhodesia," but British responsibility there has extended back to 1650. On Feb. 6, 1969, the Anguillans voted 1,739 to 4 for independence; St. Kitts and Nevis demanded that Britain uphold the integrity of the Associated State. In March, the British tried conciliation once more by sending another official contingent, but Webster's followers erected roadblocks around the British quarters and ordered the officials to leave in thirty minutes. Shots were fired into the air. One of the harassed visitors, Mr. William Whitlock, later commented that the island was dominated by thugs.

London now responded with 300 paratroopers on Mar. 19 (in a maneuver named Operation Sheepskin) and named Mr. Anthony Lee as commissioner. On Mar. 22, 23 and 28, there occurred more skirmishes, the last between pro- and anti-Websterites, but on Mar. 31 the latest British delegation announced a settlement. By its terms, the administration of the island would remain British, but the *de facto* government council would be allowed to continue. Unfortunately, this kind of arrangement may not be acceptable to the other islands of the Associated State.

LESTER D. LANGLEY
Central Washington State College

Fidel Castro displays his knack at cutting sugarcane.

Tass from Sovfoto

Up country, where the climate is delightfully cool, terraced paddies add man-made pattern to enthralling natural beauty.

Ed Lark

CEYLON

The Government of Prime Minister Dudley Senanayake exerted new efforts during 1969 to increase Ceylon's food production, diversify its agriculture and expand its industrial development. The heavy emphasis on improving the country's economy was unmistakably tied to the elections scheduled for 1970.

Economic growth during 1969 slowed somewhat from the previous year. In 1968, Ceylon's gross national product (GNP) had increased by 8.3 per cent, but in 1969 it was estimated to be about 7 per cent. Although the program to diversify agriculture was proceeding steadily, the continuing fall in prices of tea created severe economic problems. (Tea accounts for more than 60 per cent of Ceylon's foreign-exchange earnings.) Because of a glut on world tea markets, all the major tea-producing countries were facing the worst tea crisis ever. As a result, economic development was checked despite a number of grants and loans provided

by the International Monetary Fund, the World Bank, the Asian Development Bank and the like. The restraints created a source of potential political trouble for Senanayake and his Government.

The high cost of living and growing unemployment are turning a number of people toward the main opposition political parties, the Sri Lanka Freedom Party of former Prime Minister Mrs. Sirima Bandaranaike, the Trotskyite Lanka Sama Samaja Party headed by Dr. N. M. Perera, and the Moscow-oriented Communist Party of Pieter Keuneman. Senanayake is depending on his administration's effort to increase food production and improve the general economy to win another term in office for himself.

Under Senanayake's administration the basically agrarian island nation has constructed new plants producing textiles, plywood, ceramics, tires and tubes, simple steel parts, cement and rubber. Against these gains, a number of industrial strikes broke out as 1969 drew to a close. In September, government electrical workers struck against a decision to convert the Department of Government Electrical Undertakings into a corporation. The workers claimed that the Government had not compensated them for loss of security and other privileges as a result of the change. Later, petroleum workers went out on strike. The Government then proclaimed a state of emergency. Troops were called in to man the oil and electrical installations.

Nearly all of this agitation, however, was considered an effect of the impending elections. The year ended with election fever building to a frenzy.

ARTHUR C. MILLER
Senior Editor, *The Asia Letter*

CEYLON

Area: 25,332 sq. mi.
Population: 12,300,000
Capital: Colombo (pop., 511,000)
Government: Sir William Gopallawa, governor-general—1962; Dudley Senanayake, premier —1965
Gross National Product: $1,950,000,000
Monetary unit: rupee (5.9 rupees=U.S. $1.00)
Chief products: tea, rubber, coconuts, graphite
Foreign trade: exports, $342,000,000; imports, $365,000,000
Communications: 55,500 telephones, 16 daily newspapers
Transportation: roads, 11,700 mi.; 83,743 passenger cars; railroads, 939 mi.
Education: 2,620,000 elementary and secondary students, 3 universities

CHINA

October 1, 1969, should have been the occasion for a joyful and spirited celebration in the contemporary history of the world's largest nation. That date, after all, marked the 20th anniversary of the victory of Mao Tse-tung's communist forces and of the founding of the People's Republic' of China. As it turned out, China's 20th National Day observance was one of the dullest and most quiet on record. Yet the failure to greet the 20th anniversary with great fanfare and display was hardly surprising, for the Chinese leadership really had little to celebrate.

True, the communist victory in 1949 and the efforts of the early 1950's did unify the Chinese nation for the first time in decades. True, the economic-development projects initiated in the early years of communist rule seemed to point China in the right direction and lay the foundation for modernization. Also true, its national unity and economic progress allowed China to claim greater international recognition, with a louder voice in world affairs.

Yet the glory of the early years of the People's Republic lay shattered as the Chinese leaders stood on Oct. 1 on the balcony of Tien An Men (the Gate of Heavenly Peace) and reviewed the parading masses in Peking. For the facade of the marchers' smiling faces and wild histrionics could hardly hide the fact that China was now in flux. The political, social and economic prospects were far from certain.

The long-delayed Ninth Congress of the Chinese Communist Party finally was held in 1969, but its call for unity among the country's diverse and oft-warring factions was largely unheeded. Efforts to get the economy moving forward again and to recoup the losses suffered during three years of the Cultural Revolution met with lukewarm enthusiasm at best. Perhaps of greater significance, the Chinese people themselves demonstrated in many ways their mastery of the art of mouthing political dogmas while pursuing their own interests and desires. The nation's youngsters were, more or less, back in school. But the education system itself vibrated with the thrusts and counterthrusts of the effort to create a politically acceptable approach. Mao-thought was the only consistent element of school curricula.

Domestic problems, however, were not the only worries on the minds of the Chinese leaders. Several large-scale and bloody skirmishes between Chinese and Russian troops along their common 4,500-mile border kept war fever high. In remote Tibet, rebels staged running battles with the People's Liberation Army (PLA) troops. The highest-ranking Chinese diplomat ever to defect, the charge d'affaires at the Chinese mission in The Hague, sought and was granted political asylum in the United States. Even as it sent a couple of dozen ambassadors back to their posts abroad and thus attempted to restore its international contacts, the reverberations of the Cultural Revolution-generated xenophobia continued to undermine China's image abroad. Once again the United Nations defeated (48 for and 56 against with 21 abstentions) a motion to seat Peking in place of Nationalist China (Taiwan).

The Ninth Communist Party Congress (the first in 11 years) finally met on Apr. 1. It adopted a new party constitution that, unlike the 1956 document it replaced, paid tribute to Mao Tse-tung's thought and changed the official romanization of the Chairman's name to Mao Tsetung. One unusual aspect of the constitution was that it specifically named Mao's successor: Defense Minister Lin Piao.

On Apr. 24, last day of the congress, it elected a new Central Committee and 21-member policy-formulating Politburo. The new Central Committee consists of 170 full members and 109 alternate members, with Mao Tse-tung the chairman and Lin Piao the only vice-chairman (in the past there had been several vice-chairmen). Only 25 per cent of the old Central Committee was reelected, showing just how deeply the Cultural Revolution had cut into the ranks of Chinese leaders. The People's Liberation Army, which had been the only force holding the country together from 1966, was more heavily represented. Some 40 per cent of the members and alternates were drawn from the ranks of the PLA. The nonmilitary element, representing 35 per cent of the full members on the Central Committee, consisted of the revolutionary hard core of the Cultural Revolution groups, a number of elderly and more moderate individuals and a few professionals (including two ambassadors).

One of the major "fighting tasks" spelled out by the congress was to restore unity in the country and rehabilitate the badly shattered Communist Party organization. As 1969 wore on, however, it was evident that neither elimination of the factionalism dividing the nation nor reconstruction of the party machine would be easy tasks. Throughout the year, in fact, Peking complained of the continued existence of factions at virtually all levels, from factories and farms to provincial administration and even the military. The problem was clearly reflected in an incident at Taiyuan in Shansi Province. In late July the PLA had to be called in to halt civil disorders in that city. According to posters seen in Canton, Taiyuan was at the mercy of armed bands. The warring factions were given a time limit to either resolve their differences or face the wrath of the PLA.

Through the summer and into September and October the Chinese press and radio hinted at a state of anarchy existing in some areas. Reports of violence filtered into such listening posts as Hong Kong. Wide credence was given to stories of armed clashes between Tibetan guerrillas and Chinese troops. If anything positive could be said about the situation it was simply that the fighting and turmoil had lessened somewhat since 1967. The country was not about to fall apart. But the leadership no longer had the firm central control it once exercised, most decisions were being made at the local level, and central directives and policies were not always being implemented.

Half-hearted attempts to rejuvenate the Communist Party had begun as early as September 1968. The attention the matter received during the Ninth Congress was hardly overwhelming. By June only a handful of party branches had been reconstituted, judging by reports in the official press. However, a change in attitude occurred in September 1969, and Peking began to promote reconstruction of the party actively. Many of the earlier stringent requirements for party membership were relaxed, and the central leaders seemed determined to restore party rule even at the expense of absolute Maoist purity. However, the old party groups —or cadres—were reluctant to accept responsibility for fear of retribution should the political winds change again. The various factions at the lower levels often were the quickest to take control of the new party organizations and manipulate them to their own ends.

Life in China as molded by the Cultural Revolution also had a negative effect on the economy. The main campaign designed to spur production flaunted the slogan: "Prepare for

Camera Press, PIX

In a photograph dated Apr. 24, 1969, Mao Tse-tung wears his usual plain uniform and appears to be well.

war, for natural disasters and help the people." As has been China's practice from 1960, no meaningful statistics on the economy were published during 1969, though the official press often made claims of important industrial and agricultural advances. There was no visible evidence of such strides. Analysts concluded, on the basis of the skimpy information available, that the economy did not even match the production levels of the peak pre–Cultural Revolution years. It was equally difficult to assess China's trading position. The general pattern seemed to be a gradual return to the pre–Cultural Revolution levels of activity, with total two-way trade running about US$2,500,000,-000.

As far as economic policy was concerned, the Chinese leaders pressed ahead in 1969 with the Maoist scheme to make the rural areas self-supporting, with every people's commune growing its own food, producing its own fertilizer and tools, making its own electricity, running its own small factories and financing its own capital-construction projects. To some extent the peasants continued to reject the idea

CHINA

Area: 3,768,727 sq. mi.
Population: 740,300,000
Capital: Peking (pop., 10,000,000)
Government: Mao Tse-tung, chairman—1949; Chou En-lai, premier—1949
Monetary unit: yuan (2.46 yuan = U.S. $1.00)
Chief products: rice, coal, iron ore, crude steel, tin, tungsten, oil, cotton
Communications: 255,000 telephones, 7,000,-000 radios, 30,000 TV sets
Transportation: roads, 124,000 mi.; 50,000 passenger cars, railroads, 19,840 mi.
Education: 102,900,000 elementary and secondary students, 61 universities
Armed forces: 2,821,000

of giving their best to the common good, and instead were turning all their spare efforts to cultivating private plots and personally owned livestock. The same attitude, to a much larger extent, prevailed on China's industrial front. There were numerous reports throughout the year of industrial discontent. The Chinese press made reference to slowdowns, strikes, anarchy and factionalism affecting industry in several areas. With the abandonment of the old policy of cash bonuses for overfulfillment of production quotas the Chinese industrial workers simply refused to work faster or put in longer hours.

Reform of the education system and maintenance of control over the nation's youth demanded the leaders' attention. Like nearly everything else, the question of how to cope with the havoc wrought by the Cultural Revolution on the educational system remained largely unanswered during the year. Though most schools were functioning, debate continued on what to teach, on teacher-student relations and even on who should be allowed more or higher levels of education. The only general agreement was that Mao Tse-tung's "thought" must be included in the curricula at all levels.

The problem of what to do with the millions of young people who had finished school or had no opportunity to continue their education also posed difficulties. The policy of shipping young people off to the countryside where they could be gainfully employed remained in effect. An estimated 10,000,000 Chinese youngsters had been sent to the countryside by the end of 1969. Many of them, however, were beginning to drift back to their urban homes.

Internationally, events were dominated by a series of bloody border clashes between Chinese and Russian troops. Trouble began on Mar. 2 when the two sides engaged in a running battle, using tanks, artillery and armored vehicles, over an obscure island, called Chen Pao by the Chinese and Damansky by the Russians, in the Ussuri River. Several more skirmishes occurred before attempts were made to cool tempers. Neither country ever disclosed precise figures on the dead and wounded, but the announcements implied that casualties ran in the hundreds on both sides.

More serious was the strife in midyear on the border between Soviet Kazakhstan and Chinese Sinkiang. Sinkiang is the site of China's atomic-weapons and missile-testing grounds. According to Chinese accounts, Soviet tanks and armored columns twice drove several kilometers into Sinkiang, on June 10 and Aug. 13.

Tensions eased in early summer when the frozen Ussuri and Amur rivers thawed and could no longer support the armored Soviet columns. On June 18 the Sino-Soviet boundary navigation commission (set up in 1951) began talks on navigation of boundary rivers, which resulted in a signed agreement.

By early September, it was apparent that the two communist giants were moving back from a serious confrontation. To a large degree the death of North Vietnamese leader Ho Chi Minh seems to have eased tensions. In his "political will," Ho expressed disappointment over the continuing dispute between Russia and China and called on them to settle their differences. Chinese Premier Chou En-lai rushed to Hanoi as soon as word of Ho's death was received. Just as quickly as he arrived he turned around and headed home to avoid, it seemed to observers, a face-to-face meeting with Soviet Premier Aleksei Kosygin, who turned up for the funeral. A lower-ranking Chinese delegation eventually was sent to the memorial services in Hanoi.

However, after leaving Hanoi, Kosygin made a surprise side trip to Peking. There he was greeted by Chou En-lai. Their brief talks were the prelude to the start of formal negotiations over border issues at the vice-ministerial level, which began in Peking on Oct. 20.

Mao had dropped out of sight in mid-May, and his failure to attend any of the ceremonies in Peking related to Ho's death led to speculation (again) that he was either dying or dead. On Oct. 1, however, Mao surfaced—as he has on quite a few similar occasions before—at least looking well.

New ambassadors were sent to North Vietnam, Cambodia, Pakistan, Tanzania, Zambia, Rumania, Sweden, Syria, Nepal, Mauritania, Algeria, Yemen, Afghanistan and elsewhere. In October a number of foreigners, who had been imprisoned or held under house arrest for periods of up to 26 months, were released. Anthony Grey, Reuters correspondent in Peking, was the first. He was followed by a number of other British and West German and Japanese nationals. It was estimated, however, that some 25 to 30 other foreigners were still detained in China as 1969 ended.

China's reaction to the inauguration of a new American president was as expected. Richard M. Nixon, the Chinese official pronouncements maintained, would be no different from any other American president. To show that it meant what it said, on Feb. 18 Peking called off the scheduled 135th ambassadorial level meeting between Chinese and American representatives in Warsaw, Poland. The pretext for the cancellation was the defection to the United

門工會聯合總會工

慶祝建國十九週年

Propaganda is plastered over the facade of a Red Chinese hospital in Macao, the tiny Portuguese colony that China permits to stay in existence on its doorstep. Politically, Macao's situation is much like that of the nearby British colony of Hong Kong.

Camera Press, PIX

States of the Chinese charge d'affaires in the Netherlands, Liao Ho-shu, on Jan. 24. Most analysts agreed that an inability to agree on new policies was the more likely cause for calling off the meeting. To attempts by Nixon to ease Sino-American tensions, the Chinese showed no signs of responding.

While the United States was getting nowhere in establishing better relations, Canada (in May) and Italy (in secret) entered into talks with Chinese representatives on the question of exchanging diplomatic recognition. A number of issues remained to be resolved but as the year ended it appeared that agreements were not far off.

China's scientists kept the world aware of its nuclear potential by detonating two atomic devices. The Chinese delayed announcing the tests until Oct. 4. However, on Sept. 23, China detonated its first underground nuclear explosion at the Lob Nor proving grounds in Sinkiang. On Sept. 29, a hydrogen bomb was tested in the atmosphere. The tests represented the ninth and tenth nuclear explosions detected by the United States Atomic Energy Agency (although China had announced only nine explosions). It had been expected that China would make some important progress in the development of long-range missiles during 1969, but its complete silence on the subject suggested that it was having problems.

EDWARD NEILAN
China and Southeast Asia Correspondent
Copley News Service

CITIES

In contrast to the riots of previous summers, U.S. cities were somewhat calmer in 1969. But during this first year of the Nixon administration, the Federal Government did little to start curing the urban ills that it had so extensively diagnosed under President Johnson. There were, however, promising new prescriptions.

The comprehensive diagnosis of the causes of the misery and unrest in the inner-city ghettos by the National Advisory Commission on Civil Disorders, chaired by Gov. Otto Kerner, was supplemented by two further, specific reports. The National Commission on Urban Problems, headed by former Sen. Paul H. Douglas, made an impressively thorough analysis of low-cost-housing programs, land use, building and housing codes, urban government and services, urban financing and taxation—and offered a long list of specific recommendations for improvement. The President's Committee on Urban Housing, headed by industrialist Edgar F. Kaiser, emphasized that "decent housing is essential in helping lower-income families help themselves achieve self-fulfillment" and that "major efforts by the Federal Government, private enterprise, organized labor and state and local governments in creative and affirmative partnerships" must be made if massive Federal intervention is to be avoided.

The dimensions of the needed effort became apparent in the 1968 housing statistics. Only 1,548,000 new housing units of all types were built that year in the United States. Yet new families and the demolition of existing housing had generated a need for 2,100,000 new units. Moreover, of the total units built, fewer than 50,000 were for low-income families. Yet 20,000,000 Americans are living in substandard housing.

The new Secretary of Housing and Urban Development, George Romney, pointed out that "housing, more than almost any other area of the economy offers the greatest potential for job creation, business development, economic growth, environment improvement and human betterment." He launched a program, which he optimistically called Operation Breakthrough, to promote the industrialization of housing construction. It calls for inducing industry to invest in the development and testing of promising building systems by offering markets large enough to justify the investment. The markets are to be created by state and local governments which are also asked to revise obstructive and inconsistent building codes. Some of the 12 to 20 different systems to be tried have been developed in previous years in demonstration programs. These had always been too small to demonstrate actually whether mass production can significantly reduce the time and cost of building homes and apartments.

There were signs that the building-trade unions, traditionally opposed to innovation in construction methods, might relent and cooperate. The United Brotherhood of Carpenters signed a contract with the Stirling Homex Corporation, which manufactures wood-framed "Instant Housing" units. But AFL-CIO President George Meany still insisted that "you can't build houses like automobiles. Too many things go into them."

There were also doubts whether HUD's limited funds could accomplish a real breakthrough. Industry's response has been disappointing. A private experiment, organized by the Metropolitan Detroit Citizens Development Authority, for instance, had hoped that 40 to 50 companies would compete for a contract to build 800 homes. Only 3 companies bid.

John Morris Dixon, writing in *Architectural Forum,* feared that "the housing shortage may have to go even further beyond our ability to produce—to the point where the secure middle class is seriously affected—before government at all levels will put real commitment and real money behind industrialized housing systems." With the shortage of mortgage money and steadily rising building costs, however, that point may no longer be far off. And Dixon conceded that Romney's program "will at least stimulate a round of intensive research and evaluation of the many systems currently on the drafting boards."

Much-touted efforts to involve big business in inner-city problems and promote "black capitalism" proved disappointing. Despite much exhortation very few new factories found it feasible to move into the ghetto to provide more employment opportunities. On the contrary, a study showed that in St. Louis, for instance, 75,000 jobs that were in the city in 1953 were there no longer. Nor did many businesses respond to a call to train "hard core" unemployed youths for jobs. In Boston, business leaders promised in May 1968 that their Urban Foundation would raise $2,000,000 to assist black businessmen. A year later it had raised a bare $350,000 and actually lent only $200,000. And in New York, it was reported, the Urban Coalition could not even find a fund raiser for its highly advertised slum efforts. The Small Business Administration, it was charged, all but abandoned a special effort to extend loans to would-be black capitalists because, for lack of management skills and other reasons, it found them poor risks.

City services meanwhile became worse and not just for the poor. Uncollected debris fluttered in the wind. Hundreds of cars, abandoned

David W. Corson from A. Devaney, N.Y.

Though the plant remains busy, belching smoke, the mill town has long been unfit for human habitation.

in slum alleys or vacant lots, invited rats to breed in their upholstery. In Newark, police had to open fire with shotguns to defend a downtown park against a massive rat invasion. Potholes in unrepaired streets got deeper. In New York City, complaints about telephone service—disconnections, breakdowns, misdirected calls and installation delays of up to a month—tripled the number of complaints to the State Public Service Commission. Generator breakdowns slashed Con Ed's power capacity by 20 per cent in the heat of summer, enveloping the city in a "brownout" (a controlled reduction in electricity) that dimmed lights, reduced air conditioning, turned TV pictures fuzzy and hampered hospital operations. In other cities, too, citizens were asked to conserve electricity and water.

An assessment of the nation's response to racial aspects of the urban crisis found that a year after publication of the Kerner report "we are a year closer to being two societies, black and white, increasingly separated and scarcely less unequal." The assessment was made by

John Littlewood, staff photographer, "The Christian Science Monitor"

Every day most city dwellers must cope with the hazards of crowding, traffic jams and polluted air.

A. Devaney, Inc., N.Y.

Pirate's Alley, a quiet old byway in New Orleans, has been allowed to keep its mellow charm undisturbed. Today it is a haven for appreciative artists.

Urban America, Inc., and the Urban Coalition. It concluded that disorder in the ghettos and on college and university campuses was continuing and in 1968–69 struck the nation's high schools. Crime was increasing with little evidence of change or reform in the criminal-justice system. Structural change to make local government more responsive was rare. Although black immigration from rural areas into the inner city had virtually stopped, white departure to the suburbs—nearly 2,000,000 in the past ten years—had sharply accelerated, increasing the trend toward black cities and white suburbs. Black pride, identity and control and improvement of ghetto neighborhoods seemed to be increasing. But so was white resistance to slum-ghetto needs and demands.

This "backlash," according to some observers, was evidenced by the results of municipal elections in Minneapolis and Los Angeles and the primary election in New York City. Others felt, however, that race attitudes were too simple an explanation and that the outcome was more decisively determined by complex local politics. In Minneapolis the "law and order" candidate Charles Stenvig decisively defeated the liberal Dan Cohen in his bid for mayor. In Los Angeles, Thomas Bradley, a liberal Negro, after leading the field in the primary, lost out to the more conservative incumbent Mayor, Sam Yorty. In New York, Mario Procaccino won the Democratic primary over several liberal candidates, and John Marchi defeated the liberal Mayor John Lindsay in the Republican primary. Lindsay was nominated by the Liberal Party, however, and was reelected.

President Nixon's first and foremost move to aid the cities was his establishment of an Urban Affairs Council, similar to the National Security Council, and consisting of several cabinet members, "to advise and assist" his administration, specifically "in the development of a national urban policy, having regard both to immediate and to long-range concerns, and to priorities among them." He appointed the liberal Democratic urban expert Daniel Patrick Moynihan as the council's secretary. The national urban policy, a new idea in America, was slow to emerge, however. And Romney was the only council member who publicly asserted that the cities require as much attention and Federal funds as the space effort and the Vietnam war. The House Appropriations Committee, however, blaming the "inflationary spiral," chopped $384,300,000 from HUD's budget request, which was already 10 per cent lower than the previous year. This left HUD $1,600,000,000, roughly ⅟₂₀ of the annual expenditure for the war. The cut forced Romney to reduce social programs, such as neighborhood facilities, and to drop Federal financing of social work in public-housing projects. He placed greater emphasis on the role of the states in solving urban problems, notably the "model cities" program. Devised under the Johnson administration, this program, in which 150 communities participate, combines physical rebuilding with an effort to improve social services. The most promising progress, according to a HUD report, was made in Atlanta, Seattle and Dayton.

The President's proposal to Congress to help cities improve their public transportation disappointed most city mayors. They had hoped that Federal assistance for buses and rapid transit would eventually become as generous as it is for freeways. Under the Federal Highway Act the Federal Government, out of a Highway Trust Fund, pays $9.00 of every $10 spent on interstate highways. The fund is derived from gasoline taxes and related revenues. But the Federal Government pays only a theoretical ⅓ for public transportation. In practice there is not enough money appropriated for the purpose to go around. As a consequence, public transportation, desperately needed by the poor who cannot afford cars and the young and old who cannot drive, is inadequate and deteriorating. And cities have been almost forced to build more and more freeways so that suburban commuters can bring more and more cars downtown for which there is no parking.

To establish a better balance, Transportation Secretary John A. Volpe, supported by the mayors, had proposed that, after the Highway Act expires in 1973, a Rapid Transit Trust Fund be established from automobile excise taxes. Both highways and public transportation would then receive an equal one third of the total cost. Nixon, however, decided against this proposal and asked Congress only for a higher mass-transportation appropriation. When Volpe decided to withdraw Federal funds for a freeway in New Orleans on the grounds that it would have destroyed much of the charm of the old French Quarter, he raised some hope, however, that urban-freeways engineers would at last be forced to be more considerate of historic buildings and areas, public parks, neighborhoods and homes of the poor than they have been in the past. In Washington, D.C., on the other hand, a freeway-minded Congress voted to withhold authorized funds for a subway unless the city council abandoned its opposition to a six-lane freeway bridge across the Potomac at Three Sisters Islands. The National Capital Planning Commission had found the bridge unnecessary. In the end the council, rather than abandon the subway plan, reluctantly submitted to what some of its members called "blackmail."

The "revenue sharing" plan as the President proposed it to Congress may also add to the cities' quandary. Under the plan the Federal Government would, by 1976, return one per cent of the income-tax money it receives to the states to spend as they see fit. The Federal Government would insist only that the states continue to aid localities but—and here is the catch —in direct proportion to the revenues raised there. Since the big cities have a disproportionate share of poor people who pay less tax, they would thus also get less state aid.

Nixon's "family assistance system," on the other hand, may benefit the city poor. It would do away with the present widely unloved welfare system and assure all families of a minimum payment ($1,600 a year for a family of four), provided those who are able accept work or job training. The program would also expand daycare centers, improve job training and decentralize the administration of assistance to the poor.

Bay Area Rapid Transit District

Subway construction is part of mass rapid-transportation system—the most extensive of any in the United States—being built in the San Francisco area.

The most promising new prescription for a cure of urban ills was written by the National Committee on Urban Growth Policy, a group of senators, congressmen, governors and mayors, chaired by former Congressman Albert Rains of Alabama. The nation, the committee proposed, should build 100 new communities of 100,000 population each, and 10 of 1,000,-000 inhabitants. Although this seemed a tall order, these new cities would accommodate only 20 per cent of the additional Americans anticipated by the end of the century.

New towns, as they are called in Britain where more than 25 of them have been started since 1946, are largely self-contained. People not only live there, as in the "dormitory suburbs," but also find jobs, shopping, recreation, cultural activities and entertainment in them. This eliminates the need for more and more freeways. Being concentrated, the towns would preserve open country. They would also be "open" and provide housing for all income groups, thus offering the people in the ghettos a chance to escape. Few of them can afford a house in suburbia, even if open-occupancy laws were vigorously enforced. The inducement would be good, low-priced housing close to new job opportunities.

If new towns were to accommodate 75 per cent white people from suburbia and 25 per cent blacks now confined to the ghetto, argued Bernard Weissbourd, a developer, in a different study, a more desirable distribution would soon be assured. More Negroes could then take over the suburban houses vacated by the whites, reducing the ghetto population even more. This would then make room in the inner city for new housing for the Negroes who want to remain there, for whites who want to move back into the city, as well as slum clearance, new businesses, cultural facilities, parking garages and all the other things the city needs and cannot get because it cannot displace people who have no place to go.

Planning for complete new cities, furthermore, "offers us a chance to discover what we really want from an urban environment, and what we plan to bring to it," said Vice-President Spiro Agnew in his introduction to the Urban Growth Policy report. "Unlike planning for a single aspect of urban life, the planning for the new city involves fresh examination of nearly every concept we have taken for granted." Innovations in education, transportation, health care and other services can be tried out because a new town *is* fresh and new.

Nearly every industrial nation in the world has a new-town policy and the idea has been advocated for many years, in the United States notably by such urban critics as Lewis Mumford and his friends. As a result, two private new towns, Reston in Virginia and Columbia

in Maryland, have been launched. But it is doubtful that other private developers can amass enough land and investment capital to follow suit. What is more, many of the necessary social innovations involved in the creation of new towns will not yield the profits investors have a right to expect.

The Urban Growth Policy Committee therefore proposed that Congress enact a program of long-term Federal loans or loan guarantees to agencies or corporations formed by the states. They would acquire the land, draw up the plans, put in the roads and sewers, make sure subsidized low-cost housing is included, help locate employment centers, provide transportation and turn the rest over to private enterprise.

The recommendation was worked out in co-operation with the U.S. Conference of Mayors, the National League of Cities and the National Association of Counties. Only three years ago, when President Johnson suggested some tentative Federal assistance to new-town developers, the mayors were bitterly opposed for fear new towns would lure business investments away from their cities. They have now realized that the problems of the existing city cannot be solved within its boundaries and that orderly urbanization is as essential for the city as it is for the country, and suburban counties have in the past frequently refused to make the zoning changes to make comprehensive community planning possible. With this backing and with powerful advocates within its own ranks, Congress seems increasingly interested in such a national policy to counter growing urban disorders with a new urban order.

WOLF VON ECKARDT
Architecture Critic, *The Washington Post*

Fujihira, Monkmeyer Press

Trees, backyards and variety in design grace a low-cost housing project in Cleveland, the result of imaginative planning to include more than the most basic human needs.

COLORADO

At Golden the Rocky Flats plant of the Atomic Energy Commission suffered a $50,000,000 plutonium fire on Sunday, May 11, apparently as a result of spontaneous combustion. Cleaning the plant cost $10,000,000; and an estimated 330,000 cubic feet of contaminated waste was buried at the National Reactor Test Station in eastern Idaho. □ In Denver, on May 20, two liberal candidates for the school board were defeated. The vote was considered decisive against school integration; the big issue was school bussing. Champions of integration took the case to a Federal district court in June, asking that the school board be enjoined from canceling the ambitious integration program that had been adopted in 1968. □ On Sept. 10, Project Rulison, a 40-kiloton nuclear explosion, was set off underground beneath Battlement Mesa in western Colorado.

CONNECTICUT

On Apr. 6, at least 11 persons, 6 of them children, died in a fire in an old tenement in Bridgeport. □ In June the state sales tax was increased from 3.5 to 5 per cent; and the legislature killed a measure to build a bridge across Long Island Sound between Bridgeport and Port Jefferson, L.I. □ Litchfield celebrated its 250th birthday in July. □ On Nov. 4, Hartford Mayor Antonina P. Uccello (R) was reelected and Bartholomew F. Guida (D) won New Haven's mayoralty race. Richard C. Lee, the progressive mayor of New Haven since 1953, had announced in July that he would not seek reelection. It was a surprise decision.

CONSERVATION

Man has become an ecological force second only to nature in shaping the destinies of the other forms of life with which he shares the earth.

This fact was emphasized early in 1969 by a massive oil leak in the Santa Barbara Channel off the coast of California, and in June by a disastrous spill of an insecticide in the Rhine River. The oil destroyed thousands of seabirds and other forms of marine life. The insecticide turned most of the lower 200 miles of the Rhine—between Bingen, West Germany, and the river's outlet into the North Sea, in Holland —into a biological desert. German and Dutch biologists estimated that 40,000,000 fish were lost in this stretch of the river—80 per cent of the number present before the accident.

In recent years the osprey and southern bald eagle have declined sharply in numbers. The peregrine falcon, or duck hawk, has all but disappeared as a breeding species in much of North America. The number of bluebirds, once one of America's most familiar songbirds, has dwindled; and the brown pelican has become rare along the coast of the Gulf of Mexico.

In each of these cases, biologists point the finger of suspicion at extensive applications of DDT and related persistent agricultural pesticides, particularly those of the chlorinated-hydrocarbon family. These compounds are readily borne from their place of application in air and water (DDT has been found in the tissues of penguins in Antarctica), they do not decompose, and they tend to concentrate in the fatty tissues of animals that ingest them. They are immediately deadly not only to insects but to all invertebrates, many of which are essential foods for many species of valuable wildlife. Most are lethal to fish in relatively low concentrations. Vertebrates that are not killed outright absorb the substances from their foods. A two-year study by the Bureau of Sport Fisheries and Wildlife found DDT ranging up to 45.27 parts per million in 584 of 590 samples of fish taken from 45 rivers and lakes across the United States. The Government's recommended safe level for DDT is 5 parts per million. Fifteen of the rivers and lakes contained levels of dieldrin, a pesticide more dangerous to human life than DDT, higher than the FDA guideline limit for fish.

As a result of these threats to the natural environment, Wisconsin, Michigan and Arizona, in 1969, enacted laws either banning or sharply restricting the use of DDT. In Europe, Sweden and Denmark also restricted its use. The U.S. Departments of Agriculture and the Interior have adopted policies suspending the use of DDT and similar persistent pesticides in insect control on federally controlled areas. In November, HEW Secretary Robert H. Finch ordered that DDT and other "hard" pesticides be phased out for all but "essential uses" in two years.

Human pressures on the natural environment continue. A massive assault resulted from the discovery of an enormous oil field on the north slope of Alaska, one of the few remaining vast, undisturbed wilderness areas in North America. The fragile environment of the northern tundra, inhabited until recently by a relatively few Eskimos and a unique community of Arctic wildlife, now bustles with industrial activity.

Also in Alaska, the Atomic Energy Commission is conducting a series of subterranean thermonuclear explosions beneath Amchitka Island in the Aleutians, the home of the sea otter and other forms of rare Arctic marine

Nelson Tiffany

A tule-elk cow, in Owens Valley, Calif.; hunting has reduced the rare species to only some 400 animals.

wildlife. The first blast, in early October 1969, caused no serious surface damage. As a precautionary measure, however, the Alaska Department of Fish and Game, in July, had already livetrapped and transported 59 sea otters from the blast site and airlifted them for release in Washington and British Columbia. If the transplants are successful, they will help repopulate a section of the coast that has not seen the species for more than a century. Sea otters were nearly exterminated throughout their range during the mid-1800's. They have been restored by careful protection and management. The latest census in Alaska indicates that approximately 50,000 now exist in the waters along the Aleutian chain. The animals in central coastal

Among the birds vanishing from North America is the speckle-breasted peregrine falcon, or duck hawk.

Eric Hosking from National Audubon Society

California, descendants of a few that managed to escape the fur trade, now number more than 1,000. Their revival is one of the happier conservation stories.

In Florida, the Dade County Port Authority started construction of a planned supersonic jetport on a 39-square-mile tract near Everglades National Park. Conservationists, supported by a report prepared by Dr. Luna Leopold, senior scientist of the U.S. Geological Survey, fear that the project, if carried through, will result in insoluble problems of water and air pollution and change irreparably the movement of surface water into the park. As planned, the project would doom the park and its unique community of wildlife. Natural flows already have been seriously disturbed by earlier drainage and land-reclamation projects north of the park. Secretary of the Interior Walter J. Hickel strongly opposed the jetport. Secretary of Transportation John A. Volpe forbade the further use of Federal funds for the project until environmental studies were completed. They were joined by Gov. Claude R. Kirk, Jr., of Florida, who asked the county authorities to construct the proposed jetport elsewhere. Governor Kirk's decision seems to have forestalled present plans for the airport. Dr. Leopold's report stated that the park could survive if the training field now under construction is not extended farther.

A major concern of the conservationists, other than the park itself, is the loss of a unique natural area with many rare forms of wildlife. Chief among these is the alligator, harassed throughout its shrinking range by poachers, who can get from $5.00 to $6.00 per linear foot for illegally killed alligator hide. Everglades National Park and several national wildife refuges on the Gulf coast are invaded regularly by alligator poachers in spite of state and

Helen Hynson Merrick

Gnus and zebras graze in the Serengeti (Tanzania), one of the few remaining sanctuaries of vast wild herds.

Federal laws. Both the state and Federal wildlife agencies are understaffed and underfinanced to cope with the problem.

The hope of conservationists to end this situation lies in bills before Congress. H.R. 11363, enacted in November, extends the Federal protection now accorded to birds and mammals under the Lacey Act of 1900 to all forms of wildlife. Specifically, it bars interstate traffic in all reptiles, amphibians and fish or their products or parts taken in violation of state laws. Heavy penalties are provided for violators.

This and similar bills concerning endangered wildlife also would prohibit the importation into the United States for commercial use of any species of fish or wildlife threatened with extinction. In addition, other countries would be encouraged to enter into agreements to further the objectives of the worldwide wildlife-protection plan. Such agreements would provide assurance that action by the United States would not result in a shift of the damaging commercial trade elsewhere.

Many of the newly independent nations of Africa are making earnest efforts to preserve their wildlife populations. Most have engaged American and European wildlife specialists as advisers or as instructors to their own nationals. However, there was disturbing news in 1969. On July 20, Tanzania Minister for Agriculture, Food and Co-operatives D. N. M. Bryceson announced that the Ngorongoro Conservation Area would be reduced from 3,200 square miles to roughly 160 square miles and opened up to ranching and farming. If the decision is upheld, it will end one of the greatest wildlife spectacles in the world and a lucrative tourist attraction for Tanzania. In effect, the decision would block the migration route of hundreds of thousands of wildebeest, zebra and antelope, as well as lesser numbers of elephants, leopards and other wildlife, between Ngorongoro crater and Serengeti National Park. African conservationists believe that it would destroy the national park.

Other wildlife news of 1969 was more encouraging. Waterfowl in North America staged an encouraging recovery after nearly ten years of serious drought on their major breeding grounds. The trumpeter swan, once considered near extinction south of Canada, was removed from the list of rare and endangered species maintained by the Bureau of Sport Fisheries and Wildlife. The wild population of whooping cranes leaving Texas for their breeding grounds in northwestern Canada last spring reached 50, the highest number in nearly 50 years. Today, in addition to the wild birds, there are 25 cranes in captivity.

Seventeen of these are held at the Endangered Species Laboratory of the Patuxent Wildlife Research Center near Washington, D.C. Most of them were saved by an unprecedented rescue operation involving the governments of Canada and the United States. During the summers of 1967 through 1969, Federal biologists flew to the breeding grounds of the cranes near Great Slave Lake in the Northwest Territories, removing one egg of the two in each of several nests and flying them back to the laboratory. Research has disclosed that under natural conditions a pair of cranes seldom if ever succeeds in raising more than one offspring of a clutch to flying age. In any case the egg removed is usually replaced by the female. The eggs taken are incubated artificially with excellent hatching success. Eventually, birds from the growing captive flock will be released to supplement the wild population.

JAMES B. TREFETHEN
Director of Publications
Wildlife Management Institute

Le Pelley, from "The Christian Science Monitor,"
© 1969 The Christian Science Publishing Society

"There ought to be a better way to grow lettuce."

COST OF LIVING

In nearly every part of the world, prices of everything from food to furniture rose in 1969. Living costs jumped more than 5 per cent in the United States; and to worried housewives from Boston to San Diego, the rise at times must have seemed more severe than that. Prices also went up roughly 5 per cent in Japan, ending more than two decades of postwar price stability. In the Netherlands, prices shot up more than 8 per cent, and consumers organized boycotts and took to the streets in protest. Even in West Germany, which for some years has had one of the most stable of all economies, prices rose about 4 per cent and became a political issue for the first time since World War II.

Increases of 2 or even 3 per cent are usually considered tolerable; anything much beyond that is generally regarded as meaning trouble. And in 1969 there was almost no escaping the troublesome upsurge no matter where you lived. In New York City, for instance, rents continued to soar, triggering emergency legislation to limit increases. In Phoenix and Denver, angry shoppers boycotted supermarkets they felt were overcharging. In Amsterdam and Paris the newspapers were filled almost daily with letters from disgruntled consumers wondering what was behind it all and what could be done.

These indeed were the key questions. In every capital and financial center of the world, economists and politicians debated possible answers to them while, on another level, housewives muttered the questions as they watched the bills escalate. The bare cost-of-living increases—up 4, 5 or 8 per cent—actually only hinted at the full story. The strain imposed on most family budgets was far more severe than that.

Prices of meat, dairy products and other essential food items jumped nearly 10 per cent in many cities around the world. The cost of hospital rooms and other medical care spiraled across the United States. (See Medicine.) Nearly everywhere the price of services—from dry cleaning to television repairs to housekeeping—lurched upward at rates far faster than the overall cost of living.

"A 5 per cent living cost increase," said one British economist in December, "is a rather misleading figure. It has been more like double that for many of the basic bills families have had to pay. 1969 simply was the year of inflation."

Indeed it was. Writing in *Fortune,* economic analyst Lawrence Mayer used that phrase as the title for a probing article on the subject, and concluded that "inflation remains the preoccupation of practically all the advanced countries." It could, of course, hardly be otherwise. An unacceptably large dose of it—or, in other words, too fast a rise in living costs—can do more than merely raise havoc with a housewife's budget. Carried far enough, it can lead to worldwide financial problems and political discontent, to "international instability as well as internal dissension," said Mayer.

Many Latin American countries have had long histories of inflation linked to political unrest, and they experienced more of the same throughout most of 1969. But at least since World War II, the problem is fairly new for most developed countries.

France, for example, had to face the possibility in 1969 that rising living costs would produce a repeat of the May 1968 revolt, which was fueled partly by bitter factory workers who could no longer make ends meet. In the United States, meanwhile, inflation was given top priority as a national problem. Early in the year the Nixon administration labeled it, along with Vietnam, as "the nation's most pressing business."

But *what could be done about it,* and *how did it get so bad in the first place?* These questions proved, as the year wore on, to be ex-

"The Long Island Press"

As increasing prices eat into family budgets, irate housewives demonstrate against the high cost of food.

tremely vexing, not only in the United States but also in Europe and the Orient. As Japanese Vice Minister of Finance Yusuke Kashiwagi told this reporter in November: "We recognize that the increase in living costs must be contained. But it is a very complicated and troublesome matter."

This assessment clearly applies not only to Japan but to the worldwide escalation of living costs. It was brought on by a combination of economic and political developments. Two were of paramount importance. First, the United States failed in the mid-1960's to curb the domestic economy while expanding the Vietnam war effort. Second, especially in Europe, demands increased for substantially higher wages in order to live a more comfortable life.

Another factor—to the extent that higher wages forced manufacturers to raise prices—reflected what economists call *cost-push* inflation. It was a different variety—*demand-pull*—in the United States, where until recently too much money was chasing too few goods. Looked at from a worldwide viewpoint, one could blame a combination of these two forces, building in intensity over the years, for the disconcerting cost-of-living increases that earmarked 1969 as the year of inflation.

Apart from budgeting prudently and shopping with extra care, there was very little most families could do about galloping prices. Governments the world over, meanwhile, tried to check the inflation by tightening credit, cutting spending modestly, raising some taxes slightly, and, in almost every country, by appealing to business and labor to hold down wage demands and price increases. In France, the Pompidou Government clamped an official lid on price increases and negotiated furiously with unions to limit pay hikes. Britain meanwhile struggled to sell industry and labor an anti-inflationary incomes policy. In the United States, unions and businessmen were urged to exercise restraint voluntarily, and monetary officials allowed credit to become exceedingly tight. However, since much of the rise in living costs was in the service sector of the economy—where tight credit is less important than in the manufacturing sector—the effort was something less than an instant success. In fact, it was only beginning to have a mild deterrent effect on prices as the year drew to a close, and prices were continuing to rise in January 1970.

See Economy; Labor.

JOHN QUIRT
Free-Lance Economics Writer
Paris, France

CRIME

In comparison with 1968 the year 1969 was a relatively quiet year on the crime front. Except for a few mayoralty campaigns, the law-and-order rhetoric so prevalent during the 1968 U.S. presidential election was silent, and the nation was spared the trauma produced a year earlier by the assassinations of Martin Luther King, Jr., and Robert F. Kennedy.

Yet the crime rate, like economic inflation, continued to climb even as the Nixon administration unveiled a rather modest program to deal with the crime problem. As always, important trials liquidated some of the more notable crimes of the past. It was too soon to tell whether a new chief justice and associate justice would change the balance on the U.S. Supreme Court and push the court into holdings less favorable to criminal defendants than those of the Warren Court. There was a decline in the number of serious riots and public disorders, even as another government report, that of Jerome Skolnick on *The Politics of Protest,* insisted that the causes of violence were rooted in the fundamental shortcomings of American society.

The Rising Crime Rate. It is hardly newsworthy that the crime rate for the first six months of 1969 rose by 9 per cent, though the rise was far less than the 21 per cent increase recorded for the same period in 1968. The rise in suburban areas was 11 per cent, while in metropolitan and rural areas the increase was 8 per cent. The chief crime statistic to draw attention was that larcenies of more than $50 increased 17 per cent nationally. The Uniform Crime Reports, as compiled by the FBI, showed over 4,500,000 crimes in 1968, but it was obvious that the actual number of crimes committed was much higher.

Riots and Public Disorders. The United States enjoyed a comparatively quiet year with respect to riots and public disorders. Racial disorders occurred in some 85 cities in 27 states between Jan. 1 and Sept. 5, compared with more than 300 cities in 1968 and nearly 200 in 1967. In addition, the riots of 1969 affected smaller cities, such as Hartford, Conn., Ft. Lauderdale, Fla., and Dayton, Ohio, and resulted in much less human and property loss. There was no nonracial disorder comparable with the 1968 Chicago clashes of police and demonstrators during the Democratic convention. An attempt by a small number of militants representing the Students for a Democratic Society (SDS) to stage a violent demonstration in Chicago during October was repressed with little of the criticism of police voiced during the 1968 confrontations.

The Nixon Anticrime Program. Following the intense and frequently unenlightening debate on the crime problem in the 1968 presidential campaign, the winning party was under heavy pressure to offer solutions. In a series of messages and speeches throughout 1969, the President and his Attorney General, John N. Mitchell, revealed three principal concerns. One was an attack on organized crime through greater expenditures, more trained investigators, and greater cooperation between field offices and Federal, state and local law-enforcement officials. Increased immunity for witnesses and other laws directed at gambling and other racketeers were also proposed.

Drug abuse was a second major target of the administration. Measures to limit importation and to increase penalties for internal sale were introduced. Educational, research and rehabilitation programs aimed particularly at youth were also recommended to Congress. Finally, there was an extensive set of proposals directed at the crime problem in Washington.

Most items aroused little controversy. Neighborhood-housing renewal, more police courts, and prosecutors, youth assistance and similar aids were generally regarded as necessary. The novel idea in the package was pretrial detention of those whose release might present a danger to the community. This concept, familiar enough outside the United States, aroused civil libertarians who regret those few occasions, principally in wartime, when preventive detention was used by the Federal Government. Critics argued that the indigent and minority-group members are the most likely victims of preventive detention and that it violates basic principles of Anglo-American jurisprudence. Congress, for various reasons, was in no haste to adopt any substantial part of the Nixon program.

Prison Reform. After a three-year study of prisons in the United States, the Joint Commission on Correctional Manpower and Training issued its report in November. The report warned that the nation's increasing crime rate cannot be checked until U.S. prisons undergo major reform. Authorized by Congress in 1965 and headed by James V. Bennett, former director of the Bureau of Prisons, the commission further pointed out that the problem of repeat offenders would remain as long as "harsh laws, huge isolated prisons, token program resources and discriminatory practices" are prevalent. To improve the prison system, the commission urged Congress to pass legislation authorizing a minimum of $25,000,000 annually for Federal, state and local prison improvement. Following release of the report, President Nixon asked

Yippie leader Jerry Rubin pounds the desk to make a point at a press conference in Chicago. He and six others were tried on charges of conspiracy to incite mob action during the 1968 Democratic national convention.

Wide World

Attorney General John Mitchell to draw up a ten-year prison-reform plan.

The Trial of James Earl Ray. When the Rev. Dr. Martin Luther King, Jr., distinguished apostle of nonviolence and outstanding leader in the black struggle for equality, was murdered in Memphis, Tenn., Apr. 4, 1968, a worldwide search for the assassin began. It ended in London, June 8, 1968, with the arrest of an obscure Southerner, James Earl Ray, a man with a criminal record who had demonstrated strong racial prejudice. Many observers thought that it was unlikely that a man of Ray's apparently limited resources and attainments could have planned the crime, slipped through the Memphis police dragnet, and traveled to Canada and Europe without the help and guidance of others.

Speculation that there might have been a conspiracy was strengthened when Arthur Hanes, a prominent Birmingham, Ala., lawyer with a reputation for supporting segregationist causes, promptly appeared in London as Ray's counsel. After months in a Memphis jail, Ray asked for a continuance of his original trial date of Nov. 12, 1968, because he wished to discharge Hanes, with whom he had disagreed on trial strategy. Surprisingly, his new counsel was Percy Foreman, one of the most colorful and successful trial lawyers in the United States. In a lifetime of defending men and women charged with murder, Foreman had successfully avoided imposition of the death penalty in all but one case. To the outrage of leading newspapers and numerous white and black leaders, Foreman's magic worked again. Ray pleaded guilty to first-degree murder in return for a sentence of 99 years.

The prosecution seemed happy to avoid a long trial, which could hardly cast Memphis in

UPI

Apparently quite at ease, Sirhan B. Sirhan talks with a news correspondent in Los Angeles County jail after Sirhan was convicted of slaying Robert F. Kennedy.

Principals in the Green Beret case included Col. Robert B. Rheault (without glasses), former commander of Green Beret troops in Vietnam. Charges were dropped and the case never came to trial.

UPI

a favorable light. The jury, as required by Tennessee law, was given the bare bones of the case in evidence after each juror agreed to adhere to the state-defense agreement. Even then Ray spoke out at one point during the "trial" in apparent disagreement with the comment of counsel that there was no evidence of conspiracy. He was quickly straightened out by the judge. This curious proceeding ended shortly thereafter, leaving many questions about the case unanswered, perhaps for all time.

The Sirhan Trial. After a trial lasting more than three months, Sirhan Bishara Sirhan, assassin of Sen. Robert F. Kennedy (D-N.Y.), was found guilty by a Los Angeles jury and sentenced to death on May 21. The trial was notable chiefly for intensive security measures and the parade of psychiatrists for each side who gave sharply conflicting testimony on the sanity issue.

There was little that Grant Cooper, famous Los Angeles defense attorney, could do to resist the impression of carefully premeditated murder once the defendant's diary proclaiming the need to kill the Senator was placed before the jury. Another unusual touch was a plea by letter from Sen. Edward Kennedy (D-Mass.) to the trial judge, asking, in vain, that Sirhan receive a life sentence. The scheduled execution was still delayed by various legal actions as the year ended.

The Green Beret Murder Case. One of the rare cases in the military-justice system to come to the attention of the general public emerged in late summer. Col. Robert B. Rheault, the commander, five other officers and two noncom-

missioned officers of the Green Berets, a specially trained counterinsurgency Army unit, were charged with murdering an alleged Vietnamese double agent. Almost immediately it became apparent that behind the events and charges was a conflict between the Green Berets and the regular Army, as well as one between the Central Intelligence Agency (CIA) and the Army.

Some of the most distinguished trial lawyers in the United States, F. Lee Bailey, Edward Bennett Williams and Henry B. Rothblatt, were retained to defend the officers, three of whom were scheduled to be tried Oct. 20, with trial of the others to follow. The two Green Beret noncommissioned officers were expected to be the principal witnesses for the prosecution.

The potentially far-reaching effects of the trial became clearer as charges and countercharges filtered through the news media. Portions of the trials were to be closed because of the presentation of classified material involving the military services and CIA. A principal witness to be called by the defense was the commander of U.S. forces in Vietnam, Gen. Creighton W. Abrams. Then suddenly, on Sept. 29, the Army dropped charges against all eight Green Berets. The reason for this action, said Secretary of the Army Stanley R. Resor, was the refusal of the CIA to permit any of its personnel to appear as witnesses at the trial, thus making a fair trial impossible. It was announced that the eight men would receive new assignments outside Vietnam.

WILLIAM M. BEANEY
Professor of Law, University of Denver

Police and soldiers, supported by armored vehicles, guard against new demonstrations around the statue of King Wenceslas, a rallying point for anti-Soviet citizens of Prague, Czechoslovak capital.

Caron-Gamma-PIX

CZECHOSLOVAKIA

With 80,000 Soviet troops occupying key positions throughout the country, Czechoslovakia in 1969 lost by successive stages about all that had remained of the liberal conquests of the "Prague spring" of 1968.

Each time Czechoslovaks defied the invaders and their domestic backers, a new wave of repression followed. The somber mood of 1969 and the pattern of Moscow-inspired crackdowns were established when a 21-year-old student, Jan Palach, set himself afire on Jan. 16 in Prague's Wenceslas Square in a desperate protest against the occupation. Half a million mourners gave him a martyr's funeral.

Czechoslovakia had a new national hero but quickly lost some recently won liberties. Censorship over the press, radio and television was tightened, and progressives were ousted from Communist Party, state and trade-union posts.

On Mar. 28 a Czechoslovak four-to-three victory over a Soviet ice-hockey team in the Stockholm world championships set off jubilation in Prague; demonstrators ransacked and burned the offices of the Soviet airline Aeroflot. The Prague incidents brought a furious reaction

from Moscow and hastened the downfall of Alexander Dubcek, who had been first secretary of the Communist Party since the beginning of 1968.

In a plenary meeting of the party's Central Committee on Apr. 17, Dubcek was replaced as party chief by Gustav Husak. A Slovak like Dubcek, the new First Secretary had spent nine years in jail in the 1950's on charges of "bourgeois nationalism."

Husak pledged to fight "counterrevolutionary, antisocialist and right-wing opportunist forces." The terms became hard-line jargon to denounce any democratic yearnings in Czechoslovak society.

At another Central Committee meeting at the end of May, Husak emerged as a close ally of a pro-Soviet faction within the party. More purges of liberals followed.

During the world conference of communist parties in Moscow in June, Husak firmly backed the Kremlin in its controversy with Peking. Also he opposed a debate on the invasion of his country in 1968, a debate that was being sought by communist delegates from Italy and some other countries.

CZECHOSLOVAKIA

Area: 49,366 sq. mi.
Population: 14,400,000
Capital: Prague (pop., 1,030,330)
Government: Gustav Husak, Communist Party secretary—1969; Ludvik Svoboda, president —1968; Oldrich Cernik, premier—1968
Gross National Product: $26,800,000,000
Monetary unit: crown (8.5 crowns=U.S. $1.00)
Chief products: motor cars, glass, beer, ceramics, textiles, timber, coal
Foreign trade: exports, $3,155,000,000; imports, $3,115,000,000
Communications: 1,678,717 telephones, 3,200,-000 radios, 2,760,611 TV sets, 27 daily newspapers
Transportation: roads, 45,203 mi.; passenger cars, 375,000; railroads, 8,265 mi.
Education: 2,264,267 elementary and secondary students; 92,834 university students
Armed forces: 230,000

See map on page 185

At home, clandestine leaflets urged the population to observe the first anniversary of the invasion, Aug. 21, as a national "Day of Shame" by walking to work instead of riding streetcars or buses, boycotting stores and places of amusement and performing other passive gestures of mourning. The regime harshly warned the public against such "subversion," and mobilized the Army, police and People's Militia, an auxiliary force of party volunteers, to repress protests.

Two days before the anniversary, anti-Soviet demonstrations broke out in Prague's Wenceslas Square. They spread through downtown Prague the next day, and youthful demonstrators built barricades. The regime's forces used tear gas and armored cars to restore control. They fired into the protesting crowd, killing at least two teen-agers. On Aug. 21, one year after the invasion, Prague was again an armed camp with motorized troops, this time Czechoslovak, deployed throughout the city. At noon, thousands paraded in the center, shouting "Russians go home!" and "Only Dubcek!" The police reacted brutally, and almost a hundred tanks rumbled into downtown Prague, including historic Wenceslas Square.

Across the country, most of the population followed the underground instructions for observance of the "Day of Shame." Heavy clashes between anti-Soviet demonstrators and state-security forces occurred also in Brno and Liberec.

The invasion-anniversary disorders took a dozen lives and touched off furious reprisals by the regime. The communist leadership claimed it had foiled an attempt at "counterrevolution," and proceeded to tighten its grip on the country.

Dubcek lost his seat in the party Presidium and chairmanship of the Federal Assembly, in a plenary meeting of the Communist Party's Central Committee, Sept. 25–27. In an unpublished speech in his own defense, he accused Husak of slandering and muzzling him, and refused to engage in "self-criticism."

Dubcek remained a member of the Central Committee, at least in name; and in an apparent victory for the moderates, the former party chief was named ambassador to Turkey.

The Central Committee voted a resolution justifying the 1968 invasion as serving "the defense of socialism," and rejecting the view that it was aggression. Federal Premier Oldrich Cernik, a former presumed liberal who later had turned against Dubcek, remained at the head of the Government but shuffled his ministers. The state governments for Bohemia-Moravia and for Slovakia also were revamped, and the National Assembly was purged of all remaining progressives.

On Oct. 8, Prague virtually closed the country's frontiers to Czechoslovaks who wanted to travel to Western countries, and canceled 100,-000 exit visas that had already been granted. Visits of Western tourists to Czechoslovakia were also curtailed.

The restrictions were ostensibly aimed at eliminating a lively black market in foreign currencies. However, the actual purpose clearly was to prevent any contacts between Czechoslovaks and citizens of democratic countries. Above all, the Prague regime wanted to halt further emigration of skilled workers. More than 50,000 Czechoslovaks had sought asylum abroad since the invasion, and only 600 had returned home by Sept. 15, the deadline of a special amnesty.

Late in October, Husak and President Ludvik Svoboda led a Czechoslovak Communist Party and government delegation on an eight-day official visit to the Soviet Union. They failed to obtain from the Kremlin leaders even a token reduction of the Soviet occupation forces or to secure the large credits in convertible currency that the ailing Czechoslovak economy badly needed.

Moscow promised to step up deliveries of crude oil, iron ore and other raw materials, and announced that a new Soviet-Czechoslovak friendship and cooperation treaty would be signed in Prague in May 1970. By the end of 1969, Czechoslovaks were being told by their new leaders that their fate was welded to the Soviet Union "forever."

PAUL HOFMANN
Chief, Vienna Bureau
The New York Times

Ron Protas

In her "Cortege of Eagles," Martha Graham dances the role of Hecuba, queen of Troy, whose husband and children (including Paris and Cassandra) are finally slain or broken in the Trojan War of Greek myth.

DANCE

The number of dance performances in the United States increased about 200 per cent during the 1960's, with a comparable improvement in the technical training of the dancers. These are heartening developments in an art that has tended to lag behind the others in public acceptance. And yet American dance companies must constantly turn to Europe for the added performing outlets needed to make ends meet.

Even more significantly, several promising choreographers, ballet masters, and dancers have become expatriates. The principal lure has been the economic stability and more leisurely working pace of European opera houses.

Among the touring aggregations have been the City Center Joffrey Ballet and the companies of Alwin Nikolais, Glen Tetley, Don Redlich, Murray Louis, Merce Cunningham and Paul Taylor. Particular audience favorites have been the light-and-sound concoctions of Nikolais (*Echo,* for example) and the whimsy of Taylor (*Private Domain*).

England's Contemporary Ballet Trust and Israel's Batsheva and Bat-Dor companies have continued to invite Americans as guest choreographers and teachers, among them Richard Kuch, Bella Lewitzky, Norman Walker, Sophie Maslow, Mary Anthony, Talley Beatty, Donald McKayle, Robert Cohan, Yuriko, and Ethel Winter.

The Geneva Grand Theatre (Switzerland) is amassing a repertoire of Balanchine ballets under his personal supervision. He has also established former New York City Ballet dancers Alfonso Cata and Patricia Wilde as ballet master and principal teacher respectively. The Frankfort Opera Ballet, formerly directed by American choreographer Todd Bolender, is now headed by Chicago-born John Neumeier. Glen Tetley, assisted by Scott Douglas, has disbanded his company to become director of the Netherlands Dance Theatre (formerly under another American, Benjamin Harkarvy, who returned to his native land to codirect the Harkness Ballet).

The exchange has not been entirely one-sided. In June the Stuttgart Ballet, directed by

German Information Center, photographer V. Sladon

Airy leaps make a blithe interlude in the Stuttgart Ballet's exciting "Eugene Onegin," choreographed by John Cranko. Based on Pushkin's tragic poem, ballet is danced to score based on Tchaikovsky's music.

John Cranko, had a brief New York season. It returned in the fall for a triumphal cross-country tour. Particularly appreciated were Cranko's evening-long ballets *Eugene Onegin, Romeo and Juliet* and *The Taming of the Shrew,* all of which emphasized the company's flair for characterization, which exceeded its assurance in ensemble work. Special favorites were principal dancers Marcia Haydée and Richard Cragun.

Eliot Feld, a young choreographer with two distinguished efforts to his credit, was offered the Brooklyn Academy of Music as home base for a company of his own. The initial season of his American Ballet Company did not particularly enhance Feld's own reputation as a choreographer, but he did make some wise repertory selections, notably Donald McKayle's *Games* and Herbert Ross' *Caprichos* and *The Maids.* There was also a tepid revival of Michel Fokine's sixty-year-old *Carnaval.* Outstanding among the young dancers were Christine Sarry, John Sowinski and David Coll.

The birth of the Feld company was offset by the demise of Ruth Page's Chicago-based International Ballet. Its autumn assignment with the Chicago Lyric Opera was filled by the Boston Ballet; its Christmas presentation of *The Nutcracker* was absorbed by the Pennsylvania Ballet; and its national tour was turned over to a small ensemble, Thomas Andrew's Ballet Brio.

The year's creative triumph was Jerome Robbins' *Dances at a Gathering,* an exquisitely lyric utterance lightly brushed with ethnic allusion (as are the Chopin piano pieces that accompanied it). The dancers in this hour-long work looked as though they were enjoying a field, a clear sky and an untroubled afternoon. And yet there were momentary shadows, shifts of mood, perhaps to be further reflected in a sequel called *Night,* scheduled for Jan. 29, 1970.

While revivals of full-length works from the standard repertoire (among these *La Sylphide* for the National Ballet of Washington and *The Sleeping Beauty* for the Atlanta Ballet) were in the ascendancy, the exponents of non-thematic or nonstructured activity (loosely called avant-garde) were gaining support. The Connecticut College Summer School of Dance celebrated its 21st season by gearing its entire curriculum and concert series to this end. For example, Twyla Tharp's *Medley* dispersed 42 dancers over an expanse of lawn where they resembled imperceptibly moving statues. Yvonne Rainer's *Audience Piece, Continuous Projects* and *People Plane* took place simultaneously in three dance studios. Audience was free to move about watching or participating.

In the fall, Dance Theater Workshop, from which many of the avant-garde dance makers have emerged, received a Rockefeller grant to stage performances at the Manhattan School of Music. They turned out to be almost uniformly self-indulgent, as did Meredith Monk's three-part *Juice,* performed at the Guggenheim Museum, the Minor Latham Playhouse of Barnard College, and a loft on lower Broadway. Miss Monk also received a touring grant from the New York State Arts Council.

Nonprofessional dance (in the trade-union sense) received further impetus from a meeting in Boston of the Conference on Ballet in Higher Education, of which David McLain of the University of Cincinnati is chairman. The National Association for Regional Ballet also made strides by appointing a committee to plan a national festival at the Kennedy Center in Washington, D.C.

The commercial scene fared less well, with Broadway and television in a rut. There were, however, three serious dance films. Erik Bruhn and Carla Fracci, with members of the American Ballet Theatre, were filmed in the romantic ballet *Giselle.* Another film of the same ballet reached the United States from Cuba. It is a fortunate record of the great ballerina Alicia Alonso in her prime. *Isadora,* later retitled *The Loves of Isadora,* was a loving if uneven re-creation of the life and artistic precepts of America's great pioneer, Isadora Duncan. Although cutting placed too much emphasis on the artist's personal peccadillos, there were inspiring moments in the portrayal of Vanessa Redgrave and the directing of Karel Reisz and choreographer Litz Pisk.

A film was also made of Martha Graham's *Seraphic Dialogue, Acrobats of God* and *Cortege of Eagles.* Miss Graham was fortunate in having choreographer (and former Graham dancer) John Butler to supervise the production for National Educational Television. The dancing was enhanced, rather than cheated (as is too often the case), by the sensitively planned camera work. On the plus side was the eloquent record of the dancing of Mary Hinkson as St. Joan in *Seraphic Dialogue.* By the same token it was unfortunate that Miss Graham should have allowed her facsimile dancing (she is 76) to be perpetuated in the other two works.

The dance lost two valuable human beings: Maximiliano Zomosa, leading character dancer of the City Center Joffrey Ballet (and known especially for his humane yet ominous portrayal of Death in Kurt Jooss' classic *The Green Table*); and Jean Rosenthal, whose lighting concepts, especially for the New York City Ballet and the Martha Graham Company, gave dance and dancers a rich new dimension.

DORIS HERING
Associate Editor, Principal Critic
Dance Magazine

New Arts Management, photographer Robert Sosenko

Skeletal props extend the pattern of movement in "Imago," a modern abstract work by Alwin Nikolais.

At Connecticut College Summer School of Dance, Twyla Tharp's avant-garde "Medley" is danced on the lawn.

Sheldon Soffer Management

"The New York Times"

DWIGHT DAVID EISENHOWER

1890-1969

Thirty-fourth President of the United States

Shortly after noon, on Mar. 28, 1969, Dwight David Eisenhower passed away peacefully, after a long illness, in Washington. He had been both president of his country and a five-star general of the army. Leading the nation in mourning, President Richard Nixon said:

"General Eisenhower held a unique place in America's history, and in its heart, and in the hearts of people the world over.

"He was a man of great strength, wisdom and compassion. But it always seemed to me that two qualities stood out above all in both his public and private life: One was an unwavering sense of duty; the other was that whatever he did, he did because he believed it was right."

General Eisenhower's character shone forth in his own words. On D-day morning, June 6, 1944, he heartened his troops by radio: "Soldiers, sailors and airmen of the Allied Expeditionary Force. You are about to embark on the great crusade toward which we have striven these many months. The eyes of the world are upon you. I have full confidence in your courage, devotion to duty and skill in battle. We will accept nothing less than full victory. Good luck, and let us all beseech the blessing of Almighty God upon this great and noble undertaking." (At the time he had another communiqué in his pocket, taking full blame upon himself should the landings fail.)

Later speeches expressed his basic views, which remain valid.

On America: "The mission of America has been, and is, the expansion of individual liberty, self-reliance and personal responsibility within a system where a government, of conscience and of heart, is the servant of every individual, doing for him what he cannot do for himself."

On foreign relations: "The best foreign policy is to live our daily lives in honesty, decency and integrity; at home, making our own land a more fitting habitation for free men; and, abroad, joining with those of like mind and heart, to make of the world a place where all men can dwell in peace. Neither palsied by fear nor duped by dreams but strong in the rightness of our purpose, we can then place our case and cause before the bar of world opinion—history's final arbiter between nations."

At General Eisenhower's death, heartfelt tribute came from many sources, at home and abroad. President Charles de Gaulle of France, who attended the state funeral, said: "For me, I see disappear with great sadness a dear companion in arms and a friend."

On Apr. 2, General Eisenhower was buried in Abilene, Kansas (though born in Denison, Texas—on Oct. 14, 1890—he grew up in Abilene). He had written the words that are inscribed on tablets above his grave: "Give us the power to discern clearly right from wrong, and allow all our words and actions to be governed thereby, and by the laws of this land. Especially we pray that our concern shall be for all the people regardless of station, race or calling. May cooperation be permitted, and be the mutual aim of those who, under the concepts of our Constitution, hold to differing political faiths, so that all may work for the good of our beloved country and Thy glory."

While still in office, Premier Levi Eshkol died, on Feb. 26, 1969, after the second of two heart attacks within three weeks, in Jerusalem. He had led Israel since 1963.

Premier Eshkol's most valuable gifts were for conciliation and for forging working political agreements, in a country with as many as 17 political parties on election day. Through his efforts the three center labor parties were united as the Israel Labor Party.

He was born on Oct. 25, 1895, in a Jewish pale (ghetto) in the Ukraine. (His family name was Shkolnik, which he Hebraized to Eshkol—meaning a cluster of grapes—after Israel became independent.) The boy passed non-Jewish examinations for the gymnasium (high school) but because the quota for the nearby school was filled, he went all the way to Vilna, Lithuania, then a center of political and socialist activity. The new century began in Russia with riots and pogroms. By now there was much talk of Palestine, and the youth found his way there in 1914. During World War I he fought with the British against the Turks.

World leaders paid tribute. Arthur Goldberg, former U.S. associate justice and president of the American Jewish Committee, called Eshkol "one of the stalwart group of pioneers who fashioned a nation out of the wastelands of Palestine." West German President Heinrich Lübke said, "I and the whole German people have followed with continuing sympathy his tireless efforts to assure for the Israeli people a life of peace and freedom in a just society."

UPI

LEVI ESHKOL
1895-1969

HO CHI MINH
1890-1969

Ho Chi Minh, titular head of the North Vietnam Government and president of the Vietnamese Communist Party, died on Sept. 3, 1969, as his country was celebrating the 24th anniversary of its declaration of independence from French rule. He had fought for Vietnamese independence practically all his life. Though a communist agent from 1920, he was a patriot first.

"Ho Chi Minh" (which may be translated as Ho, Shedder of Light) was only one of numerous aliases he took during years of wandering. It is widely accepted that he was born Nguyen Tat Thanh on May 19, 1890, in central Vietnam. From 1911, when he left Vietnam, until after World War I, he worked at various menial jobs on ships and in London, New York and Paris.

In 1941 he returned to Vietnam, then controlled by the Japanese. He took advantage of the situation to organize the Vietminh, or Independence Front (of Communists and nationalists), and fought the Japanese with a guerrilla force of 10,000, and thus collaborated with American OSS agents. Though Vietnamese independence was proclaimed in 1945, it did not become a fact until the French were defeated in 1954. Vietnam was then divided. Ho had admired many aspects of the United States, not least its Constitution, which he partly copied. But the United States' support of the French and its thwarting of the 1954 agreement for elections only strengthened his determination—and undoubtedly that of his people—to resist the growing U.S. military might in Vietnam.

Camera Press, PIX

DEATHS

Sir Harold Alexander, 77, British general, planned Allied strategy in Middle East, North Africa campaigns in World War II; Buckinghamshire, England, June 16.

Princess Andrew of Greece, 84, mother of Prince Philip, granddaughter of Queen Victoria; Buckingham Palace, London, Dec. 5.

Ernest Ansermet, 85, conductor, founded l'Orchestre de la Suisse Romande; Geneva, Feb. 20.

Emilio Arenales, 46, foreign minister of Guatemala, president, UN General Assembly (September 1968–69); Guatemala City, Apr. 17.

Thurman W. Arnold, 78, lawyer, assistant U.S. attorney general in charge of antitrust division (1938–43); Alexandria, Va., Nov. 7.

Mitchell Ayres, 58, bandleader and composer; Las Vegas, Sept. 5.

René Barrientos Ortuño, 49, president of Bolivia (1966–69); Oruru Province, Bolivia, Apr. 27.

W. Preston Battle, 60, Criminal Court judge, presided over trial of James Earl Ray; Memphis, Tenn., Mar. 31.

Josef Cardinal Beran, 80, archbishop of Prague from November 1946, imprisoned by Nazis and then Communists for 17 years; Rome, May 17.

John Boles, 73, singer-actor (*The Desert Song*); San Angelo, Tex., Feb. 27.

Charles Brackett, 77, writer and film producer, won Oscars for *The Lost Weekend, Sunset Boulevard* and *Titanic;* Hollywood, Mar. 9.

Robert Briscoe, 74, Irish nationalist, first Jewish lord mayor of Dublin; Dublin, May 30.

Ned Brooks, 68, former journalist, moderator of radio and television program, *Meet the Press;* Washington, D.C., Apr. 13.

John Mason Brown, 68, drama critic, biographer, lecturer; New York City, Mar. 16.

Sir Lewis Casson, 93, actor, producer, dean of British stage; London, May 16.

Irene Castle, 75, ballroom dancer; Eureka Springs, Ark., Jan. 25.

Georges Catroux, 92, general of the French Army (served in Algeria and Indochina), a grand chancellor of the Legion of Honor, ambassador to the Soviet Union (1944–48); Paris, Dec. 21.

Frank G. Clement, 49, governor of Tennessee (1953–59, 1963–67); Nashville, Tenn., Nov. 4.

Bud Collyer, 61, television master of ceremonies (*To Tell the Truth*); Greenwich, Conn., Sept. 8.

Ivy Compton-Burnett, 85, British novelist; London, Aug. 27.

Maureen Connolly (Brinker), 34, U.S. tennis star (1951–54); Dallas, Tex., June 21.

Artur da Costa e Silva, 67, president of Brazil (Mar. 15, 1967–Aug. 31, 1969); Rio de Janeiro, Dec. 17.

Vicki Cummings, 50, actress, appeared as Olive Lashbrooke in *The Voice of the Turtle;* New York City, Nov. 30.

Samuel Dalsimer, 60, national chairman, Anti-Defamation League of B'nai B'rith; New York City, Aug. 22.

Amos De-Shalit, 42, Israeli nuclear physicist, director, Weizmann Institute of Science, Rehovoth, Israel (1966–68); Rehovoth, Sept. 2.

Claude Dornier, 85, German aviation pioneer, in 1929 created the DO-X, at the time the world's largest plane; Zug, Switzerland, Dec. 5.

Vernon Duke (Vladimir Dukelsky), 65, composer of popular songs (*April in Paris*) and classical works; Santa Monica, Calif., Jan. 17.

Allen W. Dulles, 75, director, Central Intelligence Agency (1953–61); Washington, D.C., Jan. 29.

Henry Francis du Pont, 88, director, Du Pont (1915–69) and General Motors (1918–44), art collector, horticulturist; Wilmington, Del., Apr. 10.

Canadian Consulate General

Pierre Dupuy, 72, Canada's ambassador to France 1958–63, organized Expo 67; Cannes, May 21.

Culver Pictures, Inc.

Judy Garland, 47, popular singer, actress ("The Wizard of Oz," "A Star Is Born"); London, June 22.

Pictorial Parade

Everett McKinley Dirksen, 73, U.S. senator (R-Ill., 1951–69), Senate minority leader from 1959; Washington, Sept. 7.

John L. Lewis, 89, president, United Mine Workers Union, 1920–60; Washington, June 11.

Joseph P. Kennedy, 81, former chairman SEC and ambassador to Great Britain; Hyannis Port, Nov 18.

PIX

Wide World

...es van der Rohe, ..., leading 20th-...ntury architect; ...icago, Aug. 17.

PIX

Wide World

...ovanni Martinelli, 83, star tenor, New York ...tropolitan Opera 1913–46; New York City, Feb. 2.

Pictorial Parade

...ew Pearson, 71, news-...per columnist ("Wash-...gton Merry-Go-Round"); ...shington, Sept. 1.

Culver Pictures, Inc.

Robert Taylor, 57, film ("Quo Vadis") and television ("The Detectives") actor; Santa Monica, June 8.

Camera Press-PIX

Franz von Papen, 89, German vice-chancellor under Hitler; Obersasbach, Germany, May 2.

Charles Edison, 78, son of inventor, secretary of Navy (1939–40), governor of New Jersey (1941–44); New York City, July 31.

Eve Zoltan Elmes, 55, created Eve of Roma cosmetics; New York City, Apr. 30.

Raoul H. Fleischmann, 83, founder and publisher, *The New Yorker* magazine; New York City, May 11.

Harry Emerson Fosdick, 91, liberal theologian, founding pastor of Riverside Church in New York City; Bronxville, N.Y., Oct. 5.

Thomas Francis, Jr., 69, developed first effective flu vaccine, directed Salk vaccine field trials; Ann Arbor, Mich., Oct. 1.

Vinton Freedley, 77, producer, Broadway musical comedies (*Anything Goes, Girl Crazy*); New York City, June 5.

William F. Friedman, 78, U.S. Army colonel, leader of task force that broke the Japanese code during World War II; Washington, D.C., Nov. 2.

Vito Genovese, 71, New York Mafia leader; Springfield, Mo., Feb. 14.

Kimon Georgiev, 87, premier of Bulgaria (1934–35, 1944–46); Sofia, Bulgaria, Sept. 28.

Adam Gimbel, 75, president, Saks Fifth Avenue (1926–69); New York City, Sept. 9.

Ramon Grau San Martin, 86, president of Cuba (1933–34, 1944–48); Havana, July 28.

Mitzi Green, 48, actress, child star of 1920's and 1930's; Huntington Beach, Calif., May 24.

Walter Gropius, 86, architect, father of modern design, founded Bauhaus school of design and architecture in Germany; Boston, Mass., July 5.

Walter Hagen, 76, professional golfer, won 17 major titles; Traverse City, Mich., Oct. 5.

Fred A. Hartley, Jr., 67, U.S. representative (R-N.J., 1929–49), coauthor Taft-Hartley Act; Linwood, N.J., May 11.

Coleman Hawkins, 64, tenor saxophonist; New York City, May 19.

Cameron Hawley, 63, novelist (*Executive Suite*); Lancaster, Pa., Feb. 9.

Gabby Hayes, 83, actor, appeared in over 200 Westerns; Burbank, Calif., Feb. 9.

Dan Healy, 80, "song and dance" man; Jackson Heights, N.Y., Aug. 31.

Sonja Henie, 57, ice-skating star, ice-show producer, movie actress; died on ambulance plane flying from Paris to Oslo, Oct. 12.

Michael F. (Pinky) Higgins, 59, manager Boston Red Sox (1955–59, 1960–62); Dallas, Mar. 21.

Conrad Hilton, Jr., 42, chairman of the executive committee, Hilton International Co., eldest son of Conrad Hilton; West Los Angeles, Feb. 5.

Martita Hunt, 69, actress, known for her stage portrayal of *The Madwoman of Chaillot;* London, June 13.

Jeffrey Hunter, 43, screen actor, portrayed Christ in *King of Kings* (1961); Hollywood, May 27.

Rex Ingram, 73, actor (*The Green Pastures*); Hollywood, Sept. 19.

Karl Jaspers, 86, existentialist philosopher; Basel, Switzerland, Feb. 26.

Henry Enoch Kagan, 62, rabbi, special consultant to Ecumenical Council, Vatican II; Pittsburgh, Pa., Aug. 16.

Boris Karloff, 81, horror-movie star (*Frankenstein*); Midhurst, Sussex, Feb. 2.

Joseph Kasavubu, 59, first president, Democratic Republic of the Congo (1960–65); Boma, Lower Congo, Mar. 24.

Jack Kerouac, 47, author (*On the Road*); St. Petersburg, Fla., Oct. 21.

Frank King, 86, cartoonist, created *Gasoline Alley* comic strip; Winter Park, Fla., June 24.

Boris Kroyt, 72, violist, Budapest String Quartet (1931–68); New York City, Nov. 15.

Rod La Rocque, 70, silent-film star, matinee idol of the 1920's; Beverly Hills, Calif., Oct. 15.

Boyd Leedom, 62, chairman, National Labor Relations Board (1955–65); Arlington, Va., Aug. 11.

Robert Lehman, 76, investment banker, bequeathed $100,000,000 art collection to Metropolitan Museum of Art; Sands Point, N.Y., Aug. 9.

Nathaniel Leverone, 84, founder, Automatic Canteen Company of America; Chicago, May 30.

D. B. Wyndham Lewis, 78, humorist, satirist and biographer; author, *The World of Goya* (1968); Altea, Spain, Nov. 21.

Willy Ley, 62, science writer, specialized in rocketry and space travel; Jackson Heights, N.Y., June 24.

Allan Haines Lockheed, 80, founder, Lockheed Aircraft Corporation; Tucson, Ariz., May 26.

Frank Loesser, 59, composer, lyricist (*Guys and Dolls, The Most Happy Fella*); New York City, July 28.

Ella Logan, 56, musical-comedy and film star (*Finian's Rainbow*); Burlingame, Calif., May 1.

Adolfo Lopez Mateos, 59, president of Mexico (1958–64); Mexico City, Sept. 22.

Bart Lytton, 56, financier, founder, Lytton Financial Corp. (1959); Los Angeles, June 29.

Ralph McGill, 70, columnist, publisher, *The Atlanta Constitution,* civil-rights champion; Atlanta, Feb. 3.

Jimmy McHugh, 74, composer (*The Sunny Side of the Street*); Beverly Hills, Calif., May 23.

Rocky Marciano, 45, world-champion heavyweight prizefighter (1952–56), undefeated in 49 professional fights; Newton, Iowa, Aug. 31.

Max Millikan, 56, director, Center for International Studies, Massachusetts Institute of Technology (1952–69); Boston, Dec. 14.

Maj. Gen. Iskander Mirza, 70, first president, Republic of Pakistan (1956–58); London, Nov. 13.

Douglas Stuart Moore, 75, composer (*The Ballad of Baby Doe*), won Pulitzer Prize for *Giants in the Earth* (1951); Greenport, N.Y., July 25.

Clinton W. Murchison, Sr., 74, oilman, multimillionaire; Athens, Tex., June 20.

Sir Edward Mutesa, 45, president of Uganda (1963–66); London, Nov. 21.

Julian S. Myrick, 88, "Mr. Life Insurance," vice-president, Mutual Life Insurance Company of New York, also instrumental in making tennis a major sport; New York City, Jan. 8.

Francisco Orlich, 62, president of Costa Rica (1962–66); San Jose, Costa Rica, Oct. 29.

Fairfield Osborn, 82, president, New York Zoological Society (1940–68), leading conservationist; New York City, Sept. 16.

Rafael Osuna, 31, Mexican tennis champion, won U.S. singles title (1963); near Monterrey, Mexico, June 4.

Tony Pastor, 62, bandleader; New London, Conn., Oct. 31.

Westbrook Pegler, 74, newspaper columnist (1933–62), won Pulitzer Prize (1941); Tucson, Ariz., June 24.

James A. Pike, 56, former Episcopal bishop of California whose controversial doctrines resulted in charges of heresy; near Jerusalem, Sept. 7.

Dominique Pire, 58, Dominican priest, won Nobel Peace Prize for helping refugees (1958); Louvain, Belgium, Jan. 30.

Eric Portman, 66, British actor (*Separate Tables*); Cornwall, England, Dec. 7.

Cecil Frank Powell, 65, British nuclear physicist, won Nobel Prize (1950); Milan, Italy, Aug. 9.

Thelma Ritter, 63, stage, screen and TV star; New York City, Feb. 5.

Red Rolfe, 60, baseball star for the New York Yankees (1934–42), Detroit Tigers manager (1949–52); Laconia, N.H., July 8.

Vincent Sardi, Sr., 83, founder, Sardi's Restaurant in New York City; Saranac Lake, N.Y., Nov. 19.

Kenny Sargent, 63, popular crooner of the 1930's, early 1940's (*For You*); Dallas, Tex., Dec. 20.

King Saud (Saud Ibn Abdul Aziz al-Faisal al-Saud), 67, ruler of Saudi Arabia (1953–64); Athens, Greece, Feb. 23.

Earl of Scarbrough (Lawrence Roger Lumley), 72, as lord chamberlain (1952–63) acted as official British censor; Yorkshire, England, June 29.

Nicholas M. Schenck, 87, founder of MGM, leader in motion pictures; Miami Beach, Fla., Mar. 3.

Harry Scherman, 82, a founder of the Book-of-the-Month Club; New York City, Nov. 12.

Ben Shahn, 70, painter, used his art to explain his social and political views; New York City, Mar. 14.

Matsutaro Shoriki, 84, newspaper publisher, chairman, Japan's Atomic Energy Commission (1956–69), introduced baseball to Japan; Tokyo, Oct. 9.

Ole Singstad, 87, civil engineer, designed New York City tunnels; New York City, Dec. 8.

Sir Osbert Sitwell, 76, British poet, essayist and novelist; Florence, Italy, May 4.

Vesto Melvin Slipher, 93, astronomer, director of the Lowell Observatory (1926–52); Flagstaff, Ariz., Nov. 8.

Otto Stern, 81, nuclear physicist, won Nobel Prize (1943); Berkeley, Calif., Aug. 17.

Josef von Sternberg, 75, motion-picture director (1920's, 1930's), discovered Marlene Dietrich; Hollywood, Calif., Dec. 22.

Gladys Swarthout, 64, mezzo-soprano, New York Metropolitan Opera; Florence, Italy, July 7.

Moise Tshombe, 49, premier, Democratic Republic of the Congo (1964–65); Algiers, June 29.

Cardinal Urbani, 69, patriarch of Venice, president of Italian Bishops Conference (1966–69); Rome, Sept. 17.

Queen Victoria Eugenie, 81, queen of Spain (1906–31), widow of King Alfonso XIII, granddaughter of Britain's Queen Victoria; Lausanne, Switzerland, Apr. 15.

Marshal Kliment Y. Voroshilov, 88, Soviet civil-war hero, chairman of the Presidium of the Supreme Soviet (1953–60); Moscow, Dec. 2.

Fred Linwood Walker, 82, major general, commander, 36th Infantry Division in North Africa and Italy during World War II; Washington, D.C., Oct. 6.

Saul Wallen, 59, labor arbitrator, president, New York Urban Coalition; New York City, Aug. 5.

James P. Warburg, 72, financier, writer on U.S. foreign policy, published over 30 books; Greenwich, Conn., June 3.

Sidney J. Weinberg, 77, investment banker, financier, "Mr. Wall Street," unofficial presidential adviser; New York City, July 23.

Josh White, 61, folk singer (*Hard-Time Blues, John Henry*); Manhasset, N.Y., Sept. 5.

Leolyn Dana Wilgress, 76, Canadian diplomat, Canada's first envoy to the Soviet Union (1942–47); Ottawa, July 21.

John Dover Wilson, 87, educator (King's College in London, and Edinburgh University), noted Shakespearean scholar; near Edinburgh, Scotland, Jan. 15.

Charles Winninger, 84, stage and screen star, created role of Cap'n Andy in *Show Boat;* Palm Springs, Calif., Jan. 19.

Robert E. Wood, 90, developed Sears, Roebuck & Co. into the world's largest merchandising concern; Lake Forest, Ill., Nov. 6.

Willard G. Wyman, 71, U.S. Army general, leader of First Division during Normandy invasion (World War II); Washington, D.C., Mar. 29.

UPI

Only the stern section of U.S. destroyer "Frank E. Evans" remains after she collided with Australian carrier "Melbourne" on June 2. Later a U.S.-Australian naval board of inquiry placed major blame on the destroyer.

DEFENSE

The year 1969 may be remembered for the start of a revolt against the Pentagon, its $80,-000,000,000 budget and the close link between the armed services and defense contractors—the "military-industrial complex." Aided by allies in Congress and the timely support of President Nixon, the Pentagon managed to stave off most of the attacks but gave ground repeatedly before a determined assault on its hitherto unquestioned weapons systems and other spending programs. The assault gave no signs of letting up as the year ended.

Under the leadership of Nixon and Defense Secretary Melvin R. Laird, a former Wisconsin congressman, the United States seemed to be moving away from dependence on large conventional forces and back toward heavy reliance on missiles, antimissile missiles and a modernized force of manned bombers. In a major policy declaration, the President said that the nation would no longer supply combat troops to help Asian countries, such as Vietnam, defend themselves from communist insurgents. Rather, U.S. policy would be to help supply military aid and equipment so the embattled nations could do their own fighting. Similarly, the President directed that studies be made to prepare for an all-volunteer Army once the Vietnam war ended. And 60,000 troops were withdrawn from Vietnam, with another 6,000 troops scheduled to pull out of Thailand by mid-1970.

In one of the great defense controversies of 1969, Nixon won Senate support for starting to deploy the 12-site Safeguard antiballistic missile (ABM) system. His victory climaxed a six-month war of words with antagonists led by Sen. Edward M. Kennedy (D-Mass.) and leading Republicans. The narrow vote in the Senate was later confirmed overwhelmingly in the House. The controversy erupted when the Nixon administration proceeded to buy land near major cities as the first step in deploying the Sentinel ABM system inherited from the Johnson administration. Under pressure from Capitol Hill and protest groups in the affected cities, the Pentagon put a freeze on land acquisition while it reviewed missile-defense plans. On Mar. 14, the President announced his decision to go ahead with a revised system designed to protect the nation's nuclear counterpunch—Minuteman missiles in silos centered in the sparsely populated Great Plains states. "There is no way that we can defend our cities without an unacceptable loss of life," Nixon said. "The only way that I have concluded that we can save lives—which is the primary purpose of our defense system—is to prevent war."

Laird and pro-ABM senators insisted that the Safeguard system would deter the Soviet Union from attempting a nuclear surprise at-

In controversy over deployment of the Safeguard ABM system, Deputy Defense Secretary David Packard uses chart in arguing for the system before the Senate Armed Services Committee, as Defense Secretary Melvin Laird listens thoughtfully.

UPI

tack, or first strike. The Defense Secretary divulged previously secret information about the Soviets' SS-9 missile, a superweapon that could carry a 25-megaton warhead more than 5,000 miles and hit a target with an accuracy of 0.6 of a mile. Opponents accused Laird of using a "technique of fear" to frighten Congress into approving the program. They also insisted the new ABM system would not work and might set back efforts to halt the nuclear arms race by negotiation with the Kremlin. As the battle continued, Laird stressed the Soviet Union's effort to surpass the United States in number of land-based intercontinental ballistic missiles (ICBM's) and catch up with the American lead in missile-firing nuclear submarines. Opponents relied heavily on the opinion of leading scientists who said that the United States already had enough nuclear muscle to deter the Soviets despite their buildup and preliminary work on a missile defense system around Moscow.

Although the ABM opponents lost that fight, they set a new pattern of thorough Congressional scrutiny of military spending programs. In the past, Congress had accepted most Pentagon requests without serious question. In the new critical mood, the Senate spent nearly six weeks in debating the $20,000,000,000 military authorization bill. Critics of the military won a series of votes to give the General Accounting Office more "watchdog" power over Pentagon contracts. The C-5A, a supertransport plane built by Lockheed, was a major target since it apparently was going to cost $2,000,000,000

more to get delivery of the planes than the Pentagon estimated. Sen. William O. Proxmire (D. Wis.) lost his bid to eliminate $533,000,000 for the C-5A from the bill. Foes of a new manned bomber and more nuclear aircraft carriers also went down to defeat. In the end, only $71,000,000 was trimmed from the spending total but the Pentagon's defenders knew they had been through a fight.

A series of mishaps added to the general skepticism about the military. A nuclear submarine sank at the dock at a California shipyard, resulting in $25,000,000 damage. Congressional investigators blamed it on a "wholly avoidable blunder" by inexperienced workmen. Skyrocketing costs, known as "overruns" in Pentagon jargon, were cited to bolster the case for those who wanted to slice billions from the defense budget. The Army's Main Battle Tank, for example, had originally been estimated to cost $86,000,000, but six years later the estimates were $303,000,000 and the tank was not yet in production. Even Chairman George Mahon of the House Appropriations Committee, a military-minded conservative, scored the generals and admirals for generating a "lack of confidence" by mistakes in procurement.

In a speech at the Air Force Academy on June 4, President Nixon deplored an "open season on the armed forces" and suggested that the critics favored unilateral disarmament. This brought a bristling reaction from liberal Democrats. Senator Kennedy said in rebuttal: "The burden of proof is on those who seek to justify

NEW U.S. SELECTIVE SERVICE LAW

On Nov. 26, 1969, President Nixon signed a bill providing for a lottery draft system. Five days later the first such lottery in a generation was held in Washington. Each day in the year was assigned a number according to the order in which it was drawn. Thus, as Sept. 14 was drawn first, it became number 1. Since January 1970, young men eligible for U.S. military service have been called in accordance with the numbers their birth days received in the Dec. 1 lottery, beginning with number 1. Unless there is a national emergency the men whose numbers do not come up before the end of the year will be free from service.

Order of birth dates:

1.	Sept. 14	62.	Apr. 21	123.	Dec. 28	184.	Sept. 8	245.	Aug. 26	306.	Jan. 7
2.	Apr. 24	63.	Sept. 20	124.	Apr. 13	185.	Nov. 20	246.	Sept. 18	307.	Aug. 13
3.	Dec. 30	64.	June 27	125.	Oct. 2	186.	Jan. 21	247.	June 22	308.	May 28
4.	Feb. 14	65.	May 10	126.	Nov. 13	187.	July 20	248.	July 11	309.	Nov. 26
5.	Oct. 18	66.	Nov. 12	127.	Nov. 14	188.	July 5	249.	June 1	310.	Nov. 5
6.	Sept. 6	67.	July 25	128.	Dec. 18	189.	Feb. 17	250.	May 21	311.	Aug. 19
7.	Oct. 26	68.	Feb. 12	129.	Dec. 1	190.	July 18	251.	Jan. 3	312.	Apr. 8
8.	Sept. 7	69.	June 13	130.	May 15	191.	Apr. 29	252.	Apr. 23	313.	May 31
9.	Nov. 22	70.	Dec. 21	131.	Nov. 15	192.	Oct. 20	253.	Apr. 6	314.	Dec. 12
10.	Dec. 6	71.	Sept. 10	132.	Nov. 25	193.	July 31	254.	Oct. 16	315.	Sept. 30
11.	Aug. 31	72.	Oct. 12	133.	May 12	194.	Jan. 9	255.	Sept. 17	316.	Apr. 22
12.	Dec. 7	73.	June 17	134.	June 11	195.	Sept. 24	256.	Mar. 23	317.	Mar. 9
13.	July 8	74.	Apr. 27	135.	Dec. 20	196.	Oct. 24	257.	Sept. 28	318.	Jan. 13
14.	Apr. 11	75.	May 19	136.	Mar. 11	197.	May 9	258.	Mar. 24	319.	May 23
15.	July 12	76.	Nov. 6	137.	June 25	198.	Aug. 14	259.	Mar. 13	320.	Dec. 15
16.	Dec. 29	77.	Jan. 28	138.	Oct. 13	199.	Jan. 8	260.	Apr. 17	321.	May 8
17.	Jan. 15	78.	Dec. 27	139.	Mar. 6	200.	Mar. 19	261.	Aug. 3	322.	July 15
18.	Sept. 26	79.	Oct. 31	140.	Jan. 18	201.	Oct. 23	262.	Apr. 28	323.	Mar. 10
19.	Nov. 1	80.	Nov. 9	141.	Aug. 18	202.	Oct. 4	263.	Sept. 9	324.	Aug. 11
20.	June 4	81.	Apr. 4	142.	Aug. 12	203.	Nov. 19	264.	Oct. 27	325.	Jan. 10
21.	Aug. 10	82.	Sept. 5	143.	Nov. 17	204.	Sept. 21	265.	Mar. 22	326.	May 22
22.	June 26	83.	Apr. 3	144.	Feb. 2	205.	Feb. 27	266.	Nov. 4	327.	July 6
23.	July 24	84.	Dec. 25	145.	Aug. 4	206.	June 10	267.	Mar. 3	328.	Dec. 2
24.	Oct. 5	85.	June 7	146.	Nov. 18	207.	Sept. 16	268.	Mar. 27	329.	Jan. 11
25.	Feb. 19	86.	Feb. 1	147.	Apr. 7	208.	Apr. 30	269.	Apr. 5	330.	May 1
26.	Dec. 14	87.	Oct. 6	148.	Apr. 16	209.	June 30	270.	July 29	331.	July 14
27.	July 21	88.	July 28	149.	Sept. 25	210.	Feb. 4	271.	Apr. 2	332.	Mar. 18
28.	June 5	89.	Feb. 15	150.	Feb. 11	211.	Jan. 31	272.	June 12	333.	Aug. 30
29.	Mar. 2	90.	Apr. 18	151.	Sept. 29	212.	Feb. 16	273.	Apr. 15	334.	Mar. 21
30.	Mar. 31	91.	Feb. 7	152.	Feb. 13	213.	Mar. 8	274.	June 16	335.	June 9
31.	May 24	92.	Jan. 26	153.	July 22	214.	Feb. 5	275.	Mar. 4	336.	Apr. 19
32.	Apr. 1	93.	July 1	154.	Aug. 17	215.	Jan. 4	276.	May 4	337.	Jan. 22
33.	Mar. 17	94.	Oct. 28	155.	May 6	216.	Feb. 10	277.	July 9	338.	Feb. 9
34.	Nov. 2	95.	Dec. 24	156.	Nov. 21	217.	Mar. 30	278.	May 18	339.	Aug. 22
35.	May 7	96.	Dec. 16	157.	Dec. 3	218.	Apr. 10	279.	July 4	340.	Apr. 26
36.	Aug. 24	97.	Nov. 8	158.	Sept. 11	219.	Apr. 9	280.	Jan. 20	341.	June 18
37.	May 11	98.	July 17	159.	Jan. 2	220.	Oct. 10	281.	Nov. 28	342.	Oct. 9
38.	Oct. 30	99.	Nov. 29	160.	Sept. 22	221.	Jan. 12	282.	Nov. 10	343.	Mar. 25
39.	Dec. 11	100.	Dec. 31	161.	Sept. 2	222.	June 28	283.	Oct. 8	344.	Aug. 20
40.	May 3	101.	Jan. 5	162.	Dec. 23	223.	Mar. 28	284.	July 10	345.	Apr. 20
41.	Dec. 10	102.	Aug. 15	163.	Dec. 13	224.	Jan. 6	285.	Feb. 29	346.	Apr. 12
42.	July 13	103.	May 30	164.	Jan. 30	225.	Sept. 1	286.	Aug. 25	347.	Feb. 6
43.	Dec. 9	104.	June 19	165.	Dec. 4	226.	May 29	287.	July 30	348.	Nov. 3
44.	Aug. 16	105.	Dec. 8	166.	Mar. 16	227.	July 19	288.	Oct. 17	349.	Jan. 29
45.	Aug. 2	106.	Aug. 9	167.	Aug. 28	228.	June 2	289.	July 27	350.	July 2
46.	Nov. 11	107.	Nov. 16	168.	Aug. 7	229.	Oct. 29	290.	Feb. 22	351.	Apr. 25
47.	Nov. 27	108.	Mar. 1	169.	Mar. 15	230.	Nov. 24	291.	Aug. 21	352.	Aug. 27
48.	Aug. 8	109.	June 23	170.	Mar. 26	231.	Apr. 14	292.	Feb. 18	353.	June 29
49.	Sept. 3	110.	June 6	171.	Oct. 15	232.	Sept. 4	293.	Mar. 5	354.	Mar. 14
50.	July 7	111.	Aug. 1	172.	July 23	233.	Sept. 27	294.	Oct. 14	355.	Jan. 27
51.	Nov. 7	112.	May 17	173.	Dec. 26	234.	Oct. 7	295.	May 13	356.	June 14
52.	Jan. 25	113.	Sept. 15	174.	Nov. 30	235.	Jan. 17	296.	May 27	357.	May 26
53.	Dec. 22	114.	Aug. 6	175.	Sept. 13	236.	Feb. 24	297.	Feb. 3	358.	June 24
54.	Aug. 5	115.	July 3	176.	Oct. 25	237.	Oct. 11	298.	May 2	359.	Oct. 1
55.	May 16	116.	Aug. 23	177.	Sept. 19	238.	Jan. 14	299.	Feb. 28	360.	June 20
56.	Dec. 5	117.	Oct. 22	178.	May 14	239.	Mar. 20	300.	Mar. 12	361.	May 25
57.	Feb. 23	118.	Jan. 23	179.	Feb. 25	240.	Dec. 19	301.	June 3	362.	Mar. 29
58.	Jan. 19	119.	Sept. 23	180.	June 15	241.	Oct. 19	302.	Feb. 20	363.	Feb. 21
59.	Jan. 24	120.	July 16	181.	Feb. 8	242.	Sept. 12	303.	July 26	364.	May 5
60.	June 21	121.	Jan. 16	182.	Nov. 23	243.	Oct. 21	304.	Dec. 17	365.	Feb. 26
61.	Aug. 29	122.	Mar. 7	183.	May 20	244.	Oct. 3	305.	Jan. 1	366.	June 8

Order of the alphabet (first letter last name) when birth dates are the same: J, G, D, X, N, O, Z, T, W, P, Q, Y, U, C, F, I, K, H, S, L, M, A, R, E, B, V.

spending two thirds of all controllable tax dollars on defense."

Another response came from Defense Secretary Laird, wise in the ways of Capitol Hill from his years on the House Appropriations Committee. He announced on Aug. 21 that he hoped to cut defense spending by $3,000,000,-000 a year even though it might cause "an inevitable weakening of our worldwide military posture." The cutbacks included a slash of 100,000 military personnel, to bring the total down to 3,300,000 men under arms, reduction of Air Force training flying hours, closing of some military bases and mothballing of more than 100 Navy ships, including the battleship *New Jersey*. The old battlewagon, taken out of mothballs at a cost of $22,200,000 for brief service in the Vietnam war, was a symbol of the wasteful practices the Senate critics had in mind.

Prodded by Chairman L. Mendel Rivers of the House Armed Services Committee, the House produced a bill that was more favorable to the Pentagon and added $1,000,000,000 for modernizing the Navy. In the Senate-House conference, many of the gains made by Pentagon critics were knocked out or watered down. For the first time, both chambers approved restrictions on the transportation and storage of chemical and biological warfare (CBW) weapons, such as nerve gas, after disclosures of open-air testing in Alabama, Utah and elsewhere. (In late November, President Nixon announced that the United States would never engage in germ warfare and would use chemical-warfare weapons only for defensive purposes.)

After the debate was over, the Air Force said it would buy only 81 C-5A's, not the 120 planes originally contemplated. Even those 81 will cost more than $3,000,000,000. The 120-plane fleet was supposed to cost $3,400,000,000 when the estimates were first presented to Congress.

Other episodes contributed to a loss of prestige for the military, including Senate hearings into scandals involving the operation of post exchanges and enlisted men's clubs in Vietnam, and the highly publicized "Case of the Green Berets." (See article on Crime.)

Another revolt, aimed against the alleged unfairness of the Selective Service System, spread across college campuses in 1969. President Nixon, responding to this sentiment, proposed a draft lottery and calling up 19-year-olds first (instead of last) to reduce the likelihood of being drafted for the whole 19–26 age bracket. He urged retention of college deferments, however, and a relaxing of the rules for

induction of graduate students. Nixon also eased out the controversial director of the nation's draft system, Lewis B. Hershey, by promoting the 76-year-old general to a "consultant" position starting early in 1970. Congress passed the draft-lottery bill despite sharp opposition to it in the past.

Even within the ranks there was dissent. The Pentagon issued a remarkable five-page directive to military commanders that set down guidelines for permissible dissent by soldiers on the Vietnam war and other matters. The directive followed a series of protests at Army stockades and the establishment of antiwar coffeehouses near major military bases. Desertions to Sweden and other foreign havens became an increasing problem. The President announced a reduction of 50,000 in draft calls for the final three months of 1969. It represented only a small cut, however, to 290,400 from the 296,000 called to the colors in 1968.

The war in Vietnam seemed to be at the heart of the widespread unrest and criticism of the Pentagon, perhaps because the military had failed to achieve a victory in Southeast Asia over the North Vietnamese and Vietcong forces. Nixon's plans to withdraw 60,000 troops by the end of 1969 did not seem to mollify the antiwar protesters, who staged a gigantic march on Washington in mid-November to demand complete withdrawal of American troops from Vietnam.

In another controversial matter, the Nixon administration agreed to hold talks with the Soviet Union in Helsinki, Finland, starting Nov. 17, to discuss strategic-arms limitation, including a mutual ban on testing of the MIRV (Multiple Independently-targeted Reentry Vehicle), a weapon that contains more than one nuclear warhead. (See Disarmament.) The debate over ABM may have foreshadowed a similar controversy over MIRV in the 1970's. Many regard a halt in the tests as critically important in arranging a slowdown or reversal in the arms race. The Pentagon awarded a contract to General Electric on June 19 to go ahead with production of the advanced missile system. Some voices in Congress, in the spirit of 1969, then suggested legislation to halt further testing to spur chances of an agreement with the Soviets on the weapon. They are conceded to be ahead of the United States in development of what some observers regard as a "terror weapon" that rivals the hydrogen bomb in potential destructive power. See Intelligence, Military.

WILLIAM J. EATON
Washington Correspondent
Chicago Daily News

DELAWARE

On Jan. 21, Russell W. Peterson, former director of research for Du Pont, was inaugurated as governor. His first step was to order National Guard troops from Negro sections of Wilmington, there since April 1968. In March, following disclosures of brutal treatment of children in the state's reform school for boys, he pledged the full power of his office to correct conditions. (In July, corporal punishment in all state juvenile institutions was abolished.) On Apr. 24, he signed an open-housing bill.

DENMARK

The possible creation of a future inter-Scandinavian customs union, to be known as Nordek, was one of the overriding issues discussed by Danes and other Scandinavians during 1969. In July a committee of 50 economic experts met for a week at Vedbaek, Denmark, and completed a draft for a comprehensive treaty. Their report, dealing with more than a thousand detailed problems, was discussed by the prime ministers of Denmark, Finland, Norway and Sweden in November. The main difficulty was the conflict of interest between industrially powerful Sweden and the less-so Finland, Norway and Denmark.

Responding to a supposed popular wish to lower the voting age, the Danish Parliament on June 5 reduced the age requirement from 21 to 18. Since the bill would be part of the constitution, the Folketing's action had to be voted on in a plebiscite. Contrary to expectations, the measure was turned down at the polls on June 24. It was evident that young people were much less interested in it than had been supposed.

In February 1967, Denmark and the Netherlands on one side and West Germany on the other brought a dispute over the continental shelf in the North Sea before the International Court of Justice at The Hague. Under a UN convention ruling of 1958, Holland, with a convex coastline, had received a larger share of the continental shelf than West Germany. Dissatisfied with this arrangement, West Germany at last took the case to the court. (The settlement would be of some consequence if oil or natural gas were found in the involved parts of the shelf.) On Feb. 20 the court ruled that the parties negotiate until they reach an agreement that would leave as much as possible to each country of the parts of the continental shelf that are a natural prolongation of the land territory of each. The ruling was considered largely in favor of West Germany.

On Mar. 11, King Frederik IX celebrated his 70th birthday and was hailed by his people.

Pictorial Parade

King Frederik meets soldiers engaged in Green Express, NATO exercise held on Danish soil in Sept. 1969. Twelve thousand soldiers from ten countries took part.

A unique anniversary, the 750th birthday of the red-and-white Danish flag, was celebrated in Denmark on June 15. According to legend, the flag fell from heaven on the Danish Army during a battle with the heathen at Lyndanisse in Estonia on June 15, 1219. As it fell, a voice from on high proclaimed: "Under this sign shall ye conquer!" Historians are not certain about the flag's actual origin.

ERIK J. FRIIS
Editor, The American-Scandinavian Review

DENMARK

Area: 16,619 sq. mi.
Population: 4,900,000
Capital: Copenhagen (pop., 1,000,000)
Government: Frederik IX, king—1947; Hilmar Baunsgaard, premier—1968
Gross national product: $12,500,000,000
Monetary unit: krone (7.5 Dkr. = U.S.$1.00)
Chief products: dairy products, beer, fish, machinery, furniture, porcelain, textiles
Foreign trade: exports, $2,638,000,000; imports, $3,224,000,000
Communications: 1,469,195 telephones, 379,-642 radios, 1,204,000 TV sets, 62 daily newspapers
Transportation: roads, 38,007 mi.; 874,311 passenger cars; railroads, 2,082 mi.
Education: 702,728 elementary and secondary students, 4 universities
Armed forces: 45,500

See map on page 185

DISARMAMENT

SALT was the word for disarmament in 1969. Diplomats, disarmament experts and international statesmen generally hailed the five weeks of Strategic Arms Limitation Talks between the United States and the Soviet Union held at Helsinki, Finland, from Nov. 17 to Dec. 22.

Delegations headed by Gerard C. Smith, director of the U.S. Arms Control and Disarmament Agency, and Vladimir S. Semyonov, a deputy foreign minister of the Soviet Union, did not reach agreement on limitation, control or elimination of anti-ballistic missiles (ABM) or Multiple Independently-targeted Reentry Vehicles (MIRV), whose development had brought the East-West arms race to a new high pitch.

The measurable gain, with each side apparently realizing that the new weapons meant destruction for itself as well as for the other, was that the Helsinki SALT discussions were held in low key, with a minimum of propaganda and an agreement to continue the search for accord in 1970.

Announcing their intention to resume the SALT talks at Vienna on Apr. 16, 1970, with the venue later changing back to Helsinki, the two superpowers said in a communiqué on Dec. 22 that as a result of their talks "each side was able to understand better the views of the other side in regard to the problems under consideration. An understanding was reached on the general range of questions which will be the subject of further Soviet-U.S. exchanges of opinion."

The choice of the site for the resumed talks was a compromise that appeared to augur well for them. The Russians, annoyed by adverse comment in Austria on the take-over of Czechoslovakia by the Warsaw Pact powers in 1968, disliked the U.S. choice of Vienna. The Americans, uncomfortable because of the lack of space and privacy in their Finnish Embassy, objected to Helsinki. Both sides objected to Geneva, the traditional neutral site for conferences. Both were concerned that the calm, realistic atmosphere of the SALT talks might be influenced by the propaganda surrounding the Disarmament Conference that has gone on there for years.

Rivaling the rosy optimism generated by the Helsinki talks was a unilateral announcement by President Nixon that the United States would never engage in germ warfare and renounced all but defensive use of chemical-warfare weapons. Specifically, Nixon said: "The United States reaffirms its oft-repeated renunciation of the first use of lethal chemical weapons [and] extends this renunciation to the first use of incapacitating chemicals. . . . The United States shall renounce the use of lethal biological agents and weapons and all other methods of biological warfare. The United States will confine its biological research to defensive measures such as immunization and safety measures."

Nixon's declaration was made despite the fact that the United States never had ratified the Geneva Protocol of 1925, which prohibits the use in war of "asphyxiating, poisonous or other gases and . . . bacteriological methods of warfare."

The President said he would urge the Senate to ratify the 44-year-old treaty. His declaration of renunciation was warmly welcomed in international circles, but the edge was taken from the glad acceptance by a White House clarification that tear gas and herbicides, both widely used in Vietnam, were not included in the presidential ban. The United States was under criticism in some quarters because it used tear gas to force the enemy into the open against U.S. gunfire, or herbicides to defoliate the jungle so that enemy troops could be more easily spotted from the air.

Further tarnishing of the Nixon statement came several days later when the Defense Department disclosed that it would continue the manufacture of toxins, which, although they cause death-dealing disease, are made from dead bacteria and cannot spread epidemics. Nixon's statement had specifically endorsed a British proposal for a convention on biological warfare which authorities in London said expressly outlawed toxins for use in warfare.

The year's third major step in disarmament was ratification by the United States and the Soviet Union of the nonproliferation treaty (NPT) designed to prevent the spread of nuclear weapons to countries not already possessing them. Coupled with the ratification by Washington and Moscow (Britain already had ratified the pact) was the signing of the treaty by the Federal Republic of Germany. This was considered a considerable step inasmuch as West Germany long had held to its status as a major country and had threatened, at least implicitly, to take steps to become a nuclear power in its own right, a development that would have upset the balance of power in Europe and perhaps the entire world.

"The opportunities, as well as the need, for halting the nuclear arms race have never been greater than at the present time," UN Secretary-General Thant said in his annual report to the General Assembly. "There now exists a rough balance between the Soviet Union and the United States where each is capable of virtually destroying the other and neither is capable, if nuclear war should ever break out, of preventing or escaping the holocaust.

"The present situation of relative stability could disappear, even if only temporarily, if new generations of nuclear weapons systems were developed and deployed. This upsetting of the balance, or 'destabilization,' would create unknown temptations and pressures and greatly increase the danger of possible miscalculation.

"Hence, there may never be a better time to put a stop to the nuclear arms race."

Thant proposed that the United Nations dedicate the 1970's, already designated as the Second UN Development Decade, as "a Disarmament Decade."

The General Assembly reacted promptly to Thant's suggestions. It declared the 1970's a Disarmament Decade by a 104 to 0 vote. It called for peaceful uses of outer space and of the seabeds and for a complete ban on nuclear testing, including experimental blasts underground.

Most of these resolutions—which, as Assembly actions, carried only the force of recommendations—were referred for further

discussion in Geneva, where the 18-nation Disarmament Committee has become the 26-nation Conference of the Committee on Disarmament with the addition of Argentina, Hungary, Japan, Mongolia, Morocco, the Netherlands, Pakistan and Yugoslavia. France, as it had done from the beginning, continued to boycott the arms talks.

The Assembly, running athwart the wishes of the Soviet Union and the United States, which warned it not to upset the Helsinki SALT talks, voted 82 to 0 with 37 abstentions to urge the two superpowers to agree to "a moratorium on further testing and deployment of new offensive and strategic nuclear-weapons systems."

In another revolt against the Great Powers— or, specifically, the United States—the Assembly decided by an 80 to 3 vote with 36 abstentions that, in effect, tear gas and defoliants are prohibited under the 1925 Geneva Protocol. The U.S. State Department said later that the vote could not be regarded as an "international consensus."

BRUCE W. MUNN
Chief UN Correspondent
United Press International

In Helsinki, Finland, after signing agreement to continue talks in 1970 on limiting strategic weapons, Soviet Deputy Foreign Minister Vladimir Semyonov (l) and U.S. chief delegate Gerard Smith exchange pens.

UPI

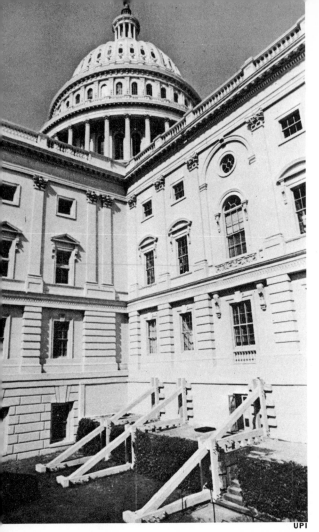

Heavy wooden props shore up the Capitol's cracked west front. Dispute rages over whether to restore (difficult) or expand (and possibly spoil) it.

DISTRICT OF COLUMBIA

President Nixon sent a special message to Congress on District of Columbia problems in April, proposing a variety of measures to increase the efficiency of the Washington government. Many of these had been suggested before, and, as before, Congress was slow to act on them.

To meet the long-debated problem of home rule for the District, Nixon suggested the creation of a special commission to investigate the matter and submit recommendations for self-government to the President and Congress. The Senate passed such a bill in October, but the House of Representatives, where there is strong home-rule opposition, did not act. Nixon also recommended approval of a constitutional amendment granting the District representation in Congress. This, too, failed to pass, as did his proposal that Congress provide for a nonvoting Washington delegate in the House as an interim measure. The Senate passed the delegate bill, but the House did not.

The President sent up a record-breaking budget for fiscal 1970 for the District, totaling $733,000,000. This was cut to $650,200,000 by Congress, but the amount voted still was an all-time high for the Washington government. Nixon recommended that the Federal Government annually provide the District with a payment of 30 per cent of the revenues raised locally, a more generous Federal payment than Congress had previously been willing to grant. The Senate agreed to this but not the House.

Mayor Walter Washington, assessing the city's problems after two years as head of the new form of District government, said that progress had been made, but that more authority was needed through some form of home rule.

Washington suffered disappointments during the year. Little progress was made in rebuilding sections of the city, largely in Negro areas, scarred and burned in riots after the assassination of the Rev. Martin Luther King, Jr., in April 1968. However, urban-renewal planning for these areas went ahead, and Nixon showed personal interest by visiting one of the most heavily damaged corridors. The Mayor also was unhappy over the steadily rising crime rates in the District. In a further effort to combat crime, Nixon proposed legislation calling for tougher crime-fighting measures and for court reorganization to bring swifter trials.

Another disappointment came in the squabbling over plans to build a model community center at Fort Lincoln, on a site formerly occupied by the National Training School for Boys, in northeast Washington. The administration indicated that the plans were too elaborate and that the project would be delayed.

The Mayor was pleased that, with strong administration help, the long freeway-subway dispute was settled. It was decided to go ahead with both. Groundbreaking for the subway took place in December.

Washington's top Republican Party official, National Committeeman Carl Shipley, called the new mayor-city council government system a failure. According to Shipley, "The schools are still terrible; the budget is still going up; the number of government employees is soaring; narcotics traffic is still high; the jail population is still increasing; juvenile delinquency is up."

JOSEPH W. HALL, JR.
Senate Staff, Washington Bureau
The Associated Press

ECONOMY

During 1969, economics and government economic policies commanded first-line attention throughout the world. It was also a year when the attention of the world was centered on U.S. efforts to curb a spiraling inflation.

United States. In the United States, the economy went through one of its roughest years of the decade. Elsewhere in the world, there was one major currency devaluation and one major upward revaluation as the international monetary system continued adjusting to the pressures of the past few years.

U.S. economic policies and the business climate were governed almost exclusively by the fight against inflation, which pushed prices up an average of 6 per cent during the year. The new Republican administration in Washington said it was determined to cut into that rate, but it did not introduce any new programs to accomplish the job. Once again, as in 1968, the chief burden of containing the business expansion fell to the Federal Reserve Board. And the Fed responded by keeping a firm lid on the amount of money available for banks to lend to finance even more expansion.

Businessmen found their costs, both labor and raw materials, rising faster than the productivity of their companies, and corporate profits rose slower than they had for several years. Late in 1969, in fact, there were clear indications that corporate earnings would drop off in 1970.

As a result of the Fed's tight-money policies, interest rates rose to their highest levels in more than 100 years. The Government itself was forced to pay more than 7 per cent to borrow money. The Fed's discount rate, the charge banks pay to borrow from the Government, rose to 6 per cent; and the bankers increased their prime rate—the charge to their biggest and best customers, usually large corporations —to 8½ per cent in the spring. Bonds issued by highly rated companies carried interest rates of more than 9 per cent, and American dollars that were out of the country, and not so restricted as domestic funds, commanded rates of more than 11 per cent.

Late in the year, economists began urging that the Fed let up on its credit stringency to forestall the risk of a recession in 1970. Despite the Fed's policies, though, price increases continued to spread through the economy, and the governors seemed determined to hold on until they had broken the back of the inflation.

The income-tax surcharge, first passed by Congress in June 1968, remained in force at the 10 per cent level throughout the year, thanks to an extension by Congress after its scheduled expiration in June 1969. The surtax was reduced to 5 per cent, and set to expire in June 1970, as part of an income-tax-reform bill passed in December.

The new Government attempted to cut some spending, but, as often happens in a change of administrations, it was pretty well committed

U.S. Treasury Secretary David M. Kennedy and Federal Reserve Board Chairman William McChesney Martin (l) confer during meeting of nation's major bankers. Martin's term on the board was to expire on Jan. 31, 1970.

UPI

to the budget prepared by the previous administration.

As business activity slowed, and prices kept rising, pressure began to build among nongovernment economists for some kind of wage-and-price controls or guidelines. Government experts echoed the sentiments of President Nixon, who said several times that he was opposed to controls, since he considered them unworkable. The President also said he would not use "jawboning" to coerce labor and management to hold the line, though the economists insisted that the policies pursued by the Government were not slowing the inflation fast enough and that additional pressure was needed.

Despite signs of wear around the edges, and flying in the face of government programs to slow business, the American economy established a string of new records in 1969.

The country's gross national product, the value of all goods and services produced, rose to an estimated $943,000,000,000 or 9 per cent above the total recorded in 1968. At year's end, economic experts were predicting that the GNP might reach the $1,000,000,000,000 level by the end of 1970.

Inflation played a big part in the growth of GNP. With prices rising by 5 per cent, only 4 per cent of the increase could be attributed to increased production. In the last quarter of the year, the Commerce Department reported that "real growth," after allowing for price inflation, had stopped completely.

Personal income rose to $767,000,000,000 from $687,900,000,000 in 1968, and disposable income climbed to $639,000,000,000 from $590,000,000,000.

The industries most seriously affected by the Government's anti-inflation policies were those in which considerable cash or outside financing is necessary. Housing, always the first to feel the pinch of tight money, was the hardest hit. By the end of November, contracts for nonresidential construction were down 21 per cent from the figures in the same month of 1968, while residential construction fell 18 per cent. Savings and loan companies, a primary source of mortgage money for the building industry, were virtually out of cash to lend.

Stock Market. The U.S. stock market, where money is the chief commodity, took a pounding. An early rally, based mostly on speculative issues, ran out in mid-May as investors finally realized that stopping the inflationary spiral would involve a tight squeeze on corporate profits. The Dow-Jones Industrial Average dropped about 100 points, or 10 per cent, in six weeks to the end of June and never recovered the rest of the year. After the final day's trading, the Dow Industrials stood at 800.36, down 143.39 points in the year.

Brokers' clerical problems kept the exchanges on shortened hours throughout the year, although trading time did expand from 4 hours a day to 5. Normal trading hours are 5½ hours a day. Partly as a result of the shorter hours and partly because of the gloomy market, volume receded on all exchanges. The New York Stock Exchange reported a total volume of 2,850,784,841 shares, which was the second best year on record but down from the pace-setting 2,931,555,941 shares in 1968. The American Stock Exchange had a total of 1,240,742,012 shares, also second to the record-setting year of 1968, when 1,435,765,734 shares were traded.

The lower volume did little to help hard-pressed brokers, however. During the year, several brokerage firms went out of business, and

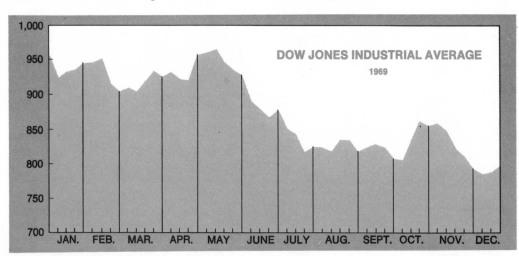

DOW JONES INDUSTRIAL AVERAGE
1969

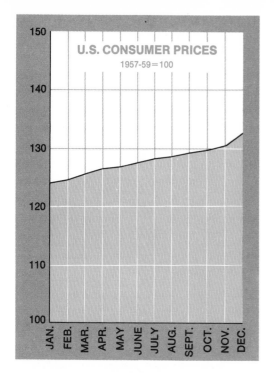

U.S. CONSUMER PRICES
1957-59 = 100

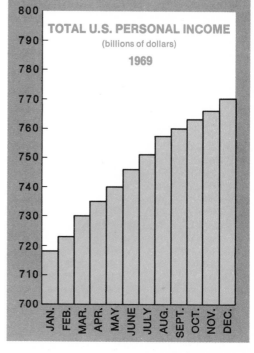

TOTAL U.S. PERSONAL INCOME
(billions of dollars)
1969

many more were merged into other firms. The New York Stock Exchange wrestled with the problem of developing a new commission-rate schedule, but no firm proposal had been sent to the Securities and Exchange Commission by the end of the year.

The NYSE also considered another problem, which could change the face of the securities industry. In May a firm, which specializes in servicing mutual funds and other investing institutions, filed a registration statement with the SEC to sell its shares to the public. NYSE member firms are currently prohibited from "going public." The exchange, however, recognizing the brokers' needs for additional capital and unwilling to force brokers out of the exchange in order to find that capital, approved public ownership in principle and offered a set of constitutional and rule changes to permit such sales. A protracted period of SEC consideration followed, which had not been completed as the year ended.

Profits continued to rise in 1969, although the rate of increase slowed noticeably. A survey by The First National City Bank of New York showed that 1,155 nonfinancial corporations reported a year-to-year earnings increase of 3½ per cent in the third quarter. For the first six months, the same companies had reported a 6 per cent earnings improvement. Most forecasts expected earnings to decline in 1970, by about 5 to 10 per cent. Estimated corporate earnings for 1969 were placed at $50,500,000,-

000, just a little above the $49,800,000,000 reported for 1968.

Big-ticket merchandise, such as automobiles and major appliances, also suffered from the credit squeeze. Auto sales fell only a little for the year as a whole—to 9,600,000 units from 9,640,000 in 1968, including imports—but advancing sales early in the year masked a slippage later on. Domestic production came to 8,460,000 cars, down from 8,600,000 in 1968. Some industry leaders were predicting that 1970 sales might fall to as low as 9,000,000 cars, while others felt sales might hold at 9,500,000.

Higher-priced merchandise in other areas also declined. Color-television sales fell; major appliances were weak. Furriers said that even mink coats, the female symbol of luxury, generated less buyer interest.

As money became dearer and interest rates moved higher, consumers generally cut back on their buying. Retail sales for the year came to nearly $345,000,000,000, a slim 1.5 per cent higher than in 1968. By contrast, 1968 sales had showed an 8 per cent increase over 1967. The slim improvement itself was attributed largely to price increases rather than higher unit sales.

Businessmen had problems in other areas too. When the Nixon administration took over in Washington, it was made clear that the Justice Department, under Attorney General John N. Mitchell, would be taking a harder look at the fast-moving merger trend. While the Democrats had insisted that present law gave them no power to control conglomerates (corporations with subsidiaries in widely diversified fields), the Republicans, and especially antitrust chief Richard McLaren, said that current law would be used to stop mergers that the Government felt might cut down on free competition. (See feature article Conglomerates, page 55.)

Earlier, in March, the Justice Department agreed to let Atlantic Richfield Company take over Sinclair Oil provided Sinclair is operated separately pending the outcome of court suits.

To some extent, however, Justice achieved its aim of cutting down on the number of mergers. With a helping hand from the slumping stock market, which cut into the value of stocks exchanged in the mergers, the growing wave of corporate combinations abated sharply. According to W. T. Grimm & Co., merger specialists, there were 1,239 merger announcements in the July-September quarter of the year, 15 per cent below the 1,455 announced in the same period in 1968. For the first six months of the year, announced merger intentions, excluding cancellations, were 75 per cent higher than in 1968.

The combination of government pressure and falling stock prices kept the lid on conglomerate mergers for the rest of the year, but combinations within industry groups picked up again. This was largely because of the credit squeeze, which forced companies to look for partners who could buttress their own operations. In the fourth quarter, Grimm reported, the number of merger announcements jumped 47 per cent, and for the full year the total was 6,132 merger reports, 37 per cent ahead of 1968.

Not all the news was discouraging in 1969. Oil reserves that had been discovered on the bleak north coast of Alaska, above the Arctic Circle, brought droves of oil companies into the market for leases. In September the state of Alaska auctioned off hundreds of parcels, taking in more than $900,000,000. While the total was less than anticipated—some optimists had forecast as much as $2,000,000,000—the receipts were the equivalent of six times Alaska's 1969 state budget, and the United States seemed on the way toward developing what might be one of the world's richest oil fields.

In the summer and early fall, Humble Oil and Refining Company sent the tanker SS *Manhattan* from Philadelphia to Prudhoe Bay, Alaska, to test the feasibility of a sea route to bring the Alaskan oil to the rich east-coast markets. Although the specially fitted ship had to make several detours, she did cut through the ice and prove that the route could be used.

The problems in the United States overshadowed events in other countries, but the Americans were not the only ones with economic headaches.

Western Europe. After trying for more than a year to overcome its economic difficulties, France devalued the franc by 12.5 per cent in

"Now?"

Oliphant from "The Denver Post"

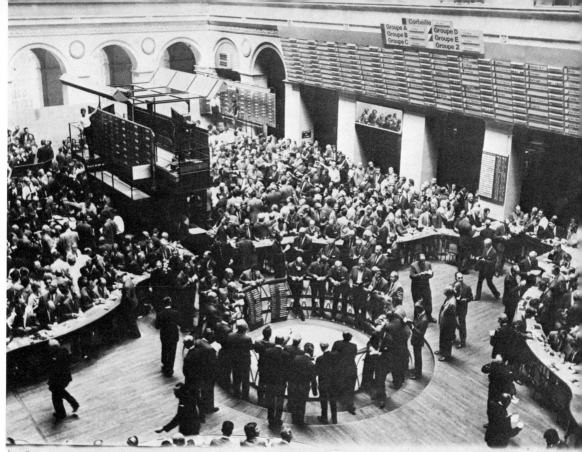

Pictorial Parade

On Monday, Aug. 11, trading on the Paris Bourse, the stock exchange, is heavy. Late on Friday, Aug. 8, the French franc had been devalued, and investors were eager to exchange their devalued cash for stocks.

August. Speculative pressure on the franc had developed in May 1968, after student riots and a general strike. Because of the work stoppage, the French balance of payments suffered a severe deficit. President Charles de Gaulle instituted strict protective measures but, at least partly for nationalistic reasons, refused to devalue the franc.

In 1969, however, De Gaulle resigned from the presidency after losing a referendum on government reform. When Georges Pompidou took over the presidency, and France continued to lose its foreign-currency reserves, the Government realized that the change had to be made.

At that, the devaluation was a well-kept secret. The reduction—pegging the franc at US$0.18, down from the old 20-cent rate—was announced over a weekend and had not been preceded by any significant speculative pressure.

After the devaluation, which was accompanied by credit and currency restrictions, the French economic picture quieted although the French bank rate was increased to 8 per cent from 7 per cent in October.

After the franc's value had been adjusted, speculative attention turned to the German mark, but for very different reasons. Since the end of World War II, West Germany had built the strongest economy in Western Europe. With a trade surplus of more than $5,000,000,000 a year, the West German mark was in strong demand in financial markets around the world.

Other members of the International Monetary Fund, whose currencies were being sold for marks, had been exerting pressure on the Germans to revalue the mark upward. The Government opposed the step on the grounds that it might trigger a depression in West Germany.

As the situation developed, the relatively stable West German economy began to reveal inflationary tendencies. On Sept. 29, just after national elections, the Government released the mark from its "peg" at US$0.25. Although the Germans made no official announcement of their plans, it was assumed that the mark would be permitted to "float" until it found its own level and would then be pegged at that rate.

On Oct. 26, the West Germans formally pegged the mark at US$0.273224, an increase of 9.29 per cent. At the same time, the Government canceled border taxes and import subsidies which had helped German companies compete in world markets.

The high-powered West German economy also produced an extremely tight labor market—even tighter than in the United States—and encouraged labor to demand large wage increases. A series of wildcat strikes in September helped win labor pay boosts of 10 to 12 per cent. Productivity of German labor increased 12 per cent in 1969.

Great Britain, which had been in the center of the world economic spotlight because of its balance-of-payments problems, receded into the background, much to the relief of British government officials. The devaluation of November 1967, combined with strenuous government efforts to cut down on imports and increase exports, helped the country attain a balance-of-payments surplus estimated at $720,-000,000. Despite this marked improvement, the British Government maintained its tight controls, including an 8 per cent discount rate at the Bank of England.

The departure of French President de Gaulle also seemed to make the way easier for Britain to enter the European Economic Community (the Common Market). In part because of his own hostility toward the British but also because he feared the possible consequences of the weak British financial position, De Gaulle had steadfastly refused to let the other Common Market members discuss British entry. When Pompidou took over, he hesitated to change that policy immediately, but he let it be known that he was willing to discuss the questions involved.

One stumbling block to consideration of British entry was cleared away late in December, when the Common Market members worked out a plan for sharing the burden of the farm surplus.

The year 1969 marked the end of the 12-year formation period planned by the founders of the market in 1958, but little progress had been made toward permanent structure. A new 14-story headquarters building was completed in Brussels, Belgium, but many technical problems remained to be solved as the year came to an end.

Currency Structure. The cooling-off in European money markets, helped by the American show of determination to control inflation—and the needs of the world's largest producer—combined to quench the speculative fire in world gold markets.

When the international monetary structure was at its shakiest in 1968, the price of gold soared to more than $44 an ounce from its official price of $35 an ounce. In March 1968 the gold-owning countries agreed to split the market, allowing the "free" or private price to fluctuate while the "official" price, used for settling international accounts, was held at $35 an ounce.

At the same time, pressure was exerted on South Africa, the world's largest gold miner, to sell its growing stockpiles in the free market and force the price lower. To add impetus, the United States said it would not buy any South African gold. The South Africans resisted, since gold is their leading export and they did not want to drive the private price down. The South Africans wanted to sell some gold in the private market, but they wanted assurances that the price would not be allowed to fall below the official level.

The member countries of the International Monetary Fund also agreed to establish Special Drawing Rights, or "paper gold," to substitute for the metal in international settlements. The plan was ratified, and the first disbursements were made at the end of the year. The SDR's are nothing but bookkeeping entries, but world economic officials hope they will not carry so much emotion as many people attach to gold itself.

Late in 1969, South Africa was forced to sell gold in the private market. From its peak at more than $42 an ounce, the price of the metal tumbled to just above $35 an ounce at year's end. Monetary officials said the dollar had won its battle against gold, and the United States agreed to guarantee the South Africans that it, and others in the IMF, would buy gold if the private-market price dropped below $35 an ounce.

If the SDR's work out as planned, gold itself will be used only as a last resort and in trade with those countries that are not members of the Monetary Fund and who insist on gold.

On both sides of the oceans, 1969 seemed to be a staging ground for even more dramatic future changes. The American economy certainly was in a state of severe flux. The fight against inflation, showing only preliminary signs of progress, promised even more hardship for businessmen. European economies, some only beginning to emerge from severe hardship, still had a long way to go.

See Cost of Living; Labor; Taxation.

PHILIP GREER
New York Financial Correspondent
The Washington Post

EDUCATION

On U.S. college and university campuses in 1969, the focus of protest was aimed at the war in Vietnam and at the relationship between the campuses and the defense effort. The organized Moratorium demonstrations, though massively supported by students, had the effect of shifting the spotlight of the rebellion somewhat from the academic administrators (who often joined the students' antiwar stance, or at least condoned it) and training it on national policy. The only exception was the continuing protest of some Negro students, often supported by white activists, over questions of admission of black students, the nature and management of Afro-American studies, and occasionally demands for all-black facilities.

In the public schools, occasional bursts of violence, sometimes with racial overtones, continued. Yet the extreme clashes symbolized by the confrontation between the teachers' union and parts of the black community in New York City during 1968 seemed to have given way to new efforts to give local communities greater control over the schools, while at the same time protecting the rights and job security of teachers and administrators. In Washington, Dr. James E. Allen, Jr., the new U.S. commissioner of education, issued an appeal for a nationwide effort to assure that by 1980 no student will leave school without a complete mastery of reading skill.

Enrollments. Total U.S. enrollments in 1969, public and private, from kindergarten through graduate school, stood at 58,600,000, according to estimates by the U.S. Office of Education. This compares with 57,600,000 in 1968. College enrollments continued to increase by almost 5 per cent, although this was more nearly stable than the 8 per cent increases of earlier annual gains. On the elementary-school level, the lower birthrates of the early 1960's were reflected in a minimal increase, only 0.3 per cent.

The elementary grades, from kindergarten through grade 8, rose from 36,700,000 in 1968 to 36,900,000. About 4,300,000 of the total attended nonpublic schools, the overwhelming majority of these Roman Catholic parochial schools.

In the secondary schools, grades 9 through 12, enrollments stood at 14,600,000, compared with 14,200,000 in 1968. Out of this total, the nonpublic schools, primarily Roman Catholic parochial schools, accounted for 1,400,000, with no change from 1968.

Colleges and universities estimated their fall 1969 enrollment at 7,100,000, compared with 6,700,000 in the fall of 1968. Graduate enrollment remained at about 700,000. About 5,100,-000 students were in public and 2,000,000 in privately financed institutions.

Expenditures and Costs. The total (fiscal 1969-70) national outlay for education at all levels, public and private, was estimated at $64,700,-000,000, compared with $58,500,000,000 in the previous fiscal year. Approximately $56,-200,000,000 was for operating budgets, a $6,-200,000,000 increase. Capital construction accounted for $8,500,000,000, or $100,000,000 more than in 1968, but was leveling off. Total expenditure for the nonpublic section stood at $12,500,000,000.

The amounts divide into $42,000,000,000 for elementary and secondary education and $22,700,000,000 for higher education.

The average U.S. public-school teacher's salary stood at $7,908 a year, compared with $7,296 in 1968, according to National Education Association statistics. In higher education, the City University of New York reached a new high for full professors' salaries with a scale that reached up to $32,000 a year.

Commissioner of Education James E. Allen, Jr., urges mastery of reading skill for all schoolchildren.

UPI

At the opening of school in September, a little girl in Bogalusa, La., expresses her opinion of integration, though her parents undoubtedly printed the sign.

Unrest. Protest on all levels of education continued to get major attention. In the public schools, however, there was some indication that the extreme disunity that had marked 1968, reaching a climax in the school shutdown in New York City and in well over 100 strikes throughout the country, was ebbing. Reports increased that earlier overtures for a merger between the two powerful teacher organizations—the National Education Association (over 1,100,000 members) and the American Federation of Teachers (170,000 members), an affiliate of the AFL–CIO—might be coming to fruition. In Flint, Mich., the local chapters of the two old rivals actually merged. In Massachusetts secret proposals for a statewide trial marriage between the two were under discussion.

For the first time in years there was practically no shortage of teachers. Although shortages persisted in some fields—mathematics, natural and physical sciences, industrial arts, special education, women's physical education and librarianship—the general supply had stabilized. The National Education Association estimated that there was a surplus of about 16,000 elementary and 22,000 secondary-school teachers, although some regional shortages were still being reported. The total number of teachers in 1969 was about 2,000,000, approximately 50,000 more than in 1968. Improved salaries were among the reasons for the increased supply. A landmark contract, for example, was negotiated by the United Federation of Teachers in New York City. It will offer, in its third year, a yearly pay scale of $9,400 to $16,950.

Equally important to the pacification of the school scene may have been the fact that the earlier conflict over school decentralization, which is an issue in many of the nation's big cities, seemed to have become less controversial in New York. An interim decentralization law went into effect that gives greater powers to local school districts with their citizen boards, and at the same time protects the job security of teachers.

On college campuses, unrest continued. However, a study by the Educational Testing Service in Princeton, N.J., indicated that the proportion of radical activists had remained the same, at about 2 per cent of the total enrollment, while another 8 per cent could usually be mobilized whenever the local issues seemed appealing. A new dimension of unrest appeared as a parallel rift among many college faculties. Even the large scholarly societies, including the American Political Science Association, the Modern Language Association, the American Historical Association, the American Sociological Association and the American Psychological Association, were confronted by caucuses that called for more or less radical departures from past policies. Moreover, not unlike the students' demands, they called for greater "relevancy" of their activities to the current socioeconomic and political scene.

A study by the American Council on Education found that violence had occurred on 145 of the nation's 2,300 campuses in the 1968-69 academic year, a total of 6.2 per cent of the institutions of higher learning. Disruptive protest took place on 624, or 22.4 per cent, of the campuses. Police were called in on about half of the campuses that experienced violence and one fourth of those that experienced disruptive protests. About 75 per cent of the institutions that were subjected to violence took major civil or disciplinary actions against some students. Such action was taken at more than one third of the colleges where disruptive protest was reported.

As for the consequences of the student unrest, the study indicated that major institutional changes were introduced on 75 per cent of the campuses that experienced violence and on 59 per cent of those that had seen disruptive protest. But the need for violence and disruption is placed in some doubt by the finding that similar changes and reforms were effected on 62 per cent of the campuses that had experienced no major incidents.

Private universities were found to have been most prone to unrest.

At the same time, student organizations themselves experienced tension and friction. A group of black students walked out of the Na-

Nonmilitant students at Harvard burn an effigy of the Students for a Democratic Society, who seized University Hall (administration building) to force demands.

UPI

UPI

Girl students take up residence at Princeton University. A male stronghold from its founding in 1746, the prestigious university is at last open to co-eds.

tional Student Association, after demanding reparation payments for allegedly inadequate support of black students' rights and needs, to form the National Association of Black Students. The NSA, in a conciliatory move, pledged itself to raise $50,000 to help the new group, and expressed the hope that the two might merge again some years hence.

In another incident of discord, the radical Students for a Democratic Society split into a nonviolent wing, which pledged help for the poor, and a revolutionary group, subsequently named Weatherman, led by Mark Rudd, the chieftain of the 1968 rebellion at Columbia University, which is committed to violent attacks on American institutions and the police. The group became identified with a brief but destructive riot in Chicago.

At the same time, the conservative Young Americans for Freedom pledged to intensify campus opposition to the radical student movements. It adopted the slogan, "Sock It to the Left."

In Washington, the moderate Association of Student Governments organized its first nationwide meeting to bring together presidents of student government and presidents of colleges and universities.

In terms of actual campus uprisings, Harvard received maximum attention when a takeover of University Hall, the administration building, by students of the SDS was followed by a bloody police raid and subsequently, a student strike. The issues at Harvard included the place of the Reserve Officer Training Corps and the future of Afro-American studies programs. One consequence of the Harvard action was the agreement to give students a greater voice in academic councils.

At Berkeley, the university's decision to fence in an off-campus university-owned two-block area, which had been taken over by "street people" and some radical students as a People's Park, led to a violent clash with police and the National Guard in which one person was killed and a number injured and arrested.

At another California campus, the University of California at Los Angeles, students and faculty rebelled against an order by the Board of Regents to dismiss Miss Angela Davis, a young Negro philosophy professor with a brilliant academic record and a radical political background, for admitted membership in the Communist Party. The courts, however, supported the student and faculty protests and demanded the teacher's reinstatement. The situation was still not resolved by the end of 1969.

At the Massachusetts Institute of Technology, radical students threatened, but failed, to shut down the Instrumentation Laboratory. It is heavily involved in defense work and has made key contributions to the moon landings. The university obtained a restraining order against violence. However, even before the protests, the institution's president, Howard W. Johnson, and a powerful panel of administrators, faculty and students had agreed to try to phase out defense work and substitute socially useful research, such as the improvement of conditions in the inner cities.

Among the most dramatic campus battles was the occupation of the student union at Cornell by a group of black students. They subsequently emerged from the building, heavily armed with rifles, but insisted that the weapons had been brought into the building

only after they learned that they might face violence at the hand of hostile whites. The students subsequently obtained faculty agreement to their demands. The resulting bitterness between liberal and conservative factions of the faculty led to the resignation of James A. Perkins, president of Cornell, who was charged by some with having been too permissive in dealing with radical and black students.

At the City University of New York, a brief shutdown forced by disaffected black and Puerto Rican students was followed by a flurry of clashes between black and white students. The university, however, replied with a promise to introduce open admission under which every high school graduate is to be offered an opportunity for some form of higher education, either in a two-year or a four-year college. Such admission policies already exist in California on a statewide basis.

Other flurries occurred, including some at Brandeis University, Vassar College and Yale.

Legislation. Congress provided added support for bank loans to students by offering subsidies for interest rates of up to 10 per cent instead of the earlier 7 per cent.

Despite growing pressure to penalize disruptive students, in accordance with the bill passed by Congress in 1968, efforts to deny funds to the educational institutions themselves failed. However, on the state level, a plethora of bills, ranging from drug control to prohibition of firearms on campus, were passed.

Under strong urging by Kingman Brewster, Jr., president of Yale University, Congress adopted a major portion of the draft-reform proposals submitted by President Nixon, including the use of a lottery among the youngest men eligible, as a means of providing Selective Service manpower.

Desegregation. When the Justice Department asked the Federal courts in Mississippi for a temporary delay in the school-desegregation plans, which had earlier been approved by the Civil Rights division of the Department of Health, Education, and Welfare, the NAACP Legal Defense and Educational Fund, Inc., took the case to the Supreme Court. The court unanimously ruled that all dual school systems must "now and henceforth" be operated as unitary ones. It thus provided a new and less permissive interpretation of the 1954 landmark ruling that holds segregated schools to be unconstitutional and ordered desegregation to proceed "with all deliberate speed."

FRED M. HECHINGER
Education Editor (Former) and
Member of Editorial Board
The New York Times

ENGINEERING, CIVIL

During 1969 a number of important civil-engineering projects were under way or completed. **Bridges.** In 1956 one of the world's longest bridges was opened to traffic across Lake Pontchartrain between New Orleans and Mandeville, La. The bridge thereafter carried so much traffic that the Greater New Orleans Expressway Commission decided to build a second lake causeway. The parallel, 24-mile, 2-lane crossing was dedicated in May 1969, some 2 months ahead of schedule. Both spans are of prestressed-concrete construction. However, the new, $29,000,000 causeway actually cost less to build than the first bridge. Savings were realized by casting the sidewalls and drainage system as a single unit with the deck span, instead of installing them separately as on the earlier bridge, and by substituting neoprene bridge pads for the usual steel expansion rollers. Other savings are attributed to general advances in prestressed-concrete technology in the past decade.

Important economies were also realized in the construction of the two-mile Newport Bridge between Newport and Jamestown, R.I., which was opened to traffic on June 28. In a major bridge-building innovation, the cables were shop fabricated in the Steelton, Pa., plant of the Bethlehem Steel Corporation and shipped to the construction site on giant spools. Seventy-six prefabricated cables were installed in two months, half the time that would have been required for conventional cable spinning. Another cost-saving first on the project was a new method of anchoring the main cables by means of embedded pipe assemblies. The new bridge cuts travel time between New York and the Cape Cod area by eliminating a ferry bottleneck over the east arm of Narragansett Bay.

Another facility for speeding East Coast traffic—the second level of the Verrazano-Narrows Bridge linking Brooklyn and Staten Island—was dedicated on June 28. Because of an unexpectedly heavy volume of traffic, the 6-lane second level was completed 11 years ahead of the schedule. In 1965, its first full year of operation, the bridge carried 17,600,000 vehicles, a figure originally projected for 1968. In 1969 it carried an estimated 30,000,000 vehicles. Completion of the lower deck has increased the annual capacity of the bridge to about 48,000,000 vehicles. With a 4,260-foot center span, the Verrazano-Narrows Bridge is the longest suspension crossing in the world. It is the key to the web of roads that forms the southerly bypass of New York City's metropolitan area.

June also saw completion of an important West Coast crossing, the $40,000,000 San Diego-Coronado Bridge. The first bridge across San Diego Bay, the 2.1-mile structure spans the wide stretch of water between San Diego on the mainland and the Coronado peninsula. The spectacular superstructure is supported on reinforced-concrete towers with tapering legs

Supported on concrete towers, the San Diego-Coronado Bridge makes a breathtaking swing across San Diego Bay.

City of San Diego

"Civil Engineering Magazine"

A joint effort by Mexico and the United States, for the benefit of both, the Amistad Dam stems the Devils River near its junction with the Rio Grande.

varying in height from 50 to 200 feet above the water. Another notable feature of the crossing is 3 orthotropic spans totaling 1,880 feet.

All 50 states have stiffened their bridge-inspection programs as a result of the Silver Bridge collapse (Point Pleasant, W. Va.). At the time of the disaster, December 1967, only 17 states had bridge-inspection programs considered adequate to ensure the safety of the traveling public. Since then, 10 more states have revised their programs to conform to Bureau of Public Roads standards, and 24 other states have initiated such programs. During inspection, President Johnson's Task Force on Bridge Safety found that 90 per cent of the nation's bridges were built before 1935.

Canals. Plans for building a $600,000,000 canal that will develop the Saar territory by connecting it to the waterways of Western Europe were announced by West Germany. The plan provides for construction of an initial 15-mile stretch from Saarbrücken northward to Dillingen. Later the Government will decide whether to continue the canal northward to the Moselle River and from there to connect with the Belgian-Luxembourg waterways leading to the port of Antwerp, or to continue the canal in an eastward direction toward the Rhine.

Another important canal, extending from Bamberg to Regensburg, is under construction in West Germany. It will connect the Rhine and Danube waterway systems.

An ambitious plan to meet the water needs of Texas for the next 50 years was proposed by the Texas Water Development Board. The key feature in the $10,000,000,000 program is an 800-mile canal running across Texas from the Louisiana border and into eastern New Mexico. The canal, together with a second proposed canal, would link all the rivers of the state. The 800-mile Trans-Texas Canal would carry more than 10,000,000 acre-feet of water annually from the northeastern part of the state and the lower Mississippi River to arid west Texas. Although voters rejected a bond issue for the initial phase of the plan, it was expected that the project would be resubmitted to the voters in 1970.

Work on Florida's $162,000,000 Cross-Florida Barge Canal was almost at a standstill because of cutbacks in Federal funds for public works. Extending in a southwesterly direction from Jacksonville on the Atlantic Coast to Yankeetown on the Gulf of Mexico, the 184-mile canal will shorten the costly movement, using the southern-tip route, of barge cargo from the Atlantic to the Gulf by 600 miles. The Corps of Engineers estimates that the shorter route will save shippers about $12,000,000 a year. It will also be a connecting link between the Atlantic and Gulf Intracoastal Waterways, providing a protected route for barge and small-boat traffic.

Dams. In October, work began on Tachien Dam, the key structure in Taiwan's huge power-and-irrigation project for developing the Tachia River basin. The dam will be a major thin-arch structure with a height of 590 feet. Portugal signed final construction contracts for another impressive project, the Cahora Bassa hydroelectric project on the Zambezi River in Mozambique. The key feature of the project will be a 508-foot-high, double-curvature concrete arch dam. It will provide 4,000,000 kilowatts of power, and irrigation for over 3,000,000 acres.

On the North American continent, construction was nearing completion on Manicouagan

(Manic) 5 Dam, the key structure in a $1,200,-000,000, 5,500,000-kilowatt project on the Manicouagan and Outardes rivers in central Quebec. The 703-foot-high dam, the highest multiple-arch in the world, is 4,310 feet long and impounds 115,000,000 acre-feet of water in an 800-square-mile reservoir, the sixth largest in the world. (It has been named the Daniel Johnson Dam, in honor of the late premier of Quebec.)

Far to the south, the United States and Mexico completed construction of Amistad Dam, a joint project on the Rio Grande near Del Rio, Tex. The $78,000,000, 6-mile-long dam is the second major international storage project to be built jointly by the 2 countries. It furnishes irrigation, flood-control and power.

The second supplement to the *World Register of Dams*, issued in September by the International Commission on Large Dams, reported that about 925 large dams were completed in the 3-year period ending Dec. 31, 1968. Once again, the United States was the major dam builder, with 370 new dams, followed by Japan with 96, India with 43 and Canada with 42.

Tunnels. New tunneling techniques were discussed in conferences held throughout the United States and Canada. The Oak Ridge National Laboratory reported that it has been investigating a promising method of tunneling through rock with ordinary water jets. The method, which involves continuous cutting of the rock by a water stream with pressures ranging from 5,000 to 12,000 pounds per square inch, offers the possibility of faster and more economical tunneling than present techniques can achieve.

In April the Bay Area Rapid Transit (BART) District sank the last section of its prefabricated Transbay Tube under San Francisco Bay. The longest and deepest tube-type underwater crossing ever constructed, the $180,000,000 facility is 3.6 miles long. It is approached by 2.4 miles of tunnel excavated through solid rock. Before the BART project is completed, construction men will have driven 36 tunnels under San Francisco, Oakland and Berkeley. There will be 12 underground stations in the 3 cities. On some routes, 2 tunnels are being bored side by side. On others, they are stacked 2 and even 3 high.

On the East Coast, test drilling began for the New York City Board of Water Supply's third great tunnel. The 20- to 27-foot water tunnel will extend 15 miles from Kensico Reservoir in Westchester County to a reservoir at Yonkers. It will cost $238,000,000.

Major links in Europe's longest intercontinental highway, the 2,249-mile E-3 Motorway connecting Stockholm, Paris and Lisbon, were forged in May with the opening of 2 important subaqueous tunnels. The John F. Kennedy Tunnel, under the Scheldt River in Antwerp, Belgium, is the world's widest tunnel. It carries 3 road lanes each way, a separate lane for cyclists, and a double railway line. Limfjord Tunnel, which connects the northern tip of Denmark with the rest of Jutland under Limfjord Strait, is a 3,120-foot, 4-lane crossing. Both tunnels consist of prefabricated-concrete sections, prepared in dry dock and sunk into channels dredged across the stream beds.

MARY E. JESSUP
News Editor, *Civil Engineering*

A link in Europe's longest highway, the E-3 Motorway, connecting Stockholm, Paris and Lisbon, passes under the Scheldt River, in Antwerp, Belgium, through the John F. Kennedy Tunnel, the widest tunnel in the world.

Institut Belge

europe

Western Europe discovered a new opportunity for broader union in 1969 with the departure of French President Charles de Gaulle, the triumph of the Social Democrats in West Germany and the fixed goal of Prime Minister Harold Wilson to link Britain with the Continent. Yet it remained to be seen as 1970 approached whether Europe's statesmen had the will and the courage to exploit the possibility.

De Gaulle had twice vetoed Britain's application to join the six-nation European Common Market, and in the public mind was to blame for the infirmity of the European ideal. The problems of enlarging on the nucleus of the EEC, however, by no means disappeared with De Gaulle. As Jacques Duhamel, the French agriculture minister, told his colleagues at an EEC gathering in July, "We have lost a general, but you have lost an alibi." The difficulties posed in forming a larger organization of Western European states could no longer be hidden in De Gaulle's shadow.

Georg Kiesinger shakes hands with Charles de Gaulle after a meeting. Before both lost power, the German Chancellor usually bowed to the Frenchman's ideas.

Wide World

Georges Pompidou, the General's successor in the Elysée Palace, indicated France was finally willing to negotiate the admission of Great Britain and three other applicants—Ireland, Denmark and Norway—if it could be shown that it would not weaken the economic community. A fresh EEC commission report in October offered the necessary assurances.

French Foreign Minister Maurice Schumann, who is considered a "pro-European," told his partners, "The clearer it becomes that none of us has any objection in principle to the adhesion of the countries that have posed their candidacies, the more indispensable it is for us to engage in fruitful negotiations." The men at EEC headquarters in Brussels had had to wait for years to hear such language from a French emissary.

Yet for all their display of flexibility on the issue of enlarging the Six, the French were not going to overlook their own vital interests. As the community's largest agricultural producer, France was insisting on an ironclad agreement for the permanent financing of EEC farm-price supports. Paris appeared willing to risk a crisis. The existing scheme was due to expire, and the French said there could be no progress on any other issues until a satisfactory farm-fund accord was achieved. Some Brussels observers wondered whether the French were trying merely to drive the best bargain possible, or whether this was another, subtler, way of blocking British entry, by imposing preconditions unacceptable to its partners.

Where the French were the principal beneficiaries of the price-support fund—which ran to $2,300,000,000 in 1969—the Germans were the largest contributors.

Accordingly, Bonn maneuvered to avoid an open-ended commitment to a fund the experts forecast would balloon to $8,000,000,000 by 1980. Germany was ready to "make sacrifices for European solidarity," her spokesmen said, but there were limits on the German taxpayers' sense of comradeship in paying for mounting French farm surpluses.

If there were any doubts about Willy Brandt's commitment to expanding European union, he moved to dispel them within a week after his Social Democrats turned Chancellor Kurt Georg Kiesinger's Christian Democrats (CDU) out of power for the first time since the war. Brandt sent his deputy, Helmut Schmidt, as an envoy to the British Labor Party's annual conference at Brighton. There Schmidt affirmed that the first priority of the Brandt Government would be to ensure that Britain enter the Common Market as soon as possible.

This represented a major change of emphasis in German policy. The CDU had consistently acquiesced in De Gaulle's blocking tactics. It was especially true of Kiesinger, who was seduced by the Gaullist notion of a Paris-Bonn axis and let the question of expanding the EEC stagnate.

Meantime, Prime Minister Wilson kept his eye on the Continent, repeating, "Europe needs Britain as much as Britain needs Europe." He said Britain accepted in advance the existing Common Market regulations, even though this would mean abandoning cheap agricultural imports from the Commonwealth countries.

Opponents of the EEC in Britain argued that Wilson's pledge would cost the British some $2,400,000,000 a year; they concluded the price was too high. Though a public-opinion poll showed most Englishmen as unfavorable to joining Europe, Wilson's men were confident that this sentiment would change as the country's economic health improved and the goal of EEC membership approached realization. The Prime Minister's hand was strengthened by the August trade figures. They put Britain in the black for the first time since the November 1967 devaluation of the pound sterling.

While the debate raged over the new forms Europe might take, only here and there was a voice raised in defense of the concept behind the Common Market's foundation: the creation of a political unit drawing on the formidable resources of the Old World and capable of dealing on equal terms with the American and Soviet superpowers. For the most part, Europe's leaders were bogged down in the details of preserving a customs union that would not damage purely national interests.

Pictorial Parade

With notable charm, Helmut Schmidt (a leader of the German Social Democrats) tells British Labor Party meeting that Common Market will welcome Britain.

New complex of buildings rising in Brussels, Belgium, is home of Common Market's Executive Commission.

EEC

Close observers of developments in "Little Europe" were Denmark, Norway, Sweden, Finland and Iceland. They postponed a final decision on establishing a Nordic Economic Union until the EEC had sorted out the problem of new members. The future of the European Free Trade Association (EFTA) was also in abeyance as leaders of the Six prepared for a difficult summit conference in The Hague where the question of the EEC's evolution was to be reviewed.

Whatever the outcome, it was clear that the center of power in Western Europe had shifted to Germany. France, which had pretended to hegemony in the mid-1960's, lost De Gaulle and foundered in economic difficulties only partially resolved by the Aug. 8 devaluation of the franc. Britain seemed to be on the path of recovery but was still a distant claimant to European leadership. Italian officials presided over the curious combination of an economic

Jan Palach, 21-year-old Czech student, publicly burned himself to death in protest against Soviet occupation.

Bureau, Gamma-PIX

miracle and profound social unrest with periodic cabinet crises thrown in. The Federal Republic, meanwhile, continued to astound its partners with balanced, efficient economic growth crowned in October by the upward revaluation of the D-mark.

It seemed only a matter of time before, in the words of former Finance Minister Franz Josef Strauss, the German "economic giant" would cease to be a "political dwarf."

Brandt intended to profit from German strength to pursue his *Ostpolitik,* a quest for an understanding with the communist East. In this he was encouraged by the Soviet Union which even before Kiesinger's defeat had begun to downplay its professed fears of German militarism and revanchism.

From the Warsaw Pact meeting in Budapest on Mar. 17 came a proposal for a Pan-European Security Conference in which the Federal Republic was offered a role. When the West Germans selected West Berlin as the place to elect Gustav Heinemann the Federal president, the Soviets appeared to be the ones trying to defuse a crisis that East German President Walter Ulbricht was bent on aggravating.

When a serious clash of arms between Russian and Chinese troops occurred on the disputed Ussuri River frontier, the Soviet ambassador took the unusual step of discussing the conflict with the Bonn Government. Bonn assured the Soviet Union that it would not take advantage of the situation.

To Poland, Brandt proposed normal relations and a hint that Bonn would accept the Oder-Neisse Line, as German investments in other Eastern European countries multiplied.

The pursuit of a *détante* continued despite accelerated Soviet repression in Czechoslovakia where the invaders systematically dismembered the Czech Government's reform program. The Russians obtained Alexander Dubcek's dismissal as party first secretary, and had him replaced with the more conservative Dr. Gustav Husak. Dubcek was later deprived of his seat in the Central Committee and Presidium as reaction against the liberal experiment solidified.

Europe was shocked when Warsaw Pact troops invaded Czechoslovakia in August 1968 and was horrified in 1969 when Jan Palach, a 21-year-old Czech student, committed suicide by fire to protest the rollback of reform. But the Western democracies learned to live with Soviet repression in Central Europe as they had come to accept the authoritarian regimes of their allies in Spain, Portugal and Greece.

STEPHENS BROENING
Correspondent, Paris Bureau
The Associated Press

EUROPE 1969: 1. Charles de Gaulle resigned as president of France and was succeeded by Georges Pompidou; 2. Willy Brandt became the first Socialist to head a German Government since 1930; 3. Italy was hit by a series of general strikes; 4. Strategic Arms Limitation Talks (SALT) opened in Helsinki; 5. Moscow was host to the first international Communist Party conference in nine years; 6. Greece withdrew from the Council of Europe; 7. Great Britain registered a trade surplus; 8. Francisco Franco designated Prince Juan Carlos as future king of Spain; 9. Gustav Husak replaced Alexander Dubcek as first secretary of the Czechoslovak Communist Party; 10. Olof Palme was sworn in as premier of Sweden; 11. British troops restored order in Northern Ireland.

Samir Sawfat, photographer, "Mademoiselle"

Gosta Peterson, photographer, "Mademoiselle"

FASHION

As no one style took center stage in 1969, fashionables could do their own thing. Among the fascinating variety of choices were (clockwise from upper left on this page): "her" and "him" matching midi-coats; two-piece knits with bare midriffs; low belt on a casual shirt-dress in a floral print; covered-top swimsuit, the bare expanse adorned with a chain; blouse and pants "borrowed" from safari outfits; several chains on a jumper with deep pockets, over a deep-cuffed blouse; and a trim outfit of blazer, finely pleated skirt, and dangling scarf.

All photos © 1969 by The Condé Nast Publications Inc.

Gosta Peterson, photographer, "Mademoiselle"

Barbara Waterston, photographer, "Mademoiselle"

David Bailey, photographer, "Vogue"

Alen MacWeeney, photographer, "Mademoiselle"

Norman Parkinson, photographer, "Vogue"

Central Press, Pictorial Parade

Finnish Pres. Kekkonen and his wife (center) are welcomed to London by the British royal family.

FINLAND

The domestic political scene remained placid throughout the year, apparently because parliamentary elections were scheduled for March 1970. Dr. Mauno Koivisto's Cabinet, a coalition of the Center Party (Agrarians), Social Democrats, People's Democrats (Communists) and Swedish People's Party, succeeded in stabilizing the economy. Threats to leave the coalition were at times heard from various party leaders. The leaders of the two largest parties, Dr. Koivisto and Dr. Johannes Virolainen, a former prime minister and currently minister of education, are likely candidates for the presidency in 1974.

FINLAND

Area: 130,120 sq. mi.
Population: 4,700,000
Capital: Helsinki (pop., 523,000)
Government: Urho K. Kekkonen, president—1956; Mauno Koivisto, premier—1968
Gross national product: $7,250,000,000
Monetary unit: markka (4.2 markkas = U.S. $1.00)
Chief products: cereal and dairy products, timber, pulp, paper, textiles
Foreign trade: exports, $1,637,000,000; imports, $1,598,000,000
Communications: 949,976 telephones, 1,622,-710 radios, 950,000 TV sets, 123 daily newspapers
Transportation: roads, 43,513 mi.; 551,198 passenger cars; railroads, 3,490 mi.
Education: 307,657 elementary and secondary students, 6 universities
Armed forces: 36,400

See map on page 185

Finnish cabinet members traveled widely during the year. The Scandinavian prime ministers met in Helsinki in February, the chief item on their agenda being the planned inter-Scandinavian customs union, Nordek. In March they met in Stockholm and discussed economic affairs. Dr. Ahti Karjalainen, the Finnish minister of foreign affairs, paid an official visit to the Soviet Union in February. President Urho K. Kekkonen, an inveterate traveler, visited Senegal in June, made a state visit to Great Britain in July, and then met with Premier Kosygin in the Caucasus. In the fall, President Kekkonen visited Rumania, Hungary and Czechoslovakia. He played host to King Baudouin and Queen Fabiola of Belgium in June, and to Nikolai Podgorny, the president of the Soviet Union, in mid-October.

The Finnish Government offered Helsinki as the site for an all-European security conference, to be attended by all NATO and Warsaw Pact members. That meeting had not materialized by year's end. However, in November, Helsinki welcomed American and Soviet representatives to the Strategic Arms Limitation Talks (SALT).

The Academy of Finland, a body of 12 outstanding men drawn from the humanities and sciences, was disbanded by Parliament at year's end. It was replaced by a central organization and six commissions for the promotion of science. In the arts the work of the academy will be done by appointed university professors.

At the beginning of 1969, Finland became a member of the Organization for Economic Cooperation and Development, which may be interpreted as a desire for closer trade relationship with the Western countries.

ERIK J. FRIIS
Editor, *The American-Scandinavian Review*

FLORIDA

On Mar. 1 the state Supreme Court ruled a 1967 law invalid that denied a permit to any retail store promoting or advertising the use or sale of prescription drugs. □ In April the state Board of Education was successful in selling a $39,000,000 bond issue at a cost below a 5.5 per cent interest-rate ceiling. □ Also in April the state legislature approved a bill giving state legislators a $12,000 yearly salary (it had been $100 a month since 1885). Later, in May, the legislature finally ratified the 19th Amendment to the Constitution (giving women the vote), although Florida women had been voting since 1920. □ On Aug. 5 an explosion and fire in a power plant resulted in a blackout for some 2,000,000 residents along the east coast.

FOREIGN AID

The United States cut back on its foreign aid in 1969 although the gap between rich nations and poor nations had widened even further. President Nixon's austerity directive and competing demands from high-priority Federal programs for the cities led to the lowest aid request to Congress since the Marshall Plan two decades earlier. Mr. Nixon emphasized American help for the "green revolution" in agricultural methods and more extensive family planning in his foreign-aid message to Congress on May 28, 1969. He also proposed the creation of an Overseas Private Investment Corporation to encourage private U.S. investment in developing nations, along with an auditor-general for the Agency for International Development to halt misuse of funds and other irregularities that had plagued the agency in recent years. By urging Congress to approve $2,200,000,000 for economic aid and $375,000,000 for military aid, Nixon cut $138,000,000 from Lyndon B. Johnson's aid package for fiscal 1970. It showed an awareness of the temper of Congress, which had slashed Mr. Johnson's fiscal-1969 request to $1,760,000,000, the lowest amount in the 21-year history of the program.

After considerable debate, Congress trimmed Nixon's request further. Just before adjourning in December, Congress passed a foreign-aid authorization bill of $1,972,000,000 for fiscal 1970 and $1,936,000,000 for fiscal 1971. Final action on the foreign-aid appropriation bill was postponed until 1970.

Secretary of State William P. Rogers, urging Congress to approve the full amount the President asked, said the real issue is "whether the East-West polarization that characterized the postwar world is going to be followed by a different polarization that divides the world into the rich and the poor."

Rogers added: "Even with great generosity in our efforts to encourage the development process in poorer parts of the world, the foreseeable prospects are for that gap to increase still further." Other countries increasingly asked if the sharp cutback in aid funds in 1968 represented a turning away by the United States from the world's needy.

In the first international study of its kind, a commission headed by Lester B. Pearson, former prime minister of Canada, reported to the World Bank that the aid effort was "flagging" just as the drive for economic development had started to pay off with visible results.

"The climate surrounding foreign aid programs is heavy with disillusion and distrust," the Pearson report began, although economic growth in the have-not nations actually is faster than the expansion achieved by industrialized nations at a similar stage in their development.

The commission recommended almost a doubling of government assistance, from the present level of 0.4 per cent of gross national product of industrial countries to 0.7 per cent of their GNP by 1975. This would translate into a foreign-aid outlay of more than $8,000,000,000.

Edward Seaga, finance minister of Jamaica, expressed the concern of the 80 poorest World Bank members at its annual meeting. While government aid of $7,000,000,000 is directed each year to the developing countries, he said, about $150,000,000,000 a year is spent on military items. In the first 6 years of the 1960's, Seaga added, per capita income in the richer

Edwin G. Huffman, World Bank

Speaking to the annual meeting of the World Bank, former Canadian Prime Minister Pearson reports on the first international study of foreign aid, by a distinguished commission that he headed.

World Bank

World Bank President Robert S. McNamara (r), on a field trip to the West Coast of Africa, tours the world's largest oil-palm plantation, in the Ivory Coast.

countries grew by $200 a year compared with only $7.00 a year in the poorer nations.

John A. Hannah, former president of Michigan State University who was appointed director of AID by President Nixon, said Congressional action forced the United States to cut its loans to India by half and slice away at assistance that had been earmarked for Pakistan and South Korea. The Alliance for Progress, Hannah reported, got just half of the funds the previous administration had requested. Overall, U.S. aid fell to about 0.4 per cent of the national wealth, which Hannah said was "among the lowest economic aid efforts of the western nations." While the United States was placing more stringent conditions on its loans, other rich nations were making "soft" arrangements for long-term borrowing at lower interest rates. Yet the United States continued to provide about half of the development assistance extended by noncommunist nations in 1969.

Manuel Perez Guerrero, secretary-general of the United Nations Conference on Trade and Development, found much wanting in the efforts by the United States and others to help their poorer neighbors. "Fundamentally the enormous inequalities that have existed for many years still persist," the Venezuelan said at a UN meeting in Geneva. Even though developing countries increased their exports by 4 per cent in 1968, he reported, their share of world trade fell even further because the industrialized countries did even better.

Robert S. McNamara, the former secretary of defense who is president of the World Bank, raised an articulate voice to promote greater efforts for help to needy nations.

"The need for development is desperate," he said in a widely publicized speech at Notre Dame University. "One third of mankind lives in an environment of relative abundance. But two thirds of mankind—more than 2,000,000-000 individuals—remain entrapped in a cruel web of circumstances that severely limits their right to the necessities of life. . . . They are caught in the grip of hunger and malnutrition; high illiteracy; inadequate education; shrinking opportunity; and corrosive poverty.

"The gap between the rich and the poor nations is no longer merely a gap. It is a chasm. On one side are nations of the West that enjoy per capita incomes in the $3,000 range. On the other are nations in Asia and Africa that struggle to survive on per capita incomes of less than $100," McNamara said. He blamed "rampant population growth" for bringing many areas of the world to the brink of famine, arguing eloquently for government-sponsored family-planning programs throughout the underdeveloped world.

"One half of humanity is hungering at this very moment," declared the man who was often said to have a computer for a brain when he ran the Pentagon. "There is less food per person on the planet today than there was thirty years ago in the midst of a worldwide depression." McNamara rejected the grim prophecy of British scientist C. P. Snow, however, who has forecast widespread famine starting sometime in 1975–80 resulting in the death of millions. McNamara, counting on the use of new, high-yield seeds and better fertilizers, said the world's leaders can in a twenty-year period, "the barest minimum of time," head off such a catastrophe.

President Nixon's first foreign-aid message had a stopgap quality, and, like most chief executives confronted with a colossal problem, he turned to a blue-ribbon commission for help. Rudolph Peterson, president of the Bank of America, was assigned to head a task force to review U.S. aid programs and recommend policies on the developing countries in the 1970's.

WILLIAM J. EATON
Washington Correspondent, *Chicago Daily News*

FRANCE

"I am ceasing the exercise of my functions as president of the Republic. This decision takes effect today at noon." With this terse statement in the early hours of Apr. 28, Charles de Gaulle proclaimed the end of an era. The charismatic leader of Free France, the founder of the Fifth Republic, the man whose name had become synonymous with that of his country quit power without a backward glance.

The immediate occasion was the defeat in a national referendum for regionalization and Senate reform on which De Gaulle had staked his presidency against the advice of his most trusted ministers. The underlying cause was evidence of economic troubles closely related to De Gaulle's management, which provoked a withdrawal of middle-class support of the President.

For most of his 10 years, 10 months and 27 days in power, De Gaulle had succeeded in maintaining the stability he boasted was the mainspring of his regime. Yet by the spring of 1969 he had lost his capacity to convince Frenchmen that his leadership was indispensable to order, progress and prosperity.

As he had done so frequently in past electoral events, he cast the issue of the April referendum in terms of "me or chaos." But the threat had lost its credibility: De Gaulle was 78 years old and in any case could not live forever. Moreover, Georges Pompidou, though deprived of the President's favor, had declared his availability, on the basis of six years as De Gaulle's premier, to guarantee an orderly succession if "the situation arises."

The deeper source of De Gaulle's downfall can probably be traced to what his critics called an inverted order of priorities. Except for the accumulation of large reserves of gold in the cellars of the Banque de France, which he apparently mistook for economic strength, De Gaulle neglected the real economic needs of the country for a high-altitude pursuit of national grandeur in a world dominated by two non-French superpowers.

The explosion came late but when it did the damage was enormous. In May and June of 1968, university students rioted; workers occupied factories; and a general strike ensued. The civil disorder belied the regime's vaunted stability, and the strike settlement—a 14 per cent wage increase across the board—ensured that French products would be that much less competitive in international markets. Public confidence in De Gaulle was deeply shaken.

The Government sought to absorb the strike's effects by rapid expansion, adding inflationary strains the economy could not bear. Trade figures worsened, reserves dwindled and the French franc, under attack, was discounted on foreign exchanges. Though the currency was clearly overvalued, De Gaulle, for prestige reasons, refused to consider devaluation.

As Georges Pompidou leaves his headquarters, Parisians take the opportunity to get a good look at their new President. Only the day before, on June 15, he had won a landslide victory for the top French office.

Wide World

This was the situation on Jan. 17 when Pompidou—relegated by De Gaulle to the "reserve of the Republic" six months earlier—announced during a Rome vacation that he would be a candidate for the presidency if a vacancy appeared. From this some observers concluded that De Gaulle was ready to retire. The President reacted almost immediately with a reminder than his term did not expire until 1972, and added, "I have the duty and the intention to fulfill my mandate."

De Gaulle professed to see "a malaise in the human relationship of modern society" which he said "gnaws at the regimes sprung from old Marxism as it shakes those abiding still by the dictates of ancient capitalism.

"Nothing is more important for the moral and social equilibrium of France than a new organization of the contacts and cooperation between those who lead and those who are led, between teachers and students, employers and their employees, the administration and those it administers," he said.

In February he revealed that the Government was preparing a vast reform that would be put before the voters Apr. 27. When the bill was published it contained little that could remedy the profound malaise De Gaulle had diagnosed. The bill provided for more administrative autonomy for France's 21 regions, but with councils lacking legislative and taxing authority. Their powers would be confined to deciding on how to spend money the central administration would allot for some local projects; the example most frequently cited by Social Affairs Minister Jean-Marcel Jeanneney was swimming pools.

The proposal would also have ended the Senate's role as a legislative body, and changed the order of presidential succession from the Senate president to the premier.

These were the principal ideas distilled from a bill more than 8,000 words long, with 68 provisions. As *Le Monde*'s political editor observed, it was expressed in language barely intelligible even to a practicing lawyer.

Voters were required to reply with a simple yes or no answer. To make the choice easier, De Gaulle announced on Apr. 10 that he would view the outcome as a question of personal confidence. "The reply the country makes" would determine "the continuation of my mandate or my immediate departure." The polls, which up to then had been showing a drop in support for the bill, changed not a whit after De Gaulle had hurled his weight into the balance.

On voting night the results confirmed the reading of the opinion polls. Just before midnight, Premier Maurice Couve de Murville threw in the sponge for the Government. "A majority of the French people has pronounced itself against the proposed reforms with all the political consequences that this rejection entails," he said. The Premier spoke vaguely of "grave troubles" threatening France because of De Gaulle's departure.

Word from the General himself, relayed from his retreat at Colombey-les-deux-Eglises, made the abdication formal.

So often had De Gaulle seemed to be the last line of defense against chaos that an undercurrent of uneasiness greeted his exit. Were the French, as he had suggested, going to be unmanageable without him? Nothing of the sort.

With the ink scarcely dry on the final referendum returns (52.87 per cent against, 47.13 per cent for), Pompidou announced his formal candidacy and got the unanimous endorsement of the Gaullist UDR party. Senate President Alain Poher, a centrist; Jacques Duclos, a Communist; socialist Gaston Defferre and three fringe candidates joined the race. An orderly struggle for succession had begun.

After promising "continuity" for the benefit of the Gaullist faithful and an "opening" to reduce Poher's centrist backing, Pompidou emerged the leader in the first round of the elections on June 1. Two weeks later he won a landslide victory against Poher, the first-round runner-up, as most of the Communists heeded the party order to boycott the choice between two "reactionaries."

With 11,064,371 votes (58.21 per cent of the turnout) to Poher's 7,943,118 (41.79 per cent) in the runoff balloting, Pompidou be-

---

FRANCE

Area: 212,766 sq. mi.
Population: 50,000,000
Capital: Paris (pop., 2,591,000)
Government: Georges Pompidou, president—1969; Jacques Chaban-Delmas, prime minister—1969
Gross national product: $120,800,000,000
Monetary unit: franc. (5.55 francs = U.S. $1.00)
Chief products: wine, foodstuffs, steel, motor vehicles, textiles, chemicals, coal, iron ore
Foreign trade: exports, $12,675,000,000; imports, $13,943,000,000
Communications: 6,999,621 telephones, 22,-000,000 radios, 9,183,644 TV sets, 168 daily newspapers
Transportation: roads, 485,983 mi.; railroads, 23,225 mi.
Education: 11,142,622 elementary and secondary students, 23 universities
Armed forces: 503,000

See map on page 185

came president of France. Not so much as a windowpane had been broken in the country.

Pompidou moved quickly to redeem his campaign pledges. He named Michel Debré, an ultra-Gaullist, as minister of defense, balanced him with several centrists, and brought the leader of the Independent Republican Party, Valery Giscard d'Estaing, back into the Cabinet as finance minister. As his premier he chose National Assembly President Jacques Chaban-Delmas, a 54-year-old Gaullist known for his flexibility.

Having come to office with the intention of devaluing the franc, Pompidou waited to act until the calm of the vacation period. On Aug. 8 France announced that the franc was worth 12.5 per cent less—5.55 to the dollar instead of 4.94.

Giscard d'Estaing prepared a recovery plan, considered mild by many economists, aiming at internal equilibrium by April 1970 and a trade surplus by the end of that year. The Finance Minister's tools were a balanced budget for 1970 after a $1,400,000,000 deficit in 1969, credit restrictions, savings incentives, surveillance but no control of prices, and prolonged exchange controls.

Success of the plan depended on three things: a certain tolerance by labor unions in formulating wage demands; limited price increases (3.2 per cent for the last half of 1969 and a ceiling of 4 per cent for all of 1970); and, since Germany was France's principal trading partner, a counterpart revaluation of the undervalued German mark.

The unions grumbled but seemed ready to hold the line; prices were staying within bounds; and on Oct. 24 Germany's new Social Democrat-Liberal coalition obligingly raised the mark's value by 9.29 per cent. Thus speculative pressure on the franc was relieved, and French goods sold across the Rhine received an added advantage.

If Pompidou considered it necessary to violate the Gaullist taboo against tampering with the franc, he gave no indication that he would undertake a global reversal of his predecessor's policies. His promised "opening" was a change of tone and of style and a reshuffling of national priorities. At his first press conference, on July 10, Pompidou described himself as "a Frenchman among others," and made it clear

Pictorial Parade, "Paris Match"

Valery Giscard d'Estaing, Independent Republican Party leader, is Pompidou's choice for finance minister.

Jacques Chaban-Delmas talks with newspapermen after Pompidou names him premier. A Gaullist, Chaban-Delmas had been president of the National Assembly.

Wide World

Jack Nisberg

Almost perfect grape-growing weather in most parts of France promised vintage wine—at appropriate prices.

that economic recovery and growth were his primary concerns. Under De Gaulle the economy had secondary consideration at best.

Premier Chaban-Delmas went a step further at a Sept. 12 meeting of Gaullist parliamentarians. He said that the quest for grandeur must wait until the health of the national economy was restored.

In mid-September the National Assembly gave overwhelming approval to the Government's program, described by the Premier as an attempt to construct a "New Society." The old one, Chaban-Delmas said, is blocked, archaic and provides for insufficient social mobility. "France," he judged, "is a country with a caste system."

To learn the details of the devaluation of the franc on Aug. 8 and how it might affect them personally, two Frenchmen are absorbed in a Paris newspaper.

UPI

The Premier also called for a dialogue between the Government and the people. "We must undertake a campaign of truth, realism and explanation on the profound reasons behind our difficulty in building a fully efficient economy and a prosperous society," he counseled.

Taking Chaban-Delmas at his word, Giscard d'Estaing revealed with disarming candor that the Banque de France's reserve figures had been cooked. Instead of the $3,593,000,000 claimed at the end of July, he said, in reality national gold and hard-currency reserves totaled a little more than $1,300,000,000, sufficient for 30 days of imports. Before the 1968 May-June events, French official reserves totaled nearly $7,000,000,000.

Because his internal problems were so pressing, Pompidou devoted most of his attention to them. His foreign policy was in low key, a mix of continuity and change in the first months similar to his home stance.

Regarding Canada he showed himself willing to prolong De Gaulle's quarrel with Ottawa over Quebec's status. He maintained De Gaulle's embargo on the fifty Mirage warplanes Israel had ordered and paid for. He affirmed that France would remain outside of NATO's integrated military command. His Foreign Minister went to the Soviet Union to pay tribute to an East-West *détente* and Franco-Soviet trade, and announced that the French President planned a later visit to Russia.

At the same time, Pompidou hastened French *rapprochement* with the United States, a process that began with President Nixon's visit to Paris (Feb. 28-Mar. 2). U.S. investments in France, discouraged by De Gaulle in the last years of his administration, were invited by the new regime. France rallied to the U.S.-backed scheme of Special Drawing Rights (SDR), or paper gold, for International Monetary Fund settlements, a device that De Gaulle had done his best to block. Pompidou sent the chief of staff of the French armed forces, Michel Fourquet, to Washington to reopen the dormant file of Franco-American military co-operation. And the President himself paid close personal attention to the details of his first visit to the United States, scheduled for February 1970.

In Europe, the near part of his international horizon, Pompidou suggested that he was more pliable than De Gaulle, who twice had categorically vetoed Great Britain's application to enter the European Common Market. France, Pompidou said, had withdrawn its veto, but before the question of new EEC members could be considered, France's five partners must have agreed to a new formula for community-wide farm-price supports, most of which go into the pockets of French farmers.

The French were taking a pragmatic view of things as 1970 approached. Pompidou's biggest political problem appeared to be how to make his businesslike approach palatable to the Gaullists who felt personal allegiance to the departed leader and were ready to see betrayal in each change of policy. However, the potent cement of power could be counted on to hold the ruling parliamentary coalition together after a shakedown period of adjustment to a new style of rule.

See Pompidou, Georges.

STEPHENS BROENING
Correspondent, Paris Bureau
The Associated Press

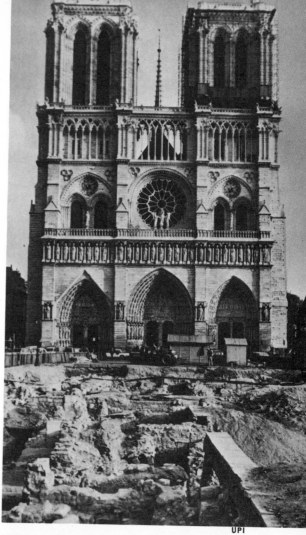

UPI

Digging up Place Notre Dame in Paris (for an underground garage), workmen uncovered a Roman hypocaust: a series of small chambers for heating rooms.

Jacques Offenbach's opera "La Périchole" was revived in Paris to mark the 150th anniversary of his birth.

Pictorial Parade, "Paris Match"

FUELS

Worldwide consumption of fossil fuels (oil, gas and coal) continued to grow at its accustomed level of about 5 per cent in 1969. As in previous years, the demand for natural gas grew most rapidly, particularly in Western Europe, with oil second and coal third. Unlike the situation in 1968, fossil-fuel supplies were not affected by any major outside event such as military action involving key oil-producing centers.

Oil. The principal events in the world oil industry in 1969 occurred in the United States. In September the state of Alaska held an auction for the right to drill for oil in the state's Northern Slope area. The oil leases yielded $900,220,590 in cash bonuses. It was the highest amount ever paid by the oil industry for this purpose, and it confirmed the fact that northern Alaska is considered by the industry to contain far more oil than has been discovered there so far. The highest single bid was made by a group of oil companies headed by Amerada Hess, of over $72,000,000, equal to $28,233 per acre, a new high for the U.S. oil industry.

According to estimates, Alaska north of the Brooks Range may well contain a total of at least 30,000,000,000 barrels of recoverable oil reserves. This would be about equal to the total proved reserves in the rest of the United States, including offshore areas, at the beginning of 1969. Production of Alaskan oil is expected to start in 1972 or 1973 when a pipeline to the southern Alaskan port of Valdez will be completed. Initially, most of the oil will be used on the West Coast of the United States. However, since Alaska's production potential is far larger than what can be absorbed by the West Coast, the industry is considering various ways of shipping Alaskan oil to the East Coast. One way would be to ship the oil by specially designed icebreaker tankers through the ice-impacted Northwest Passage, which was never commercially navigated before 1969. A trial run of the 115,000-deadweight-ton tanker *Manhattan* from Philadelphia to Prudhoe Bay, Alaska, was considered successful enough to warrant intensive further study by the principal oil companies involved.

The intention of most companies operating in Alaska is to market the newly found oil in the United States to offset the expected decline in oil production in California and the southwestern oil-producing states.

Outside of Alaska, the principal developments in the U.S. oil industry were mostly either legislative or executive. In the area of tax reform Congress passed legislation to reduce the depletion allowance for oil and gas producers from 27.5 per cent of gross revenue to 22 per cent. It was the first time since 1926 that the statutory-tax reduction, designed to

The area around Prudhoe Bay on the Arctic coast of Alaska may have the richest oil deposits in the world.

British Petroleum Co., Ltd.

compensate producers for the depletion of oil and gas deposits and to encourage them to search for and develop new reserves, had been changed. The reduction in the depletion allowance may cost the oil industry approximately $350,000,000 annually in additional income-tax payments.

Meanwhile, the President appointed a cabinet committee to review existing U.S. oil-import policy and to draft a proposal for changes. By year's end the committee's work was close to completion but its recommendations had not been revealed. There were various indications, however, that the new policy would include some form of gradual liberalization of the Oil Import Control Program in existence since 1959.

The import restrictions on oil had been imposed for national-security reasons. It was feared that without such restrictions the United States would become unduly dependent on politically unstable overseas sources for the supply of its principal energy source. During 1969 the oil industry argued strongly in favor of continuing the restrictions, while consumer groups and some government agencies held that the multibillion-dollar annual cost of the restrictions to oil consumers was excessive.

Other developments of major significance in 1969 were the entry of British Petroleum, one of the world's largest oil companies, into the U.S. market, and an increase in the price of crude oil. BP had been the only major international oil company not operating in the United States. An important factor in BP's decision to enter the U.S. market was the company's discovery of major oil reserves in Alaska. Domestic crude-oil prices registered their first big across-the-board increase since 1957. At the end of 1969 the average U.S. crude-oil price was $3.10 per barrel compared with $2.95 in 1968.

Outside the United States the most important developments occurred in South America and Indonesia. In October, Bolivia's military junta, which had come to power in September, nationalized a subsidiary of Gulf Oil, a U.S. company. The action paralleled that taken in February by a junta in Peru against the U.S.-owned International Petroleum Company.

In Indonesia a number of U.S. oil companies reported major finds during the year, both onshore and offshore. Their success attracted additional companies, making the country the most active oil-search area outside North America in 1969.

Natural Gas. In natural gas the most important development in 1969 was the announcement in the spring that the volume of proved gas re-

Major oil companies bid over $900,000,000 in competition for right to drill for oil in Alaska's Northern Slope.

serves in the United States had sharply declined during 1968. Although the ratio of reserves to production had been shrinking for a number of years, the additions to underground-gas reserves had always been larger than the volume of gas taken out of the ground for consumption. At the end of 1968, however, total proved reserves of 282,000,000,000,000 cubic feet were 11,000,000,000,000 cubic feet below those of a year earlier because the quantity of new reserves found had dropped sharply while production had increased by nearly 5 per cent to 19,300,000,000,000 cubic feet. The gas industry had been concerned for some time that a gas shortage was developing in the United States. However, the Federal Power Commission, which controls the prices of natural gas sold in interstate commerce, had dis-

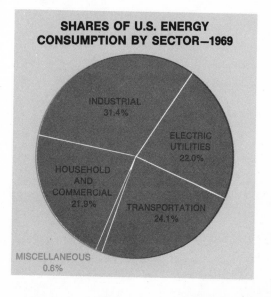

SHARES OF U.S. ENERGY CONSUMPTION BY SECTOR—1969

INDUSTRIAL 31.4%

ELECTRIC UTILITIES 22.0%

HOUSEHOLD AND COMMERCIAL 21.9%

TRANSPORTATION 24.1%

MISCELLANEOUS 0.6%

agreed with the industry's predictions. The 1968 drop in reserves apparently caused a change in the FPC's attitude. It was indicated by an extensive FPC staff report, issued in September, concluding that "evidence is mounting that the supply of natural gas is diminishing to critical levels in relation to demand. On the basis of current trends, only a few years remain before demand will outrun supply."

Another indication of a possible future shortage of domestic natural-gas supplies was the agreement concluded in October between a major U.S. gas-pipeline company and the Algerian Government for the importation of 365,-000,000,000 cubic feet annually of liquefied natural gas over a 25-year period beginning in

In view of Arabian American Oil Company's Ras Tanura refinery, marine terminal is in background; Saudi Arabia produces 3,000,000 barrels of crude oil daily.

Arabian American Oil Company

1973. A similar agreement for Venezuelan gas was concluded by a utility company located on the U.S. East Coast. The two agreements marked the first importation of liquefied natural gas into the United States on a regular commercial basis.

In Western Europe the demand for natural gas continued to increase at an extremely rapid rate. In the six Common Market countries, demand in 1969 was nearly twice that of 1967 and was equal to about a third of the six countries' coal demand. Thus, natural gas, which was an insignificant source of energy in Europe at the beginning of the 1960's, is emerging as a major source as the Continent enters the 1970's. By 1975 some 11 per cent of Western Europe's primary energy will be supplied by that source. In 1969 the share was below 6 per cent.

Coal. World coal production in 1969 amounted to approximately 2,000,000,000 tons, of which roughly 25 per cent came from the United States, 30 per cent from Eastern Europe, 18 per cent from Western Europe, 15 per cent from Communist China and 12 per cent from all other areas. Production in Western Europe continued its long-term decline. In the Soviet Union a slight increase was registered.

In the United States, production was expected to be slightly above the 1968 output of 545,000,000 tons, while domestic and export demand was expected to be at least 3 per cent above the 550,000,000-ton level of 1968. The result was a sharp tightening in U.S. coal supplies during 1969. Earlier in the 1960's, coal supplies had been quite ample in relation to demand.

A combination of factors brought about the tightening of supplies in 1969. The most important were a shortage of railroad cars to transport the coal; a sharp increase in the demand for coal by utility companies as a result of the postponement of atomic-power construction plans; reluctance by the coal industry to open new mines because of long-term uncertainty over future atomic-power and air-pollution developments; a very sharp increase in exports to Japan in both 1968 and 1969; and, finally, a series of small but effective wildcat strikes in coal mines throughout the United States. The effect of tight supplies was reported to be particularly acute for the Tennessee Valley Authority, the nation's largest user of coal. Other coal-burning electric utilities in the Southeast also reported supply problems and delivery delays during 1969.

JOHN H. LICHTBLAU
Executive Director
Petroleum Industry Research Foundation, Inc.

The brilliant Soviet chess players Boris Spassky (l) and Tigran Petrosian again faced each other in 1969; Spassky won the world championship this time.

Sovfoto

GAMES: Bridge

The 1969 World Bridge Championships were won again by Italy's apparently unbeatable Blue Team. To the dismay of North American bridge enthusiasts, the United States team, captained by Oswald Jacoby, did not qualify for the finals. Taiwan reached the finals, but lost to Italy by a wide margin.

The first professional team, the Dallas Aces, sponsored by industrialist Ira Corn, won the right to represent the United States in the World Championships to be played in Stockholm in June 1970.

Travel with Goren escorted 160 bridge players on a northern European cruise which included a visit to Leningrad and Moscow.

Winners of the 1969 U.S. National Championships were:

Blue Ribbon Pairs: Erik Paulsen, Alex Tschekaloff

Life Master Men's Pairs: Peter Pender, Harlow Lewis

Life Master Women's Pairs: Gratian Goldstein, Sylvia Stein

Life Master Pairs: Erik Murray, Sammy Kehela

Mixed Teams: Ivor and Alice Stakgold, Dan Rotman and Flo Orner, Charles Peres and Janice Cohn

Open Pairs: Robert Freedman, James Mathis

Reisinger Teams: Ira Rubin, Jeff Westheimer, Philip Feldesman, William Grieve

CHARLES H. GOREN
Bridge Authority

Chess

Chess in 1969 was marked by a reinforced domination by the Soviet Union. Boris Spassky of Leningrad, turned back in 1966 by world champion Tigran Petrosian of Erevan, won the world championship. Nona Gaprindashvili of Tiflis successfully defended her women's world championship also against a former challenger, her compatriot, Alla Kushnir. By winning the world junior championship, Anatoly Karpov of Zlatoust emerged as the first Soviet youngster of promise since Spassky won the title in 1955.

Soviet players also took the most honors in the major international tournaments. Ratimir Kholmov, Leonid Stein and Aleksei Suetin placed 1, 2, 3 at Havana. Vassily Smyslov came in first at Hastings, England, ahead of Svetozar Gligoric of Yugoslavia. David Bronstein and Wolfgang Uhlmann of East Germany shared first, followed by Suetin, at East Berlin. Smyslov and Lajos Portisch of Hungary tied for first in Monaco. Mikhail Botvinnik and Evfim Geller split first at Wijk ann Zee, Holland. Viktor Korchnoy and Paul Keres were first and second at Bad Luhacovice, Czechoslovakia. And Korchnoy led Milan Matulovic of Yugoslavia by two full points at Sarajevo.

Some, however, scored above Soviet contenders. Vlastimil Hort of Czechoslovakia was first at Venice, two full points ahead of six players who tied for second place, including Pal Benko of the United States and Mark Taimanov of the U.S.S.R. Bent Larsen of Denmark won at Busum, West Germany, topping Soviet champion Lev Polugayevski. And Dr. Max Euwe of Holland scored in front of Salo Flohr of the U.S.S.R. in a tournament of veterans at Bladel, Holland.

In the United States, Pal Benko of New Jersey won the U.S. Open Championship. Mrs. G. K. Gresser of New York won the women's championship. Kenneth Rogoff of Rochester, N.Y., became junior champion; Kimball Nedved of New Jersey, amateur champion.

JACK STRALEY BATTELL
Executive Editor
Chess Review

GEOGRAPHICAL DATA BANK, COMPUTERIZED

More and more in today's complex world the computer is helping man digest volumes of data accumulating at a rate unheard of in previous centuries. While the computer does nothing that man could not do himself, it works very much faster and more economically. Also it makes many operations extremely attractive that would be unprofitable if done manually.

A recent use is the manipulation of the vast quantity of data found on maps. Before the computer can be brought into play, however, some preliminary work is necessary. The first step is "data reduction," the process by which all information on a map is read by machine, interpreted according to certain rules, and finally represented as a very long string of numbers. This is the method of the Canadian Geographic Information System, which is currently reducing the data contained on maps representing over a million square miles of Canada.

The data are carefully drawn on topographical maps measuring about 24 by 36 inches on a scale of 1:50,000 (1 inch on the map equals 50,000 inches on land). In the Canadian system the data represent soil areas with various agricultural potentials; administrative and political boundaries; and present land use. Contiguous areas with the same classification are encircled in ink on the map, dividing it into regions called "faces." Each face bears its classification number. When all regions have been bounded and classified in this way, the map (or manuscript) is sent to the computer center, where the regional boundaries are carefully "scribed"—scratched on plastic material.

The copy of the map thus created is placed on a large rotating drum, where it is scanned by a photoelectric cell. The information is thereby fed to magnetic tape, which records about 54,000,000 bits of information, drawn from 1/250-inch squares. For practical purposes, it is necessary only to note in what squares the scribed lines appear. Thus, depending upon the density of lines on the map, the information is reduced to between 4,000 to 240,000 bits.

The location of an arbitrary point within an area on the original map is measured accurately, and the classification of that area, together with the location of the point, is recorded on magnetic tape. For each position and classification data pair, the computer determines which area on the scribed map contains the measured point. Information on the boundary and classification of this area is stored in a data bank. It has an index that allows rapid retrieval of the information by geographic location, much like the index of a book.

A major problem remains. The information on a single map amounts to about 40,000,000 items, far more than the computer can handle at one time. Most problems met in building the Canadian Geographic Information System involved partitioning the data sufficiently so that a computer *could* handle it, and reconstructing these partitions after processing.

A separate data bank has been built up for each "coverage" across Canada. A coverage represents a single classification criterion, e.g., agricultural potential of the land. One of the main uses of the Canadian Geographic Information System will be to show how agricultural land potentials, farm incomes, educational levels within a community, administrative authorities, weather factors, and even the present land use are related geographically. The size and shape of the various areas so determined can be calculated rapidly by a computer. Moreover, the computer can be programed to take nonlinear changes into account when calculating an area, and to be selective, rejecting areas too small to be of much interest or too far from transportation to be practical for immediate development, for example.

The Canadian Geographic Information System will provide a basic tool for administrators: it will tell them what Canada has, where it is, and how best to use it. Considering that in a few years the data banks will include over a million square miles of Canada, it is obvious that the system will provide a powerful tool for the wise administration of Canada's large and often sparsely populated areas. The program could also be of great benefit to underdeveloped countries which need to know much more about their land. Another fruitful possibility for the project is cooperation with satellite analysis of the land, for a similar data bank could be built up from satellite photographs of the earth. The huge task of interpreting such photographs must eventually fall to computers, particularly if speed is a factor, as it would be to note week-by-week changes as the satellite rephotographed the same area. More information will be gathered about the growing patterns of vegetation in various parts of the world, for instance. Similar techniques could extract weather information from cloud-cover photographs. The Canadian Geographic Information System is not only a very important project for Canada but for all the world.

RobERT W. Shaw
Executive Assistant, Consultation Division
Multiple Access Computer Corp.

GEOLOGY

Because the relationship between the earth and the moon is so close, the most significant event for geology in 1969 was the landing of the astronauts on the moon in July and their successful return with 48 pounds of lunar rock.

Late in 1969 the scientists at the Lunar Receiving Laboratory in Houston published the results of their preliminary examination, and it is clear that the moon's surface, at least at the landing site in Mare Tranquillitatis, differs in several important respects from any part of the earth's surface. The lunar rocks are igneous, but crystallized from a molten state between 3,000,000,000 and 4,000,000,000 years ago. The craters on the moon may have been formed at an early stage in the history of the solar system and been preserved. Similar craters could have existed at one time on earth and been destroyed.

The chemistry of moon rocks is different. There is no trace of water, which makes the likelihood of any life on the moon remote. All the analyzed rocks contain from 7 to 13 per cent of titanium oxide, which is several times the amount found in any lavas on earth. If these results are typical, it seems less likely that the moon was ever part of the earth, and more likely that it was a separate body captured long ago by the earth.

On the earth the exploration of the oceans by the Deep Sea Drilling Project and by extensive magnetometer surveys continued. The ship *Glomar Challenger* completed its initial traverses across the Atlantic Ocean, drilling 54 holes at 31 sites, and crossed the Pacific to the Philippine Sea. Some holes were over 2,000 feet

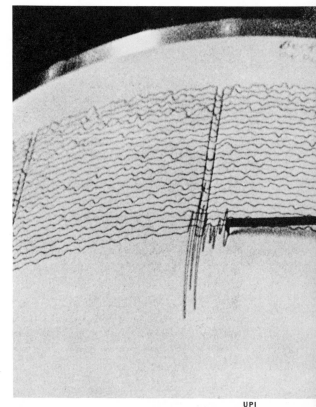

UPI

Tremors are recorded on Berkeley, Calif., seismograph from nuclear explosion on Amchitka Island, Aleutians. Effects of underground test were later said to be minor.

Thermal (heat) infrared scanning, a form of remote sensing, shows discharge pattern of the Quinault River as it flows into the Pacific Ocean at Taholah, Wash.

NASA

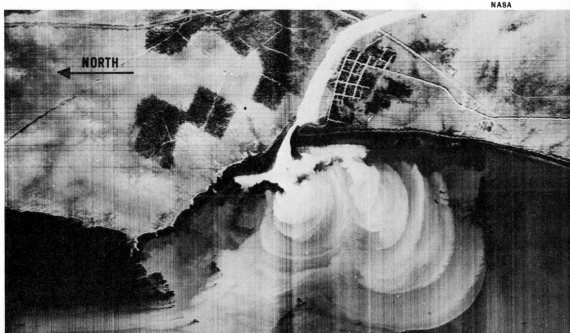

NORTH

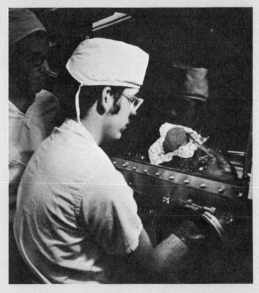

MOON SAMPLES UNDER EXAMINATION

To avoid contaminating the samples, scientists handle them in a vacuum with "port" gloves (above). A microscopic photo (l) of lunar material brings out puzzling "beads," glazed at some time by tremendous heat. Beads are about 1/100 of an inch in diameter. Under a special "rock" microscope, a crystallization pattern appears. All samples are igneous (created by heat).

Photos NASA

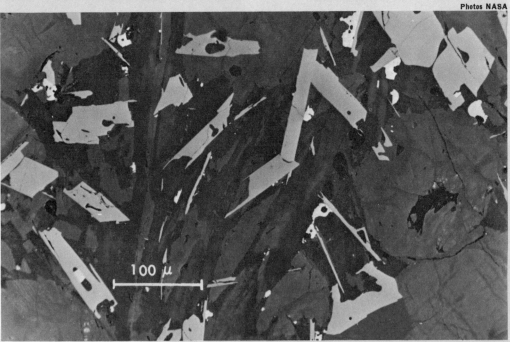

100 μ

deep, and many reached bedrock below the sediments on the sea floor. In all cases the ages of the bedrock confirmed predictions made by magnetic surveys, and supported the theory that the Atlantic sea floor has been spreading away from the Mid-Atlantic Ridge.

It now seems probable that during the Permian period, about 250,000,000 years ago, there was no Atlantic Ocean and only one great continent. It slowly split into two parts along a line through the Gulf of Mexico and between Africa and the United States to the Mediterranean. About 150,000,000 years ago Africa and South America started to separate, and even more recently Europe and North America. This growth of the Atlantic and Indian oceans led the continents to overlap the Pacific Ocean floors, which are being reabsorbed into the interior along the great trenches that rim the Pacific. The oldest large area of ocean floor lies in the western Pacific. Overriding causes earthquakes, volcanoes, mountain building and ore deposits. Their behavior can perhaps be better predicted now that their causes are becoming understood.

Discoveries on the ocean floors and on islands in the Mediterranean have provided a probable explanation for the story of Atlantis. The evidence shows that no large country could have existed in the Atlantic Ocean, but that about 1500 B.C. a tremendous volcanic eruption destroyed and buried a city on the island of Santorini and devastated the coasts of Crete. If the Pillars of Hercules were the two mountainous peninsulas at the southern tip of Greece and not those at the Strait of Gibraltar, then the islands fit the description of Atlantis given by Plato.

In paleontology the investigation of the ocean floors, the greater opportunities for travel, and the ever increasing use and understanding of microfossils are leading to better correlation between different parts of the world. Ever smaller fossils have been discovered and are being studied. They have the advantage that they are often abundant where larger fossils are lacking. More fossils of early primates bearing on the evolution of man continue to be discovered in large numbers in Africa, and new sites were discovered in Ethiopia.

The new networks of improved seismographs, whose installation began about a decade ago, are now producing a wealth of precise knowledge about earthquakes and about the movements of the earth's surface, which cause sea-floor spreading and build mountains. Seismic waves pass through the earth's interior and give information that is being combined with laboratory studies to suggest how the interior of the earth is constituted. The size of the central core of liquid iron has been found to be a few miles larger than supposed, and the layers of the mantle are being identified as various silicates.

Great instrumental progress has continued in remote sensing. This term includes radar, ultraviolet, infrared and thermal scanning and photography from aircraft and satellites. All these methods are rapid, and some are independent of weather or are useful in detecting pollution and ores. Geophysical prospecting by magnetic, electrical, gravitational, radioactive and seismic methods continued to be developed. To these older methods have been added delicate sensing or "sniffing" of vapors given off by mineralized areas. The search for economic minerals is more intensive than ever before and has led to such great successes as the discovery of vast oil deposits in Alaska, though shortages of some important minerals are foreseen within the next twenty years.

Broadly speaking, 1969 was the year in which earth scientists realized that the discovery of sea-floor spreading and the truth of continental drift gave them a far better and more powerful knowledge of the earth's behavior than was thought possible a few years before. Thus vast possibilities are open for better prediction. At the same time, scientists have recognized that man is enclosed by his environment, and that the resources of that environment are not limitless. It is delicate and is being polluted.

As a result, there is increasing awareness that the study of geology must be broadened. For a century it has chiefly dealt with rocks, minerals and fossils. In the future it must include geophysics and the study of the whole earth with special reference to its function as man's habitat—his home.

J. TUZO WILSON
Professor of Geophysics
University of Toronto

GEORGIA

On Jan. 17, Atlanta became the second city to receive a Federal model-cities grant. The plan approved was drawn up by a technical team provided by Lockheed-Georgia Company. It is one of the largest of the Defense Department contractors that are a major source of employment and revenue for the state. □ In June, Gov. Lester G. Maddox's $115,000,000 additional tax program was rejected by the state General Assembly. □ In nonpartisan elections in October, Sam H. Massell, Jr., was voted mayor of Atlanta. Massell, a liberal Democrat, had been the city's vice mayor for eight years.

GERMANY

In 1969, West Germany proved its economic strength and political resiliency, while its principal neighbors showed weaknesses in both respects. The Federal Republic's (FRG) weight in international affairs increased therefore, but thanks to the restrained and cooperative attitudes of its leaders this did not arouse the fears of German power that are always latent among its neighbors. Ulbricht's German Democratic Republic (GDR) had less solid reasons for rejoicing. While the existence of this communist state was more readily acknowledged outside the Soviet camp than before, it barely held its own economically and was put on the defensive politically. In the play of forces between the two parts of Germany, the GDR sought safety in truculent self-isolation while the FRG went out of its way to broaden political, economic and social contacts. Both parts fixed their eyes on the Soviet Union, which holds the real power in East German affairs, the GDR to reassure itself of that buttress, and the FRG to envelop and soften up the GDR in better relations between Bonn and Moscow.

WEST GERMANY

The outstanding events of the year were the upward revaluation of the D-mark and the elections that, in the spring, brought the country its first Social-Democratic president and, in the fall, its first SPD chief executive (chancellor).

Economic Strength. Some lingering concern early in the year that an economic recession might be in the offing was soon dispelled as the vigorous upswing continued. By the middle of 1969, nearly 22,000,000 wage and salary earners were employed, including 1,300,000 foreign workers (more than ever before), while 140,000 unemployed were facing 750,000 job vacancies. Two out of three enterprises were working overtime. Private consumption, investment, construction and, above all, exports were on the increase and more than made up for the continuing decline of coal mining and agricultural employment. While the domestic economy remained in fairly good balance, with prices rising only moderately compared with other countries, the balance of international payments showed an embarrassment of riches.

Rising net earnings from foreign trade and recurrent massive inflows of speculative funds (the latter stimulated by rumors of an impending appreciation of the D-mark) caused large increases in German foreign-currency holdings, partly counterbalanced by German long-term lending. France, Britain and the United States, all having payment deficits, were pressing Bonn

to revalue the D-mark. In late 1968, both SPD Economics Minister Schiller and Finance Minister Strauss, leader of the Christian Social Union (the Bavarian affiliate of the Christian Democrats), had resisted this pressure and agreed instead on a small surtax on exports and a tax rebate on imports as corrective. In March 1969, Schiller changed his mind and joined the Central Bank in proposing an appreciation of the D-mark. Strauss stuck to his position. He and Chancellor Kiesinger argued that the deficit countries were causing the trouble and should correct it by austerity or by devaluing their currencies.

This led to the sharpest conflict within the 2½-year-old grand-coalition Government, which enlivened the election campaign. The day after the election, Kiesinger gave in and ordered the Central Bank to stop supporting the 4 to 1 D-mark/dollar rate in the market. The first act of the new Brandt Government was to decree a 9.29 per cent appreciation of the D-mark, to a rate of DM 3.66 per dollar. Welcomed in international financial circles, the decision came somewhat too late to check the inflationary potential of the German boom. Also, as predicted, it exacerbated the difficulties of the European Common Market. The uniform agricultural-price system, already riddled with exceptions following the devaluation of the French franc in August, was temporarily suspended. It would now be saddled with provisions for large national (and small communitarian) subsidies to German farmers unless price uniformity were to be abandoned altogether.

Elections and New Government. On Mar. 5, the Federal Assembly, meeting in West Berlin, elected a new president. Minister of Justice Gustav Heinemann, the SPD candidate, narrowly won over Defense Minister Gerhard Schröder of the CDU, with the help of the votes of the Free Democrats (FDP). The lineup of the small and crisis-troubled FDP with the Socialists, against the latter's partner in Government, was regarded as a harbinger of the breakup of the grand coalition. The events following the general elections of Sept. 28 fulfilled this expectation.

The sixth Bundestag, elected by 87 per cent of the electorate, showed no radically different composition from its predecessor. With 46 per cent of the vote (formerly 48) and 242 (245) seats, the CDU/CSU remained the strongest party. But the SPD's share of the vote rose from 39 to 43 per cent, its seats from 202 to 224. The FDP lost 19 of its 49 seats and barely stayed above the 5 per cent threshold below which a party cannot be represented in the

Parliament. No other party won representation. In particular, the nationalist-authoritarian NPD, whose rise in previous years had spread fears of neo-nazism at home and abroad, failed to enter the Bundestag.

The defeat of the NPD and the leftward shift in the FDP under the leadership of Walter Scheel, once foreign-aid minister under Konrad Adenauer and Ludwig Erhardt, enabled SPD leader Willy Brandt to break the partnership with the CDU to form a small coalition with the FDP, and to reach the long-coveted goal of becoming federal chancellor. Although the SPD/FDP coalition held only a 12-seat margin over the CDU/CSU, Brandt was elected handily. With a disciplined party behind him, and a small coalition partner that must fear political extinction if its failure to cooperate should cause a government crisis and new elections, Brandt may well remain in power for four years. For the first time in the history of the Federal Republic, the Christian Democrats have found themselves in the opposition. Despite their numerical strength they have shown signs of wear, and their weakened leadership was easily outmaneuvered in the coalition negotiations.

The new Government bears the strong stamp of the Social Democrats. All their leading men reentered or entered the Cabinet, streamlined from 20 to 15 ministries, including the chancellery. Only the successful party strategist, Herbert Wehner, stayed outside, to assume the critical role of parliamentary whip. The three FDP ministers, headed by Scheel in the foreign office, play second fiddle. The left-center Government was welcomed widely, even by some leading industrialists. The balance of public opinion favored a new broom in Bonn.

Domestic Affairs. Brandt's policy declaration stressed domestic reforms and continuity of foreign policy. The new Government intends to lower the voting age from 21 to 18 years, thus strengthening its political base (young voters having shown a leaning in its direction) and hoping to counter the tendency among the young intellectuals to engage in sterile, demonstrative radicalism. Promised educational reforms aim in the same direction. In the field of labor, however, the trade-union demand for an expansion of workers' codetermination in industrial management, favored by the SPD, was shelved for the time being. The SPD leaders persuaded the unions to accept this concession to the FDP, and the union leaders once more demonstrated their political cooperativeness. Apart from a flurry of wildcat strikes just before the elections, which were met by wage increases, Germany's labor force re-

UPI

Poisoned fish are removed from the lower Rhine River after millions are killed by a toxic insecticide.

A German compares new exchange rates (Wechselkurse) of revalued mark with outdated money guides.

UPI

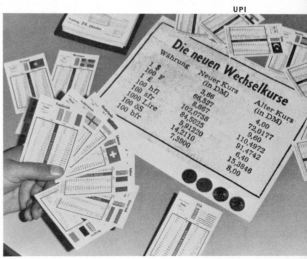

**FEDERAL REPUBLIC OF GERMANY
(WEST)**

Area: 95,700 sq. mi.
Population: 58,100,000
Capital: Bonn (pop., 140,500)
Government: Gustav Heinemann, president—1969; Willy Brandt, chancellor—1969
Gross national product: $132,000,000,000
Monetary unit: mark (3.66 marks = U.S. $1.00)
Chief products: potatoes, lignite, coal, potash, machinery, optical goods
Foreign trade: exports, $24,841,000,000; imports, $20,152,000,000
Communications: 10,321,281 telephones, 18,586,929 radios, 14,815,393 TV sets, 477 daily newspapers
Transportation: roads, 98,984 mi.; 11,682,600 passenger cars; railroads, 21,283 mi.
Education: 7,537,925 elementary and secondary students, 21 universities
Armed forces: 465,000

See map on page 185

GERMAN DEMOCRATIC REPUBLIC (EAST)

Area: 41,500 sq. mi.
Population: 16,000,000
Capital: East Berlin (pop., 1,100,000)
Government: Walter Ulbricht, chairman—1960; Willi Stoph, premier—1964
Gross National Product: $30,000,000,000
Monetary unit: ostmark (3.39 ostmarks = U.S. $1.00)
Chief products: chemicals, textiles, potatoes, sugar beets, lignite, crude steel
Foreign trade: exports, $3,784,000,000; imports, $3,388,000,000
Communications: 1,780,319 telephones, 5,880,000 radios, 4,500,000 TV sets, 40 daily newspapers
Transportation: roads, 28,174 mi.; 826,991 passenger cars, railroads, 9,618 mi.
Education: 2,439,942 elementary and secondary students
Armed forces: 137,000

See map on page 185

mained steadily at work throughout the year, in sharp contrast with several neighboring countries.

Among other domestic reforms, the Government will continue the improvement of transportation initiated under energetic Transport Minister Georg Leber and grapple with the structural difficulties of the Bundeswehr (Army). Helmut Schmidt, defense minister, intends to make the Bundeswehr a better integrated part of society. Whatever may become of specific plans, the Federal Republic is clearly continuing to consolidate itself as a state. The administrative reorganization that made the "temporary" capital Bonn a city of 300,000 on Aug. 1 symbolizes the trend. The fact that no one in the new Government has a nazi past is another.

Foreign Policy. The prescription of "continuity in foreign policy" marks the chancellor's wary realization that there are great obstacles to the changes he would like to bring and that there are many dangers on the way to his goal, "a peaceful order with greater justice in Europe." He wants to rely on the security alliance with the United States, which under his predecessor reached a new peak of cordiality, cemented by the renewal, in July, of the financial "offset" agreement for American troop expenditures. However, unlike Kiesinger, Brandt does not look on the United States as "the leader of the West." He runs the risk that the United States, for reasons of its own, will insist that the FRG bear a greater share of the responsibility for its security. Brandt would like to bring Britain into the Common Market, but the integrationist élan of the Brussels Community appears

broken, and an arrangement with Britain may be possible only by way of intra-European trade preferences, which would antagonize the United States. Finally, Brandt wants to improve relations with Russia and East Germany; but these partners may take more from him than they give.

By its Ostpolitik and Deutschlandpolitik, Bonn seeks to satisfy Soviet security interests, to liberalize the East German regime, and to deepen social intercourse with the communist-ruled societies of Central and Eastern Europe. To that end it offers nonaggression pacts, economic incentives, and acceptance of the GDR as "another state within the German nation" (but not its recognition "under international law" as Ulbricht demands). Moscow and Pankow seek to extract the economic advantages but to isolate their one-party regimes against the manifestations of the West's free society which appeal to the people under their rule, and at the same time to encourage the West Germans to loosen their political and military ties to the United States. Both sides run considerable risks in this play: one, that communist rule east of the Elbe River might be eroded; the other, that West Germany might slip into a Soviet orbit.

EAST GERMANY

With blatant self-satisfaction, Walter Ulbricht's regime celebrated its twentieth anniversary. New buildings and industrial structures testify to the productivity of its 16,000,000 subjects. East Germans now consume more bread, butter and potatoes per capita than West Germans (but still less meat, milk and eggs). Two

Wide World

Soldiers of the East German People's Army goose-step stiffly in the tradition of the old Prussian armies.

out of three households are said to have TV, and East German technology in many fields outranks that of its communist neighbors although it usually is a step or two behind that of the West.

But pride in the economic advances, which many people share, has failed to stabilize the regime. Travel abroad, not only to West Germany which the regime treats as a *hostile* nation—it cannot quite make up its mind whether the FRG is a *foreign* nation—but also to communist countries, is severely restricted. Barbed wire, mine fields and radar screens around the borders remind the citizen that he is not being trusted. Only the most ingenious and lucky manage an unauthorized crossing in the gas tank of an automobile, a homemade submarine or the like. Scientists and artists, in whom the state takes pride, are constantly being disciplined. Youth, on whom it lavishes resources, must always be admonished to love the "socialist republic" and to hate the West. The regime remains insecure, wedded to thought control and shows of military force; and the succession to Ulbricht, 76 years old, poses problems.

While the governing party, with firm support from Moscow, continues to preach and practice the "class struggle" against free Ger-

many, it readily accepts the financial favors that Bonn bestows on it in the hope of maintaining economic contacts and loosening the stranglehold on Berlin. During the year, East Germany increased its trade with West Germany (interzonal trade), which is conducted under preferences, and succeeded in levying exorbitant charges on transportation and communications.

Internationally, East Germany harvested prestige gains from the conflict between the Arab states and Israel, the dependence of the Arabs on the U.S.S.R., and West Germany's friendly relations with Israel. Iraq, Sudan, Syria and the U.A.R. took up diplomatic relations with the GDR. Since all of them had broken off relations with Bonn previously, the latter had little leverage for countermeasures under the Hallstein doctrine, which from 1955 declared recognition of the GDR by other states "an unfriendly act." But when Cambodia followed suit, a conflict developed in the grand coalition. Kiesinger wanted to recall Bonn's ambassador. Brandt, then foreign minister, opposed leaving the field to the GDR. They compromised on "suspending" relations with Pnomh Penh. The Hallstein doctrine was then said to be dead, and it was declared dead once more when the new Government took over in October. But with all its efforts to avoid giving verbal offense to Pankow—the Brandt/Scheel regime no longer uses "so-called" or quotation marks when it speaks of the GDR—Bonn soon warned again that states recognizing East Germany would "burden their relations" with West Germany as long as the East rejects endeavors for better intra-German relations.

WEST BERLIN

Twenty-five years after its political incapsulation in Soviet-occupied territory and eight years after Ulbricht built the Wall, West Berlin is not a dying city; but it remains a beleaguered city.

Industrial and construction activity in Berlin continued high in 1969 and there was a shortage of workers, though the decline of the working population was arrested. This city of more than 2,000,000 is a productive contributor to the West German economy in which it is embedded; but it requires West German subsidies to compensate for its hostile environment and its unfavorable age structure. (Some 22 per cent of the population is over 65, against 16 in Hamburg and 12 in the whole FRG.) Direct federal subsidies and tax preferences amount to DM 3,000,000,000 to 4,000,000,000 a year (around $1,000,000,000). While this is less than one per cent of West Germany's national income, some West Germans find the bill for the city's political independence high. A study of Berlin's economic and social situation, published under the auspices of the city government during 1969, pointed out, however, that DM 1,500,000,000 to 2,000,000,000 of Berliners' savings flow to West Germany, so that there are notable economic besides political compensations. (No other Western city contributes so much to the arts.)

With the permission of the three allied powers who constitute the supreme authority in West Berlin, the Federal Assembly of the FRG met in the city in March to elect the new president. Soviet and East German threats to interrupt traffic to Berlin, under the pretext of military maneuvers, caused jitters in Bonn. However, a new Berlin crisis failed to materialize when the Soviets decided to avoid a confrontation. For a short time, the East Germans obstructed traffic on the Autobahn. Then their controls returned to the sluggish norm. Hardly a week passed, however, without some chicanery of the transports or arbitrary arrests of travelers. The political links of West Berlin

Newly constructed Alexander Square in East Berlin draws throngs for the twentieth anniversary of the German Democratic Republic. Scene is a far cry from the drab, deserted-looking East Berlin of only a few years ago.

Eastfoto

to the FRG—it is the eleventh *Land* of the FRG and the seat of several Federal offices —are a special target of the Communists, who insist that the city be a "separate political entity on the territory of the GDR."

Inside the city the activity of the radical left caused periodic disturbances. Student rebels led by the SDS terrorized the Free University and staged violent demonstrations when the city authorities arrested and returned to West Germany a handful of deserters from the Bundeswehr. Under the special status of Berlin, which excludes the German military, thousands of West German draft dodgers have sought refuge in the city. The SDS went as far as to appeal to the Soviets and the East Germans to blockade the air lanes. The city government, controlled by the SPD, reacted with great restraint and sought to appease the agitation by passing a liberal university-reform law which gave students and assistants considerable influence on university management. In November, a thirty-year-old assistant was elected president of the Free University under this law.

Early in the year, President Nixon was warmly welcomed by the city, notably its industrial workers, and so was Willy Brandt in the fall when he made his first visit as chancellor. But many Berliners continue to fear that both Bonn and the Allies may be more anxious to avoid conflict with their tormentors than to resist effectively their encroachments on the city's liberty.

HORST MENDERSHAUSEN
Senior Staff Member, Social Science Dept.
The RAND Corporation

GREECE

Politically, economically and diplomatically, the Greek military Government weathered some hard knocks in 1969. Premier George Papadopoulos appeared in no hurry to restore democracy. Allies in the North Atlantic pact called for the isolation of Greece, opponents at home used bombs and leaflets to show their sentiments, and exiled politicians called for uprisings against the army officers who seized power in April 1967. The Government's response was fresh crackdowns on dissenters and undisguised displeasure at critical foreign ministers in Rome, Stockholm, The Hague and other West European capitals. Economic sluggishness persisted despite government moves to boost foreign reserves, close the export-import gap and attract foreign investors.

Facing certain suspension from the 18-nation Council of Europe, whose members are pledged to uphold democratic forms of government,

Greece withdrew from the council in late November. A few days later, Papadopoulos announced that his Government would not hold elections under international pressure and warned European nations to beware of anarchy.

If 1968 was the year for consolidating power and purging questionable supporters in the civil service, army and navy, schools and church, 1969 was the year of the backlash. Opponents at home used bombs, eight of them in central Athens one mid-October morning. About 25 persons were injured. Vocal opponents ranged from such respected figures at home as poet Georgos Seferis, the nation's only Nobel Prizewinner, to such respected figures abroad as exiled former Premier Constantine Caramanlis, who called the Government a tyrannical failure. Many political figures at home agreed, but Papadopoulos appeared more worried about foreign critics.

A few Greeks hijacked aircraft to express their feelings. A self-labeled Communist forced the crew of an Olympic Airways DC-6, carrying 102 persons, to fly from Athens to Egypt in January. Another man, his wife and two sons hijacked an Olympic Airways DC-3 in August and forced its crew to fly them to Albania. Both men requested and received political asylum.

An eight-month vacuum was filled in September with the nomination of veteran diplomat Henry J. Tasca as U.S. ambassador. The move dismayed Greeks who thought Washington's refusal to fill the post was a mark of coolness toward the Government, but Papadopoulos was heartened by the appointment. Supporters considered it a tacit U.S. endorsement of the stocky, 50-year-old former tank commander. Relations between the United States and Greece, although still formal on the surface, relaxed somewhat behind the scenes. U.S. military aid, including secondhand armor and weapons from American forces in West Germany, totaled about $47,000,000, up a couple of million from 1968 but still far below precoup levels. Greece continued to play a vital role in Western defense strategy, especially in view of Mideast instability and the largest show yet of Soviet ships in the Mediterranean.

Military and civilian tribunals were kept busy. Hundreds of persons, many of them self-labeled Communists and Leftists, were jailed after mass trials for subversion, sedition, sabotage and anti-regime activities. Angeliki Mangakis, daughter of a 1920 military dictator, was jailed for four years on charges of anti-regime activities. Former soldier Alexandros Panaghoulis, who in late 1968 was sentenced to die for his role in an assassination attempt on Papadopoulos, escaped from a high-security

GREECE

Area: 51,182 sq. mi.
Population: 8,900,000
Capital: Athens (pop., 1,875,000)
Government: Constantine II, king—1964;
George Papadopoulos, premier—1967
Gross National Product: $7,400,000,000
Monetary unit: drachma (30 drachmas = U.S.
$1.00)
Chief products: tobacco, olive oil, cotton, citrus
fruits, raisins, wine
Foreign trade: exports, $468,000,000; imports,
$1,393,000,000
Communications: 660,129 telephones, 1,380,-
000 radios, 22,019 TV sets, 87 daily news-
papers
Transportation: roads, 24,144 mi.; 122,479
passenger cars; railroads, 1,595 mi.
Education: 1,350,440 elementary and secondary
students, 2 universities
Armed forces: 159,000

prison on June 6. He was recaptured in Athens three days later, reportedly for a $16,000 government reward, offered to friends who hid Panaghoulis in an apartment. During the year, Papadopoulos announced the smashing of plots involving dozens of retired or dismissed military officers, many of whom overzealously championed the cause of exiled King Constantine. Papadopoulos announced the restoration of some civil liberties, but said paper work would delay full implementation of them for several months. He also eased censorship laws, but applied new regulations in a way that frightened most editors into self-censorship.

There was little evidence to support rumors of strife among Papadopoulos and his cabinet colleagues. Education Minister Theophylaktos Papaconstantinou resigned in June without explanation, and the Premier assumed the education portfolio in addition to those he already held for defense and foreign affairs. He remained foreign minister on a temporary basis.

The most vexing and perhaps most damaging row of the year for Papadopoulos was his confrontation with the Greek Council of State, a 25-member executive watchdog board appointed for life and protected by law from dismissal. After the board reinstated 21 senior judges purged in mid-1968 and declared more than 100 government laws unconstitutional, Papadopoulos fired Council President Michael Stasinopoulos. The Premier then announced that Stasinopoulos had resigned. Stasinopoulos denied this and other council members resigned in protest. The Government then voided all council decisions it disliked. A Greek tradition died when the Government banned, on grounds that it was "barbaric," the custom of smashing crockery in bouzoukia night clubs.

Constantine, 29, wound up his second year of exile in Rome. Exile was fretful but comfortable, with Constantine living on a $500,000 grant continued by the Government which still considers him king. Constantine maintained discreet silence on the situation in Athens, whiling away his time with riding, sailing and visits to royal kinsmen outside Greece.

Economic headaches persisted. Imports again outpaced exports by about 3 to 1, leaving a trade deficit of $910,000,000, somewhat lower than the 1968 deficit of $925,000,000. Even tourist receipts of $160,000,000, up about $60,000,000 from 1968, money sent home by Greeks working abroad, and traditionally lucrative shipping receipts did not close the trade gap. The final deficit was about $310,000,000, roughly equal to the country's foreign reserves, which edged up from the 1968 level of $262,-000,000. Bank deposits hit a post–World War II record of $512,600,000, and the Government introduced a balanced budget of $2,000,-000,000, compared with the previous year's $1,700,000,000. The Government also announced that $350,000,000 was earmarked for such rural-development projects as irrigation dams, roads and electrification schemes. The gross national product (GNP) rose by 4.5 per cent in 1968, and Bank of Greece officials optimistically predicted a growth rate of about 6 per cent in 1969. Both figures were short of the 8 per cent anticipated in the 5-year plan.

Foreign investment was a disappointment. By Aug. 31 the Government had approved investment projects valued at $125,000,000, almost one fourth of them representing American interests. But only projects valued at $30,000,-000 were actually launched. A contract with the U.S. controlled Litton International Development Corp., authorizing it to negotiate investment proposals worth $840,000,000 by 1979, was broken off by the Greek Government two years after it was signed.

CHARLES W. BELL
Reporter, Rome Bureau, United Press International

HAWAII

On Jan. 10, Haleakala National Park, on the island of Maui, acquired 4,300 more acres, gift of Laurance S. Rockefeller and the Nature Conservancy. ☐ The tenth anniversary of statehood was celebrated on Mar. 15 with the dedication of the new, $26,500,000 state capitol. Its open design reflects the island character and geography of the state. ☐ In May, Hawaii became the first state to acquire a full-time, official ombudsman (whose function is to handle the complaints of citizens).

HEINEMANN, GUSTAV

On July 1, Dr. Gustav Heinemann was sworn in as the third president of the Federal Republic of Germany. Succeeding Heinrich Lübke, a member of the Christian Democratic Union, Social Democrat Heinemann brought to the office the reputation of an outspoken man of high principles and a political maverick. He had been a prominent member of the CDU and minister of the interior in Adenauer's first Government, but had broken with Adenauer over rearmament policy and left government and party in the early 1950's to work as a corporation lawyer. In 1952 Heinemann founded the All-German People's Party which sought unsuccessfully to pursue German reunification at the price of political concessions to the Soviets. When the party broke up in 1957, he joined the SPD and, in December 1966, entered Kiesinger's grand-coalition Government as minister of justice.

Trim and fit at the age of 70—Heinemann likes to start the day with a swim in Bonn's fine public pool—he promises to be a very lively, popular and controversial occupant of the highest state office. Under the FRG's Basic Law, the president holds far less power than the chancellor. He has largely ceremonial functions. But the Germans could not have elected a more unceremonious man. Asked whether he loved the state, he replied that he loved his wife. He hates formality and stuffiness and has castigated his countrymen for their subservience to authority.

An enemy of chauvinism and a sharp critic of its manifestations in imperial, republican and nazi Germany, Heinemann said in a speech commemorating the unsuccessful rising against Hitler of July 20, 1944, that "a good German cannot be a nationalist, only a European." A prominent lay leader of the German Evangelical Church—Heinemann presided over its highest body, the Synod, for six years—his criticism did not spare the Church for its behavior under Hitler. Neither did he spare himself. Although untainted with a nazi past, the new President said, "I cannot put aside the question why I did not resist more during the Third Reich."

Heinemann's political philosophy is marked by a belief in representative democracy, the dignity of man, and continual reform. As minister of justice he undertook a large reform of the penal law. As president, he said he would never sign a law reintroducing the death penalty. But politics with him does not stop with the articulation of principles. He likes to mingle with people and debate; he wants to be a "citizens' president." This has taken him into

German Information Center

a debate with student extremists about the use of force in political opposition and amnesty for convicted rioters, after which some of his partners paid him reluctant tribute. His informality shone when he told a group of disenchanted high-school students who criticized textbooks, "If you find nonsense in your books why don't you simply tear out the pages." Needless to say, many a good German citizen has been horrified by the President's "undignified behavior."

Heinemann raised a storm of controversy when he expressed his skepticism of the German army and national security policy. He said in a newspaper interview that "every German army must be ready to have its existence called into question. Even our membership in NATO cannot be the final stage of our policy on the German problem, because it is as impossible to restore the community of our people in NATO as it is in the Warsaw Pact. We must be ready in principle to dismantle the blocs." These words drew a rebuke from Chancellor Kiesinger, and Heinemann found it politic to explain that he was no opponent of the Bundeswehr. The new Bonn Government is likely to be more receptive to his views and his preference for "a democratic order in a philosophically neutral state."

HORST MENDERSHAUSEN
Senior Staff Member, Social Science Dept.
The RAND Corporation

Swedish Information Service

A modern road swings through rural southern Sweden, one of the most motorized countries of Europe.

HIGHWAYS

Perhaps the most important highway development of 1969 was the realization that a *system* of roads is needed. A "system approach" to highway construction considers the function of roads as similar to that of great rivers. They gather together individual "streams" from various tributary points, and unite them into a strong flow that can reach a distant destination —ports, distribution centers, manufacturing

centers and the like. By the same token—and again as happened with the great waterways— roads can act as a great common denominator, mixing people and ideas into a cohesive nation or group of nations.

The Convention on Road Traffic and Road Signs, Signals and Markings—probably the greatest single step toward uniformity in highway marking—was opened for signature in 1969.

Latin America. The Pan American Highway System, which started as a road system connecting the capitals of the American republics, has evolved into a true system, including alternate international routes. The system consists of some 49,300 miles of road—of which 27,500 miles are paved or surfaced in some manner; 11,100 miles have all-weather surfaces; 2,700 miles are "dry weather" roads. Thus, less than 8,000 miles are still to be constructed or designed. With the exception of the "Darien Gap" in Panama and Colombia, the principal route of the Pan American Highway is thus already in existence. Southward from the U.S.-Mexican border, the road is paved through Mexico, El Salvador, Honduras and Nicaragua, and only a few sections remain to be paved in Guatemala, Costa Rica and Panama. Most of the route in South America either is paved or the surface has had all-weather (granular stabilized soil) treatment.

In 1969 a final study for the Darien Gap was completed. Construction is expected to require about five years, and will start when $175,000,000 in funds becomes available. The United States will probably finance two thirds of the construction costs; Panama and Colombia will contribute the remainder.

Asia. In Japan, the Tokyo-Nagoya expressway, a toll road that joins with the Nagoya-Kobe expressway, was formally opened to traffic. The entire highway is called the Tomei Expressway; it links Japan's industrial and population centers.

The Asia Highway System, which was formally organized in 1959, will be about 34,175 miles long, 20,505 miles of it international routes. Agreement has been reached concerning route and construction standards, signs and signals, and pavement markings.

Europe. A highway network that includes some 27 main arteries and 75 branch or link roads stretches from Scotland to the Turkish-Iranian frontier (where the network is to join the Asian system), and from Finland and Norway to Spain and Sicily. The length of the main international traffic arteries, including branch roads, is about 43,496 miles.

A design for Europe's longest suspension bridge—crossing the strait of Bosporus at Is-

International Road Federation

The new Mexico City-Queretaro Freeway runs straight with no demarcation, except railings, for a bridge.

tanbul—was completed during the year. Contractors were invited to bid on the actual construction.

In 1970, West Germany will launch a program to bring an autobahn within at least 31 miles of every German resident. Costing about $2,300,000,000, the plan will more than double the total mileage of the nation's autobahn system.

Africa. Roads exist in Africa solely as segments within the various nations, with little or no connection at all. There is need for both a major north-south route and an east-west route near the center of the continent. To help Africa develop a continental highway system, the International Road Federation cosponsored an African Highway Conference in Addis Ababa, Ethiopia, in October.

In 1969, highway expenditures of the 147 countries that report data to the International Road Federation (including the United States) topped $37,100,000,000, almost twice the amount spent for highways in the early 1960's. Total spending for highways outside the United States continued slightly greater than the U.S. total of about $18,200,000,000. Japan continued to spend the second highest amount for highways ($3,200,000,000); followed by West Germany ($3,100,000,000); Canada ($1,700,-000,000); Great Britain ($1,300,000,000) and Italy ($1,200,000,000). For the first time in history, U.S. motor-vehicle registration was exceeded by the total of all other noncommunist countries' registrations (more than 100,000,-000).

ROBERT O. SWAIN
President, International Road Federation

High on pillars for part of the way, the 335-mile Tomei Expressway links Japan's largest cities, Tokyo and Osaka, and has an artery west to the port of Kobe.

UPI

HOBBIES

The trend in hobbies during 1969 was toward scale-model railroading. "N"-gage, or narrow-track, model railroading has attracted well over 150,000 hobby fans and bids fair to increase its following by almost 50,000 more within the next few years.

The "N"-gage-miniature-scale railroads are small enough so that a locomotive along with its tender fits into the palm of a boy's hand. However, the age of the average railroader is about 34 years. Most of the fans are college-educated and married. Many are doctors, lawyers, engineers, and business executives. Only about 20 per cent of the railroading fans are 8 to 19 years old.

"Tiffany" lampshades made of stained glass and leading were the most popular single craft items made by the ever-increasing numbers of primarily female crafts fans. They also made thousands of costume pins, lamp bases and candleholders of stained glass.

Flowers and a myriad of other decorative items were formed by an army of hobbyists who were fascinated by the versatility of liquid plastic. Resin, the basic plastic material, lends itself to easy casting in molds and may be colored in any hue of the rainbow.

Hundreds of thousands of prints were made part of decorative motifs on furniture, trays, wastepaper containers and miscellaneous objects, transformed by the art of decoupage, as this hobbycraft climbed in popularity.

All photos Paramount International Coin Corp.

Die-cast scale-model vehicles were collected by hobby fans all over the world to the tune of about $65,000,000 in sales volume. The average enthusiast bought 15 cars during the year at an average cost of about 65 cents each. It is estimated that there are over 6,000,000 collectors of miniature cars throughout the world.

WILLIAM H. VAN PRECHT
Consultant
Hobby Industry Association

Coin Collecting

The first and foremost numismatic event of 1969 was the dedication of the new United States Mint in Philadelphia on Aug. 14, the fourth in that city since 1792. Now the world's largest and most modern mint, it stands just a few hundred feet from the site of the first United States Mint built in 1792.

The new mint facilities include the prototype of a new super coin press designed for the Government by General Motors. Still in the experimental stages, it is capable of producing 10,000 coins per minute as compared with 600 per minute with present-day coin presses. The new super presses (six are on order) will revolutionize coinage production.

As 1969 came to a close, a major coinage bill was before Congress. Endorsed by the Joint Commission on the Coinage, a bipartisan body adopted by law to advise the executive branch and Congress on silver and coinage matters, the bill would have a strong influence on coin collecting. The proposed legislation calls for the minting of a nonsilver, cupronickel half-dollar and a nonsilver, cupronickel dollar coin, and the transfer of 2,900,000 rare silver dollars now held in the Treasury to the administrator of the General Services Administration for sale to the public.

In urging Congress to pass the bill, the administration pointed out that the 40 per cent silver Kennedy half-dollar has not circulated sufficiently. Although almost 1,000,000,000 Kennedy half-dollars have been struck, there are few in circulation. The Treasury believes that if it produced a nonsilver half-dollar, the coin would circulate. In applying the same principle for a new dollar-size coin, the Treasury believes that if it contained any silver it would not circulate and would be hoarded by the public. If approved, this would be the first dollar-size coin struck by the U.S. Mint since 1935.

The biggest feature of the bill, however, is the proposed sale to the public of the 2,900,000 silver dollars being held by the Treasury. In approving a plan for the disposal of these rare coins, the Joint Commission on the Coinage recommended the following guidelines: (1) ensure a widespread opportunity for the public to obtain the coins; (2) get the maximum return on disposal for the Treasury; (3) have the Government conduct the disposal operation.

Production of 1969 proof sets was expected to set new records. Orders for the proof sets had been accepted by the San Francisco Assay Office beginning on Nov. 1, 1968, and by Nov. 6 they had received orders for more than 3,000,000 sets. The Nov. 6 cutoff date for orders was the earliest one on record. Collectors were allowed up to 20 sets per order for the 1969 sets, while a limit of 5 was placed on 1970 sets.

The obverse of the Lincoln cent underwent a face-lifting in 1969. A redesign of the master die was made, the first in the sixty years that the Lincoln cent has been produced. Details on the 1969 cent are much sharper and slightly reduced in size.

Collector interest continued to increase, and more countries introduced commemorative coins solely for collector sale. Guinea issued a series that commemorates, among other things, the 1972 Olympics in Munich (500 francs), Apollo 11 (250 francs), John F. and Robert F. Kennedy (200 francs), and Martin Luther King, Jr. (100 francs). Tunisia released a special issue of coins consisting of ten different pieces of 1 dinar value representing the ancient history of Tunisia; and Uganda issued a series of six coins to commemorate the visit of Pope Paul VI in 1969. All these coins are legal tender by government decree, but their issue is aimed directly at the U.S. coin collector.

Hundreds of different medal issues, mostly private ones, were struck to mark U.S. space achievements.

EDWARD C. ROCHETTE
Editor, *The Numismatist*

Stamp Collecting

U.S. space efforts in 1969, notably the Apollo 11 mission, not only thrilled the world but also provided the stimulus for many countries to issue stamps honoring man's first walk on the moon.

The United States took note of the feat by issuing its largest postage stamp to date—the second U.S. stamp of 1969 to honor progress in lunar exploration. Many tiny countries, with small populations and little need for a great number of stamps, came out with Apollo stamps simply for philatelic reasons. The demand for covers bearing the first-day-of-use cancellation of the U.S. stamp was so great that

FIRST MAN ON THE MOON

1/6 Gandhi Centenary Year 1969

weeks after its issuance, the Washington Post Office was still canceling covers.

Various anniversaries—the fiftieth year of the International Labor Organization, the golden jubilee of the first nonstop-transatlantic airplane flight and the centenary of the birth of Mohandas K. Gandhi—brought forth stamps from a number of countries. Great Britain presented a portrait stamp of Gandhi, making the former leader of India the first foreigner to appear on a British stamp.

Several islands under British control—including the Channel Islands of Guernsey and Jersey, and the Caribbean island of Anguilla—issued their own stamps in 1969. Biafra, which broke away from the federation of Nigeria in 1967, developed its own postage. However, since Biafra was fighting both the Nigerian Army and starvation, the new postage had limited use.

The UN postal administration arranged for its stamps to be used at the UN headquarters in Geneva, Switzerland, as well as in New York.

Almost every stamp issued in 1969 was multicolored. The U.S. Post Office Department furthered its interest in multicolored stamps by purchasing a highly efficient photogravure press to add to several intaglio multicolor presses.

The Royal Philatelic Society, London—the world's oldest organization of stamp collectors —celebrated its centennial in 1969.

DAVID LIDMAN
Stamp Editor, *The New York Times*

HONG KONG

The end of China's momentous Cultural Revolution was nowhere more welcome than in Hong Kong. Confrontation with left wingers "making revolution" along Maoist lines had provoked the worst disturbances in the colony's history in 1967. Even after the riots and bombings came to an end, the truce that ensued was uneasy. Demonstrations staged by Communists who had lost their jobs, after going on strike during the disturbances, resulted in some minor clashes with police on China's national day, Oct. 1, in 1968. The start of 1969 brought a welcome reappraisal of what China had termed "the Hong Kong problem."

Statements made by several communist spokesmen, including a leading banker, stressed the part China was playing in Hong Kong's economic prosperity and indicated that the Chinese were concerned to rebuild their valuable trade with the British colony to boost foreign-exchange earnings. With relations returning to normal, the Hong Kong government was able to dismantle the machinery set up to deal with confrontation and proceeded to release the re-

Apartment buildings, erected optimistically as if China could never be a threat to Hong Kong, make sharp contrast with the sampan homes of Chinese.

A. Devaney, Inc.

maining Communists held in detention. Emergency regulations that had empowered the authorities to detain troublemakers, for a year without trial, were suspended. In May, detainees held under this law were freed and Governor Sir David Trench announced a reduction in the sentences imposed on 13 Communists still serving jail terms. The release of the last left winger from prison in October prompted the Chinese authorities to lift the house arrest of Reuter correspondent Anthony Grey in Peking and free another five Britons from confinement in the same month.

A calmer political situation led to renewed calls for internal change. Hong Kong's colonial status, with a lack of any form of democratic representation in government, came under attack as it had done in the days before confrontation. One suggestion was that Hong Kong should drop the title "colony" and refer to itself as an "international city." In June, visiting British Minister of State Lord Shepherd was caught in the crossfire between the government and its critics. The colonial administration has long resisted demands for greater popular participation in the conduct of local affairs because it fears that this would provoke a clash between Maoist supporters and followers of Taiwan's Nationalist Party, in which Peking would feel obliged to intervene. The signs were that the government would consent to administrative change but only as a long-term process.

Economically, Hong Kong continued to make swift progress. The value of the colony's exports rose 25 per cent, the same increase as in 1968; and bank deposits were up substantially and the local stock exchange enjoyed a boom. Real-estate development, which had lapsed since a local banking crisis in 1965, proceeded at a fast pace; in November an American firm paid a record US$21,700,000 to acquire a central city site in Kowloon for hotel development. In terms of trade, sales to the United States, which takes over 40 per cent of Hong Kong's exports, showed a particularly significant rise though there was concern for the future of the colony's major textile sales following an American call for a voluntary reduction in shipments. The announcement that Britain would end quota arrangements on cotton textiles from the Commonwealth at the end of 1971 was also a blow to long-term prospects in the colony's second largest market, the United Kingdom. During 1969 a considerable breakthrough was made in sales to the European Common Market countries, notably West Germany.

DEREK DAVIES
Editor, *Far Eastern Economic Review*

HUNGARY

The Hungarians carefully cultivated their garden during 1969. Under the cautious leadership of Janos Kadar, who may not have been forgiven for his role in crushing the 1956 revolt but who has become respected for his political ability, Hungary concentrated on making its economic reforms work. To begin with, Budapest resisted, as did Rumania, pressure from Moscow to make COMECON, the East European economic group, an effective instrument of Soviet control. In fact, Hungary's official radio suggested reforming COMECON by adopting "some of the proved methods of the West European Common Market." Other recommendations urged a more liberal intra-bloc-trading policy, the abolition of quota and barter systems, and the introduction of currency convertibility, first within the bloc and later to be extended to Western currencies.

Again and again the continued need for making decentralization of the economy work was stressed by party commentators. During the second year of the New Economic Mechanism, an overall planning group organized to implement the reforms, plans were laid to reduce the workweek; to reduce subsidies to state enterprises through more efficient use of short-term credit; to broaden "free price" or market price on consumer goods; to fix annual rises of 5 to 6 per cent in national income and 2 per cent in real wages; and to establish a favorable balance of payments, last accomplished in 1961.

Throughout the year, economic problems were discussed freely. The head of the National Material and Price office urged "extensive liberalization" of foreign trade and suggested a multilateral-payments system among members of the communist bloc. There was a desire to import a smaller volume of raw materials from the Soviet Union and, also, to open up new markets in the West.

Dissatisfaction with the operation of Hungary's new profit-sharing system was evident. Under the current law, top-management officers receive up to 80 per cent of their salaries, professional and technical personnel receive up to 50 per cent, while other workers get no more than 15 per cent in profit shares. Since distribution depends on the profits of the enterprise, there is far greater disparity between workers and managers profit shares than when the state subsidized industry. Although profit sharing will continue, workers complaints about the inequities of the prevailing system may result in a reworking of the scheme.

Unlike Polish intellectuals, who must curb their tongues and dull their pens, Hungarian writers have received new concessions from the regime. Young writers have been granted an opportunity to make their views known. A conference of young writers was held in September, and the views expressed demonstrated that young Hungarian writers are restless, unsettled, nonconformist, skeptical and lack a sense of mission. Though the Government may not be able to meet the challenge of these attitudes, it was agreed that more space would be provided in literary periodicals for the new generation.

Church-state relations continued to improve. After two years of negotiations an accord was signed between Budapest and the Vatican, allowing for the investiture of new bishops and archbishops. However, the problem of Jozsef Cardinal Mindszenty remained. The Hungarian Primate, still in asylum in the U.S. Embassy in Budapest, remains in the Vatican's view the *de jure* archbishop of Esztergom. Though Austrian Cardinal Koenig again visited him in Budapest and tried to work out some arrangement between the Vatican, the Cardinal and the Hungarian authorities, nothing was settled; the Cardinal has simply refused the Pope's offer of a post at the Vatican and insists on remaining in Hungary.

JAMES CHACE
Managing Editor, *Foreign Affairs*

HUNGARY
Area: 35,902 sq. mi.
Population: 10,300,000
Capital: Budapest (pop., 1,990,000)
Government: Jenö Fock, premier—1967; Janos Kadar, Communist Party secretary—1956
Gross national product: $12,700,000,000
Monetary unit: forint (17.4 forints = U.S. $1.00)
Chief products: meats, fruits and vegetables, wine, coal, crude steel, electrical equipment
Foreign trade: exports, $1,790,000,000; imports, $1,803,000,000
Communications: 634,527 telephones, 2,478,-800 radios, 1,300,000 TV sets, 26 daily newspapers
Transportation: roads, 18,195 mi.; 116,667 passenger cars, railroads, 8,520 mi.
Education: 1,682,286 elementary and secondary students, 4 universities
Armed forces: 97,000
See map on page 185

ICELAND

Since the great "herring boom" of 1962–66, placing Iceland third among the world's nations in per capita national income (after the United States and Kuwait), catch failures and lower prices abroad have resulted in a serious economic setback. Two severe devaluations have helped little. Unemployment remains widespread. Skilled workers have been going to Scandinavia and West Germany or migrating to Australia.

A seamen's strike early in 1969 kept most of the fishing fleet in port, but the winter-fishing season ending in May still produced higher catches than for the same period in 1968. A subsequent chain of short strikes for higher wages by many trade unions and some lockouts by employers further disturbed the economy. Some forty meetings between employers and unions were required to settle the overall dispute, which was considered the most difficult to solve in the history of labor relations in Iceland. Both sides made concessions, agreeing (for one year) to: an average increase in the basic wage of 13 per cent for the lowest-paid workers and about 6½ per cent for the remainder; the introduction of state labor pensions for workers not already covered by private-pension arrangements; and an automatic increase in wages, effective Aug. 1, to parallel any rise in the cost-of-living index. Prices of various consumer goods, especially food, continued to rise throughout 1969.

Agriculture and fishing cannot absorb more manpower in the foreseeable future, and the population may reach 350,000 by the year 2000, yet the labor force is expected to grow by 34,000 by 1985. Thus the need is overriding to expand and develop Icelandic industries. With this in mind Iceland has applied for membership in the European Free Trade Association (EFTA). Some 40 per cent of Iceland's commodity trade is with Western Europe. Because Iceland's industrial production has been sheltered by high import tariffs and quantitative import restrictions, it needs a transitional period to dismantle protection. At the outset, entry of Icelandic products into the duty-free EFTA market would be of considerable help. At year's end, Iceland's prospects of joining EFTA were bright. Britain announced its intention of removing import tariffs and fixing minimum prices on frozen fish from the Nordic countries. Moreover, the Scandinavian Industrial Development Fund agreed to provide Iceland with an interest-free long-term loan of $14,000,000 to help it make necessary economic adjustments in the event of EFTA membership.

A new aluminum-reduction plant at Straumsvik, eight miles from Reykjavik, began full production on Oct. 1, an important addition to the one-sided Icelandic economy. Initial production will be 33,000 tons of aluminum per year, and the schedule calls for 75,000 tons by 1972.

In conjunction with the aluminum plant, the Icelanders built a hydroelectric power plant that is expected to produce 210,000 kw per year. The amount of electricity used by the aluminum plant equals Iceland's total electricity output before the new power plant was built.

SIGURDUR A. MAGNUSSON
Editor, *Samvinnan*

IDAHO

As one of the lumbering states, Idaho was affected by the sharp drop in lumber prices between March and June. The resulting huge stockpile of plywood was considered a possible spur to housing construction. □ Boise and its surrounding area moved toward merging some of their activities during the year. Under a new reform law, the city and Ada County united their courts in a single district system.

ILLINOIS

A Federal grand jury indicted eight persons, on Mar. 20, on the charge that they conspired to incite a riot during the Democratic national convention in Chicago, August 1968. □ On Apr. 3, the eve of the first anniversary of the assassination of Martin Luther King, Jr., violence broke out in Chicago. Gov. Richard B. Ogilvie mobilized National Guard troops. □ On June 22, in Cairo, already torn by racial conflict, trouble broke out anew as the Rev. Jesse L. Jackson, of the Southern Christian Leadership Conference, arrived to lead a rally and march in protest against local law-enforcement and employment practices. □ Everett McKinley Dirksen, the state's senior U.S. senator, died on Sept. 7. On Sept. 17, Governor Ogilvie appointed Ralph T. Smith (R) to the vacant seat.

ICELAND

Area: 39,758 sq. mi.
Population: 200,000
Capital: Reykjavik (pop., 92,000)
Government: Kristjan Eldjarn, president—1968; Bjarni Benediktsson, prime minister—1963
Gross National Product: $500,000,000
Monetary unit: krona (88 kronur = U.S. $1.00)
Chief products: hay, potatoes, fish and fish products
Foreign trade: exports, $80,000,000; imports, $134,000,000
Communications: 62,698 telephones, 50,000 radios, 27,000 TV sets, 5 daily newspapers
Transportation: roads, about 7,000 mi.; 35,991 passenger cars; no railroads
Education: 14,730 elementary and secondary students, 1 university

See map on page 185

Raghubir Singh from Nancy Palmer

With a picture of her famous father in the background, Prime Minister Indira Gandhi confers with supporters before challenging the once all-powerful organizational leaders—the Syndicate—of the Congress Party.

INDIA

In 1969 the economic recovery begun in 1968 continued. But so did the shaky political situation that began after the Congress Party defeats in the 1967 general elections. Indian foreign policy continued to move toward more intimate cooperation with the U.S.S.R. while relations with the West continued to deteriorate. The greatest change in 1969 was the dramatic split in the Congress Party, with Prime Minister Indira Gandhi risking her future by challenging the organizational leaders of the Congress Party, who had things very much their own way for many years.

Throughout the year, politics took center stage. In January former Congress President Kamaraj, no friend of Mrs. Gandhi, won a seat in Parliament in a by-election in his native state of Madras (renamed Tamil Nadu, "land of the Tamils"). From Feb. 5 to 9, there was a "minigeneral" election in the states of Bihar, Punjab, Nagaland, Uttar Pradesh and West Bengal. They resulted in astounding defeats for the Congress Party, so great as to surprise almost all observers. A 12-party United Front, led by the Left Communist Party of India, swept 210 of 280 seats in West Bengal's provincial legislature. In the Punjab, the Akali Dal, in coalition with the Jan Sangh, formed the government. In Bihar, the Congress won only 118 of 317 seats; and in Uttar Pradesh the

Congress also fell short of a majority even though it improved its position slightly. In Nagaland, the nonseparatist parties won a majority. These elections were widely seen as confirmation of the 1967 trends: the erosion of confidence in the Congress, party flabbiness at the polls, the fragmentation of the Indian parties.

From then on, the crisis deepened. In the spring the Congress Cabinet faced great difficulty in getting its proposal for a "state within a state" for the hill people of Assam ratified in

INDIA

Area: 1,258,983 sq. mi.
Population: 536,900,000
Capital: New Delhi (pop., 319,000)
Government: V. V. Giri, president—1969; Indira Gandhi, prime minister—1966
Gross national product: $40,500,000,000
Monetary unit: rupee (7.5 rupees = U.S. $1.00)
Chief products: tea, groundnuts, rice, jute, raw sugar, cotton, textiles, coal, bauxite
Foreign trade: exports, $1,754,000,000; imports, $2,510,000,000
Communications: 993,590 telephones, 8,500 TV sets, 601 daily and bi-weekly newspapers
Transportation: roads, 492,996 mi.; 377,533 passenger cars; railroads, 57,923 mi.
Education: 57,842,940 elementary and secondary students, 1,280,404 students of higher education
Armed forces: 925,000

Raghubir Singh from Nancy Palmer

Farmers from the state of Haryana shout their approval of Mrs. Gandhi's plan to nationalize the Indian banks. The plan was announced on July 19.

The Congress Party leadership threatened to withdraw their support of the Gandhi Government; Mrs. Gandhi threatened in turn to break their hold on the decision-making organ of the party, the All-India Congress Committee (AICC) Working Committee.

The stage was set for conflict at the AICC meetings, July 9 to 13. Indira Gandhi presented a statement calling for the social control of private banking, a resolution that the Working Committee adopted without enthusiasm. Mrs. Gandhi's suggestion that half of the working committee be elected and only half be nominated by the president of the Congress Party was approved but earned her the ill will of the organizational wing, the Syndicate. At every stage, Mrs. Gandhi found the Syndicate working against her; they found her attempting to capture party control. By mid-July it was clear that the Syndicate meant to force the Congress Party parliamentary members to remove her as prime minister. On July 16 she stunned the country by taking the finance portfolio from Morarji Desai, a leading member of the Syndicate faction. The resulting tumult forced the Government of India to suspend trading in bank stocks on the stock exchange, and on July 19 Prime Minister Gandhi announced the nationalization of the banks.

Having "wrapped herself in socialist glory," she then set out to undo the Syndicate's power in the party. By October, both sides were so steeled that reconciliation was impossible; and in November the Syndicate, claiming the party label, withdrew from the Prime Minister's party to become an opposition group of about 65 in Parliament. At year's end it was impossible to say how secure the Prime Minister's position in Parliament was, though the struggle had further divided and weakened the Congress Party throughout India.

The economy, on the other hand, was growing more strong. National income for the period rose more than 3 per cent with industry growing at 5 to 6 per cent and agriculture continuing to support the view that the "green revolution" had come to rural India. Record exports of about $1,620,000,000 were reported for the first ten months of the year. The record represented many new markets, the result of the continued closure of the Suez Canal.

The economy also experienced some firsts. In the last week of 1968 the first MiG-21 engine, built on Soviet license, was produced in India, at Koraput. In February the second of three nuclear reactors went into operation in the Tarapore nuclear-power plant. Coupled with the announcement in May of a French-Indian nuclear agreement, these developments

Parliament. The so-called "Naxalite" faction, a group of revolutionary militants, of the Communist Party of India, continued to gain headlines for their activities in Kerala and elsewhere in India. Amid general public skepticism, the fourth Five Year Plan made its tardy debut in April. It called for what large groups in the public considered wholly inadequate annual investment goals of $3,500,000,000.

On May 3 the President of India, Zakir Husain, died. At once a struggle began between the factions of the Prime Minister and the Congress Party organizers as to who should succeed him. In the bitter contest the Prime Minister worked against the official candidate of the Congress. V. V. Giri, the Prime Minister's choice, was narrowly elected president of India.

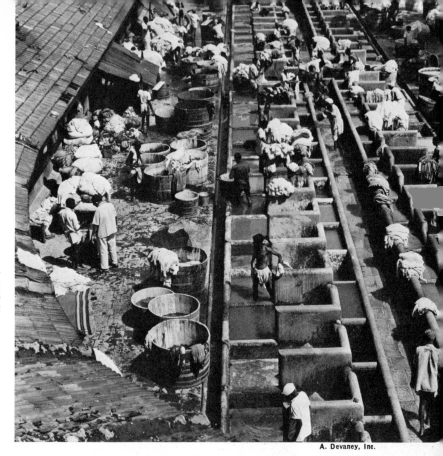

The "dhobi ghats"—an outdoor public laundry—in Bombay is nearly always busy. Indian men, especially the poor, wear white clothing at all times.

A. Devaney, Inc.

underlined India's priority development of sophisticated weapons and nuclear technology.

The Soviet Union, despite arms shipments to Pakistan, continued to play a key role in India's diplomacy. In February the Prime Minister moved Commerce Minister Dinesh Singh, generally reputed to be pro-Soviet, into the Foreign Ministry. In March, when trouble between China and Russia was entering the crisis stage, Soviet Defense Minister Marshal Grechko came to India on a state visit. The Indian Government supported the Soviet position on the Ussuri River clash, and continued to support the Arab states and Soviet positions on the "west Asian crisis." When bilateral U.S.-Indian talks were held in Washington in October, there was widespread concern that India would recognize the National Liberation Front of Vietnam, thereby exacerbating strained relations with the United States further.

On balance, 1969 was one of the most dramatic political years since independence, though the implications of the shattering of the Congress Party cannot yet be fully weighed. The steady, impressive growth of the economy, both quantitatively and qualitatively, is still threatened by the very high rate of population growth and the turbulence associated with great changes in the pattern of agriculture. India continues to find Soviet assistance and arms an important aspect of its development and diplomacy, and relations with Moscow steadily improve. At the same time, India maintains correct—sometimes good and other times strained —relations with Washington. As long as Mrs. Gandhi remains prime minister, these trends seem likely to continue.

WAYNE WILCOX
Professor of Government; Chairman, Department of Political Science, Columbia University

INDIANA

In Indianapolis on Mar. 7, some 30,000 public-school teachers were absent in a one-day boycott protesting what they called "inadequate" state funds for education. □ A Federal court ruled, on July 28, that the state's legislative districts were unconstitutional because of discrimination against urban racial minorities. □ In Gary, in August, Mayor Richard G. Hatcher took a strong stand against the city's striking firemen, who were demanding a $2,000 yearly increase in pay. They were accused of turning back fire equipment while a lumberyard went up in flames. The 275 firemen who walked off their jobs on Aug. 5 were suspended. Others returned to work late on Aug. 10.

INDIANS, AMERICAN

In 1969 many of the United States' 600,000 American Indians were engaged in the same struggles as their ancestors over a century ago: struggles to hold on to their land and to their rights as Indian Americans.

Throughout the late 1800's, as tribe after tribe was defeated by the U.S. Army, the Indians were banished to reservations and made to sign treaties with the Government in which they ceded much of their land in return for promises of money and security. When the treaties ceased to accommodate the white man, he brought his armies back and made new ones.

Unfortunately, Indian property rights are still being violated. One battle, which began more than sixty years ago for the Taos Pueblo (community) of New Mexico, is still being fought in Congress. Today the Taos people are struggling to win back the land that was taken from them in 1906, without consultation or compensation, and incorporated into Carson National Forest. Included in the acreage taken at that time was Blue Lake and the area surrounding it. The lake is the central shrine of

A wall is lettered after a group of Indians invades Alcatraz Island (San Francisco Bay), proposing that the former prison be used for an Indian cultural center.

UPI

the Taos religion, to which the Taos people travel each summer. Their journey to the lake symbolizes their return to the source of their life and spirit.

To regain the land would require an act of Congress, directing that no money need be paid to the Taos Pueblo and that title to the 48,000 acres in the vicinity of Blue Lake be restored to the tribe. A bill to that effect has passed twice the U.S. House of Representatives but has always been tabled in the Senate. Though this happened again in 1969, the Taos people are persisting in their demands.

Another instance of present-day violation of Indian property rights is a controversial water compact that poses a serious threat to the economic welfare of the Pyramid Lake Paiute tribe of Nevada. Designed to allocate the waters of the Truckee, Carson and Walker rivers and of Lake Tahoe to the states of California and Nevada, the compact would drain and destroy beautiful Pyramid Lake, the Indians' sole economic asset. The Paiutes retained legal rights to the lake under an 1859 treaty with the United States. They earn a meager living from trout fishing in the lake waters and from the sale of about $15,000 worth of sport-fishing permits each year. The compact would not only deprive the Indians of their water rights and harm their fishing grounds but would also bar them from possible new income to come from development of parts of the lake as a recreational area.

The compact was approved by the Nevada legislature and the California state senate but was held up in the California assembly. Whatever the outcome of the case, it has implications for Indian tribes throughout the western United States. The question is whether the U.S. Department of the Interior, which is the arm of the Federal Government charged with responsibility for protecting Indian land and water rights, will support the Indians, or whether their water claims will be subordinated to the regulatory powers of the states.

In 1969 the problems of Indian education were continually in the national spotlight as educators, government officials, psychiatrists, political scientists, and Indians themselves presented their views during countless hours of hearings before the Senate Subcommittee on Indian Education. Chaired by the late Sen. Robert F. Kennedy when it was formed in 1967, and later by his brother, Sen. Edward M. Kennedy, the subcommittee's task was to discover the "whys" behind the sorry state of Indian education: Why are dropout rates for Indians twice the national average? Why do most Indians average only five years of schooling?

Paul Conklin

At Many Farms, Ariz., in the Navajo Community College, an intensive course in basic English is given for Navajo matrons who previously spoke no English. Class meets every weekday morning and is attended faithfully.

Why do only 18 per cent of the students in Federal Indian schools today go on to college? Why are no books on Indian history and culture included in most Indian-school libraries? Why are Indian and Eskimo students sent all the way from Alaska and Oregon to Federal boarding schools in Oklahoma?

From the beginning, the U.S. policy for educating Indian children was to take them away from their "blanket Indian" parents and place them in faraway boarding or mission schools. It was hoped that if they were cut off from their Indian culture and background, they would more readily enter white society. In most cases this did not happen, however. As a rule, the students did not become more "white"; they merely became less Indian.

In April 1969, a Bureau of Indian Affairs report on conditions at the Chilocco Indian School in Chilocco, Okla., was released. Charging "criminal malpractice" and "physical and mental perversion" by Chilocco staff members, the report cited cases of students being handcuffed in their dormitories, jailed, or subjected to physical abuse in the counseling room.

Although the brutality charges received most of the publicity, the report was in essence a thorough study of other conditions at Chilocco which are more universal in Indian schools and, in the long run, have greater impact on the academic development of Indian children. Such conditions include limited school health services, inadequate psychological counseling and testing, and little student and community involvement in school affairs.

In November 1969, the Senate subcommittee issued a final 200-page report, *Indian Education: A National Tragedy—A National Challenge*. It labeled programs for educating American Indian children "a failure of major proportions" and "a stain on our national conscience." With 60 recommendations for improving conditions in Indian schools, the report called for the establishment of a White House Conference on American Indian Affairs to be planned and run by Indians themselves, a Senate Select Committee on Indian Needs, and a National Indian Board of Indian Education.

If many of the age-old Indian problems still remained in 1969, there was also a glimmer of hope. Indians young and old are beginning to demand a greater voice in their own destinies. Someday, perhaps, enough people will listen.

JOHN BELINDO
Executive Director
National Congress of American Indians

INDONESIA

When Indonesia President Suharto addressed his nation on its 24th Independence Day in 1969, he spoke bluntly and to the point. The country had come a long way since the unsuccessful communist attempt at a coup in October 1965, Suharto declared. The hyperinflation inherited from former President Sukarno's regime had been checked. Foreign-investor confidence in the country was being steadily restored. Creditor nations were showing a willingness to cooperate on Indonesia's need for time to repay its obligations. But, Suharto warned, all of that represented merely a first step. Much hard work lay ahead, he said, if the country were truly to lift itself from the economic morass of the past.

To Indonesia's and Suharto's credit, 1969 was indeed a year of hard work, but it did result in further progress.

The highlight was the launching on Apr. 1 of a Five-Year Development Plan which will cost an estimated US$3,500,000,000. Other targets included self-sufficiency in rice by 1973 (currently some 600,000 tons must be imported annually to make up the domestic shortage). Indonesia remains basically an agrarian nation; thus the development plan stresses agricultural development as a prelude to large-scale industrialization. Minerals—particularly petroleum, tin, bauxite, copper and nickel—also were stressed and given priority. With some US$90,-000,000 already invested in the oil industry, and prospects of new discoveries exceedingly bright, the Government hopes for total foreign investment in oil of US$280,000,000 by 1974.

Another focus of attention was trade. Clearly Indonesia hopes to improve its export position and thus improve its foreign-exchange position. As 1969 ended, it looked as if exports would reach or even pass the US$900,000,000 mark, up substantially from 1968. Even greater performance, however, is needed to help the country begin meeting its foreign debts of more than US$3,000,000,000.

In the view of most economists the Five-Year Plan was realistic. Yet, to a large degree it still depends on heavy transfusions of foreign aid, including some US$500,000,000 in 1969, as well as on foreign investment. The investment picture fortunately remained bright. By the end of 1969, total investment (encouraged by the adoption of an attractive foreign-investment law in 1967) had reached US$750,000,000. The United States was the largest single investing nation, followed by Japan.

Of equal importance with economic gains, however, was the attitude of the Government toward such serious problems as corruption and an overweight bureaucracy. On May 20,

Indonesian Army Brig. Gen. Sudharman went on trial charged with corruption. The General had been the director of a state-owned tin company. It was the first time any high-ranking official had been arrested and tried on charges of corruption since the Government launched an anticorruption drive in 1967. However, few others of any stature were brought to trial. The Suharto Government did resist pressures to swell further the ranks of the crowded civil service.

Moreover, it took measures against a number of banking institutions that had failed to maintain the necessary reserves to guarantee deposits. On Sept. 27 the Government announced the suspension of four Indonesian banks. Later, still others were suspended, and eventually several were closed. In early November the Central Bank of Indonesia shored up the private banks by setting up a special revolving fund from which the small banks could draw. The bank suspensions and the tightening of regulations impressed foreign investors with the seriousness of the Suharto regime's efforts to put Indonesia's house in order.

Many other problems, nonetheless, remained, especially for the would-be foreign investor who is so important to Indonesia's economic development. Trying to cut through Indonesian red tape or reach the right officials is still a nightmare. Taxation is arbitrary and exceptionally high. The process of incorporation is lengthy and costly. The redeeming factor is that Suharto and his associates have pledged themselves to rectify the problems.

During 1969 Suharto moved to streamline the armed-forces command and bring the military under more direct central control. On Oct. 12 he announced a military reorganization that

---

INDONESIA

Area: 576,000 sq. mi.
Population: 115,400,000
Capital: Jakarta (pop., 3,000,000)
Government: Suharto, president—1968
Gross National Product: $9,100,000,000
Monetary unit: new rupiah (350 new rupiahs = U.S. $1.00)
Chief products: rubber, tobacco, coffee, tea, spices, petroleum, tin
Foreign trade: exports, $658,000,000; imports, $649,000,000
Communications: 169,142 telephones, 785,010 radios, 17,265 TV sets, 90 daily newspapers
Transportation: roads, 50,220 mi.; 92,463 passenger cars; railroads, 4,117 mi.
Education: 9,283,737 elementary and secondary students, 41,000 university students
Armed forces: 365,000

See map on page 481

Rapho Guillumette Pictures

Though Indonesia is rich in oil, pedicabs remain a necessity for passenger transportation—here, in Jakarta.

in essence adopts the U.S. joint-chiefs-of-staff system, reduced the regional commands from 30 to 6, and created independent army, airforce and naval commands. On Nov. 10, 53-year-old Gen. Panggabean, who has worked closely with Suharto in recent years, was appointed deputy supreme commander of the armed forces directly under Suharto. Gen. Panggabean clearly would be handling the day-to-day running of the military and was the likely successor to Suharto as defense minister. Military reorganization was badly needed and could lead to the elimination of some corrupt practices in the armed forces. Earlier in the year, on Apr. 8, Brig. Gen. Sugandhi, director of the Armed Forces Information Services, announced plans to create a militia in which every Indonesian reaching a certain age would undergo one-year military training and two years of military "education."

Politically the year was dominated by two issues: the so-called "act of free choice" in West Irian (the western half of New Guinea) to decide whether this area would be officially incorporated into Indonesia; and the question of whether elections would be held by July 1971, as ordered by the Indonesian Parliament.

The West Irian "voting" (by representatives of eight consultative assemblies) took place from July 14 through Aug. 2. All eight assemblies voted to join the Indonesian Republic. On Sept. 17, President Suharto officially inaugurated West Irian as an Indonesian province. In November the United Nations, under whose observation the "act of free choice" was conducted, put its stamp of approval on Indonesia's control of the area.

The West Irian matter was child's play compared with the difficulty the Suharto Government met on the question of elections. Many prominent military officers (who hold key political positions) oppose the alliance, between the military and political parties, that would be necessary for an election. The officers regard the political parties as squabbling private-interest groups more concerned with seeking patronage than with national aims. On their part, the parties want a return to democratic rule, and fear the growing power of the military. Decision rested with the Indonesian Parliament, which passed an election bill in November so that elections could be held on schedule.

In other domestic political matters, the Government began sending large numbers of the more than 80,000 communist or procommunist political prisoners in the country to the remote island of Buru for resettlement. The first 2,500 of an estimated 10,000 who will be sent to the island left by steamer on Oct. 2. The Government also announced that in the near future it intended to release 26,000 persons who, though not hard-core Communists, are suspected of having worked with them.

In international affairs, President Richard Nixon made a brief visit to Jakarta on July 27-28 following the successful Apollo 11 mission. Nixon assured Suharto that the United States would respect Indonesia's nonalignment policy and would continue to provide economic aid.

EDWARD NEILAN
China and Southeast Asia Correspondent
Copley News Service

Airco Reduction Co., Inc.

Plastic bottles—shatter resistant, more protective and lighter than glass—are being used for olive oil.

INDUSTRY

When astronauts Armstrong and Aldrin made man's first footprints on the moon, it was as much of an accomplishment for U.S. industry as for the space program. For without the composite materials, rocket engines, life-support systems, computers and communication network developed by industry, man could not have traveled to the moon and back.

While the aerospace industry helped man explore the moon, the petroleum industry in 1969 began development of new oil fields in Alaska that will rival those of the Middle East. An ice-breaking tanker, the SS *Manhattan,* was dispatched through the Northwest Passage to prove that the oil can be brought to market.

The electronics industry found additional uses for computers; the textile industry marketed close-knit fibers for indoor-outdoor carpets; and the electrical industry planned more and bigger nuclear-power plants.

Although new industrial products made life easier, they also brought new problems. For example, the use of unbreakable, plastic polyvinyl chloride (PVC) bottles became more widespread for cosmetics, liquor and, in Europe, beer. But when, after use, these bottles are disposed of and incinerated, hydrochloric acid is released to the atmosphere. As a result, PVC bottles have been banned in Sweden and some other areas. Plastic-industry scientists are hard at work to find a PVC additive to absorb the chloride.

Pollution control was one of industry's major problems. In order to meet the new standards, industry will have to spend some $2,600,000,-000 to $4,600,000,000 between 1969 and 1973 for industrial-waste-treatment plants. In 1969 the major U.S. steel companies alone authorized expenditures of more than $329,-000,000 for air and water quality-improvement projects.

Total expenditures for capital and equipment by U.S. industry in 1969 were up some 10 per cent over 1968 and exceeded $70,000,000,000. These capital expenditures slowed down in the final months when production lagged.

With inflation boosting wages to new highs, industry bought a lot of equipment as a substitute for labor. Despite this, profits margins of U.S. private industrial companies declined. Partially this was because companies were maintaining too large a labor force.

Building. The population explosion and rush to metropolitan areas have created a worldwide housing shortage. Combined with inflation, housing was a critical problem for most families in 1969.

In Eastern Europe the waiting period for an apartment is over 5 years. In the United States, the average cost of a new house has increased 28 per cent within 3 years to about $26,000 in 1969. The inventory of completed new homes for sale reached the lowest point in 10 years.

To meet the demand for housing, industry has urgently sought new technology and new materials. But in many areas, these new approaches have been hindered by antiquated building codes and construction methods. (See article on cities.)

Although tight money reduced the rate of new housing starts from 1,878,000 per year in January to a rate of 1,336,000 at the end of the year, the number of cluster, mobile and modular homes increased sharply. The cluster town houses are usually joined together and thus save on building and land costs.

Factory-built mobile homes, per square foot, cost about half as much as a conventional house. In the United States, 220 companies were producing mobile homes in 1969. They shipped over 350,000 units, a 22 per cent increase over 1968.

Modular homes are factory-built sections, complete with plumbing, wiring and appliances. The sections are transported to the site and fastened together to produce the desired size of house.

The use of PVC piping, siding and bricks, as well as glass-fiber reinforced-plastic bathrooms, helped boost the use of plastics in building by nearly 10 per cent. At the same time, new plastic adhesives helped bring about the increase in modular construction.

Chemicals and Plastics. The year 1969 was a good one for the chemical industry in terms of sales, but a poor one for profits. While most other industries have been able to protect profits by increasing prices, competitive pressures from larger and larger production plants made this impossible for the chemical companies. As a result, increased costs of capital and labor have had to come out of profits.

The profit squeeze has led to much realignment within the industry. Large companies have acquired small ones, and chemical companies have integrated vertically with petroleum raw-material suppliers or makers of consumer products. Chemical concerns have also combined in joint ventures to produce a particular product. Many have crossed borders to obtain marketing or technical know-how. A typical example in 1969 was the purchase of Wyandotte Chemicals Corp. of the United States by West Germany's Badische Anilin & Soda Fabrik (BASF). (See feature article Conglomerates.)

Petrochemical centers have mushroomed in many parts of the world. Every oil-producing area from Venezuela to Iran has been building petrochemical plants as a means of obtaining more income from local oil. As a result, U.S. chemical exports in 1969 did not attain the 17 per cent increase achieved during 1968.

Total U.S. chemical shipments were up some 7 per cent to $49,500,000,000. The increase in sales was not so large as in previous years and was a reflection of the slight slowdown in the economy.

Plastics enjoyed a particularly good year. Demand remained strong. Not many new plants were built; as a result, prices were firm. The growing use of urethane bumpers and polyethylene gas tanks increased the amount of plastics in cars by some 15 per cent, to almost 100 pounds for the average 1970 model. Plastic refuse bags are being adopted widely and will be required as garbage-can liners in some cities in 1970.

Food and Beverage. In some high-output countries, food surpluses have become a problem. For example, the major wheat-exporting countries now have stock only slightly below the all-time peak. Wheat stocks at the end of 1969 were some 56,000,000 metric tons, compared with 37,000,000 tons in 1968. In Japan, large rice stocks now constitute a major prob-

Midvale-Heppenstall Co.

The huge grid will serve as the lower support for the core section of a nuclear reactor, for producing electric power. The grid was forged from a stainless-steel ingot 82 feet in diameter and weighing 271,000 pounds, said to be the largest ingot ever cast.

lem, and in the Soviet Union large stocks of butter have accumulated for the first time.

In the United States the increasing number of working wives and mothers has led to an emphasis on foods that can be easily prepared and readily served. This has affected the types of meat cuts that are most popular and the need for convenient packaged foods. The rise in personal income has also increased home entertaining and the demand for snack-type and specialty food. The increased use of diet foods boosted the use of artificial sweeteners in the United States to 21,000,000 pounds in 1969, an 8,400 per cent increase in 14 years. (See article on medicine and health.)

One victim of inflation in 1969 was the restaurant. After steady increases for many years, U.S. restaurant sales leveled off. Apparently consumers reacted to the high menu prices. Overall, the U.S. food industry was expected to complete 1969 with an increase in sales, to $107,000,000,000.

Iron and Steel. The dire predictions of overcapacity and depressed prices turned out to be completely wrong, making 1969 a pleasant surprise to steelmakers. The demand for steel by the construction, automotive, machinery and container industries far exceeded steelmakers' expectations. Worldwide steel production set a new record. Output soared to an estimated 565,000,000 metric tons. The demand in Western Europe and Japan paced the rest of the world.

For the U.S. steel industry, 1969's increase in exports (from 2,200,000 tons in 1968 to some 4,000,000 tons) and decrease in steel imports (from 18,000,000 tons to about 14,000,-000 tons) was an unexpected turnabout. Total U.S. steel output despite a slowdown in the fourth quarter, exceeded the 131,500,000 tons produced in 1968. Although steel production was up, profits were down. This was due to increased labor costs and capital expenditures. In 1969, for the first time, basic oxygen-furnace and electric-furnace steel output exceeded open-hearth production in the United States.

Machinery. Steady demand for consumer goods and the need to keep down production costs helped maintain a strong worldwide market for industrial machinery. The growth was particularly dynamic in Japan. In Europe and North America there was some slowing down during the last months of the year.

In the United States, industrial production in 1969 climbed steadily until August and then dipped slightly. Despite the slowdown, industry spent far more for plant and equipment in 1969 than in 1968. Nevertheless, the spending was at a declining rate. In February a Department of Commerce survey estimated that capital expenditures for 1969 would be up 14 per cent. By August, businessmen had scaled their plans down to 10.6 per cent.

Shipments of U.S. machine tools—the basic tools needed to produce thousands of metal products—declined some 10 per cent during 1969. Although total shipments were down, new orders were up, particularly for numerically controlled tools.

The machine-tool industry is looking forward to a resurgence of business as a result of new products to be introduced at the National Machine Tool Show in Chicago in September 1970.

Nonferrous Metals. Spurred by the high level of economic activity in all the industrialized countries and by the war in Vietnam, the nonferrous-metal industries enjoyed an excellent year in 1969.

Worldwide consumption of aluminum was up over 8 per cent with increased tonnage being used by the building, transportation, electrical-equipment and packaging industries. The growing popularity of pull-tab, easy-opening cans, the use of formed-foil frozen-food packages, and the growth of containerized shipping helped boost packaging applications some 10 per cent.

U.S. aluminum production, which had lagged in 1968 because of a strike, was expected to show an increase of at least 15 per cent, to over 3,750,000 tons. Had it not been for the slowdown in the construction industry, the increase would have been even greater.

During 1969 the copper industry still suffered from the 8½-month-long strike that was settled in March 1968. Some of the users, who had turned to alternative materials—primarily aluminum—during the long strike, did not return to copper. As a result, U.S. copper production in 1969 was below the pre-strike level. The disparity between the higher world copper price and the lower U.S. price was accentuated during 1969, as a result of the nationalization of copper mines in Chile and Zambia.

Zinc production in the United States during 1969 was slightly higher than the 1,333,699 tons of 1968. The main increase was in die castings. Other important zinc-consuming areas include galvanizing and brass products.

Nickel will be in short supply throughout 1970 as a result of a strike that idled the Canadian nickel industry for over four months. Due to the increasing use of stainless steel, the demand for nickel will continue at a high level.

STEPHEN W. KANN
Editor and Publisher, *Industrial World*

"U.S. News & World Report"

As unsettled auto-insurance claims continue to pile up, a new, faster system of payment has been proposed.

INSURANCE, AUTOMOBILE

Over the past decade the price of insuring an automobile has climbed sharply. At the same time, companies that do over $8,500,000,000 worth of insurance business are much more choosy than they once were about customers. As a consequence, people are finding it increasingly difficult to buy new policies, and in some instances they can't retain policies already in force. For its part, the industry says it is in a bind, caught in a squeeze between rising costs and growing numbers of reckless drivers who smash up cars. In addition, the companies say, juries are awarding larger claims in damage suits than before, and this drives the prices still higher.

What happens to people who can't buy auto insurance? Some go ahead and drive without any insurance. But generally they fall into the hands of the so-called high-risk insurance companies which specialize in insuring people with bad accident records. The high-risk companies charge usurious rates and often collapse. When Sen. Thomas Dodd investigated the activities of the high-risk firms, he found that between 1960 and 1965, 65 of these companies had collapsed, leaving 300,000 people, many of them badly injured in car accidents, with $100,000,000 in unpaid claims.

As a result of the squeeze on drivers, there is a widespread demand for a reform of the industry, and investigations of the auto-insur-

ance business are being conducted by the Congress and the administration. Sen. Philip Hart's Antitrust and Monopoly Subcommittee has brought out information that suggests the companies are not losing money, as they claim, but actually showing a profit. This is because of unusual accounting practices employed by insurance companies. In short, Hart is saying that the accounting method amounts to a sleight-of-hand maneuver calculated to distort the financial picture. In hearings in 1968, Hart introduced figures showing that in 1967 the 10 largest stock property and casualty companies reported an underwriting loss of $273,000,000. Yet when the accounting method was changed to the type generally accepted by corporations, the loss turned into a profit of $55,000,000. Neither of the figures included net income from investment by the 10. This came to $1,700,000,000. (Auto-insurance companies usually invest the premiums they collect from motorists, and the income from these investments is enormous and amounts to a major part of their business. In fact, some critics have likened these insurance companies to new types of investment banks, claiming that the investing part of the business is more important from the firms' point of view than the handling of the auto-insurance operation.)

The auto-insurance companies openly admit they are searching for the so-called preferred-risk drivers, and inquiries by the Hart subcommittee indicate the industry goes to great lengths to find them. For instance, Fred Jasper, president of Jasper Reports, Inc., a Chicago-based company that makes a business of supplying the large insurance companies with reports on prospective policyholders, told Hart how he put out a booklet on "environmental conditions" in the Chicago area. The book informed the insurance companies on various ethnic areas—Polish, Jewish, hillbilly and Negro—and advised them about the risks involved in insuring the different groups. Of the Mexicans, Jasper Reports said, "These Mexicans are for the most part well behaved, but a few do drink to excess, and many of them are illiterate, and many cannot speak English. These Mexicans should be inspected carefully for auto insurance."

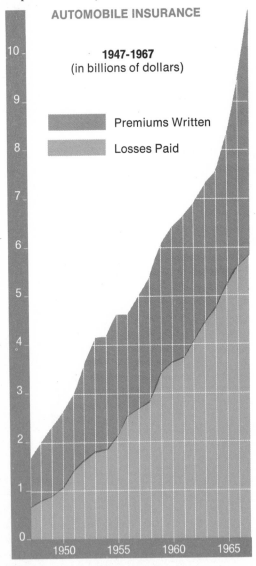

AUTOMOBILE INSURANCE

1947-1967
(in billions of dollars)

Premiums Written

Losses Paid

The big insurance companies publish their own manuals to help agents decide whether to insure a person. Hart inserted excerpts from one company's manual into the hearing record. The company warned its agents to be on the lookout for such "bad risks" as merchant seamen, oil-field employees, farm workers, waiters, janitors, painters, bellhops, unemployed persons and taxicab drivers. The manual says, "The divorced or separated male is, in our opinion, more undesirable than the man who has never married. The same is true in comparing the divorcée and the unmarried female." The manual warns the agents to shy clear of the "exhibitionist who overdecorates his car with foxtails, fender fins, mud flaps, boxing gloves, baby shoes, spotlights and other ornaments. He is not very likely to be a very conservative or considerate driver."

While people are finding it increasingly difficult to buy auto insurance because of the sort of job they hold, their marital status, looks, and other matters, the Congress also receives complaints from heretofore reliable drivers, insured for years by some company, who suddenly find their policies canceled. A man in South Carolina had his policy canceled because, according to the insurance company, his wife got a parking ticket one day. A Virginia resident, who asked to have his car towed out of a snowdrift under a clause in his insurance policy, had his policy canceled because of "loss history." Veterans complain of having great difficulty in buying auto insurance.

This sort of thing infuriates members of Congress, and there is widespread demand by both Democrats and Republicans for some sort of reform of industry policies. At the request of the powerful Senate Commerce Committee, the Department of Transportation is studying the whole automobile-insurance system, and its report, expected in 1970, may well lead to legislation. In addition, Hart's subcommittee continues to pepper the industry. The insurance companies themselves apparently are gradually moving to an acceptance of government regulation. The companies of the American Insurance Association, which write 35 per cent of the business, are not opposed to Federal regulation in principle, and they are for changing around the business to make it more efficient and fairer. One proposal made by both the industry and its critics is to institute a system whereby an accident victim can get his insurance quickly by sending a form to his company. Auto insurance then could be handled in much the same manner as health insurance.

JAMES RIDGEWAY
Contributing Editor, *The New Republic*

INTELLIGENCE, MILITARY

Push-button military reconnaissance carries with it the same perils that plagued the old cloak-and-dagger espionage agent. When the culprit is caught, he is either exterminated or made to pay a heavy indemnity.

In recent years the United States and the Soviet Union have held each other at bay in the cold war by electronically snooping on each other's aircraft activity, shipping, troop movements and military installations. Some of this "eavesdropping" is done through strategically located unmanned listening posts in areas within antenna reach of potential combat zones. These well-camouflaged installations are believed to pull in even weak electronic signals from hundreds of miles around.

Additionally, "spy" satellites have proved to be highly efficient in gathering both photographic and electronic intelligence. Modern photography has made it possible for satellites —sweeping over tens of thousands of miles of airspace—to capture on film exact details of military developments. These space-age detectors are also equipped to pick up valuable data on the production of nuclear materials and the deployment of nuclear weapons.

To back up these intelligence gatherers and fill in information gaps, the two big powers have developed reconnaissance ships and planes to peek at the military operations of potential enemies. These craft also carry electronic packages designed for sophisticated snooping.

The United States and the Soviet Union are aware of each other's ELINT (electronic intelligence) capabilities. Both nations take pains to keep their "spy" craft well out in international waters and over "open" airspace while on sleuthing missions. The Soviets and most communist nations claim that their sovereignty extends 12 miles out from their mainland and offshore islands. The United States officially recognizes only 3-mile territorial sea rights, but its reconnaissance craft are ordered to abide by 12-mile limits when surveilling the coasts of iron-curtain countries.

Electronic surveillance, via ground stations, satellites, ships and planes, is neither in accord with nor in violation of international law. In recent years the ELINT game has been played under unwritten rules of nonviolence. Since the U-2 incident in 1960, the Russians have refrained from shooting down American reconnaissance craft, and the United States in turn has done little more than mildly harass Soviet intelligence vessels, usually disguised as fishing trawlers, probing its continental waters.

But in January 1968 the unwritten rules of ELINT were suddenly challenged. The United States, becoming more and more concerned about keeping the peace in South Korea in the face of belligerent threats by North Korean Communists to rekindle the Korean war, sent out an intelligence ship to cruise along the North Korean coast and report on military operations ashore.

The USS *Pueblo*, a converted Army supply ship, ventured into the Sea of Japan with 83 men—28 of them part of her ship-within-the-ship intelligence detachment. She was virtually defenseless. She did carry two .50-caliber machine guns, but her captain was unsure whether he had the authority to use them. Also she was without dynamite or an automatic destruct system to rid herself of her cache of cryptographic equipment and secret documents in an emergency.

Just past noon, on Jan. 23, 1968, the *Pueblo* was attacked on the high seas by a North Korean submarine chaser and a trio of torpedo boats. At the time, she was lying dead in the water conducting electronic research some 16

UPI

Comdr. Lloyd M. Bucher (l) and his lawyer Capt. James E. Keys. After a two-month investigation, a Navy court of inquiry recommended that Bucher should be court-martialed for failing to defend his ship, the "Pueblo." The decision was overruled.

COURT of INQUIRY

miles from the North Korean port of Wonsan. This position—some 4 miles beyond claimed territorial waters—was confirmed by the ship's navigator, Lt. Edward R. Murphy, Jr. The *Pueblo* also intercepted a radio message from the North Korean subchaser to a command post on shore indicating that the U.S. vessel had not intruded into the 12-mile zone. Within 2 hours, the North Koreans captured the *Pueblo* and turned 82 surviving crewmen into hostages. One man was killed when the subchaser fired on the American ship. The battle was all one way. *Pueblo* skipper Comdr. Lloyd M. Bucher never fired a shot at his assailants. He later reported that he was "hopelessly outgunned and outmanned" by the North Korean gunboats. While under attack, the ship's crew did manage to disable most of the cryptographic equipment. But stacks of classified papers, which could not be burned, shredded or jettisoned in time, fell into communist hands.

The North Koreans held the *Pueblo* crew captive for 11 months. During this time, they brutally forced both officers and enlisted men to confess falsely to espionage and intrusion into territorial waters.

The men were finally released, on Dec. 23, 1968, only after the United States also acknowledged in writing acts of "espionage" against the Democratic People's Republic of Korea. The U.S. negotiators publicly denied the validity of this document even as they signed it. This is one of the most bizarre international agreements the United States has ever attested to.

Commander Bucher returned to the United States to be named a "party" to a Navy court of inquiry in a fact-finding investigation which received worldwide attention. After a two-month hearing, during which every member of the *Pueblo* crew testified, the five-admiral court recommended that the *Pueblo* skipper be court-martialed for failing to defend his ship while he still had the "power to resist" and for allowing his intelligence cargo to be captured by the North Koreans.

The Navy probers also suggested court-martial for Lt. Stephen R. Harris, chief of the ship's top-secret intelligence unit, for "dereliction in the performance of his duties" in regard to destruction of classified material. The *Pueblo*'s executive officer, Lieutenant Murphy, was recommended for a "letter of admonition" for failing to organize and lead the crew in the extermination of classified matter. R. Adm. Frank L. Johnson, commander of the U.S. Naval Forces in Japan at the time of the *Pueblo* seizure, and Capt. Everett B. Gladding, then director of the Naval Security Group, Pacific,

also received court "reprimands" for not giving adequate support to the *Pueblo*'s intelligence mission.

On May 6, 1969, Navy Secretary John H. Chafee revealed the results of the court's deliberations, but he then stated that all charges against these naval officers would be dropped and no disciplinary action taken against *Pueblo* personnel. His rationale was that everybody involved had "suffered enough."

Meanwhile, U.S. military intelligence had received another jolt, on Apr. 14, 1969. A Navy EC-121 ELINT plane, with 31 men aboard, was shot down by North Korean MiG fighters while on a reconnaissance mission over the Sea of Japan. The whole crew was lost. The aggressors claimed that the plane had violated their territorial airspace, but U.S. authorities insisted that the Super Constellation was more than 50 miles off the North Korean coast when attacked.

Almost immediately, President Nixon announced that all further U.S. intelligence sea and air forays in the Far East would be "protected." The President was clearly talking about armed air support for these craft should they be harassed or fired upon on the open seas or in international airspace.

The *Pueblo* and EC-121 incidents had certain ramifications for U.S. military reconnaissance. Before the *Pueblo* seizure, Pentagon officials were extremely reluctant to arm intelligence vessels. They feared that large guns would make these ships appear "provocative" and prod an enemy attack on them. The Navy, on the other hand, had insisted that all military craft must carry guns. But they were undecided over the type of armament intelligence ships should mount until the *Pueblo* was actually on station in the Sea of Japan. AGER (Auxiliary General Environmental Research) vessels—of the *Pueblo* class—now tote 20mm. cannon and individual armament such as grenade launchers and rifles.

During 1969 the Defense Department quietly reevaluated its entire program to ensure the protection of intelligence ships and to minimize the loss of militarily vital equipment and documents.

Changes are along these lines:

Certain types of warships, including destroyers and guided-missile cruisers, are likely to be used more extensively for military reconnaissance—especially in high-risk areas, such as the Sea of Japan.

The Navy has provided vastly improved destruction equipment for intelligence vessels. This will allow rapid demolition of security materials in an emergency. Secret documents to

"Well, let's see . . . in my case he called for new leadership."

Le Pelley in "The Christian Science Monitor" © 1969 TCSPS

In April, North Korea shot down a U.S. Navy EC-121 (similar to the plane below). As the "Pueblo" case was fresh in mind, the incident stirred considerable debate (note cartoon) over the role of U.S. reconnaissance missions.

UPI

be stowed on these ships are now being printed on water-soluble paper so they may be jettisoned into the sea.

New interior designs will make it possible to scuttle reconnaissance ships quickly. Scuttling of the *Pueblo* would have been a lengthy and involved process.

Communications procedures have been revised to make sure that intelligence-ship captains can make immediate radio contact with their superiors in the event of any possible difficulty.

Despite these improvements, there is political pressure to cut down or completely scrap U.S. sea and air intelligence missions in high-risk areas of the world.

Congressman Otis G. Pike (D-N.Y.) states: "I think we can gather 90 per cent of the intelligence we're gathering with about 20 per cent of the missions." Pike's special subcommittee held extensive hearings in March and April (1969) on the *Pueblo* incident and the loss of the EC-121.

On the other hand, President Nixon says that intelligence-gathering missions are necessary to the security of U.S. forces in the Far East.

However, many U.S. diplomatic officials are edgy about taunting North Korea's hawkish Premier, Kim Il Sung, into further belligerent action against the United States. To avoid such confrontation, in the future there is likely to be more reliance on eavesdropping satellites and unmanned listening posts for intelligence collection on the Asian front than on the more vulnerable *Pueblo*s and EC-121's.

CURTIS J. SITOMER
Staff Correspondent
The Christian Science Monitor

Bill Rothschild, photographer; Boris Klapwahl, interior designer

INTERIOR DESIGN

Bill Rothschild, photographer
Boris Klapwahl, interior designer

In a two-story-high living room (left), created in the renovation of a New York brownstone, a skylight allows natural illumination. Strips of mirror splinter the reflections in a dazzling bathroom (above). A serene office studio (below) is dramatized with a seeming illusion: the ladder and chair on the far wall are in an oil painting.

John Hill, photographer

234

Photo by James Vincent

John Hill, photographer

A contemporary apartment (above) with a balcony is accented with sculpture—the object that looks accordion-pleated. Both this living room and the one below (with a see-through fireplace) illustrate the trend toward "more floor and less rug." Right: A fabric-covered shell masks the room's rectangular shape; hard surfaces contrast with soft fabrics.

Bill Rothschild, photographer;
Arthur Witthoefft, architect

IOWA

In April, hearings—in Davenport and Council Bluffs—brought to a focus the state's opposition to the Federal Government's program for combating water pollution, especially of the Mississippi and Missouri rivers (though the state's record for fighting pollution is good). The Federal Water Pollution Control Administration insisted that Iowa follow the other 49 states in agreeing to general statewide plans for secondary treatment of waste. The Iowa Water Pollution Control Commission was equally insistent that Federal charges of Mississippi pollution had not been proved, and that it did not have the power under Iowa law to order the amount of treatment demanded.

IRELAND, REPUBLIC OF

The Republic of Ireland emerged from a year of stringent tests, with almost no harm done.

The year 1969 started with a strike of 3,000 maintenance men throughout Irish industry. Some 30,000 other workers refused to pass picket lines. The country thereby lost an estimated $20,000,000 in exports.

Members of the undercover Irish Republican Army (IRA) attacked the property of "absentee West German landlords"—owners of homes and businesses in the new international light-industry sector of the Irish economy.

During the summer, serious trouble exploded in Northern Ireland (Ulster), which is a province within the United Kingdom of Great Britain and Northern Ireland. The Irish Republican Government ordered troops to the border and sought to take the case to the United Nations. However, an announcement

---

IRELAND, REPUBLIC OF

Area: 31,846 sq. mi.
Population: 2,900,000
Capital: Dublin (pop., 537,448)
Government: Eamon de Valera, president—1959; John Lynch, prime minister—1966
Gross National Product: $3,300,000,000
Monetary unit: Irish pound (1 Irish pound = U.S. $2.40)
Chief products: woolen textiles, tobacco, beer, dairy products, potatoes, turnips, lead, zinc
Foreign trade: exports, $798,000,000; imports, $1,175,000,000
Communications: 249,473 telephones, 191,657 radios, 435,000 TV sets, 7 daily newspapers
Transportation: roads, 53,324 mi.; 314,434 passenger cars, railroads, 1,334 mi.
Education: 600,074 elementary and secondary students, 14,686 university students, 5 universities

See map on page 185

---

by the IRA that they had "sent fully equipped units" into Northern Ireland brought a strong reply from Irish Prime Minister Jack Lynch. He declared that the Government would "not tolerate any usurpation of its powers."

The IRA is illegal in Ireland. Sensing the considerable dangers in any confrontation along the border involving both regular and irregular forces, Lynch moved rapidly to take as much heat out of the situation as possible. (See the article United Kingdom.) In the fall, he ruled out any possibility of the use of force to unify Ireland. He even offered the North a form of federation under which it might keep its special economic ties with Great Britain and yet join the Republic in a federal union.

March brought the Third Irish Economic Plan. It forecast an increase in the gross national product of 7 per cent between 1969 and 1972, with industrial output up 29 per cent, and an increase in employemt of 16,000.

May, however, saw taxes on liquor and gasoline increased. At the same time social-welfare benefits were improved.

At a general election in June, many commentators expected the resurgent Labor Party to defeat Lynch's Fianna Fail. A new political figure of some stature had appeared in the person of Dr. Conor Cruise O'Brien. The college professor, famous for his work with the United Nations, particularly in the Congo, was elected to Parliament. However, outside of Dublin the Labor Party did not in the event do very well. Lynch won quite a victory. Fianna Fail increased its seats to 75. Labor took only 18 seats. Fine Gael, the second main party, has 50 seats in the Dail (Parliament).

In September a reform program was initiated by the Government. Major reorganization of public services was proposed. It was announced that an Ombudsman would be appointed, as in Great Britain and Ulster, to investigate the complaints of private citizens against the state bureaucracy.

Lynch has set some store on the prospect of a larger European Common Market, which would help to solve the Irish-unity problem. Ireland, like Britain, has applied for membership. Currently, Ireland has a free-trade area agreement with Britain. Northern Ireland, as a part of the United Kingdom, of course has total free trade, plus subsidies costing Britain something like $500,000,000 a year. According to Lynch, if all the countries involved were within a single customs union, the gulf between the two Irelands might be bridged.

JOHN ALLAN MAY
Chief, London Bureau
The Christian Science Monitor

Gamma-PIX

Sinking of Venice has reached such a perilous stage that a plan for saving it may at last be forthcoming.

ITALY

For Italians, 1969 was the year "Raf" Minichiello, who had skyjacked a TWA plane from California to Rome, came home and took their minds off almost nonstop labor strife, municipal tensions and political wrangling, which left the nation without a government for nearly a month at mid-year. Yet the turmoil of strikes and riots did not stall *Il Boom,* the upward economic surge that began in 1964, and officials reported several new financial highs. Divorce came one step nearer reality in this most officially Roman Catholic country of all. Settlement of the long, vexing, once bloody Alto Adige issue appeared certain.

Premier Mariano Rumor, a genial 54-year-old bachelor with a talent for soothing ruffled political feelings, needed all his gifts after his center-left coalition fell apart July 5, bringing down the 29th Government since World War II. The downfall was sparked by a split in the Socialist Party, one of two main partners in the Rumor-led coalition. The Socialists came apart over the issue of cooperation with the huge Italian Communist Party, beginning what some observers called the worst political crisis since 1945. But nobody, including the Communists, wanted new elections. It was only a matter of time before Rumor would come up with some sort of solution. His Christian Democrats, who filled 265 of the 630 seats in the Chamber of Deputies, could not govern alone. But both socialist factions agreed tacitly not to vote

Rumor and a Christian Democrat Cabinet out of power pending negotiations on a broader, more permanent and stable political alignment. Most of the eight parties in Parliament, ranging from neo-Fascists to Communists, had leadership or ideological quarrels during the year. The Communists publicly expelled four pro-Moscow hardliners, including three members of Parliament, because they repeatedly rebuked the Italian party's censure of the Soviet invasion of Czechoslovakia.

Rumor lost a major fight when a divorce bill, the first to reach Parliament since 1852, was approved in late November in the Chamber of Deputies over the opposition of Pope Paul VI and the Christian Democrats. The bill still faced a tough battle in the Senate, but it was expected to pass into law by mid-1970, allowing divorce for the first time in Italy. One concrete accomplishment was the all but formal agreement between Italy, Austria and 230,000 German-speaking inhabitants of Alto Adige, in the Tyrol, on the future of the Alpine province seized at the end of World War I by Italy from the Austro-Hungarian Empire. The bitter dispute that raged over it for a half century finally won the attention of the United Nations. After nine years of negotiations all parties agreed that Italy should grant the province greater autonomy in exchange for a pledge by the German-speaking political leaders to end demands for complete independence from Italy. The Italian Government approved the agreement in early December, setting the stage for formal approval in the Austrian Parliament, which still regards itself as responsible for the welfare of the inhabitants of the region that it called South Tyrol.

Although enough social and economic problems lingered on to bring down any government, Rumor did benefit from the glow of a hot economy. Italy ended 1969 with gold and foreign currency reserves totaling $4,500,000,000, the third largest reserve in the world after the United States and West Germany, and officials reported record peaks in earnings and trading. One nagging factor was the outflow of lire to neighboring countries, notably Switzerland, where investors were guaranteed higher earnings than at home. By the end of June, when the central Bank of Italy intervened, the outflow of money had reached $1,524,000,000, compared with an outflow of $1,900,000,000 for all of 1968. The Bank of Italy action included raising the official discount rate from 3.5 to 5 per cent, the first such action in 11 years.

Imports outstripped exports by $1,000,000,000. However, Italy, which is traditionally in the red on trade, more than made up the deficit with rich invisible earnings from tourism, shipping, and money sent home by 332,000 Italians working abroad. Tourism alone earned more than $1,000,000,000 again in 1969, and expatriate workers sent home a record $641,000,000. The overall balance of payments in 1968 was a record $1,071,000,000, and the Bank of Italy expected the 1969 balance to reach $1,300,000,000. The proposed 1970 budget included record revenues of $17,500,000,000 and expenditures of $20,500,000,000, but officials said the deficit would be small because of the way the ministries of finance and treasury time the spending. The gross national product (GNP) grew by only 4.5 per cent in 1969 because of massive industrial strikes.

The labor situation kept most of the country in an uproar almost all year. Union leaders called wave after wave of strikes to dramatize their fight to get sizable pay increases and a reduction of the workweek to 40 hours. When the total number of strike hours for 1969 hit 250,000,000 in mid-October, a Rome newspaper called it a record no nation would break unless it had a revolution. The total strike time compared with 73,900,000 for all 1968. During the year, three 24-hour general strikes were called, and during one of them, a policeman was killed in Milan, the first such police fatality since 1945. Most of the strikes turned on efforts by 5,100,000 of the nation's total unionized labor force of 19,100,000 to win

new two-year national contracts in such key industrial sectors as shipping, auto making, and building, although virtually no trade or profession escaped the agitation. A national mail strike lasted one month, leaving a mountain of letters requiring 90 days to clear away. Labor Minister Carlo Donat-Cattin said strikes since September had caused a 2.5 per cent drop in industrial output and cut production at the huge Fiat auto company by 172,000 cars, equivalent to four times the annual output of the Lancia car firm purchased by Fiat in mid-October.

Some of the worst rioting occurred early in the year. In April, two persons were shot dead and 140 were injured in the poor southern town of Battipaglia during a demonstration over joblessness. A chain-reaction riot swept a dozen prisons in April, leaving scores injured and reducing Milan's main jail to a smoldering shell, in a revolt to support demands by prisoners for reform of the still-used Fascist-era penal code. The small southern town of Caserta was almost torn apart in September by thousands of soccer fans enraged over a decision to punish their team for bribing another squad to lose. Not all disturbances turned violent. About fifty orphans in Novara briefly seized control of their orphanage at midyear and held out until officials agreed to meet some of their demands, including dropping the rule that boys must wear smocks.

One problem bothering authorities was the fiscal crisis of the cities—deeply in debt, lacking many essential services and enough housing and schools, and overloaded with bureaucratic machinery. Rome was worse off with a debt of

---

ITALY

Area: 116,370 sq. mi.
Population: 53,100,000
Capital: Rome (pop., 2,635,000)
Government: Giuseppe Saragat, president—1964; Mariano Rumor, premier—1968
Gross national product: $72,000,000,000
Monetary unit: lira (625 lira = U.S. $1.00)
Chief products: wheat, grapes, olives, wine, marble, natural gas, steel, machinery, automobiles, textiles
Foreign trade: exports, $10,183,000,000; imports, $10,253,000,000
Communications: 7,057,187 telephones, 11,510,447 radios, 8,324,812 TV sets, 84 daily newspapers
Transportation: roads, 174,495 mi.; 7,311,385 passenger cars; railroads, 12,823 mi.
Education: 7,698,896 elementary, secondary and vocational students, 297,783 students of higher education
Armed forces: 420,000

See map on page 185

$2,900,000,000, and it is going another $208,-000,000 into the red every year.

Raffaele Minichiello arrived Nov. 1, becoming a hero to many of his countrymen and a prolonged international legal issue for Italy and the United States after one of aviation's most bizarre skyjackings. The 20-year-old, Italian-born U.S. Marine forced the crew of a Trans World Airlines jet to fly him 6,900 miles, from California to Rome, then fled into the woods near the ancient catacombs and eluded 500 police for hours. The adventure caught the Italian imagination. Many demonstrated for his release from jail, and in Melito Irpino, where he was born, his 76-year-old father joined Italians who blamed Minichiello's act on shock suffered in Vietnam. Italians also were upset because "Raf," as he was called, faced a possible death sentence if returned to stand trial in the United States. In Italy, he faced a maximum penalty of 30 years' imprisonment. A long legal battle shaped up for the right to try Minichiello. It was not the only hijack adventure of the year in Italy. Two armed Arabs forced another TWA jet, taking off from Rome on Aug. 29, to go to Damascus. Syrian authorities released 111 of the plane's passengers and crew members but detained 2 Israeli men.

Other crime news included the winding up of the biggest trial in Italian legal history. A total of 708 persons were found guilty of complicity in a fake driving-license racket, but most escaped jail. It also was the year of an audacious theft that delighted Italians: the disappearance of 2,760,000 quarts of wine from a sealed cellar where it was under bond as Exhibit A in a fraud trial. Four men later were accused of syphoning off the wine and replacing it with colored water. Shaping up as a complex and lengthy affair was the La Scala opera house case, which opened in October with a police raid to seize all financial records. The raid followed complaints by a baritone that La Scala officials gave away or wrongfully sold sets and props worth $30,400,000. One legal case ended after 101 years in Sicily when the Government was ordered to pay the heirs of Baron Francesco Tombetta a total of $640,000,000, the value and estimated profits since 1868 of estates seized by the Government of the day.

In the business world, the biggest deal in an otherwise fairly uneventful year was the purchase by Fiat of once strong Lancia. The transaction left Innocenti as the only major private-car manufacturer in Italy not under the control of Fiat President Giovanni Agnelli. Fiat paid a token one lire for each of Lancia's approximately 1,000,000 shares, but it also agreed to assume a debt totaling $160,000,000, much of it dating back to a 1963 slump in the Italian auto market that Lancia never overcame. Lancia sold only 35,000 cars and trucks in 1968, a fraction of its sales in the late 1950's. Fiat also acquired the famous Ferrari name when Agnelli announced in June that he had purchased joint control of the sports-car firm, which still limits production to three cars a day for customers willing to pay $15,000 for the flame-red racers.

Graham A. Martin, a former Washington reporter and social-security expert, replaced Gardner Ackley as U.S. ambassador in Rome. Ackley resigned to return to teaching at the University of Michigan. One of the chores left Martin was keeping an eye on negotiations between Italy and Communist China on establishing diplomatic relations, although there was no indication of a quick decision in either Rome or Peking.

The biggest story in the entertainment world was the long-awaited arrival of *Satyricon*, the first film by director Federico Fellini in more than four years. Black-market tickets sold for $80 each at the Venice film festival, and many spectators said the film was worth the money. By the end of the year, the picture, based on the writings of first-century satirist Petronius Arbiter, had grossed $1,000,000 in Italy alone.

CHARLES W. BELL
Foreign Correspondent,
United Press International

Undelivered letters and packages accumulate in Rome central railroad station during postal strike in May.

UPI

Fujihira from Monkmeyer

Shopping district in Naha, Okinawa's chief city: the United States will return the island to Japan in 1972.

JAPAN

According to ancient custom, 1969 was the year of the *tori* (chicken) in Japan. But charming old traditions and other important developments notwithstanding, 1969 for the Japanese was in fact the year of Okinawa.

Okinawa. Early in the year, Prime Minister Eisaku Sato, at a news conference that also dealt with another major theme of the year—increased left-wing opposition to what was styled "establishment rule"—made it clear that

---

JAPAN

Area: 142,726 sq. mi.

Population: 102,100,000

Capital: Tokyo (pop., 11,050,000)

Government: Hirohito, emperor—1926; Eisaku Sato, prime minister—1964

Gross national product: $142,000,000,000

Monetary unit: yen (360 yen = U.S.$1.00)

Chief products: rice, fruit, fish and fish products, iron and steel machinery, electronics, chemicals

Foreign trade: exports, $12,973,000,000; imports, $12,989,000,000

Communications: 18,216,767 telephones, 21,-380,000 radios, 21,027,364 TV sets, 121 daily newspapers

Transportation: roads, 92,108 mi.; 2,830,000 passenger cars; railroads, 17,287 mi.

Education: 20,087,000 elementary and secondary students, 1,114,000 university students

Armed forces: 250,000

---

his major goal in 1969 would be the return to Japan of administrative rights over American-ruled Okinawa. In late November, after the conclusion of three days of talks between President Nixon and Prime Minister Sato, in Washington, D.C., it was announced in a joint communiqué that the United States and Japan would begin immediate consultations for the purpose of restoring Okinawa to Japanese control sometime during 1972.

Sato praised the new policy of the United States toward Okinawa as an action without historical precedent. The United States, in recognition of the desires of the Japanese people, would return to Japan a piece of territory that changed hands at great mutual sacrifice at the end of World War II. The accomplishment of this action, the Prime Minister added, would end Japan's special postwar relations with the United States and initiate a new era in the Japanese-American partnership in Asia. With his success in obtaining an agreement with the United States on Okinawa as his trump card, at year's end Sato called for the dissolution of the national Diet (Parliament) to renew his public mandate and his party's, the Liberal Democrats, in a general election on Dec. 27.

Domestic Politics. Undoubtedly, after having concluded successful negotiations with the United States on Okinawa, it was to Sato's advantage to call for elections. With 68.5 per cent of the electorate voting, Sato's Liberal Democrats won 288 seats in the House of Representatives, a gain of 11 over the total won in the January 1967 elections.

The entire question of Okinawa, including the method by which it is to be given back, takes in various manifestations of the sharp divisions on the Japanese political scene. Most important of these is the lack of a common, fundamental agreement among the parties on the operation and direction of Japan's representative democracy. Immediately after the United States-Japan joint communiqué on Okinawa was released, Tomomi Narita, chairman of the Japan Socialist Party, the leading opposition party in the national Diet, charged that the new Okinawan policy was designed to turn Japan into an American nuclear base.

As nationals of the only country against which nuclear weapons have ever been employed, most Japanese have what has been labeled a "nuclear allergy." As a consequence, as well as for political gain, opposition politicians go to extraordinary lengths to ensure that their views on national nuclear policy are well publicized. Prime Minister Sato has pledged his Government to the so-called "three nonnuclear principles"—nonproduction, nonpossession and nonintroduction of nuclear weapons—without prejudice to the peaceful development of atomic energy. On his return to Japan, he stated that the new arrangements with the United States on Okinawa were in complete agreement with his nonnuclear-weapons policy. Opposition-party members have a deep-seated distrust of the governing Liberal

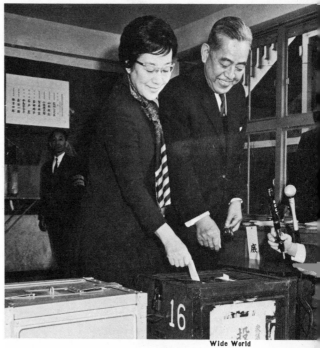

Wide World

Eisaku Sato and Mrs. Sato vote on Dec. 27. The Prime Minister won mandate for his "program for the 1970's."

Democrats, a fundamental factor in Japanese politics that prevents the formation of workable bipartisanship on ideological matters between the Socialists and the Liberal Democrats. The opposition charged that the wording of the joint communiqué on Okinawa concerning nuclear weapons was entirely too vague. It was clear as 1969 ended that Okinawa and

Tokyo, June 15: Some 25,000 people, representing about 200 organizations, demonstrate against Vietnam war.

Orion Press, PIX

A. Devaney, Inc.

Rice crop occupies 55 per cent of Japan's cultivated area; some 15,000,000 tons are produced yearly.

the political divisions its reversion emphasizes —basic disagreement in such crucial areas as defense and foreign relations—would continue to be a problem in 1970.

Foreign Relations. Since Japan's security alliance with the United States comes up for review in 1970, the year 1969 saw various political groups harden their positions regarding Japan's special relationship with the United States. For the ruling Liberal Democratic Party, the Treaty of Mutual Cooperation and Security (official title of the Japanese-American alliance) is the keystone of not only Japanese foreign policy but also of defense planning. For example, when Prime Minister Sato visited President Nixon in November 1969, he agreed that important American interests in east Asia, such as the security of the Republic of Korea and of the area around the island of Nationalist China, were very essential to Japan's own security.

A crucial factor behind the foreign policy of the Liberal Democrats is the assumption that Japan as an ally of the United States has nuclear protection, which Tokyo calls Japan's "nuclear umbrella." Under this arrangement, Japan, which spends comparatively little for defense, is assured that if the Japanese islands were attacked, the aggressor would come under the threat of American nuclear retaliation. In return, the United States has no assurance that Japan would take up arms to defend America from attack but does have the strategically invaluable right to maintain a number of military bases on Japanese territory and has the domestic cooperation of Japan's Self-Defense Forces.

In 1970 the treaty with the United States comes up for Diet review in early summer, with the proviso that it can be abrogated by either side upon one year's advance notification. It is expected that the opposition political parties will go to great lengths, including the whipping up of public emotions, to seek either modification or outright abrogation of the American alliance. For some opposition parties, especially the Socialists, the treaty has become a symbol for much of what they feel has gone wrong for Japan. To them, national policy has veered from an aloof pacifism to a participatory partnership, on unequal terms, in American "imperialism" in Asia. And, because of the alliance, Japanese capitalism is being spurred on to military-oriented production, prewar style.

Beyond the motivation of all the parties is Japanese nationalism. It is showing signs of discomfort with the kind of close identification with the United States that encourages the almost permanent stationing of American troops on Japanese soil. Every opposition party in 1969—Socialists and Communists on the

UPI

Women workers inspect mandarin oranges before they are exported to Canada, one of Japan's most important trading partners.

Left, the Democratic Socialists in the center, and the neo-Buddhist Komeito (Clean Government Party), which alternates between conservative and liberal poses—had a program that looked forward to the removal of American bases and to other modifications, drastic and otherwise, in the alliance with the United States. In late 1969 even the Liberal Democrats indicated that, though they did not favor the complete removal of the bases, they believed that Japan's Self-Defense Forces had become strong enough to play a leading role in the conventional defense of the homeland. So American military personnel and installations in Japan could be reduced further.

If the American promise regarding Okinawa set a historical precedent, of the victor freely returning captured territory to the vanquished, it certainly was an awkward one for the Soviet Union, which also holds territory it took from Japan at the end of World War II. Unlike the United States, which gave early indication that it meant to return Okinawa, the Soviet Union has so far refused to budge from its position that the "northern-island territorial issue," as the Soviet-held Kurile Islands are known in Japan, is "closed." It is unlikely that the Soviet Union will maintain this position for long, however, since it apparently wants to improve its relations with Japan. For this reason, as well as in consideration of Japanese sentiment, it appeared at the end of 1969 that the "closed" issue of the northern islands would be opened for discussion in the 1970's.

Still another foreign-policy issue was Japan's slowly growing involvement in Southeast Asian developmental-aid programs. On three notable occasions among others—at the fourth Ministerial Conference for Economic Development of Southeast Asia, at the annual meeting of the Asian and Pacific Council (ASPAC), held in Japan in 1969, and at the board of governors' meeting of the Asian Development Bank—various high-ranking Japanese officials promised to increase Japanese aid programs in proportion to Japan's own fast-moving economic development. According to Finance Minister Takeo Fukuda, Japanese economic aid to Asian countries would thus be doubled within the next five years. An even bolder step has been taken by the Japanese Government, especially the Foreign Ministry. It is quietly encouraging discussion of a Japanese unofficial proposal for a Pacific-Asia free-trade area (PAFTA). Though the concept is only visionary thus far, it is one more indication that new thrust is developing in Japanese diplomacy.

Society and the Economy. The slogan "two and twenty" was constantly used in 1969 to stress

A. Devaney, Inc.

Honda motorcycles roll off an assembly line. Flourishing factories help to keep Japan's unemployment rate (1-1.5 per cent) one of the world's lowest.

the painful contradictions between the surge of Japan's economy and the slow improvement of its social conditions. Among the free-world countries, Japan now has second place as an economic power. Yet its standard of living remains at the low level of twentieth among the world's nations. The gap shows in a critical shortage of social-overhead capital for facilities and equipment in such vital areas as housing, education, urban transportation, and sanitation. It has helped to fan the fires of the radicalism of the new Left. In 1969, with the cooperation of a number of high-school and university students and the help of a smaller number of young labor-union extremists, the new Left resorted to violent demonstrations against the "Establishment."

Rapidly unfolding government programs led to many exciting accomplishments in the 1960's, such as the construction of a new trunk line for the Bullet Express between Tokyo and Osaka, and the completion of a superhighway between the same two cities. But the Government cannot afford to rest on its laurels. Japan's internal social needs must soon be given their due, with more massive and more expensive programs than those of the 1960's.

F. Roy Lockheimer
Associate for Japan
American Universities Field Staff

JUAN CARLOS de BORBON y BORBON, PRINCE

A shy and amiable 31-year-old "student prince" named Juan Carlos became the man of the future in Spain in 1969.

Gen. Francisco Franco, who at 76 had completed 30 years of supreme power, chose Prince Juan Carlos de Borbon y Borbon as his successor, in a carefully staged presentation to the Spanish Cortes (parliament) on July 22. In 24 hours the succession was legally an accomplished fact, the Prince having sworn fealty to Generalissimo Franco and to Spanish laws. In the two decades since the Prince became a ward of the Spanish Government, the path to the threshold of power, fraught with tension and political infighting, has left few outward marks. Only some of the Prince's abrupt movements and his chain-smoking of American cigarettes signal inward tensions.

Although professionally a creature of his training, Prince Juan Carlos has maintained human traits. At his acceptance ceremony in La Zarzuela palace, where he lives with his wife, Greek Princess Sophia, and their three children, the Prince told a newsman, "Thank heaven, that's over." He lifted his naval-lieutenant's tunic and peered under it at his wet shirt.

Essentially Prince Juan Carlos is a young sportsman, although he is responsive to the demands of his position. He prefers sailing, golfing and hunting, often crewing his sailboat in races. Moreover, like his brother-in-law, King Constantine of Greece, he holds a brown belt in karate, a sport that goes well with his six feet of rugged frame. Despite a ready and shy smile and a masculine handsomeness, the Prince's personality has not engraved itself very deeply on the Spanish people.

Prince Juan Carlos may not be so simple as he seems. He is no stranger to political intrigues but has been the center of a tug-of-war between politicians and monarchists since his teens. Even his education fomented a palace revolution. He was supposed to enter law school at the University of Salamanca after completing a military education at age 22. This enraged members of the Opus Dei, a controversial Catholic lay organization that operates the University of Navarre. They talked Don Juan, Count of Barcelona, the Prince's father, into sending him to San Sebastian for tutoring by Opus Dei priests and professors. Amid violent arguments, he ended up at a small royal residence at El Escorial monastery where Augustine friars and University of Madrid professors tutored him.

Washington, D.C., debs, who danced with him during a one-month U.S. 1958 visit, remember him as a tongue-tied youth who danced well. Yet he is also a serious youth trying to grow into his job. He often said he would never take the throne without the permission of his father, who lives in exile in Portugal. By January 1969 he had made his choice. Generalissimo Franco permitted his first political interview, in which he said, "I will comply with my promise to serve in the post in which I can be most useful to the country." This was a tip-off to political experts that Juan Carlos would be Spain's next king.

Of the monarchy he said: "I believe that in our epoch it is better to speak of duties instead of rights. No monarchy—look at history—has been restored rigidly and without some sacrifices."

"I am a Spaniard," he said, "and as such I must respect the laws and institutions of my country."

This set the stage for Juan Carlos to become Spain's first Catholic monarch since 1931 when his grandfather, King Alfonso XIII, fled into exile under Republican pressure.

See Spain.

KEN DAVIS
Chief, Madrid Bureau, The Associated Press

KANSAS

In June, plans were launched for major redevelopment of the central business area of Fort Scott, once a frontier outpost, that will preserve and enhance its historic landmarks. The Federal Department of Housing and Urban Development, which approved more than $1,000,000 for the project, is working closely with the National Park Service, which is restoring the area immediately adjacent to the fort. The work is scheduled for completion in 1974. □ Wichita celebrated its 100th birthday.

KENTUCKY

Dr. Otis A. Singletary, University of Texas vice-chancellor and a historian, was named the eighth president of the University of Kentucky on May 27. □ July 4 was a day of mourning in Bardstown as Specialist 4 Ronald E. Simpson, 22, was buried. He was one of 5 young National Guardsmen killed in Vietnam on June 19. (Altogether 11 young men from the Bardstown area had been killed in Vietnam.) Simpson's death was taken up as a legal case on the grounds that it is unconstitutional to send National Guardsmen abroad. Eventually the case may reach the U.S. Supreme Court.

Camera Press, PIX

Communist journalists meet in North Korea to deal with task of fighting "aggression of U.S. imperialism."

KOREA

A startling change in South Korean domestic politics, rapid economic growth, and continued tension along the Demilitarized Zone (DMZ) with threats of war, eased somewhat at year's end, marked 1969.

Domestic Politics. Speculation that President Chung Hee Park and the ruling Democratic Republican Party (DRP) would attempt to amend the constitution to remove a two-term presidential limitation dominated political life in the first half of 1969. President Park, elected in 1963 and 1967, avoided direct comment on the issue by saying that such discussion should be deferred until 1970. On July 25, in a sudden reversal of position, President Park announced that he favored swift revision of the constitution. He declared that the required national referendum on the amendment would be considered a personal vote of confidence. He promised to resign immediately if revision was defeated.

Constitutional amendments require passage by a two-thirds vote in the National Assembly besides approval in a national referendum. The opposition New Democratic Party (NDP) centered its efforts on defeating the amendment bill in the Assembly. In a desperate bid to prevent a vote on the amendment, the NDP dissolved itself as a party, and NDP assemblymen, acting as "independents," occupied the Assembly building. On Sept. 13 the DRP held a "special session" of the Assembly in a nearby building. Proamendment assemblymen were bussed to the meeting and passed the government bill by a vote of 122 to 0. The subsequent national referendum was anticlimactic. The amendment passed on Oct. 17 by 7,553,589 to 3,636,369.

Political observers attributed Park's victory to public support of his economic policies and concern about North Korean bellicosity. Few doubted that he would run for reelection in 1971 and that the amendment had reduced public uncertainty about the future. However, many were appalled at the use of the R.O.K. CIA to intimidate newsmen and publishers, and at increased press censorship.

Economy. South Korea's economy continued its impressive growth performance. In 1968, the second year of the current five-year plan, the gross national product rose to approximately $5,000,000,000, an increase of 13.1 per cent compared with an 8.4 per cent advance in 1967. Exports topped $455,000,000, a 40 per cent increase over 1967. Manufacturing paced the economy with a 26.2 per cent growth rate. Domestic savings and per capita income also increased significantly.

Steady economic growth enabled South Korea to attract development loans from the United States, West Germany, Japan and international agencies. Foreign-exchange holdings reached a record high of $410,000,000 in May 1969, up from $157,000,000 in 1961. Foreign investments increased to $106,000,000 in April. To counter adverse comment on Korea's ability to repay foreign loans, the Government announced new restraints on foreign borrowing.

Two major economic problems persisted. Inflationary pressures had brought price rises of over 10 per cent in 1968, forcing an adjustment in the exchange rate between Korea won and U.S. dollars in 1969. Government action to control inflation had limited success.

Agriculture had lagged behind in 1968, partly because of severe droughts, with a production increase of only 1 per cent. Despite numerous government programs and investment, it was necessary to increase food imports. A renewed attack on agricultural problems was seen in a $45,000,000 loan from the World Bank, in May, for irrigation and all-weather farm projects. An additional grant of $3,291,-000, in flour from the World Food Program, was also aimed at the development of irrigation and flood-control projects. Economists predicted that these measures would increase farm production enough to make South Korea self-sufficient in food grains by 1970.

Optimistic economic predictions rested in part on continued success in birth-control programs. The rate of population growth declined to 2.3 per cent in 1969, down from 2.7 per cent in 1967.

National Security. Sensational espionage cases dominated the headlines in the first half of the year. In January a group from the Unification Revolution Party was tried and sentenced by South Korean authorities. In February a highly publicized defector (in 1967) from North Korea was caught as he fled South Korea in a bizarre double-agent case. Another espionage ring operating from Japan involved a member of the National Assembly.

Joint R.O.K.-U.S. efforts to bolster South Korean security made real progress in 1969. In

---

KOREA, DEMOCRATIC PEOPLE'S REPUBLIC (NORTH)

Area: 46,768 sq. mi.
Population: 13,300,000
Capital: Pyongyang (pop., 940,000)
Government: Kim Il Sung, premier—1948
Gross national product: $2,800,000,000
Monetary unit: won (2.6 won = U.S. $1.00)
Chief products: grains, coal, iron, chemicals and chemical fibers
Foreign trade: almost entirely with communist countries
Communications: 600,000 radios, Government Party Newspaper
Transportation: railroads, 6,200 mi.
Education: 2,356,000 elementary and secondary students, 214,000 students of higher education
Armed forces: 384,500

KOREA, REPUBLIC OF (SOUTH)

Area: 38,031 sq. mi.
Population: 31,200,000
Capital: Seoul (pop., 3,900,000)
Government: Chung Hee Park, president—1963; Chung Il Kwon, premier—1964
Gross national product: $5,200,000,000
Monetary unit: won (280 won = U.S. $1.00)
Chief products: rice, barley, wheat, beans, tobacco, cotton, tungsten, coal, fish, textiles
Foreign trade: exports, $455,000,000; imports, $1,468,000,000
Communications: 421,091 telephones, 120,000 TV sets, 36 daily newspapers
Transportation: roads, 21,375 mi.; 23,235 passenger cars; railroads, 3,164 mi.
Education: 6,422,307 elementary and secondary students, 6 national and 14 private universities
Armed forces: 620,000

---

addition to greatly improved security along the DMZ, agreement was reached on equipping a 2,000,000-man local reserve force and producing small arms in Korea, including the M-16 rifle. A long-standing Korean request for improved fighter aircraft was met with the transfer, in August, of F-4D Phantom jet fighters to the Korean Air Force. The planes were part of a squadron to be provided in 1969 under a supplementary U.S. military-assistance program. The F-4D Phantom is considered superior to the North Korean MiG 21C and eases South Korean concern over North Korean air superiority.

With fire fights along the DMZ, landings by North Korean agents in remote coastal areas, and strident threats of imminent guerrilla uprisings, North Korea pressed the South severely from late 1966. Serious incidents rose from 546 in 1967 to 629 in 1968. However, in 1969 the violence was sharply reversed, with only 96 serious incidents through mid-August.

Diplomatic Relations. President Park's August visit to the United States for talks with President Nixon marked a year of diplomatic activity mainly concerned with security questions. The Park-Nixon communiqué reaffirmed their nations' determination to "meet armed attack" in accord with the R.O.K.-U.S. security treaty.

South Korea expressed strong concern to Japan over the implications to Korea of the removal of U.S. bases from Okinawa when that island is returned to Japan in 1972. The Sato-Nixon communiqué in November recognized South Korean fears with an explicit statement of Japanese responsibility for South Korea's security.

Economic and cultural ties with Japan, reestablished in 1965 after twenty years of hostility, were significantly broadened. Exchanges of students and scholars, athletic contests, and meetings of parliamentarians demonstrated a growing understanding between them. A Korean-Japan Cooperation Council was formed in January to ease discussion of trade and related questions. Trade increased in 1969, but the 5-to-1 ratio in favor of Japan impeded further expansion.

South Korea's commitment to South Vietnam was emphasized in a May visit to Seoul by President Nguyen Van Thieu. South Korea, with over fifty thousand combat troops in Vietnam, indicated a willingness to assist that country in postwar rehabilitation programs.

See Intelligence, Military.

FRANK BALDWIN
Assistant Professor
East Asian Institute, Columbia University

LABOR

For labor and other segments of society, inflation was the key word in 1969. In the United States and most other countries, prices and wages played leapfrog. Under the impact of inflationary pressures, industrial turmoil was widespread.

United States. Price escalation in the United States carried over from 1968 into all of 1969 despite efforts by President Nixon's administration to bank the inflationary fires with fiscal and monetary measures. The Government's consumer-price index rose 6.1 per cent for the year.

The Nixon regime avoided "wage-price guidelines" or the "jawboning" techniques used by the Johnson administration in efforts to hold down prices and wages. However, President Nixon, late in the year, sent a letter to 2,200 industry and labor leaders asking "restraint" on wages and prices.

Because of price escalation, spurred by the war in Vietnam, organized labor was able to negotiate record wage gains. The Department of Labor estimated median-wage increases in negotiated contracts at over 6.6 per cent, compared with 5.2 per cent in 1968. Including fringe benefits, median-package increases were estimated at over 8 per cent, compared with 6.6 per cent in 1968. The overall average was boosted by exceptionally high increases, up to 15 per cent a year and more, negotiated by construction unions in major cities.

Secretary of Labor George P. Shultz said that while some wage settlements, notably in construction, have been excessive, "the median settlement kept barely ahead of the consumer-price level." He blamed the inflationary spiral on "past government policies," including large Federal deficits and "easy money."

Meanwhile, among rank and file workers as a whole, union and nonunion, average weekly wages rose approximately $6.65, or 6 per cent over the year. However, the average workweek declined. This factor, plus the advance in living costs, offset the wage gains; and by October the purchasing power of workers' wages had shown a slight decline.

Despite the inflationary climate the number of strikes in the United States declined in 1969, mainly because few contracts in major industries were up for renewal. Up until the big and bitter General Electric strike, which started Oct. 27, the proportion of working time lost due to stoppages was running at less than 0.19 per cent, compared with 0.31 per cent in 1968. For the full year 1969 the time lost was 0.23 per cent.

Extended strikes, over wages and other issues, occurred earlier in the year among longshore-

Walter Reuther, president of United Auto Workers, joins picket lines at GE plant in West Milwaukee.

men on the east and Gulf coasts, and among oil workers at major refineries. Also, the year was marked by many strikes of teachers, as well as local and state public employees, in struggles for both union recognition and higher pay.

In the critical transport field, wage settlements were reached mostly without strikes, except for a few on individual airlines and some in trucking. Railroads were confronted with a series of strike threats during the year, but agreements were negotiated in some disputes without nationwide strikes while other critical rail disputes carried over into 1970.

The total labor force neared the 85,000,000 mark, including the armed forces. The civilian-labor force neared 81,500,000, up about 2,000,000 over 1968. Civilian employment also rose approximately 2,000,000 to nearly 79,000,000, but the rate of employment increases fell sharply during the last half of 1969. Agricultural employment continued to decline, falling 210,000 over the year to 3,600,000.

Unemployment, under the impact of the administration's anti-inflationary efforts, increased by about 200,000 during the year to over 2,600,000. The jobless rate rose from a low of 3.3 per cent to a high of 4 per cent, then dropped back late in 1969 as many marginal workers gave up job-hunting and left the labor force. Unemployment among minority groups, particularly Negroes, remained substantially higher than among whites. The Department of Labor and other agencies, with labor and industry cooperation, sought to improve this situation through manpower-training programs and job recruiting.

Labor Secretary Shultz, in pressing for employment of more Negroes, turned particular attention to the building trades. He launched what became known as the Philadelphia Plan, which set hiring goals for minority groups on construction projects in the Philadelphia area financed with Federal assistance. Similar plans, Secretary Shultz said, would be instituted in other cities.

Organized labor and civil-rights groups formed alliances in support of battles by low-paid nonprofessional hospital workers, mostly Negroes, for recognition of their unions as bargaining agencies and for higher wages. Foremost on this front were successful strikes lasting over a hundred days at hospitals in Charleston, S.C.

Membership in national and international unions with headquarters in the United States reached 20,200,000 at the beginning of 1969, a gain of about 1,000,000 from 1967. However, as a percentage of total employment, union rolls declined. Total national union membership in the United States alone rose to 18,843,000, a gain of 903,000 or 5 per cent from 1966. Many unions lost membership in 1968 as technological changes eliminated jobs, but membership rose sharply among unions of Federal, state and local government employees, also among teachers and nonprofessional workers in hospitals and other public institutions.

Mergers among unions continued during the year. Four unions of "operating" employees on the railroads—the Trainmen, Conductors, Firemen and Enginemen, and the Switchmen—merged in the United Transportation Union, with a claimed membership of 280,000. Also, the Transportation-Communication Employees (formerly the Railroad Telegraphers) and the Railway Patrolmen's Union merged into the Brotherhood of Railway and Airline Clerks. This created a still larger union, with an asserted membership of over 300,000. Also, the Mail Handlers Union merged with the Laborers'

International Union. The two rival Bakery Workers' Unions reunited.

Divisions widened on the union front when the Teamsters and the United Automobile Workers, two of the nation's biggest unions, held a convention to give constitutional sanction to the Alliance for Labor Action (ALA) which they formed in 1968. The International Chemical Workers Union joined the Alliance and was then expelled from the AFL-CIO at the latter's convention in October on charges of "dual unionism." ALA leaders denied that their aim was "raiding" and asserted that it was "a revitalized labor movement." The AFL-CIO, at its convention, voted an increase in per capita taxes paid by affiliates of from 7 to 10 cents a member per month, partly to meet ALA competition and to offset loss of income resulting from the UAW withdrawal.

On the farm front, one of the most dramatic struggles, that of the grape pickers in California, continued. Their strike for recognition, called against table-grape growers in 1965, was supplemented by a national boycott of California table grapes, which drew support from labor, church and civil-rights groups in the United States and other lands. The Farm Bureau Federation and other conservative groups countered with a "buy grapes" drive.

In the states, 19 legislatures voted increases in unemployment and workmen's compensation benefits. Six states raised minimum wages; five voted broader bargaining rights for public employees, while three narrowed such rights. No new "right to work" laws, which prohibit union shop agreements, were adopted.

Canada. Like the United States, Canada was under inflationary pressures in 1969. At year's end, the Liberal Party Government of Premier Pierre Trudeau was striving to counteract the pressures. Actually, prices rose at an annual rate of approximately 4.6 per cent as against over 6 per cent in the United States.

Long and bitter strikes pockmarked the economic picture. At plants of International Nickel Company, a strike involving 16,000 workers lasted 128 days before a settlement was reached. At plants of the Steel Company of Canada, settlement came after an 80-day strike involving 11,500 workers. In each case, the striking union, United Steelworkers, claimed record wage gains.

The most dramatic strike of the year was a wildcat walkout by 3,700 police and 2,400 firemen in Montreal. They left their posts after an arbitration board handed down a wage award substantially less than the parity they sought with police and firemen pay scales in Toronto. (See Canada.)

Among the many peaceful settlements reached during the year were those between railway unions and the railroads, providing 6½ per cent annual pay increases, plus other adjustments, over a two-year period.

Union membership in Canada passed the 2,100,000 mark, about two thirds of the total being in international unions headquartered in the United States. Agitation continued in some quarters for strictly national unions, but leaders of the Canadian Labor Congress defended international unions as essential to protect the bargaining power of Canadian workers at plants owned by multinational corporations.

Japan. Spurred by continuing prosperity and a growing labor shortage, the 3 major labor federations, Sohyo, Domei and Churitsuroren, and their affiliated national unions pushed for record-breaking wage increases during 1969. The spring wage offensive, Shunto, reached a climax in April-May when over 1,000 disputes involving over 1,000,000 workers erupted. Out of this surge of strikes came wage increases averaging 15 per cent, highest in the postwar period. This led to demands in some circles for an income policy to curb wage escalation.

Many other strikes occurred during the year. Some of Japan's most serious continuing labor-management disputes have been sparked by dismissals stemming from rationalization; that is, automation, technological changes and structural revisions. One of the longest such disputes, which resulted in many work stoppages, followed attempts to implement a commission's recommendation for elimination of assistant engineers (firemen) on trains. On Nov. 1 rail unions reached a tentative agreement with the railways for a phased reduction of firemen. Nonetheless, "work to rule slowdowns" followed on the railways, partly to protest the removal of the assistant engineers. A further factor in the unrest was the prospect of eventual dismissal of a total of 165,000 rail workers as "redundant" under the railroads' rationalization program.

Japan's economy kept on the upgrade, with an estimated 12 per cent growth in the gross national product for 1969. The unemployment rate was one of the world's lowest, ranging from 1 to 1.5 per cent.

Europe. The nations of Western Europe, particularly Italy and France, were beset with industrial strife, including an almost unbroken series of limited and general strikes, some officially sanctioned, some "wildcat." Many were called for only 24-hour periods. Prolonged strikes were rare, partly because European unions generally do not have reserves to pay strike benefits.

Italy was hardest hit. During the year, millions of workers staged brief general strikes, as well as strikes in specific industries and government services. The issues involved wages, working conditions, pensions, high rents and a housing shortage. Most of the strikes led to negotiated agreements, or to relief legislated by Parliament.

In France, industrial unrest was also widespread, though it did not equal the 1968 level. After Georges Pompidou took over the Government in June there was a brief "honeymoon" period, but by fall turmoil gripped the industrial front as workers fought for wage increases to keep ahead of rising prices.

Great Britain was less beset with large-scale walkouts than the Continent, but wildcat strikes, led by shop stewards and other plant activists, hit the auto industry, coal mining and other fields.

West Germany was an ocean of relative industrial calm. This was attributed to a slower rise in living costs, and to a more stable labor movement. However, in the last half of 1969, strikes, some of them wildcat, erupted in various industries, yielding substantial wage increases.

In Spain, spontaneous strikes for higher wages or better conditions occurred frequently during the year, often sparked by clandestine unions. Strikes took place despite government arrests and jailing of union leaders.

Latin America. Labor found itself shackled under military regimes in many Latin-American lands, but unrest broke loose, particularly in Argentina. There a series of regional and general strikes occurred during the year, some of them suppressed bloodily by police and troops. In some cases the Argentine Government put military intervenors in control of unions, ousting elected leaders. Also, when rail workers struck in September, the Government replied by drafting them into the Army and ordering them to return or face prison sentences.

Similarly, in Brazil the Government seized control of uncooperative unions and removed many of their leaders, accusing them of "political agitation." Also, in Uruguay, once a bastion of democracy in South America, the Government declared a state of siege after a wave of strikes in May and June. Over a hundred union leaders were arrested. Unrest diminished later in the year as the Uruguayan Government took measures to bring rampant inflation under control.

RUBEN LEVIN
Editor and Manager
Labor

LAOS

After dilatory campaigns in the past, the Laotian internal struggle flared to almost a full-scale war in 1969. Overshadowing all other developments, however, was the revelation of U.S. involvement in Laos. In U.S. Senate hearings, the issue was "irregularity" of U.S. military support for the Royal Lao Government headed by Prime Minister Souvanna Phouma. After the closed hearings ended, Sen. J. William Fulbright asserted that use of massive U.S. airpower and logistical support in Laos could lead to another "Vietnam-style" involvement.

The edited versions of the testimony subsequently released, bulwarked by correspondents' accounts of American activity in Laos, revealed a sizable increase. Yet, the Nixon administration had contended, there was no evidence that U.S. combat units were involved in the ground fighting.

However, the United States was spending about $150,000,000 a year to arm, train and transport the Laotian Army, Fulbright said. Other sources showed that the entire might of the American warplane squadrons based in Thailand, once used to bomb North Vietnam, was now being directed against Laos. The armada was mounting over 12,000 sorties (single plane flights) against enemy targets in Laos every month, and the weight of bombs hurled down exceeded the destructive power rained on North Vietnam.

The targets were mainly the Ho Chi Minh trail and the road network in eastern Laos, over which Hanoi reinforcements and supplies were still moving into South Vietnam. To some, this made the trail a legitimate Vietnam war target. But the American Air Force also was increasing direct air support of Royal Lao troops fighting the communist Pathet Lao. *Its* ranks were being filled with North Vietnamese regulars.

Thus the Pentagon explanation that American aircraft were only "flying reconnaissance" over Laos, and would not fire unless shot at, was no longer being offered even tongue in cheek. Nevertheless, the U.S. Embassy in Vientiane continued to insist there were only about 500 U.S. Government employees in Laos, including no more than 70 military "attaches." The more accurate figure, unofficial sources said, was about 1,000 U.S. military personnel, plus a Central Intelligence Agency group of 300 civilians involved in clandestine work, and U.S. Air Force ground personnel who coordinate close-support bombing missions and man ground-guidance equipment.

Senator Fulbright charged that all this amounted to American participation in a war

LAOS
Area: 91,500 sq. mi.
Population: 2,900,000
Capital: Vientiane (pop., 170,000)
Government: Savang Vatthana, king—1959; Souvanna Phouma, prime minister—1962
Gross national product: $200,000,000
Monetary unit: (500 kip = U.S.$1.00)
Chief products: rice, maize, tobacco, fish, tin
Communications: 1,076 telephones, 100,000 radios, 9 daily newspapers
Transportation: roads, 3,485 mi.; no railroad
Education: 204,119 pupils
Armed forces: 65,000 Royal Lao forces, 30,000 Pathet Lao forces
See map on page 481

and without the consent of Congress. He said, "It seems to me to be most unusual and irregular, if not unconstitutional."

The United States is not alone, of course, in being accused of violating the 1962 Geneva Agreement. With Great Britain and the Soviet Union as supervisory powers, the agreement was intended to neutralize Laos, making the landlocked and backyard kingdom a sort of "fire break" to keep the Vietnam war from spreading.

North Vietnam, although refusing to admit it, has an estimated 46,000 troops on Laotian soil besides those on the move down the infiltration route. The Soviet Union and China provide economic and military aid to the Laos insurgents, at least indirectly through their support of the Hanoi Government. On the allied side, Thailand and South Vietnam supplement U.S. support, with at least some Thai troops in combat wearing the uniform of the Royal Lao Army.

Like other Geneva accords concerning Southeast Asia, the neutralization of Laos has failed.

Perhaps because of its impact on the Paris peace talks, the North Vietnamese and Pathet Lao troops were more aggressive in 1969 than in any previous year. They drove deep salients into the western third of the country (where about two thirds of the Lao people live), still controlled by the Western-backed Royal Lao forces. The enemy advance reached high water in July. In August the Royal Lao troops around the Plain of Jars and in south central Laos launched counteroffensives. Strongly supported by U.S. air power, they regained much lost ground and even entered the strategic Plain of Jars for the first time in five years.

JACK FOISIE
Correspondent, Southeast Asia
The Los Angeles Times

latin america

President Nixon moved very slowly in the inter-American field. The excuse given was that he was waiting for New York Governor Nelson Rockefeller to make a series of four trips to Latin America in order to prepare a special report on which the new administration's Latin-American policy would be based. In March, Charles A. Meyer, who had been in charge of the Latin-American operations of Sears Roebuck, was appointed assistant secretary of state for inter-American affairs and U.S. coordinator for the Alliance for Progress.

Finally, between May and July, Nelson Rockefeller undertook the four trips to Latin America to collect information for his report. The enterprise was severely criticized. Perhaps had Rockefeller made a quiet trip with no entourage, as apparently President Nixon intended, a fresh appraisal would have been possible. However, Rockefeller assembled some 25 experts. The group was a sitting duck for hostile demonstrations, and the brevity of its visits to the various countries was less than flattering. There were especially hostile demonstrations in Colombia, Honduras, Ecuador and Bolivia, where the group did not even visit La Paz, the capital, but remained for only three hours at the airport. The governments of Peru, Chile and Venezuela requested that the Rockefeller mission stay away. It was embarrassing that the dictatorial country of Haiti provided the warmest welcome.

Rockefeller's report was kept a top-level secret until after President Nixon had announced the new U.S. Latin American policy on Oct. 31. President Nixon's speech pleased Latin Americans because he promised to loosen the strings on the uses of the U.S. financial aid granted to Latin America. Moreover, he said he would ask Congress to raise the post of assistant secretary of state for inter-American affairs to the level of undersecretary, as a proof of the special concern of the United States for Latin America. However, the President implied that the Alliance for Progress had been largely an illusion, and he tried to substitute the expression "Action for Progress." Yet he suggested that the United States would no longer take a paternal attitude toward Latin-American countries but let them work out their salvation themselves. In line with this, the U.S. Government would not use pressure to encourage Latin American countries to adopt democratic forms of government but would deal with Latin American governments as they are. The main effect of this would be to accept as a fact of life the military dictatorships that control much of Latin America.

On Latin-American mission, Gov. Nelson Rockefeller is welcomed at the airport for Tegucigalpa, Honduras.

PIX

Riot police go on duty near burned-out train on the outskirts of Rosario, Argentina's second largest city. Rioting was sparked by a general strike, in September, prompting the Army to take control of the city.

UPI

When, in November, the Rockefeller report was finally released, it went even further and praised Latin American armies for allowing dedicated and intelligent officers of modest background to bring about national progress and social justice. Rockefeller recommended abandoning the U.S. policy of refusing to sell the latest (and very expensive) weapons to Latin America. Rockefeller's name in Latin America is still associated with oil and big business, and it was generally thought that his report presaged a return to the old order by which U.S. business worked in close cooperation with military dictatorships. Moreover, Rockefeller had certainly not forgotten that on his recent tours almost the only regimes that gave him cordial receptions were military dictatorships.

The Latin American economic-integration movement made some progress when, in May, Bolivia, Chile, Ecuador, Peru and Colombia signed the pact creating the Andean Common Market. However, the significance of this pact was greatly diminished as Venezuela, the wealthiest of the Andean countries, refused to join. In general the economic-integration movement, like the Alliance for Progress, had lost its impetus. The most promising subregional group, the Central American Common Market, had been paralyzed by the war between Honduras and El Salvador (see below). The Caribbean Free Trade Association (CARIFTA), the only bright light on the horizon, established the Caribbean Development Bank in October. But there was doubt that trade between the former British colonies that compose it could ever achieve much volume.

Argentina. The Government of Gen. Juan Carlos Onganía was successful in its austerity program. The peso remained stable, and U.S. investments increased proportionately higher than in any other Latin American country. At the same time, the political situation remained tense, as the country continued to operate under a military dictatorship, without any national or provincial legislatures. In the past, the Roman Catholic Church had been a solid supporter of military dictatorships, but now many of the rank-and-file clergy were supporting the restless workers, especially in the sugar plantations of Tucuman, where several inefficient mills were closed down, with resultant unemployment. There was a serious nationwide strike in May. The nation's most powerful labor leader, Augusto T. Vandor, head of the Metal Workers Union and leader of the moderate wing of the General Confederation of Labor (CGT), was assassinated in June, presumably because he was cooperating with Onganía. The Government instituted a state of siege and arrested a rival labor leader, Raimundo Ongaro.

The Government was determined to develop Patagonia, and, though neglecting the international plan to develop the River Plate basin, it began work in earnest on the Chocon-Cerrillos Colorados hydroelectric project in southwest Argentina. This plan to irrigate 2,500,000 acres in the Rio Negro valley was an old one; the Argentine Government was finally able to start it after receiving a $82,000,000 loan from the World Bank. Probably the biggest Argentine public-works project in this century, it should be completed by 1978; it will generate 6,000,000,000 kwh of electric power.

ATLANTIC
OCEAN

BAHAMA
ISLANDS

Havana

CUBA

DOMINICAN
REP.

JAMAICA   HAITI   Port-au-Prince

Kingston   Santo
Domingo

San Juan

PUERTO
RICO

ANGUILLA

8

CARIBBEAN

SEA

BARBADOS

BR. HONDURAS

GUATEMALA

HONDURAS

2

EL SALVADOR

NICARAGUA

COSTA RICA

CANAL ZONE
(U.S.A.)

PANAMA

6

Caracas

VENEZUELA

Medellín

Bogotá

COLOMBIA

ECUADOR

Guayaquil

CURAÇAO

9

Caracas   Port of Spain

TRINIDAD

Orinoco R.

Georgetown
Paramaribo

GUYANA

Cayenne

FRENCH
GUIANA

SURINAM
(NETH.)

Negro R.   Amazon R.

3

PERU

Lima

BRAZIL

1

São Francisco R.

Recife

ATLANTIC
OCEAN

5

La Paz

BOLIVIA

Brasília

Salvador

PACIFIC
OCEAN

PARAGUAY

Rio de
Janeiro

7

São Paulo

Asunción

CHILE

Paraná R.

ARGENTINA   URUGUAY

Santiago

Buenos Aires   Montevideo

LATIN AMERICA 1969: 1. After President
Artur da Costa e Silva suffered a stroke,
the military took over the Government of
Brazil; **2.** El Salvador and Honduras engaged in a five-day war; **3.** the Government of Peru granted diplomatic recognition to the U.S.S.R. and seized the remaining assets of the International Petroleum Company (IPC); **4.** in May, New York
Gov. Nelson Rockefeller arrived in Mexico
City, the initial stop on his four fact-finding missions to Latin America; **5.** Vice-
President Luis Adolfo Siles Salinas was
sworn in as president of Bolivia after President Barrientos was killed, but was later
deposed; **6.** an attempted coup against
Panama's strong man Omar Torrijos
failed; **7.** Chile and the Anaconda Company agreed on a plan for the nationalization of the company's copper mines; **8.**
British paratroopers landed in Anguilla;
9. E. O. Petronia became prime minister
of Curaçao after De Kroon resigned.

Ordeal at military concentration camp in Brazil to test caliber of antiguerrilla-warfare candidates: soldier is caged and isolated until he signs a confession.

Bolivia. In December 1968 a new party, the Bolivian Revolutionary Party (PRB), was formed to support President René Barrientos Ortuño. It proclaimed that it was following the Christian Democratic principles that had triumphed in Venezuela and Chile. It supported Barrientos' strong stand when he declared a state of siege in January 1969 in order to crush communist-led guerrillas, while the President's own party, the Authentic Revolutionary Party (PRA), opposed him and lost favor; the Minister of the Presidency, Jorge Rios Gamara, resigned. The PRA thus found itself siding with the opposition Bolivian Socialist Falange (FSB), which stated, however, that its aim was revolution. The economic situation

worsened since the United States, which had virtually been paying a part of the Bolivian budget, reduced this aid because of U.S. balance-of-payments problems.

There was a national crisis in April when President Barrientos, aged 49, was killed in a helicopter crash. Vice-President Luis Siles Salinas assumed the presidency and would have completed his term in 1970, when presidential elections are to be held. Walter Guevara Arze, Bolivian ambassador to the United Nations, announced that he would be the candidate for the PRA; while Victor Paz Estenssoro, who had been president in 1952–56 and 1960–64 but was now in exile in Lima, was selected as the candidate of the Nationalist Revolutionary Movement (MNR).

In September, Gen. Alfredo Ovando, who would probably have won the 1970 elections in any case, staged a coup and overthrew President Siles Salinas. Imitating the Peruvian seizure of the Standard Oil Company of New Jersey, President Ovando nationalized a subsidiary of the Gulf Oil Corporation. He also seized the gas pipeline that Gulf, Argentina and the Bolivian national oil company YPFB were building to Argentina. It seemed obvious that the seizure of the line would delay, perhaps indefinitely, the completion of the line. Bolivia's oil exports through the Chilean port of Arica suffered because tankers belonging to Gulf had been used. The Government had won a burst of applause from the nationalists and the Leftists, but at the end of the year it was bankrupt.

Brazil. The year opened in an unprecedentedly dictatorial atmosphere, since in mid-December 1968, President Artur da Costa e Silva had discarded the 1967 constitution he himself had helped to draft. He introduced a full-fledged dictatorship, closed Congress indefinitely, arrested hundreds of political opponents or deprived them of their civil rights, and imposed strict news censorship. In February, the Government suspended the state legislatures of São Paulo, Guanabara, Rio de Janeiro, Pernambuco and Sergipe, even though they were controlled by the Government's National Renovating Alliance (ARENA) Party, with the exception of Guanabara (i.e., the city of Rio de Janeiro), where the opposition Brazilian Democratic Movement (MDB) had a majority.

In an attempt to reduce expenditures and strengthen the cruzeiro, President Costa e Silva cut by 50 per cent the funds for the economic development of the impoverished northeast. This provoked the resignation of Gen. Alfonso Albuquerque Lima, who had been considered a likely successor to Costa e Silva, from the

NATION	POPULATION (in millions)	CAPITAL	AREA (approx. in sq. mi.)	HEAD OF STATE AND/OR GOVERNMENT, DATE INSTALLED (as of January 1, 1970)
Argentina	24.0	Buenos Aires	1,084,359	Juan Carlos Ongania, president—1966
Barbados	0.3	Bridgetown	166	Sir A. W. Scott, governor-general—1967
				Errol W. Barrow, prime minister—1961
Bolivia	4.5	La Paz	412,777	Gen. Alfredo Ovando Candia, president—1969
Brazil	90.6	Brasilia	3,287,842	Emilio Garrastazu Medici, president—1969
Chile	9.6	Santiago	286,396	Eduardo Frei Montalva, president—1964
Colombia	21.4	Bogota	439,828	Carlos Lleras Restrepo, president—1966
Costa Rica	1.7	San Jose	19,650	Jose Joaquin Trejos, president—1966
Cuba	8.2	Havana	44,218	Osvaldo Dorticos Torrado, president—1959
				Fidel Castro, premier—1959
Dominican Republic	4.2	Santo Domingo	19,129	Joaquin Balaguer, president—1966
Ecuador	5.8	Quito	108,478	Jose Maria Velasco Ibarra, president—1968
El Salvador	3.3	San Salvador	13,176	Fidel Sanchez Hernandez, president—1967
Guatemala	5.0	Guatemala City	42,042	Julio Cesar Mendez Montenegro, president—1966
Guyana	0.7	Georgetown	83,000	Forbes Burnham, prime minister—1965
Haiti	5.1	Port-au-Prince	10,714	François Duvalier, president—1957
Honduras	2.5	Tegucigalpa	43,227	Oswaldo Lopez Arellano, president—1965
Jamaica	1.8	Kingston	4,411	Sir Clifford Campbell, governor-general—1962
				Hugh Shearer, prime minister—1967
Nicaragua	2.0	Managua	57,145	Anastasio Somoza Debayle, Jr., president—1967
Panama	1.4	Panama	28,575	Demetrio Lakas Balas, provisional president—1969
Paraguay	2.3	Asuncion	157,047	Alfredo Stroessner, president—1954
Peru	13.2	Lima	514,059	Juan Velasco Alvarado, president—1968
Trinidad and Tobago	1.1	Port of Spain	2,000	Sir Solomon Hochoy, governor-general—1962
				Eric Williams, prime minister—1962
Uruguay	2.9	Montevideo	72,152	Jorge Pacheco Areco, president—1967
Venezuela	10.4	Caracas	352,141	Rafael Caldera Rodriguez, president—1969

key post of minister of the interior and chief of the Cabinet. Despite the economy measures, the cruzeiro was devalued eight times in 1969. In the northeast, Archbishop Helder Camara, of Recife and Olinda, denounced the failure of the Government to help the poor. He was one of the few people in the country who dared criticize the military junta, and he even suggested that the Catholics cooperate with the Marxists in the struggle for social justice.

Disturbed by lack of support for his regime, Costa e Silva announced that a new Government would be elected in 1970 and would come to power in 1971. However, in August a stroke incapacitated him. Constitutionally, he should have been succeeded by Vice-President Pedro Aleixo, but this unfortunate civilian was pushed aside by a junta consisting of one Army general, one Air Force general and one admiral. Under the guidance of Aleixo, a constitutional commission had just begun drafting a new authoritarian constitution with increased powers for the president and a smaller Senate and Chamber of Deputies. In October, the Army-Navy-Air Force Command named 63-year-old Gen. Emilio Garrastazu Medici as president.

ARENA formally endorsed Medici, and Congress was reconvened to rubber-stamp the appointment. Medici promulgated the new constitution and promised to restore freedom of the press, free speech, and genuine political parties. He seemed to be in no hurry to carry out this promise, which was really a recognition of the serious disaffection among the Brazilian population.

Earlier the disaffection took violent forms, and in September a terrorist group kidnapped U.S. Ambassador to Brazil C. Burke Elbrick. The ransom note demanded that the military Government free 15 rebels from prison and provide them safe-conduct to Mexico. This was done, and 13 of the 15 went on from Mexico to Cuba. Ambassador Elbrick was freed. A few days later the military junta restored the death penalty, which had been outlawed in Brazil since 1891, for acts of violence or subversion. In November, police trapped and killed Carlos Marighela, a former congressman who had become a terrorist leader dedicated to Castro-type guerrilla action. It was thought that, with his death and the flight to Uruguay of his two leading fellow terrorists, the guerrilla movement would fall apart.

Central America and Panama. For several years Central America had been mentioned widely as proof that Latin American countries could integrate their economies, thus promoting the peace and welfare of the region. The much-publicized success of the Organization of Central American States (ODECA) and of its related regional organs proved in 1969 to be an illusion; the mirror was broken. The

SOUTH AMERICAN GOVERNMENTS

■ MILITARY

■ CIVILIAN

American Treaty of Reciprocal Assistance, the so-called Rio Treaty. Despite the armistice, the two countries remained at daggers drawn, and Central America appeared more Balkanized than ever. Several Central American meetings were held in the hope of repairing the damage.

Guatemala remained tense, but there were no major upsets. The Government had its economic affairs well under control, and, in a report prepared by the First National City Bank, the quetzal, incredibly, was reported to be the hardest currency in the world. The capital inaugurated its vast new airport, the only one in Latin America, except Buenos Aires, capable of handling the Boeing-747 jumbo jets.

After some premature announcements, it was reported that British Honduras would become independent early in 1970 and take the name of its capital city, Belize. It would remain a member of the Commonwealth and have a special relationship with Guatemala.

Meanwhile, under President Jose Joaquin Trejos, democratic Costa Rica remained peaceful as it prepared for the February 1970 presidential elections. Jose Figueres, who had been president in 1953–58, was the candidate of the National Liberation Party (PLN). Mario Echandi, who was president in 1958–62, was the candidate of the Authentic Republican Union Party (PURA). His candidacy was also supported by the Republican Party (PR) of former President Rafael Calderon and the National Union Party (PUN) of former President Otilio Ulate.

Panama continued under military rule. Former President Arnulfo Arias, who had been expelled by the military junta in October 1968, stayed on in Washington to plot for his return, but the rebels who were supporting him in Chiriqui Province either were forced to flee into Costa Rica or were captured. Col. Omar Torrijos imposed one-man rule by sending into virtual exile four key officers who proposed an agrarian reform that would have affected the landed .oligarchy. He removed them from the junta and sent them to Washington to serve on the Inter-American Defense Board.

Torrijos promised to hold elections in 1970, but in October he modified this promise by announcing that in late 1970 machinery would be set up to choose a constituent assembly as a first step toward a return to constitutional government. These promises were intended to assuage local discontent and also the displeasure of the United States, with which the military regime had very cold relations. In December, while Torrijos was attending horse races in Mexico City, two disaffected colonels staged a

trouble began when the Government of Gen. Anastasio Somoza, Jr., of Nicaragua, showed its dislike of the liberal Government of Costa Rica by mistreating truck drivers and others going through Nicaragua on their way between Costa Rica and Guatemala. When a New Zealand tourist was seized by the Nicaraguan police, a diplomatic protest ensued.

These rumblings preceded an explosion between Honduras and El Salvador in June. The war was triggered by a squabble over the regional elimination games for the World Soccer Cup, but the real causes were much deeper. Honduras is five times larger than neighboring El Salvador, but it has only 2,500,-000 inhabitants, as compared with El Salvador's 3,300,000. Salvadoran peasants who have spilled over into Honduras now number about 300,000. They are resented, and the military Government of Honduras used legal pretexts to deprive them of their land and of employment. The military Government of El Salvador thought this sufficient grounds to invade Honduras. The Organization of American States intervened in July, invoking the 1947 Inter-

UPI

Living Honduran and slain Salvadoran soldiers both were pawns in the short war between their countries.

coup, but Torrijos returned and threw them in jail, thus becoming a popular hero.

The debate about the location of the new interoceanic canal dragged on. Panama and Colombia, traditionally divided by the canal issue, agreed in September to join forces and proposed the building of a sea-level canal along the boundary between the two countries. President Anastasio Somoza, Jr., announced plans to build a canal through Nicaragua, but it was not clear where he could find the money.

Chile. The governing Christian Democratic Party of President Eduardo Frei split into three groups as a result of rivalries and dissensions over the policy planks for the 1970 presidential elections. Radomiro Tomic, the leader of the left-wing faction and no friend of U.S. economic and political policies, even though he had recently served as ambassador to the United States, abandoned the race until he was assured of the support of all three factions. Only a few left the party to support Jacques Chonchol and his Movement of United Popular Action. However, even this was not enough to ensure Tomic's election, since strong candidates appeared on the extreme Left and on the Right. Tomic hoped he might capture some support from the extreme Left, which was divided between the pro-Moscow Communist Party (one of whose leaders and a candidate for the presidency was the famous poet Pablo Neruda) and the more violent Socialist Party. The Communists rejected vio-

lence and sought to win through Chile's democratic election processes. The Socialists, led by presidential candidate Salvador Allende, were prepared to follow the guerrilla example of their hero Fidel Castro. The candidate of the Right was 73-year-old Jorge Alessandri, who had served as president in 1958–64.

In the March congressional elections the conservative National Party made surprising gains, winning 20.9 per cent of the total vote; the Communist Party increased its support to 16.6 per cent; and the Socialist Party received 12.8 per cent of the total. The great loser was the Christian Democratic Party, whose share of the vote dropped from 42 per cent (in 1965) to 31.1 per cent. Chile continued to have by far the largest Communist Party in Latin America, except for Cuba, where the Communist Party had somewhat more members and controlled the Government. With 60,000 members, the Chilean Communist Party was the fourth largest in the noncommunist world, after those of Italy, France and India.

Chile has one of the most democratic traditions in Latin America, but it now found itself threatened by force from the Left and from the Right. Bombings by the small but violent Leftist Revolutionary Movement (MIR) caused grievous harm to persons and property, and even the Communists were outraged. Two Army regiments near Santiago staged a brief revolt against the Government, but its leaders said they wished merely to call attention to low Army pay. Nevertheless, there were rumors even in democratic Chile that the Army was tempted to stage a coup.

In order to arouse national opinion in favor of his regime, Frei in May announced that his Government would buy out the U.S.-owned Anaconda mining operations as part of the "Chileanization" of the copper industry which other companies had accepted earlier. Anaconda had refused to sell its huge Chuquicamata and El Salvador mines, but now, threatened with expropriation without compensation, it agreed to sell 51 per cent of its interest in the mines on Jan. 1, 1970, and the remaining 49 per cent before the end of 1981.

Colombia. The year 1968 ended with the acceptance of certain constitutional reforms proposed by President Carlos Lleras Restrepo. The year 1969 began with preparations for the 1970 elections. According to the National Front agreement, the president during 1970–74 must be a Conservative, and former dictator (1953–57) Gen. Gustavo Rojas Pinilla announced his candidacy. There were disquieting signs that Colombian generals, traditionally respectful of civilian authority, were being infected by the example of military coups in many other Latin-American countries. In February, President Lleras Restrepo fired Army chief Gen. Guillermo Pinzon from his post and from the Army for objecting to the auditing of the military budget by civilian treasury officials. The leading candidate for the Conservative nomination was Misael Pastrana, until late 1969 ambassador to the United States. Former Minister of Labor Belisario Betancur was named a presidential candidate by the Popular Conservative Convention. He announced that he would not submit his name to the official Conservative Party convention.

Ecuador. President Jose Velasco Ibarra continued to pursue an autocratic course. Encouraged by the Peruvian expropriation of Standard Oil Company of New Jersey properties, he extorted fresh concessions from the Gulf and Texaco companies, which jointly were exploring a 3,600,000-acre concession in the eastern part of the country. Gulf-Texaco had brought in 10 successful wells since coming to Ecuador in 1964, at a cost of $20,000,000, but their plan to bring the oil out via a pipeline through Colombia was opposed by Ecuador, which wanted its own pipeline to the coast, although it would cost $100,000,000 and take 10 years to build. The claim by Ecuador, Peru and Chile to sovereignty over coastal waters out to the 200-mile line and the seizure of U.S. fishing boats continued to be other sources of friction with the United States.

Velasco Ibarra attempted to show his independence of the Colossus of the North by negotiating diplomatic and trade relations with the Soviet Union. He sought to bring the restless universities to heel by abolishing university autonomy, thus provoking the resignation of the president, vice-president, most of the deans, and about twenty professors from the Central University in Quito. He then sought to win student favor by opening admission to universities without entrance examination, so that the campuses were flooded with unprepared students.

The Guianas. Early in January, approximately a thousand ranchers and their Indian farmhands in the southwestern part of Guyana staged a separatist revolt with the backing of Venezuela, which coveted part of Guyana's territory. However, the revolt was quickly put down.

Elections were held in Surinam in October. As in neighboring Guyana, although in a less violent way, the political struggle involved basically a struggle between Negroes and East Indians. The latter's United Hindustani Party won a surprising victory over the Negro-dominated National Party, which was widely accused of corruption and had left the treasury nearly empty. There were fears that violence might break out in Paramaribo similar to that which wracked Georgetown a few years before.

Paraguay. The military dictatorship of President Alfredo Stroessner was faced with a Catholic revolt against its brutalities. Even Asuncion Archbishop Anibal Mena Porta took a strong stand. As a sign of his disapproval, he suspended Sunday masses for the first time since the capital was founded in 1537. This "interdict" was remarkable, since thitherto the protest against the dictatorship had been confined to a small number of liberal priests, while the hierarchy had remained an ally of the Stroessner regime. Now the whole Church was moving Left, and the Catholic university of Asuncion had become a focus of Christian Democratic ideas. Stroessner attempted to assert the authoritarian rule of his Colorado Party by imprisoning members of the opposition Liberal Radical Party; by deporting a Spanish Jesuit (the Jesuits in the faculty of letters of the Catholic university were accused of indoctrinating the students with Christian Democratic ideas); by canceling an agreement with Caritas, which was distributing food supplied by CARE to needy Paraguayans; and by closing the Church's weekly news organ *Comunidad*. A state of siege, allowing the Government to imprison anyone indefinitely, had been in effect since Stroessner took power 15 years before. As though this were not enough, the Government now sponsored an incredibly repressive law called without irony "Law for the Defense of Democracy and the Political and Social Order of the State."

Peru. The expropriation in October 1968 by the Peruvian military Government of the International Petroleum Company, a subsidiary of the Standard Oil Company of New Jersey, virtually paralyzed U.S.-Peruvian relations during 1969. The United States did not use the Hickenlooper Amendment and stop U.S. aid to Peru, realizing that this would have given the Government of Gen. Juan Velasco Alvarado a pretext to incite the Peruvian mobs to acts of anti-Americanism and sustain the transient popularity it had won by its nationalistic refusal to submit the issue to international arbitration.

Meanwhile the Peruvian economy slumped, unemployment increased, and the military Government made efforts to attract fresh U.S. capital. It claimed it was not moving toward communism. A new university law, promulgated in February, allowed it to send police onto the campuses and thus to crush the pro-Moscow and pro-Peking factions that had won control of the student bodies of several universities and were using the University of San Marcos as their stronghold in Lima, the capital. At the same time, the junta established trade and diplomatic relations with the Soviet Union and other Soviet-bloc countries, while Castro's Cuba was loud in its praise of Peru's anti-U.S. stand.

President Nixon sent John N. Irwin 2d to work out an agreement on the oil expropriation with the junta, but his mission was not successful. Indeed, the Velasco Alvarado regime made another move against U.S. capital when, in August, it seized the sugar plantations of the W. R. Grace Company located in the area of Paramonga, two hundred miles north of Lima. The Government justified this move as part of its agrarian reform, saying that large estates belonging to Peruvian plantation owners would likewise be broken up and distributed among the peasants.

In May, Velasco Alvarado announced that his Government planned to nationalize communications, a move that would affect the telephone and telegraph installations belonging to Swedish, Swiss, British and U.S. interests. Peru is today the world's largest producer of fish meal, and the Government said that it would assume greater participation in running that industry, whose executives seemed ready to cooperate in order to avoid outright confiscation. In protest against the Peruvian seizure of U.S. fishing boats, the United States suspended the shipment of military equipment in February, but resumed it in July. In September, Velasco Alvarado warned U.S. mining cor-

UPI

In Haiti, civilians of all ages —and security guards—wait to greet Governor Rockefeller during his stop at the island.

Ford Foundation

Venezuelan engineering students talk with refinery employee in university-sponsored vacation-work project.

porations (the biggest being Anaconda, Cerro de Pasco, and Southern Peru Copper Corporation) that they must make new capital investments or lose their concessions to operate.

Uruguay. The Government of Jorge Pacheco Areco continued to adopt severe measures in its campaign to suppress the rebel Tupamaros. The police were successful in capturing some of the leaders, and in March the security measures, which had been in force for nine months, were lifted. The economic measures adopted by the Government likewise had some success, and a freeze on wages and prices slowed down the inflation. However, in June, half of the nation's organized workers staged a strike against the wage freeze, and again security measures were imposed. Like Chile, with which it has much in common, Uruguay succeeded in maintaining its democracy, although it was caught between the two most powerful military dictatorships of Latin America, Argentina and Brazil.

Venezuela. Following the electoral victory of the COPEI (Christian Democratic) Party over the governing Democratic Action (AD) Party, whose forces were divided, Rafael Caldera Rodriguez took office as president in March for a five-year term. It was the second Christian Democratic government in Latin America, but its base was narrower than that of President Frei in Chile. AD, which had governed since 1959, still controlled Congress and had the general support of peasants and workers.

In December 1968, former dictator Marcos Perez Jimenez, who had been in exile in Spain, won a seat in the Senate and settled in Lima while the constitutionality of his election was discussed in Caracas. The Supreme Court's verdict was negative, and Perez Jimenez remained in Peru. He praised the military juntas of Brazil and Peru and obviously hoped to win their support in overthrowing the democratic regime in Venezuela. Nevertheless, he supported COPEI against AD, which had overthrown, imprisoned and exiled him. In the mountains and even in the cities, the pro-Castro National Liberation Front continued its terrorist activities.

In order to offset his minority position in Congress, where COPEI had only 57 of the 210 seats in the Chamber of Deputies and 17 of the 52 Senate seats, Caldera patched together a colorful coalition of COPEI, the left-wing popular electoral movement (MEP), the left-wing Popular Democratic Front (FDP), and Perez Jimenez's National Civic Crusade (CCN). He legalized the Communist Party of Venezuela (PCV), hoping thus to persuade the communist guerrillas to lay down their arms. However, they rejected the bait, since most of them were pro-Castro and pro-Peking, while the PCV was pro-Moscow.

Venezuela has a long tradition of militarism (Bolivar said it was a barracks), and the danger is always present that the Army will overthrow the democratic regime so painfully established by former President Romulo Betancourt. It was this danger that prompted President Caldera, in August, to arrest Gen. Pablo Flores and a group of officers who were accusing him of being "soft on communism." Despite predictions that he would be overthrown, Caldera remained in office.

See Caribbean Islands; Mexico; Organization of American States.

RONALD HILTON
Professor, Stanford University;
Executive Director,
California Institute of International Studies

LAW

It was observed more than a century ago that in the United States, great public issues invariably work their way to the surface in the form of legal issues. As Alexis de Tocqueville put it, the crucial questions all eventually find their way to the Supreme Court. This was evident in the legal developments of 1969. Crime, protest demonstrations, students' free-speech rights, selective-service procedures, welfare, civil rights, school desegregation, marijuana, and obscenity were among the subjects stirring the nation, and all were prominent in the development of the law.

The course of the law was undoubtedly affected—although only time would tell how much—when two of the Supreme Court's most liberal and influential members left the bench. Within the span of five weeks Chief Justice Earl Warren retired, and Abe Fortas resigned. With their departures, combined with President Nixon's pledge to appoint "strict constructionists" to any and all Supreme Court vacancies, it seemed almost inevitable that the conservative tendencies in the law would be accentuated. By the end of 1969 it was still too soon to gauge the extent of this conservative current, but it seemed likely that the departure of these two justices would hasten the advent of a more restrained, conservative legal climate.

Criminal-suspects' rights continued to expand, capped by a rousing final day for Earl Warren on the Supreme Court. On June 23, 1969, the Court issued three decisions that enlarged the rights of defendants and limited the authority of the state in criminal matters. In *Chimel v. California* the Court ruled that police may not ransack a suspect's home as an incident to his arrest, but must obtain a search warrant before any area beyond the suspect's immediate surroundings may be searched. It also held in *Benton v. Maryland* that the Fifth Amendment's prohibition against double jeopardy is binding on state courts to the same extent that it has traditionally applied in Federal courts. Finally, the Court declared in *North Carolina v. Pearce* that a convict who has had his conviction overturned cannot be given a stiffer sentence at a second trial unless the trial judge can present concrete reasons for doing so.

The Warren Court's final liberal fling was characteristic of its criminal decisions throughout the year. The Court had ruled earlier that fingerprints obtained after an illegal arrest cannot be used in evidence (*Davis v. Mississippi*), had held that police must warn suspects of their rights immediately after their arrest, even if they are arrested in bed (*Orozco v. Texas*); and had given defendants the right to see transcripts of any conversations overheard by illegal police eavesdropping (*Alderman v. United States*).

For the most part, there was little public enthusiasm for decisions of this stripe, since crime continued to rise and some people continued to blame it on the courts. Yet in one respect, a consensus seemed to be developing about crime. There seemed to be a growing feeling that the punishments for marijuana violations were too strict. By 1969 it was apparent that many young people were using marijuana, and there was some evidence that it was no more harmful than liquor or tobacco. Yet penalties for smoking it ranged up to mandatory ten-year prison sentences.

Against this background, the Supreme Court struck down the conviction of Dr. Timothy F. Leary, an outspoken advocate of hallucinogenic drugs, who had been found guilty of smuggling marijuana into the country from Mexico. The decision cast doubt on virtually all of the Federal Government's marijuana laws. Because they and the "hard-narcotic" laws were based upon taxes levied upon the traffic and possession of outlawed drugs, the Court found that the entire legislative scheme tended to violate the Fifth Amendment's privilege against self-incrimination. This made the laws on the books suspect, but it left the way open for Congress to pass new laws. Initially, President Nixon hinted that he would ask for the same harsh penalties in the new laws, but soon lower-level

"What do you know, things seem to balance."

Le Pelley in "The Christian Science Monitor" © TCSPS

government officials were telling Congress that perhaps the penalties were too strict, and it seemed that penalties might soon be reduced.

However, a major effort to achieve this by court action failed. In Massachusetts, where a test case had been brought to prove that marijuana was so harmless that the stern penalties were unconstitutional, the state's highest court ruled that any reductions must be made by legislative action (*Massachusetts v. Leis*).

Protest demonstrations continued to disturb and stir Americans, and the Supreme Court strengthened the hands of those who protest peacefully. It overturned the conviction of Negro comedian Dick Gregory, who had been convicted of disorderly conduct when white hecklers caused a row at one of his civil-rights demonstrations. The police told him to move on. He refused and was arrested. This, the Court found, was the hecklers' doing—not his.

The Court also ruled for the first time that students' peaceful protest rights are protected by the First Amendment. It ruled that students could wear black armbands to protest the Vietnam war, whether school officials liked it or not (*Tinker v. Des Moines School District*). The ruling prompted a wave of lawsuits to establish the right, if any, of students to wear their hair long and their skirts short. Most lower courts found this a form of expression that was not protected by the Constitution.

The Vietnam war also produced protests in the form of refusals to perform military service, and a wave of litigation resulted over the selective-service laws. Many young men balked

for moral, rather than the traditional religious, reasons. A young Harvard graduate named John H. Sisson, Jr., raised their hopes when he won a lower-court ruling that a nonreligious person could legally be a conscientious objector to a particular war without opposing all wars. The Government argued that the country could be crippled if young men could pick and choose the wars they would fight, and the Supreme Court planned to rule on the case in 1970.

On the domestic scene, 10,000,000 people were on welfare, the costs were rising, and taxpayers were in revolt. The welfare system was caught in a painful squeeze: welfare recipients were having wide success in persuading the lower Federal courts to extend to them many of the constitutional rights against welfare officials that the Supreme Court had already granted to criminal defendants. The Supreme Court's initial response was to encourage this trend in the lower courts. It ruled that states could not cancel children's benefits because their mother was living with an able-bodied man; and held unconstitutional the one-year-residency requirements that many states had used to discourage people from moving to a high-benefit state to get on the welfare rolls.

But as the lower courts pressed forward, there was the possibility that the Supreme Court might have second thoughts. In New York a lower court ruled that welfare clients must be given trial-like hearings before benefits could be canceled. Also in New York, the legislature cut back on the amounts of benefits to dependent children, in a controversial economy move. In Maryland, a Federal court declared unconstitu-

tional a $250-per-month-per-family limit on welfare. The Supreme Court agreed to review all of these actions, creating the possibility that when the Burger Court announces its decisions in 1970, it might discourage Federal judicial intervention in welfare matters.

The law continued to be plagued by the thorny problem of civil rights, and one of its most visible protagonists, Rep. Adam Clayton Powell, Jr., of Harlem, was the subject of a major legal development. Powell had been barred from his seat in the 90th Congress for alleged misconduct. He contended that his race was a major reason for the move, and pointed out that some suspect activities by white congressmen had gone unpunished. Traditionally, Congress had been considered supreme within its own chambers, but the Supreme Court ruled, in Earl Warren's final judicial opinion, that it did have jurisdiction to review the action, and that the House had acted illegally. Later, a trial judge in Washington declined to order the House to give Powell his back pay and restore his seniority, and the matter seemed headed for the Supreme Court.

In late October, the Supreme Court ruled unanimously that school districts must end segregation "at once" and must operate integrated school systems "now and hereafter." Three things about the ruling were of interest: it was the first major decision of the Burger Court; it superseded the Court's 14-year-old "with all deliberate speed" desegregation doctrine; and contradicted the Nixon administration's policy of allowing desegregation delays in some districts.

Another major civil-rights development seemed to be in the making concerning racial discrimination by private clubs. The Supreme Court ruled that the Civil Rights Act of 1964 bars large recreation areas from excluding Negroes under the subterfuge that the facilities are "clubs," which only white members of the community may join. In a more difficult case, the Court agreed to decide soon if a community club that sells memberships to all white residents of a neighborhood may refuse to let a Negro resident join. If a club cannot do so, an important inroad will have been made into the traditional freedom of private clubs to discriminate quite arbitrarily against anybody for any reasons.

Finally, the Supreme Court struck a blow for the privacy of the home when it ruled that no person can be punished for possessing pornography on his own premises (*Stanley v. Georgia*). In keeping with the recent trend toward a generous interpretation of the Constitution's free-speech clause, several lower courts held that female entertainers may not be convicted for dancing "topless," since their performance was said to be a form of expression protected by the First Amendment. In Los Angeles, a municipal-court judge carried this principle to its ultimate—if not logical—extreme by declaring that girls who performed a nightclub act in the absolute nude were also protected against prosecution by the Constitution. The judge's name was Earl Warren, Jr.

FRED P. GRAHAM
Supreme Court Correspondent
The New York Times

SUPREME COURT DECISIONS

CHIEF JUSTICE

Earl Warren (retired June 23, 1969)   Warren E. Burger (sworn in June 23)

ASSOCIATE JUSTICES

Hugo L. Black (1937)   William J. Brennan, Jr. (1956)   Abe Fortas (resigned May 14,
William O. Douglas (1939)   Potter Stewart (1958)   1969)
John M. Harlan (1955)   Byron White (1962)   Thurgood Marshall (1967)
                                                                 (One vacancy)

CASE	DATE	DECISION
Hunter v. Akron, Ohio	Jan. 20	Limits the authority of cities to repeal fair-housing laws through popular referendums. Vote 8–1 (Black).
Allen v. State Board of Elections; Fairley v. Patterson Bunton v. Patterson; Whitley v. Williams	Mar. 3	Holds that states covered by the Voting Rights Act of 1965 cannot change their election laws in ways that would adversely affect Negroes. Vote 7–2 (Black, Harlan).
Citizen Publishing Co. v. United States	Mar. 10	Rules that competing daily newspapers violate the Sherman Antitrust Act when they share circulation and advertising departments. Vote 7–1 (Stewart; Fortas not participating).
Wells v. Rockefeller	Apr. 7	Declares New York's Congressional districts unconstitutional and orders the state legislature to reapportion them prior to 1970 elections. Vote 6–3 (Harlan, Stewart, White).
Kirkpatrick, Heinkel v. Preisler	Apr. 7	Declares Missouri's Congressional districting law unconstitutional. Vote 6–3 (Harlan, Stewart, White).
Street v. New York State	Apr. 21	Rules that the Constitution protects those who denounce the American flag in words. Vote 5–4 (Warren, Black, Fortas, White).
Shapiro v. Thompson; Washington, D.C., v. Legrant; Reynolds v. Smith	Apr. 21	Holds that states cannot constitutionally deny welfare payments to the poor simply because they have recently moved from another state. Vote 6–3 (Warren, Black, Harlan).
McDonald v. Board of Election Commissioners	Apr. 28	Rules that persons in jail awaiting trial do not have the right to vote by absentee ballot. Vote 9–0.
National Board of Young Men's Christian Association v. United States	May 19	Holds that the Federal Government is not financially responsible for damage to private property occupied by Federal troops during a riot. Vote 6–2 (Black, Douglas).
McKart v. United States	May 26	Rules that a man is entitled to exemption from the draft as a "sole surviving son" even after his parents have died. Vote 8–0.
Sullivan v. United States	May 26	Holds that the states have the right to collect sales and use taxes from servicemen even if the servicemen are permanent residents of other states. Vote 8–0.
United States v. Montgomery County Board of Education; Carr v. Montgomery County Board of Education	June 2	Rules that the Montgomery, Ala., school board may be required to eliminate traces of racial segregation by having the same ratio of white to Negro teachers (approximately 3 to 2) in each school as exists in the county-school system as a whole. Vote 8–0.
Gaston County v. United States	June 2	Upholds a lower court decision that Gaston County, N.C., must comply with the Voting Rights Act of 1965. The argument was that Gaston County had used a literacy test to discriminate against Negroes because the county, prior to 1954, had segregated Negroes in inferior schools resulting in many illiterate pupils. Vote 7–1 (Black).
Daniel v. Paul	June 2	Rules that a privately owned boating and swim club in rural Arkansas is covered by the Public Accommodations Act of 1964 and must admit Negroes. Vote 7–1 (Black).
O'Callahan v. Parker	June 2	Holds that servicemen cannot be court-martialed in peacetime for a crime committed off a military base within the United States unless the crime is "service connected." Vote 5–3 (Harlan, Stewart, White).
Sniadach v. Family Finance Corporation	June 9	Declares Wisconsin's wage-garnishment law unconstitutional. Vote 7–1 (Black).
Brandenburg v. Ohio	June 9	Rules that Ohio's criminal-syndicalism law is unconstitutional since it violates the First Amendment's guarantee of free speech. Vote 8–0.

RED LION BROADCASTING COMPANY INC. v. FCC; UNITED STATES v. RADIO TELEVISION NEWS DIRECTORS	JUNE 9	Upholds as constitutional the Federal Communications Commission's fairness doctrine and its equal-time doctrine. Vote 8–0.
POWELL v. McCORMACK	JUNE 16	Rules that the House of Representatives violated the Constitution in excluding Rep. Adam Clayton Powell, Jr., from the 90th Congress. Vote 7–1 (Stewart).
KRAMER v. UNION FREE SCHOOL DISTRICT No. 15	JUNE 16	Declares unconstitutional a New York law restricting voting in some school-district elections to parents of schoolchildren, property owners or lessors. Vote 5–3 (Black, Harlan, Stewart).
BEATRICE ALEXANDER v. HOLMES COUNTY BOARD OF EDUCATION	OCT. 29	Rules that all school districts must desegregate "at once." "The obligation of every school district is to terminate dual school systems at once and to operate now and hereafter only unitary schools." Vote 8–0.

Names of dissenting justices appear following vote.

LEGISLATION

Major bills passed by Congress in 1969 and signed by the President

SUBJECT	PURPOSE
PRESIDENTIAL COMPENSATION	Increases the annual salary of the president from $100,000 to $200,000. Signed Jan. 17, Public Law 91-1.
PUBLIC DEBT	Raises the permanent public-debt limit to $365,000,000,000 and the temporary limit to $377,000,000,000. Signed Apr. 7, Public Law 91-8.
VICE-PRESIDENTIAL AND CONGRESSIONAL LEADERS COMPENSATION	Increases the annual salary of the vice-president and the Speaker of the House of Representatives from $43,000 to $62,500 and raises the yearly compensation of the majority and minority leaders of the Senate and House and the president pro tempore of the Senate to $49,500. Signed Sept. 15, Public Law 91-67.
CHILD PROTECTION AND TOY SAFETY	Gives the secretary of health, education, and welfare the authority to prohibit the sale of all toys containing electrical, mechanical or thermal hazards. Signed Nov. 6, Public Law 91-113.
HUNGER	Increases authorization for the food-stamp program for fiscal 1970 from $340,-000,000 to $610,000,000. Signed Nov. 13, Public Law 91-116.
SPACE PROGRAM	Authorizes $3,715,000,000 for the National Aeronautics and Space Administration for fiscal 1970. Signed Nov. 18, Public Law 91-119.
DEFENSE	Authorizes $20,700,000,000 for defense-procurement programs for fiscal year 1970, including the Safeguard ABM system. Signed Nov. 19, Public Law 91-121.
DRAFT	Repeals a 1967 law prohibiting a draft-lottery system. Signed Nov. 26, Public Law 91-124.
NATIONAL PARK SERVICE	Establishes the William Howard Taft National Historic Site in Cincinnati, Ohio; provides for the development of the Eisenhower National Historic Site in Gettysburg, Pa.; establishes the Lyndon B. Johnson National Historic Site in Johnson City, Tex. Signed Dec. 2, Public Laws 91-132, 91-133, 91-134.
WILDLIFE	Prohibits the importation of endangered species of wildlife and fish into the United States and forbids the interstate shipment of reptiles, amphibians and other wildlife taken contrary to state law. Signed Dec. 5, Public Law 91-135.
NATIONAL CAPITAL TRANSPORTATION ACT	Authorizes funds (up to $1,147,044,000) for a rapid-transport system for Washington, D.C., and suburbs. Signed Dec. 9, Public Law 91-143.
DEFENSE	Appropriates $69,600,000,000 for the Department of Defense. Signed Dec. 29, Public Law 91-171.
TAX REFORM	Reduces individual income taxes by an estimated $9,100,000,000 annually; increases income-tax collections by $6,600,000,000 annually; raises social-security benefits by 15 per cent; increases personal exemptions and standard deductions; extends income-tax surcharge at a 5 per cent rate through June 30, 1970. Signed Dec. 30, Public Law 91-172.
MINE SAFETY	Establishes new Federal standards for the nation's coal mines. Signed Dec. 30, Public Law 91-173.
FOREIGN AID	Authorizes Congress to appropriate $1,972,000,000 in foreign-aid funds for the fiscal year 1970, and $1,936,000,000 for fiscal 1971. Signed Dec. 30, Public Law 91-175.
POVERTY	Extends Economic Opportunity Act for two years. Signed Dec. 30, Public Law 91-177.
TRADE	Replaces Export Control Act of 1949; permits expanded trade with communist countries as long as national security is not endangered. Signed Dec. 30, Public Law 91-184.
ENVIRONMENT	Establishes a three-member Council on Environmental Quality. Signed Jan. 1, 1970, Public Law 91-190.

LIBRARIES

It was probably inevitable that uprisings on campuses and in cities, stimulated by opposition to the war in Vietnam and by real or presumed racial hostility, should leave their mark on some libraries across the United States. Fortunately, only a relatively small number were directly affected, but in these the damage ranged from moderate to severe. One of the worst hit was the University of Illinois library, where some 16,000 cards were removed at random from the public catalog and destroyed. It was estimated that their replacement would cost some $50,-000. Other libraries vandalized included those of Queens College, New York, where catalog cases were overturned and cards dumped out, and Brandeis University, Waltham, Mass., where books were thrown about. As a precaution many libraries are now duplicating their main catalogs on microfilm.

At Beloit College (Wisconsin), music-listening equipment was damaged, furniture was slashed and water drains were plugged. One of the worst calamities was experienced by Indiana University, whose library was ravaged by two fires within three months. They resulted in the loss or damage of some 67,000 volumes, and half of its strong collection in German literature was totally destroyed.

The report of the National Advisory Commission on Libraries, submitted to President Johnson in 1968, received wide publicity in the library press in 1969. It recommended, among other things, a permanent commission for long-range library planning; and a bill, known as the National Library Commission Act of 1969, was introduced to provide for its establishment.

The trend toward economy in government noted in 1968 received new emphasis, reflected at the Federal level in budgeting provisions for library purposes. Title II of the Elementary and Secondary Education Act, providing for library materials and other instructional aids, originally called for an appropriation of $42,000,000, but this was eliminated entirely in President Nixon's budget, as was the proposed $9,100,000 for public-library construction (in the Library Services and Construction Act). These and other suggested reductions and eliminations from President Johnson's proposed budget would reduce the Federal appropriation for major library programs from $134,500,000 to $46,-200,000. Even if some of the proposed cuts are restored, a sharp overall reduction in Federal support seems inevitable.

At the local level the most disturbing event of the year was the threatened closing of the Newark Public Library, when the city council voted to cut off all funds. Protests were immediately raised, by individuals, academic institutions, organized groups and businesses, with the result that the council reversed its action, and the library remained open. Its financial problems remain, however. A grant of $200,000 has been authorized by the Longwood Foundation to be used for the purchase of land for a new library building; but the grant is conditional on the success of the Newark Library Commission in obtaining funds for site development, construction and equipment.

The New York Public Library, faced with the prospect of curtailing services at its research centers, received $1,000,000 from city and state to supplement its income from private sources. The public protest against reducing periods of operation was highlighted by a rally led by noted writers and actors.

Many important appointments were recorded in 1969. Paxton P. Price returned to Missouri from the Office of Education to become head of the St. Louis Public Library. Kenneth F. Duchac was named deputy director of the Brooklyn Public Library. Keith Doms left Pittsburgh to succeed Emerson Greenaway at Philadelphia. Doms in turn was followed in Pittsburgh by Anthony A. Martin. The new director of the Cleveland Public Library is Edward A. D'Alessandro. Frances Henselman was appointed librarian of Long Beach, Calif. Rutherford D. Rogers left Stanford University to become librarian of Yale University; Richard H. Logsdon was appointed dean of libraries for the City University of New York; and his place at Columbia was taken by Warren J. Haas of the University of Pennsylvania. William S. Budington was named executive director and librarian of the John Crerar Library, Chicago, succeeding Herman H. Henkle, who retired. Thomas Mott, Jr., succeeded retiring Neal Harlow as dean of the Rutgers University Graduate School of Library Science.

A number of new library buildings were completed or under construction. The University of Minnesota dedicated its new O. Meredith Wilson Library, to house the social-sciences and humanities collections; Princeton is constructing an addition to the Harvey S. Firestone Memorial Library; the University of Dayton has broken ground for a $4,800,000 library. Yeshiva University (New York) dedicated its $5,000,000 Mendel Gottesman Library, its first central library.

Librarians continued to participate internationally through such organizations as the International Federation of Library Associations (IFLA) and the International Council on Archives. IFLA met in Frankfurt in 1968 and in Copenhagen in 1969. Resolutions adopted at

Frankfurt looked to the creation of a working group for the national and university libraries of Western Europe, and to a request for financial aid from the Council of Europe to establish a European central collection of publications of developing countries.

In 1969 the International Council on Archives (ICA) undertook work in five major fields: started a third series of guides to the sources of national histories; issued a handbook on conservation and restoration of archival documents; organized a round table on community archives; established a group to study developments in microphotographic techniques; and established relations between ICA and associations of archivists working in business enterprises.

In May the first Japan–U.S. Conference on Libraries and Information Science was held in Tokyo, attended by 18 delegates from the United States. It explored library cooperative possibilities between the two countries and undertook to encourage the airing of ideas of mutual library interest. It also considered prospects for the exchange of personnel between the libraries of Japan and the United States.

LIBRARY ASSOCIATIONS

The ALA held its annual convention in Atlantic City, in June. Its general theme, "Mobilizing Resources for Total Library Service," became submerged in the lively debates that ensued over a proposed, later adopted, new dues structure, and over a demand for a thorough examination of the program and operations of the national association.

But even before the convention, a group of library-school students held a conference in Washington, called Congress for Change, in which library education, library service to the disadvantaged, and broader recruitment policies were discussed. The aim is actively to involve more younger people in library affairs.

Sen. Clifford P. Case (R-N.J.) addressed the opening ALA session. He discussed the nuclear arms race, and urged action to stop flight tests of Multiple Independently Targeted Reentry Vehicles (MIRV). At the concluding general session, incoming President William S. Dix chose as his theme "Libraries and the Need for Understanding." He emphasized the importance of understanding the nation's educational needs, and particularly the role that libraries must play through providing the relevant literature in bringing about better understanding of such national concerns as the war in Vietnam, racial conflicts and inequalities, and the inflationary spiral.

During the convention the Council approved a petition to Congress for restoration of Federal funds for library and education programs, and appointed a committee to study possibilities of aid to librarians who become involved in intellectual-freedom conflicts. A committee was also authorized to restudy the goals, policy and structure of the association, to see where it can be made even more relevant to needs.

The Canadian Library Association selected St. John's, Newfoundland, for its annual conference. Problems of organization loomed large in the general discussions. In addition, the public librarians considered the library-system concept, and the Canadian Association of College and University Libraries conducted workshops in library management.

LEON CARNOVSKY
Professor, Graduate Library School
University of Chicago

Indiana University Library

The handsome new library of the University of Indiana, at Bloomington, has windowless walls of native limestone, used so as to give the expanses a sculptured appearance.

literature, north american

For all the vast spate of books published by Americans in 1969 about contemporary problems—Vietnam, race relations, and the new youth subculture—it is noteworthy that many of the finest books of the year dealt with old problems and timeworn themes. In both fiction and nonfiction, for instance, the nazi nightmare continued to haunt the dreams of writers who perhaps saw a new relevance in the violence and guilt of that bloody epoch.

A whole new literature of the holocaust—a literature attempting to come to grips with the experience of the European Jews during World War II—had finally emerged nearly a generation after the fact. Historians and biographers in 1969 continued to sift the facts and try to interpret them. Imaginative writers and theologians were using them as increasingly pertinent metaphors with which to describe or discuss the human condition.

Television, once considered the mortal enemy of literature, aided these writers by bringing live atrocities into every American living room. In a more benign way, television aided the cause of a more traditional literature, as the 26-part BBC series based on Galsworthy's *Forsyte Saga* began screening in America after achieving success in Europe. It brought new life to a long dormant literary reputation, and made the Victorian Forsytes seem more alive than the characters in many more recent books.

Fiction. By a rare coincidence, the runaway best seller of 1969 was also the most distinguished novel published by an American: Philip Roth's hilarious and ferocious *Portnoy's Complaint.* Highly touted before publication and then almost universally praised and damned for the wrong reasons, Roth's third novel was not only the Ultimate Jewish Novel and the Ultimate Sex Novel, but a beautifully sustained high comedy of bad manners between parents and children, between patient and analyst (although Alexander Portnoy's long-suffering analyst doesn't speak until the last line of the book), and between our base instincts and the thin veneer of civilization.

Like *Lolita, Portnoy's Complaint* infuriated the few surviving bluenosed smut-hunters, who failed to see that, like Nabokov's *succès de scandale,* Roth's novel displayed a stylistic control, an accuracy of dialogue and an inventive wit that raised it far above the merely pornographic. But then, Nabokov didn't like it either.

The old master of black sex-comedy himself produced his fifteenth novel, *Ada, or Ardor: A Family Chronicle,* which turned out to be a big disappointment. Twice as long and ten times as complex as any of his earlier novels, *Ada* was a self-parody of Nabokov's stylistic fireworks and metaphysical themes.

The incestuous love of Ada and Van Veen was buried under such a weight of multilingual puns, anagrams, in-jokes and chess problems that anyone reading it for the wrong reasons was quickly bored and baffled. Unfortunately, even Nabokov's most ardent fans—who read it for all the right reasons—had the same reaction to a novel too clever and self-indulgent for its own good.

Yet black comedy continued to dominate quality fiction in 1969. An old hand at it, Kurt Vonnegut, Jr., produced his finest work to date in *Slaughterhouse-Five: or the Children's Crusade,* an appropriately searing account of the wanton fire-bombing of the open city of Dresden toward the end of World War II. The Candide-like hero, Billy Pilgrim, learns that the nazis have no exclusive patent on atrocity. Like Swift, Vonnegut turns his deadpan ferocity on man's inhumanity to man, regardless of national borders.

A less bitter but equally accomplished black comedy, Julian Moynahan's *Pairing Off,* dealt with its hero's attempts to find love in the stacks of a great but ill-managed big-city library, only to be plunged into a series of comic misadventures reminiscent of *Lucky Jim* and *The Ginger Man.* Where Nabokov's characters inhabit a complex mirror image of the world called anti-Terra, and Billy Pilgrim travels through the fourth dimension to the remote planet Tralfmadore, Moynahan's novel is more firmly rooted in mundane reality. The villain here is simply the oldest one of all: Death.

Biography and Autobiography. Literary biography in 1969 suffered from a depressing tendency to bury the subject under a welter of irrelevant facts. This factual overkill marred what should have been three of the best biographies of the year: John Unterecker's *Voyager: A Life of Hart Crane,* Carl Bode's *Mencken* and Carlos Baker's long-awaited official biography *Ernest Hemingway.*

Thus the most doomed poet, the most rambunctious critic and the most significant novelist of the American 1920's and 1930's were obscured rather than revealed by their biographers' inability to see the forest for the facts. Unassimilated laundry lists and high-school report cards don't by themselves constitute biography, and they turned out to be no substitute for psychological insight, coherent point of view and clear organization.

These are precisely the qualities that distinguished Leon Edel's fourth volume in his epic life of *Henry James: The Treacherous Years: 1895–1901*. Begun in 1953, this mammoth work now has just one volume to go. While Edel obviously knows more about James than James himself did, he never lets his massive accumulation of data about the great American novelist get in the way of his clear and absorbing narrative flow.

The most recent installment takes James through the difficult period when he was forced to realize that he was no playwright and consequently went into a spiritual funk that produced his weakest mature fiction. Undaunted by the placid surface of James' life, Edel probed to the inner man and produced the most fascinating biography of the year.

Another superbly vivid but authoritative and well-documented biography was T. Harry Williams' *Huey Long*. Largely sympathetic to the Louisiana Kingfish who might have become president if he had not been shot down in his own capitol, Williams had the full cooperation of Huey's son, Sen. Russell Long, and was thus able to interview surviving friends of the egalitarian semidictator of Depression Louisiana. The result was a portrait in depth of a crude but complex man.

A rather more creative man of the people was Beethoven, whose 200th birthday in 1970 was anticipated in a scholarly but highly readable biography by George Marek. And a composer who died in 1869 provided perhaps the most fascinating autobiography of 1969. He was Hector Berlioz, whose *Memoirs* were newly translated by David Cairns to reveal for the first time in English all the sparkle and imaginative fervor of one of the most characteristic of romantic geniuses.

History and General Nonfiction. For some reason this was the year for histories of the fall of France in 1940. Guy Chapman's *Why France Fell*, Alistair Horne's *To Lose a Battle* and William L. Shirer's *The Collapse of the Third Republic* all tried to account for France's ignominious defeat by the nazi army. Shirer,

Pictorial Parade

Camera Press-PIX

Novels by Philip Roth (top) and Vladimir Nabokov (dressed for another interest, butterfly collecting) won the serious attention of both critics and readers. Though otherwise quite different, Roth's "Portnoy's Complaint" and Nabokov's "Ada" were both comedies.

FICTION

John Cheever, *Bullet Park,* a symbolic allegory about father and son in suburban Cheeverland

Richard Condon, *Mile High,* sour view of making it in America by the author of *The Manchurian Candidate*

Evan S. Connell, Jr., *Mr. Bridge,* Kansas City Babbitt husband to the *Mrs. Bridge* of a decade ago

Andrew Field, *Fractions,* pseudo-Nabokovian adventures of a hung-up book reviewer

Leonard Gardner, *Fat City,* an authentic whiff of the boxing game

Cecelia Holland, *Until the Sun Falls,* brilliant evocation of the medieval Mongol invasion of Russia

Joyce Carol Oates, *them,* history of a family in slums of a Midwestern city

Robert Deane Pharr, *The Book of Numbers,* the policy racket in the Depression South

Chaim Potok, *The Promise,* sequel to the best-selling *The Chosen,* whose two heroes now enter the adult world

Mario Puzo, *The Godfather,* this year's Mafia novel

L. Woiwode, *What I'm Going To Do, I Think,* a quietly moving novel about the problems of a young marriage

BIOGRAPHY

Miriam J. Benkovitz, *Ronald Firbank,* the fullest treatment yet of the fey English novelist

Louis O. Coxe, *Edwin Arlington Robinson,* a fine account of a sorely underrated New England poet

Gordon Haight, *George Eliot,* the authoritative biography of the great Victorian novelist

Lillian Hellman, *An Unfinished Woman,* the famous playwright reminisces about Dorothy Parker, Dashiell Hammett and others

Jack Newfield, *Robert Kennedy,* a memoir by a man close to the Senator's last campaign

HISTORY

Dan T. Carter, *Scottsboro,* definitive account of the famous 1930's Southern rape case

Abba Eban, *My People,* the history of the Jews by Israel's most articulate statesman

Eric F. Goldman, *The Tragedy of Lyndon Johnson,* What Went Wrong—by LBJ's ambassador to the intellectuals

Chadwick Hansen, *Witchcraft at Salem,* the witches really *were* guilty!

Robert F. Kennedy, *Thirteen Days,* the Cuban missile crisis as experienced by the late Senator

William Manchester, *The Arms of Krupp,* a bitter look at the German munitions dynasty

Edgar B. Nixon, *Franklin D. Roosevelt and Foreign Affairs,* definitive scholarly account of FDR's foreign policy in 1933–37

Theodore H. White, *The Making of the President 1968,* journalistic once-over-lightly of the Nixon-Humphrey campaign.

POETRY

Elizabeth Bishop, *The Complete Poems,* collection by a distinguished American poet

Robert Penn Warren, *Audubon: A Vision,* a long poem about the great bird-portraitist

Philip Whalen, *On Bear's Head,* poems in the Buddhist tradition

RELIGION

Frederick Buechner, *The Hungering Dark,* religious meditations by the author of *A Long Day's Dying*

Robert Farrar Capon, *The Supper of the Lamb,* a unique combination of gourmet recipes and Episcopal theology

Martin E. Marty, *The Search for a Usable Future,* problems facing American Churches

GENERAL NONFICTION

Michael J. Arlen, *Living-Room War,* the best television criticism of the year

Henry S. Cooper, Jr., *Apollo on the Moon,* how the astronauts got there

Benjamin DeMott, *Supergrow,* essays on what ails us (mostly egoism) by a with-it professor

James Simon Kunen, *The Strawberry Statement,* a very funny account by a Columbia student of the recent ruckus on campus

Dan McCall, *The Example of Richard Wright,* about the famous black author of *Native Son*

Ellen Moers, *Two Dreisers,* concentrates on the writing of *Sister Carrie* and *An American Tragedy*

Flannery O'Connor, *Mystery and Manners,* ruminations on fiction by a fine practitioner who died in 1964

Harold Peterson, *The Last of the Mountain Men,* about Buckskin Bill, the Robinson Crusoe of Idaho

Andrew Sarris, *The American Cinema,* criticism by the provocative movie man for *The Village Voice*

C. L. Sulzberger, *A Long Row of Candles,* memoirs of a veteran reporter for the *Times*

---

because of his previous success with *The Rise and Fall of the Third Reich,* received the most publicity, but his account was the most disappointing. Lacking the grand scope of the earlier book, Shirer resorted to padding and scapegoat-hunting right back to 1870. The question of who betrayed whom in the 1930's to produce the debacle of 1940 was explored less journalistically by Chapman and Horne.

The German side of the events that led to 1940 was scrupulously examined by Richard M. Watt's *The Kings Depart: The Tragedy of Germany,* a brilliant study of the botched peace treaty of Versailles. And another major trauma

of World War II, the terrible siege of Leningrad, received full treatment in Harrison E. Salisbury's *The 900 Days.* More than a million Russians died horribly between 1941 and 1944, when the nazi Army was finally forced to release its stranglehold on the beleaguered city. Salisbury, long a Russian correspondent for *The New York Times,* produced a gruesome but compassionate account of those heroic days.

The *Times* itself came in for quite a lambasting in *The Kingdom and the Power,* a gossipy account by former *Times* reporter Gay Talese of the infighting that went on between the Good Gray Lady of 43rd St. and her

Washington Bureau. It made the lady grow considerably grayer, but armchair executive-suite generals chortled at all the corporate carryings-on.

A veteran upsetter of pompous apple carts is John Kenneth Galbraith, the prolific and versatile Harvard economist, whose *Ambassador's Journal* was a witty and yet rather pathetic account of his diplomatic mission to India during the Kennedy years. The wit came from his encounters with diplomatic officialdom, both American and Indian. The pathos arose from the messages he sent back to Camelot warning of the disastrous course the United States was then beginning to pursue in Vietnam. Since Vietnam was officially none of Galbraith's business, his advice was largely ignored. With benefit of hindsight, we can see that it should have been heeded. As usual, there is no question of who is the hero of a Galbraith book.

Poetry. To no one's surprise, 1969 was a weak year for the Muse. There was evidence on campuses, however, of a burgeoning interest in poetry among the nation's youth, so there may be hope for the future. But meanwhile, the best poetry was a thin trickle from some fairly old hands.

Age had even caught up with Allen Ginsberg, whose *Planet News,* published in 1968, bemoaned, among other things, the dean of hippiedom's lost youth. With the death in 1969 of Jack Kerouac, Ginsberg was the last major survivor of the original Beat Generation, and, at 43, he had become mellow and almost avuncular. The *Howl* that made his reputation had become an elegiac chant, and the blend of Whitman and Hindu mantras was whipped up as beguilingly as before, but had somehow lost its kick.

On the other end of the poetic spectrum were the real oldsters, one of whom, Mark Van Doren, celebrated his 75th birthday with a new volume of rural lyrics, *That Shining Place.* With Robert Frost gone, Van Doren has established himself as the ranking transported-New Englander, finding the eternal verities in apple blossoms and rocking chairs.

If a poetic voice was tuning up in 1969 to take over from the Frost-Van Doren generation, or even from the Kerouac-Ginsberg generation, it had not as yet made itself heard.

RICHARD FREEDMAN
Assistant Professor of English
Simmons College

literature, international

Of the world's various literatures, each presents national characteristics determined by the physical and social environment and historical traditions. In addition, however, there are esthetic and ideological tendencies and theories that defy national boundaries and the contingencies of space and time. Modern communication media spread ideas and artistic fashions rapidly. Where once impulses took years to travel from one country to another, they now spring up almost simultaneously in the remotest areas.

In recent years this universality of artistic direction has been particularly apparent as widespread interest in linguistic formalism and structuralism. The predominant feature of 1969 was the growing involvement of writers in experiments with language and in verbal research. The best illustration of this phenomenon is offered by France, a country that for three centuries has been the spawning ground of literary trends. However, non-French writers have played an important part in these developments. The 1969 Nobel Prize in Literature was awarded to Samuel Beckett, an Irishman whose misanthropic novels and plays are written in sophisticated French. He himself translates them into English.

In France during 1969 the general public avidly read entertainment fiction: *Papillon* (Butterfly) by Henry Charriere, a fugitive from the penal colony in French Guiana (half a million copies); and *Piaf,* a romanticized biography of the popular singer Edith Piaf by her sister and close friend Simone Berteaut (over 300,000 copies).

Un adolescent d'autrefois (A Youth of Former Times), by the octogenarian François Mauriac, is the story of a Catholic youth torn between carnal passions and the search for God. *Les Garçons* (The Boys), by the septuagenarian Henry de Montherlant, glorifies the sense of duty and sacrifice in a proud boy in a Jesuit college. In 1969, these represented the traditional novel. The transition between the old and the new was achieved by L.-F. Céline's posthumous *Rigodon.* It evokes Germany among the ruins and fires of defeat in a raving soliloquy expressed in an extravagant idiom.

The break with realism and Freudian psychology was represented by Claude Simon, whose name has been mentioned for the Nobel Prize. His *La Bataille de Pharsale* (The Battle of Pharsalus), a plotless succession of images, impressions, associations and quotations that

AFRICA

Yambo Ouologuem (Mali, writes in French), *Le devoir de violence* (The Duty of Violence), historical novel

Ralph Uwechue (Biafran in exile), *Reflections on the Nigerian Civil War* (written in English)

ASIA

Ichiro Kawasaki (career Japanese diplomat; book written in English but translated into Japanese), *Japan Unmasked,* critical probing of Japan and the Japanese

EUROPE

Simone Balazard (French, Algerian-born), *L'Histoire d'Emile,* novella collection

Carlo Castellaneta (Italian), *Gli Incantesimi* (The Spells), novel

Ramon Hernandez (Spanish), *Palabras en el muro* (Words on the Wall), novel

Siegfried Lenz (German), *Deutschstunde* (German Lesson), novel of youth under Hitler

Thomas Mann, Heinrich Mann: Briefwechsel [An Exchange of Letters] *1900–1949,* ed. by Hans Wissling

Alexander Mitscherlich (German), *Die Unfähigkeit zu trauern* (The Inability to Mourn), psychology

Michel Mohrt (French), *L'Ours des Adirondacks* (The Bear of the Adirondacks), novel

François Nourissier (French), *Le Maître de maison* (The Owner of the House), novel

Baltasar Porcel (Spanish), *Las Sombras chinescas* (Chinese Shadow Pictures), experimental novel

Renate Rasp (German), *Eine Rennstrecke* (Distance to Be Run), poetry collection

Giose Rimanelli (Italian), *Tragica America,* examination of the United States in crisis

Carlos Rojas (Spaniard in exile), *Auto de fe,* recreation of reign of Bourbon monarch Carlos II

Françoise Sagan (French), *Un peu de soleil dans l'eau froide* (A Little Sun in Cold Water), novel

Bernard Teyssèdre (French), *Foi de Fol* (A Fool's Faith), a brew of contemporary art and literature

EUROPE, EAST

Artur London (Czech-born, writing in French), *L'Aveu* (The Confession), self-accusation under Stalinism

LATIN AMERICA

Manuel Puig (Argentine), *La Traicion de* [The Betrayal of] *Rita Hayworth,* novel

MIDDLE EAST

Sadeh Galal al Azm (Arab, book pub. in Beirut), *Self-Criticism after the Defeat,* unusual objective analysis of Arab defeat in June 1967

---

must be sorted out by the reader, is conceived as a verbal symphony, a linguistic construction. Following this direction, younger writers sometimes lapse into sterile tricks (*La Disparition* [The Disappearance], a 352-page narrative by Gorges Perec, eliminates the letter "e").

A similar situation exists in Italy. Literary prizes still go to traditional novels such as *Le parole tra noi leggere,* by Lalla Romano, which depicts an Italian-style beatnik or hippie, as seen by his mother, which won the Strega Prize. *L'Airone* (The Heron), by Giorgio Bassani, a psychological study of the motives that lead a landowner and lonely bachelor to suicide, published in late 1968, was awarded the Viareggio Prize in 1969.

The younger generation is taking a different road. Elsa Morante offers fantastic dreams in her poetic and farcical *Il mondo salvato dai ragazzi* (The World Saved by the Young), written half in verse and half in prose. *Super Heliogabalo,* by Alberto Abrasino, is a surrealistic extravaganza in the guise of an exuberant, pseudohistorical tale of a Roman emperor who has four mothers. Works by Tommaso Landolfi, Dino Buzzati and Luigi Malerba represent various aspects of "magic symbolism" and imaginative flights combined with the search for a new style.

German literature offers a more complex picture. In East Germany, socialist realism is the official style, and in 1968 *Vertrauen* (In Confidence), by Anna Seghers, a novel about social conditions in a provincial factory and the demonstrations of 1953, was hailed as a typical work of communist persuasion. Less dogmatic is *Impressum* by Hermann Kant. Off the beaten path is *Nachdenken über Christa T.* (Reflections on Christa T.), by Christa Wolf, a beautifully written portrait of a sincere, talented woman trying to find the meaning of the individual in society. Though East German censors limited its circulation, it was much more widely distributed in West Germany on publication there in the fall of 1969.

Of course, writers have more creative freedom and evince more variety in West Germany, even though they are deeply involved in politics. The literary event of the year was *Ortlich Betäubt* (Local Anesthesia), a best-selling, controversial novel by Günter Grass. In parody and grotesqueries, he describes the clash between middle-aged conformists and foolish but sincere young rebels. An anthology of novels, plays and essays by Peter Handke, a 27-year-old avant-garde writer, who combines political commitment with attempts at linguistic renovation, also had great success. *Schattengrenze* (Shadow-Border), by Dieter Wellershoff, a widely discussed attempt at "new factology" in fiction, and *Der Fall d'Arthez* by H. E. Nossack are also worth mentioning.

Works by young Dutch writers included: *Vriendelijke vreemdeleng* (Kindly Stranger), by Adriaan van der Veen, a frank autobiog-

Henry Charriere, author of French best seller "Papillon" (Butterfly), talks with Indian tribe of Venezuela, who had adopted him, on trip back to French Guiana. His book is story of his life in and escape from old penal colony once there.

Günter Grass (r), German writer, chats with Federal Minister of Economy Karl Schiller during the election for West German president. A highly political work, Grass' 1969 novel "Ortlich Betäubt" (Local Anesthesia) became a best seller.

D.P.A.-Pictorial Parade

"Paris Match," Pictorial Parade

Of both literary and political interest in 1969 was the defection of Russian writer Anatoly Kuznetsov from the Soviet Union. He said that he could no longer work under repression—a feeling that was strengthened by the occupation of Czechoslovakia—and charged that his work was distorted by Soviet censors. He found asylum in Great Britain.

"The New York Times"

raphy; *De vingerwijzing* (The Key) by Ed. Hoornik, who writes in a style reminiscent of Nabokov; and *De avonturen van Kim Miller* (The Adventures of Kim Miller) by J. Bernlef.

In Spain, *San Camilo,* the new novel about the beginning of the Civil War by Camillo Cela, stories by Ana Maria Matute (who was awarded the Spanish Academy prize); and, in Portugal, *O segredo e amor,* by Sebastido de Gama, and *Alegria Breve* (Brief Joy), by Vergilio Ferreiro, were among the few more significant works of 1969.

Latin-American fiction and poetry are possibly the most inventive and flourishing on a world scale, and in the context of language completely eclipse that of Spain and Portugal. In the last decade the works of Jorge Luis Borges, Pablo Neruda, Miguel Angel Asturias, Mario Vargas Llosa and many others have revealed the wealth and diversity of Latin-American literatures. Two books emerged as masterpieces in 1968-69: *Cien Años de Soledad* (A Hundred Years of Solitude), by Gabriel Garcia Marques, a vast mythological narrative often compared with Joyce's *Ulysses;* and *62 Modelo para armar* by Julio Cortazar.

In 1969, political restrictions still crippled literary production in Spain, Portugal and Greece. Many Greek writers are publishing their works abroad, as happened with *Les Photographies* by Vassilis Vassilikos, author of

Z; and *La fontaine de Skopélos,* a warm, amusing tale by Clément Lépidis. Both were issued in French.

Censorship and oppression are responsible for the dullness and monotony of fiction in the U.S.S.R. Among the few works that succeeded in breaking away were *Kubik,* an imaginative tale by Valentin Katayev, and the fantastic historical novel *Bedny Avrosimov* (Poor Avrosimov) by the poet Bulat Okudzhava. Great interest was provoked in the West by the outspoken essay, smuggled abroad, *Intellectual Freedom and Convergence* (between communism and capitalism) by the eminent scholar Dimitry Sakharov. Svetlana Alliluyeva's second book, *Only One Year,* published in various languages, tells about her escape from Russia and gives interesting details on Stalin, her father, and his associates.

Young Hungarian authors such as Terenc Yugasz in his surrealistic poem *The Flood of Fire,* and Djula Illys in his symbolic *Charon's Ferryboat,* and the Rumanians Sanziana Pop (*Serenada na trompetu*), Marin Preda (*Intrusul*) and Marin Sorescu (*Jonas*) are strongly influenced by West European avant-garde movements. So also are Yugoslav writers Slobodan Novak and Peter Selenic. Czechoslovak writers, silenced in 1969, must publish their works abroad. These included the ironical, sharp *Diary of a Counter-Revolutionary* by

Pavel Kohout, and *The Road to the Cemetery* by Ota Filip.

Japanese literature is gaining an international audience as more works are translated and become popular, such as those of 1968 Nobel Prizewinner Yasunari Kawabata (*Kyoto, Snow Country, Dancer*). Books by Mishima, Abe Kobo and Morio Kito, a middle-aged writer of fantasies, will also soon be available in Western bookstores.

In the parts of Africa and the Middle East that were once under French control, French remains the literary language. The Association of French-Language Writers has 600 members from 29 African countries. They include the Algerians Kateb Yacine, who wrote *Nedyma*, a novel, and Rachid Boudjedra, whose violent, half-ironic, half-political *La Répudiation* was a sensation in 1969; the Moroccan Francis Morsy; the Cameroun novelists François

Evembé (*Ici Essouna*) and Francis Bebey, whose *Le fils d'Agatha Muano* won the Great Prize of Black Africa; the Nigerian Boubou Hama, author of *Kotia Nima*, a novel of childhood; and the Lebanese Andrée Chedid, whose *L'Autre* was also hailed in 1969.

In the Middle East, stories and novels in Arabic by Egyptian writers Abou an Naga (collection *Men and Love*), Al Busat (*Big and Small*) and Mustafa Mahmoud (who was awarded the state prize for his science-fiction *Spider* and *Man with Below-Zero Temperature*) found an appreciative audience. In Israel, *Mont Michel*, a novel of frustrated love and solitude set in Jerusalem, by the Jewish writer Amos Oz, sold 40,000 copies. The figure is an indication of Israel's high degree of literacy.

MARC SLONIM
Writes "European Notebook,"
The New York Times Book Review

literature, juvenile

The 50th anniversary of children's book publishing, as a special branch of the general book trade, as well as the 50th annual celebration of Children's Book Week (the third week of November) went forward with all honors due the founders. Macmillan Co. created the first juvenile-book department under Louise Seaman Bechtel in 1919, and part of its anniversary celebration included the publication of *Books in Search of Children*, a collection of Mrs. Bechtel's essays. Across the country, public and school librarians honored those responsible for the first official Children's Book Week: Mrs. Bechtel; Anne Carroll Moore, who long served as supervisor of work with children at the New York Public Library; and Frederick G. Melcher, who was president of R. R. Bowker Company.

However, children's-book specialists in publishing, bookselling, library service and education faced the golden-anniversary year gravely concerned about the heavy reduction in Federal funds for schools and libraries in the Nixon administration's first budget. At year-end, the Senate gave every indication of joining the House in recommending the restoration of the funds, which have acquired a great influence on the numbers and kinds of new children's books published. From its beginnings fifty years ago, the major market (amounting to between 75 per cent and 95 per cent of sales in juvenile-publishing houses) for children's books has been schools and public libraries. Any reduction in library book budgets immediately

affects the revenues of publishers and book wholesalers.

Despite their concern over the unresolved budget cuts for the four-year-old Education Act programs affecting book purchases, the publishers brought out most of the titles previously scheduled for 1969 publication in the spring and fall, the two seasons in which new children's books have always been bunched. The 1969 juvenile-book count was therefore expected to hold at the level of the previous three years: between 2,700 and 3,000 new titles.

Rising prices for children's books continue to be the factor that prevents the general trade children's-book publishers and the bookstores from attracting a mass audience of individual book buyers as significant to hard-cover book sales as the institutional buyers are. From 1960 to the beginning of 1969, the average cost of a children's book rose from $2.75 to $3.47, an increase of 26 per cent, reflecting the rapidly increasing costs of printing and binding, as well as the heavy costs in the mechanics of color printing. Most books for the youngest children rely heavily on illustrations, and their multicolor reproduction in quality picture books makes them at once the most beautiful and relatively the most expensive of general trade books.

The more than 4,000 juvenile paperbacks in print are expected to offer booksellers the best opportunity to capture the regular attention of individual buyers of children's books. In

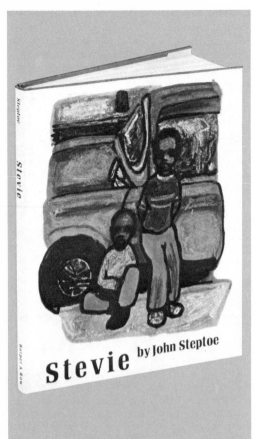

Harper & Row

steadily increasing numbers, school and public libraries are turning to collections of paperbacks as the best method of extending inadequate book budgets, to the delight of their younger patrons who appear to prefer paperbacks to books in standard, often clumsy library bindings.

Representation of contemporary social and political concerns in juvenile novels drew the most critical attention from educators, librarians and bookmen during 1969. Dominating the discussion of children's books at each reading level from preschool through junior high school was the issue of race relations and civil rights with the emphasis on clear and honest portrayals of black-ghetto conditions and the history of Negroes in America. The fact that a picture book such as Ezra Jack Keats' *Goggles* drew praise for showing in words and pictures slum street life without polishing up the neighborhood, and that an early-grade story such as Janice Udry's *What Mary Jo Wanted* was applauded for illustrator Eleanor Mill's ability to reflect typical Negroid features indicates factors long missing in books for children. Since textbooks have until recently

The bold lines of John Steptoe's illustrations give perfect support to his story "Stevie," about a lad's mixed reactions when a younger boy comes to board.

In "Thy Friend, Obadiah," Brinton Turkle tells in words and pictures about a young Quaker in old Nantucket.

Viking Press

NEWBERY MEDAL

Lloyd Alexander, *The High King*

CALDECOTT MEDAL

Uri Shulevitz, illustrator, *The Fool of the World and the Flying Ship*

FOR OLDER READERS

William H. Armstrong, *Sounder*
Vera and Bill Cleaver, *Where the Lilies Bloom*
John Donovan, *I'll Get There. It Better Be Worth the Trip*
Constance C. Greene, *A Girl Called Al*
Gil Rabin, *False Start*
Theodore Taylor, *The Cay*

FOR INTERMEDIATE READERS

Geraldine Flanagan, illustrated with photographs, *Window into an Egg*
Paula Fox, illustrated by Eros Keith, *The King's Falcon*
E. W. Hildick, illustrated by Jan Palmer, *Manhattan Is Missing*
Anne Rockwell, illustrated by the author, *Temple on a Hill*
George Selden, illustrated by Garth Williams, *Tucker's Countryside*
Mary Q. Steele, illustrated by Rocco Negri, *Journey Outside*
Harvey Weiss, illustrated with photographs, *Motors and Engines and How They Work*
Harve Zemach, illustrated by Margot Zemach, *The Judge*

FOR YOUNGEST READERS

Marcia Brown, illustrated by the author, *How, Hippo!*
Rebecca Caudill and James Ayars, illustrated by Glen Rounds, *Contrary Jenkins*
Janina Domanska, illustrated by the author, *The Turnip*
Ellen Raskin, illustrated by the author, *And It Rained*
William Steig, illustrated by the author, *Sylvester and the Magic Pebble*
John Steptoe, illustrated by the author, *Stevie*
Brinton Turkle, illustrated by the author, *Thy Friend, Obadiah*

---

given little or no space to the Negro's historic role in the United States, pressure has been increasing to close this knowledge gap with supplementary histories and source materials, with Janet Harris' and Julius Hobson's *Black Pride* and Arnold Adoff's *Black on Black* as the outstanding recent nonfiction titles published for older children.

Then there are the books that attempt to deal with sex problems and the drug scene. John Donovan's well-written *I'll Get There. It Better Be Worth the Trip* gained instant attention as the publicity focused on a first encounter with homoerotic attraction between two junior-high-school boys, the first time any juvenile novel ventured to deal with this common experience. Paul Zindel's *My Darling, My Hamburger* is all about a high-school pregnancy and an illicit abortion, while A. E. Johnson's *A Blues I Can Whistle* takes on the whole late-adolescent scene of political and philosophical unrest and indecision.

While these and other titles with the same subject matter or themes have been generally well received in printed critical appraisals, such books continue to be a source of unease among librarians, teachers and parents because of potential problems with vocal conservative groups, which often oppose the idea that sex, drugs or politics are necessary or proper concerns for younger readers. Library-book collections offer a sitting target for such attacks, which have risen in direct proportion to the organized drive during 1969 against sex education in the schools. However, the responses of children to books with contemporary issues in contemporary terms indicate that their ultimate audience is ready and eager for more.

Teachers and librarians have expanded their fields of instruction and service to children to include nonprint, audio-visual materials, such as records, films and filmstrips. This resulted in numerous gloomy predictions about the death of the book in our time. But many publishers scrambled away from the grave by coordinating their standard titles with the newer media and selling these sets as packaged units. The year 1969 saw a rash of these, which have been especially well received by classroom teachers. Their early reports indicate that the combined materials have definite value to the teaching of reading to children born in the Age of McLuhan.

A wider general recognition of books for children, their art, their uses, their costs, their content and their readership has been the unsolved problem of the juvenile-book trade in its fifty years. But in 1969 a giant step was taken toward catching and holding public attention with the presentation of the first $1,000 children's-book prize by the prestigious National Book Committee. Its judges chose Meindert De Jong's *Journey from Peppermint Street* from among the following 1968 outstanding candidates: Lloyd Alexander's *The High King*, which also received the 1969 American Library Association Newbery Medal; Patricia Clapp's *Constance;* Esther Hautzig's *The Endless Steppe* and Milton Meltzer's *Langston Hughes.*

LILLIAN N. GERHARDT, Executive Editor
School Library Journal Book Review
R. R. Bowker Co. Juvenile Projects

LOUISIANA

In Monroe, white politicians gained control of the city's antipoverty program. They had bitterly opposed its presence and policy for three years. In March the Federal Office of Economic Opportunity called the seizure "deliberately subversive." ☐ On Mar. 18, northern offshore winds and high seas fortunately dissipated an oil slick in the Gulf of Mexico near the state shore. A well 18 miles offshore had blown out on Mar. 16. Farther west in the gulf, a natural-gas well was also out of control.

LUXEMBOURG

The long government crisis in the Grand Duchy of Luxembourg ended on Jan. 27, 1969, when the Christian Social Party and the Liberal Party agreed to form a coalition. The previous coalition between the CSP and the Socialists split in October 1968. The new Cabinet was headed again by Pierre Werner, the outgoing prime minister. Members of the coalition parties hold 32 of the 55 seats in the Luxembourg Parliament.

LUXEMBOURG

Area: 999 sq. mi.
Population: 300,000
Capital: Luxembourg (pop., 77,100)
Government: Jean, grand duke—1964; Pierre Werner, prime minister—1959
Gross National Product: $800,000,000
Monetary unit: Belgian franc (50.2 BF = U.S. $1.00)
Chief products: oats, potatoes, wheat, fruit, wine, iron, steel
Communications: 93,767 telephones, 50,700 TV sets, 7 daily newspapers
Transportation: roads, 3,063 mi.; 78,097 passenger cars; railroads, 211 mi.
Education: 44,074 elementary and secondary students, 6,463 vocational and university students
Armed forces: 560

See map on page 185

In local elections in October the strength of the Liberals was confirmed, although for the first time in some years the Communists also made gains.

Luxembourg has the highest standard of living in the European Common Market, if that standard is measured in terms of cars, TV sets, telephones, home ownership and bank balances.

Steel still accounts for 25 per cent of the gross national product and employs 18 per cent of the people. The substantial dependence on heavy industry probably holds the growth rate below what it would be otherwise. At a steady 3.5 per cent it remains, however, quite creditable.

With the merger of the three executives of the European Communities (Economic, Atomic, and Coal and Steel) Luxembourg lost its main political magnet, the High Authority of the European Coal and Steel Community, the first of all the European "communities." However, in exchange, Grand Duke Jean's duchy gained the Common Market's Court of Justice, the European Investment Bank and the Statistical Office. Meanwhile the Council of Ministers meets in Luxembourg for three months of every year, in April, June and October.

Also a center of commercial broadcasting and for investments through Eurodollars and Eurobonds, Luxembourg gave indications in 1969 of becoming "the Services Capital of Western Europe."

JOHN ALLAN MAY
Chief, London Bureau
The Christian Science Monitor

MAINE

On Jan. 26 the scenic coastal community of Trenton rejected a $160,000,000 bond issue for an industrial park including an aluminum smelter and a nuclear power station. ☐ The controversial proposal to create a foreign-trade zone in Maine won Federal approval at the subcabinet level on Feb. 10. Advocates claimed that it would help New England by reducing fuel and power costs and promoting economic growth. ☐ Portland was chosen on Feb. 15 as the terminus for new ferry service from Yarmouth, Nova Scotia. ☐ On July 1 state personal and corporate income taxes went into effect.

MALAYSIA

At the end of 1969, Malaysia, as far from democracy as it had ever been since its creation in 1963, was slowly picking up the pieces after a dream-shattering few days in May when as many as five hundred people may have died in racial violence. Still nominally the country's leader, the once "smiling Prime Minister," Tunku Abdul Rahman, had become little more than an onlooker as his longtime pupil and Deputy Premier, Tun Abdul Razak, ran the nation's emergency Government, the National Operations Council. Economically the country had lost little in trade, only a few days in production and some foreign investment. Politically, at least on an official level, the nation was at a standstill. Unofficially, the Malay Peninsula remained a hotbed of intrigue al-

UPI

A street in the Chinese quarter of Kuala Lumpur, capital of Malaysia, shows the ugly result of the violence that flared up there in May between Chinese and Malays; several hundred persons probably lost their lives.

though emergency measures had all but ended racial violence. To the north, in the mountain jungles along the West Malaysian-Thai border, Chin Peng, longtime leader of the Malay Communist Party, and his followers continued to harass both Malaysian and Thai security patrols.

In East Malaysia—Sabah and Sarawak on Borneo—it was a quiet year, with the electorate showing surprising patience, though it missed a chance to go to the polls. (Voting in East Malaysia, scheduled after West Malaysia's general election on May 10, was postponed

Abdul Razak was the actual head of Malaysia in 1969.

UPI

after the racial bloodbath which started in the capital, Kuala Lumpur, on May 13.)

The year started quietly. Two months before, the Alliance Party—the dominant United Malays National Organization (UMNC), the Malaysian Chinese Association (MCA) and the Malaysian Indian Congress (MIC)—Government had carried out a purge of Labor Party leaders, judged to be the main threat to the Alliance's continuing in power. The purge had been made on the allegation that the Labor Party, or at least elements of it, was linked with the Malaysian Communist Party. Many Labor leaders were jailed, and the persecuted party boycotted the May 10 elections. In fact, having lost its key men, it was in no condition to offer a serious challenge.

The first signs of racial tension, which had flared on a lesser scale on the island state of Penang in late 1967, came as the election campaign began to warm up. With plans for the external security of the country very much up in the air in the light of Britain's intended military withdrawal from east of Suez by the end of 1971, and the Philippine claim to Sabah virtually dormant, the campaign was based mainly on domestic issues. To the fore came the questions of the rights of Malays and Chinese, the country's two dominant ethnic groups. While the Malaysian economy is controlled, first, by European and, second, by Chinese interests, the Malays form the basic work force, either in government service or as agricultural or other labor.

Tension resulted when a UMNO worker on Penang was killed, allegedly by Labor Party supporters. A few days before the election a Labor Party worker was shot dead by police, and on the eve of the election four thousand persons, the body borne among them, marched through the streets of Kuala Lumpur. Although many carried banners hailing the Thoughts of Chairman Mao Tse-tung, the demonstration was peaceful.

When election results began to come in, it became clear that though the Alliance would remain in control it had lost its two-thirds majority (and thereby its power to push through constitutional changes). Thereupon, panic seemed to seize the country. Many Malays, their faith pinned on the Alliance's capacity to work economic miracles, feared the trend marked a major step toward Chinese consolidation of their grip on the economy. Young Chinese, exhilarated by the Democratic Action Party's success in winning an unprecedented 13 seats in West Malaysia, took to the streets in victory parades.

Malays claimed that they were insulted by the Chinese and Indians. On the evening of May 13 they gathered outside the home of the UMNO chief minister of Selangor, in Kuala Lumpur. Some were armed with the traditional Malay knife, the parang. Rumors spread that Malays had been attacked by Chinese, and the killing started. Malay mobs headed for Chinese areas of the capital where they burned houses, shops and vehicles. Chinese groups, crudely armed, were dispersed by gunfire.

Allegations that Malay regiment troops had fired on Chinese and ignored roaming bands of armed Malays seemed to have some substance. But the official report on the week of burning, looting and killing did not criticize the Army. It said that 196 persons had died during the riots: 143 Chinese, 25 Malays, 13 Indians and 15 of indeterminate origin. But some unofficial estimates went as high as 2,000. (A more accurate figure is thought to be about 500 dead.) Foreign journalists, some time after the flare-up, discovered mass graves just outside the city. A month after the riots, Malay wrath turned on the minority Indians, and 20 died before security forces brought the situation under control.

A state of emergency was proclaimed on May 15, not to be lifted until harmony and mutual trust between the ethnic groups had been restored. At year's end they were still thoroughly suspicious of each other.

Handsome ministry buildings in Kuala Lumpur show strong Islamic influence; most of the Malays are Muslims.

Inger Abrahamsen from Rapho Guillumette Pictures

MALAYSIA

Area: 128,000 sq. mi.
Population: 10,700,000
Capital: Kuala Lumpur (pop., 322,000)
Government: Ismail Nasiruddin, shah, head of state—1965; Tunku Abdul Rahman, prime minister—1963; Tun Abdul Razak, head of National Operations Council—1969
Gross national product: $3,300,000,000
Monetary unit: Malaysian Dollar (3.1 MD = U.S. $1.00)
Chief products: rubber, tin, palm oil, rice, tea, pepper
Foreign trade: exports, $1,383,000,000; imports, $1,204,000,000
Communications: 145,425 telephones, 450,000 radios, 120,000 TV sets
Transportation: roads, 9,573 mi.; 182,447 passenger cars; railroads, 1,335 mi.
Education: about 2,000,000 elementary and secondary students, 1 university
Armed forces: 44,750

See map on page 481

Razak strengthened his grip on the country's leadership when the Tunku went into hospital for an eye operation soon after the disturbances. Though the Prime Minister soon returned to the political scene, it was only to tour the country establishing goodwill committees. In the hospital Tunku wrote a book *May 13—Before and After,* and its publication did little to heal the wounds. He blamed the success of the opposition parties and the riots on the Communists despite the fact that an earlier charge blaming the Communists had been withdrawn by the Government. Chin Peng probably was as surprised as anyone by the charge but far less concerned. Although the MCP's propaganda that followed still advocated ethnic harmony, it emphasized that it was mostly Chinese who had suffered during the violence.

The Tunku was more active on the international scene. He attended the Muslim summit conference at Rabat, Morocco. While speaking against a multilateral defense pact of Southeast Asian nations, he advocated "interlocking arrangements." Relations between Singapore and Malaysia, only fair since Singapore's 1965 withdrawal from the federation, did not prevent a growing cooperation on defense.

Trade statistics for the first 6 months of 1969 showed a US$100,000,000 increase on the US$1,500,000,000 earned from exports in 1968, indicating that the racial upheavals had barely affected the nation's thitherto excellent economic progress. The GNP growth rate was maintained at 5 per cent, and per capita income was expected to show a further improvement.

Gross imports for the first 6 months were US$1,650,000, a decrease of US$66,000,000 from the first half of 1968. Malaysia continued to enjoy good prices and a steady demand from the United States, Soviet Union, China and Japan for its tin. The U.S. decision to hold its rubber and tin stockpiles in Malaysia also helped the nation's major export commodities. Trade with the Soviet Union received a boost with a well-attended Soviet exhibition in Kuala Lumpur in September.

Agriculture continued to employ more than half of the nation's work force and to produce about a third of the GNP. Rubber production in the first eight months at 749,400 tons established a record, and timber production also reached an all-time peak at over 3,500,000 tons.

DEREK DAVIES
Editor, *Far Eastern Economic Review*

MARYLAND

Vice-President-elect Spiro T. Agnew resigned as governor of Maryland on Jan. 7. To fill the office a joint session of the legislature at once elected Marvin Mandel, a Democrat and Speaker of the state House of Delegates. (By the end of its seventy-day session the legislature had enacted practically all of Mandel's program.) □ On Feb. 10, state authorities announced plan for a $10 bounty to be paid to citizens or automobile wreckers for every car body delivered to a scrap dealer. The state thereby hoped to rid itself of thousands of junked or abandoned cars cluttering streets and highways.

MASSACHUSETTS

Boston's new, $26,000,000 City Hall opened on Feb. 10. It is part of a growing Government Center. □ Snowfall on Boston broke all records for the month of February, at least 36 inches. □ At a public hearing on air pollution in April, strict enforcement of a 1914 law was advocated. It bars excessive emission of smoke from automobiles. □ During the summer the state tested a computerized traffic-merging system for the Federal Department of Transportation. □ In September, Michael J. Harrington, a liberal Democrat, defeated State Sen. William L. Saltonstall for the Congressional seat left vacant by the death of Rep. William H. Bates. □ In July, Sen. Edward M. Kennedy was involved in an auto accident on Chappaquiddick Island in which Mary Jo Kopechne, a 28-year-old secretary, was killed. An inquest was planned for early 1970.

MEDICINE AND HEALTH

Human-heart transplants—so widely hailed as a medical miracle when they were first undertaken in 1967 and 1968—fell from favor during 1969 as heart-transplant surgeons around the world curtailed the operation sharply. Many in the medical profession and elsewhere began to have second thoughts about the value of heart transplants as the mortality tables started to rise.

These doubts were underscored on Aug. 17 with the death of Dr. Philip Blaiberg, the South African dentist who had the longest survival record among the world's 140 transplantees. And then, on Oct. 17, came the sudden death of the man who had taken over from Dr. Blaiberg as the longest transplant survivor, a Dominican priest, Father Damien Boulogne. Dr. Blaiberg had lived nearly 20 months with his new heart, while Father Boulogne survived 17 months after his transplant operation.

Dr. Christiaan Barnard, the South African heart surgeon who operated on Dr. Blaiberg and who performed the first human-heart transplant, defended the procedure and remained optimistic about its use in the future. "I can't understand why Dr. Blaiberg's death should make any difference," said Dr. Barnard after his patient's death. "Dr. Blaiberg did much better than we anticipated, or than anybody anticipated. People were predicting that he wouldn't last 14 days, 17 days, 2 months, 3 months, a year."

The autopsy on Dr. Blaiberg revealed the presence of high concentrations of cholesterol, indicating that the cause of death was atherosclerosis. One renal artery and both femoral arteries were occluded. The discovery of the atherosclerosis was not surprising. In the early stages of heart transplantation, Dr. Richard Lower of the Medical College of Virginia found in animal experiments that transplanted hearts tend to develop atherosclerosis. Dr. Lower explained the phenomenon as a form of rejection of the new heart by the recipient. His theory was supported by postmortems that established atherosclerosis as the cause of death among human-heart transplantees around the world.

Critics of heart transplants pointed out that Dr. Blaiberg had not enjoyed steady good health after his operation. He suffered two acute rejection episodes and was hospitalized for a considerable amount of time. Other critics pointed out that most heart-transplant recipients died relatively soon after the operation.

A child is immunized against measles using a jet injector instead of a hypodermic. Though the injection may still sting a little, there is no sight of a needle on the injector to frighten a youngster.

Educational Media Branch Training Program, NCDC

Still other critics questioned whether the high costs of transplants—a heart transplant can cost as much as $75,000—were worth it and whether the financial resources might not be better used in other medical endeavors. Dr. M. G. Candau, director general of the World Health Organization, was highly critical of heart transplants at the July meeting of the World Health Assembly in Boston. "Heart transplants are the craziest thing anybody can talk about," he said at that time. "You have no right to talk about such sophisticated and expensive medical care for the few when so many are suffering."

In the face of the discouraging results in heart transplants, the surgeons turned more and more during 1969 to immunologists for help and guidance. The immunologists responded by urging more emphasis on tissue typing: testing for biochemical differences and similarities between donors and recipients. Immunologists studying heart transplants found that tissue-antigen mismatching was associated with early rejection and mortality. Conversely, those operations with the closest tissue matches between donors and recipients were the most successful. Dr. John J. Nora, a cardiologist in Houston, Tex., reported that the best donor-recipient match among 16 heart-transplant cases he had studied had the longest survival record, while all of the recipients who had poor matches had died soon after their operations.

But close donor-recipient matches are difficult to find, and this restricts the number of acceptable candidates for human-heart transplantation. Thus it was only natural that interest in the development of artificial hearts increased during 1969. The interest was spurred by government estimates that 400,000 Americans could be helped to near-normal lives if a reliable artificial heart were available.

The drive to develop a man-made heart continued on several fronts: in medical schools, hospitals, governmental institutions, and industry. The coordinator of the program is Dr. Frank W. Hastings, a surgeon who heads the Federal Government's heart program at Bethesda, Md. Toward the end of 1969, Dr. Hastings was encouraged enough to say: "We're making rapid progress—more than I thought we would—toward developing an artificial heart."

Essentially, Dr. Hastings' team is approaching the problem from two directions. The short-range goal is to develop and improve heart-assist devices, like pacemakers and ventricular-bypass pumps. The long-range goal —and, of course, the more difficult to achieve —is to develop a totally implantable artificial heart for mass production.

Actually, an artificial heart was implanted in a human on Apr. 4 in Houston. The plastic heart was installed by Dr. Denton Cooley into Haskell Karp, an Illinois businessman. Karp survived 65 hours with the device, and then, when he was given a human heart, he lived another 32 hours. Dr. Cooley called the operation "a milestone in the relentless battle waged by man against the diseases which threaten his life."

A dispute arose in the case, however, when the National Heart Institute questioned whether Dr. Cooley had followed Federal guidelines when he implanted the plastic heart. In the end, Dr. Cooley settled the controversy by resigning his post at the Baylor College of Medicine.

In another area, Robert H. Finch, secretary of health, education, and welfare, dropped a medical bombshell when he restricted the use of the artificial sweetener called cyclamate. Most Americans had been consuming cyclamate in one way or another—usually in the form of low-calorie soft drinks—and Finch's decision to order them removed from the market stunned many users.

Actually, the use of cyclamate had been under attack for months. Originally the substance had been approved by the Food and Drug Administration solely for use by diabetics and others who are required to reduce their sugar intake for medical reasons. Yet cyclamates became popular with the public and worked their way into general usage. Ironically, Dr. Frederick Stare, chairman of Harvard's Department of Nutrition, had pointed out that there is no reliable evidence that cyclamates have ever helped anyone lose weight. More important, perhaps, was the fact that Dr. Stare was among the first to sound the alarm about the potential hazards of cyclamate. Dr. Stare had visited Dr. Ryozo Tanaka, of the Iwate Medical College in Japan, whose experiments had attracted the attention of the Harvard scientist. The Japanese scientist had tested cyclamate on pregnant mice and found that the artificial sweetener killed or retarded mice fetuses when it was administered to mothers early in pregnancy.

More conclusive and damning evidence against cyclamates was produced by the Institute of Experimental Pathology and Toxicology at Albany Medical College. It discovered that humans can convert cyclamate into cyclohexylamine, a compound that raises blood pressure and causes vascular constriction in some people. It follows that cyclamate rep-

After I quit smoking—you will remember—I developed hyper—

tension + heart trouble from the weight I'd gained—so my doctor...

...put me on a diet which contained many artificially......

...sweetened things and now, well, I know that you'll understand

resents a potential hazard to at least some cardiac patients, particularly those with high blood pressure who sought to keep their weight down by using cyclamate.

The evidence against cyclamate continued to pile up. FDA investigators found that cyclohexylamine can also bring about genetic damage in animals. In Austria a group of scientists revealed that cyclamate can harm the liver and the blood-coagulation process in rabbits and guinea pigs. Finally, the crowning blow came when it was learned that cyclamate was causing bladder tumors in rats. It was at this point that Secretary Finch moved against cyclamate and restricted its usage. He said, however, that he anticipated some diet foods containing cyclamates would be relabeled by the Food and Drug Administration and made

available to persons who, for medical reasons, must reduce their intake of sugar.

Cyclamate was not the only compound to be placed under renewed and vigorous scrutiny by the FDA. A three-year study of oral contraceptives completed during the year raised some questions about the safety of the Pill. Supported by the FDA, the study examined the records of 48 hospitals in the northeast United States. They disclosed that women using a sequential product run a greater risk of embolic disorders than women using a combination product. The report stated that there is an added risk of morbidity for women who use oral contraceptives.

The evidence, however, was not regarded as serious enough to move the FDA to action, at least not on the findings that had been submitted by the end of 1969. "The findings of the report are favorable," said FDA Commissioner Herbert Ley. "The benefits both to the individual user and to society outweigh the risks involved in Pill use."

In assessing the blood-clotting risk to Pill users, the FDA study committee generally agreed that estrogen is linked with blood-clotting disorders. It was also observed that less and less estrogen is being used in oral contraceptives. Nevertheless, the report prepared for the FDA—and a British report that also questioned the safety of the Pill—was disturbing to many. The American report called for continued research on the adverse effects connected with oral contraceptives. The American scientists who prepared the report seemed particularly interested in learning more about any possible metabolic and cancer-causing effects of the Pill.

In Japan a young dermatologist achieved successful results with the use of an antibiotic called bleomycin in treating some patients suffering from a difficult skin cancer called squamous-cell carcinoma. The dermatologist, Dr. Masayasu Goto of Kyushu University School of Medicine, was able to eliminate the cancer tumor totally in 9 patients and almost totally in another patient. "I have been working with anticancer drugs for 10 years and with bleomycin for 2 years," said Dr. Goto. "For squamous-cell carcinoma, this is the best drug

I have found." Unfortunately the antibiotic was not universally successful. The drug is not yet available in the United States, although it is under study for possible use in a few years.

For many Americans, 1969 was the year of Hong Kong flu. The flu reached epidemic proportions and spread rapidly across the country, infecting more than 20,000,000 people. The National Communicable Disease Center, in Atlanta, reported that Hong Kong flu was responsible for the death of several thousand Americans—an indication that the disease was much more serious than had at first been expected. At one point in the epidemic, when the Communicable Disease Center sampled 122 cities, it found some 1,700 deaths in one week that could be attributed to Hong Kong flu.

The drive to conquer cancer continued as unrelenting as ever in 1969, but remained as frustrating as ever. No significant breakthroughs in the fight could be claimed, although the theory that viruses cause many cancers gained as more scientists established links between cancer and viruses.

Spurred by a growing body of evidence that viruses cause both leukemia and sarcoma in a wide variety of animals, scientists and medical researchers broadened their studies in the field. One new suspect came as a surprise: cats. They are under suspicion as carriers of the oncogenic virus that may cause human leukemia. This possibility is supported by a

As use of the Pill steadily climbs, Pill containers have been taking on the look of cosmetic compacts. Research continues on the Pill's possible ill effects, though for most women it appears to be safe.

"The New York Times"

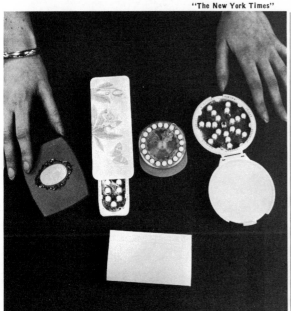

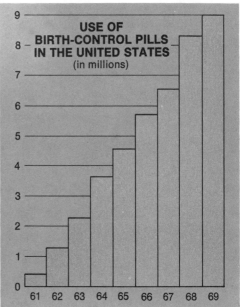

USE OF
BIRTH-CONTROL PILLS
IN THE UNITED STATES
(in millions)

number of studies made around the world. The studies were conducted at such diverse places as the National Cancer Institute in Maryland, the University of Glasgow in Scotland and the University of California at Davis. Some veterinarians attacked the findings sharply, as did others who jumped to the defense of cats. The defenders observed that the studies were not conclusive and that no scientist had produced any definite proof that cats are spreading leukemia among humans. At year's end, however, the theory was still being investigated.

As far as the virus-cancer link is concerned, a mass of new evidence was presented that strengthens the idea that many human cancers are caused by viruses. And as a possible cure, many medical men turned their attention increasingly to interferon. This is a virus-fighting molecule that, if properly activated, could trigger the body's defense against foreign elements, including possible cancer viruses. At the U.S. Government's National Institutes of Health, scientists are most intrigued by the possibility that interferon may one day be effective in combating solid, slow-growing tumors like those of the colon and the lung.

During 1969 the distribution of medical care in the United States took on new importance as it became apparent that in some sectors the system is near collapse. Indeed, President Nixon predicted that there would be a "massive crisis" in the country's health care unless firm steps were taken to improve the system. A report prepared for the President by the Department of Health, Education, and Welfare (HEW) called for immediate action.

"This nation," the report stated, "is faced with a breakdown in the delivery of health care unless immediate, concerted action is taken by the Government and the private sector. Expansion of private and public financing for health services has created a demand for services far in excess of the capacity of our health system to respond."

Is the overloading of the medical-delivery system having any effect on medical care itself? Most medical experts would answer yes to this question. Among the nations of the world, the United States ranks 13th in rate of infant mortality—a high rate for a country with such vast resources. Worse, as Dr. René Dubos of Rockefeller University reported in 1969, the infant-death rate is actually rising in parts of the United States, particularly in the southern states east of New Mexico. The United States also ranks high on rates of maternal mortality and on deaths from heart-artery diseases and cirrhosis of the liver.

One problem is clear: hospital costs. They have been skyrocketing and show no sign of leveling off in the near future. In 1965 the cost of one day's stay in a hospital was $44. By 1969 the figure was $70. It is predicted that the figure will be $100 by 1972 or 1973.

The medical system is also handicapped by a shortage of doctors. Many physicians have turned to group practice as one way to alleviate the acute scarcity. The group usually consists of a general practitioner and several specialists. As a rule, the patient sees the general practitioner first, who then steers the patient to the specialists he needs.

Early in 1969, a Maryland classroom is left almost empty because of students ill at home with Hong Kong flu.

George Tames, "Medical World News"

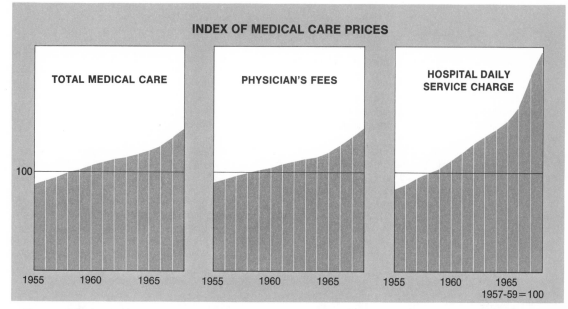

INDEX OF MEDICAL CARE PRICES

TOTAL MEDICAL CARE | PHYSICIAN'S FEES | HOSPITAL DAILY SERVICE CHARGE

100

1955 1960 1965 | 1955 1960 1965 | 1955 1960 1965

1957-59 = 100

For a while in 1969, it seemed that the nation's top health post, assistant secretary for health and scientific affairs, would go to Dr. John H. Knowles, the general director of the Massachusetts General Hospital. It was expected that he would lead the battle to reorganize the country's sagging health system. Though under serious consideration for the post, after five months of behind-the-scenes bickering and maneuvering in Washington, his appointment was blocked. The job went to Roger O. Egeberg of California. The American Medical Association, which has long resisted most proposed changes in the country's medical-care system, was credited with blocking Dr. Knowles' appointment. He was regarded as too liberal and progressive for the AMA. (Dr. Egeberg actually is hardly less liberal.)

As the year wore on, the Medicaid program came under increasingly sharp attack. In July the Federal Government set up a Medicaid task force with an eye to reorganizing the troubled program. Another purpose of the task force, which is headed by HEW Undersecretary John G. Veneman and Blue Cross President Walter J. McNerney, is to advise on the future of HEW's health-services delivery programs. "One of the main new thrusts of the department," stated one government report, "will be to use Medicare and Medicaid as major tools to obtain changes in the delivery system."

While many complained of serious problems plaguing the Medicaid program, others rushed to defend it. In New York and other large cities, some physicians and other public-

health officials pointed out that the Medicaid program had made it possible for millions of Americans to see physicians for the first time in their lives. Without Medicaid, they argued, there would have been no medical care at all for many people except in a hospital emergency room.

One possible answer to the need—a universal health-insurance plan—gained during the year. A group called the Committee for National Health Insurance predicted that, by 1972, Congress would approve a comprehensive health-insurance program that would cover most Americans. The committee is headed by UAW President Walter P. Reuther.

Reuther and his fellow committee members hammered away on the theme that the United States is the only industrial nation in the world without some form of compulsory health care. In the proposed new program, the insurance premiums would be two thirds financed by a payroll tax shared by employers and employees, the other third to be paid by the Federal Government. Besides the program proposed by the Reuther Committee, several other national health-insurance programs were promoted. There seemed to be a consensus that improvements in the country's health care are needed across the board. Although no certain answers were produced during 1969, at least there were thoughtful proposals that could prepare the way for hard solutions.

W. DAVID GARDNER
Medical Writer
Contributor to Medical Journals and
General Magazines

MEIR, GOLDA

"She's tough and everyone knows she's tough," commented an Israeli army officer on the choice of Golda Meir, a 70-year-old grand-mother, as his country's prime minister. How-ever, when she was sworn in as the fourth premier of Israel, on Mar. 17, 1969, following the sudden death of Levi Eshkol, it was rather generally assumed that her leadership would be temporary, only until the general elections in October.

Instead, on Oct. 28, her ruling coalition (Labor and Mapam parties) was returned to power, though without its previous majority, and Mrs. Meir began a full four-year term. How had an elderly, ailing woman, in one of the world's most deeply troubled areas, won such confidence from her people?

Her "toughness" includes an "iron deter-mination that . . . after three wars, we will not accept any arrangement that is not true peace." She is a realistic, extremely skillful politician (she had much to do with unifying the Labor Party) and as a speaker can hold audiences spellbound. Moreover, what she says in public and in private are the same. Yet she has remained feminine and down to earth. Cabinet meetings are often held in her kitchen when she serves endless cups of coffee she brews herself.

Golda Meir (Hebraicized in 1956 from Goldie Myerson) was born in Kiev, in the Ukraine, on May 3, 1898, at a time when Jews were suffering terrible pogroms. She remem-bers her father nailing boards across the door to protect the family from raiding Cossacks. She was brought to the United States in 1906 and grew up in poverty in Milwaukee. She taught school there for a time but, more sig-nificantly for her future, she became active in the Zionist Labor Party. Her intense devotion to the Zionist cause and, later, to the State of Israel has never wavered.

Married to Morris Myerson in 1917, she and her husband migrated to Palestine four years later. From secretary of the Histadrut's Wom-en's Labor Council in 1928, she became a leading member of the entire organization of Histadrut, which is still the most powerful joint labor organization in Israel. She was, of course, one of the signers of Israel's declaration of in-dependence. Among other government posi-tions she has served as Israel's first minister to the Soviet Union, as minister of labor and, from 1956 to 1966, as foreign minister.

For ten days, beginning on Sept. 25, Pre-mier Meir visited the United States. Besides re-ceptions and dinners given in her honor, she had private discussions with President Nixon, UN Secretary-General U Thant and Gov. Nel-son Rockefeller. New York City capped her tour with an official dinner on Sept. 30—part of the Hebrew harvest festival of Succoth.

See Middle East.

To the pupils' obvious delight, Mrs. Meir visits the elementary school she attended as a child in Milwaukee.

"The New York Times"

METEOROLOGY

The quest for improved weather forecasts and ways of combating hostile weather conditions was maintained on many levels.

International Cooperation. The global community of nations continued to cooperate through the World Weather Watch, a program initiated in 1967 for the purpose of improving international weather services, research and education. The first voluntary assistance project of the World Weather Watch, a group fellowship for training Congolese meteorologists, was completed in April 1969. Other programs ranged from new equipment for establishing upper-air observations in Tunisia, to additional fellowships for university study of meteorology. For 1969, the financial support for such projects was expected to exceed $3,000,000.

In March, a meeting was held in Melbourne, Australia, to outline plans for a "constant level balloon" system, a technique in which weather balloons are designed to float at essentially fixed altitudes in the atmosphere. Tests have shown that such balloons will remain in the air for long periods of time; one launched from New Zealand in September 1967 drifted for nearly two years at an altitude of about 50,000 feet. As a consequence of similar successful tests, the Melbourne meeting evolved a program for establishing a multiballoon, operational system in the mid-latitudes of the southwest Pacific. Radio-direction-finding stations would be used to track the balloons. The measurements, processed by electronic computers, would provide information on high-level winds and temperatures for aviation and other space-age uses.

International aeronautical meteorology was the subject of a meeting in Montreal, Canada, from Apr. 9 to May 2. The International Civil Aviation Organization and the World Meteorological Organization joined to examine the problems that will arise when the supersonic transport (SST) aircraft goes into use. Especially critical for SST operations will be accurate meteorological information for climb-out, transonic acceleration and deceleration, and final descent. The conference emphasized the importance of data obtained from meteorological satellites, and stressed the worldwide coordination of aviation-weather information through the World Weather Watch program.

A research counterpart of the World Weather Watch is the Global Atmospheric Research Program. The first major undertaking of this activity was the Barbados Oceanographic and Meteorological Experiment (BOMEX), which concluded three months of extensive observa-

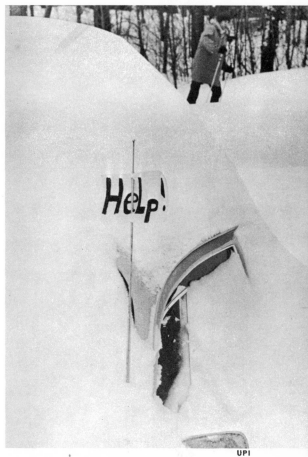

UPI

A motorist leaves an SOS sign on his car after it was buried in the snow heaped on Vermont in December.

tional work on July 28. From May 1 to July 2, BOMEX made detailed measurements of the energy exchange between the sea and air in a 90,000-square-mile area over the Atlantic east of Barbados. Later in July, the emphasis shifted to airborne investigations of tropical cloud systems.

Meteorological Satellites. Launched from the Western Test Range at Lompoc, Calif., on Apr. 14, a research weather satellite, Nimbus III, provided a major breakthrough in weather observing. The satellite carried an infrared sensor, which measures the energy emitted from carbon dioxide in the earth's atmosphere. From these measurements, the vertical temperature profile of the air below the satellite can be computed. Although only about 70 balloon soundings of the atmosphere are now made in the southern hemisphere, more than 5,000 temperature soundings may be obtained from the new satellite technique. Furthermore, future improvements aimed at measuring other atmospheric properties, such as moisture, may eventually result in eliminating completely the costly and somewhat inadequate balloon-sounding methods.

Other meteorological satellites launched during the year included spacecraft designed for operational day-to-day weather observing and forecasting. ESSA 9, orbited from the Eastern Test Range at Cape Kennedy, Fla., on Feb. 26, provided cloud photographs and other data throughout the year. A new generation of operational satellites called ITOS was under construction, but unexpected problems with the launch vehicle delayed a planned orbiting of the first of these satellites until some time in 1970.

Weather Modification. Project Stormfury, an ESSA-Air Force-Navy hurricane-modification effort, carried out its first full-scale experiments in 1969. On Aug. 18 and 20, aircraft of the 3 agencies bombarded hurricane Debbie with silver iodide. Over 2,000 cannisters of the chemical were dropped into clouds surrounding Debbie's center, where the strongest winds were located. The purpose was to determine whether the violence of such winds may be alleviated

In Biloxi, Miss., hurricane Camille blew out the interiors of some houses but left exteriors intact.

UPI

and to modify the accompanying heavy rainfall. Although some encouraging results were observed, more experiments will be required to prove the success of the technique.

The international nature of weather-modification problems was highlighted in 1969 with the visit to the United States of six Soviet specialists. The group was headed by academician E. K. Federov, director of the Soviet Union's Hydrometeorological Service. During their stay, from mid-September to mid-October, the party visited the National Meteorological Center in Washington, D.C., and other ESSA facilities throughout the country.

Weather Highlights. The year 1969 opened with a series of severe storms in North America. In the northwestern United States and western Canada, record snowfall during January closed roads and inflicted serious damage on buildings and other structures. Severe flooding occurred in California; at least 91 persons were drowned or buried in mudslides and damage was estimated to exceed $35,000,000. Blizzard conditions closed schools and highways in the Midwest, and disrupted power and communications lines in New England. Temperatures were well below normal; the thermometer fell to −52° F. in Havre, Mont., on Jan. 24, the lowest temperature recorded there in more than 50 years. In Canada, −67° was registered at Fort Selkirk, Yukon Territory.

In February, snow continued to fall over the western United States, reaching near record depths in the mountains of Washington, Oregon and California. Heavy snow also fell in New England near the end of the month, closing roads and schools in Vermont, New Hampshire and Massachusetts. In Canada, relatively dry weather prevailed, although a snowstorm in Manitoba and Saskatchewan near the end of the month produced twice the normal snowfall in that area. Temperatures were above normal in the middle and eastern portions of both the United States and Canada, but were well below normal in the west. It was the coldest February of record in Calgary, Alberta.

The cold weather spread over much of the area east of the Rocky Mountains in March. Regions as far apart as Aberdeen, S.D., and Tallahassee, Fla., suffered the coldest March weather of record, while subzero temperatures spread well southward into the Mississippi Valley. In Canada, cold weather was general over the southern prairies, with the thermometer dropping to −15° at Winnipeg on Mar. 29. Heavy snow fell in New England, closing schools and roads and delaying air and surface transportation. An accumulation of snow in southern Canada and the upper plains of the

UPI

High waves, generated by a storm in the Arctic Ocean, batter a fishing pier near San Diego, Calif., on Dec. 13. Normally there is 14 feet between the sea's surface at high tide and the top of the supporting pillars.

United States created a threat of severe flooding later in the spring.

Above-normal temperatures early in April caused rapid thawing of deep snows, producing record floods in the Missouri and Mississippi valleys. Timely warnings, issued more than a month in advance, sparked unprecedented efforts to alleviate flood damage. The Corps of Engineers alone spent $19,000,000 to construct and reinforce levees. Despite these efforts, however, the flood damage was estimated to exceed $100,000,000. In Canada, above-normal temperatures were general in the central prairies, but it was cold and wet on both coasts.

May weather showed a gradually warming trend in both the United States and Canada. Sporadic tornadoes occurred in the area from Texas to the Ohio Valley; four deaths and up to $7,000,000 in property damage were reported. A freak storm in Manitoba near the end of the month produced one-inch hailstones.

Summer weather was near normal over most of North America. However, unusually cold temperatures occurred in Alberta, Canada; Edmonton reported 21° on June 11. Tornadoes in Oklahoma, Kansas and Missouri killed 4 persons and caused extensive damage. Early in August, tornadoes resulted in 15 deaths and over $15,000,000 in damage in Minnesota. In mid-August, hurricane Camille moved inland over Mississippi. The most severe storm to hit the Gulf Coast in recorded history, it was accompanied by 190 mph winds. Some 292 deaths were attributed to the storm. Damage, including later severe flooding in Virginia, West Virginia and Kentucky amounted to nearly $1,000,000,000. Cold polar air began to flow into southern Canada and the northern United States in mid-September and, at the end of the month, the first significant snowfall occurred as far south as the central Rockies.

A major storm near the middle of October brought cold weather and heavy snow to a nine-state area of the western plains. As the storm moved eastward, it caused flash floods in Oklahoma, Missouri and Illinois, and the heaviest snowstorm of record in parts of New England. In Canada, also, intermittent snow and cold weather were general from Alberta eastward to the Maritime Provinces. Temperatures as low as 10° were reported at Armstrong, Ont., near the end of the month.

November opened with a severe storm along the middle Atlantic coast. Considerable damage occurred in the Carolinas and Virginia, as coastal winds up to 80 mph were reported. At Myrtle Beach, S.C., nearly 10 inches of rain fell in 24 hours. Around the middle of the month, snow and cold rain spread across the mountains of the western United States and Canada, closing some roads and delaying air transportation. However, fair but cold weather prevailed over most sections from the Thanksgiving holidays to the end of the month.

JACK C. THOMPSON
Professor of Meteorology
San Jose State College

MEXICO

During 1969 Mexico had made substantial economic progress and had enjoyed a period of sustained political stability, declared President Gustavo Diaz Ordaz in his fifth State of the Union message which he delivered to the Mexican nation on Sept. 1, 1969. Although admitting that there were still some unresolved social and economic problems, he said that in the past 12 months there had been a 7.1 per cent increase in goods and services and a 4 per cent growth in per capita income, and cited other gains: a stable currency, a sound credit structure, significant strides in the fields of tourism, petroleum, livestock, construction, manufacturing and electric power. Although agriculture had increased at the rate of 4 per cent, it had failed to come up to predicted growth, said Diaz Ordaz. Thus it remained Mexico's most pressing problem, in spite of the efforts that his administration had made in the distribution of land, expansion of rural electric power, construction of dams, and extension of farm credits.

The tone and character of the 1969 message was thus entirely different from that of a year before, which came after more than a month of student demonstrations protesting government corruption, one-party rule, police brutality, and unjust judicial procedures. At that time, President Diaz Ordaz, obviously concerned about the forthcoming Olympic Games, denounced the demonstrations as the work of a small, misguided group inspired by anarchistic forces both inside and outside Mexico, and declared that his administration was not going to allow student rioting to interfere with the games. Shortly after, on Oct. 2, 1968, there took place what has been called "the massacre of Tlaltelolco," a bloody affair between students and police during a student protest of the military occupation of the National Polytechnic Institute. Mexican army units stationed nearby were called in to restore order and to help put down the student unrest which threatened to sabotage the Olympic Games. The students then agreed to remain quiet during the games. Since then, outwardly at least, all has been calm, with the Diaz Ordaz administration in firm control of the situation.

During 1969 two important developments involving the border between Mexico and the United States directly affected relations between the two countries. One was the completion and dedication of the $78,000,000 Amistad Dam early in September. A phenomenal engineering feat 12 miles upstream from Del Rio, Tex., and Ciudad Acuña, Coahuila, the dam was a cooperative effort to provide flood control, water

MEXICO

Area: 760,300 sq. mi.
Population: 49,000,000
Capital: Mexico City (pop., 3,500,000)
Government: Gustavo Diaz Ordaz, president—1964
Gross National Product: $24,112,000,000
Monetary unit: peso (12.5 pesos = U.S. $1.00)
Chief products: silver, sulphur, oil, corn, cotton, wheat, coffee
Foreign trade: exports, $1,254,000,000; imports, $1,943,000,000
Communications: 1,044,415 telephones, 10,-900,000 radios, 2,240,000 TV sets, 192 daily newspapers
Transportation: roads, 38,985 mi.; 917,384 passenger cars; railroads, 14,772 mi.
Education: 9,133,569 elementary, secondary, vocational and special students, 141,514 university students
Armed forces: 67,000

See map on page 253

conservation, hydroelectric power, and recreational facilities for the entire area. At dedicatory ceremonies at the site of the dam, President Nixon of the United States and President Diaz Ordaz met for the first time. There were eloquent expressions of what the two countries had been able to achieve in a spirit of cordiality, cooperation and mutual trust.

The ideals expressed at Amistad Dam, however, soon received a serious setback as a result of the second problem relating to the border. In an effort to reduce the volume of the marijuana traffic coming into the United States from Mexico, the United States Government, late in September, announced Operation Intercept for the entire 2,500-mile border. At every port of entry, cars and trucks were subject to the most intensive inspection. It soon caused agonizing traffic tie-ups that stretched for several blocks and resulted in overheated engines, exasperated drivers, interminable delays, and at length serious dislocations to the economy on both sides. Although most people agreed with the overall objective, many came to have serious misgivings about the net gains, especially when measured against the acute problems and the ill will that the policy was generating. President Diaz Ordaz even mentioned the matter to Apollo 11 astronauts Armstrong, Aldrin and Collins on their visit to Mexico City. Late in October the policy was greatly relaxed, and gradually conditions along the border returned to normal.

Perhaps the most spectacular construction project completed in 1969, and certainly one that has captured the imagination of the residents of Mexico City with all its traffic problems, is the Metro—the new subway system the first section of which was dedicated in August. The entire system, scheduled for completion late in 1970, will involve more than 22 miles of track in 3 connecting sections, and will accommodate about 3,500,000 passengers during its 20-hour operating day. Its engineers proudly claim that it will be the highest and safest in the world, and that its stations will be the most beautiful. Some of them will have murals painted by Mexican artists; one station, in the downtown area, is built around an Aztec pyramid-temple uncovered during excavation. Actually, some 5,000 pieces of Aztec art have been unearthed during construction, all now being evaluated and catalogued by the staff of Mexico's magnificent Museum of Anthropology and History. Archeologists eagerly anticipate even richer discoveries in the next few months as construction enters the area of the Zocalo, the National Palace and the National Cathedral, all of which were built on the ruins of the great Aztec capital Tenochtitlan.

Because of the nature of Mexico's unique political system, it is already known who the president will be for the six-year term beginning in 1970, although the presidential election will not be held until early in July of that year. This is because Mexico is still virtually a one-party state, and the naming by the ruling Partido Revolucionario Institucional (PRI) of its presidential candidate is tantamount to his election. Late in 1969 the PRI selected Luis Echeverria Alvarez, the secretary of government, roughly the equivalent of the secretary of the interior in the United States but traditionally the most important cabinet post in any Mexican administration. It is significant that 8 out of the last 9 presidents of Mexico have served in the post just prior to their elevation to the presidency. There are other political parties, the most important of which is the Partido Accion Nacional (PAN); and although the campaign promises to be spirited, it is generally conceded that the PRI will win this one by a large margin, as it has every election in the last 40 years.

Luis Echeverria is 47 years old, the father of 8 children, a lawyer and political scientist by training, and is reported to be an extremely efficient administrator and politician. During the past 6 years he has been the top-ranking, most influential figure in the Diaz Ordaz administration. It was he who was chiefly responsible for suppressing student activities in October 1968 and restoring order. He states his political position as "neither to the right, nor to the left, nor in a static center, but onward and upward." Barring any unforeseen devel-

UPI

On the Mexican side of the border, cars and pedestrians wait for the intensive U.S. inspection for drugs.

opments, his election in July 1970 may be viewed as certain; but just how successful he will be in coping effectively with such problems as agriculture, the unequal distribution of wealth, a rapidly growing population, and student demands for political, social and economic reforms remains to be seen.

WILBERT H. TIMMONS
Professor of History
University of Texas at El Paso

MICHIGAN

In January, Gov. George Romney was appointed to President Nixon's Cabinet; and Lt. Gov. William Milliken assumed the governorship. □ Some $2,000,000 in loans and grants was raised by Detroit's Inner City Business Improvement Forum to promote black capitalism in the slums. □ On Apr. 16 the State Agricultural Commission voted to cancel all registrations for sale of DDT, which had been harming sport and commercial fishing. □ A 42-ton stabile, called *La Grand Vitesse* (Great Speed), by sculptor Alexander Calder, was dedicated at the new Vandenberg Center in Grand Rapids on June 14.

J. Allan Cash from Rapho Guillumette Pictures

New highway snakes through the rugged mountains near Mecca; the road makes connections that link Red Sea port of Jidda with towns on or near the Persian Gulf.

middle east

The clash of arms along embattled Israel's borders roused new fears of an imminent fourth round of all-out war in the Middle East in 1969. Although this did not occur, the steady escalation of conflict, emphasized by artillery duels and aerial dogfights high above the so-called cease-fire established by the United Nations in 1967, made prospects for peace more remote than ever. Even more dangerous than the brinkmanship practiced by both the Arab states and Israel was the terrorism of the Palestinian commando organizations. Disunited though they were, and incapable even of effective guerrilla warfare, their determination to block any settlement that would not include a reconstituted Palestine Arab state compounded the problem of negotiations. As a result, the region remained in a state of "neither war nor peace," a twilight zone whose only rules were tension and insecurity.

Under these circumstances neither the UN nor the major powers had, or were willing to exercise, the necessary authority required even to bring the combatants to the conference table. The UN presence, in the form of observers in blue berets stationed along the Suez Canal, failed to dampen the enthusiasm of Arab and Israeli gunners for their favorite targets. Secretary-General U Thant described the observer force as defenseless targets in a shooting gallery. He warned the Security Council that the pattern of violence along Israel's frontiers proved that a state of war again existed there. But the UN took no further action other than resolutions of censure against Israel.

Faced with UN ineffectiveness the major powers could no longer avoid direct involvement. The U.S.S.R. reversed its traditional opposition to international peace-keeping forces and urged a UN force for Palestine. The United States continued to press for a big-four guarantee of a settlement negotiated under the terms of the Nov. 22, 1967, resolution. The Soviet Union was concerned about its overcommitment to the Arabs, while the United States, although continuing to support Israel's overall position, also sought to disengage itself and to keep the conflict localized. After much hesitation, the Nixon administration approved

UPI

Acrid black smoke billows from a blazing oil pipeline in the port area of Haifa, Israel, after an explosion believed to be set off by Arab commandos.

the sale of fifty Phantom jets to Israel; the sale was justified as necessary to preserve the arms balance in the region. In November the United States proposed bilateral Egyptian-Israeli peace talks as a first step toward an overall settlement. However, U.A.R. spokesmen rejected the proposal as a piecemeal approach to the problem, though to others the proposal seemed to make basic good sense.

The inability of the major powers to mediate in the twenty-year-old conflict and the negative attitudes of both the Arabs and Israel toward negotiation contrasted sharply with the progress elsewhere in the Middle East in finding solutions to age-old problems. Iran made impressive economic gains. The first year of the new Iranian Five-Year Plan resulted in a record 13 per cent increase in GNP. The Iranian per capita income reached $266 although this was far from being evenly distributed. The readiness of Iranian businessmen, many of them former landlords, to invest in domestic projects set a good example for the region. Agreement with the consortium of oil companies that supervises Iran's oil industry would guarantee an additional $1,000,000,000 in revenues through an obligatory 10 per cent increase in oil production.

Turkey, Afghanistan and Israel all held national elections during the year. In contrast with the treatment meted out to the opposition in such countries as Iraq, where all newspaper licenses were revoked and even former cabinet ministers known for their integrity were jailed on espionage charges, the Turkish and Israeli elections might have served as models for their neighbors in less hectic times. Eight Turkish parties competed. They ranged from the extreme right-wing National Action Party, modeled on the Nazis even to the clenched-fist salute and armbands, to the Marxist-oriented Labor Party. The election results reaffirmed Turkey's commitment to representative democracy. The voters gave the ruling Justice Party a clear majority of 253 out of 450 seats in the Grand National Assembly. The Republican People's Party won 147 seats, gaining 13. The 6 minority parties collected 50 seats altogether, setting the stage for a genuine two-party system.

Israel's elections, although hotly contested, proved that representative political activity could be preserved even in times of supercharged tension. The Labor (Mapai) Party lost its absolute majority in the Knesset (Parliament), retaining 56 seats out of 120. Sixteen

NATION	POPULATION (in millions)	CAPITAL	APPROX. AREA (in sq. mi.)	HEAD OF STATE AND/OR GOVERNMENT, DATE INSTALLED (as of January 1, 1970)
Cyprus	0.6	Nicosia	3,572	Archbishop Makarios II, pres., 1960
Federation of Gulf Emirates	0.5	Abu Dhabi	36,531	Zayed ibn Sultan al-Mihayan, pres., 1969
Iran	27.9	Teheran	630,000	Mohammad Riza Pahlevi, shah, 1941
				Amir Abbas Hoveida, prem., 1965
Iraq	8.9	Baghdad	168,040	Ahmed Hassan al-Bakr, pres. and prem., 1968
Israel	2.9	Jerusalem	8,050	Schneor Zalman Shazar, pres., 1963
				Mrs. Golda Meir, prime minister, 1969
Jordan	2.3	Amman	37,000	Hussein I, king, 1952
				Bahjat al-Talhouni, prem., 1967
Kuwait	0.6	Kuwait	6,000	Sabah al-Salem al-Sabah, head of state, 1965
				Jaber al-Ahmed al-Jaber, prem., 1965
Lebanon	2.6	Beirut	3,927	Charles Helou, pres., 1964
				Rashid Karami, prime minister, 1969
Saudi Arabia	7.2	Riyadh	618,000	Faisal ibn Abdul Aziz, king, 1964
Southern Yemen (People's Rep. of)	1.3	Aden	112,000	Salmin Rubaya, chairman, Presidential Council, 1969
				Mohammad Ali Haitham, prime minister, 1969
Syria	6.0	Damascus	66,063	Nureddin al-Attassi, pres., 1966; and prem., 1968
Turkey	34.4	Ankara	296,185	Cevdet Sunay, pres., 1966
				Suleyman Demirel, prime minister, 1965
United Arab Republic	32.5	Cairo	386,198	Gamal Abdel Nasser, pres., 1952
Yemen	5.0	Sana	75,000	Abdul Rahman al-Iryani, president, 1967
				Abdullah al-Karshumi, prem., 1969

parties presented slates of candidates to Israel's 1,750,000 voters in an atmosphere even calmer than the mood that prevailed in Turkey. Despite orders for a boycott and threats from Palestinian terrorist organizations, over 9,000 Arabs in Jerusalem, about 25 per cent of the city's electorate, cast their ballots.

The tragedy of the Arabs was their inability to come to terms with themselves. From Morocco to the Arabian Peninsula, men talked of Arab unity, but their approach to it was essentially negative. More than anything, the Arab lands needed time to concentrate on their own problems, even to experiment peacefully with different political and social systems on their own, free from foreign influence.

Yet the development of a unified and stable Arab community requires a willingness to forget the past that seems beyond Arab capabilities. "We have reached a decisive stage in the history of the wounded Arab nation," said the leader of Libya's revolutionary Government after a coup had overthrown King Idris. Unfortunately the obsession with revenge against Israel and its "imperialist creators" absorbs Arab energies. The 52d anniversary of the Balfour Declaration, which in Arab eyes was ultimately responsible for the Jewish homeland in Palestine, was marked by riots in various capitals. Demonstrators in Tripoli sacked the British Embassy.

The Libyan coup highlighted internal rivalries in the Arab world. There were similar attempts to overthrow the traditional regimes in Saudi Arabia, Jordan and Kuwait, in each case inspired by the vague but popular revolutionary socialist doctrines of the Baath Party. The Baathist regime in Iraq, which had seized power in 1968, pursued its opponents relentlessly. Newspapers were suspended, foreign schools nationalized, and a series of spy trials followed by public executions linked even officials known for their integrity, such as former Prime Minister Bazzaz, with alleged Israeli or imperialist subversion.

Despite the political uncertainties, foreign aid continued to flow to the Arab lands, although in reduced amounts. Jordan signed its first aid agreement with the U.S.S.R. for hydrological research. The Soviet Union also granted Iraq $70,000,000 for expansion of its North Rumailah oil fields. For the first time in history there was a grain surplus in the U.A.R. With the Aswan High Dam almost completed, the prospects for Egypt's 32,500,000 patient citizens, at least in economic terms, were brighter than in many years.

Arab-Israeli Conflict. The thunder of six hundred Egyptian heavy guns over the Suez Canal inaugurated a new phase of the Arab campaign to oust Israel from territories seized in the June 1967 war. Although Israeli counterattacks across the canal demonstrated that the U.A.R. was still not ready for all-out war, the revival of Egyptian confidence provided by new equipment and the training by Soviet advisers was very much in evidence. While their artillery hammered at Israeli fortifications and supply convoys, Egyptian commandos in rubber boats carried out night amphibious land-

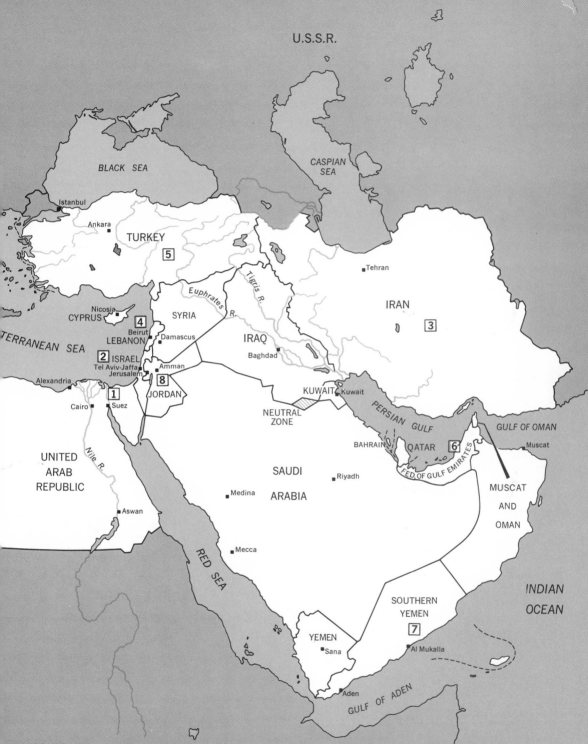

MIDDLE EAST 1969: 1. Arab and Israeli soldiers exchanged fire almost constantly under a "virtual state of active war"; 2. Mrs. Golda Meir was installed as prime minister of Israel after the death of Levi Eshkol; 3. during the first year of a new five-year plan, Iran's gross national product increased by 13 per cent; 4. Lebanon faced a serious government crisis and suffered a series of attacks by Arab guerrillas; 5. Turkey's ruling Justice Party won a solid majority in elections to the Grand National Assembly; 6. a new Arab state, the Federation of Gulf Emirates, was proclaimed formally on Oct. 22; 7. a five-man presidential council, headed by Salmin Rubaya, came to power in Southern Yemen; 8. Jordan's King Hussein reappointed Bahjat al-Talhouni premier.

ings. Several of the raids were in company strength, and one was accomplished by volunteer units from Algeria who had learned their trade in the prolonged war in Algeria against the French.

U.A.R. strategy was to involve Israel in a war of attrition; the premium placed on lives by Israeli commanders made them reluctant to engage the enemy except when forced to. Nevertheless, Israel counterattacked often and massively. A raid in September, described as the largest since the June war, overran Egyptian positions. Israel's strategy not only against the U.A.R. but on all fronts was to keep the Arabs off balance with sudden assaults. The intent was to make "canal-hopping" unprofitable in terms of equipment; Egyptian lives were expendable in view of their obsession with the recovery of Sinai and the Gaza Strip. It was a costly business: Israeli casualties for the two years of escalating conflict were 2,100 with 400 killed, while total casualties for the six-day war were 778 dead and 2,458 wounded.

The bulk of these casualties came from a sort of "third front" opened against Israel by the Palestinian Arab commandos. Being accountable only to themselves, the commandos (or fedayeen, "freedom fighters," as they styled themselves) pursued their objective of a sovereign Palestinian state without regard for the niceties of international behavior. Even the Arab governments that nourished them felt the sting of fedayeen hostility; they were the kingmakers of the modern Arab world.

Chauvel, Gamma-PIX

Yasir Arafat, chief of Al Fatah, largest Arab guerrilla organization, studies a map in planning another raid.

Undergoing intense training in Jordan, a group of Arab commandos, with guns at the ready, fords a stream.

UPI

G. Sipahioglu, PIX

After a Christian zealot sets fire to the Al Aksa Mosque (right) in Jerusalem, arousing wild anger among Muslims, an Israeli court (above) at once begins hearings on the crime. Defendant Rohan sits in a plastic booth.

Morris Teichman, Black Star

The two pillars of commando strategy were dramatization of the Palestinian cause abroad and weakening of the Israeli state through terrorism and detachment of Israel's own Arab population. The first showed up in a series of dramatic attacks on Israeli property. Commandos shot up an El Al airliner at Zurich Airport, threw bombs at Israeli Government missions in Bonn, Brussels and The Hague, and hijacked a TWA airplane headed for Tel Aviv, forcing it to fly to Damascus. The Popular Front for the Liberation of Palestine (PFLP) claimed responsibility for these exploits, and in consequence stole headlines as well as recruits (some of them 12- and 13-year-old *ashbal,* "tiger cubs") from the better-known Al Fatah.

The real tragedy of the commando campaign was its effect on the Arab governments that had sheltered the commandos as a means of revenge against Israel. On two occasions, fedayeen blew up the oil pipeline from Saudi Arabia to Lebanon's Sidon refinery, resulting in losses of $23,000,000 to Jordan, Syria and Lebanon from lost transit fees. Although these governments were the chief source of funds (one of the new Libyan regime's first actions was to send the commandos $250,000), a payroll checkoff system for Palestinian Arabs working elsewhere in the Middle East ensured protection for the fedayeen from domination by any one government. It also fostered a sense of Palestinian identity and the emergence of a Palestinian political community, one of the only groups left in the region without a separate homeland. All of this, of course, served to foster high morale.

UPI

Biblical Nablus, second largest of Arab towns occupied by Israelis on the west bank of the Jordan River, appears deserted in the noonday sun save for patrolling Israeli soldiers carrying submachine guns.

Arab terrorism forced Israel to adopt drastic security measures reminiscent of the Palestine Mandate when the British tried to keep peace between Arab and Jewish communities. Israeli courts imposed sentences of up to twenty years for illegal border crossing or possession of arms. The massive reprisal policy of Israeli security forces hit hardest at Arab civilians. Whole blocks of houses dynamited on suspicion of harboring the fedayeen, mass arrests, curfews, and brutal prisoner interrogations attested to the vigor of Israel's pursuit. But it left little room for accommodation and risked further alienation of the Arab minority of 300,000, despite their assurances of support. The prompt identification of Australian Michael Rohan as the arsonist responsible for setting fire to the Al Aksa Mosque in Jerusalem averted not only an outbreak of communal violence but the condemnation of Muslim nations. Israel put Rohan on trial. The Australian, a member of the Christian fundamentalist Church of God, readily admitted his guilt but claimed he had received orders from God to set the fire. (The sect later denied Rohan's membership and expressed regret for the fire.)

Thus the view of the Middle East's future both from within the region and outside foresaw an indefinite period of tension, at least insofar as Israel and the Arabs were concerned. It seemed impossible for any power or group of powers to impose a settlement, however desirable. Israel's clear military superiority was balanced by Arab dexterity in turning military defeat into political stalemate. But even reasonable Arab leaders, such as Jordan's King Hussein, feared to speak of concessions in the presence of the Palestinian commandos. In early December the big four reconvened at the UN for another round of talks aimed at finding an acceptable basis for a settlement, but without much hope.

Lebanon. The backwash of the guerrilla campaign against Israel nearly inundated Lebanon. The Lebanese Government, in a state of shock since the raid on Beirut Airport, staggered through one crisis after another. Fearing that the presence of strong fedayeen bases in southern Lebanon would tempt Israel to invade its territory, the Government tried desperately to expel or at least limit the freedom of action of the guerrillas. This produced violent demonstrations in Lebanese cities. Mobs rioted in Beirut; schools and universities were closed; while Israeli forces made sporadic raids across the border.

A more serious crisis erupted in October as the guerrillas demanded a total Lebanese commitment to their cause. Riots and strikes paralyzed the country. Lebanese Army units surrounded villages that sheltered the fedayeen and were in turn surrounded by other fedayeen groups infiltrating from Syria. After nearly two weeks of inconclusive fighting, a cease-fire was arranged by mediators from the U.A.R. General Bustani, the Lebanese army chief, agreed to recognize the rights of the fedayeen in Lebanon, while Yasir Arafat, chief of Al Fatah, the largest guerrilla organization, promised to reduce fedayeen units in the country

UPI

Necessary work may bring together those whom politics divides: a Jew and an Arab labor side by side on the construction of the Harry S. Truman Center for the Advancement of Peace, on Mount Scopus in Jerusalem.

to manageable proportions. However, the cease-fire was not observed fully. Lebanon's basic problem vis-à-vis the Palestinians, that of coexistence with a xenophobic Arab world, remained unsolved.

Federation of Gulf Emirates. The newest Arab state in the Middle East was born on Oct. 22 with the formal proclamation of the Federation of Gulf Emirates. Its members, nine small states all located in eastern Arabia near the Persian Gulf, had joined together informally in 1968. But their inability to reconcile their differing views on a common flag, currency, capital and constitution delayed the formal establishment of the federation for a year. With the approaching withdrawal of British military and naval forces from the area (set for early 1971), the pace of unification quickened. The announcement in Aden, capital of the Republic of Southern Yemen, that a "front for the liberation of Arab peoples of the Gulf" had been formed to unite all the Arabs of the peninsula under a revolutionary socialist regime had the desired effect as the nine ruling sheiks moved quickly to submerge their differences.

The federation began its existence with numerous assets. The nine members—Bahrain, Qatar, and the seven former Trucial States of Abu Dhabi, Dubai, Sharjah, Ras al-Khaimah, Ajman, Umm al-Qaiwain and Fujeira, so called because of their treaty relationship with Britain —collectively have enormous wealth. A major oil strike with a production of 3,000 barrels a day was reported in Abu Dhabi, one of the federation's 4 oil producers. Dubai, in the oil business since 1966, signed contracts with British firms for a $60,000,000 harbor, a jetport, and a 375-bed hospital, all payable in cash. Qatar inaugurated a chemical-fertilizer plant designed to utilize gas wastes from its Dukhan oil field. The Sheik of Sharjah, ever hopeful, granted a concession to Shell to search for a means to augment his income under the barren wastes of his principality.

The federation chose Abu Dhabi as its temporary capital until a permanent one could be built. Cost estimates ran as high as $500,-000,000. Other committees began work on a federal constitution, a flag, a common currency and laws. Saudi Arabia and Iran, the principal neighbors, recognized the federation, and the Shah of Iran agreed not to press historic Iranian claims to Bahrain. While it faced the familiar problem of adjustment to a revolutionary world, the federation's chances for survival were far more promising than those of Southern Yemen, its immediate predecessor. The latter state, cut adrift from Britain through its own mindless violence and without tangible resources, had nothing to export except revolution. The rulers of the federation, all men of traditional Arab dignity and prudence, had a rare opportunity to demonstrate to other Arab states the possibilities of good government, under a system that does not require revenge against Israel as its constant nourishment.

WILLIAM SPENCER
Professor of History,
Florida State University

MINING:
Coal-Mine Health and Safety

Historically the mining of coal underground has been one of the world's most hazardous occupations. According to the records of the U.S. Bureau of Mines, since 1906, some 90,000 men have been killed mining coal.

Although the number of men killed annually fell from 548 in 1952 to 314 in 1968, the sharp decrease is apparently due to the smaller number of men required to mine coal. With the development of mechanized mining, the number of underground coal miners decreased from over 400,000 in 1950 to 144,000 in 1968. As a result, the fatality-frequency rate has remained relatively constant at approximately one fatality per million man-hours of work.

The major causes of coal-mine fatalities have been falls of the roof and face, and gas explosions. About 50 per cent of the fatalities since 1906 have resulted from falling coal and rock. Gas and dust explosions are responsible for between 10 and 15 per cent of the deaths and are the causes of most of the major disasters.

A recently discovered major health hazard plagues the coal-mining industry. It is called coal-worker's pneumoconiosis, or, more familiarly, "black lung." Coal-worker's pneumoconiosis is a respiratory disease caused by the constant breathing of respirable coal dust. It results in many years of short breath and ul-

Senate subcommittee members Williams (center) and, to his left, Schweiker and Saxbe visit Mathies Mine, near Pittsburgh, which has an excellent safety record.

Consolidation Coal Co.

timately death. It is also believed to cause heart failure. No cure exists for the disease, which is estimated to have afflicted, in its simple or complicated form, more than 100,000 active and inactive miners. The incidence of the disease has risen greatly with improvements in mechanized mining. Since coal dust is created by the cutting of coal, the higher speed of cutting brought about by replacing picks and shovels with machines has increased the amount of coal dust miners inhale.

Several times in the past, the U.S. Federal Government enacted legislation to improve safety in the coal-mining industry. In 1910, in response to a series of coal-mine disasters, Congress created the Bureau of Mines to investigate the problems of coal-mine safety. In 1941 the Federal Coal Mine Inspection and Investigation Act was passed, giving the Bureau of Mines authority to inspect coal mines but not the authority to enforce safety standards. This defect was cured in part by the 1952 Coal Mine Safety Act which gave the Bureau enforcement authority. However, the laws in existence still had many deficiencies.

Prompted in part by a major disaster in November 1968 at Farmington, W. Va., in which 78 coal miners died, and by public awareness of the extent and seriousness of coal-worker's pneumoconiosis, Congress wrote a major, comprehensive coal-mine health-and-safety statute in 1969. The bill became law in December. It establishes health-and-safety standards to reduce significantly the causes of accidents and disease, and it gives the executive branch authority to promulgate improved standards and a broad array of enforcement powers. In addition, it provides for disability benefits for coal miners who have been disabled by coal-worker's pneumoconiosis.

SEN. HARRISON A. WILLIAMS, JR., Chairman
Senate Subcommittee on Labor

MINNESOTA

Charles S. Stenvig, police detective, was elected mayor of Minneapolis by a margin of almost two to one on June 10. He ran on a "law and order" campaign. Although the vote was considered a backlash triumph, one of his first appointments was of a Negro. □ On July 24, U.S. Sen. Eugene J. McCarthy, a presidential candidate in 1968, announced that he would not seek reelection to the Senate on any ticket in Minnesota or any other state in 1970. □ Tornadoes swept the state's north-central resort area on Aug. 6, especially around Lake Roosevelt near Outing. At least 14 persons were killed and 40 injured.

UPI

An artist's drawing shows the layout of a missile-site radar, with its associated Spartan and Sprint missiles; also included are two remote Sprint launching sites and certain support facilities within the ABM complex.

MISSILES AND ROCKETS

For missiles and rockets the highlight of 1969 was a series of events involving the controversial antiballistic-missile system (ABM). The first major defense decision by the Nixon administration was a reorientation of the ABM program. Instead of the "light" ABM system, which would have afforded limited protection for U.S. cities and military bases, the purpose of the new system is to protect the nation's prime retaliatory force, the silo-based ICBM's. Named Safeguard, the reoriented ABM system would employ the same hardware as the earlier-proposed Sentinel. The hardware includes a battery of radars and computers for the detection and tracking of incoming warheads and for steering a defending missile to an intercept; and 2 types of interceptors: one for long-range, high-altitude "kill" in space, and a second for close-in attack within the atmosphere.

Both the 55-foot, 3-stage Spartan, the long-range member of the missile team, and its 27-foot companion, Sprint, kept their advanced-testing status during 1969. Although Safeguard encountered a storm of opposition from many who felt that any kind of ABM system repre-

sents an escalation of the arms race, the program survived its initial Congressional hurdles. Early in November the necessary funds were approved, and the Department of Defense began preparing to initiate operational-hardware production in 1970.

During 1969 the Army began upgrading the performance of both nuclear-tipped missiles of the Safeguard system. In development was an Improved Spartan, with a range greater than the 400 miles of the initial version, and an Improved Sprint, which features a maneuverable upper stage called Upstage. At the same time, DOD authorized both the Army and the Air Force to continue developmental investigations of nonnuclear ABM's. The USAF system is based upon the Minuteman ICBM. The Army was researching a multiple-warhead ABM.

The newest U.S. ballistic missiles, the Air Force's Minuteman 3 and the Navy's Poseidon, also retained advanced-test status throughout the year. Each averaged about 1 test flight every 5 weeks, and each scored a high rate of success. Equipped with Multiple Independently-targeted Reentry Vehicles (MIRV's), Poseidon was scheduled to arm 31 of the 41 Fleet Ballistic

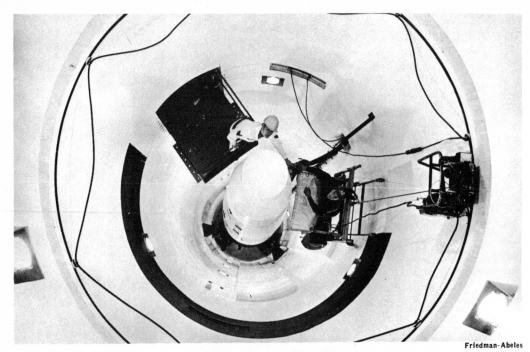

Friedman-Abeles

In its underground silo a Minuteman is serviced; a thousand Minutemen are scattered across the U.S. prairies.

Missile submarines starting in 1970. Also MIRV-equipped, Minuteman 3 is scheduled to go into operational service in 1971. Then it is gradually supposed to become the chief missile in a 1,000-weapon Minuteman force composed of Minuteman 2 and 3. At the end of 1969, Minuteman 2 filled most of the silos in a 1,000-missile Minuteman 1 and 2 mix. The ground-based ICBM force also included 54 liq-

The gantries fall away as the manned Soviet spacecraft Soyuz 8 is launched on Oct. 13, 1969.

Sovfoto

uid-fueled Titan 2's. The Navy's sea-launched-ballistic-missile arsenal amounted to 656 weapons of the Polaris A-2 and A-3 variety aboard 41 submarines.

On Sept. 15, after a hiatus of almost a year, the Soviet Union resumed flight testing of its Fractional Orbital Bombardment System (FOBS), a hybrid missile-spacecraft system that seeks to delay radar detection by flying a suborbital path at lower-than-customary ICBM trajectories. As usual the FOBS was disguised as a Cosmos "scientific" satellite. The September launch was designated Cosmos 298, and it was followed on Oct. 23 by Cosmos 305, another FOBS. The latter marked the 15th test of the series.

Two new American missiles made successful first flights during the year. On July 29, at White Sands Missile Range, N.M., the USAF made the first firing of SRAM (Short Range Attack Missile) from a B-52H bomber, and declared that "all primary test objectives" had been met in a 71-second flight. SRAM is a "standoff" missile to be used by B-52's and later bombers. Congress, however, was not impressed by the flight, and cited "developmental difficulties" as the reason for withholding SRAM production funds in the budget for fiscal 1970.

The other new missile to take to the air was Maverick, a USAF air-to-surface weapon guided by television and designed for use against small targets such as tanks and field fortifications. Maverick was launched for the first time on Sept. 19, from an F-4 fighter over Edwards AFB, Calif.

Though the Navy's Phoenix and Condor missiles remained in advance-test status, Congress postponed plans to begin buying them in quantity. Phoenix is a long-range, very-high-performance air-to-air missile. Condor is a standoff weapon, designed to fly long distances under its own rocket power so that Navy aircraft may remain out of heavily defended target areas.

With many of its major missile systems growing rather old, the Department of Defense had in study and early test stages a number of completely new concepts planned for service introduction in the 1970's. Among them were the Air Force's Airborne Ballistic Missile Intercept System (ABMIS), and the Navy's Sea-based AntiBallistic Missile Intercept System (SABMIS), which is based on the Poseidon missile. CAMS (Coastal AntiMissile System) would employ both ABMIS and SABMIS together with other air-, sea- and land-launched weapons in a mixed force. It is designed to destroy enemy missiles launched at sea.

Also on the Navy's planning board were ASMS (Advanced Surface Missile System) and ULMS (Underwater Long-range Missile System). The former would be an ultramodern replacement for a variety of ship-based anti-aircraft missiles now in use. The latter involves not only a very advanced underwater missile but also a high-performance, quieter submarine to launch it.

The Air Force was studying CASW (Close Air Support Weapon), a missile with greater accuracy than anything yet achieved for close support of ground troops. Both the Air Force and the Navy initiated design studies on a new "dogfight" missile for their advanced F-15 and F-14 fighters. This missile system, designed for air-to-air use in close, maneuvering air combat, is known in the USAF as SRM (Short Range Missile) AIM-82A and in the Navy as AAAM (Advanced Air-to-Air Missile). The Army was studying contractors' designs for a MARS (Multiple Artillery Rocket System), an intermediate-range bombardment system involving a mobile launcher carrying a number of rockets launched in several waves.

In the field of space-launch vehicles, the world's biggest booster, Saturn 5, made 4 flights in 1969, bringing its total to 7. (Few people realized that the 2 manned lunar-landing flights of 1969 were launched after only 5 flights of Saturn 5.) The long-awaited Soviet superrocket, reportedly more powerful than Saturn 5, failed to make its appearance in 1969, but the U.S.S.R. did provide one rocketry spectacular in October. It launched 3 separate manned spacecraft by 3 separate boosters at 24-hour intervals, a launch-pad capability not enjoyed yet by the United States.

JAMES J. HAGGERTY
Editor, *Aerospace Year Book*

MISSISSIPPI

Charles Evers, nationally known civil-rights leader, won the Democratic primary race, tantamount to election, for mayor of Fayette, on May 13. (He took office in a joyous ceremony on July 7.) At least a dozen other Negroes won the primary for lesser offices in various state localities. □ On Aug. 17, Mississippi was in the direct path of hurricane Camille, one of the most violent hurricanes in years. Fatalities and damage from winds and floods were especially severe in Pass Christian and Gulfport.

MISSOURI

On Mar. 20 the railroad car in which former President Harry S. Truman whistle-stopped across the country in the 1948 campaign, was bought for $77,000 by Alex J. Barket, a Kansas City banker, to preserve as a historic relic. □ Democrat A. J. Cervantes was reelected mayor of St. Louis on Apr. 1. □ On the campus of Westminster College in Fulton, the Church of St. Mary, Aldermanbury (England), was dedicated on May 7 in memory of Winston Churchill's famous iron-curtain speech in Fulton in 1946. The stones of the church, burned out in World War II, were transported and reconstructed.

MONTANA

After the voters of Anaconda had approved a special tax to provide $65,000 in public funds to pay salaries of lay teachers at a Roman Catholic high school, a district judge ruled in June that the funds could not be collected until the state Supreme Court had decided on the constitutionality of the procedure. □ On June 24, for the first time since 1958, a Democrat, John Melcher, was elected to the House of Representatives from the state's Second Congressional District. □ In July, at Glasgow, where Air Force base was closed in 1968, the Defense Department was testing an aid program in effort to make up loss of $25,000,000 that the base had poured into the local economy. Program included training in new skills that would attract commercial manufacturing.

Culver Pictures, Inc.

Jon Voight (l) as Joe Buck—anxious, dim-witted, would-be cowboy—and Dustin Hoffman as Ratso—Buck's ill, dirty pal, who knows only squalor—form a bizarre but oddly tender friendship in "Midnight Cowboy."

motion pictures

In 1968, audiences watched the movies get more and more volatile and wondered what they would be showing next.

In 1969, moviemakers filled in the blanks.

The screen in 1969 was the most vigorous site of expression except perhaps for the very streets. Motion pictures often reflected the tensions of their country, political and private. Nudity on the screen became a commonplace. More and more young people than ever before, the movie industry said, paid increasing prices for cinema tickets. Whatever filmgoers in 1969 were looking for, one picture or another would supply it.

Comments on the Vietnam war were many. Action on the riot-torn streets of Chicago turned up in *Medium Cool* to the distinct sound-track crunch of a police nightstick. The Western, that most sanctified of American film products, returned—sort of. *True Grit* was a classic of the type, but something like *The Wild Bunch* took the species into places it had never been before, and used the Western as a means to show new highs (or lows) of cruelty and mayhem.

Partway through 1969, the motion-picture industry's self-policing ratings system, which pastes a G, M, R or X on films as an index for anxious parents, had scanned some 294 films. It found only 16 of them too indelicate for anything but the lowest, X, rating. Criteria for the X rating were not always clear, but it quickly became obvious that more than one quick-buck producer was striving for his X by drumming up a salacious scene, just enough to get audiences lining up at the box office.

The criteria were explained in the trade press by the Code and Rating Administration in Hollywood, which said that an X rating was given for "sexuality and related scenes," sometimes because of dialogue, but not because of violence and "never has a picture been rated X because of it."

The year saw the strong emergence of "the personal film," a cliquish term that nonetheless came to stand for earnest work like John Cassavetes' *Faces*. *Faces* was probably the most overpraised picture of the year, a grainy but seemingly honest little picture with no "name" stars, which depicted suburban married life

Allied Artists
United Artists Corp.

Cathy Burns, seated, is tormented in "Last Summer," which underlined youth's capacity for cruelty. The extremely original "Alice's Restaurant," with Arlo Guthrie, made a point of youth's grace and gentleness.

harshly. Arthur Penn, of *Bonnie and Clyde,* directed the very young Arlo Guthrie in a very young picture, *Alice's Restaurant.* Youngsters seized on it as a gonfalon, a gentle comic property they could hold high as their own. *Easy Rider* was made on a shoestring by Peter Fonda, was directed by Dennis Hopper and starred both young actors. It was the ultimate motorcycle picture thus far; but more than that, it was the odyssey of two marijuana-powered youths plunging across beautiful American landscapes to tragedy.

The charm of some of these movies was their makers' apparent desire to get away from the Super Hollywood Effects school and tackle the basic facts of film making. John Schlesinger, for instance, in *Midnight Cowboy,* put his camera on Jon Voight, as a desperate Texas stud in New York City, and on Dustin Hoffman as his foul pal, Ratso Rizzo, and left it there. The result was one of the finest movies of 1969, a journey high and low around Manhattan that showed vermin, terror, hunger, love, and a little of what they used to call the human comedy.

Many of the films, admittedly, were made for the ballooning youth market. The statistic that about half the U.S. population is under age 25 made the movie industry suspect that perhaps a larger per cent than that could be lured away from the family TV set. *Last Summer* was a beautiful film about young people, made by the knowing Frank and Eleanor Perry. It pointed up how cruel beauty can sometimes be to the less beautiful, not a bad lesson perhaps for privileged youth in an affluent society. *Putney Swope* satirized Madison Avenue, as if it needed any more satirizing, though this time put a young Negro in charge of matters. *The Sterile Cuckoo* gave Liza Minnelli opportunity for a very sympathetic portrayal of a young girl in love. Youthful trends like the "singles' bar" meeting places got a nod in *John and Mary* in which Dustin Hoffman meets Mia Farrow, has a love affair, and learns her name later. Besides being a superlative job of photographic ingenuity by Haskell Wexler, *Medium Cool* inserted drama into the Chicago riots. For extra piquancy it included one of the most airy and extensively photographed nude sequences of the year.

Nudity was, seemingly, everywhere in the movies. A plastic piece of Hollywood smuggery called *Bob & Carol & Ted & Alice* got two men and two women into the same bed at once. It might have been interesting except that the entire picture was built up to just that moment and the ultimate effect was rather boring. Even a Gregory Peck picture had a nude scene. It

Culver Pictures, Inc.

Ali MacGraw and Richard Benjamin play the young Jewish lovers in the funny-appalling "Goodbye, Columbus."

was not Peck but Julie Newmar in a gratuitous swimming scene in a mountain stream. *Goodbye, Columbus* had flashes of nudity—Ali MacGraw's, in a shower—but it had much more, chiefly a performance by Richard Benjamin that marked him as a major screen talent. The film came from Philip Roth's bittersweet tale of a Jewish boy in love with a wealthy, suburban Jewish girl.

For older ticket buyers, abysmally tired of long dirty hair and of pictures about disaffected youth, there was always Hollywood to fall back on. A new James Bond appeared, as George Lazenby replaced Sean Connery as 007 in *On Her Majesty's Secret Service*. Big, earnest pictures came one after another, among them *Ice Station Zebra* and *Krakatoa, East of Java,* two Cinerama releases, both huge, both doleful.

For a near-miss such as the romantic comedy *The April Fools,* with Jack Lemmon and Catherine Deneuve, there was a fine tragicomedy *The Prime of Miss Jean Brodie,* in which lovely Maggie Smith starred as a fascinating, eccentric schoolteacher.

From the superb Swedish director Ingmar Bergman came one of his best films, *Shame*. It starred Liv Ullmann and Max von Sydow in a scarifying and realistic parable about the visitation of war. Also Swedish was the drab but notorious *I Am Curious (Yellow),* an ex-

plicit, junky and joyless piece of work about a girl, her views on socialism, and her sex life, all portrayed relentlessly. In France, Jean-Luc Godard kept up his antiwar stand with *Weekend,* the work of a virtuoso director. François Truffaut made *Stolen Kisses,* and it was lovely.

Transfers from stage to screen yielded Sidney Lumet's version of *The Sea Gull,* a scenic, emotional and rather dull film. However, the film version of *The Royal Hunt of the Sun,* a sensational pageant on the stage, was an even more exciting spectacle on the large screen, with Christopher Plummer as an Inca ruler.

Some of the interest in the latter part of 1969 was stimulated not by what was happening, but by what was about to happen. It implied much about the immediate future of motion pictures, for public interest in the movies was high during 1969. Time Inc. released word of its intention to start a magazine devoted to film. Huntington Hartford said he would revive his glossy *Show* magazine, which this time would deal chiefly with movies. There would be no lack of material. Mike Nichols, for instance, was filming Joseph Heller's maddeningly funny book, *Catch-22*. Gore Vidal's precious novel *Myra Breckenridge* was somehow being turned into a film, involving those screen all-time all-timers Mae West and Raquel Welch. Federico Fellini offered *The Satyricon* and was getting

Culver Pictures, Inc.

Culver Pictures, Inc.

In "The Prime of Miss Jean Brodie" (above), Maggie Smith holds forth on womanhood. Liza Minnelli (with Wendell Burton) is the endearing tough-sweet heroine of "The Sterile Cuckoo" (upper r). The musical of the sentimental classic "Goodbye, Mr. Chips" was redeemed by the acting of Peter O'Toole (with Petula Clark joining in for the late-blooming romance).

stranger and stranger. Michelangelo Antonioni's sequel to *Blow-Up*, a picture entitled *Zabriskie Point*, was being made in the United States amid great secrecy and mystery.

Multimillion-dollar musicals were shunned. The so-called native Hollywood product was to have been the bonanza of 1969. The industry painfully learned otherwise. The 1968 film *Funny Girl* has been earning magnificent amounts of money on its $10,000,000 cost, because of Barbra Streisand's personal gifts. In contrast, the 1969 musical *Paint Your Wagon*, a $20,000,000 enterprise, was disappointing. It starred three people, Lee Marvin, Jean Seberg and Clint Eastwood, who cannot sing. *Hello, Dolly!*, with Streisand again, began a reserved-seat engagement in New York City at Christmastime.

Although the future of the million-dollar comedy *Darling Lili*, starring Julie Andrews, remained questionable in 1969, it was booked by Radio City Music Hall early in 1970. Plans for *Mame* and *Fiddler on the Roof* were in abeyance. *Oh! What a Lovely War*, a sizable undertaking, was a version of a British stage

MGM

Paramount Films Inc.

As an old, fat marshal, John Wayne (carrying Kim Darby) gives the performance of his life in "True Grit."

musical about the futility of World War I. It seemed to include every colorful British performer from Sir Laurence Olivier to (in a newsreel) Harold Wilson. *Goodbye, Mr. Chips* became a musical, with Petula Clark chiming in. However, the hapless experiences of Hollywood musicals were nowhere better illustrated than in *Those Were the Happy Times.* It

starred Julie Andrews of *The Sound of Music,* and advertisements trumpeted it as having "the sound of Julie!" Actually it was nothing but a reissue of *Star!,* which had been a mess the first time around and still was.

In two pictures, the Western lived. *True Grit* was John Wayne, classic as an old marshal running to fat who triumphs over evil and four bad guys in one fell swoop. *Butch Cassidy and the Sundance Kid* in the persons of Paul Newman and Robert Redford showed the gunslinger as antihero, kidded him a while, then killed him off. Dramatic and funny, the picture was ultimately false to itself in its joy over violence.

The Oscars in 1969 were won by Katharine Hepburn and Barbra Streisand in a historic tie for best actress. After winning her third Oscar, Hepburn went right out and demonstrated that practice doesn't always make perfect in *The Madwoman of Chaillot,* one of the great artistic calamities of the year.

Increasingly the big Hollywood studios seemed to be in states of flux. Metro-Goldwyn-Mayer changed hands; Warner Brothers was being run after a fashion by a parking-lot chain; Paramount fired 75 to 100 employees at one stroke, later put its studio property up for sale. M-G-M reported that its tax loss for the fiscal year ending Aug. 31 was at least $25,000,000. "The winds of change," reported the Associated Press, "are blowing through movieland." Hope for the motion-picture industry seemed to lie in smaller, independent producers, men who are adventurers and are unburdened by heavy overhead and costly inventory. The moguls—Zanuck, Mayer, Warner—are gone.

LAWRENCE DeVINE
Drama Editor and Film Critic
Detroit Free Press

Cinema Centers Film Production

Christopher Plummer, as the Inca ruler Atahualpa, and Robert Shaw, as the Spanish conqueror Pizarro, confront each other in "The Royal Hunt of the Sun," notable chiefly as a spectacle.

"The New York Times"

Members of the Metropolitan Opera orchestra and the chorus put on a protest performance. Because of the bitter disagreement with management, the great opera company came close to having no 1969–70 season.

MUSIC, CLASSICAL

The difficulty that confronts American cultural activities was brought into shocking focus in the fall of 1969, when the Metropolitan Opera failed to open its doors on Sept. 15 for the start of its new season, and stayed shut for weeks thereafter.

The difficulty can be described in a single word: money. It has long been known that there is very little money to be made out of music. For every major solo artist or conductor who has waxed rich from his musical activities, there are thousands who quite literally starve. The financial difficulties confronting a solo performer are multiplied many times over when it comes to producing an opera. A single night's performance at the Metropolitan Opera can cost close to six figures, far more than could be earned even with every seat sold at a $15 top. By the end of the 1968–69 season, the Metropolitan's annual operating deficit reached $3,500,000, which was made up only by assiduous fund-raising on the part of the company's private and commercial patrons. The company was walking a financial tightrope. Then, during the summer of 1969, it was presented with

new contract demands by the 14 unions representing its diverse staff, from singers to floor-sweepers. The issues at stake were pay scales, first of all, and such matters as rehearsal time. Finally, in mid-December, the Metropolitan and the 14 unions agreed to a new contract. The 1969-70 season, now shortened to 16 weeks, opened on Dec. 29 with Verdi's *Aïda* and Leontyne Price singing the title role.

The Metropolitan's difficulty was the most dramatic evidence of the financial crisis that overshadows all American cultural production. Though well known to participants, it is often lost sight of by the public in the glamour of the proceedings. Clearly, the ultimate solution must be some more rational and dependable source of financial support for such expensive and money-losing productions as an all-star opera company. For centuries, governmental subsidy has been the salvation of the arts in most European and even in some Western Hemisphere countries. Canada now has a national theater. Yet in the United States the idea proceeds at a snail's pace.

A crisis of somewhat more manageable proportions affected another part of the musical

"The New York Times"

"The New York Times"

Symphony conductors bow in and bow out: far left, Seiji Ozawa, called to lead the San Francisco orchestra; and Leonard Bernstein, at the end of his last concert as New York Philharmonic conductor.

establishment during 1969. When Leonard Bernstein announced, in the fall of 1966, that he would retire from the conductorship of the New York Philharmonic in three years, another problem arose that has since become acute. Not only the Philharmonic but all the major orchestras would soon need to find new leaders, simply because many of the current leaders were nearing retirement. Moreover, these jobs would be difficult to fill because the pool of available talent is not large.

Bernstein's final concert as the Philharmonic's music director came in May 1969. It was an emotion-packed probing of the long Third Symphony by Gustav Mahler, a composer Bernstein ardently championed during his ten years as conductor of the Philharmonic. (He now became the orchestra's conductor laureate, thus retaining some connection with it.) At about the same time, podiums were also vacated in Boston, Chicago, Cincinnati, Houston and San Francisco. As for the Philadelphia and Cleveland orchestras, their conductors were in their seventies. Where were the men to fill these posts?

The phenomenon of the commuting conductor came into being. To replace Erich Leinsdorf, Boston engaged the venerable William Steinberg, though he retained his post with the Pittsburgh Symphony. The young Seiji Ozawa was tapped to lead the San Francisco Symphony when Josef Krips retires. At the same time, Ozawa will continue to direct the Toronto Symphony and the summer activities of the Boston Symphony at Tanglewood. New York made a daring but lauded choice in Pierre Boulez. He is an admired avant-garde composer but has had only five full years of conductorial experience. Yet Boulez would remain the director of the BBC Symphony in London and "principal guest conductor" of the Cleveland Orchestra.

If the musical year can be said to have produced a single star, it would beyond any doubt be Beverly Sills, the Brooklyn-born coloratura soprano. Her rise to glory has not been meteoric in the romantic sense. She has been a respected member of the New York City Opera Company since her debut in 1955. But in the past few years, Miss Sills, now in her late thirties, has strengthened the virtuoso aspects of her singing. In April 1969 she made her debut at Milan's august La Scala in Rossini's fiercely difficult dramatic opera *The Siege of Corinth*. Her reception by press and public alike was of the sort reserved for only a handful of legendary singers in each century. What New York audiences had realized for at least six years was now recognized by the whole world of music. Miss Sills thus achieved true international star status. She also won hearts in her hometown in a new, uncut production of *Lucia di Lammermoor* mounted by the New York City Opera in the fall.

The City Opera also revived two much-discussed but little-performed works from the past during the year: Borodin's *Prince Igor* in the spring and Boito's *Mefistofele* in the fall, both with considerable success. Another little-known masterwork from the past which is far more often spoken about than heard, the melodramatic *Jenufa* by the Czech composer Leos Janacek, was revived in the fall by the San Francisco Opera.

It was, in fact, a year for exhuming almost-forgotten scores from the romantic era. Erich Leinsdorf and the Boston Symphony joined the American pianist Earl Wild to revive the Piano Concerto by one Xaver Schwarenka, a late-nineteenth-century Polish composer who wrote in the extravagant, virtuoso style associated with Franz Liszt. The young pianist Raymond Lewenthal has made something of a specialty of reviving examples of the flamboyant romantic repertory. In New York he played a great favorite of two generations ago, Anton Rubinstein's D Minor Piano Concerto.

During the summer, members of the Metropolitan Opera Studio (the junior training group of the Metropolitan Opera) joined a group of instrumentalists, including Lewenthal, for a

Beverly Sills' rave debut at Milan's La Scala, in Rossini's "The Siege of Corinth," made her a living legend.

John Reardon (on the cross) sang Father Grandier in the Santa Fe production of the difficult, avant-garde opera "The Devils" by the Polish composer Penderecki.

Santa Fe Opera Co.

Edgar Vincent Associates

week of still more little-known virtuoso music from the nineteenth century. The festival was given in the most appropriate settings imaginable: several magnificent, ornate mansions at Newport, R.I.

In the area of *new* new music, the avant-garde Polish composer Krzysztof Penderecki continued moving to the fore among contemporary creators. His opera *The Devils,* based on Aldous Huxley's novel *The Devils of Loudun,* had its American premiere at the summer opera festival in Santa Fe. A difficult, mystic, introverted work, it was accorded a somewhat introverted reception. However, his *Passion according to Saint Luke,* regarded by most listeners as his masterpiece to date, was hailed enthusiastically at its Carnegie Hall premiere under the direction of Stanislaw Skrowaczewski with the Minneapolis Symphony Orchestra and a large chorus. Another major work by Penderecki, *Threnody for the Victims of Hiroshima,* joined the repertory of several major symphony orchestras during the year.

Other major new pieces heard in 1969 included Milton Babbitt's *Relata II* and Leon Kirchner's *Music for Orchestra* (both commissioned for and introduced by the New York Philharmonic), and the Ninth Symphony by William Schuman, performed by the Philadelphia Orchestra.

In 1968 a manuscript was discovered in the city of Graz, Austria, of a piano piece whose lyrical beauty and overall style proclaimed it unmistakably as a work by Franz Schubert. The date on the 13-minute fantasy indicated that it was created by the composer at the age of twenty. Although it is not quite a masterpiece, its grace, charm and fire made a strong appeal when it was introduced in the United States by the pianist Lili Kraus on a nationwide television program in November 1969.

After seven years of piecemeal inaugurations, New York's Lincoln Center was finally completed in the fall of 1969, when the last of the five buildings, housing the Juilliard School, was officially dedicated. Students and visitors found the school's new appointments and facilities magnificent. The building also includes a public hall for chamber-music concerts, named after its benefactor Alice B. Tully. The hall's comfort and acoustic qualities seemed to satisfy everyone.

ALAN RICH
Music Critic, *New York* Magazine

Alice B. Tully Hall, already famous for its acoustics, completed the Lincoln Center, New York, complex.

UPI

Friedman-Abeles

Described as "the American tribal love-rock musical," the Broadway show "Hair" continued to be extremely popular for its score. The hit song, "The Age of Aquarius," was taken over as a label for 1969 pop music.

MUSIC, POPULAR

For pop music, 1969 was, quite literally, the Age of Aquarius. The most pervasively popular music of the year came from Galt MacDermot's score for *Hair,* the startlingly successful and controversial Broadway show that was called "the American tribal love-rock musical." Leading this score on its way to wide acclaim was the song *The Age of Aquarius,* although several other songs from the show—*Easy to Be Hard, Let the Sunshine In, Where Do I Go, Good Morning Starshine, Hare Krishna, Frank Mills* and the title tune *Hair*—were recorded and performed over and over again in almost every imaginable manner.

Surprisingly, despite the publicity that heralded this show as Broadway's first rock musical, the songs were less apt to be performed in a rock treatment than they were as middle-ground "easy listening," as jazz, or in treatments by the year's big new musical toy, the Moog Synthesizer. Actually, there was nothing intrinsically "rock" about the score, since rock, like jazz, essentially implies a manner of playing rather than a style of composition. The tunes themselves, even as performed in the show, were melodically traditional. This fact permitted them to be played and sung in ways sufficiently familiar to reach a very broad audience.

The music's success was slow in arriving. The show had been playing on Broadway for more than a year before the score began to catch on. An opening wedge was a recording of *The Age of Aquarius* by the Fifth Dimension, a popular nightclub act. Soon the original-cast album of *Hair* reached the top of the best-selling LP charts and stayed there for weeks on end, one of the few original-cast albums ever to reach the No. 1 position.

Then the bandwagon rush to record the tunes began in earnest. The fresh, imaginative quality of MacDermot's music combined with the young, contemporary outlook of the lyrics by Gerome Radni and James Rado made an appeal to audiences of all ages and of many different musical tastes.

That this was a musical Age of Aquarius was indicated even more positively by the proliferation of huge pop-music festivals. The climax was a three-day, so-called Aquarian Exposition at Bethel, N.Y., which attracted an audience estimated at between 300,000 and 400,000. Like similar but not quite so huge gatherings at Atlanta, Ga., Lewisville, Tex., Atlantic City, N.J., Tenino, Wash., and on the Isle of Wight in the English Channel, the basic attraction at Bethel (officially known as the Woodstock Music and Art Fair because it was originally scheduled to be held at Woodstock, N.Y.) was

At the rock-music festival at Bethel, N.Y., in August, some of the 300,000 to 400,000 young people make camp right in the road. In spite of rain and other discomforts, it was a strikingly peaceful assembly.

UPI

a long list of popular musical groups: rock, blues and folk. In practice, however, the main appeal of these festivals proved to be the opportunities they provided for young people to live briefly in what amounted to communities of their own, listening to their kind of music and following their own social practices relatively unhindered by traditional or adult concepts.

The contemporary penchant for "telling it like it is" produced a new popular superstar during the year in Johnny Cash, a country singer who had had a long and speckled career before 1969. His performances for inmates of Folsom Prison and at San Quentin, recorded and released on LP's, found an enthusiastically responsive audience in the same youngsters who trekked to the pop-music festivals to "live it like it is." Cash's major success during the year was a long story ballad, *A Boy Named Sue*.

Cash's success and the emphasis it gave to country music served to some extent to sidetrack the further development of the popularity of soul music. Spurred by such popular figures as Aretha Franklin and Ray Charles, soul music had become increasingly influential in popular music for several years past.

The new attention Cash brought to country music was supplemented by his musical cross-fertilization with Bob Dylan with whom he recorded. Dylan made an LP collection of his own kind of country material, called *Nashville Skyline*. Dylan was also the focus of the pop-music festival on the Isle of Wight where he made his first scheduled public appearance in several years. Earlier he had dropped in un-

announced on a Mississippi River festival at Edwardsville, Ill.

The turning cycle of interest in pop-music fashions also resulted in the renewed appeal of early rock 'n' roll, particularly the part of it that had been most strongly influenced by country music. Elvis Presley made an unprecedented personal appearance for several weeks at Las Vegas, scoring a tremendous success both with those who had once been his teen-age fans and others whose tastes had been molded by the steady changes in popular music during the intervening years. An early rock 'n' roll team, the Everly Brothers, made a successful return, building on their early hits with a new, more sophisticated approach.

A potential new direction for current pop music was suggested by the British group The Who, whose extended vocal-and-instrumental work *Tommy* they called an opera. It was acclaimed not only by followers of pop music

Country singer Johnny Cash performs for inmates of Folsom Prison, Calif.; his big hit is "A Boy Named Sue."

Pictorial Parade

Camera Press-PIX

but even by *The New York Times'* drama critic Clive Barnes, who saw in it the beginnings of a new approach to musical theater.

Aside from the tunes from *Hair,* relatively few songs were able to build and maintain a steady position of popularity as indicated by the popularity charts kept by the music-business trade papers. Most songs that reached the charts stayed on for less than two months, and in any given week it was unusual to find more than two or three songs that had been on the charts for as long as three months.

One of the few songs to break through and show signs of becoming a standard was Joni Mitchell's folk-tinged *Both Sides Now.* Other songs that made a strong impression during the year were *Spinning Wheel,* sung by its writer, David Clayton-Thomas, with Blood, Sweat and Tears, a very important factor in making that group one of the most popular of the new performing outfits to appear in 1969; *Honky Tonk Woman,* a hit for the Rolling Stones; *Lay Lady Lay,* a Bob Dylan composition which was picked up by a number of other singers; and *My Cherie Amour,* which helped to reestablish the onetime child star Stevie Wonder as an adult entertainer.

Broadway, except for *Hair,* was barren of successful new popular songs, and film scores provided relatively little. One surprising success from the movies was Nino Rota's *Love Theme from Romeo and Juliet;* the film made a tremendous appeal to youth. Rod McKuen's *Jean,* the main theme of *The Prime of Miss Jean Brodie,* was also raised to the hit category, through a recording by a singer singularly named Oliver.

JOHN S. WILSON
Popular-Music Reviewer
The New York Times

A British group, The Who, goes into action before a sea of fans (above). Singing the theme from "The Prime of Miss Jean Brodie," Oliver (below) makes it his own.

Penguin Photo

NATIONALISM

Throughout 1969, in both the communist and noncommunist worlds, nationalism continued to be one of the most powerful motives of political behavior in domestic as well as foreign affairs. Although many of the 1969 expressions of nationalism were familiar, there was a marked intensification of the new regional-ethnic nationalism that, in recent years, has been evolving *within* established nation-states and threatening their disruption.

Defined as a political, social and psychological force arising from unique cultural and historical conditions, nationalism has long been recognized by scholars as being ambivalent in its effects. It is benign when it enhances the unity and stability of a political community, encourages the young to emulate the deeds of their forebears, or inspires creative artists to expand the scope of their aesthetic interests. It becomes harmful when it breeds extreme xenophobia, overemphasizes the separateness and differences between groups, or provokes international conflicts such as the two world wars.

Until about the time of World War II, nationalism was most often linked to sovereign nation-states, and within a given country it was a centripetal, integrating and unifying force. Since World War II, on the other hand, nationalism has assumed a new guise: a kind of "infranational" form that is more regional and more culturally homogeneous than the traditional forms. Specifically, this new regional-ethnic nationalism reflects the spirit and aspirations of ethnic subcultures within existing nation-states. Its chief significance is that it drives its proponents to assert a kind of extreme regionalism and, in some instances, total independence.

In Western Europe, it was perhaps most prominent in France, where the nationalists of Brittany intensified their campaign for greater regional autonomy within the French state. Basing their movement on their isolated location, ancient Celtic language, and unique culture, the Breton nationalists were in part responsible for one of the outstanding events of 1969 —the resignation of Charles de Gaulle as president of France.

Belgium was likewise disturbed by the new nationalism as a result of the continuing agitation of Flemish nationalists for increased Flemish autonomy within a new decentralized, federal Belgium. Their nationalism is founded upon the Flemish language (a close relation of Dutch), ethnic homogeneity, and a culture that is much closer to that of the Netherlands and of Germany than to the culture of France, to which the Belgian Walloons are linked.

Spain, too, is a focus of the new nationalism as evidenced by the propaganda of the Basque and Catalonian separatists. These ethnic minorities aspire to regional autonomy in the short run and to total separation from Spain in the long run. Their activities in 1969 were confined to agitation in their churches, universities and labor unions.

Britain has three minorities propagating the new nationalism: Scottish Nationalists (through the Scottish National Party); Welsh Nationalists (through the Welsh National Party); and the Northern Ireland "Eiranns." The first and second groups base their movements on unique linguistic and cultural factors, while the Eiranns base theirs on Irish ethnicity and Roman Catholicism. Scottish and Welsh nationalists have generally campaigned for "federal devolution" for Scotland and Wales, but they hope ultimately to gain full independence. In July of

The words on the illicit poster mean "Long live the Basques"—a defiant cry for freedom from Franco's Spain.

PIX, Camera Press

1969, the more militant of the Welsh Nationalists tried, unsuccessfully, to disrupt the investiture of Britain's Prince Charles as Prince of Wales at historic Caernarvon Castle. The Northern Ireland Nationalists have one goal: political union with the Republic of Ireland (Eire). In 1969 their street demonstrations forced a change in the Northern Ireland Government.

In Africa the most prominent, and tragic, example of the new nationalism is that of the Biafrans, who in 1969 were still trying to secede from the West African republic of Nigeria. With a secessionist ideology derived from their cultural uniqueness and tribal homogeneity, since 1967 the Biafrans have been locked in a civil war with the Nigerian Federal Government, the consequences of which have been catastrophic for the country.

Even the United States has not escaped the pressures of the new nationalism. In the southwestern states, especially New Mexico, certain Spanish-American groups, stressing their distinctive language and culture, have stepped up their demands for the return of ancient lands and privileges. Rather similar demands have been voiced by several Indian groups. Also in 1969 the Black Power separatists continued to agitate for a wholly black nation that would be carved out of a number of southern states and that would be supported by foreign aid and reparations from the United States Government, corporations and churches.

Because of its authoritarian political system, the U.S.S.R. has generally been able to mute the voices of its regional minorities. Yet in 1969 there were several reports of agitation by the Ukrainians, long noted for their separatist aspirations, and by the Muslim Crimean Tatars, who constitute the last remnant of the Tatar empire in Russia. In fact, in Moscow in the spring of 1969, six Crimean Tatars were arrested for demonstrating in behalf of their right to return to their ancestral homes in the Crimea, from which they had been deported to Soviet Central Asia by Stalin as long ago as 1944.

In Latin America, Asia and Eastern Europe, the manifestations of nationalism in 1969 were chiefly of the old centripetal sort. There the nationalists were not demanding the break-up or unified countries but the end of foreign imperialism. This was shown by the Latin-American nationalists' reaction to the tour of Gov. Nelson Rockefeller (on a mission for President Nixon); the increasing attacks on the United States by Asian nationalists; and the growing anti-Russian sentiment in Czechoslovakia, which led to the ouster of Alexander

UPI

In Londonderry, Northern Ireland, an angry mob surges through a narrow street, hurling stones at the police.

Dubcek and his replacement by pro-Soviet Gustav Husak.

It now appears that the spread of the new regional-ethnic nationalism stems from four converging factors: the revolution of rising expectations; the dissolution of the old European empires; a growing search for ethnic identity by minority groups; and the United Nations' stress on universal self-determination. It would be premature to describe traditional integral nationalism as obsolescent. Yet it seems certain that in the coming years the emerging regional-ethnic nationalism will play a major role—both for good and evil—in the politics of the world's nation-states.

FRANCIS M. WILHOIT
Professor of Political Science
Drake University

NEBRASKA

Lincoln (state capital) elected its first black city councilman, Harry Peterson, in the spring. In a city of 152,000 people, where only 2,100 were black, the election indicated a broadening in the political views of white citizens. □ A stringent self-defense law went into effect in June. It allows any citizen, without legal jeopardy, to use any means to protect himself or anyone else from "imminent danger of criminal attack." Gov. Norbert Tiemann had vetoed the bill, calling it "legalized murder," but the legislature overruled him. □ Racial rioting broke out in Omaha at the end of June, resulting in property damage of more than $900,000.

NETHERLANDS, THE

The year opened with tax increases and a credit squeeze. The European Common Market's value-added tax (VAT) was introduced on Jan. 1, 1969 (see article on Belgium). This snowballing turnover in company taxes gave a sharp upward thrust to prices. In March the legal minimum wage was increased from 140 to 142 guilders per week, an increase of about $.55. In April a complete price freeze was imposed and the main discount rate increased from 5 to 5.5 per cent. Came August this was hiked again, to 6 per cent. The cost of living rose 8 per cent in 6 months.

In April a TV documentary sparked riots in slum areas; it is reckoned that 10 per cent of the Netherlands' housing is in urgent need of renewal. On Apr. 30 another riot developed out of a refusal of the broadcasting authorities to allow the occasion of Queen Juliana's

---

THE NETHERLANDS

Area: 12,860
Population: 12,900,000
Capital: Amsterdam (pop., 865,000)
Government: Juliana, queen—1948; Piet J. S. de Jong, prime minister—1967
Gross National Product: $23,900,000,000
Monetary unit: guilder (3.6 guilders = U.S. $1.00)
Chief products: dairy products, flower bulbs, grains, ships, machinery, textiles, chemicals, cut diamonds, precious metals, ceramics
Foreign trade: exports, $8,341,000,000; imports, $9,293,000,000
Communications: 2,715 telephones, 2,800,000 radios, 2,717,416 TV sets, 77 daily newspapers
Transportation: roads, 28,607 mi.; railroads, 1,000 mi.; navigable waterways, 3,952 mi.
Education: 1,975,959 elementary and secondary students, 13 universities
Armed forces: 124,000

See map on page 185

---

sixtieth birthday to be used for critical commentary on social conditions. The University of Tilburg was occupied by students. Later, troops had to be called in to control student demonstrations at Amsterdam University. Following these demonstrations, summonses were issued against 543 students.

A significant political development was the gain by the New Left of 9 of the 21 seats on the board of the Dutch Labor Party.

However, things are not always exactly as they seem. In September, according to a public-opinion poll, 85 per cent of the Dutch people were happy with the monarchy, while 91 per cent said they thought Queen Juliana herself was doing a good job.

Prices were unfrozen in the same month. Income taxes were slightly reduced, while the VAT was somewhat increased. The Government began to budget for a deficit of 2,200,-000,000 guilders ($611,000,000) from a total spending of 29,000,000,000 guilders ($805,-500,000). Enlarged programs for urban renewal and housing were announced; and measures were introduced for modernizing the country's universities. A plan to give employees greater participation in company management was also outlined. The Government declared its intention of stabilizing aid to developing countries at 1.0 per cent of gross national income.

In spite of everything, Dutch exports surpassed the most optimistic estimates. Those to the United States were very slightly down, but in mid-1969 it was disclosed that exports to the rest of Europe were already up 21 per cent over 1968.

The devaluation of the French franc and the upward revaluation of the West German mark acted to help Dutch exports. Patchwork though it may be, the EEC's Common Agricultural Policy has maintained a comfortable economic temperature for Holland's dairy-farming industry. (Agriculture is still responsible for 27 per cent of the Netherlands' total exports.) It looked more and more likely that the Groningen natural-gas field may become Europe's most important single source of energy. Moreover, it was reported that uranium had been found in southwest Holland, at Shouwen Duiveland.

Rotterdam has established itself as Europe's major port. The country's main shipping interests have been rationalized through a series of mergers. The official expectation in this area is that, in 1970, wages will rise 7 per cent.

Prime Minister Piet de Jong and Foreign Minister Joseph H. Luns visited the United

States in May. Luns, who, with 17 years in office, is Europe's longest-serving minister, announced his probable retirement from politics in 1970.

At a Benelux summit meeting in late April, further steps were taken toward completing the economic union of the Netherlands with Belgium and Luxembourg. It was agreed to abolish all nontariff barriers to trade by Nov. 1, 1970.

A Benelux court was established. A six-man intergovernmental committee was set up to further integration. Also, it was agreed to hold summit meetings of top ministers on a regular schedule in the future.

Benelux has been a customs union since 1948. It was originally intended that it should became a full economic union by Nov. 1, 1967. Differences in taxes and in national economic policies have been the main barriers to achieving the union.

JOHN ALLAN MAY
Chief, London Bureau
The Christian Science Monitor

NEVADA

The Nevada organization of industrialist Howard Hughes informed the Atomic Energy Commission in March that it was prepared to bring suit to halt future atomic tests in the state that his experts considered unsafe. (The AEC is responsible for making underground tests in the United States of nuclear rocket warheads of up to two megatons.) □ The world's largest resort hotel, the International, opened in Las Vegas on July 2. It cost $60,000,000 and has 1,519 rooms; its swimming pool is the second largest man-made body of water (next to Lake Mead) in the state. □ On Sept. 2 the U.S. Department of Commerce reported that Nevada's population had grown from 285,000 in 1960 to 457,000 in 1969—an increase of 60.2 per cent. □ At least 2 persons were killed and 142 persons were arrested during 3 days of rioting by Negro youths in the West Side of Las Vegas in October.

NEW HAMPSHIRE

In 1969, New Hampshire remained the last of the fifty states to have neither sales nor state income taxes. Levies on liquor, tobacco and racing accounted for two thirds of general funds, but from all sources taxes were becoming inadequate. Gov. Walter R. Peterson approved a bill setting up a task-force program to study the needs of workers and to establish priorities for state needs. On July 3, New Hampshire became the first state to adopt an airport-departure tax, effective on Aug. 31, which might yield $100,000 a year.

NEW JERSEY

Gov. Richard J. Hughes signed a bill on Jan. 13 providing for the development of 18,000 acres of the Hackensack Meadowlands, across the Hudson River from Manhattan. □ At least sixty planes, worth about $3,000,000, were destroyed in fire on Apr. 15 that razed the main hangar and terminal of Mercer County Airport. □ In May the legislature authorized a referendum for a state lottery (approved overwhelmingly in November), and in July passed two waterfront-anticrime bills designed to combat organized rackets on the piers. □ On Nov. 4, Rep. William Cahill (R) was elected governor; an amendment lowering the voting age to 18 years was defeated; and a $271,000,000 bond issue for reservoir development and water-pollution control was approved.

NEW MEXICO

After dropping out of the Medicaid (health-care) program, for which the Federal Government pays 70 per cent of the costs, New Mexico returned to it for the balance of 1969. □ A liberalized state abortion law went into effect in June. □ On Aug. 5, delegates began meetings in Santa Fe (capital city) to draft a new state constitution. The old one prohibited women, Indians and absentee voters from casting ballots. The constitution proposed would have lowered the voting age to 20 years and made such positions as secretary of state, state treasurer and attorney general gubernatorial appointments instead of elected offices. In elections on Dec. 9, voters rejected the new constitution.

NEW YORK STATE

During its spring session the legislature passed bills (later signed by Gov. Nelson Rockefeller) covering the following: more severe penalties for striking public-service employees; strengthened court and police procedures for handling child-abuse cases; for New York City—school-decentralization plan, and $600,000,000 for improving and expanding the subways; cut welfare and Medicaid funds in order to balance the budget; increases in pay for top appointed officials; and four additional long holiday weekends besides the Labor Day weekend, effective in 1971. □ In November, John V. Lindsay was reelected mayor of New York City.

S & G from Pictorial

Keith J. Holyoake, prime minister of New Zealand from 1960, was reelected to another three-year term in 1969.

NEW ZEALAND

A timely economic revival in 1969 carried New Zealanders to a more soundly based prosperity than they had enjoyed in years. The upsurge resulted primarily from a sharp improvement in overseas trade and the release into the economy of greater returns from exports. Business confidence was restored as the enhanced cash flow, to farmers and other export-oriented producers, augmented by increased government spending and a general lift in wages and salaries, induced remarkably buoyant conditions. Manufacturers had an exceptionally good year, and building activity was stepped up. The rate of increase in the cost of living slowed appreciably as general prices showed greater stability. Unemployment returned to minimal levels. In the general election on Nov. 29, the National Party, in office since December 1960, scored a solid victory in spite of some electoral disadvantages arising from redistricting.

In the 12 months to June 30, 1969, income from exports showed a 20 per cent increase to NZ$1,000,000,000 (US$1,100,000,000). Sales of meat rose to NZ$316,000,000

(US$348,000,000), reflecting larger shipments and improved prices. The United States was the principal market. Returns from wool rose to NZ$226,000,000 (US$249,000,000) as stock-piled wool was sold at improved prices. Only dairy products were at depressed levels, earning NZ$211,000,000 (US$232,000,000). Imports, NZ$772,000,000 (US$849,000,000) were at their highest level for some years, but a favorable balance of NZ$229,000,000 (US$252,000,000) was recorded.

Most analysts attributed the striking economic turnabout to the continuing benefits of the devaluation of November 1967.

During the year, the Government reduced the list of import items subject to strict volume control. The relaxation, combined with continued restocking and expanded consumer demand, resulted in a further rise in imports, but export earnings were sufficient to sustain a favorable balance of payments.

The budget recorded total government outlays in the 12 months to June 30, 1969 of NZ$1,346,000,000 (US$1,480,000,000)—a 4.5 per cent rise over the previous year—with NZ$109,000,000 (US$120,000,000) coming from loans. Estimated expenditure for 1969–70 was 7.5 per cent higher at NZ$1,449,000,000 (US-$1,594,000,000), including NZ$136,000,000 (US$150,000,000) loan money.

The budget was designed to pave the way for major economic expansion in the 1970's on lines set out in the National Development Conference's ten-year proposals, released in May. Accepting full employment and accelerated economic expansion as basic objectives, the conference recommended that a 4.5 per cent

NEW ZEALAND

Area: 103,700 sq. mi.
Population: 2,800,000
Capital: Wellington (pop., 140,000)
Government: Sir Arthur Porritt—governor-general—1967; K. J. Holyoake, prime minister—1960
Gross national product: $4,775,000,000
Monetary unit: New Zealand dollar (NZ $1 = U.S. $1.10)
Chief products: wool, meat, dairy products, pulp, paper
Foreign trade: exports, $1,010,000,000; imports, $895,000,000
Communications: 1,119,422 telephones, 656,-968 radios, 600,000 TV sets, 41 daily newspapers
Transportation: roads, 36,140 mi.; 817,656 passenger cars; railroads, 1,933 mi.
Education: 623,250 elementary and secondary students, 6 universities
Armed forces: 13,135

See map on page 481

GNP annual growth be made the overall target. Guidelines were set for agriculture, forestry, fisheries, manufacturing, minerals, and tourism. The Government approved them as indicating the soundest use of the nation's resources. A priority export target would be a doubling of earnings from farm products in the 1970's. A 14-member National Development Council was set up to advise on the necessary restructuring of the economy.

In spite of the economic resurgence the drift of people from New Zealand continued, with more leaving than arriving, for the third year. The Government's goal of 3,000 new settlers a year was criticized as "unrealistic" by private interests, including the manufacturers' spokesman who stressed the need to bring in skilled workers.

In the election campaign Prime Minister Keith Holyoake relied on a record of sound management of the economy and active pursuit of regional security in international affairs. He promised to encourage and support constructive development of national resources. The Labor Party campaigned hard on the issue of immediate withdrawal of the 500-man military force from Vietnam. In domestic matters it stressed overhaul of the social-security system and subscribed generally to expansionist objectives. Voters, concerned about the likely results to the economy in the event of Britain's admission to the EEC, felt safer with the Nationalists and returned them to power.

For the first time there was nationwide TV electioneering. A linkup between all main centers was completed by the broadcasting authority in time for leaders to present their policies, live, to the country's voters. Also the election was the first held since the voting age was lowered to include 20-year-olds, resulting in the enrollment of 47,000 young people.

In foreign affairs and defense, Holyoake pursued a policy of active involvement in the regional security of Southeast Asia. He underscored support of the ANZUS and SEATO treaties, and stood firmly behind the United States in the matter of phased withdrawal from Vietnam. In February, Holyoake announced that New Zealand military forces would remain in Malaysia and Singapore after Britain's withdrawal in 1971.

New Zealand subscribed to the Nuclear Nonproliferation Treaty when, in August, Holyoake signed the ratification, thus "formally reaffirming a long-standing policy of renouncing any intention to acquire nuclear weapons."

Agreement was reached with Australia on joint action in defense planning and purchase of equipment as a means of making the two countries "logistically self-sufficient in the event of war."

There was undiminished support for foreign aid, official and private. Directed with a regional emphasis based on proximity, need and traditional ties, the aid went mainly to Asian and Pacific areas.

In a concerted effort to reduce dependence on imported minerals, the Government encouraged prospecting by companies and individuals. Significant discoveries of natural gas and oil were made, and a vast deposit of high-grade silica was identified.

On the industrial front, steel was produced for the first time in September when a plant near Auckland opened to process iron sands and turn out galvanized products. Plans were advanced for construction of a US$93,000,000 aluminum smelter, to be opened in 1971 with an initial capacity of 70,000 tons a year.

R. M. YOUNGER
Author, *Australia and the Australians*

Auckland Harbor Bridge is expanded; prefabricated sections of girders saved ten months in construction time.

UPI

UPI

The President drives former President Lyndon B. Johnson to the western White House (San Clemente) for a luncheon in honor of Johnson's 61st birthday.

NIXON, RICHARD M.

In his inaugural address, Richard Milhous Nixon called on the American people to lower their voices. He seemed to promise an era of calm and goodwill. To a great many of his fellow citizens this offered a welcome relief from the turbulent Johnson years. Here was a new president with a new style.

But even as he took the oath of office there were shadows on the horizon that threatened uncertain weather. He was the first president since Zachary Taylor, in 1849, to come into office with both houses of Congress controlled by the opposition party. He was a minority president, the victor in a three-cornered race with 43.4 per cent of the vote. And above all, the Vietnam war, which had forced Lyndon Johnson to withdraw his candidacy for a second full term, was increasingly unpopular as the total of American war dead approached the 40,000 mark.

One of the President's first ventures was a tour, in February and March, of Western Europe. On a friendly mission to the NATO countries, he wished to assure them of America's intentions to remain steadfast in defense of the Atlantic world. One objective was to prepare them for negotiation on arms control and limitation with the Soviet Union. The mission was a modest success, the President showing himself adroit both in the ceremonial and the substantive phases of a summit tour.

Pressures were constantly building to conclude or at least to begin to de-escalate the war in Vietnam. In June the President announced the withdrawal of 25,000 combat troops. In a later press-conference remark he expressed the hope that he would exceed the target date for complete withdrawal by the end of 1970 that had been set by former Secretary of Defense Clark Clifford. Training of the South Vietnamese army had been accelerated and the forces of America's Asian ally supplied with the newest weapons. This was in contrast, Nixon noted, with the record of the Johnson administration. He was careful, however, to refrain from direct criticism of his predecessor. On Johnson's birthday, Aug. 27, Nixon invited him to the summer White House at San Clemente, Calif., for a celebration and a joint public appearance.

The pace of withdrawal (65,500 by year's end) did not satisfy critics of the war and particularly those on the Left who began organizing large-scale demonstrations. In the first of these demonstrations, in mid-October, large crowds assembled in the principal cities on the east and west coasts. Nixon said he would not be moved in any way by such manifestations. In mid-November, 300,000 demonstrators converged on Washington in what was said to be the largest showing of its kind ever. The President and his aides were persuaded that an abrupt withdrawal would result in a communist takeover in Vietnam and a wholesale massacre, and with this disaster neighboring Cambodia, Laos and Thailand would also fall to communism. The President put his case for a phased and orderly withdrawal in a speech on Nov. 3 appealing to the great middle mass of Americans. As shown in the polls taken just after the November demonstration he apparently convinced an increasing number of Americans of the sincerity of his intentions.

Two fierce controversies occupied much of the time and attention of the President and his chief aides. The first resulted from Nixon's decision not merely to continue research and development of an anti-ballistic missile system (ABM), called Safeguard, but to provide funds as well to deploy it around 12 missile sites. In the lengthy Senate debate that followed, opponents argued that deployment would make it much more difficult to come to any agreement with the Soviet Union on curbing the spiraling arms race. Nevertheless, by a vote of 51 to 49 the Senate approved funds to deploy ABM.

The second controversy stirred even deeper feelings. The President nominated Clement F. Haynsworth, Jr., a Southerner serving on the Fourth Circuit Court of Appeals, to the vacancy on the Supreme Court left by the resignation of Justice Abe Fortas. Organized-labor and civil-rights groups lobbied intensively against Haynsworth for what they considered to be his antilabor and anti-civil-rights decisions. White House lieutenants worked equally hard to counter the opposition. In the course of extended hearings and debate it was shown that Haynsworth had authorized stock transactions and had served as a director of a company having indirectly, at any rate, an issue before the court. Nixon continued to insist on his faith in the integrity of his nominee and he refused repeated appeals from members of his own party to withdraw the nomination.

Haynsworth was rejected by a vote of 55 to 45 with 17 Republicans voting in the negative and against the President.

Despite this defeat the President was reported as his first year neared an end to be in good spirits. In the Gallup poll 68 per cent approved his handling of the presidency, the highest rating he had received. Many indicated, according to Gallup poll-takers, that their response was based on the belief that the President could bring the war in Vietnam to an orderly conclusion. The preliminary phase of the long-delayed strategic arms limitation talks (SALT) had begun in Helsinki with hopeful signs that this most vital conference could go forward. The President had said in accepting the nomination of his party that the era of confrontation should give way to the era of negotiation and he appeared to be trying, with however slow a beginning, to live up to this pledge.

MARQUIS W. CHILDS
Contributing Editor
St. Louis Post-Dispatch

A surprise for Father's Day: His daughters present President Nixon with a shocking-pink model of a surfboard (to arrive later) for riding the waves near San Clemente. He laughed but said, "I'll never ride it."

UPI

SAMUEL BECKETT

MURRAY GELL-MANN

ODD HASSEL

DEREK H. R. BARTON

RAGNAR FRISCH

JAN TINBERGEN

DAVID A. MORSE

MAX DELBRUCK

SALVADOR E. LURIA

ALFRED D. HERSHEY

NOBEL PRIZES
1969

The award in each category, extended to economics in 1969, is a gold medal, a diploma, and cash in the amount of about $75,000. Multiple winners share the cash award.

Samuel Beckett, 63, winner of the prize in literature, was cited "for his writing, which—in new forms for the novel and drama—in the destitution of modern man acquires its elevation." His best-known play is *Waiting for Godot.* He was born in Dublin but lives in Paris and writes in French, though he does his own translating into English.

Murray Gell-Mann, 40, of the California Institute of Technology, won the physics prize. A theoretical physicist, he was cited "for his contributions and discoveries concerning the classification of elementary particles and their interactions." Some of this work was published when he was only 24 years old. Most recently he has contributed the concept of the quark, in theory the smallest of all particles.

Odd Hassel, 72, and **Derek H. R. Barton,** 51, shared the prize in chemistry. They were cited "for their work to develop and apply the concept of conformation in chemistry." Conformation analysis is an essential tool in current chemical research. The work was begun by Professor Hassel, at Oslo University, Norway, and followed up by Dr. Barton, of the Imperial College of Science and Technology, London. They have shown how certain heavy molecules and their compounds, which are linked together in a closed ring, relate—or conform—to the ring in three dimensions.

Ragnar Frisch, 74, and **Jan Tinbergen,** 66, were awarded the first Nobel Prize in economic science. (The new prize, established in 1968 under a donation by Sweden's national bank, is dedicated to the memory of Alfred Nobel and carries the same cash award as the other prizes.) Professor Frisch, long associated with Oslo University, and Professor Tinbergen, of the Netherlands School of Economics and chairman of the UN Committee for Development Planning, were honored for the development of mathematical techniques in the analysis of economic activity—which has become a specialty called econometrics.

The International Labor Organization (ILO), represented by its Director General, **David A. Morse,** a 62-year-old American, was awarded the Nobel Peace Prize. The ILO was honored for fifty years of international activity and, especially since World War II, its work "in the enormous problem of solving unemployment in the poor world combined with the birth explosion." The ILO, a hardy survivor of the League of Nations and now a specialized agency of the UN, has worked quietly but persistently for social justice all over the world.

Max Delbruck, 63, **Salvador E. Luria,** 57, and **Alfred D. Hershey,** 60, shared the prize in medicine for their discoveries about viruses and viral diseases. German-born biology Professor Delbruck is at the California Institute of Technology; Italian-born Dr. Luria is Sedgwick Professor of Microbiology at Massachusetts Institute of Technology; and Dr. Hershey is director of the Carnegie Institution's genetics-research unit, Cold Spring Harbor, Long Island. They were cited for having "set the solid foundation on which modern molecular biology rests."

NORTH ATLANTIC TREATY ORGANIZATION

In the late 1940's Stalin's rejection of Marshall Plan aid, the communist coup d'etat in Prague and the Soviet blockade of Berlin signaled the beginning of the cold war, and created a crisis of desperation among the leaders of Western Europe.

Out of this desperation emerged the North Atlantic Treaty, signed in Washington on Apr. 4, 1949, by 12 nations. (The original signers were Belgium, Canada, Denmark, France, Iceland, Italy, Luxembourg, the Netherlands, Norway, Portugal, the United Kingdom and the United States. Later, Greece, Turkey and the Federal Republic of Germany were admitted.) Its aim was to forestall aggression from the Soviet Union and its satellites, a consideration uppermost in Western consciousness at the time.

Massive economic, technical and manpower resources of the West were committed to correcting the imbalance of military forces in Europe, tipped perilously in favor of the Soviet bloc. This was the top priority, and the allies adopted it without second thoughts.

Twenty years later, U.S. officials considered it imperative to reassure the Europeans that American troop strength on the Continent would be maintained as long, they said, as Congress could be persuaded to provide appropriations.

And the alliance, formed as a shield against Soviet aggression and long condemned by the Russians as an instrument of aggression, was talking more about the prospects of an East-West political settlement than of a bristling defense. The North Atlantic Treaty Organization (NATO) entered its third decade in quest of a détente.

At the center of NATO consultations in 1969 was the Warsaw Pact invitation to a European Security Conference, offering to discuss the renunciation of force, and to consider commercial, technical and scientific exchanges as well as "general and complete disarmament."

During their anniversary meeting in Washington in April 1969, the NATO allies pledged themselves to maintain their "defense posture," but also agreed to "explore with the Soviet Union and the other countries of Eastern Europe the concrete issues which best lend themselves to fruitful negotiation and an early resolution."

Allied interest in such negotiations was plainly tempered by caution. Several of the major NATO members, with the United States in the lead, counseled against hasty acceptance of the Warsaw Pact bid. They said that unless the real causes of East-West tension in Europe were discussed with a reasonable prospect of finding solutions, the Soviet Union would profit from the mere convening of the conference and the West would have gained nothing.

They argued that even a conference that ended in failure would benefit Russia by making Soviet domination of Eastern Europe legitimate and by putting East Germany on the same juridicial plane as Bonn.

Consequently, at their year-end meeting in Brussels, the NATO foreign ministers decided to test how serious the Soviets and their allies were about a Pan-European settlement.

In the NATO Council session, U.S. Secretary of State William Rogers, with broad support, pointed out that the Warsaw Pact offer to conclude a nonaggression agreement was unneces-

UPI

Manlio Brosio, secretary-general of North Atlantic Treaty Organization, and Adm. Thomas H. Moorer, U.S. Chief of Naval Operations, review NATO's striking fleet from aboard the "Saratoga."

sary as UN members were already committed to it, and that the proposal to discuss commercial and scientific dealings avoided the root issues of tension.

To the Warsaw Pact's shadowy proposal of general disarmament the allies replied that serious discussion on "mutual and balanced force reductions" in Central Europe "could serve as a starting point for fruitful negotiations."

In addition, the NATO allies approved the *Ostpolitik* of Chancellor Willy Brandt's Bonn Government and stated that a "positive response" by the Eastern powers to Brandt's offer of normalization could "substantially facilitate cooperation between East and West on other problems."

Finally, in the event of a Pan-European Security Conference, NATO tied to it the success of other bilateral or multilateral negotiations planned or already under way.

This was meant to include U.S.-Soviet negotiations on strategic-arms limitation—the SALT talks; consultations on keeping the ocean beds free of arms; and the big three's efforts to settle Berlin's status.

Progress along these lines would help to ensure the success of any eventual conference —in which, of course, the North American members of the alliance would participate—on the substantial problems of cooperation and security in Europe.

Secretary Rogers made it plain in Brussels, however, that the United States did *not* intend to link a decision on a European Security Conference with progress in the Vietnam peace talks.

The allies emphasized the notion of "mutual and balanced" reductions of forces in Central Europe. Rejecting a "man-for-man" trimming of opposing forces in the region, they sought an agreement on balanced "capabilities."

The states pegged for inclusion in this first step toward disengagement were West Germany, Belgium, the Netherlands and Luxembourg on the NATO side; and East Germany, Poland and Czechoslovakia on the Soviet side. First proposed by NATO in June 1968, the force-reduction scheme had extracted no Warsaw Pact response by the end of 1969.

To some observers the reasons seemed clear. For budgetary reasons, Canada and Great Britain had already reduced their troop commitment on the Continent, and there were strong Congressional pressures on the White House to do the same. Why, some realists asked, should the Russians negotiate for something that may in any case be inevitable?

STEPHENS BROENING
Paris Correspondent, The Associated Press

	1969 Defense Expenditures	Defense Expenditure per capita 1968	1968 Defense Expenditure as a Percentage GNP
NATO			
Belgium	$ 519,000,000	$ 52	2.4
Britain	5,438,000,000	98	5.3
Canada	1,678,000,000	77	2.5
Denmark	336,000,000	60	2.3
France	5,586,000,000	121	5.3
Germany	5,301,000,000	87	3.9
Greece	382,000,000	36	4.3
Iceland	No Army or Navy		
Italy	1,930,000,000	37	2.7
Luxembourg	8,000,000	22	1.0
Netherlands	940,000,000	71	3.9
Norway	344,000,000	84	3.8
Portugal	321,000,000	32	6.2
Turkey	510,000,000	14	3.9
U.S.	78,475,000,000	396	9.2
WARSAW PACT			
Bulgaria	$ 234,000,000	$ 27	2.9
Czechoslovakia	1,576,000,000	105	5.7
East Germany	1,873,000,000	100	5.7
Hungary	457,000,000	36	2.9
Poland	2,080,000,000	57	4.8
Rumania	574,000,000	28	3.0
U.S.S.R. (Declared)	42,140,000,000	169	9.3

Source: The Institute for Strategic Studies

NORTH CAROLINA

On May 6, Howard Lee was elected mayor of Chapel Hill, the first Negro to become mayor in a predominantly white North Carolina city since Reconstruction days. In Raleigh (capital) another Negro, Mrs. Elizabeth Cofield, dean of women at Shaw University, led 8 candidates for 4 seats on the school board. □ Violence broke out later in the month at Burlington and Greensboro resulting in the death of 2 Negro youths, one a college honor student, and injuries to at least 2 other Negro youths and 5 policemen. □ On June 26 the legislature passed the state's first cigarette tax, 2 cents a pack, effective Oct. 1.

NORTH DAKOTA

On May 10, at Zap, home of the state university, more than 2,000 revelers, many of them students, from as far away as Florida, invaded the village and made a shambles of its business section. To restore order, 500 National Guardsmen were called in. Damage amounted to some $5,000. The wreckage was cleaned up largely by volunteers, many of them high-school students. □ During the summer a huge land reclamation and development project, involving about 1,000,000 acres, started to take shape in the extremely dry west-central part of the state. Eventually the land is expected to yield field crops.

NORWAY

Quadrennial elections for a new Parliament were held on Sept. 7 and 8. The Labor Party polled the greatest number of votes by a single party; it gained 6 seats, just 2 seats short of unseating the incumbent coalition Government. The coalition, consisting of Conservatives, Liberals, the Center Party (Agrarians) and the Christian People's Party, won 76 seats in the 150-member Storting. For the third consecutive time, the Communist Party failed to gain representation in Parliament. The election results guaranteed that Prime Minister Per Borten and his Cabinet would continue in office. Borten has headed Norway's government since 1965.

New tax laws, including a 20 per cent added-value tax on a whole range of commodities and products, were passed. A 9-year comprehensive school law was also adopted, the final step in a reform initiated in 1959. (In 1959 the 9-year elementary school was introduced on a voluntary basis.) The new obligatory 9-year school supersedes the 7-year school and represents an important improvement, especially in rural areas.

Norwegian Embassy

In Parliament, Prime Minister Borten (who remained in office in 1969) discusses Norway's foreign relations.

The Norwegian economy enjoyed a good year; a moderate upward trend continued throughout 1969.

Apr. 11 marked the centenary of the birth of Gustav Vigeland, the only Norwegian sculptor of international fame. Vigeland died in 1943 after a long career in which he created numerous busts, statues and large monuments. He is best known for the statuary in Oslo's Frogner Park, for which he had received a special commission from the city.

ERIK J. FRIIS
Editor, *The American-Scandinavian Review*

NORWAY

Area: 125,000 sq. mi.
Population: 3,800,000
Capital: Oslo (pop., 490,000)
Government: Olav V, king—1957; Per Borten, prime minister—1965
Gross national product: $8,500,000,000
Monetary unit: krone (7.15 kroner = U.S. $1.00)
Chief products: fish, woodpulp, paper, dairy products, metal ore, steel pyrites
Foreign trade: exports, $1,937,000,000; imports, $2,713,000,000
Communications: 987,292 telephones, 734,605 TV sets, 81 daily newspapers
Transportation: roads, 42,341 mi.; 569,199 passenger cars; railroads, 2,630 mi.
Education: 685,842 elementary and secondary students, 22,422 students of higher education
Armed forces: 38,000

See map on page 185

NUTRITION

Human nutrition continued to be a subject of worldwide concern in 1969. Malnourished children in Biafra, cut off from food because of the war with Nigeria, were seen in photographs throughout the world. The mortality rate of these children was high, and the protein-deficiency disease kwashiorkor was seen with great frequency. The name "kwashiorkor" comes from an African word meaning "second born" and refers to an infant who is being weaned from high-protein breast milk to a low-protein diet when a new infant is born. The disease results in retarded growth, poor muscle development, mental apathy, changes in texture and color of the hair, a protruding abdomen, swelling of the skin due to accumulation of fluid, and death if untreated.

Developments in other countries offered more hope, as agricultural advances resulted in the introduction of new varieties of grain, multiple crops and the use of fertilizers and pesticides. For the first time since 1903, the Philippines is now self-sufficient in the production of its staple food, rice. Iran has increased its wheat crop to the point where it is now exporting wheat. Ceylon's rice harvest climbed 13 per cent, and Pakistan's wheat crop rose 30 per cent above previous records. India's total yield of food grains was 12 per cent above the previous record and 32 per cent above the 1967 drought-depressed crop. In spite of these advances, however, undernutrition continues to be the single most formidable threat to child health throughout the world. Unfortunately, gains in crop production are frequently offset by lack of population control.

Nutritional deficiencies in the United States aroused considerable concern in 1969. After studying nutritional problems in over two dozen underdeveloped countries since 1955, the U.S. Public Health Service was directed by Congress to survey the United States' nutritional status. An initial report of the survey on 12,000 low-income Americans was presented to the Senate Select Committee on Nutrition and Human Needs by Dr. Arnold Schaefer, a career public-health officer. Very few cases of acute hunger or starvation were found, but anemia and vitamin deficiencies were present with surprising frequency. One third of the children under the age of 6 years in this group had hemoglobin levels in an unacceptably low range. Vitamin A deficiency was present in 33 per cent, and vitamin C deficiency was found in 16 per cent. Minority groups are the most severely affected, including Spanish Americans, Negroes, and American Indians. A second report, from Colorado, stated that 182 of 300 preschool Spanish-American migrant children were deficient in vitamin A. Vitamin A deficiency is associated with night blindness and alterations in the skin and mucosal linings, such as are found in the respiratory tract, which allow secondary infections to develop. Deficiencies in vitamins C, D and folic acid were also found. In a third U.S. report, 17 cases of kwashiorkor and 27 cases of marasmus, or generalized calorie undernutrition, were described among Arizona Navajo infants. Previously, kwashiorkor was not believed to exist in the United States. Vitamin C deficiency, or scurvy, which is associated with tender, bleeding gums and fragility of small blood vessels, is also prevalent among the Navajo children. These findings tended to verify both the late President John F. Kennedy's statement in 1960 that 17,000,000 Americans go to bed hungry every night, and a controversial 1968 report, *Hunger U.S.A.*, which estimated 10,000,000 Americans to be hungry and malnourished.

Only 6,400,000 of the nation's 25,000,000 poor currently receive assistance through food-stamp programs or free commodities. It is estimated that $4,000,000,000 per year rather than the present $1,300,000,000 spent for the overall food effort will be necessary to close America's hunger gap. The Nixon administration's approach to easing the United States' hunger problem is linked to the huge problem of overhauling the nation's entire welfare system, on which Congress failed to act in 1969.

The influence of undernutrition on mental development also continued to receive attention. Dr. Fernando Mönckeberg of the University of Chile Medical School in Santiago told the Western Hemisphere Nutrition Conference that deficient cranial growth and low intelligence quotients were closely related to undernutrition in children. A four-year follow-up study by the University of Colorado Medical Center demonstrated that the longer undernutrition lasts in the first year of life the greater the likelihood of impaired mental development later. This study and others concerning underdeveloped countries appear to demonstrate a solid link between undernutrition in the first year of life and subsequent intellectual impairment. The studies have great socioeconomic importance, as the underdeveloped countries in which a high percentage of the population is undernourished are likely to have a related high incidence of low mental capacity. Thus economic development is retarded and the vicious circle continues.

Work continued on the development of inexpensive high-protein substitutes for use in underdeveloped countries. "Incaparina" is the

Agency for International Development

Among the variety of new high-protein foods and beverages (above) is Saci (right; advertisement is in Portuguese), enriched with vitamins as well as extra protein.

name given by the Institute of Nutrition in Central America and Panama (INCAP) in Guatemala to vegetable mixtures containing 25 per cent or more protein. The enriched flour is prepared from cottonseed, soy and sesame seeds, and ground corn, with vitamins and minerals added. It is used as a supplement to other foods and is available as a popular drink called *atole* or *colada*. Incaparina is being distributed commercially in Latin America at about one eighth the cost of powdered milk. Guatemala alone uses over 100,000 pounds per month. Other supplemental foods under trial include "Bontrae," which is made from soybean meal, and "Cerealina," which is made from soy flour, cornstarch and dry milk. The latter is being marketed in Brazil at approximately four cents per serving. Trials of fish-protein concentrate also show promise; however, the concentrate has not yet achieved popular acceptance. Initial trials in Ghana, Burundi and the Republic of South Africa have failed, primarily for political reasons. However, the U.S. Food and Drug Administration accepted fish-protein concentrates in 1967 as acceptable as a household diet additive. Also, the Agency for International Development of the U.S. Federal Government ordered $900,000 worth of fish-protein concentrate so as to determine its acceptance in underdeveloped countries.

Overeating without regard to proper nutrition is likely to be a more common problem in technically developed countries than is undernutrition, but it receives considerably less attention. Some evidence suggests that adult obesity is related to infant obesity, wherein a greater than normal number of fat cells are formed in the infant. The rarer adult onset of obesity is ap-

Tâmos aí!

Deliciosa Energia

Saci chocolate

Para tôdas as pessoas modernas e dinâmicas, a mais fácil e prática maneira de recuperar as energias na hora do lanche é o saboroso Saci, o lanche completo e refrescante.

enriquecido com 7 vitaminas

proteína extra

Coca-Cola Export Corp.

parently not related to an increase in fat cells but rather to an increase in the size of present cells. An eight-year study, concluded in 1969, pointed out that arteriosclerosis (hardening of the arteries) and nutrition appear to be closely linked. In this study, 422 men over the age of 55 on a standard U.S. diet were compared with 424 men of similar ages on a diet high in unsaturated fatty acids. The incidence of heart attacks, sudden death due to coronary heart disease, and strokes due to closure of vessels to the brain were compared. There were 96 such incidents in the control group compared with 66 in the group on the unsaturated-fat diet. Fatalities from arteriosclerosis numbered 70 in the control group and 48 in the experimental group. Although the etiology of both heart attacks and strokes is multifaceted, nutrition appears to play a significant role.

H. PETER CHASE, M.D.
Assistant Professor of Pediatrics
University of Colorado Medical Center

UPI

After exploring the Gulf Stream, the "Ben Franklin" makes a landfall in New York (tallest man, Dr. Piccard).

OCEANOGRAPHY

Two unifying concepts—plate tectonics and sea-floor spreading—promise to revolutionize the sciences of oceanography and geology. Plate tectonics hypothesizes that the earth's crust consists of huge plates that move as rigid bodies, carrying continents, forming oceans and resulting in the creation of oceanic ridges, island arcs and other geologic features.

Most of the earth's surface is divided into 6 large plates. The entire western Atlantic Ocean, for example, is moving as 1 plate, carrying both American continents with it. Another example: 20,000,000 years ago the Arabian Peninsula was joined to Africa. Today these two land bodies are moving away from each other; between them are two embryonic oceans: the Red Sea and the Gulf of Aden.

As two plates spread apart, new crust develops between them. This forms the underwater ridges, or mountain ranges, that are found beneath the oceans. The speed of spreading on each side of a mid-ocean ridge ranges from 0.4 to 4 inches a year. The fastest rate is found along the East Pacific Rise; the slowest rates are along the Mid-Atlantic Ridge and the Carlsberg Ridge of the Northwest Indian Ocean.

The thickness of these plates is unknown; some geologists suggest they are between 40 and 60 miles thick. Little is known about their behavior, especially at points where two plates meet and one overlaps the other.

As mentioned above, new ocean floor is formed as two plates move apart. Thus the ocean floor is much younger than the ocean that covers it. But the age of the seabed varies, becoming progressively older as one moves away from the edge of a plate. This has been substantiated by drillings performed by the *Glomar Challenger* as part of the 18-month Deep Sea Drilling Project begun in August 1968. Drillings in the Atlantic showed that sediments become increasingly younger as holes are drilled closer to the Mid-Atlantic Ridge.

The *Glomar Challenger* has drilled holes in the seabed beneath waters 5,000 to 20,000 feet deep. At the end of its first year it had recovered more than 10,000 feet of core samples from the Atlantic and Pacific oceans and from the Gulf of Mexico. The oldest ocean floor it found lies east of the Marianas-Bonin islands and north of the Caroline Islands; core samples from this area were 140,000,000 years old.

Another major research project of 1969 will greatly increase man's understanding of the interactions between the oceans and the atmosphere. The BOMEX project (Barbados Oceanographic and Meteorological Experiment) studied heat and energy exchanges between sea and air in a 90,000-square-mile area east of Barbados. The program utilized earth-orbiting satellites, airplanes, balloons, deep-sea buoys, and ships. One of the most unusual vessels was FLIP (Floating Laboratory Instrument Platform), a "ship" 355 feet long and only 12½ feet in diameter. It is towed to its desired location; there its ballast tanks are flooded, causing it to flip into a vertical position. Its 55 feet above water serve as a laboratory and living quarters. BOMEX was the first of a series of such projects to be carried out under the Global Atmospheric Research Program and directed toward the development of a world weather watch.

In his search for knowledge, man is leaving the hospitable land surfaces of his planet and moving farther and farther into inner and outer space. On July 14, 1969, as three astronauts prepared to leave on man's first visit to another heavenly body, six other men left the Florida coast to explore the world's major ocean current. Aboard the 50-foot, 130-ton research submarine *Ben Franklin,* they spent 30 days drifting some 1,500 miles along the Gulf Stream, an underwater ocean "river" first charted by Benjamin Franklin some 200 years ago. The voyage, under the direction of Swiss oceanographer Dr. Jacques Piccard, studied marine life, photographed the ocean floor and studied man's reactions to long periods of isolation in an alien environment. Several interesting discoveries were made. The Gulf Stream flows faster and is much more turbulent than scientists had previously believed. There are strong vertical waves within the current, caused by previously uncharted coral formations and other obstacles looming up from the ocean floor. The men were surprised at the small number of fish living in the stream and at the almost complete lack of a deep scattering layer (a vast horizontal sheet of minute marine organisms that rises and falls periodically during the day).

Physiological and psychological studies of men living underwater for prolonged periods of time were a major purpose of another mission: Project Tektite. For 60 days, beginning on Feb.

15, 1969, four marine scientists lived 42 feet beneath the ocean's surface in Great Lameshur Bay, St. John, Virgin Islands. The men were under continual observation by land-based behavioral and biomedical teams. Their base of operations was a four-room habitat; they had access to the surrounding waters through a hatch in the laboratory. Each "aquanaut" spent an average of 2½ hours a day in the water, conducting studies of marine life, testing equipment, mapping the ocean bottom and so on. Early reports indicated that man can survive in such an environment for long periods without major changes in physiological function. And he can be performing useful work. This has significance not only for oceanographic expeditions but also for manned space missions.

A similar project in the Pacific was to have tested diving equipment and techniques needed for salvage and rescue operations on the continental shelf. Named Sealab 3, the 340-ton habitat was located approximately 600 feet beneath the ocean's surface off San Clemente Island near Long Beach, Calif. But the project was indefinitely postponed after being struck by tragedy on its first day, Feb. 17, 1969. Aquanaut Berry L. Cannon died while preparing to enter the habitat. His death was attributed to a faulty breathing apparatus.

As man gains access to greater and greater depths in the ocean, he reaches the resources that are awaiting discovery and exploitation there. Offshore wells now supply 20 per cent of the world's oil and gas. Production is moving steadily into deeper, rougher waters and more remote areas; it is only a matter of time and perseverance until drilling can be done at any

General Electric Co.

Drawing depicts habitat of Project Tektite, in which four marine scientists lived in the sea for two months. At lower right is entrance, open to the sea at all times. Vertical structure on right houses engine room, environmental-control system, food-storage area and wet laboratory. In structure at left, connected by a bridge, are the main laboratory and the crew's living quarters.

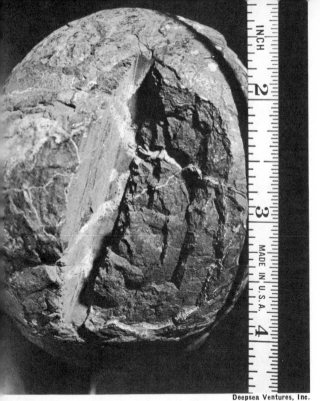

Deepsea Ventures, Inc.

Manganese-dioxide nodule: plentiful on all the ocean beds, nodules are promising new source of metals.

depth. Several companies are designing submerged systems that could be used in waters too deep for surface platforms.

Deposits of metal ore, in the form of nodules, cover large areas of the ocean floor. Manganese-dioxide nodules are among the most numerous; it is estimated that the supply is sufficient to meet man's manganese needs (at the present rate of consumption) for the next 400,000 years. In 1969 an American firm, Deepsea Ventures, Inc., began to "mine" these nodules; in a few years it hopes to be recovering more than a million tons of ore each year.

The waters in our oceans contain enormous quantities of dissolved minerals. Processes for extracting all the major inorganic components of seawater have been developed. But only salt, bromine, magnesium and fresh water are being commercially extracted at the present time; economic factors have so far made extraction of other substances unfeasible.

Many experts view the oceans as an important source of additional food for the world's rapidly increasing population. This food would be obtained by aquaculture: farming the sea rather than randomly hunting for fish.

But while man is beginning to realize the great role that the oceans will play in coming years, he continues to pollute these bodies. Some pollution, such as the Santa Barbara oil leak in early 1969, is spectacular. Equally dangerous, though less dramatic, is the daily dumping of untreated sewage, insecticides, atomic wastes, and other substances into the oceans or the rivers that empty into them. The vast wealth of the oceans may well be the key to man's survival on earth. Will man, through his ignorance and greed, destroy this great resource?

JENNY TESAR
Associate Editor, *The Book of Popular Science* and *Encyclopedia Science Supplement*

Scripps Institution of Oceanography

From the "Glomar Challenger," in the Deep Sea Drilling Project, holes have been drilled in the sea floor at depths of as much as 20,000 feet below the water's surface. Ship is first of a new kind especially designed for drilling in the open ocean.

OHIO

In Lima, on the night of Jan. 14, fires and explosions from a broken oil pipeline forced some 6,000 persons to evacuate a 110-block area. In Cleveland, in June, the Cuyahoga River, saturated with pollutants, caught fire. □ Woodville Mall, an enclosed and climate-controlled shopping area of 100 acres, including 87 stores, opened on the outskirts of Toledo in the autumn. □ Though the legislature passed measures covering a $30,000,000 pay increase for state employees, $421,000,000 for water-pollution control and various facilities, a proposal for a constitutional amendment lowering the voting age to 19, it failed to settle the overriding issue of tax reform.

OKLAHOMA

The giant General Electric and Western Electric companies joined forces to promote small businesses—and jobs—to be managed by various minority groups: in Oklahoma City; in Tulsa, mostly for Creek Indians; in Okemah, run by blacks; and in Stilwell, run by Cherokee Indians. □ The State Supreme Court upheld an earlier ruling making corporate farming constitutional; it was viewed as a threat to small farmers.

OREGON

A number of court decisions were reactivating a 1909 corrupt-election-practices act, which puts severe limits on campaign spending. □ The legislature passed what could be the state's first sales tax, rewrote the state constitution and proposed reducing the voting age to 19—all to be voted on in 1970. □ In Portland, Apr. 10–13, a thousand politically concerned undergraduates, representing various nonmilitant groups, met for the National Student Symposium on Foreign Policy. They discussed the Vietnam war and Arab-Israeli strife.

ORGANIZATION OF AMERICAN STATES

In 1967 the Organization of American States approved a new charter to make it a more effective body, but the charter was not to become operative until it was ratified by at least 16 nations. By the end of 1969 the required number of ratifications had still not been obtained. There was even some question as to the number of ratifications required, since Cuba's membership in the OAS was suspended, while three English-speaking nations, former British colonies, became members: Trinidad-Tobago, Barbados and Jamaica.

In May, President Nixon appointed Joseph J. Jova, a career diplomat, as U.S. ambassador to the Organization of American States. The appointment was interpreted as a sign that President Nixon did not intend to glamorize the OAS. The belief was confirmed when President Nixon chose in October to announce his new Latin American policy to the Inter-American Press Association rather than to the OAS, which had assumed that it would be selected for this purpose. The Nixon administration may well have been displeased that representatives of the Latin American governments had met in Chile and drafted the "Consensus of Viña del Mar," which was presented to the U.S. Government as the collective demands of Latin America on the United States.

Perhaps the only fields in which the OAS could show any progress were education and science. The Inter-American Cultural Council held its sixth meeting in Port of Spain, Trinidad. A broad program for educational development was adopted, but Galo Plaza, the secretary general of the OAS, pointed out that relatively little could be done because most Latin American countries had made little or no contribution to the OAS fund for education, science and culture.

Credit should be given to the OAS for its role in ending the war between El Salvador and Honduras. However, the net result of this war was the virtual collapse of the Central American Common Market, which was generally regarded as one of the most promising features of the Inter-American system.

The Inter-American Committee on the Alliance for Progress (CIAP) continued its activities under the chairmanship of Carlos Sanz de Santamaria. At the June meeting of the Inter-American Economic and Social Council (IA-ECOSOC) it was expanded from seven to ten members. However, the whole future of the Alliance for Progress remained in question. The U.S. House of Representatives made a sharp cut in Alliance funds, and the speech by President Nixon in October suggested that the mystique of the Alliance had disappeared. Although President Nixon proposed to channel more U.S. aid to Latin America through international agencies, he deliberately left in doubt whether the CIAP would be a chosen vehicle.

Secretary General Galo Plaza continued his efforts to vitalize the OAS, and he spoke bluntly of the problems facing it. He was credited with suggesting to Nixon the Rockefeller mission.

RONALD HILTON
Professor, Stanford University;
Executive Director
California Institute of International Studies

PAINTING

Painting no longer dominates art. Until very recently "art," for all practical purposes, meant "painting." But the heroic abstract-expressionist paintings of Jackson Pollock, Willem de Kooning and Franz Kline, among others, have been followed, with few exceptions, by pale exercises in "color field" sonorities and "stain painting." Too long neglected, sculpture is now the main area of artistic innovation. In some cases—particularly in the pioneer "combine" paintings of Robert Rauschenberg and in the works of Jasper Johns, which provide the bridge between abstract expressionism and pop art—the two traditional modes of painting and sculpture are indistinguishable or overlap to such a degree that one is forced to question the categories.

Rauschenberg, like Andy Warhol, now uses photo silk screens for his image production, but —unlike Warhol, who has abandoned his "art" to his helpmates at his "factory" to concentrate upon his remarkable film productions—has ventured into the realm of Technological Art. Utilizing motion mechanisms and lighting effects, his works go far beyond painting and require the assistance, if not the collaboration, of engineers.

Pop artist Roy Lichtenstein's retrospective in 1969 at the Guggenheim Museum in New York strengthened his art-historical position. He is best known for his Benday dot and blown-up versions of comic-book frames, the latter of which are witty, elegant and, to some, infuriating. Most recently he has been producing Lichtensteinizations of Art Deco. It is also interesting to note that some of his most successful work involving this 1930's subject matter has been his sculpture that imitates coatracks and railings of the period.

Although painting seems once again to have reached a dead end, particularly in terms of pure abstraction, certain post-painterly (i.e., post-abstract-expressionist) painters have held their own, notably Frank Stella and Kenneth Noland. In shaped canvases and horizontally striped canvases respectively, they have expanded their coloristic concerns to produce some of the most beautiful, decorative paintings that late modernism has to offer.

Although painting in some form or another will undoubtedly continue, sculpture currently seems to offer more possibilities for innovation. The number of new categories for sculpture is some evidence for its increased vitality. Excluding such self-explanatory category-defini-

Jasper Johns' "Flag" is an encaustic (melted wax mixed with paint and then fixed by heat) collage on canvas.

Leo Castelli Gallery

Whitney Museum of American Art;
Geoffrey Clements, photographer

In "Door to the River," Willem de Kooning was not aiming to paint a door—the suggestion of one is a happy accident.

"Pilgrim" by Robert Rauschenberg is a combination of abstract expressionism and pop art. Chair is part of the painting.

Leo Castelli Gallery

Frank Stella used fluorescent acrylic (a plastic) on canvas to create "Hatra II." The color of the 120-by-240-inch work has a mathematical precision.

Leo Castelli Gallery

tions (categories are useful, if annoying, fictions) as Environments, Technological Art, Kinetic Art and Light Art, we are left with three important new kinds of sculpture: Minimal Art, Earth Art and Anti-form Art.

Minimal Art (or Primary Structures) involves the use of simple, three-dimensional, geometrical forms, usually manufactured to order and constructed of industrial materials. Some artists who work in this mode are Tony Smith, Carl Andre, Robert Morris (but only until recently), Dan Flavin, Ronald Bladen and Donald Judd. Earth Art, to generalize, is an art that uses earth materials in the gallery or involves the creation of large outdoor works —often inaccessible—by rearranging the landscape slightly or by inscribing it in some way. Some artists who have worked in this mode are Walter de Maria, Michael Heizer, Dennis Oppenheim, Robert Smithson and Robert Morris. Anti-form Art involves the exploitation of the effects of gravity upon nonrigid materials. To some extent this direction has been influenced by pop artist Claes Oldenburg's discovery (as embodied by his giant soft fans and other works) that sculpture need not be self-supporting. The other artists, such as Richard Serra, Bill Bollinger, Eva Hesse, Keith Sonnier, Allan Saret and, again, Robert Morris, who work in this vein are totally nonrepresentational.

To this must also be added even-more-extreme forms of new art, forms that are not two-dimensional or three-dimensional but non-dimensional: Invisible Art, Systems Art, Conceptual Art. Some have referred to these new kinds of art as Impossible Art, impossible because there is nothing to buy—how can one buy an idea?—and because they have further diminished the boundary line between art and nonart to the extent that thinking or reading is equivalent to seeing. Some examples of this new art are a newspaper ad quoting a thesaurus entry (Joseph Kosuth); the release of gas into the atmosphere (Robert Barry); "an object thrown from one country into another" (Lawrence Weiner); a restaurant used to generate information (Les Levine); a series of secret works (Stephen Kaltenbach).

In comparison with the above, painting offers little that is new. The only new painting style to emerge is a style called Super-realism or Post-pop. It is a figurative style that at its best continues pop art's satiric coolness, as in the paintings of paintings and of photographs by such artists as John Clem Clark and Malcolm Morley. At its worst it descends into academic figure painting of the worst sort.

JOHN PERREAULT
Lecturer, The School of Visual Arts
Art Critic, *The Village Voice*

Kenneth Noland calls his horizontally striped canvases "Via Flow" (l) and "Via Token" (twenty feet long).

Lawrence Rubin Gallery; Eric Pollitzer, photographer

PAKISTAN

The date Mar. 25, 1969, is likely to go down in Pakistan's history as one of the most important since the founding of the Islamic Republic on Mar. 23, 1956. For on Mar. 25, the man who had guided Pakistan for over 10 of those 13 years, Field Marshal Mohammad Ayub Khan, bowed to public pressure and stepped down from the presidency. It was a sad, ironic end to the career of a man who had helped Pakistan achieve one of the most impressive economic-growth rates of any developing nation, and who had once been considered politically invincible, "Asia's strongest president."

Ayub Khan, to be sure, did not leave the presidency willingly. Five months of steadily mounting political and economic turmoil lay behind his decision. So, too, years of growing corruption, nepotism, favoritism in his administration and, by far the saddest aspect of all, an increasing detachment from the realities of life in Pakistan were responsible. It was symptomatic of the problems of Ayub's rule that every measure he took to deal with unrest led to greater political repression and more blatant economic and social injustices.

The trouble for Ayub Khan began to take on serious proportions in November 1968. A series of public speeches by former Foreign Minister Zulfikar Ali Bhutto, a radical but popular leader, sparked student agitation against Ayub's Government. The Government responded by cracking down on the students and placing Bhutto under arrest in Lahore on Nov. 13, 1968. The agitation built up into such a frenzy that Ayub's industrialist son, Gauhar Ayub, narrowly escaped death while attempting to speak at a charity appeal in a Karachi mosque. By December the trouble, which had started in West Pakistan, had spread to East Pakistan.

The new year brought an even more rapid deterioration of the situation. Some of the worst rioting in Pakistan's history occurred in late January. By early February, Ayub Khan was trying to contain the disorders and hold on to power. He offered to meet with the eight principal opposition parties, which had combined into a Democratic Action Committee, to discuss government reforms. In a dramatic gesture on Feb. 21, Ayub Khan announced in a nationwide broadcast that he would not be a candidate in the presidential election scheduled to be held in mid-1970.

Not even that, however, was to be allowed. Rioting and bloodshed continued, and on Mar. 25, Ayub Khan (again through a nationwide broadcast) stepped down from the presidency.

UPI

In February, militant students in Dacca, East Pakistan capital, display an effigy of President Ayub Khan.

As his successor he named a fellow Pathan, Army Commander in Chief General Mohammad Yahya Khan. (See Yahya Khan.) A tough, bushy-eyebrowed, 52-year-old, British-trained military officer, Yahya moved into the chaotic situation with confidence. Like Ayub Khan before him, his first move was to place the nation under martial law and scrap the constitution, which Ayub had given the nation in 1962 and which was due to be drastically reformed to permit a parliamentary system of government.

Denying any political ambition and terming his military rule an interim measure, Yahya Khan quickly restored order in the country. He immediately took steps to halt corruption by appointing a high-level committee to investigate corrupt practices. He ordered all Pakistanis, under threat of a 14-year prison term and con-

President Yahya Khan attends Islamic conference in Rabat, Morocco; it represented some 450,000,000 Muslims.

fiscation of their property, to declare their assets in foreign countries by June 15 and to surrender all unlawfully held or acquired foreign exchange by May 15. Widespread corruption and illegal dealings in foreign exchange were two of the major charges against the Government of Ayub Khan.

Carrying out his pledge to work toward restoration of parliamentary democracy, Yahya, on July 28, announced the appointment of Justice Abdus Sattar as chief election commissioner to "commence the work of preparing for elections." He indicated then that elections might be held in 12 to 18 months. During the same broadcast, Yahya Khan also announced that he was going to appoint a civilian Cabinet.

PAKISTAN

Area: 365,037 sq. mi.
Population: 131,600,000
Capital: Islamabad (pop. 60,000)
Government: Agha Mohammad Yahya Khan, president—1969
Gross national product: $13,800,000,000
Monetary unit: Pakistan rupee (4.8 PR = U.S. $1.00)
Chief products: rice, wheat, sugar cane, cotton, jute, natural gas, chromite
Foreign trade: exports, $720,000,000; imports, $996,000,000
Communications: 162,642 telephones, 50,000 TV sets, 289 newspapers and magazines
Transportation: roads, 70,915 mi.; railroads, 7,039 mi.
Education: 9,430,286 elementary and secondary students, 10 universities
Armed forces: 324,000

Answering demands from East Pakistan, the more populous region though smaller in area, President Yahya, by the end of the year, had given five top positions in the central Government to persons from the eastern provinces. Under Ayub Khan, only one cabinet post was held by a person from East Pakistan.

On Aug. 16, Yahya appointed new governors for both West and East Pakistan. The western wing of the country was placed under Air Marshal Malik Noor Khan, while Vice Admiral S. M. Ahsan was given authority over the eastern section. Both men had been serving as deputies to Yahya since his martial-law administration took control. The appointments of Noor Khan and Ahsan, in effect, dissolved the four-man administrative council (of which they were a part) that had been running the country. This represented another step in phasing out the martial-law administration and returning to a constitutional system. Ironically, the greatest hindrance to returning to democratic rule was the continuing discord on the shape of a new constitution among Pakistan's vociferous political parties. Nevertheless, preparations for elections went ahead, and on Oct. 16 Yahya Khan was the first to enroll as a candidate in the projected national elections. Preparations were to be completed by June 15, 1970. Then, in a dramatic move on Nov. 28, Yahya announced that full political activity would be allowed, beginning Jan. 1, 1970. Elections to the National Assembly were scheduled to be held on Oct. 5, 1970, on the democratic basis of "one man, one vote."

President Yahya, meanwhile, continued his reform program. Early in November he set up a committee to examine ways of eliminating inefficiency, red tape and other causes of public resentment against the Government. The nine-member committee was headed by Law Minister A. R. Cornelius. About the same time, Yahya restored the right of workers to strike. That right had been taken away by former President Ayub Khan in 1958 and had been one of the grievances aired during the trouble that forced Ayub Khan to step down.

While Yahya Khan moved with impressive speed and efficiency to restore political order, he was not without his problems. The fires of unrest continued to smolder, and occasionally crackled into flame again, especially in trouble-some East Pakistan. On Nov. 1, rioting broke out in the Mirpur District of East Pakistan, the result of a dispute between Bengali and Indian (Mujahirs) refugees over the use of Urdu and Bengali languages on electoral forms. A few weeks before, some 60,000 millworkers in the East walked off their jobs demanding more pay. Restiveness among militant students and political factions also tended to keep the situation uneasy.

Another problem facing the Government of Yahya Khan was the economy. The Government continued to receive large doses of economic assistance (an estimated US$500,000,-000 for fiscal 1969-70), and overall the economy seemed to have recovered from the earlier disturbances. Progress, however, clearly slowed. Growth during the fiscal year 1968-69 was an estimated 5.2 per cent, down from about 8 per cent during the previous 12 months. Exports declined early in 1969, largely the result of the troubles. The problem continued of inducing Pakistani financiers to make meaningful capital investments. And, of course, the problem of a concentration of wealth in a few hands was as starkly evident as ever. About 22 families control ⅔ of the country's industry, almost all of its insurance and ⅘ of its banking. Despite promises of agrarian reform, 60 per cent of the land is still owned by 12 per cent of the population.

The worst economic problems harassed East Pakistan, which frequently (and accurately) is described as one of the most impoverished areas in the world. The sole cash crop, on which millions of peasants depend for a living, is jute. World demand for jute, however, has plummeted. At the same time, crop failures and losses due to lack of pesticides have caused rice prices to leap by more than 25 per cent, thus threatening mass starvation. Only emergency shipments of rice and wheat (some 1,700,000 tons) from the United States, Japan and West Germany kept the situation from getting further out of hand. The Government tried to ease the pressure by ordering wage increases of 25 per cent a month, to a basic minimum of 125 rupees. Prices, however, have continued to rise.

Pakistan's third Five-Year Plan ends in June 1970, and it is presumed that the Government will introduce a fourth Five-Year Plan. But the setbacks of 1969 were serious, and the Government will be hard pressed to continue the rapid economic growth of the past, while it also deals with the serious food and other shortages.

In its international affairs, Yahya Khan's Government found the going easier. All three major powers concerned with Pakistan—the United States, Russia and Red China—recognized the new regime. The Russians invited Yahya to Moscow; Chinese Premier Chou En-lai sent assurances of Chinese friendship and support; and President Nixon made the South Asian nation one of the stopping points during his Asian tour. Yahya Khan made his first trip abroad as president when he visited Morocco for the Islamic summit conference. Although relations between India and Pakistan remained somewhat frayed, unofficial talks on a ministerial level were held on a wide range of outstanding problems.

ARTHUR C. MILLER
Senior Editor, *The Asia Letter*

By degrees, new apartment buildings are replacing the wretched, unauthorized squatters' shacks in the Golmar Bridge district of the seaport of Karachi.

United Nations

Editorial Photocolor Archives—NY

Among the ramparts of the Southern Alps, Mount Cook soars to 12,349 feet, highest peak in New Zealand and center of a vast national park. Its attractions include glacier-hopping ski-equipped planes.

PARKS, NATIONAL

During 1968, 150,835,600 persons visited the National Park System of the United States. The 1967 figure was almost 140,000,000, and 162,000,000 visitors were expected in 1969. The rapid rise in park visits in recent years reflects increased leisure, income and mobility of Americans, as well as added knowledge of the recreational opportunities within the national parks. Increased use of the park system, while serving to increase the public's awareness of its environment and its historic heritage, has caused some concern within the National Park Service that the citizen's opportunity to enjoy his parks will become limited as the country's population increases.

In the last four months of the Johnson administration (October 1968–January 1969), 9 new units were added to the National Park System, including Redwood National Park and North Cascades National Park (California and Washington respectively), 2 National Recreation Areas in the state of Washington, 2 National Historic Sites (North Carolina and Florida),

2 National Monuments (Florida and Arizona) and the Appalachian National Scenic Trail System. The last unit is the first of its kind to be included within the park system and runs through 14 eastern states. The acreage of 3 National Monuments—Katmai (Alaska), Arches and Capital Reef (both in Utah)—was also increased. As of Aug. 31, 1969, the National Park System included a total of 272 units: 71 natural areas, 168 historic and 32 recreational sites plus Washington, D.C.'s National Capital Parks. These units make up a total of 28,385,103 acres. By the end of 1969 two new park additions had been made by the Nixon administration.

During 1969 several celebrations and commemorative events were held. Grand Canyon National Park commemorated the 50th anniversary of its creation and the 100th anniversary of the exploration of the canyon by a band of 9 men, led by the one-armed Civil War veteran Maj. John Wesley Powell. From the 1869 Powell expedition and from his explorations in later years came most of our basic geographical and geological knowledge of the Grand Canyon of the Colorado. The Centennial Salute to Powell was celebrated over several months in a series of events planned by the Powell Centennial Commission. As part of the August celebration at Grand Canyon, a crew of boatmen reenacted a portion of the Major's journey down the Colorado.

In public statements and in a major policy memorandum made public June 18, 1969, the new Secretary of the Interior, Walter J. Hickel (former Alaska governor), emphasized the prospect of creating new recreational opportunities for city dwellers in the form of additions within urban areas to the National Park System. Hickel also mentioned the need for revision of the National Park Service's master-planning procedures so as to provide for more public meetings at which interested citizens may comment upon proposals that affect the National Park System. The Secretary expressed a preference for the operation of park campgrounds by the National Park Service rather than by concessioners, as has been the case in some areas. He stated that the private automobile ". . . is impairing the quality of the park experience" and asked for studies of alternative means of access and transportation of park visitors.

Another serious concern within the National Park Service relates to reductions in the operating budget resulting from the exercise of national priorities such as the war in Vietnam. As a consequence of these budgetary limitations, reductions have been made in park personnel or in visitor hours or both. In dealing with lower budgetary allowances, Director of the National Park Service George B. Hartzog, Jr., elected to maintain ". . . quality service during the time that we are able to operate the areas of the National Park System." In accordance with this philosophy, certain visitor centers and campgrounds were shut down rather than attempt to operate them with reduced staff. In some cases, entire park operations were placed on reduced operating schedules. Also, as of midsummer 1969, annual appropriations for the Land and Water Conservation Fund (from which monies for new park purchases are obtained) were lowered from $164,500,000, in 1969, to $124,000,000, in fiscal 1970, which made further additions to the National Park System unlikely in the near future.

The National Park concept is worldwide. The most recent tally of national parks and their equivalent reserves indicated 1,205 such units in 93 countries. Outside of their own national parks, the areas most familiar to U.S. citizens are the national parks of Canada. That country

National Park Service

Visitors start through the rapids of the Colorado River where it rushes between sheer walls in Marble Canyon. The gorge, in Arizona, is just above Grand Canyon.

has 19 National Parks and 44 major National Historic Parks and Sites, with a total area of 29,000 square miles. In the visitor year 1968–69 (Apr. 1 to Mar. 31), Canada's parks and historic sites received about 14,500,000 visits. In terms of numbers of visits, Banff National Park in Alberta is most popular, with 1968–69 visitors totaling over 2,100,000. Many U.S. citizens frequent Canadian National Parks, which are generally less crowded than those in the United States. On the Alberta-Montana border lies Waterton-Glacier International Peace Park, formed by agreement between Canada and the United States in 1932. The Peace Park was the first of its kind in the world. It symbolizes the friendship between the two nations and encompasses some of the finest mountain scenery and wildlife habitats in existence. As in the United States, Canadian parks are carefully managed to prevent environmental damage and thus provide opportunity for enjoyment by visitors for generations to come.

The United States established the world's first national park (Yellowstone—1872) and

now has more national-park units than any other nation. New Zealand is the country with the largest proportion of its land area devoted to national parks (8 per cent). Dahomey, in Africa, is second with 7 per cent. Several other African nations lead the United States on the basis of this criterion.

Perhaps the most valid criterion by which the sophistication of a country's national-park concept may be judged is the degree to which the land, the plants and animals within the parks are protected. At times, the attitude toward national-park management and environmental protection is reflected in official discussions of park policy such as the statement recently made by Canada's former Minister of Indian Affairs and Northern Development, Arthur Laing. He noted that the country's national parks should be maintained ". . . as sanctuaries not only of nature, but for nature." While most nations embrace this attitude to some extent, the official posture toward national parks is also affected by such factors as the economic importance of national-park tourism and the pressure of population upon the country's natural resources.

JACK HOPE
Senior Editor, *Natural History*

Sparkling water laps a beach in Islandia (the northern Florida Keys)—Biscayne National Monument since 1968.

From the lip of Murchison Falls, in the park of the same name in Uganda, East Africa, the Victoria Nile's raging waters drop 400 feet through a narrow cleft.

National Park Service

Helen Hynson Merrick

PEACE CORPS

In March, President Nixon named Joseph H. Blatchford, a 34-year-old Southern Californian, the third director of the Peace Corps. He succeeded Jack Hood Vaughn. Blatchford, who was confirmed May 1 by the Senate, had been a founder and director of a privately financed development organization of volunteer workers in Latin America, ACCION. In 1968 he ran as the Republican nominee for Congress in the 17th California district but was narrowly defeated.

Blatchford told the Senate Foreign Relations Committee in June that he believed the Peace Corps had been an outstanding success in its eight years of existence with 40,000 volunteers sent overseas. But he conceded that the Corps now faces serious problems, some of them reflected in a decline in the number of young college graduates willing to volunteer for service. "To a large extent," he said, "the problems of the Peace Corps are intertwined in the painfully obvious predicament of this country: turmoil on the campuses with no end in sight; a polarization of our society; America's disillusionment with America's role in the world, symbolized by the reduction of foreign assistance; increasing distrust of the motives of our government; and frustration at the apparent inability of any government to solve basic problems."

In reply to questions from Chairman J. William Fulbright (D-Ark.), Blatchford said that it was obvious that many young Americans were concerned over the "prolonged and agonizing struggle" in Vietnam, and that the war had colored their opinion of the Peace Corps. "I could only say," he went on, "that from my point of view and from the Peace Corps' that we would hope, as all Americans would hope, that the present administration would be able to bring the war to an end and, therefore, to enlarge our ability to serve at home and abroad."

The Director further testified that he believed that more professional and skilled persons should be enlisted in the Corps. Further, such experienced persons should be able to take their families with them to overseas stations. In the past, he said, more than 90 per cent of the Corpsmen had been recent college graduates with no particular skills. He said that there now was less demand for this kind of volunteer from the countries receiving aid. Later, in September, Blatchford announced new programs to carry out this concept, including efforts to involve the foreign countries more closely in selecting and training volunteers, and emphasizing such categories as union craftsmen,

Joan Larson

New Peace Corps Director Joseph H. Batchford (r) tours a Kenya school with volunteer Rick Graham.

experienced farmers, and vocational-education specialists. Some Peace Corps members publicly labeled the new direction as vastly unpopular and misguided. But Blatchford replied, "I know of no member of my staff, past or present, who disagrees with me that we must open up the Peace Corps to wider participation." The old policies, he said, deprived the organization "of access to an enormous pool of those very skills that are currently requested by our host countries."

The Senate Foreign Relations Committee voted a substantial cut in the Corps' budget request, from $101,100,000 to $92,800,000, the largest such reduction in the organization's history. But this later was raised to $98,400,000 and signed by the President.

JOSEPH W. HALL, JR.
Senate Staff, Washington Bureau
The Associated Press

PENNSYLVANIA

In July, Pennsylvania became the sixth state to pay state bonuses to Vietnam veterans. □ The world's largest mint opened on Aug. 14 in Philadelphia, at the north end of the mall leading to Independence Hall. The new building, which cost $39,400,000, is the fourth one to house the Philadelphia Mint. □ In September a program of state subsidies to nonpublic schools was launched, amounting to $1,200,000 for the first quarter of the school year.

When he was 14, Dan Bullock of Brooklyn, N.Y., lied about his age and enlisted in the U.S. Marine Corps. Nine months later, on June 7, 1969, Pfc Bullock was killed in Quangnam Province, the youngest American serviceman to die in Vietnam. Helen D. Bentley, 45-year-old maritime editor of "The [Baltimore] Sun," was named chairman of the Federal Maritime Commission.

All photos UPI unless otherwise indicated

people
in the 1969 spotlight

Anthony Grey (top), 31-year-old British journalist who spent two years under house arrest in China, was released in October. Clifton R. Wharton, Jr., 43-year-old Negro economist, was elected president of Michigan State University. For the first time, a woman, Mrs. Cynthia C. Wedel (r), was chosen president of National Council of Churches. John Fairfax of Great Britain was the first man ever to row alone across the Atlantic.

At year's end, Bernadette Devlin (above), 22-year-old, Catholic member of the British Parliament from Ulster, was sentenced to six months imprisonment for her part in riots in Northern Ireland on Aug. 13. Mathematician Dr. Mina S. Rees (r) was selected as president (for 1971) of the American Association for the Advancement of Science. Turi Wideroe, 30-year-old Norwegian, was accepted as a trainee jet pilot by Scandinavian Airlines System.

Arthur Avedon

Sir Learie Nicholas Constantine (l), 67, was the first Negro to be installed as a member of the British House of Lords. The Spanish Government granted Pablo Picasso (below) permission to return to his native Spain if the famous painter so desires. In October, Prince Karim Aga Khan IV married Sarah Croker Poole, one of the world's most beautiful women.

PHILIPPINE REPUBLIC

For the Philippines, 1969 ended with probably greater hope than any other year since independence in 1946. It had a President, Ferdinand Marcos, who was the first to seek and win reelection.

There were those, mostly embittered supporters of defeated presidential candidate Liberal Sergio Osmeña, Jr., who believed that Marcos' second term would be stagnant with continuing corruption. Yet the evidence suggested that Marcos would at last come to grips with some of the problems that had been too politically delicate for him to tackle earlier.

Peasants looked to Marcos to make his much-vaunted land-reform program more meaningful than it had been in his first term. During these years, Marcos had been subject to pressures from the "landed gentry," which is reluctant to give up the country's almost feudal system of land tenure. Those fanning an ever intensifying fire of nationalism among the country's young looked to Marcos to fulfill his campaign promises: to guard against "excessive" foreign investment; to bring home the boys of the 1,200-strong Civic Action Group (Philcag) from the fighting in South Vietnam; to demand Philippine jurisdiction over crimes committed by U.S. military stationed in the Philippines; and to gain for his Government a greater say over U.S. military bases scattered across the nation.

As the year began, President Marcos launched yet another offensive against the nation's Communists, the Hukbalahaps (or Huks). Although decimated since the 1950's, the Huks still held considerable sway in central Luzon provinces, north of Manila. In several pitched battles in January, government security forces reported killing 20 Communists. However, by midyear it was being reported that Huk influence had surfaced in the southern provinces. Army intelligence claimed that if the Huks were not getting direct aid from Peking, at least they were receiving direct encouragement.

Throughout 1969, Hukbalahap liquidation squads, with both politics and crime in mind, continued their work. In the six-month period ending in April, it was estimated that Huks had assassinated well over 100 persons. However, it seemed clear that the Hukbalahaps themselves were suffering from serious internecine strife and that they no longer constituted a major threat to security. Many guerrilla squads had degenerated into simple bandit gangs, with no strong ideologies.

In January, Marcos gave the first clear indication that he was intent on leading the Philippines away from foreign entanglements. He announced that the country was no longer tied to U.S. apron strings: "The time has come for us to start looking out for ourselves, because no one else will." His remarks suggested that harder times were ahead and that U.S. assistance could not always be relied upon. Although Marcos changed his tune slightly before and after President Nixon's stopover in Manila in July, he returned to his theme of greater independence and a tougher approach to the United States concerning investment and military issues by the time the November-presidential-election campaign had reached a critical stage. Nevertheless, Marcos remained eager to maintain trading preferences enjoyed under the U.S.-Philippine Laurel-Langley Agreement.

Growing restlessness among Filipino students had been obvious in 1968. But by February 1969 their mood had taken a surprising turn. No longer were students demanding withdrawal from Vietnam, and curbs on foreign investment, and staging anti-American demonstrations. Now they were looking inward and challenging the Philippine establishment.

Spurred by teachers' demonstrations for improved conditions and higher wages, students began protesting high education fees and living costs, incompetent instructors and substandard educational facilities. Normally relatively peaceful, some groups resorted to violence and arson.

Labor dissatisfaction spread quickly during the spring, with market vendors protesting high fees. Vehicle owners challenged the Government's right to inflict heavy taxes and registration fees on them. At the end of April, peasants marched on the capital, demanding better re-

---

PHILIPPINE REPUBLIC

Area: 115,707 sq. mi.
Population: 37,100,000
Capital: Quezon City (pop., 490,000)
Government: Ferdinand E. Marcos, president—1966
Gross national product: $7,100,000,000
Monetary unit: peso (3.9 pesos = U.S. $1.00)
Chief products: Manila hemp, copra, sugar cane, rice, maize, tobacco, lumber, chromite, copper, iron ore
Foreign trade: exports, $848,000,000; imports, $1,280,000,000
Communications: 207,593 telephones, 1,230,000 radios, 340,000 TV sets, 18 daily newspapers
Transportation: roads, 34,832 mi.
Education: 5,640,282 elementary and secondary students, 28 universities
Armed forces: 32,500

See map on page 481

Campaign smiles follow the nomination of President Marcos for reelection: (l to r) the President's wife, Vice-President Lopez, President Marcos, the President's mother, and Vice-President Lopez' wife.

UPI

turns for their produce and more concrete measures in the land-reform program. Marcos shrewdly persuaded them to return to their homes. However, the Opposition wanted to know where Marcos would find the money to implement the promised land reform. At the end of the year the question remained unanswered.

The Manila Government, pressed by balance-of-payments problems and a widening trade deficit, has never set aside the money to turn its words into substantial action. However, it was thought at year's end that Marcos might be persuaded to take tougher steps with the 10 per cent of the population that owns 90 per cent of the nation's land.

More serious than domestic unrest was the Philippines' chronic struggle to maintain the value of the peso. Torn between defending its value and making political capital, the Government wavered between tighter credit and slight easings to appease frustrated traders and businessmen. In March the Central Bank increased its restrictions on the movement of peso and dollar funds. In April there was talk of credit relaxation. In June the Central Bank asked commercial banks voluntarily to suspend letters of credit on the grounds that the reserve situation was "not comfortable." Loan payments that were due and slow exports made the situation even more perilous. By August, payment and trade deficits were increasing alarmingly. To meet legitimate foreign-exchange demands, U.S. standby credits were renewed and efforts were made to tap further Eurodollar resources. Yet, throughout the year, Marcos

claimed he was determined to avoid devaluation. Osmeña agreed and there was no devaluation before the election. But as soon as he knew he had won a second term, Marcos tightened credit further, and fear grew that devaluation was inevitable.

Once the Nacionalista Party (Marcos') and Liberal Party conventions nominated their candidates in midyear, no legislation was passed. Osmeña incessantly accused the administration of corruption and claimed that he had evidence showing that Marcos was involved in under-the-table deals regarding Japanese war-reparations payments. Although Marcos painted an equally dirty picture of Osmeña as a wartime Japanese collaborator, he based his campaign mainly on his own record.

Marcos was able to boast of having built well over 5,000 kilometers of roads, 500 bridges, 100 new seaports and 22 airports. He spoke with pride of his land-reform program (despite its lack of progress), his medicare program and prospects of improved export markets (albeit with communist countries).

The election results were doubtful until the last minute. But when the votes were counted, Marcos was home with a majority greater than Ramon Magsaysay's record. There was talk and evidence of ballot-box stuffing by Marcos' men, but the margin of victory left no doubt that he would have been reelected anyway. For the first time the Philippines had a president with his hands untied. It remained to be seen what he would do with that freedom.

DEREK DAVIES
Editor, *Far Eastern Economic Review*

During an extremely active year for photographic exhibitions, the controversial "Harlem on My Mind," shown at New York's Metropolitan Museum of Art, attracted 413,679 persons.

"St. Louis Post-Dispatch" from Black Star

PHOTOGRAPHY

Photo Expo 69, the largest product and picture show ever held in the United States, was the leading single photographic event of the year. Occupying all four floors of the Coliseum in New York City in June, it devoted more space to exhibits of photographic prints and movie and slide shows than had ever been seen at a U.S. exhibition before.

More than three thousand photographs, both color and black-and-white, from many sources, were on display, drawing constant streams of visitors throughout the nine-day event. The pictures ranged from camera-club work to experimentation and professional output, as well as press, technical photography, and documentation of the space flights. These shows were supplemented by several slide and film screenings in temporary "theaters" that used the latest techniques in projection, such as multiple-image devices.

New products indicated a cautious trend toward a revival of interest in 120 roll-film cameras, specifically in the single-lens reflex design, as well as advances in the design of super 8mm movie cameras that in some cases approach professional needs.

Bell & Howell introduced an automatic-focusing principle for its Focus-Matic movie-camera line. Bolex demonstrated its Multimatic movie projector that can be loaded with six cartridges at a time and project the cartridges in automatic succession.

Among several innovations were two by companies that offered lip-synchronization sound systems for home movies. An unusually large number of small electronic flash units were displayed at prices ranging from as little as $15 and $20. The Honeywell Rapid Charger phenomenally decreased the recharging time for its electronic flash units, from overnight (about 18 hours) to only 15 minutes; and Sylvania's rapid-charge portable Sun Gun is designed to re-charge in 60 minutes.

Other items announced during the year include a new line of Polaroid cameras highlighted by the $30 Colorpack II that uses regular 3¼ x 4¼-inch color or black-and-white packs, and the Polaroid Model 360 that has a clip-on electronic flash unit, and an electronic timer that automatically times the developing period. Automation reached the smallest camera in the field, the Minox C (8 x 11mm), which operates by computer exposure action.

It was an unusually active year for photographic exhibitions, particularly in New York City, San Francisco and Rochester, N.Y. The most controversial, and probably the largest, was "Harlem on My Mind: The Cultural Capital of Black America, 1900–1968," which was shown at the Metropolitan Museum of Art in New York from Jan. 18 to Apr. 6. Financed through a grant by the Henry Luce Foundation, Inc., and organized by Allon Schoener, visual-arts director of the New York State Council on the Arts, the show pictorially traced Harlem's development as a community over the course of seven decades.

Supplementing the picture displays, some of them greatly enlarged, there was a continuous program of projected slides and films, and past recordings were heard as well as taped interviews, music, and street sounds. Some white as well as black critics felt that the show, which was well attended, did not truly represent the black viewpoint.

The Gallery of Modern Art in New York City has been renamed the New York Cultural Center following a change of ownership when Huntington Hartford turned the gallery over to Fairleigh Dickinson University, with Dr. Peter Sammartino, the founder of the university and its present chancellor, as director. Alfredo Valente, onetime leading theatrical photographer, now an art collector, was named curator. He said that photography would definitely have a place in the gallery's show schedules in the years ahead.

New small galleries devoted to the exhibition and sale of original photographic prints were being started in several parts of the United States. Among them is the Witkin Gallery, which is run by Lee D. Witkin. He gave up a job as photographer for a construction company to become a free-lancer so that he could devote all his time to the gallery venture. The place consists of two small rooms, a reception room and a terrace, all of which, the last in

"Bay View Marina," a photograph by Mark Packo. For a portfolio of photographs, Mr. Packo, a 17-year-old student at Cardinal Stritch High School, Oregon, Ohio, won a $1,000 college-scholarship grant.

Courtesy, Scholastic Photography Awards sponsored by Eastman Kodak Company

Jacob Deschin

Lee D. Witkin at his New York City photo gallery. During 1969 quite a few small galleries devoted to the sale and exhibition of original photographic prints were launched.

good weather, are devoted to the display of photographs. Within four months the gallery was already paying for itself.

Most shows dealt with the contemporary world. Some, like "The Black Panthers: A Photographic Essay by Ruth-Marion Baruch and Pirkle Jones," had a social or political content. The show originally opened at the M. H. de Young Memorial Museum in San Francisco, drawing large crowds, and later came to New York.

The exhibition "600 Faces by Beaton, 1928–69" tracing Cecil Beaton's career as a photographer, principally in London, came to the Museum of the City of New York after a run at the National Portrait Gallery in London. The largest one-man photographic show ever held in New York, it displayed Beaton portraits of many if not most of the outstanding personalities of the past four decades.

Most shows were on the level of fine art. Color was shown more frequently; and frames, with prints under glass, were back in favor. Some of these, designed to be assembled easily by the photographer, were being sold in bookstores, and were available in wood, metal and plastic, the last complete with glass.

With the prevalence of exhibitions, the publication of large-format picture books, the spread of galleries designed to sell prints, and a growing public appreciation of the place of photography among the arts, there were signs that collecting prints as one does graphics or

drawings was being recognized as both valid and satisfying. In consequence, the prices of prints were increasing to as much as $75 or $100 and more for black-and-white and $75 to $150 and higher for color. Rare prints, such as signed originals by the late Edward Weston, have brought as much as $350 each.

This activity has encouraged the printing of facsimiles of rare, out-of-print volumes. One particularly significant volume issued during the year was William Henry Fox Talbot's *The Pencil of Nature* (New York: Da Capo Press), which was originally issued between 1844 and 1846 as the first book to be illustrated photographically. At that time, original prints were tipped into the book individually.

The Sierra Club of San Francisco was doing well with a series of illustrated volumes on preservation themes selling at $25 a copy. The series did even better in reprints at $3.95 through Ballantine Books.

Numerous picture books on social themes, with minimum text, were being issued. Among them were such volumes as *America in Crisis* (New York: Holt, Rinehart and Winston, Inc.) with photographs from Magnum; *Black in White America* (same publisher) with pictures and text by Leonard Freed; and *The Concerned Photographer* (same publisher), a book version of a large exhibition of that name.

JACOB DESCHIN
Photography Editor
The New York Times

PHYSICAL SCIENCES

The brotherhood between pure mathematics and down-to-earth physics is sometimes uncanny. Mathematics is a fantasy, an expression of man's unbridled imagination. Yet, time and again, abstract mathematical reasoning directs physicists to look for unsuspected facts about nature that can be seen, heard, felt or otherwise measured. Einstein's relativity theory, for example, at first seemed too strange to be true, but it has proved extremely useful for explaining gravity, the odd behavior of objects traveling at enormous speeds, and many other happenings.

Another outstanding triumph for mathematical physics seems to have been scored in 1969 when a group of Australian physicists from the University of Sydney announced they had probably observed the "quark." Some five years earlier two Caltech physicists, George Zweig and Murray Gell-Mann (the winner of the 1969 Nobel Prize in physics), reasoned that there ought to be "a most fundamental particle of matter existing not yet identified." The quark, as it was called, would have an electric charge either one third or two thirds as large as an electron's, and three quarks would combine to make one proton. Ever since then, physicists the world over have been searching for quarks, chiefly in showers of cosmic rays.

Gell-Mann himself insisted that he had devised the quark merely as a mathematical con-

University of Sydney

The first track to be photographed, by Australian physicists, of what was probably a quark shows as a faint line (l); strong line (center) is of a normal particle.

A maze of apparatus is required in connection with Tokamak, most successful magnetic bottle thus far devised to control hydrogen fusion, on which Russian and British scientists are working at Kurchatov Institute, Moscow.

Tass from Sovfoto

venience to round out a theory. And many other physicists doubted whether quarks really exist. The Australian group had enough faith in pure theory to search through the tracks of 66,000 charged particles generated by cosmic-ray showers. Out of this vast number, they discovered five trails that corresponded to those that would in theory be created by a quark.

Another success for pure reasoning was the first observation of gravity waves. According to relativity theory, gravity forces should travel in enormously long waves, yet such waves had never been detected. In 1968, Joseph Weber, of the University of Maryland, set up 4 detectors, or "gravity aerials," 3 on his campus, the other at the Argonne National Laboratory near Chicago, 600 miles away. The fourth one was to eliminate the chance of just a local effect. The strategy was to watch for waves that would occur at the same time at the 2 stations. Over a period of almost 12 weeks, Weber observed several coincidences and concluded that not all of them could be accidental.

After fruitless attempts for several years, nuclear chemists have finally managed to create element number 104 (not yet named). The biggest natural element is uranium; its atomic number 92 indicates that it contains 92 protons in its nucleus, plus a good many more neutrons. The creation of element number 104 had been reported back in 1964 by Russian scientists at the Dubna Laboratory, but they never obtained enough of the element for a conclusive chemical analysis. The recent work, done by a group at the University of California headed by Albert Ghiorso, produced enough of number 104 for a thorough study of its chemical properties.

For twenty years now, physicists of many nations have been trying to find ways to con-trol the enormous power generated by the hydrogen bomb. If they could regulate the process of fusing hydrogen atoms so that the explosion would be slowed to a steady flow of power, most of mankind's needs for energy could be satisfied cheaply. The problem is to heat hydrogen atoms to a temperature of about 100,000,000°, but obviously no simple container could long hold a gas this hot. And so physicists have been experimenting with a variety of "magnetic bottles." At high temperatures, hydrogen becomes a plasma, an electrically charged cloud that is repelled by magnetic fields. Unfortunately, all the simple designs of bottles develop serious leaks, and the hydrogen escapes before it can yield its energy. In 1969 there was new reason to hope that the problem will eventually be solved. British and Russian scientists working in Moscow have demonstrated a doughnut-shaped magnetic bottle, called a Tokamak, that contains hot hydrogen better than any hitherto devised.

Astronomers began to share the benefits of the U.S. space program with the first observations from Orbiting Astronomical Observatory 2. Launched in December 1968, this satellite carries 11 telescopes with a weight of two tons, including equipment for radioing messages back to earth. The advantage of this kind of observatory is that it can see kinds of radiation that are ordinarily screened out by the atmosphere, notably X rays and ultraviolet light. The most striking early result is that some old galaxies of stars, including our neighbor Andromeda, which is presumably much like our own galaxy, emit a great deal of ultraviolet radiation. No one yet knows why this is so, but this fact is fuel for the great debate between theorists who believe that the universe originated

Rockefeller University

Dr. Gerald Edelman explains a poppit-bead model of the gamma-globulin molecule, which he and his associates deciphered. An immunity agent, it is also the largest molecule, consisting of 1,-320 amino acids in several chains, ever to be described.

with one "big bang" and those who assume that it is steadily being regenerated everywhere. If the steady-state advocates are right, the universe should appear the same everywhere, but the orbiting observatory shows this is not the case.

Chemists continued to acquire knowledge about the scanty matter that drifts between stars. Molecules of water and formaldehyde were definitely identified. The existence of formaldehyde has a special significance. It suggests that methane gas must also be fairly common in space. And methane and water, together with ammonia, which has already been found in interstellar space, are presumably the ingredients from which life on earth first evolved. Thus there is further support for the theory that life—and probably intelligent forms of life—may exist on planets circling stars other than our sun.

Space astronomy may be due for an even bigger boost in the next few years. A committee of the Space Science Board of the National Academy of Sciences strongly recommended the launching of a 120-inch telescope, larger than almost any in earthbound observatories. This instrument might be kept in a satellite orbit, or it might be stationed on the moon. In either case, it would be able to study objects 100 times fainter than can be seen from the earth and at nearly 10 times the distance.

Striking progress was made also in solving a number of important chemical jigsaw puzzles. For years chemists and biologists have been trying to determine the structure of gamma-globulin proteins, the substances in the blood that confer immunity to disease. Finally Gerald Edelman and his colleagues at Rockefeller University, New York, deciphered the contents and geometry of this protein. Consisting of 1,320 subunits of amino acids, it is the largest molecule ever to have been completely described.

In related work, David G. Marsh at Caltech has been studying what he calls "allergoids." Allergens are potentially harmful proteins to which the body responds by creating antibodies to combat them. Allergoids are artificially altered protein allergens. The alteration is just sufficient to eliminate the harmful effects but not enough to stop the production of antibodies. Although allergoids have not yet been tested on human beings, they may eventually prove to be safe and effective vaccines.

In 1969 a team of Harvard Medical School scientists isolated a gene, the unit of heredity, for the first time. Earlier, under the direction of Dr. R. Bruce Merrifield of Rockefeller University and Dr. R. G. Denkewalter of Merck Sharp & Dohme Research Laboratories, several scientists simultaneously synthesized ribonuclease for the first time, using different techniques. The latter discovery is expected to open up entirely new research areas lying at the very core of life.

The chemical armament against disease may have been greatly enhanced also by Hans H. Muxfeldt, of Cornell University, who in 1969 synthesized the common antibiotic sold under the trade name of Terramycin. Synthetic Terramycin may never prove useful in itself: there are easier and cheaper ways to make the drug. But the principle is important. "It opens broad possibilities for the development of new synthetic and semisynthetic antibiotics," said Albert J. Frey, executive vice-president of research for the pharmaceutical firm Sandoz, Inc. At this stage of history, with microbes devel-

"The New York Times"

Researchers smile happily with model of ribonuclease, which they synthesized—the first enzyme to yield to synthesis. From l to r (seated) Drs. Ralph F. Hirschmann and Robert G. Denkewalter, (standing) Bernd Gutte and R. Bruce Merrifield.

oping resistance to most of the common antibiotics, it would obviously be helpful to "surprise" them with an endless variety of compounds that have germ-killing power slightly different from any of the compounds in use today.

Insulin is another drug whose structure was completely deciphered in 1969. To the chemist, insulin is a relatively simple protein, one that can be synthesized from simple compounds. To the physician it is still a somewhat mysterious piece in the diabetes puzzle. Physicists have now added their own view with a complete analysis of the three-dimensional shape of the insulin molecule. The work was done by Dorothy C. Hodgkin of Oxford University, a Nobel Prizewinner. She used beams of X rays to study the crystal structure of insulin, and found that it consists of three pairs of molecules bound in a triangular shape by two central zinc atoms. This research represented a stupendous effort for Dr. Hodgkin: seven years spent making thousands of X-ray reflections. Although it is scientifically gratifying to learn the structure of insulin, her research may have even greater significance in biology and medicine. The action of insulin in sugar metabolism remains something of a mystery, and it is suspected that insulin's role may depend as much on its geometry as on its chemical composition.

The extremely arduous job of solving chemical jigsaw puzzles—that is, synthesizing compounds as complex as insulin or figuring out their chemical compositions and shapes—will probably become a great deal easier in years to come. Groups at Harvard, Caltech and elsewhere are working hard to turn over most of the drudgery to computers. No really difficult problems of this sort have yet been solved by a computer, but the general strategy has been well worked out. Roughly, it consists of the following procedure. The computer is given the molecular formulas plus other information, such as spatial relationships among atoms, symmetries, and the role of various groups of atoms. From that point, the computer is programed to run through all the possibilities—perhaps millions of them—and come up with a few possible answers. In this way projects that have taken dedicated scientists several years may be reduced to a few minutes.

A chemical oddity that may or may not have practical significance is the research done in 1969 on a strange substance known as polywater or Russian water. Several years ago the Russian chemist B. V. Deryagin reported a new form of water, and almost no other scientist believed him. It does not freeze but hardens into a brownish glasslike substance at much lower temperatures than the freezing point of ordinary water. It boils at a much higher temperature. He had made it by letting ordinary water be soaked up by capillary action through extremely thin tubes of quartz. At first most of the scientific world supposed that the peculiar qualities of polywater were caused by impurities absorbed from the quartz tubes. Now that polywater has been studied more thoroughly, it appears that Deryagin discovered a real freak of nature. Whatever impurities were introduced by his manufacturing process seem to be insignificant. Polywater is very likely a long-chain molecule consisting of many water molecules strung end to end.

Scientists are beginning to wonder whether polywater may not be fairly common in nature: for instance, in quartz quarries. It may also be present in living cells; and if it is, physiologists will have to revise their calculations on the energy exchange within cells.

Of course, not all advances in chemistry and physics are on a highly theoretical level. In any year—including 1969—scientists spend some of their time making purely practical discoveries and inventions. At least a couple such discoveries of 1969 are worth mentioning. A research team headed by Carl Heinrich Krauch, of Badische Anilin & Soda Fabrik in West Germany, produced a new cast fabric. Spinning and weaving account for most of the expense in producing cloth. The new material is simply poured out as a liquid and forms a porous cloth. If the process proves commercially feasible, the cost of clothing could be greatly reduced.

Another simple development is heralded by an experiment conducted by the U.S. Bureau of Mines. Everywhere in the world, invaluable resources of topsoil and humus, the fertile layer of earth that best grows crops, are being depleted seriously. An extremely plentiful and cheap material, brown coal, may help to offset the depletion. Brown coal is a term used to describe various materials that are not quite hard enough to be burned in furnaces. Yet they may prove to be a boon to agriculture. The Bureau of Mines has been dumping brown coal on farmland near Grand Forks, North Dakota. The result: a 28 per cent increase in the yield of potatoes, and more vigorous growth of soybeans.

From theories about quarks to facts about potatoes, chemistry and physics in 1969 covered a lot of ground.

See Astronomy, Geology and Meteorology.

GEORGE A. W. BOEHM
Free-Lance Science Writer

POLAND

All signs of disunity continued to be repressed in Poland. Under the Moscow-oriented leadership of Wladyslaw Gomulka, Polish intellectual life followed the party line with little deviation. Students who participated in the March 1968 protests were still being prosecuted and imprisoned; major writers either emigrated or kept silent. The writers' congress in February proved that the regime had been successful in its efforts to change the direction of things. No "pro-revisionists" were elected as delegates to the congress. At least 3 liberals were dropped from the executive board and 4 of the 5 members of the colleagues court (the group that refused to expel 3 prominent dissident writers in 1968) were replaced.

Delegates to the congress generally echoed the party slogans in their discussions. The result was a major resolution that was in sharp contrast to the proposal by the June 1967 conclave calling for censors to make public their reasons for censorship rulings. The first outward sign of conflict between the writers and Gomulka had begun in 1957 when ten prominent writers defected from party ranks. The number of the disenchanted grew year by year, culminating in an April 1964 letter, signed by 34 Polish intellectuals, to Premier Cyrankiewicz protesting censorship. Despite the party's control over the congress in 1969, protests against the regime's policies by writers who did not attend the congress may well surface again.

Another manifestation of Gomulka's subservience to the U.S.S.R. was his speech after his return to Warsaw from the June world communist conference in Moscow. The party first secretary praised the "unity" the conference allegedly attained and sharply criticized those parties that did not fully accept the views adopted. These included the Chinese, Albanian, Yugoslav, Italian, Japanese and Rumanian parties. He also tried to justify Poland's role in the 1968 invasion of Czechoslovakia.

Gomulka's only serious rival within the party, Gen. Mieczyslaw Moczar, was reelected, presumably with Gomulka's backing, as head of the Polish veterans' organization. Moczar, an alternate Politburo member and leader of a group within the party known as the Partisans, declared that changes taking place in Poland "have erased those things that, in the past, have divided us." He eliminated his usual references to "Zionists," "rotten liberals" and "cosmopolitans," indicating his desire to find a broader base for his growing power.

A somewhat brighter note was sounded by high church authorities who saw new opportunities for warmer church-state relations.

POLAND

Area: 120,000 sq. mi.
Population: 32,500,000
Capital: Warsaw (pop., 1,300,000)
Government: Marian Spychalski, chairman, council of state—1968; Wladyslaw Gomulka, Communist Party secretary—1956; Josef Cyrankiewicz, premier—1954
Gross national product: $38,000,000,000
Monetary unit: zloty (15.9 zloty = U.S. $1.00)
Chief products: grains, potatoes, copper, sulphur, ships, textiles, steel, cement, chemicals
Foreign trade: exports, $2,858,000,000; imports, $2,853,000,000
Communications: 1,530,479 telephones, 6,000,000 radios, 3,450,000 TV sets, 41 daily newspapers
Transportation: roads, 73,034 mi.; 313,547 passenger cars; railroads, 22,740 mi.
Education: 6,012,370 elementary and secondary students; 8 universities
Armed forces: 275,000

See map on page 185

A foundation for a new church was put down after a delay of over four years in granting the permit, and a series of articles in a liberal Catholic weekly indicated that a rapprochement was likely. A leading Polish Catholic deputy declared that "there is a growing conviction in the communist camp that religion and the church are permanent features of Polish life, and the theory of their reactionary function is losing ground." Such reports became more and more common as the 1960's drew to a close.

Otherwise the Polish scene was black indeed. However, Polish nationalism has long been perhaps the most explosive force in Eastern Europe and a new outbreak similar to the demands of 1956 should not be discounted.

JAMES CHACE
Managing Editor, *Foreign Affairs*

POMPIDOU, GEORGES

On June 15, Georges Jean Raymond Pompidou was elected the second president of the Fifth French Republic, capping a meteoric rise that was aided by neither wealth nor family position in a nation where both still count for a great deal.

The grandson of an Auvergnat peasant and the son of a teacher of Spanish, Pompidou was born July 5, 1911, in the hilltop village of Montboudif in backward central France. At the age of 24 he earned the equivalent of a doctorate in French Literature. Had it not been for World War II he probably would have finished his life as a brilliant, but obscure, professor.

G. Sipahioglu, PIX

The style of President Pompidou's press conferences is more relaxed, informal and democratic in contrast with former President de Gaulle's, who was aloof and answered only a few carefully planted questions.

On the morrow of the liberation of France, an old university friend introduced Pompidou to Charles de Gaulle. And though he had sat out the Resistance, Pompidou was taken on as a low-echelon staff member, drafting reports for De Gaulle.

This association deepened as Pompidou won the General's confidence. The former teacher often performed sensitive missions for De Gaulle after the General quit power in 1946. He served briefly as chief of the General's personal cabinet when De Gaulle returned to power in 1958.

To the surprise and displeasure of many of his wartime followers, De Gaulle made Pompidou his premier in April 1962, defying an unwritten rule that premiers should be chosen from among men who have held elective office. Pompidou had never run for office, and so never proved himself politically.

The once-shy outsider remained head of government for more than six years, growing in stature and gradually building a power base of his own.

He emerged from the student-labor upheaval of May–June 1968 as the only man in or out of office whose prestige had not been diminished. Almost alone he gained credit for the unprecedented Gaullist legislative victory in the strike's aftermath, earning him De Gaulle's disfavor.

The 77-year-old President dismissed him, explaining that Pompidou, 57, needed a rest. De Gaulle said he was putting his Premier "in reserve for the Republic."

For seven months Pompidou appeared to accept his fall from grace with saintly resignation. Then, on a vacation trip to Rome in January, he announced he would be available to replace De Gaulle "if the situation arises."

Pompidou's enemies in the Gaullist camp viewed this as a bid to force the question of presidential succession, with De Gaulle's term still having three years to run. Their fears were given substance when De Gaulle insisted on staking his presidency on a national referendum that need not have been held. When voters rejected his bill to reform the Senate and establish limited regional authority, De Gaulle resigned, Apr. 28.

Pompidou moved immediately to claim the inheritance. As a candidate for the presidency, he presented himself to De Gaulle's followers as the defender of "continuity," and to eventual center allies he promised an "opening."

Since his election—as his campaign posters said he would—Pompidou has kept his promises. He has maintained much of what has been identified as Gaullist doctrine, stripping it, however, of the language of grandeur. At the same time, he has sought pragmatic solutions to pressing national-housekeeping problems, unafraid of violating Gaullist taboos. His first major act in office, after all, was to devalue the franc, a decision De Gaulle had made a point of honor to refuse.

"France is not the same without De Gaulle," a senior government official remarked a few months after Pompidou's election, "but it does make more sense."

See also France.

STEPHENS BROENING
Correspondent, Paris Bureau
The Associated Press

PORTUGAL

The year 1969 was for Portugal a time of cautious change, an interim period in which Premier Marcelo Caetano consolidated his power and created his own image as the nation's strong man.

It was the first full year since 80-year-old Antonio de Oliveira Salazar, austere dictator for nearly four decades, suffered a brain hemorrhage and his disability pushed Caetano into leadership and confronted him with the need to stamp his own personality on the Portuguese Government. Moreover, the 63-year-old lawyer-educator had to walk a political tightrope between the unremitting conservatism of the armed forces and entrenched political leaders and the harassing liberalism of students and Salazar opponents. Without the former he could not govern now, and without the latter he might not be able to govern later.

While moving crabwise politically, now toward liberalism, now toward conservatism, Caetano set out like a U.S. politician to woo the nation. He instituted a series of unprecedented television fireside chats. He toured the countryside, dropping into hamlets where a Portuguese leader had never been seen in the memory of most. He plunged, smiling, into the crowds, shaking hands and chatting with peasants, politicians and businessmen.

Whereas Salazar lived as a hermit, Caetano made a successful trip to Portugal's African territories of Mozambique and Angola. He later made a state visit to Brazil, and planned other foreign forays, including a 1970 visit to West Germany. He also represented Portugal at the funeral of General Eisenhower in Washington, and met with President Nixon.

As a former rector of Lisbon University and a brilliant corporation lawyer, Caetano moved naturally in circles unknown to Salazar and drew personal power from them. He carefully and quietly pruned away some key Salazar appointees and replaced them with his own, younger technocrats.

PORTUGAL
Area: 34,216 sq. mi.
Population: 9,600,000
Capital: Lisbon (pop., 825,000)
Government: Americo Thomaz, president—1958; Marcelo Caetano, premier—1968
Gross national product: $4,900,000,000
Monetary unit: escudo (28.7 escudos = U.S. $1.00)
Chief products: olive oil, Port wine, sardines, cork, coal, copper, textiles, resin
Foreign trade: exports, $733,000,000; imports, $1,039,000,000
Communications: 615,965 telephones, 332,000 TV sets, 29 daily newspapers
Transportation: roads, 18,253 mi.; railroads, 2,243 mi.
Education: 1,036,527 elementary and secondary students, 3 universities
Armed forces: 182,000

See map on page 185

His success in plaiting his own lifelines was illustrated dramatically in the parliamentary election of Oct. 26. Although the government opposition was given more freedom (carefully curbed), including access to voter lists, than under Salazar, the ruling União Nacional Party won every one of the 130 seats in the house. One reason was public apathy. Abstentions ran as high as 40 per cent, and as only 18 per cent of the total population could vote in the first place, the Caetano Government won the actual approval of only 10 per cent of the populace.

With Caetano vowing never to give up the country's African lands, Portugal continued to pour nearly one half of the national budget into the war against the native rebels. It budgeted $45,100,000 to support its military, which has 60,000 troops in Angola alone.

War expenditures were the key to other policies. Caetano retained press censorship on the grounds that the country was technically at war. He could move only slowly on needed social and economic changes.

Yet apparently there was some progress. The Government announced an end to terrorism in Mozambique with the unconditional surrender of Lazaro Kavandame, the rebel chieftain. In Portuguese Guinea, 92 nationalist leaders, including Rafael Barbosa, former Independence Party president, signed allegiance pledges and were freed from jail.

At home, students plagued the peace. After an examination boycott and disorders, the Government closed down Coimbra University. There were student demonstrations also in Oporto and Lisbon.

KEN DAVIS
Chief, Madrid Bureau, The Associated Press

Haynie, "The Courier-Journal"

"If we can get men to the moon. . . . Who knows?
We may even learn to get the mail across town."

POSTAL SERVICES

Several times during the first year of the Nixon administration, President Nixon and Postmaster General Winton M. Blount both described the U.S. postal service as completely inadequate. In September, the President said that the postal system "has broken down; it is not what it ought to be for a nation of 200,-000,000 people and a nation that will be 300,-000,000 within 30 years."

To meet this situation, Nixon and Blount proposed a wide-reaching series of postal reforms. But the Democratic-controlled Congress showed very little interest in any of the proposals, and they remained in limbo as the 1969 session adjourned. Powerful opposition was mounted against the recommendations at the Capitol by the postal unions—particularly the National Association of Letter Carriers and the United Federation of Postal Clerks. These organizations have important influence with the Post Office and Civil Service Committees of the House and Senate. They argued that the setting of wage rates for the 750,000 postal employees should continue to be handled by Congress. Nixon's major reform proposal was to remove postal operations from supervision by a cabinet department and put them under a new government-owned corporation. Responsibility for the basic decisions on postal rates, wages, personnel and capital expenditures would pass from Congress to a corporation with a mere nine-member board of directors. Seven of the directors would be named by the president and confirmed by the Senate. Two others would be named by the board to act as operating managers of the system.

Under the plan, Congress would have the right to review rate increases but no authority over wage scales. Nixon said that the plan would make the system self-supporting, bring much greater efficiency and sharply improved mail service. It would also take postal matters out of politics.

On Sept. 2, Nixon sought to generate support for it by meeting at his San Clemente, Calif., home with Blount, former Postmaster General Lawrence F. O'Brien and former Sen. Thruston B. Morton (R-Ky.). O'Brien, who favored the government-corporation idea when he was in the Johnson administration, and Morton served as cochairmen of a citizens group set up to back the plan. At this conference, Nixon predicted further deterioration in postal service if Congress rejected his proposal. Nevertheless, the Senate Post Office and Civil Service Committee remained uninterested. Though the House panel considered the plan, it was shelved in favor of some revisions in the present system.

Not all of the opposition to the administration postal reforms came from the unions. Some Republicans in Congress were angered by the President's proposal to end political appointment of postmasters and thus remove patronage plums that congressmen have enjoyed since the beginning of the nation. The Senate did pass a bill to carry out one recommendation, ending Senate confirmation of postmasters; but the House refused to consider it. However, by nominating not a single postmaster, the President moved on his own to stop political selection for that post.

Congress also ignored a Nixon plea to raise the letter-stamp rate from 6 to 7 cents. Former President Johnson had backed such a plan, and the new administration supported it too. Blount, in arguing for it, said that the postal deficit in fiscal 1970 would be $1,200,000,000. His department was faced with a 3.1 per cent increase in mail volume to 85,000,000,000 pieces for 1970 and must have more revenue, he declared. He claimed the rate increases sought would bring in an additional $638,000,000. Nixon pointed out that in all but 17 years since 1838, the department had run at a loss. He added that $16,000,000,000 will be diverted from the Treasury in the next 10 years at the present rate of postal deficit, and no funds would be available for badly needed government programs. But some members of Congress insisted that the first-class letter rate already bears too big a share of postal costs. They emphasized that the last increase, to 6 cents, took effect only in 1968 and that in early 1958 the rate had been 3 cents.

JOSEPH W. HALL, JR.
Senate Staff, Washington Bureau
The Associated Press

PRIZES AND AWARDS

ART, ARCHITECTURE, DANCE AND MUSIC

American Institute of Architects Critic Medal: ADA LOUISE HUXTABLE, architecture critic, *The New York Times*

American Institute of Graphic Arts Medal: ROBERT L. LESLIE, The Composing Room, Inc.

National Academy of Recording Arts and Sciences Awards (Grammy Awards)
  Album: BY THE TIME I GET TO PHOENIX, Glen Campbell
  New Artist: JOSE FELICIANO
  Record: MRS. ROBINSON, Simon & Garfunkel
  Song: LITTLE GREEN APPLES, Bobby Russell, songwriter
  Vocal performance by female, contemporary-pop: DO YOU KNOW THE WAY TO SAN JOSE, Dionne Warwick
  Vocal performance by male, contemporary-pop: LIGHT MY FIRE, Jose Feliciano
  Vocal performance by female, country: HARPER VALLEY P.T.A., Jeannie C. Riley
  Vocal performance by male, country: FOLSOM PRISON BLUES, Johnny Cash
  Vocal performance by female, rhythm and blues: CHAIN OF FOOLS, Aretha Franklin
  Vocal performance by male, rhythm and blues: THE DOCK OF THE BAY, Otis Redding

National Council on the Arts Award for "lifelong contribution to American letters" ($7,000 each): KENNETH BURKE, literary critic; REED WHITTEMORE, poet, critic and editor

National Institute of Arts and Letters Awards
  Brunner Award in Architecture ($1,000): NOEL MICHAEL MCKINNELL
  The Gold Medal for Graphic Art: LEONARD BASKIN
  Award for Distinguished Service to the Arts: LEOPOLD STOKOWSKI
  Grants in art ($2,500 each): LENNART ANDERSON; WILLIAM CHRISTOPHER; FRANK GALLO; LEONEL GONGORA; RED GROOMS; SIDNEY HURWITZ; BEN KAMIHIRA; ALICE NEEL
  Grants in music ($2,500 each): MICHAEL BROZEN; JACOB R. DRUCKMAN; NICOLAS ROUSSAKIS; CLAUDIO SPIES
  Marjorie Peabody Waite Award ($1,500): HERBERT ELWELL
  The Traveling Fellowship (about $9,000): ROBERT STONE
  The Rosenthal Award for Painting ($2,000): NICHOLAS SPERAKIS

JOURNALISM

Albert Lasker Medical Journalism Awards ($2,500 each): C. P. GILMORE, free-lance magazine writer, for article, *Instead of a Heart, a Man-made Pump*, The New York Times Magazine; NBC NEWS, LEN GIOVANNITTI, for documentary, *The American Alcoholic;* BARBARA YUNCKER, medicine and science writer, the New York Post, for series, *The Human Brain*

Dumont Award for International Journalism ($2,500): THOMAS A. JOHNSON, The New York Times, series on the American Negro in Vietnam

Overseas Press Club Awards
  Asia Magazine Award for best article or report on Asia: BERNARD KALB, CBS, for television program, *The Viet Cong*
  Book on foreign affairs: GEORGE BALL, *The Discipline of Power*
  Cartoon on foreign affairs: DON WRIGHT, The Miami News

Daily-newspaper or wire-service interpretation of foreign affairs: ROBERT S. ELEGANT, The Los Angeles Times, for articles on Communist China; STANLEY KARNOW, The Washington Post, for series, *China-Watcher*

Daily-newspaper or wire-service photographic reporting from abroad: EDWARD T. ADAMS, The Associated Press, for photograph, *Street-Corner Execution*

Daily-newspaper or wire-service reporting from abroad: PETER REHAK, The Associated Press, for reporting before, during and after the Czech crisis

E. W. Fairchild Award for best business news reporting from abroad ($500): CLYDE FARNSWORTH, The New York Times, for coverage of West European economic and monetary problems

George Polk Memorial Award for best reporting in any medium, requiring exceptional courage and enterprise abroad ($500): PETER REHAK

Magazine interpretation of foreign affairs: JAMES THOMSON, The Atlantic, for *How Could Vietnam Happen?*

Magazine reporting from abroad: J. ROBERT MOSKIN, Look, for *Israel—20 Years of Siege and Struggle*

Photographic reporting or interpretation from abroad in a magazine or book: DAVID ROBISON, Life, for *Starving Children of Biafra;* ROMANO CAGNONI, PRIYA RAMRAHKA, Life, for *The War of Extinction*

Radio interpretation of foreign affairs: ELIE ABEL, NBC, *De Gaulle Faces His Creditors*

Radio reporting from abroad: BERNARD REDMONT, Westinghouse Broadcasting Company, for *Vietnam Peace Story*

Robert Capa Award for superlative still photography requiring exceptional courage and enterprise abroad: JOHN OLSON, Life, for his photographs of *The Battle That Regained and Ruined Hue*

Television interpretation of foreign affairs: CHARLES COLLINGWOOD, CBS, for *Visit to Hanoi*

Television reporting from abroad: LIZ TROTTA, NBC, for Vietnam reports

Vision Magazine/Ed Stout Award for best article or report on Latin America ($500): HENRY GINIGER, The New York Times

LITERATURE

American Academy of Arts and Letters Awards
  Award of Merit ($1,000): VLADIMIR NABAKOV, novelist and short-story writer
  Traveling Fellowship ($9,000): ROBERT STONE, novelist

American Library Association Awards
  John Newbery Medal for the "most distinguished contribution to American literature for children": LLOYD ALEXANDER, *The High King*
  Randolph J. Caldecott Medal for the "most distinguished American picture book": URI SHULEVITZ (illustrator), *The Fool of the World and the Flying Ship*
  Grolier Award for "great contribution to children's reading and librarianship" ($1,000): ANNE REBECCA IZARD, children's consultant, Westchester Library System, Mount Vernon, N.Y.

Bancroft Prizes for "the best books in American history in its broadest sense, American diplomacy, and American international relations" ($4,000 each): WINTHROP D. JORDAN, *White over Black: American Attitudes toward the Negro, 1550–1812;* N. GORDON LEVIN, JR., *Woodrow Wilson and World Politics: America's Response to War and Revolution;* REXFORD GUY TUGWELL, *The Brains Trust*

Bollingen Prize in Poetry ($5,000 shared): JOHN BERRY-MAN, *His Toy, His Dream, His Rest;* KARL SHAPIRO, *Selected Poems*

Canadian Governor-General's Literary Awards ($2,500 each)

English fiction: MORDECAI RICHLER, *Cocksure* (novel), *Hunting Tigers under Glass* (essays); ALICE MUNRO, *Dance of the Happy Shades* (short stories)

English poetry: LEONARD COHEN, *Selected Poems*

French fiction: HUBERT AQUIN, *Trou de memoire;* MARIE-CLAIRE BLAIS, *Les manuscrits de Pauline Archange*

French nonfiction: FERNAND DUMONT, *Le lieu de l'homme*

Dutton Animal Book Award for book-length work of adult fiction or nonfiction related to animals ($10,000): STERLING NORTH, *The Wolfling: A Documentary Novel of the 1870's*

George Freedley Memorial Award: LOUIS SHEAFFER, *O'Neill, Son and Playwright*

Mystery Writers of America Awards (Edgar Awards)

Fact crime book: JOHN WALSH, *Poe the Detective*

First mystery novel: E. RICHARD JOHNSON, *Silver Street;* DOROTHY UHNAK, *The Bait*

Juvenile mystery: VIRGINIA HAMILTON, *The House of Dies Drear*

Mystery novel: JEFFERY HUDSON, *A Case of Need*

National Book Awards ($1,000 each)

Arts and letters: NORMAN MAILER, *The Armies of the Night*

Children's literature: MEINDERT DEJONG, *Journey from Peppermint Street*

Fiction: JERZY KOSINSKI, *Steps*

History and biography: WINTHROP D. JORDAN, *White over Black: American Attitudes toward the Negro, 1550–1812*

Poetry: JOHN BERRYMAN, *His Toy, His Dream, His Rest*

Science: ROBERT JAY LIFTON, *Death in Life*

Translation: WILLIAM WEAVER, *Cosmocomics*

National Medal for Literature: CONRAD AIKEN

National Institute of Arts and Letters Awards

Grants ($5,000 each): JOHN ASHBERY, poet; ALLEN GINSBERG, poet; GEORGE P. ELLIOTT, novelist; HUGH KENNER, essayist and critic; L. E. SISSMAN, poet

Richard and Hinda Rosenthal Foundation Award ($2,000): FREDERICK EXLEY, writer

MOTION PICTURES

Academy of Motion Picture Arts and Sciences Awards (Oscars)

Actor: CLIFF ROBERTSON, *Charly*

Actor (supporting role): JACK ALBERTSON, *The Subject Was Roses*

Actress: BARBRA STREISAND, *Funny Girl;* KATHARINE HEPBURN, *The Lion in Winter*

Actress (supporting role): RUTH GORDON, *Rosemary's Baby*

Direction: SIR CAROL REED, *Oliver!*

Foreign-language film: WAR AND PEACE, U.S.S.R.

Picture: OLIVER!

Song: THE WINDMILLS OF YOUR MIND by Michel Legrand, from *The Thomas Crown Affair*

Writing (screenplay—based on material from another medium): THE LION IN WINTER, James Goldman

Writing (story and screenplay—written directly for the screen): THE PRODUCERS, Mel Brooks

Jean Hersholt Humanitarian Award: MARTHA RAYE, for "devoted and often dangerous work in entertaining troops in combat areas"

Special awards: JOHN CHAMBERS, for creating the makeup for the cast of *Planet of the Apes;* ONNA WHITE, for choreography, *Oliver!*

Cannes International Film Festival Awards

Actor: JEAN LOUIS TRINTIGNANT, Z, France

Actress: VANESSA REDGRAVE, *The Loves of Isadora,* Great Britain

Director: GLAUBER ROCHA, *Antoniodas Mortes,* Brazil; VOJTECH JASNY, *Moravian Chronicle,* Czechoslovakia

Film: IF, Great Britain

Grand Jury Prize: ADALEN 31, Sweden

Jury Prize: Z

PULITZER PRIZES

Journalism ($1,000 each except for public-service gold medal)

Cartoon: JOHN FISCHETTI, The Chicago Daily News

Editorial writing: PAUL GREENBERG, The Pine Bluff (Ark.) Commercial

Feature photography: MONETA SLEET, JR., Ebony magazine

International reporting: WILLIAM TUOHY, The Los Angeles Times, for coverage of the Vietnam war

Local reporting (general): JOHN FETTERMAN, The Louisville (Ky.) Courier-Journal, for story about how "the body of Pfc James Thurman (Little Duck) Gibson came home from Vietnam"

Local reporting (special): ALBERT L. DELUGACH, the St. Louis Globe-Democrat, and DENNY WALSH, Life magazine, for their exposé of fraud and abuse of power in Local 562, St. Louis Steamfitters Union

Meritorious public service: THE LOS ANGELES TIMES, for exposing "wrongdoing within the Los Angeles city government commissions"

National reporting: ROBERT CAHN, The Christian Science Monitor, series on the necessity of saving national parks

Spot-news photography: EDWARD T. ADAMS, The Associated Press

Letters and music ($1,000 each)

Biography: THE MAN FROM NEW YORK: JOHN QUINN AND HIS FRIENDS by Benjamin L. Reid

Drama: THE GREAT WHITE HOPE by Howard Sackler

Fiction: HOUSE MADE OF DAWN by N. Scott Momaday

History: ORIGINS OF THE FIFTH AMENDMENT by Leonard W. Levy

Music: STRING QUARTET NO. 3 by Karel Husa

Nonfiction (general): THE ARMIES OF THE NIGHT by Norman Mailer; and SO HUMAN AN ANIMAL: HOW WE ARE SHAPED BY SURROUNDINGS AND EVENTS by René J. Dubos

Poetry: OF BEING NUMEROUS by George Oppen

SCIENCE

Albert Lasker Medical Research Awards ($10,000 each)

Basic research: BRUCE MERRIFIELD, Rockefeller University

Clinical research: GEORGE C. COTZIAS, Brookhaven National Laboratory

American Chemical Society Awards

Anselme Payen Award for "professional contributions to the science and technology of cellulose and its applied products" ($1,000): STANLEY G. MASON, McGill University, Montreal

American Heart Association Awards

Louis N. Katz Basic Research Prize for Young Investigators ($1,500): ERIC O. FEIGL, University of Washington Medical School

UPI

NBC

Laurels were bestowed on (clockwise, from above): Bill Cosby, for his delightful TV special; Norman Mailer, for "The Armies of the Night"; James Earl Jones and Julie Harris, best actor and actress; Duke Ellington, here receiving the Medal of Freedom from President Nixon; and TV correspondent Charles Collingwood, singled out for his interpretation of foreign affairs.

Friedman-Abeles

CBS News

UPI

Research Achievement Award ($1,000): OTTO KRAYER, formerly Harvard Medical School

Arches of Science Award ($25,000): GERARD PIEL, *Scientific American*

Atoms for Peace Awards ($15,000 each): AGAE N. BOHR, Nordic Institute for Theoretical Atomic Physics, Copenhagen; FLOYD L. CULLER, JR., Oak Ridge National Laboratory, Oak Ridge, Tenn.; M. S. IOFFE, I. V. Kurchatov Institute of Atomic Energy, Moscow; HENRY S. KAPLAN, Stanford University School of Medicine; BEN R. MOTTELSON, Nordic Institute for Theoretical Atomic Physics; COMPTON A. RENNIE, England; ANTHONY L. TURKEVICH, University of Chicago

Bronfman Prize for public-health achievement ($5,000 each): WILLIAM HADDON, JR., president, Insurance Institute for Highway Safety; FELIPE HERRERA, president, Inter-American Bank; EDWIN H. LANNETTE, California State Department of Health

Dreyfus Medical Foundation Award ($75,000): TRACY JACKSON PUTNAM, Cedars of Lebanon Hospital, Los Angeles

Louisa Gross Horowitz Prize for outstanding research in biology ($25,000 shared): MAX DELBRUCK, California Institute of Technology; SALVADOR LURIA, Massachusetts Institute of Technology

U.S. Atomic Energy Commission Enrico Fermi Award ($25,000): WALTER H. ZINN, Combustion Engineering Corporation

U.S. National Medal of Science
Biological sciences: HORACE A. BARKER, University of California, Berkeley; BERNARD B. BRODIE, National Institutes of Health; DETLEV W. BRONK, president emeritus, Rockefeller University; JAY L. LUSH, Iowa State University; BURRHUS F. SKINNER, Harvard University

Engineering sciences: JOHN P. ECKERT, Sperry Rand Corporation; NATHAN N. NEWMARK, University of Illinois; JERRY NEYMAN, University of California, Berkeley

Physical sciences: PAUL D. BARTLETT, Harvard University; HERBERT FRIEDMAN, Naval Research Laboratory; LARS ONSAGER, Yale University; EUGENE P. WIGNER, Princeton University

TELEVISION AND RADIO

George Foster Peabody Awards
Radio education: LEONARD REIFFEL, THE WORLD TOMORROW, WEEI-CBS (Boston)

Radio entertainment: STEINWAY HALL, WQXR (New York City)

Radio news: SECOND SUNDAY, NBC

Radio public service: KALEIDOSCOPE, WJR-CBS (Detroit)

Television education: ROBERT CROMIE, BOOK BEAT, WTTW (Chicago); AMERICAN BROADCASTING COMPANY, for its creative documentaries

Television entertainment: NATIONAL EDUCATIONAL TELEVISION PLAYHOUSE

Television news: CHARLES KURALT, ON THE ROAD, CBS

Television promotion of international understanding: AMERICAN BROADCASTING COMPANY, for televising the 1968 Olympics

Television public service: WESTINGHOUSE BROADCASTING COMPANY, for *One Nation Indivisible*

Television special award: CBS REPORTS: HUNGER IN AMERICA

Television youth or children's programs: MISTEROGERS' NEIGHBORHOOD, NET

National Academy of Television Arts and Sciences Awards (Emmy Awards)
Comedy series: GET SMART, NBC

Continued performance by an actor in a leading role in a comedy series: DON ADAMS, *Get Smart*

Continued performance by an actor in a leading role in a dramatic series: CARL BETZ, *Judd for the Defense*, ABC

Continued performance by an actor in a supporting role in a series: WERNER KLEMPERER, *Hogan's Heroes*, CBS

Continued performance by an actress in a leading role in a comedy series: HOPE LANGE, *The Ghost and Mrs. Muir*, NBC

Continued performance by an actress in a leading role in a dramatic series: BARBARA BAIN, *Mission: Impossible*, CBS

Continued performance by an actress in a supporting role in a series: SUSAN SAINT JAMES, *The Name of the Game*, NBC

Cultural-documentary and "magazine-type" program or series
Programs: DON'T COUNT THE CANDLES, William K. McClure producer, *CBS News Hour*; JUSTICE BLACK AND THE BILL OF RIGHTS, Burton Benjamin producer, CBS News Special; MAN WHO DANCES: EDWARD VILLELLA, Robert Drew and Mike Jackson producers, *Bell Telephone Hour*; THE GREAT AMERICAN NOVEL, Arthur Barron producer, *CBS News Hour*

Individuals: WALTER DOMBROW, JERRY SIMS, cinematographers, "The Great American Novel"; TOM PETTIT, producer, "CBW: The Secrets of Secrecy," *First Tuesday*, NBC; LORD SNOWDON, cinematographer, "Don't Count the Candles"

Daytime programing: THE DICK CAVETT SHOW, Don Silverman producer, ABC

Directorial achievement in drama: DAVID GREENE, "The People Next Door," *CBS Playhouse*

Dramatic program: TEACHER, TEACHER, *Hallmark Hall of Fame*, Henry Jaffe executive producer, NBC

Dramatic series: NET PLAYHOUSE, Curtis Davis executive producer, NET

International documentary: THE LAST CAMPAIGN OF ROBERT KENNEDY, Swiss Broadcasting and Television, Zurich

International entertainment: A SCENT OF FLOWERS, CBC-TV FESTIVAL SERIES, Canadian Broadcasting Corporation, Ottawa

News documentary
Programs: CBS REPORTS: HUNGER IN AMERICA, Martin Carr producer; LAW AND ORDER, Frederick Wiseman producer, Public Broadcasting Laboratory

Individuals: PERRY WOLFF, ANDREW A. ROONEY, writers, "Black History: Lost, Stolen or Strayed," *CBS News Hour*

Regularly scheduled news program: WALLACE WESTFELDT, executive producer of special coverage of hunger in the United States, *The Huntley-Brinkley Report*, NBC; CHARLES KURALT, correspondent, JAMES WILSON, cameraman, ROBERT FUNK, sound man, for "On the Road," *CBS Evening News with Walter Cronkite*; JOHN LAURENCE, correspondent, "Police after Chicago," *CBS Evening News with Walter Cronkite*

Single performance by an actor in a leading role: PAUL SCOFIELD, "Male of the Species," *Prudential's on Stage*, NBC

Single performance by an actress in a leading role: GERALDINE PAGE, *The Thanksgiving Visitor*, ABC

Special events: ROBERT WUSSLER, ERNEST LEISER, DON HEWITT, BURTON BENJAMIN, executive producers, coverage of the assassination of Dr. Martin Luther King, Jr., CBS News Specials

Sports programing: 19TH SUMMER OLYMPIC GAMES, ABC

Trustees award: WILLIAM R. MCANDREW, NBC News president; ASTRONAUTS OF APOLLO 7, 8, 9, 10

Variety or musical program: THE BILL COSBY SPECIAL, ROY SILVER executive producer, NBC

Variety or musical series: ROWAN AND MARTIN'S LAUGH-IN; GEORGE SCHLATTER executive producer, NBC

Writing achievement in comedy, variety or music: ALLAN BLYE, BOB EINSTEIN, MURRAY ROMAN, CARL GOTTLIEB, JERRY MUSIC, STEVE MARTIN, CECIL TUCK, PAUL WAYNE, CY HOWARD, MASON WILLIAMS, *The Smothers Brothers Comedy Hour*, CBS

Writing achievement in drama: JP MILLER, "The People Next Door," *CBS Playhouse*

THEATER

Antoinette Perry Awards of the American Theater Wing (Tony Awards)

Actor (dramatic): JAMES EARL JONES, *The Great White Hope*

Actor (dramatic featured or supporting): AL PACINO, *Does a Tiger Wear a Necktie?*

Actor (musical): JERRY ORBACH, *Promises, Promises*

Actor (musical featured or supporting): RONALD HOLGATE, *1776*

Actress (dramatic): JULIE HARRIS, *Forty Carats*

Actress (dramatic featured or supporting): JANE ALEXANDER, *The Great White Hope*

Actress (musical): ANGELA LANSBURY, *Dear World*

Actress (musical featured or supporting): MARIAN MERCER, *Promises, Promises*

Choreographer: JOE LAYTON, *George M!*

Costume designer: LOUDEN SAINTHILL, *Canterbury Tales*

Director (musical): PETER HUNT, *1776*

Director (play): PETER DEWS, *Hadrian VII*

Musical: *1776* by Peter Stone

Play: THE GREAT WHITE HOPE by Howard Sackler

Scenic designer: BORIS ANDERSON, *Zorba*

Special awards: LEONARD BERNSTEIN; CAROL BURNETT; REX HARRISON; NEGRO ENSEMBLE COMPANY; SIR LAURENCE OLIVIER

Drama Desk Awards

Choreography: GEORGE DALE, *Billy*

Composer: AL CARMINES, *Peace*

Costume design: TANYA MOISEIWITSCH, *The House of Atreus*

Direction: EDWIN SHERIN, *The Great White Hope*

Lyrics: GEORGE HAIMSOHN, ROBIN MILLER, *Dames at Sea*

Musical book: PETER STONE, *1776*

Performance: JAMES EARL JONES, *The Great White Hope*; LINDA LAVIN, *Little Murders*

Scenic design: MING CHO LEE, *Invitation to a Beheading*

New York Drama Critics Circle Awards

Musical: *1776*

Play: THE GREAT WHITE HOPE

Village Voice Off-Broadway Awards (Obies): THE LIVING THEATRE, *Frankenstein;* JEFF WEISS, *The International Wrestling Match;* JULIE BOVASSO, *Gloria & Esperanza;* JUDITH MALINA, *Antigone;* JULIAN BECK, *Antigone;* ISRAEL HOROVITZ, *The Honest-to-God Schnozzola;* JULES FEIFFER, *Little Murders;* RONALD TAVEL, *The Boy on the Straight-Back Chair;* NATHAN GEORGE, RON O'NEAL, *No Place to Be Somebody;* ARLENE ROTHLEIN, *The Poor Little Match Girl;* THEATRE GENESIS, sustained excellence; OPEN THEATRE, *The Serpent;* OM THEATRE, *Riot;* PERFORMANCE GROUP, *Dionysus in '69*

UNITED STATES AND WORLD SCENE

Albert Einstein Commemorative Awards: JOHN W. GARDNER, The Urban Coalition; JACQUES LIPSCHITZ, sculptor; JOSEPH I. LUBIN, investor and philanthropist; MARSHALL W. NIRENBERG, National Heart Institute

Big Brothers of America Big Brother of the Year Award: EDWARD W. BROOKE, U.S. senator (R-Mass.)

Brotherhood-in-Action Awards: KENNETH B. CLARK, psychologist; SAMUEL HAUSMAN, Brotherhood-in-Action; JOHN MACCRATE, former justice, New York State Supreme Court; GEORGE ROMNEY, U.S. secretary of housing and urban development; HOWARD A. RUSK, New York University Medical Center; ED SULLIVAN, television entertainer

Canada's Royal Bank Award for humanitarian achievement ($50,000): PAUL-EMILE CARDINAL LEGER, former archbishop of Montreal

Freedom Award: EARL WARREN, former chief justice, U.S. Supreme Court

National Institute of Social Sciences Gold Medals for "distinguished service to humanity": FRANK BORMAN, U.S. astronaut; THE REV. THEODORE M. HESBURGH, president, Notre Dame University; LADY JACKSON (BARBARA WARD), British economist and writer; LESTER B. PEARSON, former prime minister of Canada

Rockefeller Public Service Awards for "distinguished service to the Government of the United States and to the American people" ($10,000)

Administration: ARTHUR E. HESS, deputy commissioner, Social Security Administration, Department of Health, Education, and Welfare

Foreign Affairs or International Operations (shared): JOHN FREDERICK THOMAS, director-general, Intergovernmental Committee for European Migration, Geneva; PHILIP C. HABIB, U.S. delegation, Paris peace talks on Vietnam

General Welfare or National Resources: WILLIAM T. PECORA, director, U.S. Geological Survey, Department of the Interior

Law, Legislation or Regulation: ASHLEY FOARD, deputy legal counsel for legal affairs, Department of Housing and Urban Development

Science, Technology or Engineering: JOHN W. EVANS, director, Sacramento Peak Observatory, Department of the Air Force

At-Large: ROBERT R. GILRUTH, director, Manned Spacecraft Center, National Aeronautics and Space Administration

U.S. Presidential Medal of Freedom (Conferred by President Johnson): EUGENE R. BLACK, former president, World Bank; CLARK M. CLIFFORD, presidential adviser and secretary of defense; W. AVERELL HARRIMAN, diplomat; CYRUS R. VANCE, presidential troubleshooter; DR. MICHAEL E. DEBAKEY, heart specialist; DAVID DUBINSKY, former president, International Ladies Garment Workers Union; HENRY FORD II, Ford Motor Company; RALPH ELLISON, Negro writer; BOB HOPE, entertainer; EDGAR KAISER, industrialist; MARY LASKER, philanthropist; GREGORY PECK, actor; LAURANCE S. ROCKEFELLER, conservationist; WALT W. ROSTOW, presidential adviser; MERRIMAN SMITH, White House correspondent, United Press International; WILLIAM S. WHITE, columnist; ROY WILKINS, executive director, National Association for the Advancement of Colored People; WHITNEY M. YOUNG, JR., director, National Urban League; MCGEORGE BUNDY, president, Ford Foundation; JOHN W. MACY, JR., chairman, Civil Service Commission

U.S. Presidential Medal of Freedom (Conferred by President Nixon): COL. EDWIN E. ALDRIN, JR., NEIL A. ARMSTRONG, COL. MICHAEL COLLINS, Apollo 11 astronauts; DUKE ELLINGTON, jazz musician

PSYCHIATRY AND PSYCHOLOGY

Traditional Freudian or more recent neo-Freudian psychoanalytic theories have argued that neurotic behaviors are only symptomatic of underlying deep emotional disturbances. These therapists say that unless the deep problems are brought to the surface and recognized by the patient, he cannot be considered cured. In contrast, the new trend in clinical treatment, *behavior therapy,* is to claim that all behavior—normal, neurotic and even some psychotic actions—is learned and can be modified. This method of treatment is a direct application of a method—called operant conditioning—that has been developed in various experimental laboratories.

Behavior therapy, more often called behavior modification, is a process aimed at changing or controlling behavior by means of positive or negative reinforcement. The behaviorist focuses on the patient's immediate behavior problem and attempts to modify it, helping the patient learn to do the things that will bring him rewards and encouragement in his social environment.

Token economy is a good example of the recent application of operant conditioning to human problems. The token system is based on the idea, confirmed by B. F. Skinner in the mid-1930's, that laboratory animals learn to perform tasks when the desired behavior is positively reinforced; that is, behavior is determined by its consequences.

Today, in a mental hospital, for instance, a catatonic patient who has vegetated for thirty years—being force-fed and dressed—can learn in less than a month to groom himself and select his own food in a cafeteria. While many Freudian theorists would have considered such a psychotic patient beyond hope, behavior therapists demonstrated that the patient could learn to make a particular response when it was rewarded. Behaviorists say they have also disproved the Freudian argument that psychotic behavior is unpredictable; rather, under operant conditioning, the patient's responses to stimuli are stable and regular.

During the patient's initial treatment, the reinforcement may be candy, cigarettes or something else the patient strongly desires. After a while, the therapist substitutes a token —a metal slug, poker chip or even a symbolic mark in a record book—for the earlier reinforcement. The idea is similar to the monetary system, and the patient comes to understand that he may exchange his tokens for specific reinforcements: the favorite foods, special dining facilities or entertainment privileges on which he may "spend" his tokens.

The hospital staff chooses the behavior patterns for which the patients will be awarded tokens; the staff's long-term goal for the patient is social reinforcement. The patient's responsible behavior will earn him social approval first in the institution, and then, it is hoped, in the outside world. Dr. Leonard Krasner, of State University of New York, who has done extensive research in behavior modification, is best known for his development of the first token-economy treatment program, at the Palo Alto Veterans Administration Hospital. Today many hospitals, schools and penal institutions are using the token-economy system successfully.

Modern knowledge of operant conditioning also permits behavior therapists, notably Dr. Joseph Wolpe, to help patients "unlearn" phobias and other neurotic fears. Laboratory psychologists can teach animals to relax in an environment that formerly caused anxiety—by slowly making a safe environment more similar to the fear-producing one. Likewise, behavior therapists can desensitize human beings to an anxiety-producing stimulus, be it fear of cats, high places or the opposite sex. The therapist has his patient relax and imagine proximity to the feared stimulus by slow degrees. Wolpe decidedly improved his method by employing E. Jacobson's technique for progressive relaxation of the body, since relaxation is the essential desired response in the face of anxiety.

Perhaps the most startling advances in experimental psychology have grown out of recent research findings in physiological memory transfer. Behavior therapists, as noted, apply to human behavior the scientific premise that learning is the result of conditioning. Current work in the laboratory has exciting—and unsettling—implications for the future of applied psychology in the field of learning.

Physiological psychologists, such as Dr. David Krech, are building evidence that mind and matter are not the distinct entities that most people, including psychotherapists, thought they were. Laboratory research with rats—and even with flatworms and goldfish (by, respectively, James McConnell and Bernard Agranoff of the University of Michigan) —indicates that the basis of memory and learning may lie in the chemical and anatomical circuitry of the brain.

Recent research indicates that memory may be transferred from one brain to another, and experiments with rats have already paved the way. Untrained rats prefer dark chambers to light ones and will invariably jump through a hole leading to a dark chamber from the light one in which they are placed. After a laboratory worker trains rat A to avoid a dark chamber that gives him an electric shock, the worker extracts fluid from A's brain and injects it into the brain of B, an untrained rat. Rat B is then placed in the light half of a box with light and dark chambers. Rat B hesitates before entering the dark chamber, even though he desires to be there and there is no electric shock; finally entering the dark room, rat B shows anxiety and jumps back and forth between the two chambers.

Rat C, also untrained but without the "memory injection," will jump into the dark chamber, showing little or no reluctance, and remain there. The conclusion is that memory of the dark room and its shock was transferred from rat A to rat B, thus producing a fear response in rat B to a stimulus he had never before experienced.

Findings from several other experiments suggest that therapists may use chemical therapy in the future to modify behavior and enhance learning. Although the implications for man's intellectual development stagger the imagination with miraculous, as well as frightening, possibilities, memory-transfer research is still at the experimental stage, and the possibilities of application remain.

More widely publicized and popularized than the clinical behavioristic developments, and far removed from the laboratory, is the encounter-group phenomenon in psychology. Groups of individuals, numbering 10 to 15, simply get together and talk, reacting to each other not on the basis of their pasts or assumed roles but on an immediate emotional level. Encounter groups were originally called T groups ("T" standing for training) and were organized under the National Training Laboratories (NTL) to promote better interpersonal relations in the field of industry.

Soon people associated in such other fields as education, medicine and religion began to form new groups. The idea has expanded to include intensive-group experiences for families, married couples, divorcées and bachelors, as well as for individuals who are unacquainted and have no backgrounds or interests in common.

T groups are also called basic encounter groups and sensitivity-training groups. Sensory-awareness, or body-awareness, groups, as emphasized at Esalen Institute, usually stress physical expression; some groups have recently experimented with nudity as a catalyst for emotional spontaneity. Synanon groups, or "games," initially restricted to treatment of drug addicts, rely heavily on the encounter-group approach.

Dr. Carl Rogers, one of the major proponents of intensive-group therapy, says that the process is in one way "a cultural attempt to meet the isolation and alienation of contemporary life." Furthermore, intensive-group therapy makes available a means of improving "basic gut-level communication" for people whose everyday relationships are characterized by conflict, bad faith and boredom.

The goal of the intensive-group process is to foster greater personal flexibility, openness and freedom. The future of the encounter-group phenomenon is uncertain. Some critics think that many group leaders are not properly trained and so will miss danger signals within the groups. If or when psychologists learn to measure the changes in attitudes expressed in group encounters in terms of human learning and motivational processes, sensitivity training may become a tool permitting prediction and eventually may then be brought into the scientific fold.

RICHARD L. ROE
Psychology Editorial Director
CRM Books

PUBLISHING

In 1968, U.S. newspaper readers spent $2,300,-000,000 for daily newspapers, while Canadians spent $162,000,000 for their papers. The combined figure was expected to reach $2,500,-000,000 in 1969.

Book publishers reported record sales; while advertisers poured billions into the mass media, debating just where the money for cigarette ads should be spent.

Books. Suspense and sex dominated the book scene in 1969. Americans had the opportunity to read more books: 23,321 new titles appeared in 1968, up 5.6 per cent over 1967. In addition, 7,066 new editions of older books appeared.

With a better educated public having more leisure time for reading, and with more students in colleges and universities, publishers could look forward to a continued upward turn in sales. The Commerce Department estimated 1969 book sales at $2,664,000,000, up 5 per cent over 1968.

In late 1969, *The Love Machine* and *Portnoy's Complaint* were still extremely popular. *Naked Came the Stranger* stirred the reading public when it was revealed that its author was no "Penelope Ashe," but a group of newspapermen who had set out to write the worst sex-oriented book they could with "true excellence in writing quickly blue-penciled into oblivion."

Hemingway remained popular, while *The Money Game* had many followers. *Between*

© 1969 by The New York Times Company. Reprinted by permission.

To announce one of the greatest of human feats, "The New York Times" used the biggest headline type it had ever displayed: one inch high (or, in the term printers use, 72 points).

Parent and Teenager attracted older persons seeking to close the generation gap. A study of *The New York Times—The Kingdom and the Power*—also was a best seller.

Movie tie-ins helped sales, especially of paperback editions of *Myra Breckinridge* and *Rosemary's Baby. Peanuts* continued well in front, with total sales of the cartoon books approaching 40,000,000 copies.

Censorship caused concern when the Supreme Court in 1968 ruled that states have the right to impose "variable censorship." Parents struck back at publishers of obscene material mailed to their teen-agers; the Post Office made it possible for parents to get their children's names removed from the publishers' mailing lists.

The book trade expanded. Some publishers added magazines to their business; others acquired bookstores. More "integrated" books appeared: ethnic groups joined the all-white world of Dick and Jane. Some larger cities, such as New York and Los Angeles, published their own books about the Negro in American history.

The Johnsons were busy writing. The first article by the former President, a 30,000-word essay "Agenda for the Future," appeared in an encyclopedia book of the year.

Magazines. The Curtis saga came to an end in 1969 when *The Saturday Evening Post* folded, ending a career that dated from 1821. Losses had totaled more than $62,000,000 since 1961. Under the ownership of Cyrus H. K. Curtis and the editorship of George Horace Lorimer, the *Post* became an American institution, reaching its zenith in the 1920's. Efforts to orient the *Post* to the newer generation helped some, yet the editors had too little time to convince skeptical advertisers that it was on the road to recovery. *Advertising Age* said the *Post* "wandered, for decades, all over the lot," and forgot about "today's scheme of Marketing."

Edward R. Downe, Jr., who owns *Family Weekly* and acquired *Ladies' Home Journal* and *American Home* from Curtis, was named the Consumer Magazine Man of the Year by *Magazine Industry Newsletter*. In the business-publications field, Norman L. Cahners was so honored. Albert L. Cole, long associated with *Reader's Digest,* won the 1969 Fisher award for outstanding achievement in magazine publishing.

For the fifth consecutive year, advertising revenue surpassed the billion-dollar mark, again in the $1,200,000,000 area in 1969. Stephen E. Kelly, president of the Magazine Publishers Association, said in late 1969 that the industry "is healthy, vital, viable, more full of potential than ever before." The Commerce Department estimated that periodical publishers' revenues would amount to some $2,775,000,000 for the year 1969.

Newsweek and *Time* struggled for ad-page leadership, with *Newsweek* continuing a trend it started in 1968. *Newsweek* was threatened with expulsion from Vietnam for unfriendly articles about the Government there. At home, *Time* added a "Behavior" section and announced plans to spend $17,000,000 to get the "hard news" in 1969. Both magazines used more signed articles than in the past.

Business Week led consumer magazines in ad pages, replacing the longtime leader *The New Yorker*. With its higher circulation and ad rates, *Life* continued to dominate the advertising dollar, as it had for more than 25 years.

Time Inc. was in the limelight. After a dismal first quarter, profits were higher for the second period in 1969 when net income reached $15,400,000 on revenues of $292,800,000 for the six-month period. The trend toward higher revenues and lower profits was also evident elsewhere in the industry. The *Magazine Industry Newsletter* said Time Inc. had "grown fat and a bit drowsy on its profits." A revival followed after *Life*'s advertising decline. The magazine's circulation had moved upward, reflecting the many *Saturday Evening Post* subscribers it had acquired. *Life* turned to greater use of exposé articles.

Time Inc. acquired a group of suburban weekly newspapers in Chicago and was considering adding more. It also bought several CATV outlets and expanded other projects. Circulation and ad income rose on *Time, Fortune* and *Sports Illustrated.* Near the end of the year a second-generation leadership instituted many changes in management and editorship.

New magazines continued to appear, but were highly specialized, seeking the attention of specific age groups, ethnic units, and business leaders. Many appeared in the health field.

Circulation leaders remained practically the same as in recent years. *Reader's Digest,* with some 17,800,000 copies sold in the United States, was No. 1. *TV Guide* continued in the 14,500,000 category. *McCall's,* at 8,500,000, led its competitor, *Ladies' Home Journal,* which had more ad pages but only 7,000,000 circulation. *Better Homes and Gardens* reached 7,700,000; *Woman's Day* and *Family Circle* had 7,600,000 each. *National Geographic* moved into the 6,000,000 bracket; *Good Housekeeping* went to 5,700,000; and *Playboy* continued to grow, reaching 5,500,000. *Life* went ahead of *Look,* 8,500,000 to 7,800,000.

Newspapers. The two big stories of the summer were the triumph of man's moon landing and the tragedy of the Ted Kennedy–Mary Jo Kopechne accident. Newsmen adapted to a new President; some found more freedom working with Richard M. Nixon than they had with Lyndon B. Johnson. *Time* noted that the coverage of Nixon was "more regular, less exciting and, for those trying to report in depth, much more difficult."

The bigger publishers grew bigger. The Los Angeles Times-Mirror Co. had record profits in 1968 and higher returns for early 1969. Expansion continued, including plans to acquire the Dallas *Times Herald* and its radio-TV affiliates in a $91,000,000 stock deal.

The New York Times also reported higher profits, acquired *Golf Digest* and Quadrangle

In the heyday of the "Post," during the 1920's, its folksy covers by Norman Rockwell were almost a trademark; its last cover, of Feb. 8, 1969, indicates the efforts it made to appeal to a younger generation.

UPI

Frank Senyk

I. W. Abel (center), United Steelworkers president, shows his union's support of a strike by the Wire Service Guild against the Associated Press, in January, one of the few strikes affecting newspapers during 1969.

Books, Inc. Its news service was expanded, and staff changes sent James Reston back to his favorite news center, Washington, D.C. The Gannett Company paid $15,500,000 for the Pensacola, Fla., newspapers, while the Knight Newspapers Inc. purchased the Macon, Ga., *Telegraph* and *News.*

Editor & Publisher noted that the typical 250,000-circulation daily had higher profits in 1968, continuing the upward trend. The National Newspaper Association reported that weeklies too were in better condition, with their net income in 1968 at 9.2 per cent compared with 7.4 per cent in 1967.

Marshall Field V followed in his father's footsteps and became publisher of the Chicago *Sun-Times* and *Daily News.* In that city *The American* was killed, replaced by the tabloid *Chicago Today.* Several new dailies were started in the suburbs. Press critics found an outlet for their views in the monthly *Chicago Journalism Review.*

In New York the *Daily News* celebrated its 50th birthday with a 288-page special edition and a salute in a Radio City Music Hall extravaganza.

Disturbed by probings of the Senate Subcommittee on Antitrust and Monopoly, publishers supported a proposed Newspaper Preservation Act. The Supreme Court ruled that joint operating arrangements, such as those in operation in Tucson, Ariz., since 1940, are in violation of the antitrust laws because of price fixing, profit pooling and market control. Publishers in more than twenty cities were affected.

This Week, a Sunday newspaper supplement founded in 1935, died in 1969. It reached its peak in 1963 when circulation passed 14,-000,000. *Parade* continued to top this field, with 14,300,000 copies in some 90 newspapers. *Family Weekly,* which appears in more than 225 smaller newspapers, has a circulation of 6,100,000. However, local newspapers now tend to develop their own Sunday supplements.

Late in October it was disclosed that Knight Newspapers, Inc., had bought the *Philadelphia Inquirer* and the *Philadelphia Daily News* from Walter H. Annenberg's Triangle Publications for a record price of about $55,000,000.

Major strikes were avoided in 1969. Other problems did arise, such as what to do about cigarette advertising. Several newspapers, including the *Boston Globe,* declined such ads. However, the majority of the papers looked forward to a greater shift of such ads from broadcasting to print.

WILLIAM H. TAFT
Professor of Journalism
University of Missouri

PUERTO RICO

On Jan. 2, Luis A. Ferre was sworn in as governor, marking the end of the 28-year rule of Luis Muñoz Marin's Popular Democratic Party. Mr. Ferre's New Progressive Party favors statehood for Puerto Rico. In his inaugural address Governor Ferre affirmed his support for statehood but he also indicated that the question should be decided in a special plebiscite rather than through general elections. He also announced his desire to build *la nueva vida* (a new life) for the thousands of Puerto Ricans who have not yet benefited from the island's recent economic development. The new Ferre Cabinet includes Puerto Rico's first woman cabinet member, Mrs. Julia Rivera de Vicenti. Mrs. Vicenti holds the post of secretary of labor.

The cultivation of sugar was once the mainstay of Puerto Rico's economy, but in recent years drought, rising costs and low productivity have taken their toll. In March the government announced an $80,000,000 modernization plan for the industry. The plan is designed to restore production to a million tons a year, raise wage levels from $.70 to $1.00 an hour, and promote extensive mechanization.

The long-neglected southwest corner of Puerto Rico has been marked for development by the Ferre government. In October a major development program for the region was announced. The program includes a new jet airport between Ponce and Mayaguez; a dam near Villalba; new highways; tourist facilities; and development of copper mining and petrochemical plants.

In March a government-sponsored report on tourism revealed connections between organized crime in the United States and the tourist-oriented gambling casinos in Puerto Rico. Tourism is one of Puerto Rico's largest sources of income—1968 tourist revenues approached $250,000,000. The major hotels on the island earn approximately a quarter of their income from the casinos. The government promised an investigation and corrective measures to protect the tourist industry.

Operation Bootstrap, Puerto Rico's industrial-promotion scheme, announced in July that the 1968–69 fiscal year set a record for new projects and jobs. The number of new jobs promised by the projects was 75 per cent higher than in 1967–68.

Puerto Rico was the scene of several anti-United States bombing incidents during 1969. It appeared that the bombings might be connected with extremists in the independence movement. In June a new political party, the Puerto Rican Union, was established to seek independence for Puerto Rico by nonviolent methods.

Economic development has received the major share of attention in Puerto Rico in recent years, but now the government has decided to devote a program to cultural aspirations. Operation Serenidad promotes, among other things, the restoration of fine historical buildings, the annual Casals Festival and the Puerto Rico Symphony Orchestra.

NORA ANN SMYTH
Associate Editor, *Lands and Peoples*

UPI

New Puerto Rican Governor Luis A. Ferre, addressing the AFL–CIO Maritime Trades Department, asks the union's support of changes in the Federal coastwise-marine-shipping laws.

RADIO

With predictions that 1968 would be commercial radio's first billion-dollar revenue year confirmed, the medium entered 1969 with renewed strength and awareness. FM broadcast continued to pace the growth with the largest increase in new stations, some 150.

Revenues continued strong throughout the year, and broadcasters centered their interest on programing. There was a conviction that post-television radio, all music or all fact-talk, had come of age and into its own.

The fact orientation was in concept simply a news and public-service orientation, with the latter involving a considerable degree of editorializing, both in essay fashion and through news documentaries. The kind of closer community ties encouraged by this was further enhanced by the many awards granted stations both from within and outside the industry.

The Columbia Broadcasting System recognized the trend late in the year with a complete reorientation of the radio service offered its network affiliates. It dropped numerous programs to concentrate instead on a news format with many short programs offering wide coverage. (A year earlier the American Broadcasting Company had in effect split into four radio services, one offering nothing but news and factual coverage.)

In music programing, dispute raged over what rock 'n' roll really is, with many all-music stations softening the "hard rock" formula to appeal to a wider-age and more-affluent audience. A few years before, much of that audience would simply have been left to TV.

As radio got more attention from the public, so it did from the experts. For a considerable fee, program specialists would study a station's audience, policy and potential and recommend change, often quite basic. Their work was sometimes abetted by technical development: a kind of electronic automation permitted a station to program a full 24 hours, with a staff available for only part of this time; this contributed to a certain sameness among stations.

U.S. Government officials, including the members of the Federal Communications Commission, looked at radio closely. In part, the scrutiny was a reflection of other activities, such as the radio aspect of the coming ban on cigarette broadcast advertising. But it also included closer examination of renewal applications—sometimes goaded by public protests. Such a case was the Miami station that, in changing hands, also changed programing from Negro-market orientation to country music.

CHARLES S. JULES
Librarian, Triangle Broadcasting

RAILROADS

At Promontory Summit, Utah, on May 10, 1969, the United States marked the 100th anniversary of its first transcontinental rail line. Federal and industry officials participating in the Golden Spike ceremony agreed that "the past is prologue," and that the railroads "are just beginning to roll" as a force in the U.S. economy.

An outstanding feature of the year's effort to put the railroad house in order for the 1970's and later was the attention given to passenger service. Obviously, long-distance travel by rail is dwindling rapidly. At the same time, rail-passenger service came into new prominence relative to mass transportation. Commutation in urban areas and comparatively short intercity routes were being expanded and improved, for example in the Northeast Corridor—Boston-New York-Washington.

Federal or state aid, once anathema to the railroad industry, now is being called into play in both phases of passenger service. New York-Washington speedliner service, Federally sponsored, was an immediate success and led to consideration of similar services between major points elsewhere in the country. Such services take their cue in part from the highly successful "bullet train" on the Tokaido line in Japan, a government-owned operation. In the United States, operations are expected to continue on a private-enterprise basis, though backed by Federal protection against losses.

Problems of railroad safety loomed large in both passenger and freight traffic. Compared with other means of transportation, the passenger-safety record remained the best. Numerous train accidents involving hazards to persons and property, however, led to creation of a new industry-wide safety division of the Association of American Railroads, to concentrate on preventive measures. The industry also worked with the Department of Transportation on legislation proposing new regulations and cooperation in transportation safety.

Derailments of passenger trains, one in high-speed territory, and repeated accidents involving hazardous materials in freight cars focused attention on the need to upgrade and maintain track in keeping with present operating conditions. Larger and heavier equipment and higher train speeds on track built for less demanding use appear as major contributing causes of rail mishaps.

In an effort to eliminate or at least reduce safety hazards ascribed to track conditions, the railroads spent almost $2,000,000,000 in 1969 to improve and maintain roadway facilities and structures. Maintenance expenditures increased

UPI

Two locomotives (one eastbound, the other westbound) met in Utah on May 10, 1869, to mark completion of the first U.S. transcontinental rail line (drawing at l). The event was reenacted on its 100th anniversary (above).

New York Public Library

Container cars (above) are transferred intact between trains, trucks and ships, saving time and money.

Bozell & Jacobs, Inc.

The hauling of deadly materials (right) cross-country is causing deep concern. New laws may result.

"The Register and Tribune," Des Moines

DO NOT REMAIN ON OR NEAR THIS CAR UNNECESSARILY

POISON GAS

PHOSGENE

Gary Settle, "The New York Times"

Government officials inspect the rusty spikes, crumbling ties and worn rails of a dangerous stretch of track, with a view to drawing up regulations for improving the safety of rail travel.

by $100,000,000 over 1968; and capital outlays for roadway and structures neared $450,000,-000 against $368,000,000 in 1968.

With labor contracts expiring at the end of 1969, the railroads were threatened by higher costs throughout the year. Management-union negotiations broke down completely late in the year, and a presidential emergency board was created to intervene in the dispute. The United Transportation Union—representing some 280,000 firemen, conductors, trainmen and switchmen—sought a 15 per cent wage increase for 1970 and 1971, a cost-of-living adjustment, and changes in holiday, vacation and overtime benefits.

A particularly thorny problem in the labor dispute springs from efforts of rail firemen to force reinstatement of firemen on diesel locomotives in freight and yard service. For the most part such jobs had been eliminated by a Federal arbitration award in 1963. Rail management calculated that restoration of such "featherbedding" jobs would cost the industry an immediate $200,000,000 a year and even larger sums in the future.

Threatened repeal of the Federal 7 per cent investment tax credit for all industry, including the railroads, brought up the possibility that carriers might limit severely their purchases of new equipment for modernization and growth.

The industry continued to advocate changes in Federal law that would permit the railroads to create streamlined transportation companies embracing all modes: rail, highway, air, water, and pipeline. To the extent that diversification is already allowed, several railroads joined in conglomerates, forming holding companies in which railroad operations are only one element.

Southern Pacific and Union Pacific, two of the largest rail companies, followed earlier examples set by Penn Central, Chicago & North Western, Illinois Central and others. Acquisition of companies far outside of transportation is designed to offset frequently marginal earnings from transport alone.

Efforts to rationalize the nation's rail system by the merger route continued. At the year's end, several major consolidation plans were already far advanced along the tortuous route of the Interstate Commerce Commission and court proceedings. These included: a union of Norfolk & Western and Chesapeake & Ohio to form a giant competitor for Penn Central in the East; the long-standing (since 1959) Great Northern-Northern Pacific-Burlington plan; the North Western-Milwaukee Road merger; and the involved Midwest squabble over control of the Rock Island.

In spite of a slowdown in some sectors of the economy, rail-freight traffic continued through most of the year at levels slightly above the record total of ton-miles set in 1968. Rate of growth in this index, as well as in piggyback loadings of trailers and containers on rail cars, was somewhat under that of 1968.

Looking to the future, the railroads embarked in 1969 on an expanded and accelerated research program. In addition to continued work on the physical aspects of railroad plant, the new program will delve deeply into problems of operations, economics and marketing of rail transportation. One tool for such research will be the newly authorized computer "model" railroad to simulate the workings of an entire railroad operating network.

FRED B. STAUFFER
Specialist on Transportation

Soul City

Rock, particularly rock groups, dominated popular music in 1969. With their recordings of "The Age of Aquarius" and "Wedding Bell Blues," The 5th Dimension remained a favorite group throughout the year.

RECORDINGS

The major events and developments in recordings in 1969 were technical or commercial rather than musical. The principal technical advance was the introduction of four-channel stereo, first demonstrated by Acoustic Research (an equipment manufacturer) and Vanguard Records.

Variously called "Surround Stereo," "Quadriphonic Stereo" or "Quadrasonic Stereo," the four-channel system requires four separate recorded signals, each of which must go through its own separate amplification chain and emerge from its own separate speaker. As demonstrated at the Los Angeles High Fidelity Music Show in October by Acoustic Research, Telex and H. H. Scott, the system worked best with tapes of Boston Pops Orchestra performances engineered to reproduce the acoustics of Boston's Symphony Hall in the listening room. It provided considerably more depth than is possible with conventional two-channel stereo. Experimental tapes of popular music, in which different instruments were channeled to each of the four speakers, gave listeners the impression that they were sitting in the middle of the band, which many found unnatural and somewhat disquieting.

By the end of the year several manufacturers were marketing tape decks that would play four-channel tapes, and H. H. Scott had introduced the first integrated four-channel amplifier. Vanguard announced the release of its first four-channel recordings on reel-to-reel tape, including the Berlioz *Requiem* and Mahler's Ninth Symphony.

Recording four-channels on tape is comparatively simple, but pressing them into a disc presents numerous problems. However, several companies were at work on solving them, and the Audiodata Company of Rochester, N.Y., gave an impressive demonstration of a four-channel-stereo disc, but did not reveal when it might be available to the public.

Aside from the new four-channel tapes, interest in prerecorded tapes in the traditional reel-to-reel format dwindled in 1969, but sales of prerecorded tape cartridges climbed dramatically. It was impossible to prophesy which of the three types of cartridge would ultimately prevail—the four-track or eight-track cartridge or the cassette—but the future looked brightest for the cassette. RCA, which had formerly backed the eight-track cartridge, began manufacturing prerecorded cassettes, and the musical repertoire available on cassettes expanded in all directions. London Records even issued a complete opera on two cassettes: *La Traviata* with Pilar Lorengar, Giacomo Aragall and Dietrich Fischer-Dieskau. Discs outsold prerecorded tapes by a wide margin, but sales of tape cartridges reached an estimated $500,000,000 during 1969, more than twice the total for 1968.

Rock continued to dominate popular music. One new rock group after another appeared, but few of the new groups managed to stay together long enough to record more than one album. Few of the old groups besides the Beatles, Jefferson Airplane, and the Rolling Stones seemed stable.

Artistically and commercially 1969 was a poor year for classical recordings. Record companies complained that sales were down and costs were up. The higher fees demanded by American orchestras made it difficult for companies to fulfill their contractual obligations to the orchestras, and there were some surprising shifts in affiliations. The Philadelphia Orchestra left Columbia Records and went to RCA, which dropped the Boston Symphony and the Chicago Symphony. Curiously, European companies seemed to think it was economically feasible for them to record American orchestras. Deutsche Grammophone Gesellschaft, of Hamburg, Germany, contracted the Boston Symphony, and two British companies agreed to share the Chicago Symphony.

There was greater interest in classical music on budget-priced records. Such records sold well and offered a wide variety of new stereo recordings and mono reissues of older items long out of the catalogue. Angel led in the mono reissues by bringing out on its Seraphim label ($2.49) a number of its Great Recordings of the Century, formerly available at premium prices. These reissues included performances by such artists of the past as Alfred Cortot, Artur Schnabel, Wanda Landowska, Aksel Schiotz, Fritz Kreisler, Elisabeth Schumann and Lotte Lehmann. On its Victrola label ($2.98), RCA reissued recitals by Lily Pons, Ezio Pinza, Richard Crooks, Ernestine Schumann-Heink and others, and such complete operas as *Manon Lescaut* with Licia Albanese and Jussi Bjoerling, and *Aïda* with Bjoerling and Zinka Milanov. DGG made similar reissues on Heliodor ($2.98), as did Columbia on Odyssey ($2.98).

Since the United States still has not extended copyright protection to sound recordings, piracy continued to plague record companies. The pirates' favorite booty consisted of best-selling popular recordings, such as Broadway shows and Beatles albums. Some were issued in unauthorized tape cartridges manufactured in the United States, and others were pirated on discs or tapes manufactured in Southeast Asia, Europe or the United States.

The high quality of small portable tape recorders has led to a new kind of pirating of live performances. A pirate takes a recorder to a concert or to the opera, makes a tape of the performance, and then issues it on discs without paying royalties to the performers. Among such pirated performances issued in 1969 were Donizetti's *Anna Bolena* with Maria Callas; Montserrat Caballe's recital in Philharmonic Hall; and Beverly Sills' debut at La Scala (Milan) in Rossini's *The Siege of Corinth*.

WILLIAM LIVINGSTONE
Managing Editor, *Stereo Review*

"Age of the Great Instrumentalists Six Concertos" was a popular reissue on Angel's new Seraphim label.

The W. C. Fields recording based on his films was a big seller, especially with teen-agers and young adults.

Seraphim

Decca

SOME MAJOR RECORDINGS OF 1969

Classical

Barber, *Knoxville: Summer of 1915*, Price (RCA)
Beethoven, *Symphony No. 6*, Leinsdorf (RCA)
Berlioz, *Harold in Italy*, Trampler/Prêtre (RCA)
Berlioz, *Roméo et Juliette*, Davis (Philips)
Berlioz, *Symphonie Fantastique*, Bernstein (Columbia)
Billings, *The Continental Harmony*, Smith (Columbia)
Britten, *Billy Budd*, Glossop/Pears (London)
Catalani, *La Wally*, Tebaldi (London)
Chausson, *Poème for Violin and Orchestra*, Grumiaux (Philips)
Chopin, *Twenty-four Études*, Anievas (Seraphim)
Copland, *Short Symphony, Dance Symphony*, Copland (Columbia)
Delibes, *Lakmé*, Sutherland (London)
Gilbert and Sullivan, *The Pirates of Penzance*, Godfrey (London)
Glinka, *Jota Aragonesa and others*, Svetlanov (Melodiya/Angel)
Handel, *Italian Cantatas*, Baker (Angel)
Handel, *Theodora*, Somary (Vanguard Cardinal)
Handel, *Twelve Concerti Grossi*, Marriner (London)
Haydn, *The "London" Symphonies*, Jones (Nonesuch)
Haydn, *Symphonies No. 88 and No. 102*, Bernstein (Columbia)
Hindemith, *Die Sieben Kammermusiken*, Concerto Amsterdam (Telefunken)
Mahler, *Symphony No. 4*, Kubelik (DGG)
Mascagni, *L'Amico Fritz*, Pavarotti/Freni (Angel)
Mendelssohn, *Symphony No. 3 "Scotch" and Symphony No. 4 "Italian"*, Abbado (London)
Mozart, *Le nozze di Figaro*, Böhm (DGG)
Mozart, *Requiem*, Richter (Telefunken)
Mozart, *Symphony No. 40, Serenade No. 6*, Britten (London)
Prokofiev, *Symphony No. 5*, Von Karajan (DGG)
Rachmaninoff, *Piano Concerto No. 3*, Weissenberg (RCA)
Ravel, *Gaspard de la nuit and others*, Browning (RCA)
Saint-Saëns, *Piano Concerto No. 2;* Schumann, *Carnaval*, Sokolov (Melodiya/Angel)
Schubert, *Der Hirt auf dem Felsen and other songs*, Ameling/Demus (RCA Victrola)
Strauss, *Salome*, Caballe (RCA)
Szymanowski, *Violin Concerto No. 1;* Wieniawski, *Violin Concerto No. 2*, Wilkomirska (Heliodor)
Tchaikovsky, *1812 Overture;* Rachmaninoff, *Spring Cantata*, Buketoff (RCA)
Vaughan Williams, *Symphony No. 1*, Boult (Angel)
Vaughan Williams, *Symphony No. 4, Serenade to Music*, Bernstein (Columbia)
Wagner, *Siegfried*, Von Karajan (DGG)
Wolf, *Italian Song Book*, Schwarzkopf/Fischer-Dieskau (Angel)

Classical Collections

Montserrat Caballe/Bernarbe Marti, *Zarzuela Love Duets* (RCA)
Placido Domingo, *Romantic Arias* (RCA)
Nelson Freire, *Piano Concertos* (Columbia)
Igor Kipnis, *Mozart and Haydn on the Harpsichord* (Columbia)
Christa Ludwig/Walter Berry/Gerald Moore, *A Most Unusual Song Recital* (Seraphim)
Orchestre de Paris, *Favorite French Showpieces* (Angel)
Christopher Parkening, *In the Classic Style* (Angel)
Luciano Pavarotti, *Verdi and Donizetti Arias* (London)

Beverly Sills, *Bellini and Donizetti Heroines* (Westminster)
Fritz Wunderlich, *Opera Arias* (Seraphim)

Popular

Joan Baez, *Any Day Now* (Vanguard)
Beatles, *The Beatles* (Apple)
Blood, Sweat and Tears, *Second Album* (Columbia)
James Brown, *James Brown Sings Out of Sight* (Smash)
Maxine Brown, *Sugar Cane County* (Chart)
Julie Budd, *Wild and Wonderful* (MGM)
Petula Clark, *Portrait of Petula* (Warner Bros.)
Cream, *Best of the Cream* (ATCO)
Julie Driscoll/Brian Auger/The Trinity, *Streetnoise* (ATCO)
Bob Dylan, *Nashville Skyline* (Columbia)
Don Ellis, *Autumn* (Columbia)
Jose Feliciano, *Feliciano/10 to 23* (RCA)
The 5th Dimension, *The Age of Aquarius* (Soul City)
Bobbie Gentry and Glen Campbell, *Bobbie Gentry and Glen Campbell* (Capitol)
Joel Grey, *Black Sheep Boy* (Columbia)
Isaac Hayes, *Hot Buttered Soul* (Enterprise)
Incredible String Band, *Wee Tam; The Big Huge* (Elektra)
Ketty Lester, *Ketty Lester* (Pete)
Sergio Mendes/Brasil '66, *Fool on the Hill* (A&M)
Joni Mitchell, *Clouds* (Reprise)
Mothers of Invention, *Uncle Meat* (Bizarre)
New York Rock and Roll Ensemble, *The New York Rock and Roll Ensemble* (ATCO)
Phyllis Newman, *Those Were the Days* (Sire)
Nilsson, *Harry* (RCA)
Pentangle, *The Pentangle* (Reprise)
Rolling Stones, *Beggars Banquet* (London)
Peggy Seeger, *Anthology of London Songs* (ARGO)
Dinah Shore, *Country Feelin'* (Decca)
Barbra Streisand, *What about Today?* (Columbia)
Sweetwater, *Sweetwater* (Reprise)
Joanne Vent, *The Black and White of It Is Blues* (A&M)

Jazz

Gary Burton Quartet, *Country Roads and Other Places* (RCA)
Miles Davis, *Filles de Kilimanjaro* (Columbia)
Roland Kirk, *Left and Right* (Atlantic)
Carmen McRae, *The Sound of Silence* (Atlantic)
Jimmy Rushing All Stars, *Gee, Baby, Ain't I Good to You* (Master Jazz Recordings)
Nina Simone, *To Love Somebody* (RCA)
Martial Solal Trio, *On Home Ground* (Milestone)

Theater, Films, TV, Spoken

Woody Allen, *The Third Woody Allen Album* (Capitol)
Mart Crowley, *The Boys in the Band* (A&M)
Dames at Sea, Original Cast (Columbia)
W. C. Fields, *Original Voice Tracks from His Greatest Movies* (Decca)
Richard Kiley/Julie Harris, *The Greek Myths* (Spoken Arts)
James Jones, *James Jones Reads James Jones* (CMS)
Laugh-In '69, Original Cast (Reprise)
Man of La Mancha, London Cast (Decca)
Midnight Cowboy, Original Soundtrack (United Artists)
Max Morath, *At the Turn of the Century* (RCA)
Paul Scofield, *Murder in the Cathedral* (Caedmon)
Howard Sackler, *The Great White Hope* (Tetragrammaton)

UPI

Pope Paul VI speaks to the Synod of Bishops, beneath Michelangelo's "Last Judgment" in the Sistine Chapel.

RELIGION

Two questions dominated the religious issue in 1969: authority and race.

Catholic, Orthodox, Protestant, Jewish, Muslim and Eastern faiths were faced with the turmoil attendant on reconciling past tradition with a revolutionary world. The persistence of revolutionary rhetoric, campus demonstrations, and the emergence of a moon age together with a new humanism, which sets no limits on man's capabilities, further strained the ties with traditional religion. Other trends grew during the year: concern for the have-nots,

calls for more honesty and straightforwardness in the church, and a youth culture with radical new styles.

The "floating parish," which can even meet in a park, holds a discussion during Mass and is an example of the trend toward relevance and honesty. Five new schools to train married deacons to assume many of the functions of the priesthood (except for hearing confessions and saying Mass) were started in the United States.

In Holland, Bishop Martinus Jansen had his 76-year-old Rotterdam Cathedral torn down because it was "ugly," in need of repairs and expensive to maintain. He redistributed $1,400,000 to three new parishes and remodeled a convent chapel for the former cathedral parishioners.

The Issue of Authority. For Roman Catholics, the issue came to a head at the second Synod of Bishops in Rome. Stirring the debate was Leon-Joseph Cardinal Suenens, primate of Belgium. He argued that the national hierarchies should be consulted before a pope issues encyclicals and other documents. He also suggested that eventually popes should be elected through the hierarchies rather than by the Italian-based college of cardinals.

The Synod of Bishops succeeded in moving along "collegiality," the concept of shared authority. Pope Paul adopted the bishops' proposal that the Synod meet at least every two years. But he said in opening and closing Synod speeches that there could be no challenge to his authority. However, he promised "maximum" consideration of nearly a dozen other proposals suggested by the bishops; among them, that the pope consult with the bishops of the world before he makes crucial decisions.

Delegates to the National Federation of Priest Councils, meeting in New Orleans, were told that 3,000 priests had left the active ministry during 1968, and that twice as many were prepared to leave in 1969. The Most Rev. James Shannon, auxiliary bishop of St. Paul-Minneapolis and the most popular American bishop, resigned from his see. Shannon, who later married, said he could not reconcile his conscience with the papal encyclical of a year earlier, *Humanae Vitae,* which continued a rigid ban on artificial birth control. Other defecting clergymen included a South American bishop, a monsignor in the papal household in Rome, a former Illinois diocesan-chancery official, and a leading Jesuit.

In Rosario, Argentina, more than 200 priests resigned because of a disagreement with their Archbishop, Guillermo Bolatti. The priests accused the Archbishop of being indifferent to the poor. In Spain, some priests were arrested as the result of involvement in separatist, anti-Franco movements in Catalonia and the Basque provinces.

Unrest in the Jewish community was also evident. In a study, for the first time a U.S. rabbinical body, the Central Conference of American Rabbis, raised such questions as: "Can you envisage a rabbinate unrelated to the synagogue?" and "Could you envisage a team rabbinate which would provide for greater specialization?" CCAR President Rabbi Levi Olan of Dallas said that its complaint committee was one of the busiest, and that the loss of 8 to 10 rabbis a year from its membership of 1,000 was one reason for the study.

According to Rabbi Martin Freedman, of Paterson, N.J., the chairman of CCAR's commission on justice and peace, "The synagogue is undergoing the same pressure as the church and will change in 30 years. The congregation as an extension of the family is dying or is dead." Changing patterns and youth unrest were prime sources of discussion at the general assembly of the Union of American Hebrew Organization Congregations meeting in Miami in late October.

The Issue of Race. Regarding race relations, the Black Economic Development Conference (BEDC), launched in Detroit in April, issued a "black manifesto." The document criticized capitalism, favored social reforms and warned of violence. James Forman, the first BEDC spokesman, taking the Riverside Church in New York City by surprise at a Sunday morning service, asked for reparation for past injuries to blacks. From all churches and synagogues he first requested $500,000,000, and then $3,000,000,000.

Although some of the BEDC demands (which included a Southern land bank, black publishing firms and audio-visual networks and a black university) were accepted as valid across the United States, churchmen generally hesitated to give any funds directly. However, before the year ended, the Episcopalians agreed to grant $200,000 to the National Committee of Black Churchmen (NCBC). And the National Council of Churches, at its general board meeting in Indianapolis in September, asked its member denominations to help raise $500,000 for the NCBC and the predominantly black Interreligious Foundation for Community Organization. In so doing, it was understood that the money would help underwrite five NCBC regional conferences and also BEDC projects.

Ecumenical Developments. The Consultation on Church Union moved ahead with its plan to

Pictorial Parade

Seeking financial reparations for injustice to blacks, James Forman "campaigns" in a church in New York.

unite nine denominations to form a single church with 25,000,000 members. The plan will be presented for discussion to representatives of the denominations meeting in St. Louis in 1970. In Atlanta, at the 1969 meeting of the seven-year-old Consultation, a new structure was proposed for the merged church. It would be organized into multicongregational parishes.

In England a proposed reunification of Methodists and Anglicans failed by a narrow margin. In the United States, the Presbyterians U.S. (Southern) and the Reformed Church of

Religious News Service

An ecumenical doxology is celebrated by (l to r) Carpatho-Russian Orthodox Bishop Martin, Catholic Archbishop Cooke and Greek Orthodox Archbishop Iakovos.

America failed to ratify their merger attempt, but merger talks were reopened between the U.S. (Southern) Presbyterians and the United Presbyterians. The proposed Church of Christ in New Zealand revealed a plan to unite New Zealand's Anglicans, Congregationalists, Churches of Christ, Methodists and Presbyterians. In Japan, 100 individuals, led by the Rev. Joseph Spae of the Immaculate Heart Fathers and Ryuzo Hara of the United Church, formed the Japan Ecumenical Association.

In Geneva, in June, Pope Paul VI visited the headquarters of the World Council of Churches. WCC President Eugene C. Blake told him, "You remind the whole world of the rapidly developing joint efforts of the Roman Catholic Church and the World Council of Churches in the interest of justice and peace." Closer Roman Catholic and Protestant ties were seen

in the United States as the Texas Catholic Conference and the Texas Council of Churches merged as the Texas Conference of Churches. A sixth Roman Catholic, the Rev. Richard Rousseau, was added to the executive staff of the National Council of Churches; and the Rev. David Bowman, S.J., became special deputy to NCC General Secretary R. H. Edwin Espy.

Eastern Orthodox Christians felt continued pressure to put aside ethnic differences and unite into one Orthodox church in America. The Standing Conference of the Canonical Orthodox Bishops in the Americas recognized the "obvious urgency for a Pan-Orthodox discussion of the jurisdictional situation in America" and authorized a commission to bring the matter before the world Pan-Orthodox conference.

Moon Landing and Church-State Relations. The landing on the moon in July had many religious implications, particularly in the field of theology. According to Leslie Dewart of St. Michael's College (University of Toronto): "A deed with the magnitude of the moon landing certainly forces man to consider himself and his relationship to all reality." In August, Mrs. Madalyn Murray O'Hair, an atheist, asked a Federal court to forbid Bible reading and other religious practices by U.S. spacemen. The Apollo 11 astronauts had left religious objects, including a plaque in Latin from Pope Paul, on the moon. Col. Edwin Aldrin, Jr., a Presbyterian, had read Bible passages and celebrated Communion privately on the moon.

There were increasing demands for the Federal Government to levy taxes on church-owned business projects. The NCC and the U.S. Catholic Conference, in a joint statement to the House Ways and Means Committee, recommended that churches pay taxes on unrelated business incomes. In a separate state-

Religious News Service

During a New York crusade, at Madison Square Garden, evangelist Billy Graham (r) welcomes those coming forward to make personal "decisions for Christ."

ment, the NCC said further that employees or leaders of churches should not enjoy any special tax benefits, and that churches should pay a "just share" of the cost for municipal services. The movement to add a school-prayer amendment to the U.S. Constitution continued, though less strongly. Seventy-four congressmen held a caucus supporting the legalization of school prayer.

Evangelist Billy Graham, during a ten-day period in 1969, preached to 200,000 people in New York City's Madison Square Garden. He also was among the clergymen who conducted private Sunday services in the White House. Others included Rabbi Louis Finkelstein of New York and Terence Cardinal Cooke, archbishop of New York. Theologian Reinhold Niebuhr criticized the White House services as a violation of the provision in the Bill of Rights separating church and state.

Other Developments. On Mar. 29, Pope Paul named 35 new cardinals, bringing the college of cardinals to a record high of 136. Of the 33 announced nominees (2 were kept secret), 8 were Italians and 4 were Americans. The Pope also appointed Jean Cardinal Villot of France as the Vatican's secretary of state.

In Germany, attention centered on Auxiliary Bishop Matthias Defregger of Munich. In a magazine article it was revealed that the former German Army captain had been connected with the execution of 17 Italian villagers in 1944.

In Moscow a 13-day summit meeting of world communist leaders recommended cooperation between Communists and Christians, particularly Roman Catholics. "The Catholic Church and some other religious organizations are experiencing an ideological crisis which is shattering their age-long concepts and existing structures. . . . The mass of the religious people can become an active force in the anti-imperialist struggle and in carrying out far-reaching social changes," the leaders said. Despite the pronouncement, two Orthodox churchmen, daring to criticize the lack of full religious liberty in the Soviet Union, were arrested by Soviet authorities.

To help the American Jew better understand himself and his role in the community, the American Jewish Committee published *Not Quite at Home: How an American Community Lives with Itself and Its Neighbors*. In April the National Jewish Community Relations Advisory Council released its second report in 15 years on anti-Semitism. The report stated: "Notwithstanding some acute manifestations of overt anti-Semitism, including the appearance of such manifestations among some Negroes

UPI

President and Mrs. Nixon stand with Rabbi Louis Finkelstein after a private service in the White House.

and intellectuals within the New Left, overt anti-Semitism continues at low ebb, as it has been for a number of years."

Meeting in Minneapolis, the U.S. Congress on Evangelism brought together 4,600 evangelists from 93 denominations. A growing concern about social issues was evident during the conference.

In Kuala Lumpur, Malaysia, Muslim scholars from 23 nations convened to seek ways to update their faith. The conference sessions dealt with such modern themes as human organ transplants, which were found to be consistent with the Islamic doctrine of preserving life. In addition, the conference initiated talks between the Shiite and Sunnite Muslim groups, and refused to sanction a holy war against Israel as called for by Arab Al Fatah guerrillas.

HILEY H. WARD
Religion Writer, *Detroit Free Press*

RHODE ISLAND

On June 28 the 2.1-mile Newport Bridge opened. A suspension bridge, with its roadway 200 feet above the water, it is the largest span in New England. □ For some five weeks during June and July, Newport Beach was fouled by an invasion of millions of clams borne in on the tide, possibly from an overcrowded ocean bed. □ By a new law, Rhode Island will hold its presidential primaries on the first Tuesday in March. Thus it joined New Hampshire in leading off presidential primaries.

RUMANIA

Wary of the Russians, insistent on maintaining their independent course, the Rumanians defied Moscow in word if not in deed. To Rumania, Moscow's worst doctrine was "limited sovereignty." Concocted by Soviet theorists to justify the invasion of Czechoslovakia in 1968, the terms of the formula were phrased in such a way as to allow the U.S.S.R., acting alone, to intervene in the affairs of any nation that dropped out of the Eastern Europe communist bloc. Rumanian party chief Nicolae Ceausescu spoke out on the issue shortly after his meeting with Yugoslavia's Marshal Tito in February. "Attempts to justify mistakes," Ceausescu declared, "as well as the emergence of some new theses like that of limited sovereignty, are damaging Communist unity."

Resistance to Russian interference was also evident in the Rumanian refusal to implement Moscow's desire to merge the national economies of Eastern Europe under a Soviet master plan. Though Eastern Europe's economic group, COMECON, had been devised to assign the "socialist division of labor" within the bloc according to Moscow dictates, Rumania had refused since 1964 to accept the place assigned it. Ceausescu saw in Russia's new emphasis on limited sovereignty a new effort to impose economic vassalage on Rumania. To combat this, the Rumanian party leader called for an "open" COMECON: one that other communist and noncommunist countries could join. This was hardly what Moscow intended.

In Moscow, in late spring, at the long-delayed World Conference of Communist and Workers' Parties, Ceausescu refused to ally himself with either side in the Sino-Soviet struggle. And Rumania expressed oral discontent with the final communiqué, which balanced support for noninterference in the affairs of individual parties with declarations that each party had a duty to the unity of communism.

At their own party congress, in the summer, the Rumanians affirmed Rumania's independent line; Moscow showed its displeasure by sending a low-level representative. Ceausescu not only reiterated his stand that relations among communist parties must be based on "national independence and sovereignty, equal rights, noninterference in internal affairs," but also denounced his predecessor, Gheorghe Gheorghiu-Dej, for the purges during the Stalinist era.

There is no doubt that Ceausescu is solidly in command of the Rumanian party. He is popular with the rank and file, and during the year he removed old-line party leaders and replaced them with men who are absolutely loyal

RUMANIA

Area: 91,675 sq. mi.
Population: 20,000,000
Capital: Bucharest (pop., 1,420,000)
Government: Nicolae Ceausescu, chief of state —1967, Communist Party secretary—1965; Ion Maurer, chairman, council of ministers—1961
Gross national product: $18,100,000,000
Monetary unit: lei (9.4 lei = U.S. $1.00)
Chief products: oil, timber, wine, fruit, coal, steel, methane gas
Foreign trade: exports, $1,469,000,000; imports, $1,609,000,000
Communications: 550,000 telephones, 3,020,000 radios, 580,000 TV sets, 33 daily newspapers
Transportation: roads, 7,270 mi.; railroads, 6,415 mi.
Education: 3,268,707 elementary and secondary students, 5 universities
Armed forces: 193,000

See map on page 185

to him. Almost no one from the Stalinist days of Gheorghiu-Dej now retains a top post within the party hierarchy. Ceausescu can take this attitude toward Russia in part because there is little liberalization in internal Rumanian affairs. All facets of production and the news media are tightly controlled by the party.

JAMES CHACE
Managing Editor, *Foreign Affairs*

SCOTT, HUGH DOGGETT

In what was considered a victory for the liberal or moderate wing of the Republican Party, Hugh Scott, Pennsylvania's senior senator, was elected (Sept. 24) Senate minority leader, succeeding the late Sen. Everett McKinley Dirksen. By a vote of 24–19, Scott defeated Dirksen's son-in-law, Howard H. Baker, Jr., a conservative-backed senator from Tennessee. Only nine months earlier Scott had been chosen over Nebraska Sen. Roman Hruska as minority whip, the number two party post in the Senate.

Scott had been his party's national chairman (1948–49), and in 1952 he was very active in the Eisenhower presidential campaign. Prior to entering the Senate in January 1959, Scott had served eight terms in the U.S. House of Representatives. Up for reelection to the Senate in 1964, Scott was one of the few Pennsylvania Republicans to survive the Johnson landslide.

Born in Fredericksburg, Va., on Nov. 11, 1900, Hugh Doggett Scott received his bachelor's degree from Randolph-Macon College in Ashland, Va. After obtaining a law degree from the University of Virginia in 1922, the future legislator practiced law in Philadelphia.

SCULPTURE

While nothing vastly new was added to the world of sculpture in 1969, certain tendencies and directions became more distinct. Especially explicit, though it has been developing over many years, was the substantial fragmentation of the very idea of what constitutes sculpture.

The vast middle ground of sculpture in the gallery-museum-critic complex of approval could be seen in the Whitney Museum's sculpture biennial which opened in mid-December 1968. The middle ground runs the gamut, from the figurative work of Baskin, Gallo, Segal to the direct metal works of Roszak and Lipton, to the suspensions of Snelson—which are Buckminster Fuller engineering feats. It includes 71-year-old Calder and 23-year-old Gary Wojcik; and it ends either hard or soft: hard, the minimalists Judd and Morris; and soft, Claes Oldenburg. All they have in common is that they are object-oriented.

The middle ground, enormous in its variety, is being attacked from two directions. At the rear are the figurative sculptors who are the natural descendants of the Academy (especially Beaux-Arts), the idealists and the realists. Their position might more properly be defined as entrenchment, for they do not deign to attack but rest on their solidly felt, time-honored values of craftsmanship, literary content, and metaphorical power. Their work is not seen primarily in galleries but is closer to the people as distinct from connoisseurs. It appears as monumental-decorative sculpture commissioned for governments and big business by architects of similar persuasion. More-intimate works can be seen in group shows, the most prestigious of which are mounted by the National Academy of Design and the National Sculpture Society, both in New York City. Prizes in 1969 were presented to Edward Fenno Hoffman, III, Bashka Paeff, Kristin Lothrop, Charlotte Dunwiddie, Karl Gruppe, Jose de Creeft, Frances Lamont, Cleo Hartwig and Richard Frazier.

The American Academy of Achievement in Dallas chooses the sculptor of the year from among this group. In June 1969, Michael Lantz was selected. He also won the Saltus award of the American Numismatic Society, the top honor given to medalists.

The entire area of bas-relief sculpture for art medals is dominated by the great technical skill of these figurative artists. Ralph Menconi, chosen to create President Nixon's official inaugural medal, also designed the medal commemorating the Apollo 11 landing on the moon. Abram Belski did the official SCLC medal of Dr. Martin Luther King, Jr. The newest of the Hall of Fame series of medals

The Solomon R. Guggenheim Museum, New York City

In Brancusi's "The Beginning of the World" (marble, steel and stone), "thought and form are inseparable."

honors Washington Irving and was sculptured by Adolph Block.

In the memorial category, Donald de Lue. won the sculpture competition for the design and erection of a monument to the Louisiana Confederate Soldier at the battlefield at Gettysburg, Penn. Henry Van Wolf's 11-foot sculpture of an Indian in gilded bronze dominates a mall in Van Nuys, Calif. Una Hanbury's metaphorical *Spirit of Male Compassion* adorns a park in Arlington County, Va.

Advance-guard action on the middle-ground establishment emanates from a group of artists who produce what is variously called Impossible Art, Earth Art, or Concept Art. Two

Realistic, perceptive portraiture is achieved in Richard Frazier's prizewinning bust "Stephen Galatti."

An idealistic torso by Cleo Hartwig; light reflected from the lustrous ebony wood accents the exquisite modeling. The sculpture won two prizes in 1969.

Soichi Sunami, photographer

National Sculpture Society

exhibitions epitomize this group. The first, sponsored by the Philip Morris Company of Europe, was organized in Bern, Switzerland, by Harald Szeemann, director of the Künsthalle, and has toured the Continent and Great Britain. The second was the "Anti-Illusion" exhibition at the Whitney Museum in New York. Non-object-oriented, these artists look upon art as instrument, concept, intention, not as a possessable thing. One example is Les Levine's show in which he used two yellow sodium-vapor lights which drain color from anything they illuminate. The spectator becomes participant, and the result looks very much like a black-and-white photograph. The "object," here the sodium light, is of no direct importance; it is the uncontrollable environment that brings the event into congruence with anti-form art.

When the Establishment decried the "literary" idea, it demolished words and asked that attention be centered in the object. Consequently the new group presents (to quote Norbert Lynton) "creative action rather than objects." Dennis Oppenheim's snow projects shown in January are an example. They exist only in documentation, that is, in photographs, map details and models. His projects are shown as changes in the snow's surface, resulting from snowmobile, shovel and foot; and his relocations of landmasses are recorded with pseudo-scientific exactness.

Within the Establishment, the late David Smith's retrospective at the Guggenheim and assorted galleries around New York was the key event of 1969. There was no reevaluation of his work, but the thunder of lagging critics jumping on the bandwagon completed Smith's apotheosis. The open linear pictorial works did take on a classical elegance warranting the praise.

Rudolph Burckhardt, photographer

The precision and balance of Roy Lichtenstein's "Modern Sculpture with Loop" (brass, marble) hold the eye.

Fashioned out of steel and nickel-silver, Theodore Roszak's "Thorn Blossom" conveys the idea of thorniness by both its overall shape and its rough surface texture.

Geoffrey Clements, photographer; Whitney Museum

More than a hundred sculptures by Claes Oldenburg were seen in a major show at New York's Museum of Modern Art from September through November. Oldenburg's soft sculptures—the typewriter, the light switch and so on—are familiar by now. What was new was his dramatization of scale. "Giant" objects and a section devoted to scale models for colossal monuments—the enormous lipstick for Yale, to illustrate—brought a further horror to his celebrations of the commonplace.

The Jewish Museum's exhibition "Inflatable Sculpture" invited punning disparagement; and the "Machine" show at the Modern Museum was elaborately installed but somewhat beside the point. The Metropolitan Museum's first exhibition of its centennial year, "New York Painting & Sculpture, 1940–1970," left out as many important sculptors as it included, but Mark di Suvero, Tony Smith and John Chamberlain were nicely represented.

Work of the Establishment's grand old master Brancusi was seen, in a fine traveling exhibition, at the Philadelphia Museum of Art and later at the Guggenheim. The purity of Brancusi's later sculpture, its suppression of all but the most essential detail, its Platonic idealism make it seem totally abstract. But Brancusi is not an abstract artist. As Sidney Geist, the exhibition's organizer, observes in his text for the catalogue of the exhibition: "The characteristic unity of a sculpture by Brancusi is not that of its formalist reputation, but rather a poetic unity in which thought and form are inseparable. . . . Refined, rigorous and esthetical as Brancusi's art may be, he is attentive to a large world which he engages with humor and his own rare sweetness."

CLAIRE A. STEIN
Executive Secretary
National Sculpture Society

SHIPS AND SHIPPING

President Richard Nixon's long-awaited message to Congress to secure appropriations for rebuilding the American merchant marine received favorable response among legislators and in some quarters of the steamship and shipbuilding industries. In essence, the President proposed a long-range ten-year building program, costing upward of $3,800,000,000 in subsidies.

The White House proposal suggested the construction of about 30 ships a year for fiscal 1972, beginning July 1, 1971, compared with 27 ships for fiscal 1971, which begins July 1, 1970, and 20 ships in the fiscal year ending June 30, 1970.

Construction and operating subsidies will be distributed alike to all American-flag ship operators. It is interesting to note that the Washington administration projected decreasing subsidies for ships' operating and building costs, which were roughly estimated at $200,000,000 annually for the operating differential and a projected construction subsidy of about $200,000,000. The operating subsidy on new ships would be based only on insurance and higher wage costs for American seamen.

The shipbuilders' construction differential would be trimmed in the White House formula from 55 per cent to 45 per cent. Mr. Nixon observed that costs of American-built ships are about twice those of foreign yards, but he ignored the prime reason for the cost differential: that wages abroad are about 45 per cent of those paid to U.S. labor. This accounts for the 55 per cent differential paid so far for building in the United States.

Warning shipbuilders that they must reduce construction costs, President Nixon suggested that if this challenge were not met the administration's commitment to a shipbuilding program would not be continued.

Strike Threat Raised. At the end of a lengthy strike of longshoremen on the Atlantic and Gulf coasts of the United States early in 1969, it seemed reasonably sure that a period of three years' peace had been assured in waterfront employment. Regrettably, toward the end of the year another labor halt loomed as T. W. (Teddy) Gleason, president of the International Longshoremen's Association, embraced the socialistic approach of urging direct worker sharing in the profits from containerization of ocean-freight shipments. Mr. Gleason raised the issue that freight consolidators and forwarders had found ways to circumvent clauses in an agreement on freight containers. He saw a strike as inevitable.

Advent of Lash Ship. The newest innovation in ocean shipping, a Lash-type vessel, was placed in service during the fall of 1969 between U.S. Gulf ports and Europe. Approximately 12 Lash vessels, together costing between $250,000,000 and $300,000,000, were being built principally for American owners. The Lash plans and design were drawn up in the United States, but Japan is credited with building the first of the new craft for a Norwegian owner, with responsibility entrusted to an American steamship operator.

The name "Lash" is derived from Lighter Aboard Ship. The MS *Acadia Forest,* world's first Lash ship, has a carrying capacity of 27,000 long tons, contained in 73 barges. A 510-ton lift-capacity crane is located amidship of the vessel for loading barges.

Lykes Steamship Co. of New Orleans, with more than a half century of operation behind it, pioneered in the design of the Lash-type freighter. It has been estimated that three of Lykes' new ocean leviathans, designated *Seabees,* will have an annual cargo capacity equal to that of 12 or more conventional freighters built during the 1940's. Construction of the *Seabees* was under way at Quincy, Mass., at a cost of $135,000,000. The new tonnage was expected to enter service during late 1971 and early 1972.

Instead of being subsidized by the Government, United States Lines' containerships may soon be chartered.

United States Lines Co.

AMERICAN LANCER

Pictorial Parade

The supertanker "Manhattan," equipped as an ice-breaker, crunches through the Northwest Passage (map at r) in pioneer attempt to open the far northern route to commercial oil shipping.

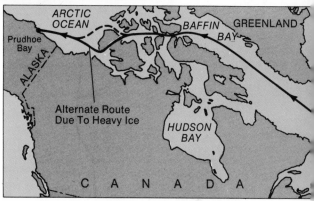

ARCTIC OCEAN — BAFFIN BAY — GREENLAND — Prudhoe Bay — ALASKA — Alternate Route Due To Heavy Ice — HUDSON BAY — C A N A D A

Containerization. Containerization in ocean shipping offered much hope at the beginning of 1969. It has worked well insofar as foreign-flag lines are concerned, but some American-flag owners apparently were having difficulties. At this point it should be mentioned that owners abroad resorted to pooling capital—or entering into consortiums—in order to meet the challenge of ship replacements and operations.

In the United States it would be difficult to accomplish these goals so quickly and successfully. Subsidies, governmental control and the like do not permit business operations to function normally.

The United States Lines Co., a subsidiary of W. A. Kidde Co., indicated a willingness to turn over its modern fleet of 16 containerships to Sea-Land Service Inc., an unsubsidized operator, on a time-charter basis of $10,500 per ship per day for a period of 20 years, usually regarded as the lifetime of a ship, at a 5 per cent write-off per year. The transaction would require approval of the Federal Maritime Commission.

The significant point in the U.S. Lines and Sea-Land proposed charter transaction is the fact that subsidization may very well be on the way out as a prerequisite for operation of American-flag tonnage in foreign trade.

Mention of the corporate title United States Lines Co. immediately brings to mind the outstanding symbol of the American merchant marine, the SS *United States*, holder of the Atlantic Blue Ribbon. The SS *United States* was prematurely retired at the end of 1969 be-

cause of a lack of patronage. The U.S. Government provided $12,000,000 in subsidy for the vessel's operation during 1969, and the vessel's owner took an additional loss of more than $4,000,000 in operating expenses.

Adventure. Mention must be made of the Arctic voyage of the ice-breaking super tanker *Manhattan*, from the U.S. Atlantic coast through the Northwest Passage, to open a navigation route for the delivery of petroleum to U.S. Atlantic seaboard oil-refinery terminals. In an assessment of the *Manhattan*'s adventurous voyage, Humble Oil & Refining Co. revealed that terminal facilities, which may cost as much as $500,000,000, will be needed at Prudhoe Bay, Alaska.

The positive view has been advanced that the Prudhoe terminal facilities can be built. Inasmuch as petroleum is highly competitive with other fuels, there is some doubt that it can be delivered from Alaska at a cost comparable with that of competitive sources.

JOHN DUFFY
Editor, *Shipping Digest*

Vegetable market in Chinatown—though Chinese are in the majority in Singapore there is racial harmony.

UPI

SINGAPORE

Area: 225 sq. mi.
Population: 2,100,000
Capital: Singapore (pop., 1,970,600)
Government: Inche Yusof ibn Ishak, president —1959; Lee Kuan Yew, prime minister—1965
Gross national product: $1,200,000,000
Monetary unit: Singapore dollar (3.1 SD = U.S. $1.00)
Chief products: steel products, chemicals, plastics, cement, fish, fruits and vegetables
Foreign trade: exports, $1,271,000,000; imports, $1,661,000,000
Communications: 106,124 telephones, 175,126 radios, 109,049 TV sets, 11 daily newspapers
Transportation: roads, 1,138 mi.; 118,846 passenger cars; railroads, 28 mi.
Education: 530,079 elementary and secondary students, 2 universities
Armed forces: 14,250

See map on page 481

SINGAPORE

For the Lion City of Singapore, 1969 marked the 150th year since the founding of the city by Sir Stamford Raffles. National Day, Aug. 9, stressed Singaporeans' ability to stand alone. The young republic, which drew out of federation with Malaysia in 1965, put its new armed forces on parade. Pride of place went to 18 French-made tanks, the first of 50 purchased from the Israeli Army, while 2 of the 3 infantry brigades, which will form the basis of the Singapore Army, took part in the celebration march. The third brigade was formed during 1969, and agreement was reached on purchasing surface-to-air missiles from the British for defense needs after 1971; training for Singapore's forces came from a 40-strong detachment of Israeli military advisers.

Defense arrangements after the British "east of Suez" withdrawal remained a major concern for Prime Minister Lee Kuan Yew and his governing People's Action Party. Five-power ministerial level defense talks were held with Malaysia, Britain, Australia and New Zealand in Canberra in June, and in November there were lower level meetings in Kuala Lumpur. Meanwhile the Government curbed some expenditures in its 1969 budget to allow for extra spending on defense.

Abroad the Singapore Government pursued its policy of "positive neutrality." In September, Foreign Minister S. Rajaratnam declared that the republic would avoid involving itself in big-power rivalries that might endanger the region's security. Singapore refused to consider membership in ASPAC on the grounds that it was basically an anticommunist alliance.

With its multiracial population, the city could not remain uninvolved by the rioting that erupted in neighboring Malaysia. A few weeks after Kuala Lumpur's May 13 outbreak, clashes occurred between Malays and Chinese in Singapore's Geylang Serai district, which resulted in six deaths. Security forces moved quickly to avert further trouble and the Government held "outsiders" responsible for the violence. The People's Action Party, firmly entrenched following the 1968 elections in which it won all 58 parliamentary seats, ruled without opposition. It felt strong enough to release prominent left winger Lim Chin Siong, of the Barisan Socialis party, after more than six years in detention.

Progress was evident in the Singapore economy, and the volume of both foreign trade and the major entrepôt trade showed substantial increases. Tourism figures also rose fast, and during the year construction was started on no less than 30 new hotels. With unemployment assessed at 44,000 and the need to find 25,000 jobs annually for those leaving school, the Government continued to make strenuous efforts to attract foreign investment in the city's developing industries.

DEREK DAVIES
Editor, *Far Eastern Economic Review*

SOUTH AFRICA

In 1969 the ruling Nationalist Party was split, after 21 years in power. The right-wingers, known as the *verkramptes* (narrow-minded ones), are led by Dr. Albert Hertzog, a member of Parliament and former minister in the Vorster Government. The *verkramptes* feel that the *verligtes* (enlightened ones), led by Prime Minister John Vorster, are diluting the policy of apartheid. The split was caused partly over the question of allowing Maoris on New Zealand's rugby team to enter South Africa and travel as whites. In September, Vorster, fearing a further challenge to his policies, called for an election in 1970, a year ahead of time. Hertzog was read out of the party several weeks later, and then formed the Reformed National Party, which he said would run candidates in the 1970 elections.

In December, Alan Paton, the well-known novelist, announced his retirement from politics, and indicated that he would devote all his time to writing. Paton was the leader of the Liberal Party, which has not existed officially since 1968 when the Government banned multiracial political organizations. However, Paton made it clear that his retirement does not affect his opposition to apartheid.

Heart-transplant pioneer Dr. Christiaan Barnard lost his position as a national idol in South Africa when he said in a speech that the apartheid policy of the Government had embarrassed him on his overseas travels.

When the two-tier gold-price system went into effect in 1968, central bankers agreed that there was no need for them to buy newly mined gold. This was acknowledged to be an effort, led by the United States, to force the South Africans to dump their gold on the free market and drive the price down to or below the official price of $35 per ounce. In July 1969 it was revealed that South Africa had been selling gold to a consortium of Swiss banks which later fed it into the free market. By the end of the year, South Africa was being forced to sell more of its rapidly mounting gold reserves on the free market. The price fell to almost $35 per ounce. The United States said that it and other International Monetary Fund members would agree to buy South African gold on the free market if the price fell below $35 an ounce.

The controversial BOSS bill became law on June 30. It gives the Bureau of State Security the right to forbid a person being investigated by the bureau to give evidence in his own behalf if the evidence is considered prejudicial to the public interest of the state. The law also forbids giving the press news of the bureau's activities if the news is prejudicial to the security of the bureau.

In February the Government introduced the South-West Africa Affairs bill into Parliament. The bill would give the Government the power to apply any South African law to the territory.

On July 10 the editor in chief of the *Rand Daily Mail*, Laurence Gandar, was found guilty of publishing information about alleged brutal conditions in South African prisons without making enough of an effort to verify it.

NORA ANN SMYTH
Associate Editor
Lands and Peoples

SOUTH AFRICA

Area: 472,733 sq. mi.
Population: 19,600,000
Capital: Cape Town (pop., 812,000)
Government: J. J. Fouché, president—1968; Balthazar J. Vorster, prime minister—1966
Gross national product: $13,730,000,000
Monetary unit: rand (1 rand = U.S. $1.40)
Chief products: gold, wool, maize, sugar, livestock, fishing, chemicals, petroleum
Foreign trade: exports, $2,105,000,000; imports, $2,638,000,000
Communications: 1,322,101 telephones, 1,457,739 radios, 18 daily newspapers
Transportation: roads, 206,680 mi.; 1,126,000 passenger cars, railroads, 14,000 mi.
Education: elementary and secondary enrollment: white, 810,226; non-white, 2,853,837, 11 universities
Armed forces: 39,700

See map on page 75

SOUTH CAROLINA

In Charleston a strike by unskilled Negro hospital employees, which began on Mar. 20, lasted more than three months. It was supported by Mrs. Coretta King and the Rev. Ralph D. Abernathy and brought nationwide attention, especially as it was the first time in the South that civil-rights and labor forces were allied. Settlement included union recognition and a guaranteed minimum wage of $1.60 an hour.

SOUTH DAKOTA

A project was begun to reclaim and develop some 1,000,000 acres of arid land in North and South Dakota. The area sweeps eastward from Garrison Dam (N.D.) and then southeast into northeastern South Dakota. It gets little more than a few inches of rain a year and at present has extremely limited agricultural use. When the project is completed some years hence, the area is expected to produce feed crops.

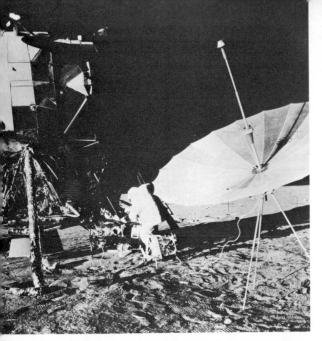

Apollo 12 astronaut unpacks equipment from storage place at bottom of lunar module. Behind him, communications radar, like a big parasol, has been set up.

From Apollo 9 a thunderhead—a cumulus-cloud mass heralding a storm—is shot over South America.

SPACE

The landing of man on the moon, a dream of centuries and a specific goal of the United States from 1961, became a reality in 1969, by far the most dramatic and successful year of the space age. Three times during the year the U.S. National Aeronautics and Space Administration sent Apollo spacecraft to the moon, and two of the missions climaxed in lunar landings.

Man's first landing on the ancient satellite began on July 16 with the launch from Cape Kennedy of Apollo 11, crewed by Neil Armstrong, spacecraft commander, Edwin Aldrin and Michael Collins. Boosted into lunar trajectory by a Saturn 5 launch vehicle, Apollo 11 negotiated the distance to the moon in 75 hours and 50 minutes Ground Elapsed Time (GET) and went into lunar orbit. At 100 hours 15 minutes GET, the lunar module *Eagle*, carrying Armstrong and Aldrin, separated from the command module *Columbia* and started its descent to the moon. After a hair-raising final approach to the landing site, in which Armstrong had to wrest control from the automatic system and manually guide *Eagle* clear of a boulder-strewn area, the lunar module settled on the surface of the moon at 102 hours 45 minutes GET.

After a rest period and a lengthy series of necessary preliminaries, Neil Armstrong descended *Eagle*'s ladder and became the first man to set foot on the moon at 109 hours 24 minutes GET on July 20. Aldrin followed 18 minutes later.

During a 2-hour-and-21-minute moon stay, the astronauts planted the American flag on the moon, set up 3 scientific experiments and filled 2 specially designed containers with lunar rock and soil samples for scientific analysis on earth. At 124 hours 22 minutes GET, they blasted off from the moon in the ascent stage of the lunar module and rejoined Collins and *Columbia* in lunar orbit. Following a return flight that brought overall mission time to 195 hours 18 minutes, *Columbia* splashed down in the Pacific, where the astronauts and the command module were picked up by the recovery ship USS *Hornet*. (See feature article Man's First Step on the Moon, page 38.)

Apollo 12, the second lunar-landing flight, followed the same general pattern of Apollo 11 except that overall mission duration, 244 hours 36 minutes, was some 50 hours longer. This was due in part to the relative earth-moon positions at launch, which dictated longer outbound and inbound trajectories, but primarily to a longer stay time in the vicinity of the moon.

All photos NASA

Indentations in the dust show that Surveyor 3 bounced when it landed in a moon crater in 1967. On the rim of the crater, about 600 feet away, the lunar module "Intrepid" waits for the Apollo 12 astronauts.

Crewed by Charles Conrad, Jr., spacecraft commander, Alan L. Bean and Richard F. Gordon, Jr., Apollo 12 was launched Nov. 14. After separation from the command module *Yankee Clipper,* Conrad and Bean in the lunar module *Intrepid* dropped to the moon's Ocean of Storms, about 950 miles west of the Sea of Tranquility, the site of the Apollo 11 landing. *Intrepid*'s landing was a masterpiece of precision. The craft touched down within 600 feet of the aiming point, the unmanned Surveyor 3 spacecraft, which had landed on the moon on Apr. 19, 1967.

On Nov. 19, 115 hours 27 minutes after launch, Conrad became the third man to step onto the moon, and Bean followed a half hour later. The Apollo 12 moon men made a more thorough investigation of the lunar surface than had Armstrong and Aldrin. Instead of the latter's 2½-hour moon walk, Conrad and Bean took 2 "walks," each of about 4 hours duration. In the course of their exploration, they ventured as far as 1,300 feet from *Intrepid* and covered a circuit of about a mile and a half which took them to the Surveyor 3 site and 6 other craters. They collected a greater variety of samples (including some components of the Surveyor) and deposited on the surface a more comprehensive lunar-experiments package. It included 5 instruments and a nuclear-power source designed to keep them operating for at least a year.

At 142 hours 4 minutes GET, on Nov. 20, Conrad and Bean ignited the ascent engine of the lunar module and climbed to lunar orbit for docking with *Yankee Clipper*. Reunited with Gordon, they jettisoned *Intrepid* and sent it crashing to the lunar surface in a moonquake impact experiment recorded by the seismometer left on the moon. Then they fired the main Apollo engine to escape from lunar orbit and return home to a Pacific recovery by the *Hornet*. The venture came off with almost clockwork precision except for its color TV.

Prior to the 2 lunar-landing missions, NASA conducted 2 other manned Apollo flights in 1969. Apollo 9, launched Mar. 3, and crewed by spacecraft commander James A. McDivitt, David R. Scott and Russell Schweickart, was the final test of the lunar module, extensively checked out in a 10-day earth-orbital flight. Apollo 10 was a dress rehearsal for the lunar landing; manned by Thomas P. Stafford (commander), Eugene A. Cernan and John W. Young, it was launched May 18. In 8 days and 3 minutes, Apollo 10 made a 577,000-mile round trip to the moon, which included 31 revolutions in lunar orbit. Stafford and Cernan paved the way for the lunar landings by making a partial descent in the lunar module to within 9.4 miles of the lunar surface.

The Soviet Union was also active in manned space flight during the year, flying 2 earth-orbital rendezvous missions, the first involving 2 spacecraft, and the second 3 ships.

The first mission started on Jan. 14 with the launch from Tyuratam space complex of Soyuz 4, crewed by a single cosmonaut, Lt. Col. Vladimir Shatalov. On the following day Soyuz 5 was launched from the same base; it carried a crew that comprised Lt. Col. Boris Volynov, Lt. Col. Yevgey Khrunov and Aleksei Yeliseyev. The latter spacecraft was directed into an orbit closely approximating that of Soyuz 4, and on Jan. 16 Shatalov maneuvered his craft to a docking with Soyuz 5. In a simulation of emergency rescue, Khrunov and Yeliseyev spent 1 hour outside their spacecraft, then transferred to Soyuz 4. On Jan. 17, after 48 orbits, Soyuz 4 reentered and landed with 3 of the 4 cosmonauts aboard. Alone in Soyuz 5, Volynov completed 49 orbits and landed on Jan. 18.

The second Soviet manned spectacular got under way on Oct. 11 with the launch of Soyuz 6, piloted by Lt. Col. Georgi Shonin and civilian Dr. Valery Kubasov. Less than 24 hours later, the Soviets sent up Soyuz 7, carrying Lt. Cols. Anatoly Filipchenko and Viktor Gorbatko and civilian flight engineer Vladislav Volkov. Again within 24 hours, on Oct. 13, Soyuz 8 went into orbit, crewed by Shatalov and Yeliseyev, veterans of the Soyuz 4–5 docking.

The Soviets demonstrated extreme precision in directing the 3 spacecraft into compatible

NASA

As photographed by Mariner 7, the south polar cap of the planet Mars has many different sizes and shapes of craters. The cap, which appears seasonally, may be a layer of carbon-dioxide ice (Dry Ice) or an extremely thin film of water ice.

UPI

After the largest mass flight thus far, in three Soyuz craft, the Soviet cosmonauts march across Moscow airport (l to r): Col. Vladimir A. Shatalov, Col. Georgi S. Shonin, Col. Anatoly V. Filipchenko, civil engineer Valery N. Kubasov, Col. Viktor V. Gorbatko, and civil engineers Aleksei S. Yeliseyev and Vladislav N. Volkov.

orbits, but the mission was something of a let-down to observers expecting another dramatic space breakthrough. Soyuz 6 accomplished the first welding in space, an experimental prelude to the someday assembly of space stations in orbit. All 3 craft conducted geological-geographical surveying experiments. On Oct. 15, Soyuz 7 and 8 maneuvered to within 500 yards of each other; while Soyuz 6, close enough for visual observation by its crew, served as flight director. But nothing else happened. Soyuz 6, 7 and 8 landed on Oct. 16, 17 and 18 respectively. Western observers could conclude only that the Soviets had planned a multiple docking as a preliminary to assembling a space platform in orbit consisting of 2 more spacecraft units and that, for unexplained reasons, the mission had failed.

Both the United States and the U.S.S.R. flew successful missions of planetary spacecraft during the year, the United States to Mars and the Soviets to Venus. Both employed the twin-spacecraft approach to increase the chance of getting data.

The Soviet Venera 5 and 6 reached Venus in mid-May after having been launched on Jan. 5 and 10 respectively. Each spacecraft ejected instrumented capsules equipped with rocket-braking devices and parachutes to slow the descent through the atmosphere and produce longer reporting time. Venera 5 trans-mitted Venusian-atmosphere data for 53 minutes, Venera 6 for 51 minutes. Their reports, the U.S.S.R. announced, permitted the first precise determination of the chemical composition of the Venusian atmosphere and its temperature, density and pressure profile.

The American Mars explorers were Mariners 6 and 7, launched Feb. 24 and Mar. 27 into a trajectory that took them within photographic distance of the Red Planet when it was some 59,000,000 miles distant from earth. Both spacecraft made planetary "flybys" (close approach but no landing) of Mars, providing the closest-range photos ever taken of the planet. Mariner 6 reached its closest point (2,130 miles) on July 31; Mariner 7 came within 2,190 miles on Aug. 5. (Although the latter was launched a month later, it was sent into a slightly different trajectory allowing it to catch up with Mariner 6.) The pictures returned were not duplicatory, because Mariner 6 flew directly over the Martian equator while Mariner 7 approached from the Martian South Pole. The twin flights provided exceptionally valuable photographs, particularly those of the polar ice cap and the mysterious rills or "canals," together with additional data on pressures, temperatures and densities telemetered by instruments aboard the spacecraft.

In other unmanned activity, the Soviet Union launched 2 lunar probes, Luna 15 and Zond 7.

Launched July 13, Luna 15 was designed to obtain lunar-gravity and perturbation data, presumably as a preliminary to manned flights. It orbited the moon concurrently with Apollo 11 and crashed on the moon July 21 while the American astronauts were still on the surface, but nowhere near their landing site. Zond 7, launched Aug. 8, apparently was a test of space navigation and earth reentry at lunar-return velocity. It flew a circumlunar course and returned to an on-land touchdown in the northern part of Kazakhstan on Aug. 15.

Other Soviet unmanned launches included 2 meteorological satellites and the customary lengthy series of Cosmos spacecraft. The weather satellites were Meteor 1 and 2, launched on Mar. 26 and Oct. 6. The new designations apparently indicated operational status for the weather-reporting network, since the U.S.S.R. had launched a number of experimental metsats under Cosmos designations. Cosmos is a catchall designation for a variety of unmanned spacecraft, among them purely scientific satellites, experimental-applied spacecraft and military-intelligence-gathering vehicles. The high rate of Cosmos launches, approximately 1 a week, started in 1967 and continued through 1968 and 1969.

On Oct. 14 the Soviets launched Intercosmos 1, a cooperative spacecraft designed to allow participation of Soviet-bloc nations in space research. The spacecraft was launched by a Soviet booster, but the experiments were provided by East Germany and Czechoslovakia. Hungary, Rumania and Bulgaria participated on an "observer" basis.

Aside from the Mariners, other major U.S. unmanned flights of the year included 3 launches of "observatory-class" spacecraft, a flight of a monkey-carrying biological satellite, and the successful orbiting of an advanced weather satellite.

On Jan. 22 and on Aug. 9, NASA launched Orbiting Solar Observatories (OSO) 5 and 6. The 600-plus-pound spacecraft studied solar radiation and reported on evolutionary changes in various features of the sun. On June 5, the U.S. space agency sent into orbit OGO 6, the sixth and last of the Orbiting Geophysical Observatory series, which investigated the upper atmosphere and ionosphere, the auroral regions surrounding the poles and the edges of the regions of trapped radiation surrounding the earth.

A biological satellite, Biosatellite 3, was launched June 28 in what was to have been a 30-day orbital experiment in the effects of weightlessness on a 14-pound pig-tailed monkey. It ended, however, after only 9 days, when the monkey became ill. (It later died.) By ground command, the monkey's capsule was ejected from the spacecraft. An attempt to retrieve the craft by the "midair snatch" technique pioneered by the U.S. Air Force failed.

The advanced weather satellite was Nimbus 3, launched Apr. 14. Nimbus 3 carried cloud-cover cameras as its predecessors did, but it was also equipped with a series of sophisticated instruments to take the first "vertical soundings," readings of atmospheric composition and conditions from the ground up. The success of Nimbus 3 heralded near-future availability of the long-sought space platform capable of providing the data necessary for two-week weather forecasts.

The U.S. Air Force continued to launch about one reconnaissance satellite every six weeks, although all details of such launches were classified. It also launched a series of scientific satellites investigating such fields as solar radiation, ionospheric electric fields and radio interference and the hazards of radiation to humans. A major military launch came on Feb. 9 when the USAF sent into orbit Tacsat 1, a supersized satellite designed to make possible long-range communications to small troop units carrying only a one-foot-diameter receiving antenna.

In the operational applied-satellite field, the Environmental Science Services Administration (ESSA) launched the ESSA 9 weather satellite on Feb. 26 as a replacement for the U.S. weather-observation network for ESSA 7, which was no longer functioning. Communications Satellite Corp. added three Intelsat 3 Comsats to the international network, bringing to four the number in service.

Among U.S. international-cooperation ventures, NASA provided launch services for Isis 1, a Canadian ionospheric-research satellite, on Jan. 30; for ESRO 1B, an eight-experiment package designed to investigate the polar ionosphere for the European Space Research Organization, on Oct. 1; and Azur 1, Germany's first satellite, a tool for further study of the earth's radiation belts, on Nov. 7.

Japan failed for the fourth time to become the fourth nation with complete space capability; that is, the ability to orbit a satellite of its own design by means of a home-developed launch vehicle (only the U.S.S.R., the United States and France had this capability at year-end). On Sept. 22, after what looked like a good launch, Japan's Lambda 4S rocket developed control difficulties in its third stage, and the 56-pound satellite failed to go into orbit.

JAMES J. HAGGERTY
Editor, *Aerospace Year Book*

SPAIN

After 30 years as the supreme Spaniard, 76-year-old Gen. Francisco Franco announced his successor in 1969: Prince Juan Carlos de Borbon y Borbon, the next king of Spain.

The unique political event capped an exciting year in Spain. It included a national state of emergency, the biggest reshuffle of the Franco Government since the end of the Spanish Civil War, controversy over U.S. military bases on the peninsula, and an export-loan scandal that shocked the nation.

Selection of 31-year-old Prince Juan Carlos was no surprise, though the Prince's father, 56-year-old Don Juan, Count of Barcelona, and dynastic heir to the Catholic throne, bitterly assailed Generalissimo Franco from exile in Portugal. Carlists—monarchists who back Prince Carlos Hugo de Borbon-Parma, a French citizen—protested mildly but did not stage the expected public demonstrations.

On Jan. 20, Enrique Ruano Casanova, 21, a Madrid University student, jumped from his apartment window while police searched for evidence that he was a political activist. Students protested so vigorously that Generalissimo Franco declared a national state of emergency on Jan. 24. Ostensibly aimed at students, the emergency suspended civil rights, imposed news censorship and gave police broad powers of arrest and exile. These measures were used against clandestine labor organizations, Basque nationalists who want to split the three Basque provinces from Spain, and liberal lawyers. By the time the emergency ended by decree on Mar. 25, several hundred Basques, members of underground *comisiones obreras* (worker committees) and students had been arrested. A score or more of lawyers critical of the regime were exiled to remote villages.

After more than a year of controversy, Spain and the United States agreed to continue U.S. military bases on the peninsula until Sept. 26, 1970, when the bases revert to Spanish control.

Spain closed its land border with Gibraltar on June 8 in a continuing cold war aimed at wresting the rock back from Great Britain after 265 years of British occupation. On June 27, the Franco Government stopped ferry service between Algeciras and Gibraltar, isolating it except by air. Later, telephone and electric services were suspended.

The Spanish economy continued to rebound in 1969 but there was a threat of inflation, and the Government retained wage and price controls.

Six persons were arrested in what newspapers called Spain's biggest financial scandal.

PIX

Wearing an army captain's uniform with a blue sash, Prince Juan Carlos (l) speaks to the Cortes after taking oath to become king when Franco (r) steps down.

It involved $142,500,000 in official export credits made to Maquinaria Textil del Norte de España (Matesa), manufacturer of textile machinery with roots in more than a dozen countries. It was alleged that the credits were partly used for imaginary transactions, and many credits went to buy shares in foreign concerns.

See Juan Carlos, Prince.

KEN DAVIS
Chief, Madrid Bureau
The Associated Press

SPAIN

Area: 194,400
Population: 32,700,000
Capital: Madrid (pop., 2,610,000)
Government: Francisco Franco, chief of state —1939
Gross national product: $28,100,000,000
Monetary unit: peseta (70 pesetas = U.S. $1.00)
Chief products: olives, cereals, grapes, citrus fruits, wine, fish, iron, coal, textiles
Foreign trade: exports, $1,589,000,000; imports, $3,497,000,000
Communications: 3,378,865 telephones, 3,000,-000 TV sets, 123 daily newspapers
Transportation: roads, 82,906 mi.; 3,148,000 passenger cars; railroads, 11,744 mi.
Education: 5,451,000 elementary and secondary students, 13 universities
Armed forces: 289,500

See map on page 185

UPI

Fans live it up after Mets win World Series. Shea Stadium turf was considered an appropriate souvenir.

SPORTS HIGHLIGHTS

It was the year of the Jets and the Mets.

That is how 1969 will be described forever more by sports followers. It did not seem possible in mid-January that any sports event could happen in the remainder of 1969 that would equal the surprise victory of the New York Jets in the Super Bowl. Underdog was hardly the word to describe how the public felt about the Jets' status in regard to the heavily favored Baltimore Colts, despite the brash predictions of success by the New Yorkers' Joe Namath. The cocky quarterback made good his boasts, however, and passed the Jets to a 16–7 triumph.

In the months to come there were dramatic events in other stadiums, and on courts, fields, links and tracks, but another group of New York upstarts—baseball's amazing Mets—was to pull off an upset that in some ways was more astonishing than the Jets' win.

The Mets had been lovable clowns to their fans since their birth as an expansion team in 1962, but in the summer of 1969 young pitching arms matured, and an assortment of stars and nonstars at other positions blended their talents to win it all.

Some of the other sports had surprises too. In the National Basketball Association, for instance, Bill Russell, the Boston Celtics' player-coach, summoned one last burst of brilliance as he led his green-clad mates to the championship play-offs against the Western champion Los Angeles Lakers. It took seven games, but the Celts defeated LA to bring Boston its eleventh title in Russell's 13-year reign. After the series, Russell retired from professional basketball.

There was no surprise in college basketball as Lew Alcindor led UCLA to its third straight national championship. Then Alcindor, in effect, took Russell's place as a pro attraction by signing a million-dollar contract with the NBA's Milwaukee Bucks.

Hockey followed form. The Montreal Canadiens fought off the Boston Bruins, 4 games to 2, in the Stanley Cup semifinals, then brushed off the St. Louis Blues 4 straight for the championship.

In golf the unexpected became the expected as long shots won the major tournaments. George Archer took the Masters, Orville Moody the U.S. Open and Ray Floyd the PGA. Moody's 2-day total of 141 was good enough to win $50,000 in the World Series of Golf.

Majestic Prince galloped to victory in the Kentucky Derby and gave jockey Bill Hartack his fifth triumph in the 95th run for the roses at Churchill Downs.

On another type of track, Mario Andretti steered a turbocharged Ford to first place in the Indianapolis 500, averaging 156.867 mph.

College football seemed certain to be dominated by an Ohio State squad that had begun the year with a 27–16 Rose Bowl victory over Southern California. However, in Ohio State's final appearance Michigan gained a 24–12 upset that gave the Wolverines a share of the Big Ten crown with the Buckeyes.

It was a shocker, all right, but after the Jets and Mets a sports fan could no longer be stunned.

BOB BROEG
Sports Editor, *St. Louis Post-Dispatch*

UPI

"The New York Times"

'The New York Times'

THE AMAZING METS

Tom Seaver (top l), Mets' star right-hander, won 25 regular-season games, a play-off and a series game; Jerry Koosman (above with Seaver) won two series games; and Donn Clendenon (lower l) hit three homers in the series. Gil Hodges (with Mets principal owner Mrs. Joan Payson) was voted National League manager of the year.

UPI

UPI

A Ford GT 40, driven by Ickx and Oliver, wins the Le Mans 24-hour endurance race; a Porsche finishes second.

Automobile Racing

Mario Andretti and Jackie Stewart, two of the brightest young stars in auto racing, dominated the sport in 1969.

Italian-born Andretti, who had survived a fiery crash that destroyed his racer on May 21, scored a crushing victory in the Indianapolis 500-Mile race on May 30. Andretti led for 114 of the 200 laps, set a record speed of 156.867 mph and finished more than 2 laps ahead of second-place Dan Gurney. Andretti's payoff for 3 hours and 11 minutes of driving was $205,727. By winning, the diminutive (5′ 6″, 138 lb.) Italian-American ended a 23-year famine in the 500 for car-owner Andy Granatelli. Andretti went on to take the United States Auto Club driving title for the third time in 5 years.

Stewart, who lost the 1968 world title to Graham Hill in the final race, was almost unbeatable in 1969. The Scot, who lives in Switzerland, won six of the first eight Grand Prix races to clinch the championship. However, Austrian Jochen Rindt won the United States Grand Prix. It was his first Formula One racing triumph.

In one of the closest finishes of the 1969 racing season, Lee Roy Yarbrough, driving a Ford, passed Charlie Glotzbach, in a Dodge, on the final lap to take the Daytona 500-Mile Stock Car race by less than a car length.

Italian star Lucien Bianchi was killed at Le Mans, France, on Mar. 30, when his car went off the course and hit a pole. Bianchi, who won

the 1968 Le Mans 24-hour endurance race with Pedro Rodriguez as codriver, was practicing for the 1969 program. Jackie Ickx of Belgium and England's Jackie Oliver captured the 1969 Le Mans event. Ickx, a promising newcomer to Grand Prix racing, also captured the Grand Prix races of West Germany and Canada.

Cars built by Bruce McLaren of New Zealand dominated the $1,000,000 Can-Am sports-car series for the second year in a row. Driven by McLaren and Denis Hulme, the McLarens finished first and second in 8 of the first 9 races.

BOB COLLINS
Sports Editor, *The Indianapolis Star*

AUTOMOBILE RACING

World Champion: Jackie Stewart, Scotland
USAC National Champion: Mario Andretti
NASCAR National Champion: David Pearson
Can-Am Series Champion: Bruce McLaren-Denis Hulme, New Zealand
Trans-Am Series Champion: Mark Donohue

Grand Prix Circuit

South African Grand Prix: Stewart
Spanish Grand Prix: Stewart
Monaco Grand Prix: Graham Hill
Dutch Grand Prix: Stewart
French Grand Prix: Stewart
British Grand Prix: Stewart
West German Grand Prix: Jackie Ickx
Italian Grand Prix: Stewart
Canadian Grand Prix: Ickx
U.S. Grand Prix: Jochen Rindt
Mexican Grand Prix: Denis Hulme

Baseball

In major-league baseball, the 1969 season will be remembered as the year of the Mets, the miracle team that told the world no odds are too forbidding, no task is impossible. The little team that had never finished better than ninth in its seven-year history became champion of the baseball world.

Written off in early September as the team that had made a courageous run in the National League's Eastern Division but would finish second to the Chicago Cubs, the Mets persevered. They capitalized on a sudden slump by Leo Durocher's Cubs and started a 9-game winning streak of their own, clinched the Eastern Division title and then dispatched Atlanta, Western Division champions, in 3 straight play-off games to qualify for the World Series.

Even with such superior pitchers as 25-game-winner Tom Seaver and Jerry Koosman (17–9), the Mets were rated as over their heads in the World Series. The Mets' opponents, the Baltimore Orioles, had won the American League play-off by beating Minnesota, Western Division champions, in 3 straight. When the Orioles won the first World Series game, 4 to 1 on Mike Cuellar's 6-hitter, the Mets appeared doomed to speedy death. But it was the Orioles who were quickly eliminated in a dramatic turnabout by the Mets which won the next 4 games and the series.

Game 2 saw the Mets even the series with Koosman and Ron Taylor holding the Orioles to 2 hits; Al Weis drove in the run that won it, 2–1. In game 3, Gary Gentry and Nolan Ryan combined to shut out the Orioles on 4 hits, 5–0. Tommy Agee's superb catches in the outfield cut off 5 potential Baltimore runs. Seaver, the first-game loser, came back in game 4 to win, 2–1, with a 6-hitter. A wild throw by Baltimore relief pitcher Pete Richert figured in the winning run.

The Mets came from behind, 3–0, to win the fifth and final game, with the help of Donn Clendenon's third home run of the series, and Al Weis' first home run of the season in Shea Stadium. The final score was 5–3. Weis, regarded mostly as a defensive asset, led the series in hitting with a .454 average.

The effect of the Mets' World Series victory was electric. One national television commentator, taking note of the great excitement, ob-

BASEBALL

FINAL MAJOR-LEAGUE STANDINGS

AMERICAN LEAGUE	WON	LOST	PER CENT	GAMES BEHIND	NATIONAL LEAGUE	WON	LOST	PER CENT	GAMES BEHIND
Eastern Division					**Eastern Division**				
Baltimore	109	53	.673	—	New York	100	62	.617	—
Detroit	90	72	.556	19	Chicago	92	70	.568	8
Boston	87	75	.537	22	Pittsburgh	88	74	.543	12
Washington	86	76	.531	23	St. Louis	87	75	.537	13
New York	80	81	.497	28½	Philadelphia	63	99	.389	37
Cleveland	62	99	.385	46½	Montreal	52	110	.321	48
Western Division					**Western Division**				
Minnesota	97	65	.599	—	Atlanta	93	69	.574	—
Oakland	88	74	.543	9	San Francisco	90	72	.556	3
California	71	91	.438	26	Cincinnati	89	73	.549	4
Kansas City	69	93	.426	28	Los Angeles	85	77	.525	8
Chicago	68	94	.420	29	Houston	81	81	.500	12
Seattle	64	98	.395	33	San Diego	52	110	.321	41

Baltimore defeated Minnesota in play-offs, 3 games to 0.

New York defeated Atlanta in play-offs, 3 games to 0.

AMERICAN LEAGUE		NATIONAL LEAGUE
American League 3	All-Star Game	National League 9
Rod Carew (.322) Minn.	Batting Champion	Pete Rose (.348) Cinc.
Dennis McLain (24-9) Det.	Cy Young Award	Tom Seaver (25-7) N.Y.
Mike Cuellar (23-11) Balt.		
Harmon Killebrew (49) Minn.	Home-Run Leader	Willie McCovey (45) S.F.
Ted Williams, Wash.	Manager of the Year	Gil Hodges, N.Y.
Harmon Killebrew (140)	Runs Batted In	Willie McCovey (126)
Harmon Killebrew	Most Valuable Player	Willie McCovey
Lou Piniella, Kans. City	Rookie of the Year	Ted Sizemore, L.A.
Baltimore, 1 game	World Series	New York, 4 games

UPI

After receiving a "most fantastic" financial offer, former Boston Red Sox star Ted Williams returned to baseball in 1969 as manager of the Washington Senators.

Baseball operated with a new Commissioner, Bowie Kuhn, a Wall Street attorney, who succeeded William D. Eckert. Kuhn showed himself to be a forceful figure. His term began in the year of the 12-team major league, with the American League expanding into Seattle and restoring a team in Kansas City, and the National League moving into San Diego and Montreal.

Attendance set a new record, with Montreal, despite its last-place finish, drawing 1,212,608 and boosting National League attendance to 15,094,946, a rise of 3,309,588 over 1968. American League attendance was up 806,627 to 12,124,014, with Washington showing the largest increase.

The year marked Ted Williams' return to baseball as manager of the Washington Senators. He was named manager of the year, after his team finished 10 games above the .500 mark. In 1968 the Senators finished 31 games below .500.

The innovation of two divisions in each of the major leagues proved highly successful, both from an attendance standpoint and in sustaining fan interest. With the World Series teams cutting up the spoils for division play as well as the series, new records were set for both winners and losers. Each member of the Mets drew a check for $18,338, and each member of the Orioles received $14,904.

Before the year was over, every manager in the AL's Western Division had been fired or had resigned. Billy Martin, despite winning the division pennant with Minnesota, was fired and replaced by Bill Rigney. Harold (Lefty) Phillips had succeeded Rigney with the California Angels early in the season. At Oakland, Hank Bauer was fired, and replaced by John McNamara. Joe Gordon was replaced at Kansas City by Charlie Metro. Seattle fired Joe Schultz and replaced him with Dave Bristol. Al Lopez resigned from the White Sox and was succeeded by Don Gutteridge. In the AL East, the Red Sox fired Dick Williams and hired Eddie Kasko as their 1970 manager. In the National League, Danny Murtaugh replaced Larry Shepard at Pittsburgh; Frank Lucchesi took over for Bob Skinner with the Phillies; and the Reds hired George Anderson to replace Dave Bristol.

After the season, the Cardinals and Phillies swung one of the biggest trades of several years. Richie Allen, long-discontented slugger of the Phillies, went to the Cardinals for outfielder Curt Flood, catcher Tim McCarver and lesser players.

SHIRLEY POVICH
Sports Editor, *The Washington Post*

served "The Mets have done more to unite the nation than any other national event." The Mets were given a ticker-tape parade in New York.

To win the Western Division title in the National League, the Braves outlasted 4 other teams in a close race. At various points San Francisco, Los Angeles, Cincinnati and Houston had glowing chances to win. In the American League East, the Orioles took an early lead and were scarcely threatened. Minnesota beat off a challenge from Oakland, which slumped badly after mid-August.

Basketball

For an unprecedented third straight year UCLA emerged from the college-basketball season as the national champion. To the surprise of no one, Lew Alcindor, UCLA's great center, was named college player of the year—also for the third consecutive time.

In the professional ranks, the NBA enjoyed a banner year and the most exciting play-offs in a decade. To the surprise and admiration of everyone, Boston won its eleventh world title in 13 years by beating a powerful Los Angeles Lakers team in the seventh and final game of the play-off series. The Celtics accomplished what no other team in play-off competition had ever been able to do: come from a two-game deficit to capture the title.

Coached by Alex Hannum, the Oakland Oaks won the crown in the struggling American Basketball Association. The Oaks defeated the Indiana Pacers in the final play-offs, 4 games to 1.

COLLEGE BASKETBALL

Excluding the dominance of UCLA and the emergence of Spencer Haywood of Detroit as a possible successor to Alcindor as the outstanding college player, the 1968–69 college season stood out for the high scoring of many outstanding shooters. Shooting stars included Louisiana State University's Pete Maravich (the nation's top scorer, with an average of over forty points per game), Rick Mount of Purdue and Calvin Murphy of Niagara.

To a certain extent, it was a foregone conclusion that UCLA would be the outstanding team and that everyone else would be competing for the number two position. The finals of the national-championship tournament held in Louisville, Ky., told the story of the season. Such highly ranked teams as Drake, with its star guard Willie McCarter, and Purdue, led by Rick Mount and Herman Gilliam, were no match for the height, strength and overall team play of the Bruins. The championship once again proved the old adage that one or two great players cannot beat a solid team. Although no one discounted the presence of Alcindor in the pivot, he was certainly complemented by as fine a supporting cast as has ever been seen on a college-basketball floor.

In the semifinal round of the championship, Drake slowed down the ball and worked for the good shot against UCLA. It was the same tactic that had enabled Southern California to defeat the Bruins, 46–44, a few weeks earlier. The plan was almost successful for Drake too, as they lost to UCLA by only 3 points, 85–82. In the other semifinal game, which saw Purdue against

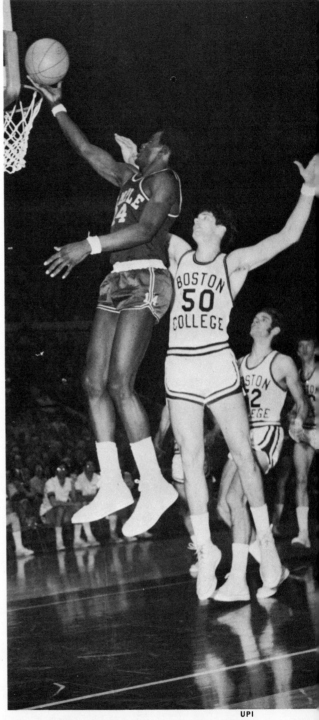

UPI

National Invitation Tournament Final: Johnny Baum scores 2 of his 30 points as Temple, coached by Harry Litwack, defeats Boston College, 89–76. Terry Driscoll (50), the tournament's most valuable player, is unsuccessful in his attempt to block the shot.

North Carolina, it was simply Mount vs. Scott. Rick Mount scored 36 points to Charlie Scott's 16, and Purdue won by a score of 92 to 65.

For the final, Purdue coach George King retained his plan of getting the ball to Mount. However, the pressure of the game and the presence of Lew Alcindor blocking the driving lanes were too much for Mount and Purdue. During the first half, Rick made only 3 of 8 field-goal attempts, and the game was virtually over. The only uncertainty was how badly UCLA would beat Purdue. The final score was UCLA 92 and Purdue 72.

Meanwhile in New York City's Madison Square Garden, Harry Litwack's Temple Owls beat a spirited Boston College club, 89 to 76, to capture the National Invitational Tournament. After the tournament Bob Cousy retired as BC's coach.

PROFESSIONAL BASKETBALL

The 1968–69 professional-basketball season marked the debut of two new superstars, Wes Unseld and Elvin Hayes. Playing for the San Diego Rockets, Hayes was the NBA's top scorer. Unseld elevated his Baltimore Bullets team, a last-place club in 1968, to first place in the East. As a result of this tremendous contribution he was named rookie of the year by the sportswriters and sportscasters who cover the NBA, and most valuable player by his fellow players.

The Philadelphia 76ers, the New York Knicks and the Boston Celtics were the runners-up to the Bullets in the East. In the West the Los Angeles Lakers, led by Elgin Baylor, Jerry West and Wilt Chamberlain, finished first; the Atlanta Hawks were second, followed by the San Francisco Warriors and the San Diego Rockets. The

---

BASKETBALL

COLLEGE

Conference Winners

Atlantic Coast: North Carolina	**Pacific Eight:** UCLA
Big Eight: Colorado	**Southeastern:** Kentucky
Big Ten: Purdue	**Southern:** Davidson
Ivy League: Princeton	**Southwest:** Texas A. & M.
Metropolitan: St. Peter's, Manhattan (tie)	**West Coast Athletic:** Santa Clara
Mid-American: Miami (Ohio)	**Western Athletic:** Brigham Young
Missouri Valley: Drake, Louisville (tie)	**Yankee:** Massachusetts

PROFESSIONAL

National Basketball Association (Final Standings)

Eastern Division

	Won	Lost	Pct.
Baltimore	57	25	.695
Philadelphia	55	27	.671
New York	54	28	.659
Boston	48	34	.585
Cincinnati	41	41	.500
Detroit	32	50	.390

Western Division

	Won	Lost	Pct.
Los Angeles	55	27	.671
Atlanta	48	34	.585
San Francisco	41	41	.500
San Diego	37	45	.451
Chicago	33	49	.402
Seattle	30	52	.366
Phoenix	16	66	.195

American Basketball Association (Final Standings)

Eastern Division

	Won	Lost	Pct.
Indiana	44	34	.564
Miami	43	35	.551
Kentucky	42	36	.538
Minnesota	36	42	.462
Milwaukee	27	55	.329
New York	17	61	.218

Western Division

	Won	Lost	Pct.
Oakland	60	18	.769
New Orleans	46	32	.590
Denver	44	34	.564
Dallas	41	37	.526
Los Angeles	33	45	.423
Houston	23	55	.295

ABA All-Star Game: West 133, East 127
ABA Championship: Oakland Oaks
NBA All-Star Game: East 123, West 112
NBA Championship: Boston Celtics
NBA Coach of the Year: Gene Shue, Baltimore
NBA Most Valuable Player: Wes Unseld, Baltimore
NBA Rookie of the Year: Wes Unseld

Western Division play-offs saw the Lakers hold off a determined San Francisco club and also defeat Atlanta in the division finals. Atlanta had beaten the Rockets in the first round, 4 games to 2. And so, as predicted, Los Angeles sat back and waited to see who would represent the East for the world title.

In the Eastern Division play-offs, the New York Knicks surprised everyone by taking the Bullets in 4 straight games. At the same time, a "tired and old" Celtics team used their trademark of good defense and got by a very sound Philadelphia team, 4 games to 1.

Everyone then concluded that the Knicks with their momentum would make short work of the Celtics. With a little luck and a lot of determination, the fourth-place Celtics emerged after 6 games as the Eastern Division champs. The "luck" was a groin injury to the Knicks playmaker Walt Frazier, and the determination was player-coach Bill Russell playing defense like a man possessed.

Boston had little time to savor its victory. For after 2 games with the Lakers the Boston team found themselves back home down by 2 games. Jerry West of the Lakers had a little something to do with winning the first 2 games: he scored 53 and 41 points respectively. From then on the tide turned, and 4 games later the series was tied at 3 games apiece. On Monday evening, May 5, before a sellout crowd in the Los Angeles Forum, and one of the largest television audiences of the year, the stage was set for one of the most dramatic games in the history of the NBA.

Boston once again called on balanced offense with Em Bryant, John Havlicek, Sam Jones and Don Nelson carrying the load. Their team defense was brilliant, and individually Bill Russell kept Chamberlain from getting to the boards. Boston so dominated the first three quarters that going into the fourth quarter it was leading by 15 points. Then due to carelessness on the part of the Celtics and a valiant effort on the part of Jerry West, the Lakers were back in the ball game trailing by a mere point. The Celtics then double and triple teamed West and managed to hold on and win the most important game by 2 points, 108–106.

It was truly one of the greatest moments in sports! After the game, though Russell and his team were overjoyed, they could hardly believe that they had won their 11th championship in 13 years and their 2d under Russell. To the regret of all basketball fans, Boston's player-coach later announced his retirement.

JACK TWYMAN
Sportscaster
American Broadcasting Company

"Los Angeles Times"

Completely disregarding the Lakers' Wilt Chamberlain, Boston's player-coach Bill Russell taps one in. The Celtics defeated the Los Angeles Lakers in 7 games to win their 11th NBA championship in 13 years.

Boxing

Joe Frazier fought only twice but solidified his stature as the major claimant to the world-heavyweight-boxing championship during 1969. He is rated the king of the ring in only six states while Jimmy Ellis is recognized by the World Boxing Association as the successor to the repudiated Muhammad Ali, born Cassius Clay.

Frazier's rise and Ellis' decline, and the professional debut of George Foreman shared the year's dim fistic spotlight. Foreman, 1968 Olympic heavyweight champion, quit the amateurs in May and by year's end had produced an 13-0 record as a professional.

Madison Square Garden, June 23: Joe Frazier (l) retains a share of heavyweight crown by defeating Jerry Quarry. The fight was stopped after seven rounds.

UPI

Frazier knocked out Texas' Dave Zyglewicz in less than 2 minutes of the first round of a colossal mismatch in Houston on Apr. 22 before sending Jerry Quarry into semiretirement with a 7-round technical-knockout triumph in New York's Madison Square Garden on June 23. The referee and ringside physician stopped the action after the seventh round because Quarry's right eye had swollen shut.

It was on this program that Foreman made his professional debut. The Hayward, Calif., boxer, who paraded around the ring after his Olympic triumph with a tiny U.S. flag clutched in his huge paw, disposed of Don Waldhelm of Freeport, N.Y., by a knockout at 1 minute, 54 seconds of the third round.

There was one other battle on Frazier's program for the year, but it will never show on the record books. After he and Clay, formerly friends, had finished a television interview in Philadelphia, they swung at each other when they reached the street. By common consent it was rated a draw. So meager was the talent in the heavyweight division that Frazier spent the remainder of the year as a singer and would-be entertainer.

Ellis spent the entire year in ring idleness and virtually evaporated from the scene. He refused a chance to fight Frazier because of the purse, giving Quarry the chance to earn an estimated $250,000. Much of the summer was spent in negotiating a bout against the aging Henry Cooper of London. Although the details were ironed out, the fight had to be canceled when doctors insisted upon an operation for the venerable Briton's right knee.

There also was a tragic oddity in the sport. Rocky Marciano, who retired in 1956 as the unbeaten heavyweight champion, was killed in an Iowa plane crash the night before his 46th birthday. In October, Al Weill, who managed the Brockton, Mass., native through his 49-bout career, died at age 75 in Miami Beach, Fla. Prior to Marciano's death on Aug. 31, trainer Charley Goldman passed on, as did Marciano's closest friend and adviser, Allie Columbo. Thus, the quartet that dominated the boxing world through the early 1950's was gone.

While boxing lacked attractions of international interest during the year, there were indications of better things to come. There was intense activity among the smaller men throughout the world, and Madison Square Garden, generally regarded as the capital of the sport, was averaging three fight shows a month as the winter season began.

HAROLD (SPIKE) CLAASSEN
Assistant General Sports Editor
The Associated Press

Football

College football entered its second hundred years in 1969, and, for the first time ever, the No. 1 team in the nation, Texas, was so designated by the president of the United States. On the professional side, it marked the end of the American Football League as an autonomous entity. In 1970, all of pro football would amalgamate.

PROFESSIONAL FOOTBALL

For the second year in a row, the American Football League achieved an upset of major proportions when the Kansas City Chiefs trounced the Minnesota Vikings, 23–7, before 80,998 fans in the 1970 Super Bowl game in New Orleans.

In 1969 the pro game made more news in the off-season than ever before. The pros regarded 1969 as an anniversary year too, the National Football League's fiftieth year.

The year started with George Allen, coach of the Los Angeles Rams, being fired by owner Dan Reeves because of a "lack of communication." Then, after a revolt by the Ram stars, including Deacon Jones and Roman Gabriel, he was rehired. The Rams, as if to prove they had to vindicate their involvement in the case, won their first 11 games; and Gabriel himself was named in most polls as the Player of the Year. But there followed three straight losses, and then elimination in the semifinal round of the play-offs against Minnesota.

Joe Namath, quarterback of the New York Jets and chief architect of the AFL's first Super Bowl triumph, was directed by Commissioner Pete Rozelle to sell his interest in a Manhattan restaurant. The reason given was that shady characters frequented the bar. Namath reacted by announcing his retirement rather than sell. This was, in a way, the most serious challenge to Rozelle's authority, but after six weeks, Namath recanted. He sold as directed and reported to the Jets' training camp in time to prepare for the new season.

One of the stickiest problems in the off-season was how to balance the two leagues for 1970. The NFL had 16 teams, the AFL 10. Rozelle had to find 3 NFL teams agreeable to a transfer into what would be the American Conference of the NFL. In May, he found acceptance in Pittsburgh, Baltimore and Cleveland, for which each of these old-line clubs would be paid a reported $3,000,000. Each conference in turn would be divided into three divisions, one of five teams and two of four teams each. By the end of 1969, the National owners had yet to agree on their divisional makeup.

UPI

Kansas City coach Hank Stram gets a triumphant ride to the dressing room after winning AFL championship.

The races in both leagues were almost totally lacking in suspense, particularly in the NFL where Dallas, Cleveland, Los Angeles and Minnesota easily won their divisional titles. Despite the drab races, attendance in the NFL rose again (6,293,243 as compared with 5,882,313 in 1968). It was the ninth consecutive year on the upbeat. AFL attendance also went up, from 2,610,278 to 2,988,069 for 70 games, due in part to O. J. Simpson's arrival.

Simpson made his pro debut rather reluctantly. The former Southern Cal star, possibly the most-talked-of college-football hero of all time, was picked first in the college draft by Buffalo of the AFL. He held out until one third of the training season was over before signing.

And with Simpson a holdout, other top draft choices waited to see how O. J. would fare. Simpson's rookie year was good but hardly up to expectations. He was clearly outdistanced for Rookie of the Year honors by Greg Cook, the Cincinnati quarterback, and Carl Garrett, a running back out of obscure New Mexico

Washington Redskins' new coach Vince Lombardi works with quarterback Sonny Jurgeson during training camp. Lombardi joined the Redskins in 1969 after highly successful career with Green Bay.

UPI

Highlands. Garrett joined Jim Nance in the Boston backfield.

In the NFL, the leading rookies were Calvin Hill, a first draft choice by Dallas from Yale, and tackle Joe Greene. Hill led the NFL's ground gainers through most of the season, then fell back because of a foot injury.

In the AFL, it was decided that the first two teams in each division would enter into a play-off, and thus the Oakland Raiders and the Kansas City Chiefs made it easily in the Western Division, the New York Jets and the Houston Oilers in the Eastern Division.

Super Bowl. Against Minnesota on Jan. 11, 1970, the Chiefs jumped off to a 9–0 lead on field goals of 48, 32 and 25 yards by Norwegian-born, soccer-style kicker Jan Stenerud. As the teams went to their dressing rooms at half time, it was 16–0.

Early in the second half the Vikings put together their only touchdown drive, 69 yards, with Dave Osborn crossing the goal line. There were visions of a Minnesota comeback, but the Chiefs kept their cool. On the next series of downs, quarterback Dawson passed short to Otis Taylor, who broke free from his defender, Earsell Mackbee, going 40 more yards for the score.

Dawson, plagued by reports that he was involved in a nationwide gambling investigation the week preceding the Super Bowl, had an outstanding afternoon and was voted the game's No. 1 player.

NFL Championship. On Sunday, Jan. 4, 1970, the Minnesota Vikings, with the best record in the NFL, opened with a quick burst against the Cleveland Browns in the deep freeze of Metropolitan Stadium, Bloomington, Minn., to win the title, 27–7.

The Vikings, only nine years old, had scored the most points in the regular season and had given up the fewest. And against the underdog Browns, on a field made playable by blowing hot air through an insulated blanket underneath the tarpaulin, and then by the use of flame-throwers after the tarp had been removed, the Vikings moved quickly.

They scored on their first march upfield. Quarterback Joe Kapp climaxed the drive by trying to hand off to Bill Brown from 7 yards out. After running into the fullback, he took it over himself. Then he passed to Gene Washington for a 75-yard score. And after a field goal by Fred Cox, rushing star Dave Osborn ran for 20 yards to make it 24–0 at half time. In the second half, the Vikings got a second field goal from Cox, and then finally the Browns scored on a pass from Bill Nelsen to Gary Collins. But the game was really won in the line where Minnesota's famed front four, the Purple People Eaters, harried Nelsen to distraction.

To qualify for the title game, Minnesota had defeated Los Angeles, 23–20, and Cleveland had trounced the Dallas Cowboys in the Cotton Bowl, 38–14.

NFL Regular Season. The NFL's four-division setup, four teams in each division, was not nearly so pulsating as it had been the year before, when it all began. One team in each division clearly dominated its field.

Gale Sayers of Chicago, coming off knee surgery, regained his stature as the league's top runner, but the Bears' season ended on a note of dissension. Quarterback Virgil Carter blasted the coaching staff and in turn was fined $1,000. Kicker Fred Cox of Minnesota led the league in scoring.

The Coach of the Year, even before the play-offs, was Minnesota's Bud Grant. Grant had spent most of his professional career playing for and coaching Winnipeg in the Canadian Football League.

AFL Championship. Also on Jan. 4, underdog Kansas City qualified for the Super Bowl for the second time in four years by whipping the Oakland Raiders on the West Coast, 17–7. The Chiefs had dropped two regular-season games to Oakland, and in the three seasons that Daryle Lamonica had led the Raiders to Western Division titles, Kansas City had beaten Oakland only once in seven games.

But this time Kansas City's front four, led by defensive end Aaron Brown, put a strong rush on Lamonica, forcing him out of the pocket. Brown, on one charge, jammed Lamonica's hand early in the third quarter, and the Oakland quarterback was ineffective the rest of the way.

The Raiders scored first on a four-yard burst by Charlie Smith. However, before the first half ended, Kansas City's Wendell Hayes went over from the 1 and the score was tied. In the third quarter, the Chiefs marched 94 yards for the go-ahead touchdown, Robert Holmes scoring from the 5. A field goal by K.C.'s Jan Stenerud from the 22 clinched the victory.

Len Dawson, who was spared the surgeon's knife at midseason when coach Hank Stram called off knee surgery, guided the Chiefs to the erratic triumph. In semifinal play-offs, Kansas City had defeated New York, 13–6,

---

FOOTBALL

COLLEGE

Conference Winners

Atlantic Coast: South Carolina
Big Eight: Missouri and Nebraska (tie)
Big Ten: Michigan and Ohio State (tie)
Ivy League: Princeton, Dartmouth, Yale (tie)
Mid-American: Toledo
Missouri Valley: Memphis State
Pacific Eight: Southern California
Southeastern: Tennessee
Southern: Davidson and Richmond (tie)
Southwest: Texas
Western Athletic: Arizona State
Yankee: Massachusetts

BOWL GAMES

Astro-Bluebonnet: Houston 36, Auburn 7
Cotton Bowl: Texas 21, Notre Dame 17
Gator Bowl: Florida 14, Tennessee 13
Orange Bowl: Penn State 10, Missouri 3
Rose Bowl: U.S.C. 10, Michigan 3
Sugar Bowl: Mississippi 27, Arkansas 22
Sun Bowl: Nebraska 45, Georgia 6

PROFESSIONAL

AMERICAN FOOTBALL LEAGUE FINAL STANDINGS

Eastern Division	Won	Lost	Tied	Per Cent	Western Division	Won	Lost	Tied	Per Cent
New York	10	4	0	.714	Oakland	12	1	1	.923
Houston	6	6	2	.500	Kansas City	11	3	0	.786
Boston	4	10	0	.286	San Diego	8	6	0	.571
Buffalo	4	10	0	.286	Denver	5	8	1	.385
Miami	3	10	1	.231	Cincinnati	4	9	1	.308

NATIONAL FOOTBALL LEAGUE FINAL STANDINGS

Eastern Conference

Century Division	Won	Lost	Tied		Capitol Division	Won	Lost	Tied	
Cleveland	10	3	1	.769	Dallas	11	2	1	.846
New York	6	8	0	.429	Washington	7	5	2	.583
St. Louis	4	9	1	.308	New Orleans	5	9	0	.357
Pittsburgh	1	13	0	.071	Philadelphia	4	9	1	.308

Western Conference

Coastal Division	Won	Lost	Tied		Central Division	Won	Lost	Tied	
Minnesota	12	2	0	.857	Los Angeles	11	3	0	.786
Detroit	9	4	1	.692	Baltimore	8	5	1	.615
Green Bay	8	6	0	.571	Atlanta	6	8	0	.429
Chicago	1	13	0	.071	San Francisco	4	8	2	.333

UPI

Fayetteville, Ark., Dec. 6: In final minutes of play, Texas halfback Jim Bertelsen carries the ball over the goal line to score winning touchdown against Arkansas.

and Oakland had overwhelmed Houston, 56–7, with Daryle Lamonica throwing six touchdown passes.

AFL Regular Season. Rookie coach John Madden of Oakland was selected as the AFL Coach of the Year. Sid Gillman of San Diego, one of the AFL charter coaches, retired in midseason because of an ulcer, and was replaced by an assistant, Charley Waller. Kicker Jim Turner of New York was the league's top scorer, and Dickie Post of San Diego led the ground-gainers. Lamonica's 34 touchdown passes was also tops.

COLLEGE FOOTBALL

The Ratings. Ohio State, as defending champions, held on to the No. 1 pinnacle until their final game, against Michigan. The Buckeyes were favored by 15 points, but lost 24–12 in the year's major upset. This loss catapulted Texas to the top, and as an extra fillip in the ratings game, President Nixon flew to Fayetteville, Ark., for the meeting between Texas and second or third ranked Arkansas. He had with him a plaque for the winning team, proclaiming it as No. 1.

Texas won the game, 15–14, closing out the regular season, 10 and 0. The President made the postgame presentation on national televi-

sion to the dismay of Penn State and all its rooters, since the Nittany Lions were also 10 and 0. In the final UPI poll of writers and broadcasters across the country, the Nixon decision was amply supported. However, The Associated Press decided to hold off on its final poll until the bowl games were out of the way, and the President wondered out loud if he had not been premature.

Attendance at college games again increased, from 27,025,846 to 27,626,160, and so did scoring, from 42.4 a game to 43.2. Steve Owens of Oklahoma rewrote the record book. The hard-running back rushed for a three-year all-time high of 3,867 yards on a record number of carries, 905, and he also scored the most points in three varsity seasons, 336.

Bowl Games. The postseason classics did nothing to change the mood of the country insofar as Texas was concerned. The Longhorns met Notre Dame in the Cotton Bowl, and with 1:08 left to play, sub-back Billy Dale plunged across from the 1 to score the touchdown that put Texas ahead 21–17 in a thrilling come-from-behind victory. It was Notre Dame's first bowl game in 45 years.

Thus the Longhorns nailed down No. 1 on all polls, despite the fact that second-ranked Penn State defeated No. 6 Missouri in the Orange Bowl, 10–3. It was the Lions' 22d victory in a row, the nation's longest winning streak. Coach Joe Paterno of Penn State continued to challenge the ratings, and losing coach Dan Devine of Missouri supported Paterno's stand.

In the Rose Bowl, the University of Southern California upset Michigan, 10–3. The losing Wolverines played without head coach Glenn (Bo) Schembechler, hospitalized a few hours before game time. Schembechler, in his first year at Michigan, had been voted by his peers Coach of the Year.

In the Sugar Bowl, Mississippi rocked Arkansas, 27–22, behind the quarterbacking of Archie Manning.

Award Winners. Steve Owens won the Heisman Trophy as college football's outstanding player. Mike Phipps of Purdue was runner-up.

Yale beat Harvard in what has been called The Game, 7–0, and Army shut out the Navy, 27–0. The original college combatants in 1869, Rutgers and Princeton, met again, and Rutgers was an easy winner.

A consensus of All-America backfields showed Phipps at quarterback, Owens and Jim Otis of Ohio State as the set backs, and sophomore Carlos Alvarez of Florida as the flanker.

FRANK GIFFORD
Director of Sports, WCBS-TV

Tony Jacklin putts on the 13th green during first round of the British Open. Jacklin went on to become the first Briton to win his country's Open since 1951.

UPI

Golf

When peace came to the embattled professionals with the naming of Joseph C. Dey, Jr., the longtime, serene but sagacious executive director of the U.S. Golf Association, as the commissioner of the players division of the PGA, the links world embarked on a year of unparalleled growth and wealth. Never before had so many pro golfers shared in so much money as in 1969 when approximately $6,000,000 was available in official purses. In addition, an estimated equal sum was available from such unofficial activities as endorsements, personal appearances and special clinics.

Dey forsook the USGA in late January to become the healing factor in the festering split between the traveling professionals and the far greater number of teaching pros. Once peace came, golf was off on a year of huge purses, huge collapses and huge comebacks, with the U.S. forces dominating the game everywhere except in the British Open and the U.S. Women's Amateur. Tony Jacklin, sharpened by two years of play in the United States, was the first Briton to win his country's Open since 1951, and France's stocky Catherine Lacoste triumphed in the Women's Amateur.

The Masters, annually held in Augusta, Ga., early in April, is the sport's grand entrance each year and often gives an indication of what lies ahead. This time its forecast came true. Bill Casper, golfer of the year in 1968, led through the first 3 rounds, but he skied over par on 5 of 7 early holes in the fourth and final trip around the flower-bedecked National course. Only a furious rally on the closing holes brought him into a tie for second with George Knudson of Canada and Tom Weiskopf at 282.

George Archer, a 6-foot-6-inch former cowboy, was the winner at 281.

Casper, however, got financial revenge late in the year when he won the Alcan Golfer of the Year tournament and its massive $55,000 first prize by a single stroke from Lee Trevino, 1968 Open champion. It is the sport's greatest dollar reward for first place. Leading by 6 strokes with 3 holes to go, Trevino ran into trouble while Casper was under par on the final 4 holes. The shaken Texan received a check for $15,000.

Trevino was succeeded as the Open champion by Orville Moody, who earned his nickname of Old Sarge by 14 years of Army service. Moody came within a stroke of not qualifying for the Open in both the preliminaries, but in the tournament itself his score of 281 was 1 over par for the 72 holes.

The devout Moody uncorked what he called the best shot of his career to eke out another close triumph in the World Series of Golf. It was a low-flying No. 2 iron that saved his par on the third hole of the last round and enabled him to beat Archer for the $50,000 first prize by 2 strokes.

Ray Floyd zoomed to a 74 in the final 18 holes of the PGA tourney, after previously posting nothing higher than a 69, but beat out Gary Player for the title. The tourney probably will be remembered longer by the fact that Arnold Palmer, the idol of millions, shot an 82 on opening day and had to withdraw because of a throbbing hip. It is the only major crown the Pennsylvania millionaire has never won.

Tommy Aaron won his first major tourney after 8 years of trying. He defeated the 57-

year-old Sam Snead by 2 strokes in a play-off for the Canadian Open.

A spectacular 35-foot putt for an eagle 3 by Jacklin on the final hole of the final match in the Ryder Cup competition gave the British a 16-16 deadlock. Jack Nicklaus was the victim of the spectacular tap, but the tie score let the defending U.S. Cup team keep the trophy for the 14th time in 18 meetings.

U.S. amateurs won the Walker Cup from their British cousins for the 20th time in 22 encounters, but again the score was close. The Americans won at Milwaukee, 10 matches to 8, but only pressure-packed play by Vinnie Giles and Dick Siderowf in 2 of the final single matches kept the British from getting at least a draw.

Giles again was second in the U.S. Amateur, decided this time over the demanding Oakmont, Pa., layout. Steve Melnyk, a University of Florida senior, built up a 3-stroke lead in the early rounds and relegated Giles to the runner-up role for the third straight year by getting a 32 on the opening 9 holes the last day.

Miss Lacoste, 1967 winner of the U.S. Women's Open, defeated Shelley Hamlin of Stanford University for the amateur crown, while the Ladies PGA laurels went to Betsy Rawls by 4 strokes over Kathy Whitworth.

HAROLD (SPIKE) CLAASSEN
Assistant General Sports Editor
The Associated Press

GOLF

INDIVIDUAL

MEN

Alcan: Bill Casper
Australian Open: Gary Player
British Open: Tony Jacklin
Canadian Open: Tommy Aaron
Masters: George Archer
Pro Golfers' Association: Ray Floyd
Tournament of Champions: Gary Player
United States Amateur: Steve Melnyk
United States Open: Orville Moody
World Series of Golf: Orville Moody

WOMEN

Canadian Open: Sandra Haynie
Pro Golfers' Association: Betsy Rawls
Tournament of Champions: Carol Mann
United States Amateur: Catherine Lacoste
United States Open: Donna Caponi
World Amateur: Catherine Lacoste

TEAM

MEN

Ryder Cup: Great Britain and United States (tie)
Walker Cup: United States
World Cup: United States

Horse Racing

Hardly anything can stir more arguments than a good horse race. The Kentucky Derby, the Preakness and the Belmont Stakes of 1969 stirred many discussions as two great colts, Arts and Letters and Majestic Prince, faced one another.

Early in the year, Top Knight, winner of the Flamingo and Florida Derby, dominated the three-year-old picture. Then, on the West Coast, Majestic Prince worked his way into favor by staying unbeaten for seven races before entering the Kentucky Derby. When Majestic Prince had just galloped to win the Santa Anita Derby, everybody gasped at the thought that he might be a superhorse.

Meanwhile, back in Florida, trainer Elliott Burch watched Arts and Letters show great promise with mostly second-place finishes to Top Knight. "At one time in Florida," Burch said, "I thought I might have the Triple Crown winner." These were bold words because Citation was the last Triple Crown winner (1948).

Three days before the Kentucky Derby, Arts and Letters' regular jockey, Willie Shoemaker, was hurt. It never helps to have a rider who does not know the horse. Although Braulio Baeza proved to be an able substitute, Bill Hartack and Majestic Prince got the better of the argument. The Prince stayed unbeaten by winning over Arts and Letters by a neck. The thrilling race was seen by President Nixon and thirty governors.

In the Preakness, Majestic Prince did it again. He won by a head. Trainer Johnny Longden did not want to run Majestic Prince in the Belmont because "he doesn't act just right." Owner Frank McMahon did. Arts and Letters, a chestnut son of Ribot, won the Belmont by 5½ lengths. Majestic Prince was second.

Majestic Prince was retired for the year because of an osselet (bone ailment) problem. Arts and Letters went on to greater honors. After Arts and Letters won the Travers and took a good lead in the race for horse-of-the-year honors, Burch commented: "Arts and Letters is not only the best horse I ever trained, but he may be the best horse anyone ever trained." Whether Burch is right remains to be seen, but he missed the Triple Crown by a neck and a head.

Night racing came to a major track when Fast Hilarious led all the way to win the American Derby at Arlington Park, near Chicago. Actually it was the first race on a night program but was run without lights. Mrs. Marjorie Everett, executive director of Arlington, turned to night racing after twilight racing failed to boost attendance.

Dean Eagle

Arts and Letters wins Belmont Stakes by 5½ lengths.

HORSE RACING

Horse of the year: Arts and Letters
Best 3-year-old: Arts and Letters
Best 3-year-old filly: Gallant Bloom
Best 2-year-old colt: Silent Screen
Best handicap mare: Gamely

TOP RACES

Arlington Classic: Ack Ack
Arlington-Washington Futurity: Silent Screen
American Derby: Fast Hilarious
Belmont Futurity: High Echelon
Belmont Stakes: Arts and Letters
Brooklyn Handicap: Nodouble
Flamingo: Top Knight
Florida Derby: Top Knight
Hollywood Derby: Tell
Hollywood Juvenile: Insubordination
Haskell Handicap: Verbatim
Jersey Derby: Al Hattab
Kentucky Derby: Majestic Prince
Kentucky Oaks: Hail to Patsy
Preakness Stakes: Majestic Prince
Santa Anita Handicap: Nodouble
Suburban Handicap: Mr. Right
Travers Stakes: Arts and Letters
Yankee Gold Cup: Jean-Pierre

At the conclusion of the Arlington meeting, Mrs. Everett said: "Racing has been suffering alarming decreases in attendance, and this increase for the final night of racing shows me night racing definitely has a future."

DEAN EAGLE
Sports Editor, *The Courier-Journal*
Louisville, Ky.

Ice Hockey

"We had something to prove." The statement was by Claude Ruel, coach of the Montreal Canadiens, and he had just supplied proof as capably as any district attorney. His team had just captured the Stanley Cup by sweeping four consecutive games from the St. Louis Blues in the best-of-seven series between the East and West Division champions of the National Hockey League.

The impressive bulk of Ruel's evidence had been provided earlier. That was when the Canadiens fought off the challenge of a fierce and fired-up Boston Bruin team to win the regular-season crown and then repel the same Bruins in the East Division play-off final. Many observers regarded Montreal's disposal of the Blues, runaway champions of the expansion division, as anticlimactic.

Ruel had felt unusual pressure in the 1968–69 NHL season because he was in his first season as coach of the Canadiens, and he was just thirty years old. "There were a lot of people who said we couldn't do it—meaning that I couldn't do it—because of my lack of experience," said Ruel. "The only way we could convince them they were wrong was by winning it all."

There were many times during the season when it appeared that Ruel's critics were wise. In late December, Boston, which had finished in the NHL cellar six times in the previous eight years, began a streak that threatened to leave the Canadiens hopelessly behind in the East race. With center Phil Esposito scoring points at a record pace, the Bruins went 18 games without a defeat. Boston finally suffered a loss on Feb. 6, 3–1 at the hands of the Blues in St. Louis. A series of injuries to key players, including Bobby Orr and John McKenzie, hampered Boston in the weeks after that. Montreal, which had stayed within range, regained first place two weeks later and nipped Boston by three points in the final standings.

In the early rounds of the East play-offs, Montreal disposed of third-place New York, and Boston ousted fourth-place Toronto, each without the loss of a game.

Coach Scotty Bowman's St. Louisans, winners over second-place Oakland by 19 points in the West, took four straight from third-place Philadelphia and then did the same to Los

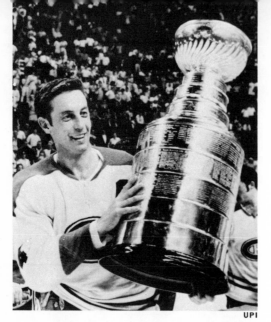

Montreal's Jean Beliveau proudly accepts Stanley Cup.

UPI

tying goal with 56 seconds remaining. Ralph Backstrom's first shot of the game, in the opening minute of sudden-death overtime gave Montreal a 3–2 victory.

The Canadiens came from behind in game No. 2, with defenseman Serge Savard scoring with 1:09 to go to tie Boston at 3–3. Mickey Redmond's shot in overtime put Montreal two-up.

Esposito, who had cracked the NHL record with 126 points in the regular season, had two goals and three assists as the series switched to Boston and the Bruins won 5–0. Boston evened the count at two victories apiece with a 3–2 victory, with the Bruins scoring their first two goals while shorthanded in the opening period.

Boston's fun was over, however. Montreal gained a 4–2 triumph and then ended the series with a 2–1 overtime victory, with Beliveau firing in the decisive goal after 11:28 of the second extra period.

As the Canadiens and Blues prepared to open the final Stanley Cup series, a headline in the Montreal *Gazette* read: "St. Louis Improved, but Not Enough to Make It Close." The words stung the proud Blues, but unfortunately they appeared to be true. A year before, the Blues had lost four straight to the Canadiens, but each was by a one-goal margin. This time Ruel's Canadiens ruled the ice.

St. Louis' chief offensive threat was Red Berenson, whose feats had included a six-goal

Angeles. Jacques Plante, who shared the Vezina Trophy honors with fellow St. Louis goaltender Glenn Hall by allowing just 157 points in the regular season, did all the net minding in these series because of an injury to Hall. Plante permitted eight goals in the eight play-off contests.

While the Blues were breezing, the Canadiens were up to their necks in Bruins. In the opening game, Boston had a 2–0 lead with only seven minutes left. But then John Ferguson scored for Montreal, and Jean Beliveau flicked in the

---

ICE HOCKEY

COLLEGE
NCAA Championship: Denver

PROFESSIONAL
National Hockey League
All-Star Game: East 3, West 3

Final Standings

Eastern Division	W.	L.	T.	Pts.	Western Division	W.	L.	T.	Pts.
Montreal	46	19	11	103	St. Louis	37	25	14	88
Boston	42	18	16	100	Oakland	29	36	11	69
New York	41	26	9	91	Philadelphia	20	35	21	61
Toronto	35	26	15	85	Los Angeles	24	42	10	58
Detroit	33	31	12	78	Pittsburgh	20	45	11	51
Chicago	34	33	9	77	Minnesota	18	43	15	51

Stanley Cup: Montreal Canadiens

Art Ross Trophy (scoring): Phil Esposito, Boston
Calder Trophy (rookie): Danny Grant, Minnesota
Georges Vezina Trophy (goalie): Jacques Plante and Glenn Hall, St. Louis
Hart Trophy (most valuable player): Phil Esposito
Lady Byng Trophy (sportsmanship): Alex Delvecchio, Detroit
Norris Trophy (defense): Bobby Orr, Boston
Smythe Trophy (play-off performance): Serge Savard, Montreal

performance against Philadelphia early in the season, but he and the other Blues were throttled by the hard-checking Canadiens, who won by scores of 3–1, 3–1, 4–0 and 2–1. This gave Montreal its fifteenth Stanley Cup, and it gave coach Claude Ruel a heaping measure of satisfaction. "Winning this series from St. Louis was my second best thrill," said Ruel. "The best was winning the East Division title. They said we couldn't do it."

BOB BROEG
Sports Editor
St. Louis Post-Dispatch

Rowing

During 1969, Harvard, with most of its 1968 Olympic eight intact, again dominated the U.S. college rowing scene. Yet they were not undefeated. The University of Pennsylvania ended Harvard's string of victories, unbroken from 1963, by beating them for the Adams Cup at Philadelphia in May. Harvard bounced back, however, to show a clean stern to Penn and everyone else in the Eastern Sprints at Worcester, Mass., the following week. Harvard's lightweights were also undefeated during the season.

In the Intercollegiate Rowing Association Regatta at Syracuse in mid-June, generally considered the U.S. collegiate championships, Penn's varsity eight fought off a strong challenge to beat Dartmouth. Cornell's junior varsity won handsomely, while the University of

---

ROWING

European Championship (Klagenfurt, Austria)
  Double sculls: John VanBlom and Tom McKibbon, U.S.
  Eights: East Germany
  Four with coxswain: West Germany
  Four without coxswain: Russia
  Pair with coxswain: Czechoslovakia
  Pair without coxswain: Tony Johnson and Larry Hough, U.S.
  Singles: Demiddi, Argentina

Royal Henley Regatta (Henley-on-Thames, England)
  Diamond sculls: Hans Joachim Bohmer, S.C. Dynamo-Berlin, East Germany
  Grand Challenge Cup for eights: Einheit, East Germany
  Princess Elizabeth Cup: Washington-Lee High School, Arlington, Va.
  Thames Challenge Cup for lightweight eights: Leander Club, England

U.S. Youth Championships
  Eights without coxswain: Litchfield Rowing Association, Kent, Conn.
  Four without coxswain: Litchfield Rowing Association

Washington frosh caught Penn for a dead heat, the first in the IRA's 67-year history. Harvard's varsity was not present. They were on the Thames at New London giving the Yale eight a lesson to remember in their annual four-mile classic.

In August, under the leadership of Bill Stowe, head rowing coach at Columbia University, an entire team of 35 boys under 19 years of age flew to Naples, Italy, to race in the World Youth Championships. The U.S. eight took third—an encouraging step in the direction of matching the Europeans' systematic development of rowers.

Perhaps the most significant development in international rowing is the increasing attention paid to physiology. Aware of the enormous publicity advantages, the East Germans are particularly active in this research. According to Bill Stowe, public-relations director of the National Association of Amateur Oarsmen, it is not unusual to see an entire crew take their pulses within ten seconds of the end of a race. The coxswain calls the time, and each oarsman feels a vein in his neck.

MOULTON H. FARNHAM
Editor, *Boating*

Soccer

The year 1969 was an ironic one for soccer in the United States. While the game had been making tremendous advances on the lower levels from juvenile up, the nationwide professional circuit, the North American Soccer League, saw its active membership dwindle to five teams in as many cities. Although many non-U.S. teams toured the country, the crowds ranged from good to poor and left no definite pattern.

The regular North American League season went right down to the wire before the Kansas City Spurs, which had joined the circuit in 1968, wound up titlist to succeed Atlanta. Victory was won by a single point under the league's unusual point-scoring system adopted to encourage more goals. This, too, provided an ironic touch, since Atlanta had been a prime mover for the system. Under the regular system prevailing in soccer, the Chiefs would have retained the honors by the same margin of a single point.

The Greek-Americans of New York made soccer history by becoming the first team to capture the National Challenge Cup, symbolic of the U.S. Open championship, for the third consecutive time. They accomplished it by downing the Montabello Armenians of Los Angeles, 1–0, in overtime in Los Angeles.

The Wolverhampton Wolves of England, representing Kansas City in the NASL's month-long, pre-regular-season International Cup competition whereby the league cities had British teams fronting for them, won this tournament.

Among the many other foreign teams who played in the United States during 1969 and enjoyed varying successes were West Ham United and Aston Villa of England; Dundee United and Glasgow Celtics of Scotland; Eintracht Braunschweig of Germany; Inter Bratislava of Czechoslovakia; Atlas, Guadalajara and Club America of Mexico; Dynamo Kiev of Russia; West Bromwich Albion of England; Dukla of Czechoslovakia; Fiorentina, Juventus, Inter Milan and A. C. Milan of Italy; Setubal of Portugal; Barcelona of Spain; Barcelona of Ecuador; Kilmarnock of Scotland; Sparta of Prague, Czechoslovakia; Legia of Poland; Portuguesa and Corinthians of Brazil; Olympiakos of Greece; M.T.K. of Hungary; River Plate of Argentina; TSV Ottobeuren, Phoenix Durmersheim and 1896 Mainaschaff of Germany.

After surviving the first preliminary round, the United States was eliminated by Haiti in the World Cup zone play. The American eleven lost, 2–0, and then, 1–0. Erwin Single of Tappan, N.Y., was elected president of the U.S. Soccer Football Association to succeed Robert Guelker of St. Louis.

MILT MILLER
Editor
Soccer News

Swimming

The United States' dominance in swimming has rarely been broken in recent years, and the Americans—led by such tested competitors as Debbie Meyer, Mark Spitz, Mike Burton and Susie Atwood—were out in front again in 1969. Yet it was also a year in which a West German, Hans Fassnacht; an East German, Roland Matthes; a South American, Jose Fiola; and a Russian, Nikolai Pankin, began to dull the American edge.

Fassnacht, a student at California State College at Long Beach, broke Burton's 1,650-yard freestyle American record with a clocking of 15:54.2, before Burton took over again with a 15:40.1. Hans swam another American record, 4:07.7, in the 400-yard individual medley, before Gary Hall, a 17-year-old from Garden Grove, Calif., bettered that with a 4:00.8. But Fassnacht held one world record: his 4:04 in the 400-meter freestyle.

Matthes set a world mark of 2:07.4 in the 200-meter backstroke, and Pankin established two standards: 1:05.8 in the 100-meter breaststroke and 2:25.4 in the 200-meter breaststroke. Teen-ager Hall had a brilliant year, adding records in the long-course 400-meter individual medley (4:33.9), the 200-meter individual medley (2:09.6) and the 200-meter backstroke (2:06.6). Burton set a new men's record for the 1,500-meter freestyle (16:04.5).

Among the women, Susie Atwood of Lakewood Aquatic Club was the star, establishing world records in the 100- and 200-meter backstrokes (1:06.0 and 2:21.5). Debbie Meyer added one in the 1,500-meter freestyle (17:19.9) and was accorded an unusual honor. She won the annual Sullivan Award (outstanding amateur athlete in the United States), the first woman to do so since track star Wilma Rudolph in 1961.

Indiana University defeated USC, 427 points to 306, for the NCAA swimming championship; and the University of California at Irvine, behind a record five firsts by Mike Martin, took NCAA college-division honors. Eastern Michigan was the NAIA champion.

DWIGHT CHAPIN
Sportswriter
Los Angeles Times

Tennis

Turmoil and Rod (Rocket) Laver shared the tennis spotlight in 1969. The confusion created in 1968 when the governing fathers of tennis permitted amateur and professional players to compete together continued to simultaneously bewilder and enthrall galleries in the United States and around the world.

The carrottop Australian Rocket individually dominated the racket sport as no other man had previously. When Laver pocketed $16,000 at Forest Hills, the highest prize for a winner in the sport's history, he became the first man to capture two grand slams (Australian, United States, French and Wimbledon championships).

Laver's triumph on this occasion was more meaningful than his slam in 1962. In 1969 he had to survive the best of all categories of competitors: amateurs, "registered players" and professionals alike. Since Arthur Ashe, as an amateur in 1968, had helped destroy the myth that the touring professional was superior by winning the U.S. Open, respect for Laver's performance against all comers was enhanced enormously.

A report of individual accomplishment would be incomplete without mention of the venerable war-horse Pancho Gonzales, who at the age of 41 won the Pacific Southwest and Howard

Hughes Opens in successive weeks. Pancho's incredible accomplishment came at the end of an arduous season over a magnificent field that included Laver, Ashe, John Newcombe, Ken Rosewall, Tony Roche and Tom Okker. Gonzales once again talked of retirement after his triumphs, but his legion of followers know better.

Just as Laver ruled individually, the United States dominated team competitions by capturing the Davis Cup, the Federation Cup and the Wightman Cup. For the first time in 22 years, the United States successfully defended the trophy that Dwight Davis donated in 1900 for an event symbolic of international tennis supremacy. The surprise challengers were Rumania's Ilie Nastase and Ion Tiriac, who defeated England, Russia, Spain and Brazil on the way to a showdown with the booming services of Ashe and Stan Smith.

New Yorker Julie Heldman was the heroine of the Wightman (United States against Britain) and Federation Cup (woman's version of Davis Cup). Nancy Richey and Billie Jean King continued their global rivalry, with Nancy having a distinct edge in head-to-head meetings.

Of primary interest among American players was the acceptance in the United States of the

Although a veteran, popular Pancho Gonzales won the Pacific Southwest and Howard Hughes Opens in 1969.

Pictorial Parade

TENNIS

Davis Cup: United States
Federation Cup: United States
Wightman Cup: United States

AUSTRALIA (Open)

Men's Singles: Rod Laver (Australia)
Men's Doubles: Roy Emerson-Laver (Australia)
Women's Singles: Margaret Court (Australia)
Women's Doubles: Court-Judy Tegart (Australia)

FRANCE (Open)

Men's Singles: Rod Laver (Australia)
Men's Doubles: John Newcombe-Tony Roche (Australia)
Women's Singles: Margaret Court (Australia)
Women's Doubles: Françoise Durr-Ann Jones (France-England)

WIMBLEDON (Open)

Men's Singles: Rod Laver (Australia)
Men's Doubles: Newcombe-Roche (Australia)
Women's Singles: Ann Jones (England)
Women's Doubles: Court-Tegart (Australia)

UNITED STATES (Open)

Men's Singles: Rod Laver (Australia)
Men's Doubles: Ken Rosewall-Fred Stolle (Australia)
Women's Singles: Margaret Court (Australia)
Women's Doubles: Durr-Darlene Hard (France-United States)

UNITED STATES (Clay Court)

Men's Singles: Zeljko Franulovic (Yugoslavia)
Men's Doubles: Bill Bowrey-Clark Graebner (Australia-United States)
Women's Singles: Gail Chanfreau (Australia)
Women's Doubles: Chanfreau-Leslie Bowrey (Australia)

UNITED STATES (Grass Court)

Men's Singles: Stan Smith (United States)
Men's Doubles: Dick Crealy-Allan Stone (Australia)
Women's Singles: Margaret Court (Australia)
Women's Doubles: Court-Wade (Australia-England)

UNITED STATES (Amateur)

Men's Singles: George Butch Seewagen
Men's Doubles: Tom Leonard-Erik Van Dillen
Women's Singles: Linda Tuero
Women's Doubles: Emilie Burrer-Pam Richmond

concept of the "registered player," whereby top tennis stars, such as Ashe and Clark Graebner, could maintain their eligibility for Davis Cup competition and be free to accept prize money, endorse products and generally make a living from the game. The only difference between Laver and Graebner is that the latter accepts the authority of the United States Lawn Tennis Association, while Laver's boss is a professional promoter, George MacCall.

The USLTA promoted a series of prize-money tournaments for their "house pros," among whom was Stan Smith, who collected $4,000 plus a new car for winning the Eastern Grass Court Championship. However, no promoter or "contract" pros were allowed to enter. Accordingly, the disagreements between promoters and national associations around the world solidified. The center of the storm revolves around Davis Cup rules which prevent a half dozen of the world's best players (including Laver, Okker, Roche and Newcombe) from competing.

Many associations outside the United States are losing prime, young tennis athletes to the touring-professional organizers who offer the apparent security of a long-term contract. But the promoters may be consuming players faster than they can be sold to the public. The administrative stalemate is likely to be resolved only when the finances of the promoters are exhausted, leaving players to participate freely in any tournament, as in golf, without guarantees or employers to contend with.

EUGENE L. SCOTT
Captain, International Lawn Tennis Club

Eli Attar

Willie Davenport, who set 3 records in 1969, wins 110-meter high-hurdles event in meet against the U.S.S.R.

Track and Field

There is usually a letdown in track and field after an Olympic year, and that was partially true in 1969. Such old favorites as Jim Ryun and Gerry Lindgren were bothered by injuries and the rigors of competition, and both had disappointing years. Nonetheless, 1969 was a big year for several other performers.

It will be remembered as the year Curtis Mills, the Texas A & M sophomore and the first Negro athlete it has ever had, ran the 440-yard dash in 44.7 seconds, clipping 0.1 second off Tommie Smith's world mark. It will also be remembered as the year veteran John Pennel of the Southern California Striders soared higher than any man ever had before in the outdoor pole vault, 17 ft., 10¼ in., and as the year Bill Toomey set a new world decathlon record.

It will be recalled as the year that both the U.S. men's and women's teams scored victories over the U.S.S.R. and Britain in a three-way meet at the Los Angeles Coliseum. The women's triumph over the Russian women, 70–67, was the first such victory in history.

And 1969 will be thought of as the year in which Willie Davenport won 15 straight indoor-hurdle tests and set several records in the process: 45-yard highs (5.3), 50-yard highs (5.8) and 70-yard highs (7.8).

DWIGHT CHAPIN
Sportswriter, *Los Angeles Times*

TRACK AND FIELD

Some Indoor Records Set in 1969

  100-yard dash: Lennox Miller, USC (9.4)
  500-yard dash: Larry James, Villanova (55.4)
  880-yard run: Ralph Doubell, Australia (1:47.9)
  Pole vault: Bob Seagren, USC (17-6)
  3-mile run: George Young, Casa Grande, Ariz. (13:09.8)
  2-mile relay: Villanova (7:22.8)

Some Outdoor Records Set in 1969

  3-mile walk: Ron Laird, New York AC (20:49.4)
  5,000-meter walk: Ron Laird (21:33.8)
  Distance medley relay: Kansas (9:33.0)
  Hammer throw: Anatoly Bondarchuk, U.S.S.R. (245 ft.)
  Javelin: Jorma Kinnunen, Finland (304-1½)

NCAA Indoor: Kansas
National AAU Indoor: Tennessee State
NCAA Outdoor: San Jose State
NCAA College Division Outdoor: Cal Poly, San Luis Obispo
NAIA Outdoor: Prairie View A&M
IC4A: Villanova

Nigel Dowden

Dick Carter's "Red Rooster" won the Admiral's Cup Fastnet Race and the New York City Cup in 1969.

Yachting

Though yachting in 1969 lacked the excitement of an America's Cup competition or an Olympics, the year was rich in the variety and number of competitive events available to the racing skipper.

He could have started in late winter with the Southern Ocean Racing Conference's six-race series and matched himself against Jack Powell and Wally Frank's winning *Salty Tiger.* The winner, a new 46-foot aluminum yawl, was designed and built by Bob Derecktor of Mamaroneck, N.Y. Then, in June the racing skipper might have entered the Transatlantic Race from Newport, R.I., to Cork, Ireland, to help celebrate (a year in advance) the 250th anniversary of the Royal Cork Yacht Club, the world's oldest. In this placid race the winner was John B. Kilroy's 73-footer *Kialoa II,* from Los Angeles, Calif.

Many racing skippers, however, bypassed the 2,790-mile transatlantic event in favor of the 26th TransPac, a 2,250-mile race from San Pedro, Calif., to Honolulu. By so doing they caught one of the roughest TransPacs on record. The record-breaking overall and Class C winner was *Argonaut,* a Cal 40 piloted by 23-year-old Jon Andron. Cal boats, fleet fiberglass racers designed by Bill Lapworth and built by Jensen Marine, dominated the race by taking 7 of the first 10 overall places.

> **YACHTING**
>
> **Admiral's Cup Series (England):** United States **North American Yacht Racing Union Championships**
> > **Adams Cup (Women's):** Mrs. Jan Chance O'Malley, Mantoloking, N.J.
> > **Mallory Cup (Men's):** Graham Hall, Fort Schuyler, N.Y.
> > **Sears Cup Junior Championship:** Noroton Yacht Club, Darien, Conn.

Americans dominated the international-racing scene with a team victory over 10 other nations in the Admiral's Cup series in England. This victory hinged on the brilliant performance of Boston yacht designer Dick Carter, with his own new 41-foot sloop *Red Rooster.* She won the 600-mile Fastnet Race, one of four Admiral's Cup contests. Of the American team's 496 total points, *Red Rooster* accounted for 213. Dick Nye's new 48-foot aluminum Mc-Curdy-Rhodes sloop *Carina* contributed 177, and Tom Watson's 58-foot cutter *Palawan* added 106.

For 1970, an America's Cup year, the prospects are bright. Although England has dropped out as a candidate for the challenge, Australia and France will descend on Newport, R.I., in late summer to face each other in an elimination series. The winner will have the honor of challenging the United States in the 22d contest for the America's Cup.

MOULTON H. FARNHAM
Editor, *Boating*

"Skiing" magazine

Gertrud Gabl, twenty-year-old Austrian skiing star, wins the women's 1969 World Cup title with 131 points.

SPORTS

SUMMARY OF WINNERS NOT INCLUDED ON PAGES 398–419

ARCHERY—World Champions
Men: Hardy Ward, Mount Pleasant, Tex.
Women: Dorothy Lidstone, Vancouver, B.C.

BADMINTON—All-England World Champions
Men's Singles: Rudy Hartano, Indonesia
Women's Singles: Hiroe Yuki, Japan

BOBSLEDDING—World Champions
Two-man: Italy
Four-man: West Germany

BOWLING—American Bowling Congress Champions
All-events (classic): Larry Lichstein, Hartford, Conn.
All-events (regular): Ed Jackson, Cincinnati
Doubles (classic): Jim Stefanich, Joliet, Ill., Dan McCune, Munster, Ind.
Doubles (regular): Bob Maschmeyer, Charles Guedel, Indianapolis
Singles (classic): Nelson Burton, Jr., St. Louis
Singles (regular): Greg Campbell, St. Louis

CANOEING—U.S. Champions
Canoe Singles (1,000 meters): Andy Torro, Ann Arbor, Mich.
Kayak Singles (1,000 meters): Peter Weigand, Newport Beach, Calif.

CASTING—U.S. Champion
All-round: Edward Lanser, St. Louis

CURLING
U.S.: Superior, Wisc.
World: Canada

CYCLING
U.S. Sprint: Tim Mountford, Sherman Oaks, Calif.
World Amateur Sprint: Daniel Morelon, France
World Professional Sprint: Patrick Sercu, Belgium

DOGS—Best-in-Show Winners
International (Chicago): Ch. Arriba's Prima Donna, fawn boxer
Westminster: Ch. Glamoor Good News, Skye terrier

FENCING—World Champions
Epée: Bohdan Andrzejewski, Poland
Foil: Friederich Wessel, West Germany
Saber: Alex Orban, New York

GYMNASTICS—U.S. National AAU Champions
All-round: Mauno Nissinen, Seattle
Team: Husky Gym Club, Seattle

HANDBALL—U.S. Handball Association 4-Wall Champions
Singles: Paul Haber, Milwaukee
Doubles: Lou Kramberg, Lou Russo, New York

HORSESHOE PITCHING—World Champions
Men: Danny Kuchcinski, Erie, Pa.
Women: Vicki Winston, La Monte, Mo.

HORSE SHOWS—U.S. National Horse Shows Association Champions
International: William Steinkraus

ICE SKATING—World Champions
Men's Figure: Tim Wood, Bloomfield Hills, Mich.
Men's Speed: Dag Fornaess, Norway
Women's Figure: Gabriele Seyfert, East Germany
Women's Speed: Lasma Kauniste, U.S.S.R.

JUDO—U.S. National AAU Champions
Open: Taizo Noguchi, New York
Team: New York

LACROSSE
Club: Long Island A.C.

POLO
Intercollegiate: Yale
Open: Tulsa Green Hills

RUGBY
Eastern U.S.: Boston
European: Wales
World: New Zealand

SKIING—World Cup
Men: Karl Schranz, Austria
Women: Gertrud Gabl, Austria

SOFTBALL—U.S. Amateur Association
Men's Fast Pitch: Raybestos, Stratford, Conn.
Men's Slow Pitch: Copper Hearth, Milwaukee
Women's Fast Pitch: Lionettes, Orange, Calif.
Women's Slow Pitch: Converse Dots, Miami

SURFING—U.S. Champions
Men: Corky Carroll, Dana Point, Calif.
Women: Sharron Weber, Hawaii

VOLLEYBALL—U.S. National AAU Champions
Men: U.S. Armed Forces
Women: Rebels, Mayor Daley Youth Foundation, Chicago

WATER POLO
NCAA: UCLA

WEIGHT LIFTING—World Champions
Heavyweight: Joe Dube, Doctor's Inlet, Fla.

WRESTLING—World Free Style Champions
Unlimited: Aleksandr Medved, U.S.S.R.

Sweden's new Premier, Socialist Olof Palme, poses happily with his attractive wife and three children.

UPI

SWEDEN

The Erlander era ended in September 1969. Having served as prime minister for the previous 23 years, Tage Erlander resigned as chairman of the Social Democratic Party in September, and on Oct. 1 was succeeded by Olof Palme. On Oct. 14, Palme was sworn in as the new prime minister at a king-in-council meeting at the Royal Palace. Fifteen members of the Erlander Cabinet retained their posts in the new Government.

Olof Palme, who was born in 1927, had been looked upon as one of Erlander's "crown princes." He attended college in the United States, took a law degree in Sweden in 1951, and for some time served as Erlander's private secretary. He was appointed minister without portfolio in 1963, minister of communications in 1965, and became minister of education in 1967.

In February the two-chamber Swedish Parliament (Riksdag) voted to replace itself with one house on Jan. 1, 1971. There were 274 votes in favor and only 15 in opposition. The new single-chamber Riksdag will have 350 members elected for a period of 3 years. To secure a seat a party must win at least 4 per cent of the votes cast. National and municipal elections will be held on the same day.

In early January, Sweden became the first Western European nation to grant diplomatic recognition to North Vietnam. A Swedish Foreign Ministry communiqué stressed that the step was motivated by both political and practical reasons. A statement by Foreign Minister Torsten Nilsson pointed out: "We were among the first to recognize the People's Republic of China and the Republic of Algeria. Those who are interested in history may recall that Sweden was also among the first to recognize the United States of America in 1783. In all these cases the decision taken was a realistic one."

Johannes Edfelt, poet and critic, and Justice Sture Petren were elected to the Swedish Academy. They succeeded the late poet Erik Lindegren and the late Birger Ekeberg, marshal of the realm.

ERIK J. FRIIS
Editor, *The American-Scandinavian Review*

SWEDEN

Area: 173,600 sq. mi.
Population: 8,000,000
Capital: Stockholm (pop., 780,000)
Government: Gustaf VI Adolf, king—1950; Olof Palme, prime minister—1969
Gross national product: $26,500,000,000
Monetary unit: krona (5.17 kronor = U.S. $1.00)
Chief products: dairy products, grains, wood products, iron ore, lead, zinc
Foreign trade: exports, $4,944,000,000; imports, $5,084,000,000
Communications: 3,934,694 telephones, 2,934,-795 radios, 2,325,834 TV sets, 152 daily newspapers
Transportation: roads, 60,454 mi.; 1,966,600 passenger cars; railroads, 8,002 mi.
Education: 1,284,900 elementary, secondary and vocational students, 96,932 students of higher education
Armed forces: 750,000

See map on page 185

ILO/Jean Mohr

In Geneva, once a Calvinist stronghold, Pope Paul VI is introduced to International Labor Organization.

SWITZERLAND

In April, Geneva celebrated the fiftieth anniversary of the decision to set up the League of Nations there. Though the League failed, it made Geneva the acknowledged center of many international organizations. During the ceremonies, which were attended by UN Secretary-General U Thant, a plaque was placed in the Palais Wilson. The Palais, formerly a hotel, served as League headquarters until the Palais des Nations was completed in 1936. Today the Palais des Nations is the European headquarters of the United Nations, and the Palais Wilson houses the International Education Office of the United Nations Educational, Scientific and Cultural Organization.

SWITZERLAND

Area: 15,944 sq. mi.
Population: 6,200,000
Capital: Bern (pop., 170,000)
Government: Hans Peter Tschudi, president—1970
Gross national product: $16,900,000,000
Monetary unit: franc (4.3 francs = U.S. $1.00)
Chief products: wheat, potatoes, cheese, sugar, clocks
Foreign trade: exports, $3,973,000,000; imports, $4,514,000,000
Communications: 2,533,684 telephones, 1,725,341 radios, 990,000 TV sets, 128 daily newspapers
Transportation: roads, 11,004 mi.; 979,267 passenger cars; railroads, 1,807 mi.
Education: 720,042 elementary and secondary students, 7 universities
Armed forces: 644,500

See map on page 185

Foreign Minister Willy Spühler announced in June that Switzerland would not "at this time" join the United Nations. However, Switzerland will continue to develop its relations with the UN. Switzerland is a member of specialized UN agencies such as the World Health Organization and the International Labor Organization, and has contributed to UN peace-keeping operations. The decision not to join the United Nations followed the findings of a government report that revealed little popular support in Switzerland for joining the world body. A Swiss government decision to join would have to be approved by a national referendum.

In August the Swiss Government awarded contracts for the construction of the world's longest road tunnel. It will connect northern and southern Europe year-round through the Swiss Alps. The 10-mile-long St. Gotthard Tunnel will run from Göschenen to Airolo and relieve the increasing congestion in the existing rail tunnel under the St. Gotthard Pass. The pass is closed by snow for several months each winter, while the road tunnel will be usable all year round. Preliminary work has already started on the tunnel, and it is expected that 7 years and 306,000,000 francs (US$71,160,000) will be required to complete the work.

On June 10, Pope Paul VI made a one-day visit to Geneva, the center of Calvinism since the Reformation. The official purpose of the visit was his address to the annual meeting of the International Labor Organization. But during his stay he also spoke before a meeting of the World Council of Churches and participated in an ecumenical service. During his address to the churchmen, he reaffirmed the Catholic doctrine of papal infallibility.

On Mar. 5, President Ludwig von Moos announced that the Government would propose a constitutional amendment granting women full voting rights and the right to be elected to Federal offices. Thus far, only men who have served in the military are permitted to vote.

Like almost all Western countries, Switzerland was faced with the threat of increasing inflation in 1969. Exports rose 12 per cent above the 1968 rate, and the total rate of inflation was expected to reach 3 per cent by the end of 1969. In August the Swiss National Bank and the Swiss Bankers' Association agreed on measures to limit credit, and in September the National Bank raised its discount rate from 3 to 3¾ per cent. It was hoped that both moves would help slow down the inflationary spiral.

NORA ANN SMYTH
Associate Editor
Lands and Peoples

TAIWAN

In 1969 the Nationalist Chinese regime on Taiwan marked its 20th year in exile from mainland China. Though the Nationalists might continue to bemoan their exile, they could rejoice in the healthiest economy and most stable political situation they had enjoyed since 1949.

The booming economy, the product of the most successful economic-development program in developing Asia, continued to set impressive marks. Exports soared to the magical US$1,000,000,000 mark, up from US$850,-000,000 in 1968. Imports for the year were expected to be about the same as, or perhaps slightly more than, exports, thus making two-way trade of more than US$2,000,000,000. With new foreign investment for the year estimated at US$112,000,000 (compared with US$104,000,000 in 1968) the basis for continued economic growth seemed assured. The growth rate for the year, which had been projected at about 8 per cent, in fact hit 10 per cent, making it one of the highest growth rates in the world.

Although personal incomes remained low by the standards of developed nations, the people of Taiwan were clearly beginning to enjoy the benefits of the booming economy. Per capita income climbed to US$237, compared with US$218 in 1968. Taiwan industry needs greater variety and sophistication. The Government has begun tailoring its economic policies to that end and promoting technical education to provide the skilled workers needed.

The political spotlight was focused on Chiang Ching-kuo, the 59-year-old elder son of President Chiang Kai-shek. Although the President continues active, it became evident during 1969 that Chiang Ching-kuo was handling day-to-day matters and was destined to succeed his father as Nationalist leader.

During the Tenth National Party Congress of the ruling Kuomintang (Nationalist Party) held in Taipei between Mar. 29 and Apr. 9, Chiang Ching-kuo received the most votes of any of the 99 members of the policy-making Party Central Committee. Even more significant was the promotion, on June 25, of Chiang Ching-kuo from defense minister to vice premier. Thus Chiang Ching-kuo entered the government bureaucracy, the ultimate source of power. Through earlier appointments, including years as defense minister from 1965 to June 1969, Chiang Ching-kuo still controls the military, the security and intelligence organizations, the 130,000-member Youth Corps and the 180,000-strong retired servicemen's organization. On July 31 Chiang Ching-kuo also was appointed to head the Council for International Economic Cooperation and Development (CIECD), the body that oversees Taiwan's economic development.

In the view of many observers, these changes augur well for Taiwan. Chiang Ching-kuo is considered strong, and a strong leader probably will be needed when 82-year-old Chiang Kai-shek dies. In addition, Chiang Ching-kuo's recognized ability to get things done should help the island-nation's industry as it begins to produce finished, complicated articles.

EDWARD NEILAN
China and Southeast Asia Correspondent
Copley News Service

Chiang Ching-kuo is the elder son of Chiang Kai-shek.

Camera Press, PIX

TAIWAN

Area: 13,886 sq. mi.
Population: 13,800,000
Capital: Taipei (pop., 1,225,000)
Government: Chiang Kai-shek, president—1950; C. K. Yen, premier—1963
Gross National Product: $3,960,000,000
Monetary unit: New Taiwan dollar (40 NT dollars = U.S. $1.00)
Chief products: rice, sugar, bananas, textiles, flour, tobacco, cement
Foreign trade: exports, $850,000,000; imports, $903,000,000
Communications: 230,229 telephones, 1,370,-000 radios, 300,000 TV sets, 31 daily newspapers
Transportation: roads, 10,398 mi.; 27,375 passenger cars, railroads, 2,852 mi.
Education: 3,115,146 elementary and secondary students, 9 universities
Armed forces: 555,000

See map on page 481

TAXATION

The most extensive reform of U.S. income-tax laws since their original adoption in 1913, and one of the biggest reductions in income taxes ever put into effect, were voted by Congress in the Tax Reform Act of 1969.

The reform provisions of the bill were designed to make the tax laws fairer: to assure that individuals in similar financial circumstances pay similar amounts of tax. There has been general agreement that the legislation, in fact, achieved this objective; that although the tax laws are still not perfectly fair, they are fairer than they were before the 1969 reform act was passed. The legislation did not completely eliminate any one of the hundreds of special provisions of the tax law that permit persons with certain kinds of income or certain kinds of expenditures to avoid large amounts of Federal income tax legally. But it did reduce, in some cases quite drastically, the amount of income that could be sheltered from Federal income taxation through the use of these various special preferential provisions.

The relief provisions of the legislation reduce the taxes paid by persons in every income group, upper, middle and lower. But proportionally, the greatest tax relief by far was given the lowest-income groups. The middle-income group got the next largest amount of tax relief, and the upper-income the least. In fact, when the tax-reform provisions of the bill are taken into account, the highest-income individuals, taken as a group, will actually be paying more in Federal income taxes. This is because they are the ones who tend to be able to take advantage of the special-preference provisions in the tax law; what they gain from the tax-relief provisions they will lose from the tax-reform provisions.

The tax-relief provisions of the bill, which will save taxpayers a total of $9,100,000,000 annually, involve a number of changes in the tax laws, most of which were specifically tailored to bring tax reduction to a specific group of taxpayers.

Minimum Standard Deduction. This is aimed at helping the poor. Until the passage of the 1969 act, the minimum standard deduction was $200 per tax return, plus $100 for each person covered by the return. Under the new law, the minimum standard deduction will be raised to a new, permanent level of $1,000, regardless of the number of individuals in the family, by 1972.

Standard Deduction. To be increased, it will help reduce the taxes mainly of middle-income individuals, especially those who are not homeowners. (Persons who own their own homes usually have sufficiently large deductions for interest on their mortgages and real-estate taxes to make it worthwhile itemizing their deductions rather than using the flat figure in the standard deduction.) The standard deduction has long been 10 per cent of income or $1,000, whichever was lower. Under the 1969 act, it will be raised, in a series of steps, to 15 per cent of income or $2,000, by 1973.

Personal Exemption. To be increased, it will reduce taxes for everyone, but will be of most benefit to those with the largest families. Until the passage of the 1969 act, the personal exemption, for some years, had been $600 for each person covered by the tax return. Now it is to be raised, in a series of steps, to $750 by 1973.

Single Individuals. They have long been discriminated against by the income-tax laws in the view of most experts in the field. The 1969 act provides a whole new schedule of tax rates

The following table shows the effects of the 1969 act on different income groups when all of its reform and relief provisions are fully in effect, which will not happen until 1979. Most of the major provisions will be in effect by 1973 at the lastest, however.

Income group	Number of taxpaying families and single individuals in each income group (in 1,000's)	Total tax paid under old law (in 1,000,000's)	Change in tax paid under 1969 act	Per cent change
0 to $3,000	10,053	$ 1,169	$− 816	−69.8
$3 to $5,000	9,562	3,320	−1,101	−33.2
$5 to $7,000	9,779	5,591	−1,112	−19.9
$7 to $10,000	13,815	11,792	−1,859	−15.8
$10 to $15,000	13,062	18,494	−2,327	−12.6
$15 to $20,000	3,852	9,184	− 791	− 8.6
$20 to $50,000	2,594	13,988	− 715	− 5.1
$50 to $100,000	340	6,659	− 128	− 1.9
$100,000 and over	95	7,686	+ 557	+ 7.2

for single persons, which will ensure that none pay more than 20 per cent above the Federal income taxes that a married couple pays with the same taxable income. This provision will help all single persons but especially those well above the middle-income level, from about $15,000 to $50,000, who have been the most discriminated against compared with married couples at the same income levels.

Maximum Tax Rate on Earned Income. This is a wholly new provision of the tax law and is aimed at helping upper-income individuals, such as doctors, lawyers and corporate executives, who work for their money. "Earned income" basically means salaries, professional fees or commissions. It would be subject to a maximum rate of tax of 50 per cent by 1972. Taxes on "unearned income," such as dividends, interest, rents, capital gains and so on, would remain subject to a maximum tax rate of 70 per cent. Tax rates of more than 50 per cent start at the $52,000-a-year mark, for a married couple, so all those with earned income above that level would benefit.

Reform. The reform side of the 1969 act contains literally hundreds of provisions, related to corporations as well as individuals. Its most novel provision is the "minimum tax." The minimum tax provides in effect that regardless of any other preferential provisions that are in the tax law, some tax will have to be paid by most individuals and companies that manage to escape large amounts of tax because of the preferences.

Under the minimum tax, a list of 10 tax preferences is enumerated, among them the one half of capital gains that is not taxed; the extent to which the depletion allowance on oil and other minerals exceeds the cost of developing the mineral-producing property; and the amount by which accelerated depreciation on real estate exceeds the actual rate of depreciation. The amount of income shielded from tax by these preferences is added together and is made taxable, under the minimum tax, if it exceeds $30,000. The tax rate on the amount of income subject to the minimum tax is a flat one, 10 per cent, rather than a progressive one, that is, a rate that rises as the amount of income rises. This is considered a defect in the minimum tax by many of those who wanted to see tax preferences sharply reduced.

An even more serious defect in the minimum tax, in the eyes of ardent tax reformers, is the fact that not all kinds of tax-sheltered income are included. Most notably, the interest on bonds issued by state and local governments remains completely tax-exempt under the bill. In addition, some of the key tax preferences accorded the oil and gas industry, notably its ability to deduct from taxable income the expenses of drilling that are really long-term capital costs, are also excluded from the coverage of the minimum tax.

Nevertheless, the minimum tax will make taxpayers out of many individuals and some corporations that have paid little or no Federal income tax in recent years.

Among the other major reform provisions of the bill are these:

Capital Gains. Under the old law, these were taxed at one half the taxpayer's tax rate for other income, except that the rate never went above 25 per cent. Under the new law, the special 25 per cent ceiling will be eliminated by 1972, except for the first $50,000 of any individual's capital gains each year. Thus the rate of tax on capital gains will be a progressive one, which will affect incomes all the way to the top of the scale.

Wide World

Edwin Cohen, assistant secretary of the treasury, explains differences between administration's tax-reform plan and a tax bill passed by House of Representatives.

PERCENT MORE TAX A SINGLE PERSON PAYS THAN A MARRIED COUPLE WITH SAME TAXABLE INCOME

% MORE TAX

40

30

20

10

Present Law - Single Person

Treasury - Single Person

HRl3270- Single Person under 35

HRl3270- Single Person 35 and over

UPI

Rep. Wilbur D. Mills, chairman of the House Ways and Means Committee, welcomes Treasury Secretary Kennedy to hearings on tax reform.

Oil and Gas Industry. The depletion allowance of 27½ per cent of gross income from oil and gas wells that was allowed to be deducted from income before figuring tax was cut to 22 per cent. Some complex deals that had allowed the oil industry to bunch expenses in one year and special deductions in the next—to wind up with no taxable income in either year—were outlawed.

Real Estate. Complicated arrangements that had allowed owners and operators of commercial buildings to combine interest payments on their loans with doubled-up deductions for depreciation to offset all their taxable income were severely restricted.

Hobby Farmers. An effective end was put to the ability of wealthy individuals to buy farms, report paper losses on them under the imprecise bookkeeping methods that farmers are permitted to follow, and use those "losses" to wipe out taxable income from other sources.

Tax-exempt Foundations. The ability of individuals to set up foundations, allegedly for charitable purposes but use them as personal tax-avoidance schemes instead, was ended. Even foundations that perform a legitimate charitable, educational or community purpose were put under some new restrictions requiring nonpartisan uses of their funds and imposing a fee to cover the Government's costs of supervising their activities.

Churches. For the first time, the profits made by ordinary businesses that are owned by religious organizations will be taxed.

Many individuals and organizations had a hand in the shaping of the Tax Reform Act of 1969. A number of the basic provisions of the bill were worked out by the tax experts in the Treasury Department during the Johnson ad-

ministration. President Johnson, for reasons he never explained, refused to submit these proposals to Congress, and they were made available to Congress for study only after he left office. The Treasury officials of the Nixon administration modified some of these proposals, accepted others and came up with some entirely new ones. Other portions of the legislation were born in the minds of either the members of the House Ways and Means Committee or the Senate Finance Committee or of their staffs of experts. They were hammered into their final form mainly by the senior members of these two committees, which have jurisdiction over all tax matters, with the help of Treasury and Congressional staff experts.

To a significant extent, however, the real origin of the Tax Reform Act of 1969 was in the fury of the average American taxpayer. Feelings that the tax law was unfair, that too many persons, especially individuals of considerable wealth, were not paying their fair share, had been mounting over a period of years, with more and more publicity over the special-privilege sections of the tax law.

The imposition of the 10 per cent tax surcharge in mid-1968, which added 10 per cent to everyone's tax bills, greatly heightened and sharpened this resentment. If the law was already unfair, then adding 10 per cent to the taxes paid under the same old law made things just that much worse.

This was the message tens of thousands of Americans transmitted to their elected representatives in early 1969: a demand for tax reform, to which Congress responded.

EILEEN SHANAHAN
Financial Reporter, Washington Bureau
The New York Times

TELEVISION

There was one overriding event on television in 1969, a broadcast for the ages: live and direct coverage of the first landing of man on the moon. For several hours during a night in July, countless millions of televiewers watched the incredible scene as astronauts Neil Armstrong and Ed Aldrin set foot on the lunar surface, walked around, planted the American flag, gathered research material and spoke to earth.

Despite the distance, the pan shots of the moon—with its harsh, striking, even splendid desolation—were received with remarkable clarity on television. The sound too, for the most part, was good. Overall, the commercial video networks offered 31 hours of continuous coverage of events surrounding the astronauts' arrival on and departure from the moon.

While exhilaration marked the astronauts' time on the moon, the hours immediately preceding their first steps on the lunar surface were a tense television experience. There had been color-video transmissions from space as the voyagers journeyed to their destination. Finally the spacecraft sat down on the moon—a feat televiewers could only hear about but not see live and direct. That was in the afternoon. Later came one of the most dramatic stage waits in history, as Armstrong prepared to step out of the craft, a step that would also start the moon telecast.

Televiewers saw the step that ushered in a new age for mankind. Although the appreciation of historic import was paramount on video, there was also a more immediate, human relief at the safety of astronaut Armstrong as he felt his way onto the moon. For televiewers, the first mooncast gave the promise of the wonders of the universe being accessible at home. And a second manned American lunar trip was launched on Nov. 14, with two more moon-walk telecasts on tap before the end of the year. Unfortunately a malfunctioning color camera made it impossible for viewers to see more than a short period of the moon walks.

Curiously, aside from the monumental moon-shot achievement, 1969 was a rather conservative and even regressive year for most of commercial television. It was no accident. To begin with, some of the conservatism was well founded, a manifestation of the reaction against violence that followed the 1968 assassinations of Sen. Robert F. Kennedy and the Rev. Martin Luther King, Jr. One result was that the 1969–70 television schedule, for the first time in memory, included no new Western or private-eye series. In order to get some gore of a more respectable nature on video, the networks fell back on several series about doctors:

Lloyd Haynes portrays a public high-school teacher, Pete Dixon, on popular new series "Room 222."

20th Century-Fox Television

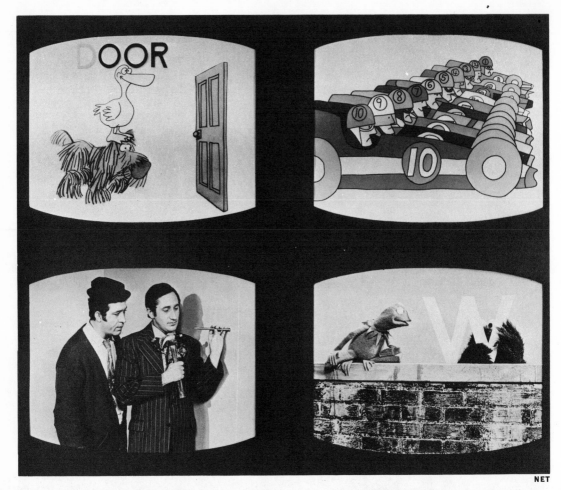

NET

"Sesame Street," a daily series for preschoolers, won high acclaim. Using advertising techniques, the program tries to give children skill in the alphabet, number concepts and logical reasoning.

ABC-TV's *Marcus Welby, M.D.,* CBS-TV's *Medical Center* and NBC-TV's *The Bold Ones.*

In addition, public and printed uproar over the violence shown on television's Saturday-morning children's cartoons reached a crescendo and had some effect. NBC-TV led the way, offering a new fantasy show, *H. R. Pufnstuf,* along with two other year-old antiviolence children's series, *The Banana Splits Adventure Hour* and *Untamed World,* a show about animals and nature. CBS-TV, meanwhile, scheduled a daytime *Children's Hour* series of original dramas for Saturdays. In November, National Educational Television launched a notable daily series for preschoolers—particularly disadvantaged ones—entitled *Sesame Street.* Budgeted at $8,000,000, it was offered an hour each weekday. It emphasized the alphabet, numbers, and development of concepts.

Some of the new conservatism, however, was more controversial. It stemmed in great part from the quietly growing revolt of "the silent majority" against increased salaciousness in all the arts. Since television is the most steadily visible, if the least guilty, of the arts, it was video—with its nervous concern for the mass audience—that felt the reaction most of all. Emerging as a symbol of this reaction was Sen. John Pastore, whose subcommittee launched a widely publicized further assault on television sex and violence, even after the networks on their own initiative had begun to tone down unnecessary video brutality.

Violence, however, was only one target of the reaction. The networks felt the impact of many average Americans who suddenly expressed their antagonism against what they felt was too much attention being given to militants, revolutionists, irreverence toward Establishment values, and hippie types. All this was an outgrowth of the national swing back to conservatism. Many viewers still were rankled by the riots at the 1968 Democratic national convention, which some people seemed to blame on video simply because it covered the story that was happening.

In November, television news in general came under fire. The controversy was sparked by an address by Vice-President Agnew in which he severely questioned the objectivity of television news as well as, to him, the excessive power of those who put it together. (See Agnew, Spiro; United States.)

Pastore, in his antiviolence campaign concerning entertainment, even inspired an attempt to get the networks to accede to general prescreenings of their shows by the code authority of the National Association of Broadcasters. Dr. Frank Stanton, president of CBS, refused, arguing that such a move was a seed of censorship, and stating that his network had its own screening practices. Soon afterward, CBS-TV became the first major commercial network to adopt a general policy permitting advance reviews of its shows by professional television critics. Many observers interpreted this as, in part, a shrewd move to cut off threatened censorship by allowing public arbiters—outside the network—to render judgment on program taste, without bringing in official authorities.

The peak of controversy over television entertainment in 1969 broke out over the firing by CBS-TV of the Smothers brothers, whose weekly variety series was frankly youth-oriented, irreverent, and politically and socially liberal. The brothers, along with NBC-TV's enormously popular and racy *Laugh-In* series, had become representative of video's new freedom. As a result, they had not only many admirers but also detractors because of their puncturing of sacred cows, and their suggestiveness. To the sophisticated viewer, the Smothers brothers' allegedly questionable material might well have seemed rather unexciting. For example, British television, which bought the series, canceled it quickly, contending, in part, that it was very mild stuff and no one could understand what all the shouting was about.

Technically, CBS-TV fired the brothers because, among other corporate reasons, they delivered their show too late for perusal by the network's program-practices department and by affiliate stations. But it was clear that other, deeper matters prompted the split. There was definite conflict over the series' content and taste. And there was sharp personal antagonism between the brothers and CBS-TV. Furthermore, the show undeniably had become more preachy and heavy-handed in making its points. Perhaps worst of all, to cynics, the ratings had dropped—or, some say, the network might have tolerated its headache.

MGM-Television

Michael Parks is Jim Bronson, a young man who gives up a newspaper career to travel across the country on a motorcycle, on "Then Came Bronson."

At any rate, the Smothers brothers wound up by suing CBS for $31,000,000, charging infringement of their constitutional rights of free speech; violation of antitrust laws; and breach of contract. They also wound up with a one-hour special scheduled for early 1970 on an opposition network, NBC-TV. One of the mainstays of their series, deadpan satirist Pat Paulsen, also landed his own show for early 1970: a weekly series on another competition network, ABC-TV. Meanwhile CBS-TV replaced the Smothers brothers on the 1969–70 schedule with Negro songstress Leslie Uggams in a variety series that also tried to be topical. It was, however, very mild if pleasant entertainment, and the series was soon canceled. Its replacement was a hillbilly copy of *Laugh-In* called *Hee Haw*, the precise kind of provincial show that television's young bloods were trying to overcome when the reaction set in.

Some progress, nevertheless, continued to be made on video in contemporary themes such as racial relations. ABC-TV's series *Summer Focus, 1969*, for instance, dealt with racial matters in a documentary way. Healthy, self-aimed ethnic humor was widespread in television's entertainment shows. And two new series starring black performers—Bill Cosby in an NBC-TV situation comedy, and Lloyd Haynes as a high-school teacher in ABC-TV's *Room 222*—were immediate hits, while the year-old show *Julia*, featuring Negro actress Diahann Carroll as a nurse, remained successful.

One 1969 decision, however, upset some television craftsmen who are sensitive to the endless pressures on video creators. Early in the year, ABC-TV canceled, after one performance, a new half-hour series called *Turn-On* that tried to show the impersonality of modern life by using a computer as host, electronic impulses as music, and a visual assault on the senses that employed media techniques from graphics to film. It was also spicy and jabbed at popular institutions. Some viewers and stations found it dirty or too outspoken or just plain bad. When ABC-TV killed the show instantly instead of quietly doing away with it after several weeks, various television observers felt it opened the door for pressure groups (and some network officials) to attack and criticize other controversial shows, such as the Smothers brothers series and *Laugh-In*, with more hope of results.

The quick cancellation of *Turn-On* under apparent pressure was the year's first major setback for video's "new freedom." It was followed shortly by the Smothers brothers' cancellation. Before the year was out, the producer of *Laugh-In* quit, telling the show-business trade paper *Variety* that he left because the series was "slanted and vulgar, dirty." But *Laugh-In* maintained high ratings and seemed safe until they drop.

There were other attention-getting series in 1969. In addition to *Marcus Welby, M.D.*, *Room 222*, *Sesame Street* and the Bill Cosby show, they included *First Tuesday*, a news-magazine of the air; the Dick Cavett program, a thrice-weekly summertime talk-and-variety entry; *Love, American Style*, a humorous anthology of contemporary romance; *Then Came Bronson*, about a young man who motorcycles around the nation in search of himself; Johnny Cash's summer, country-folk musical series, which was set to return early in 1970; and *The Forsyte Saga*, based on the John Galsworthy novels and imported from Britain by National Educational Television, which began a coast-to-coast network operation during October.

Michael Caine and Anna Calder-Marshall star in "Male of the Species," a moving British drama.

ITC

The outstanding entertainment specials of 1969, meanwhile, included two other British imports: *A Midsummer Night's Dream* produced by the Royal Shakespeare Company; and *Male of the Species,* a charming modern tale about a young woman's encounters with three very different men (Sean Connery, Paul Scofield and Michael Caine). There was an adaptation of Edgar Lee Masters' *Spoon River Anthology;* a drama, *Color Me German,* about a Negro-American teacher who visits his German-born, black nephew in Munich; and a well-done, spicy melodrama, *Shadow Game,* about a group of persons trapped overnight in a business office during a power blackout. Jack Paar had two fine hours, one about Africa, the other about lions. And there were noteworthy variety shows by Woody Allen, Frank Sinatra and Dinah Shore, as well as a Julie Andrews-Harry Belafonte musical hour.

Documentaries in 1969 offered these highlights: *The Making of the President: 1968; The Ordeal of Anatoly Kuznetsov,* a talk with the writer who defected from Russia; *Confrontation,* which focused on politically embattled San Francisco State College; *From Here to the Seventies,* a look at the last decade, with an eye to the next; and *Three Young Americans in Search of Survival,* about a trio of humanists who work at conservation—from people to wildlife. In December, former President Lyndon B. Johnson was interviewed in the first of a series of broadcasts about his career.

To lure some of the late-night television audience (estimated at 18,000,000) from Johnny Carson and Joey Bishop, CBS, in August, replaced its *Late Show* with *The Merv Griffin Show.* David Frost, a favorite on British television, took over the Griffin talk show for the Westinghouse Broadcasting Company. In November, ABC announced that Dick Cavett would succeed Bishop. At the time, the Bishop show was running third in the Nielsen ratings behind Carson and Griffin.

Signs of the future were indicated in 1969. The days of cigarette advertising on television seemed numbered as legislation suggested the ban would take effect by the end of 1970. One star, Debbie Reynolds, quit her series briefly when it used a cigarette ad. Antismoking commercials had great impact on the home screen.

More contemporary movies with adult themes, such as *A Man and a Woman* and *Georgy Girl* were seen on video's national networks. Two massive developments seemed clearly in the offing. First, the growth of cable and community-antenna television will mean

NET

Susan Hampshire is the idle, self-centered Fleur and Eric Porter her father in the 26-installment television version of John Galsworthy's "The Forsyte Saga."

more stations, with specialized program material and audiences. As with the current radio pattern, an example of this might well be all-news stations. Second, there will be an increased growth of home family-entertainment centers as prices drop for do-it-yourself videotape machines, and programs-via-cassettes become more available as alternatives or complements to network shows. In this area, instructional and informational programs seem certain to be widely used. In short, televiewers will be able to program their own broadcasts.

RICK DU BROW
Television Critic
United Press International

TENNESSEE

In January a major discovery of sphalerite (a zinc ore) in central Tennessee was announced. Estimates varied from 13,000,000 to 50,000,000 tons of ore averaging 5 to 10 per cent pure metal. □ On Apr. 4, in Memphis, where Martin Luther King, Jr., was slain just a year before, memorial services for him were almost broken up by window-smashing and looting by Negro youths. □ In June a thunderstorm dropped 7 inches of rain on Red Boiling Springs and the vicinity. Resulting floods left 2 persons dead, 1 missing, 40 to 50 families homeless and the "town cut in half."

TEXAS

Former President Lyndon B. Johnson and his wife dedicated the 190-acre Lady Bird Johnson Municipal Park, three miles south of Fredericksburg, on May 11. It is the only recreation center in Texas' hill country. □ The Lyndon B. Johnson State Park opened on June 1, across the Pedernales River from the LBJ Ranch. □ On Aug. 6, voters rejected a plan to borrow $3,500,-000,000 for a water-development plan but approved an increase in the welfare ceiling.

THAILAND

The year 1969 was mainly a period of adjustment for the staunchly anti-Communist, avowedly pro-Western Government of Thailand. The cause of the adjustment, and of long-range underlying problems, were the U.S. moves leading to eventual withdrawal from Vietnam.

Despite growing concern and uncertainty over the future role of the United States in

---

THAILAND

Area: 198,500 sq. mi.
Population: 34,700,000
Capital: Bangkok (pop., 1,609,000)
Government: Bhumibol Adulyadej (Rama IX), king—1946; Thanom Kittikachorn, prime minister—1963
Gross National Product: $5,400,000,000
Monetary unit: baht (20.8 baht = U.S. $1.00)
Chief products: rice, teak, rubber, tapioca, tin, manganese, lignite and iron ores
Foreign trade: exports, $660,000,000; imports, $1,188,000,000
Communications: 98,390 telephones, 370,000 TV sets, 18 daily newspapers
Transportation: roads, 7,610 mi.; 67,261 passenger cars, railroads, 2,230 mi.
Education: 4,091,610 elementary and secondary students, 8 universities
Armed forces: 126,400

See map on page 481

Southeast Asia and Thailand's mounting military and security needs, Thailand began 1969 on a confident note. In the February elections for the 219-seat House of Representatives, the pro-Government United Thai People's Party gained control. On Mar. 7, military strongman Field Marshal Thanom Kittikachorn was reappointed prime minister by King Bhumibol Adulyadej and instructed to form a new government.

The Vietnam war, however, remained the dominating factor. In mid-1969, after the United States indicated that it would reduce its military forces in Southeast Asia, the Thai Government voiced strong opposition to the move, recalling U.S. pledges to "stand proudly" with Thailand against external and internal threats and a secret U.S. agreement to help defend the country. Dismay over the U.S. pullback was later replaced by a hard-nosed determination to strengthen the country's ability to stand alone. In mid-August the Government announced a budget of about US$1,210,000,-000, almost one fourth of it for defense. On Aug. 22, Thai Foreign Minister Thanat Khoman announced that Bangkok would begin negotiations with the United States on the withdrawal of the 49,000 American troops based in Thailand. On Sept. 30 the United States and Thailand made public their agreement that about 6,000 U.S. Air Force and Army troops would be withdrawn from Thailand by July 1, 1970.

None of this meant a sudden U.S. withdrawal. Indications were that the United States would help the Thais as much as required, particularly with material support to combat the local rebellions in the northeastern, northern and southern areas of the country. While they did not worsen during the year, they remained a constant problem for the Government.

The mounting defense costs had an understandably adverse effect on Thailand's economy. While the gross national product grew by an estimated 7.6 per cent during 1969, a disproportionate share of the nation's resources had to be devoted to counter-insurgency operations (25 per cent of the national budget, an estimated 75 per cent of all U.S. aid). A steadily growing trade deficit undermined the Thai balance of payments. Although foreign aid and spending by U.S. troops helped cover the deficit, gold and foreign-exchange reserves (still a substantial US$1,000,000,000) declined somewhat. Nevertheless, the country remained on a fairly stable economic footing.

EDWARD NEILAN
China and Southeast Asia Correspondent
Copley News Service

As Benjamin Franklin, Howard da Silva looks with concern at Billy Daniels as John Adams in the musical "1776."

Martha Swope

THEATER

The American theater in 1969 was fragmented and frightened; otherwise, its course cannot easily be summarized. On Broadway, the most notable innovation was, rather improbably, the successful revival of old plays. Importations from Europe provided some of the most resounding commercial triumphs, but not much help was forthcoming from Broadway's native sources of new blood. The off-Broadway writers who tried to make the great leap to the larger audience generally failed, and plays transferred from regional theaters in other cities fell far short of the astounding precedent set by *The Great White Hope* in 1968. One of New York's two principal repertory theaters, the Vivian Beaumont of Lincoln Center, pursued a conservative course. The other, the APA-Phoenix, disintegrated and temporarily disappeared from the New York scene. Two Broadway musicals won clear and emphatic commercial success. One of them, *1776,* broke all the rules but charmed both critics and audiences. The other, *Coco,* had so

much advance publicity that its opening was anticlimactic. Nevertheless, the first-night audience was enthusiastic.

Off-Broadway's new courses were easier to chart: nudity, black drama, and pop musicals with minimal plots (or none at all) and one-word titles (like *Hair*). Some early, hesitant ventures into nudity were succeeded by *Oh, Calcutta!,* which made nudity its *raison d'être.* Though Actors' Equity began to make stern rules for nude auditions, the influence began to creep uptown, and the leading man of the Broadway musical *Jimmy* was seen for an instant in the altogether. Black drama—that is to say, drama about blacks (as Negroes prefer to call themselves) but not necessarily by blacks—was relatively absent from Broadway. However, it burgeoned off-Broadway, producing two of the most admired plays of the year, Charles Gordone's *No Place to Be Somebody* and Lonne Elder III's *Ceremonies in Dark Old Men.* Other black plays moved perceptibly in the direction of militant antiwhite partisanship of black power. Among the one-word-title

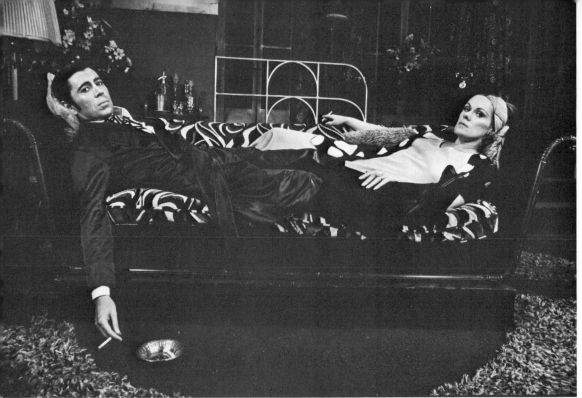

Carl Samrock

Tammy Grimes and Brian Bedford cavorted with charm in Noël Coward's sophisticated, 1930's "Private Lives."

pop musicals, *Promenade* and *Salvation* won more admirers than *Stomp* and *Sambo,* but together they established a tendency.

1776, which had a book by Peter Stone and songs by Sherman Edwards (who originally conceived this historical musical), was unquestionably the favorite musical of the year. Its popularity came as a surprise. Austerely omitting intermissions, it dealt with an austere subject: the writing and ratification of the Declaration of Independence. The angry industry of John Adams (vigorously played by William Daniels) enlivens the drama, and the voting tests and necessary compromises generate suspense. The songs, strictly in character, contain little of the usual ingredients of Broadway musicals, save for a slightly overstressed reunion between Thomas Jefferson and his wife. Some took *1776* and *The Great White Hope* to be signs of a new American-historical trend on Broadway, but, although a musical about Columbus was in the works, nothing else of the sort appeared, unless one counts *Jimmy.* With book by Melville Shavelson and songs by Bill and Patti Jacob, *Jimmy* is a desperately jazzy musical about New York's "night mayor," Jimmy Walker. Possibly helped by the dearth of new musicals, *Jimmy* lasted out the hostility of the critics and won a popular audience.

Coco ranked high as a historic event but low as a musical. Because it brought Katharine Hepburn back to Broadway in the role of "Coco" Chanel, the Parisian dress designer, it had enormous advance publicity and a huge advance sale of tickets. When it finally opened in mid-December, Miss Hepburn proved herself to be, as always, a matchless stage personality, but she seemed unequal to the talk-singing required of her. Even in the early performances, her voice was noticeably hoarse. Still, anyone who wanted to see a 1953 fashion show (designed by Cecil Beaton, not by "Coco" Chanel) was bound to be pleased. The words and music by Alan Jay Lerner and André Previn, respectively, came alive twice during the evening, and that was twice more than in Lerner's book, which was enlivened only by the peculiar authority that Miss Hepburn gave to Coco's aphorisms. Among the other musicals, *Canterbury Tales* came from London and was frail but good-natured; *Celebration* was a pointless fable about a girl compelled to choose between a rich old man and a poor young man; and *Dear World,* a disastrously unsympathetic adaptation of Jean Giraudoux's *The Madwoman of Chaillot,* wasted the talents of Angela Lansbury in the lead.

Straight plays that ran on Broadway were few indeed, and that no doubt is why 1969 was a year for revivals. *The Front Page* (1928), by Ben Hecht and Charles MacArthur, a comedy of journalism and crime in the corrupt

Friedman-Abeles

With her radiance and energy, Katharine Hepburn made a triumphant success of rather limp material in "Coco."

Nathan George and Ron O'Neal argue in the vigorous, sardonic "No Place to Be Somebody" by Charles Gordone.

Friedman-Abeles

city of Chicago, scored a deserved hit in spring with a stellar cast led by Robert Ryan. It returned in the fall with much the same cast but adding MacArthur's widow, Helen Hayes, in a supporting role. The farcical *Three Men on a Horse* (1935), by George Abbott and John Cecil Holm, directed by Abbott, returned with Sam Levene playing the role he originated. Broadway celebrated Noël Coward's seventieth birthday by reviving his highly stylized comedy *Private Lives* (1930), featuring Tammy Grimes and Brian Bedford in a small but expert cast. This production had originated with the APA after it broke away from the Phoenix. A limited but well-received run of William Saroyan's comedy of insistent optimism, *The Time of Your Life* (1939), inaugurated the Vivian Beaumont Theater's all-American 1969–70 season. Thornton Wilder's nostalgic, sentimental view of smalltown life, *Our Town* (1938), with

Henry Fonda as the Stage Manager, was the Plumstead Playhouse's entry in a series of plays from regional theaters sponsored by the American National Theater and Academy and financed by a Federal grant. The series had begun with three productions from the American Conservatory Theatre of San Francisco, all very stylized and not to the advantage of the plays: Edward Albee's *Tiny Alice,* Georges Feydeau's *A Flea in Her Ear,* and Chekhov's *The Three Sisters,* in an astonishingly free adaptation. They were followed by Michael Kahn's antiwar, semi-Brechtian production of Shakespeare's *Henry V,* from the American Shakespeare Festival of Stratford, Conn.

As for new and native plays on Broadway, a few comedies made it, while some serious plays of interest did not. Neil Simon's *Last of the Red Hot Lovers* consisted of three one-act comedies about the same man, a hapless middle-

Joseph Wiseman plays scientist of title in "In the Matter of J. Robert Oppenheimer," based on the famous case.

Penguin Photo

aged would-be Lothario, agreeably played by James Coco, an off-Broadway find of early 1969. While the first and third acts had astringent moments, the play as a whole was closer to one-line gag comedy than it was to Simon's best work. Woody Allen's *Play It Again, Sam,* which starred its author, was a fairly obvious gag-filled farce about a timid soul who, goaded by the ghost of Humphrey Bogart, fulfills himself by sleeping with his best friend's wife. Leonard Gershe's *Butterflies Are Free* was less frenetic than either of the other two hit comedies. This story of a blind young man who wins a girl and fights free of his bossy mother's influence adroitly steers clear of bad taste, and punches enough funny lines across. It had the incidental merit of introducing a winning young actress, Blythe Danner. Among the plays that stayed briefly but deserved a better fate were Don Petersen's *Does a Tiger Wear a Necktie?,* a biting drama of hope and despair among drug addicts in a rehabilitation center; Lyke Kessler's *The Watering Place,* about a soldier's destructive influence on a friend's family; Lanford Wilson's *The Gingham Dog,* the drama of an interracial marriage that is breaking up; and John Guare's *Cop-Out,* a program of two far-out one-act plays probably better suited to off-Broadway.

Importations that made a hit were an English play, Peter Luke's *Hadrian VII* (adapted from Frederick Rolfe's novel of the same name), about an impoverished writer who imagines that he has become the Pope, with Alec McCowen performing brilliantly in the title role; and a German play, Heinar Kipphardt's *In the Matter of J. Robert Oppenheimer,* which was part of the 1968–69 season at the Vivian Beaumont Theater. Kipphardt's play presented the essence of the 1954 investigation into the loyalty of the atomic physicist who is considered the father of the atomic bomb. It touched upon two main issues: McCarthyism and the responsibility of the scientists who created the bomb. Even though this was a German play of American life, written several years before, it was still quite impressive. Gordon Davidson's expert staging, with Joseph Wiseman as Oppenheimer, was based upon an earlier production at Davidson's own repertory theater in Los Angeles. John Osborne's *A Patriot for Me,* an English play concerning a homosexual Austro-Hungarian officer who is blackmailed into spying for the Russians, had a more ambiguous reception. It demonstrated that, as in his *Luther,* Osborne was still using history as a backdrop for his dramatic accounts of personal eccentricity. *Hamlet* might legitimately be considered a foreign play, especially since it

Penguin Photo

Thornton Wilder's nostalgic 1938 play "Our Town" was revived with Henry Fonda as the Stage Manager.

Gifted British playwright Harold Pinter had a double bill, "Landscape" and "Silence," on in London.

Penguin Photo

came to Broadway in an English production, with Nicol Williamson giving an extremely distinctive and rather personal interpretation of the title role. Odd as Williamson occasionally was as Hamlet, he was a considerable improvement over Ellis Rabb's haphazard portrayal in the APA-Phoenix series early in the year.

For *Oh, Calcutta!* off-Broadway, Kenneth Tynan selected and Jacques Levy directed several short plays by celebrated authors, including 1969's Nobel Prize laureate Samuel Beckett. Still, words did not avail, and the best sequence was a nude *pas de deux,* choreographed by Margo Sappington. The nude play that ran second in the attention it attracted was Lennox Raphael's murky and quite undistinguished political parable *Che!,* which, it was claimed, the police had unjustly censored.

While black drama was primarily an off-Broadway phenomenon, it did reach Broadway briefly in a thinned-out musical adaptation of an interesting off-Broadway play of the previous year, Joseph Dolan Tuotti's *Big Time Buck White.* The chief interest of this musical revival lay in the presence of the heavyweight boxer billed as "Muhammad Ali also known as Cassius Clay" in the title role. His performance was certainly a historic event, but it was just as certainly no histrionic triumph. Of much greater consequence were the off-Broadway *No Place to Be Somebody* and *Ceremonies in Dark Old Men.* The former play, presented by Joseph Papp in his municipally supported series at the New York Shakespeare Festival Public Theater (and by far the most striking of the year's offerings there), made good use of comedy, pathos and melodrama in its portrait of a black opportunist vainly trying to rise in an environment dominated by white gangsters. *Ceremonies,* which began in the regular series of the Negro Ensemble Company but later started an independent off-Broadway run in a new production, showed the disintegration of a Harlem family. Later in the season came two plays more in line with black nationalism. *The Ofay Watcher,* by Frank Cucci (a white, oddly enough), was a brief parable of a white scientist who turns black skin white and is murdered—or, more exactly, executed—by a mysterious black. LeRoi Jones' *Slave Ship* was a chronicle of black history in America, expressing contempt for whites and for black integrationists. Equally concerned with racial relations but occupied with a different race was a Broadway play, Arthur Kopit's *Indians,* which had come to New York from the Washington Arena Stage. Kopit used Buffalo Bill, well played by Stacy Keach, to introduce us to the whites' guilt toward the red man. Unfortunately, he drained his play of much of the humor and incident that it had when it was staged by the Royal Shakespeare Company in London in 1968. *Indians* became a lecture in history, and Gene Frankel's elaborate production only partially compensated for what was lost.

At least one off-Broadway play unrelated to the important trends and categories must be mentioned here: the short-lived *In the Bar of a Tokyo Hotel* by Tennessee Williams. A minor work by a major dramatist, the play is the legend of a dying artist tormented by a shrewish, unfaithful wife. Another leading American dramatist, Arthur Miller, was represented in 1969 only by two one-act plays acted in informal circumstances and consequently not reviewed. On the other hand, a brilliant popular success was scored off-Broadway by two hilarious short plays that Elaine May directed: Miss May's own *Adaptation,* in which life is seen as a board game, like Monopoly; and Terrence McNally's *Next,* with James Coco as the middle-aged assistant manager of a film theater incomprehensibly called up to take a physical examination for military service.

In the London year, many of the younger dramatists were represented by highly characteristic plays, but only one of the acknowledged masters, Harold Pinter, contributed a major piece of work. With his double bill, *Landscape* and *Silence,* Pinter had two little dramas of people who speak but do not communicate. Both were sensitively directed by Peter Hall for the Royal Shakespeare Company, and *Landscape,* the second to be performed and the more poetic of the two, was acted with particular spirit by Dame Peggy Ashcroft. Other new plays of distinction included a farce by the late Joe Orton, *What the Butler Saw;* Peter Nichols' black comedy of hospital life, *The National Health* (at the National Theatre); Charles Wood's antiwar play, *H or Monologues at Front of Burning Cities* (also at the National); Peter Barnes' political satire, *The Ruling Class;* David Storey's tense and telling family drama, *In Celebration;* and Peter Terson's bitter comedy of student life, *Fuzz.*

In Paris, Jean Anouilh contributed his best-received play in a very long time, *Dear Antoine,* in which an aging dramatist writes a play-within-a-play concerning the aftermath of his death. Fernando Arrabal was represented by two new plays, *The Garden of Delights* and *The Tale of Barabbas,* and Eugene Ionesco by an evening of short works.

See feature article Sex in the Performing Arts.

HENRY POPKIN
Professor of English
State University of New York at Buffalo

TRADE

World trade in 1969 showed what the General Agreement on Tariffs and Trade (GATT) called "an exceptionally strong increase" for the second consecutive year. The increase was expected to exceed the 11 per cent growth in world trade registered in 1968, when total trade among noncommunist nations was valued at $224,500,000,000.

The GATT administration attributed the sustained trade growth to a sharp increase in the imports of the six members (France, West Germany, Italy and the Benelux nations) of the European Economic Community or Common Market. During the first half of 1969 their imports grew by 25 per cent. Among all industrialized nations, exports increased 16 per cent during that period, and imports rose 14 per cent. The Common Market was expected to show an overall trade deficit of $250,000,000 for 1969, after three years of surpluses.

The steady and substantial increase in world trade in 1969 came as a surprise, because most forecasts had indicated that the "cooling off" of the U.S. economy would have a slowing effect in the growth of world trade. In fact, growth of U.S. imports declined to 7 per cent in the first half of the year as compared with a rate of 24 per cent in the same period in 1968. But this relaxation was more than offset by the performance of the Common Market countries.

The European Common Market strengthened its position as the world's largest trading unit. Figures in the third quarter of 1969 indicated that the total of the imports and exports would substantially exceed the $76,400,000,000 forecast for the United States. Nonetheless, because the Common Market lacks complete internal cohesion, the United States remained the key nation in international-trade negotiations.

In another major development, the United Kingdom began to enjoy the benefits of its devaluation of the pound sterling in November 1967. This measure made imports into Britain more expensive and lowered the price of British goods in foreign markets. By the latter part of 1969, the United Kingdom was showing a steady trade surplus.

In August the French franc was devalued and in November the German mark was revalued upward. Both measures were intended to influence international-trade patterns. Although the German move was designed to slow exports and increase imports, it was accompanied by reinstitution of border taxes, suspended a year earlier, which will somewhat counteract the expected trade impact of the revaluation.

Pictorial Parade

With Japanese compact cars becoming increasingly popular on the world market, Japan's motor-vehicle production increased by 23 per cent in fiscal 1969.

Japan continued to perform on the world stage as a major force in trade. It ranks fourth in the world, behind the United States, the United Kingdom and West Germany. Japan became the world's leading steel exporter in 1969.

Steel. Because of the sharp increase of American steel imports in 1968, the United States negotiated voluntary limitations on imports with Japan and the European Community, which together account for 82 per cent of

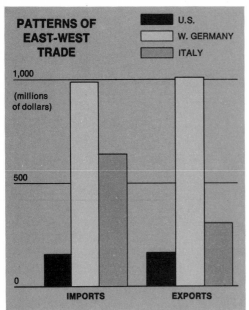

"The New York Times"

PATTERNS OF EAST-WEST TRADE

U.S.
W. GERMANY
ITALY

1,000

(millions of dollars)

500

0

IMPORTS   EXPORTS

American purchases from abroad. In 1968, steel imports totalled 17,500,000 tons; the 1969 limits allowed for imports of not more than 14,000,000 tons. Part of the pressure was removed because of increased European demand for steel which meant that less remained available for export to the United States. But Japanese producers felt the effects of the cutback. The voluntary limitations are scheduled to remain in effect, with a 5 per cent annual increase, through 1971.

Textiles. Throughout the year, the United States sought an international agreement placing voluntary limits on exports to the American market of woolens, synthetic fibers and fiber blends. During the first six months of the year, U.S. textile imports rose 13 per cent as compared with the same period in 1968. If voluntary quotas were not adopted, some American congressmen promised that legislation would be passed imposing limits. The Japanese indicated their reluctance to open their relatively highly protected domestic market, if the United States imposed new tariffs on Japanese exports. At the same time, American officials argued that much of the pressure on the U.S. market could be relieved if the European Community accepted more Japanese goods. In November, the Common Market agreed to consider liberalizing its trade with Japan.

East-West Trade. Although the Nixon administration was reluctant to push for freer trade with the Soviet Union and its Eastern Euro-

pean allies, Congress, in December, passed a more liberal Export Control Act. Debate had centered on rules restricting "strategic" exports to those countries. Under current rules, more than 1,000 items cannot be sold to Soviet-area countries. But both houses of Congress asked the president to loosen controls, although they refrained from adopting rules forcing him to do so. The new rules may make it more difficult to justify the exclusion of nonmilitary items from East-West trade.

In another development, the European Community agreed that after Jan. 1, 1970, no single member would conclude an agreement with an Eastern European country without the agreement of a majority of Common Market members.

Rumania applied for participation in the General Agreement on Tariffs and Trade, which provides for a gradual lowering of trade barriers through negotiation.

U.S. Trade Legislation. Much of the world looked to the United States for leadership in trade liberalization. The American position depends on its trade legislation; and in November, President Nixon submitted to Congress a proposal asking for limited authority to reduce tariff protection. He asked that Congress approve the removal of the American Selling Price (ASP) system of customs valuation used principally for imports of benzenoid chemicals. This system often results in unusually high levels of protection. During the Kennedy round of trade negotiations, which ended in 1967, many European nations agreed to remove similar nontariff barriers to trade and to reduce chemical tariffs if ASP were repealed. A large portion of the American chemical industry opposes the ending of this special form of protection. In addition to his specific proposal, President Nixon asked Congress to express its support for the removal of other nontariff trade barriers.

The Nixon administration also asked for greater authority to increase protection when imports increase under certain conditions or when U.S. farm exports meet foreign discriminatory protection. The President asked for rules making it easier to extend financial and other help to American industries and workers when they suffer from an increase in imports. But even before Congress could take any action on this proposal, the Tariff Commission, the agency responsible for determining whether an industry has suffered injury from imports, adopted a less restrictive approach and began to issue decisions under existing legislation, which eased the granting of adjustment assistance to firms and workers.

Trade with Developing Countries. In November, proposals by several developed countries to reduce protection on imports from developing nations were submitted to the United Nations Conference on Trade and Development. In general, these proposals called for the reduction or abolition of protection on manufactured and semimanufactured products produced by the poor nations. This preferential treatment would last for at least ten years. The developed nations submitted individual proposals because they had not been able to come to an agreement on a common approach.

The United States supported the suggested trade liberalization. The Nixon administration indicated, however, that the United States would not extend the benefits of reduced protection to all developing nations unless other developed countries did the same. In the event they failed to do so, President Nixon indicated that the reduced American protection would be offered only to Latin America. This position also reflected American disapproval of the association agreement between the European Common Market and 18 African countries. The agreement, renewed in 1969, provides that the developing nations will reciprocate trade benefits given them by lowering their protection on imports from Europe alone.

Trade Groups. In December the European Common Market agreed to open membership negotiations with the United Kingdom, Denmark, Ireland and Norway. These talks were expected to begin in mid-1970. They would result in the enlargement of the Common Market's customs union and might radically transform, if not end,

London "Daily Express," Pictorial Parade

A possible new British export: British rail experts demonstrate their 150-mile-an-hour Advanced Passenger Train, which will be in commercial service by 1974.

the European Free Trade Association in which three of the four (not Ireland) are members. A full customs union (no tariffs among members, a common tariff on imports from nonmembers) already exists among the Six.

At the same time, the four Scandinavian countries—Denmark, Finland, Norway and Sweden—held talks for the creation of Nordek, a customs union.

GORDON L. WEIL
Twentieth Century Fund

The United Nations Commission on International Trade Law, established by a General Assembly resolution in December 1966, begins its second session in Geneva, Switzerland, in March.

United Nations

TRAVEL

In 1969, travel headlines went to cut-rate flights across the Atlantic. The regularly scheduled airlines found they were losing more and more tourist traffic to charter flights, especially since 1968 when the U.S. Congress began permitting nonscheduled supplemental airlines to engage in the charter business. The Boeing 747 superjets, scheduled to go into service in early 1970, seemed likely to accentuate the problem of empty seats, with their 362-to-490-passenger capacity.

In September 1969 the Italian national airline, Alitalia, announced that it would no longer abide by the fares established at the last International Air Transport Association (IATA) meeting, held in Dallas in February.

IATA rules provide that if one member abandons the tariffs agreed on, none of the members are bound by the agreement. Therefore within a month most other transatlantic airlines announced price cuts ranging from 10 to 26 per cent for individual tickets, provided the traveler stayed abroad at least 22 days and came home by May 15, 1970. The 22-day minimum was intended to eliminate the business traveler, who usually stays less than two weeks; the May 15 date was to allow the airlines to evaluate the success of the lower fares before the 1970 peak vacation season. Until then the new New York–Rome round-trip fare is $299, compared with $409 previously.

Travel Conglomerates. While the regularly scheduled airlines were wrestling with the problem of empty seats, the nonscheduled or supplementary lines were rapidly expanding their activities. Several of these lines belong to conglomerate companies that seek to offer customers "a complete travel experience." Such companies own, in addition to an airline, a chain of hotels, a car-rental system and the computer that ties reservations together for an entire trip.

At the Lille Fair in France, a computer program was demonstrated that has startling ramifications. In an experiment, "customers" were asked to fill out an electrostatic form giving their vacation preferences by area, budget, type of accommodations desired, and favorite activities. The form was fed into a computer which then "suggested" several possible vacations. In practice, such a computer set-up will of course suggest the airline, hotels and rental cars of the conglomerate owning the computer. Small travel agents and privately owned hotels will be forced to affiliate with such systems in order to enjoy the business so generated.

The individual traveler can have his vacation planned by a computer in three seconds. But if he is fussy about his arrangements, he

"I have a feeling we've already seen the Uffizi Gallery—but just forgot to cross it off the list."

© 1969 Saturday Review, Inc., by John Ruge

McFadden Air Photo

A $5,000,000 terminal accommodates the sleek liners that are making the Port of Miami the cruise "capital."

will have even more of a problem than he had under the old system. While he is asking about various hotels in one city, the agent could be selling dozens of trips at three seconds each; the agent will naturally charge extra for fussiness.

The travel conglomerates are willing to let the fussy man fuss, while they concentrate on the first-time traveler. Since more than half the population of the United States has never journeyed more than 200 miles from home, they have an ample market if they can find ways to tap it. One device used by the conglomerates, and by the large travel agents and scheduled airlines too, is the vacation club. Members pay dues of $30 to $50 a month.

Under one plan, after a year they are entitled to a trip to Europe; at the end of the second year, they are entitled to a trip to Mexico; then the process repeats. During the year members can attend monthly meetings of local club chapters to talk about travel, see slides and movies, and make plans. They get acquainted with other members, so they do not set out on a trip as a group of strangers. The clubs sponsored by one large travel agent have adopted hospitals and charities in the countries they visit; when they arrive they have a person-to-person contact already established.

The travel-club method allows the sponsoring company to allocate plane seats and hotel rooms efficiently for maximum occupancy, since it knows who is going where (and has

the money in hand) well in advance of the trip. That efficiency makes possible the bargain rates that seem to be the incentive most effective for the first-time traveler.

Cruises. The cruise business continues to grow overall but in ways that mean distress for some areas. Los Angeles is developing as a departure point for Westerners, whose choice until recently was limited almost entirely to expensive Pacific trips to Hawaii or the Orient. Now cruises are available from Los Angeles to Mexico and South America, and, as a result of a surprisingly heavy demand, to the Caribbean through the Panama Canal. The canal apparently exerts a strong appeal and one line has put a ship on a sort of shuttle service between Los Angeles and Port Everglades, Fla., for four round trips from January to May. Most of the passengers go one way by ship and the other way by air.

Port Everglades and Miami have taken a large share of the cruise business away from the Port of New York. The logic is simple: people go on cruises for sun, so why should they sail from congested New York and spend a total of four days in the wintry North Atlantic. The Port of Miami has built five new piers for the cruise business and has a site ready for five more; 500,000 passengers are expected to use these futuristic facilities in 1970.

U.S. shipping companies have not been able to share in the cruise boom. Even with heavy subsidies meant to cover the difference in wages paid by U.S. and foreign carriers, American passenger ships have been losing money. First the American Export Isbrandtsen Lines laid up the *Independence* and the *Constitution*. Then Moore-McCormack laid up the *Argentina* and *Brasil* at least until June 1970. Even the *United States,* holder of the blue ribbon for speed on the North Atlantic, was laid up "indefinitely."

Cunard's new liner, the *Queen Elizabeth 2* or *QE 2,* entered service in 1969, after her maiden voyage had to be postponed because of a defect in one of her turbines. The popularity of the *France* of the French Line was not hurt at all when *The New York Times* food expert Craig Claiborne pronounced her probably the best restaurant anywhere in the world, on land or sea.

U.S. Travel and the Balance of Payments. The major travel story of 1968 was the possibility of government restrictions on travel abroad by U.S. citizens—restrictions intended to reduce the annual U.S. "tourist deficit" of $2,000,-000,000. The restrictions were not approved by Congress and were subsequently rejected by the new Republican administration. Secretary of Commerce Maurice H. Stans traveled through Western Europe and Japan in 1969, and repeatedly said: "Given the alternative of restricting American travel overseas or encouraging others to travel in America, the Nixon administration has made its choice. It will not restrict American travel to other countries; we want more visitors to discover America."

Travel continued to increase everywhere, although not all areas maintained the huge rate of growth of the years just past. For the 1969 fiscal year, the Port of New York showed an 8.6 per cent increase in international air arrivals over the previous year and the month of August showed a 21 per cent increase over August 1968. Most of these arrivals were returning U.S. citizens, of course, but overseas visitors in the first six months of 1969 totaled 715,507, an increase of 13.4 per cent compared with the same period in 1968. In January-June 1969 the top ten sources of overseas visitors to the United States were the United Kingdom, Japan, Germany, the Bahamas, France, Italy, the Dominican Republic, Australia, Venezuela and Colombia. Japan moved ahead of Germany into second place, and the Dominican Republic and Australia exchanged seventh and eighth places.

France made a splendid recovery from the tourist drought caused by the strikes and riots of 1968. The French National Railroads introduced several new trains, including a new version of the Paris-to-Nice *Mistral* with all new equipment, and the *Palatino* (in cooperation with the Italian State Railways) an overnight train from Paris to Rome that makes the trip in 15 hours, and includes meals in the cost of a ticket.

In Africa the most popular destinations were Morocco, Kenya, Uganda and Tanzania—Morocco for resort life with an Arab flavor, and East Africa for animal watching. In South America, which has some of the great spectacles of the world, every government has now enacted legislation to encourage the tourist trade.

Expo '70 and the Pacific. In Japan, Osaka will be the scene of Expo '70, a fully accredited international exposition running from Mar. 15 through Sept. 13. By the end of 1969, 77 nations were scheduled to have exhibits on an 815-acre site. Japan's own exhibits will enable visitors to contemplate that nation's genius for good design, and the reasons why it is now the second-ranking industrial country of the world.

Expo '70 will undoubtedly attract a number of Americans to Asia. For a few hundred dollars more than the cost of a ticket from New York to Osaka, they can continue on to Hong Kong and Bangkok; and from Bangkok they can continue on around the world as cheaply as they can backtrack across the Pacific.

School's Out. For many years, U.S. schools have closed for vacation in the summer, a throwback to the time when children worked on the family farm. Atlanta and several other cities have now recognized the big changes in agriculture and how silly the old vacation arrangement is. The new idea is that students may take their vacation in any quarter of the year, and attend classes the other three quarters. For the schools it means a great increase in the number of classrooms available, since fewer will stand empty in the summer. It means that families can take their vacations in the winter to go skiing, or in the spring or the fall when highways, airlines and resorts are not jammed. For the travel industry it means a smoothing out of the peaks that cause customers to be turned away, and the valleys that cause staff to be let go. The plan for more three-day holiday weekends was approved by nearly all the states. In the near future, therefore, Memorial Day, Washington's Birthday, Columbus Day and Veterans Day will always be observed on Monday.

See Aviation and Shipping.

JOHN R. ROBERSON
Senior Editor, *Holiday*

TRUDEAU, PIERRE E.

On Oct. 18, 1969, Canada's Prime Minister Pierre Elliott Trudeau was 50 years old. "But 50 for *him*," as a newspaper cartoonist explained, sketching a dialogue between two teenage victims of Trudeaumania, "isn't 50 like for your father."

The most eligible playboy of the Western democracies started his first full year as prime minister by breaking away from the Commonwealth leaders' conference in London to date a German divorcée, Mrs. Eva von Rittinghausen. Later—a few hours later—she told the press that it was "love at first sight." Trudeau wasn't amused. Commenting on the "crummy behavior" of journalists, he warned that "if you are entitled to pry into my private affairs, I don't see why I wouldn't be able to pry into yours."

It was a sign that Trudeau was beginning to tire of the swinger's image that had helped to elect him the previous year. As friends were aware, the image related to only a fraction of his activities. During most of his career, he had been a scholarly, hard-working and somewhat aloof professor of international law whose life rarely reflected the fact that he was a bachelor with a family fortune estimated at $7,000,000.

After the Rittinghausen affair, Trudeau projected a quieter image. This was evident in March during his first visit to Washington, rated by all concerned as one of the dullest state occasions in memory. But it did create, during a conference at the National Press Club, a memorable description of relations between Canada and the United States.

"Living next to you is in some ways like sleeping with an elephant," the Prime Minister told his audience. "No matter how friendly or even-tempered is the beast, if I may call it that, one is affected by every twitch and grunt."

In May, a poll by the *Toronto Daily Star* revealed that Trudeau's popularity had waned since the election-year adulation of 1968. The proportion of Canadians who were "very satisfied" with his performance declined from 28 to 18 per cent. Most approved of his domestic reforms ("liberal" changes of the Criminal Code and divorce law) and international moves (reduction of Canadian NATO forces in Europe and progress toward diplomatic recognition of Peking). But they were critical of his record on poverty, farm problems, inflation, housing and taxes. The Prime Minister encountered his first hostile crowds during a July tour of western Canada when farmers greeted him with placards saying "Hustle Grain Not Women" and labeling him a "rich playboy."

"London Daily Express," Pictorial Parade

In London for Commonwealth Conference, Prime Minister Trudeau makes a dashing appearance—which is combined with high intelligence and deep seriousness.

"If you want to see me in future," retorted Trudeau, "don't bring signs saying that Trudeau is a pig and don't bring signs saying that I hustle women. . . . I didn't get into politics to be insulted."

Always an advocate of Federalism, the Prime Minister made a fierce attack on French-Canadian separatists in October. Linking the relatively low rate of foreign investment in Quebec with political uncertainty in the French-speaking province, he said that "the folly of the past years has lasted long enough." He warned that the Federal Government would not tolerate the use of the Federal radio and television networks in Quebec to spread separatist doctrines.

Trudeau's pragmatic approach to government, his intelligence and obvious enjoyment of life seemed to suit the mood of Canadians on the eve of the 1970's.

"Despite the fact that many of his policies fill me with unease," wrote syndicated columnist Charles Lynch from Ottawa, "my own feeling is that he is the right man, in the right place, at the right time for Canada."

PETER DESBARATS
Associate Editor, *Saturday Night*

UPI

Summertime in Siberia: Children play in a rivulet feeding Lake Baikal, world's largest volume of fresh water. Pollution from industries has become a problem.

union of soviet socialist republics

External affairs dominated the Soviet scene in 1969. In the spring the long-smoldering Sino-Soviet conflict reached a climax that brought the two communist giants to the brink of war. In the fall, however, the two sides agreed to attempt a negotiated settlement of their explosive border dispute. By year's end, the Soviet Union, in a dazzling burst of diplomatic activity, had also opened negotiations on major security issues with its two principal Western opponents, the United States and the Federal Republic of Germany. In domestic affairs, by contrast, the Soviet leadership displayed a massive unwillingness or inability to innovate despite fresh evidence that existing institutions and practices for managing the economy had exhausted their creative capacities.

Written off as a "caretaker regime" by foreign observers when it deposed the garrulous Nikita Khrushchev in 1964, the "collective leadership" headed by Leonid I. Brezhnev and

Aleksei N. Kosygin completed its fifth year in office in 1969. Despite rumors that deep cleavages had been created in the leadership during the 1968 Czechoslovak crisis, there were no changes in the composition of the ruling 11-member Politburo of the Party Central Committee. A new test of the post-Khrushchev leadership's stability was expected at a Party Congress (the 24th) due to be held in 1970, according to party statutes, but not yet announced at year's end.

Brezhnev continued in 1969 to receive the deference due him as ranking party secretary, but there was no sign that the leadership was becoming any less "collective" than before. As party general secretary, Brezhnev enjoyed the limelight in June at the international conference of communist parties in Moscow. Premier Kosygin won diplomatic honors with a dramatic peacemaking flight to Peking in September. The annual October Revolution anniversary speech was delivered by the titular "President" of the U.S.S.R., Nikolai V. Podgorny.

In 1969, economic enterprises throughout the Soviet Union participated in a special all-union socialist competition in honor of the 100th anniversary of the birth of the founder of the Soviet state, Lenin (V. I. Ulyanov), scheduled to be celebrated in April 1970. The results were disappointing. The Soviet Union's industrial growth rate slowed to about 7 per cent, still respectable by world standards but lower than in any peacetime year since 1928. The planned goal for 1969 was technically achieved, but only because the original target had been "corrected" earlier in the year, due to "adverse weather conditions and other natural calamities." Deputy Premier Nikolai K. Baibakov, chairman of the State Planning Commission, told the U.S.S.R. Supreme Soviet in December that industrial goals for the next year had also been cut back below the original targets of the Five-Year Plan that ends in 1970.

As usual, performance among industrial branches was uneven. The construction and transportation industries, which registered growth rates of less than 3 per cent, came in for especially strong criticism. Defense-related industries, such as instrumentation, and automation and guidance systems, made their customary strong showings.

The industrial sector's poor 1969 performance was particularly discouraging news for Premier Kosygin and others prominently associated with the economic reforms instituted in 1965. By the end of the year, three fourths of all industrial enterprises, accounting for 83 per cent of total industrial output and more

than 91 per cent of profits, were operating under the new system. It was designed to raise industrial productivity by increasing plant managers' autonomy and enhancing the importance of profit as a criterion of success. But labor productivity grew at a rate of only 4.4 per cent in 1969, compared with a 5 per cent increase in per capita national income. At midyear, profits in the aggregate economy showed a sharp drop from the mid-1968 level (from 17 to 7 per cent). Bureaucratic inertia and fear of spontaneity had combined to rob the modest economic reforms of their promise.

A severe winter, late spring, dust storms and floods conspired to produce the worst year for Soviet agriculture since the disastrous harvest failure of 1963. For the first time since that year there was an absolute decline in agricultural production; farm output was down 3 per cent below 1968. While the grain harvest was

At the height of spring fishing on the lower Volga River, a big catch is sorted. Fish in foreground are sturgeon, from which caviar (salted roe) is obtained.

UPI

UPI

Janos Kadar (l), Hungarian Communist Party leader, and his wife are welcomed to Moscow by Soviet party chief Leonid Brezhnev (2d l) and Premier Aleksei Kosygin.

not so poor as to require massive emergency grain purchases abroad as in 1963, the reported yield of 160,500,000 tons was a long way from the 190,000,000- to 200,000,000-ton harvest that was the goal of the Five-Year Plan. The adverse weather conditions led to particularly heavy livestock losses which were reflected in meat shortages in Soviet cities throughout the year.

The poor harvest and the livestock losses provided a bleak backdrop for the long-postponed third All-Union Collective Farm Congress. It met in Moscow in November to adopt a new Model Statute for Collective Farms, drafted after more than three years of deliberations by a select 149-member special committee chaired by Brezhnev. The standpat congress

U.S.S.R.

Area: 8,599,776 sq. mi.
Population: 241,000,000
Capital: Moscow (pop., 6,700,000)
Government: Nikolai V. Podgorny, president of presidium—1965; Aleksei N. Kosygin, premier—1964; Leonid I. Brezhnev, Communist Party secretary—1964
Gross national product: $430,000,000,000
Monetary unit: ruble (1 ruble = U.S. $1.11)
Chief products: grains, livestock, coal, iron ore, oil, textiles, clothing, timber, furs
Foreign trade: exports, $10,634,000,000; imports, $9,410,000,000
Communications: 9,100,000 telephones, 40,-000,000 radios, 20,000,000 TV sets
Transportation: roads, 931,500 mi.; railroads, 82,546 mi.
Education: 49,000,000 elementary and secondary students, 5,000,000 students of higher education
Armed forces: 3,300,000

See map on page 185

dashed the hopes of reform-minded economists and collective-farm leaders who had argued vigorously during the precongress discussions for the creation of a national union that would increase the weight and authority of collective-farm organizations vis-à-vis the Ministry of Agriculture, and for charter reform that would strengthen the weak collective-farm incentive system by assigning land and machinery for long periods of time to small teams or "links."

In the cultural field the struggle between "conservatives" and "modernists" continued in the literary press, with the party maintaining an uneasy balance between them but shifting the center of gravity steadily in the direction of ultraorthodoxy. Conservative demands for the resignation of Alexander Tvardovsky from the liberal monthly *Novy Mir* were successfully resisted; but three other liberals, including the poet Yevgeny Yevtushenko, were dropped from the editorial board of the popular youth magazine *Yunost*. To the embarrassment of the Soviet Government, the young writer Anatoly V. Kuznetsov, one of the new editors named to replace the deposed *Yunost* liberals, dramatically defected to Britain while on a visit in July after deceiving the KGB (secret police). At year's end, Russia's most celebrated living writer, Alexander Solzhenitsyn, charged with permitting his works to be published abroad for anti-Soviet purposes, was formally expelled from the Union of Soviet Writers and invited to leave the country.

Political dissidents continued to make public protests in 1969 despite repressive police action and a new conservative press campaign to stir up anti-intellectual sentiments in the Soviet working class. In May, 55 dissidents signed an appeal to the United Nations Commission

UPI

Sportsmen stride through Red Square in the May Day parade; poster back of them extols communist virtues.

on Human Rights for an investigation of "repression of basic civil rights in the Soviet Union." Several members of the group, which included Pyotr I. Yakir, son of the Red Army General executed in the 1937 Red Army purge, were subsequently arrested on charges of anti-Soviet activity. Also arrested in 1969 for "slandering the U.S.S.R." were a number of Soviet citizens who publicly protested Soviet intervention in Czechoslovakia.

As the year began, Czechoslovakia was still very much the central concern of Soviet crisis managers. In August 1968 the Soviet Union had demonstrated with unmistakable force its determination to keep Eastern Europe within its orbit and to define for its Warsaw Pact allies the limits of their autonomy in internal as well as external affairs. Yet Soviet intervention had not produced a rapid restoration of communist orthodoxy in Prague. Having failed initially to find suitable quislings with whom to replace Alexander Dubcek and his liberal associates, the Soviet leaders decided to make Dubcek himself the instrument of Soviet-style "normalization," a tactic also calculated to drain his popularity by obliging him to preside over the freezing of the "Prague spring."

The very fact that Dubcek remained in office, however, and particularly his stubborn refusal

Ira Yakovlinaya, considered the U.S.S.R.'s leading woman editor, runs east-Siberia edition of "Pravda."

UPI

Novosti from Sovfoto

"Cosmonaut Vladimir Komarov," research motor ship of the U.S.S.R. Academy of Sciences, prepares for a long voyage at Odessa, on the Black Sea. Construction (including the "globes") and specific purpose are secret.

to condone publicly the Warsaw Five's armed intervention, kept alive in Czechoslovakia a mood of defiant optimism that proved intolerable to Moscow. In April, after a surprise visit by Soviet Defense Minister Marshal Andrei Grechko, Dubcek was deposed as party first secretary and replaced by Gustav Husak, leader of the Slovak party organization. This was the prelude to a massive purge of the Czechoslovak Communist Party, culminating in the removal of Dubcek and his group from the Central Committee Presidium. In August, the first anniversary of the Soviet occupation, the extent of the U.S.S.R.'s success in restoring reliable leadership in Prague was poignantly expressed by the brutal suppression of student demonstrations in Wenceslas Square by Prague police, with no Soviet soldiers in sight.

By that time, however, the Soviet leaders had a far more urgent problem engaging their attention thousands of miles to the east. On the morning of Mar. 2, Soviet and Chinese border guards clashed on a disputed, barren and usually uninhabited island in the frozen Ussuri River near the eastern end of the long Sino-Soviet border. Although border incidents are known to have occurred frequently since the early 1960's, neither side had wished to risk a grave aggravation of their relations by publicizing them widely. This time, however, the Soviet Union unleashed a massive and highly inflammatory propaganda campaign, charging that 31 of its soldiers had been killed and their

bodies mutilated in a Chinese ambush. Domestic anti-Chinese passions were brought to a white heat when it was announced on Mar. 15 that a second incident had occurred at the same site. This clash, unlike the first, was generally believed to have been Soviet-initiated.

One objective of the Soviet campaign was evidently to mobilize foreign communist opinion against Peking on the eve of the international conference of communist parties in Moscow. The most that the Soviet party could get, however, were speeches by individual delegates echoing Brezhnev's attack on the Maoists. The Soviet Union was held to an earlier agreement to avoid criticism in formal conference documents of any other party, including the Chinese CP, which was not represented. The conference itself, convened finally after four years of postponements and wrangling over ground rules, was an anticlimax. A semblance of communist unity was achieved when most of the delegations signed a patchwork compromise document that was minimally acceptable to them only because it ignored or hedged on all the critical questions agitating the world movement.

The Soviet effort to compel the Chinese Communists to reopen border negotiations with the U.S.S.R. was crowned with greater success, but only after Moscow applied menacing military pressure. As a precondition to resuming border talks, which had been broken off in 1964, the Chinese had insisted upon public

UPI

Some 100,000 Russians march past Chinese Embassy in Moscow to protest the Ussuri River incident of Mar. 2. On Soviet side of river boundary (below), it is thought that some 300,000 troops are concentrated.

UPI

Soviet acknowledgment that all existing treaties dating from czarist times were "unequal," a demand that Soviet leaders flatly rejected. At the end of April, the Soviet Union offered the Chinese a face-saving first step toward resuming full border negotiations by proposing to reconvene an existing Sino-Soviet commission, inactive since mid-1967, which had jurisdiction over navigation on the rivers that serve as borders between the two states in the Far East. With large Soviet military reinforcements appearing along the entire length of the Sino-Soviet frontier, Peking agreed to the new Soviet proposal. On Aug. 8, after several interruptions in negotiations punctuated by new incidents, a one-year navigation agreement was signed at Khabarovsk.

Having gained the diplomatic initiative, Moscow quickly raised the ante. Five days after conclusion of the navigation agreement, heavy fighting erupted between Soviet and Chinese forces on the central Asian border between Soviet Kazakhstan and the vulnerable Chinese province of Sinkiang. Simultaneously, rumors of an impending preemptive Soviet air strike against Chinese nuclear and missile test facilities in Sinkiang swept the world. These rumors, largely Soviet-inspired, were clearly intended to add bite to renewed Soviet demands upon China to reopen border negotiations without preconditions.

The turning point came on Sept. 11 when Soviet Premier Kosygin, homeward bound after attending Ho Chi Minh's funeral in Hanoi, suddenly detoured to the Chinese capital to confer at the Peking airport with Chinese Premier Chou En-lai. The first high-level Sino-Soviet meeting since 1965, it bore fruit a month later when Peking announced that it was prepared to begin negotiations with the U.S.S.R. to end their border dispute. In a major concession, the Chinese quietly dropped their demand for prior Soviet acknowledgment that existing treaties were "unequal." As the year ended, Sino-Soviet border talks, which opened in Peking on Oct. 20, were temporarily recessed, reportedly without having achieved any substantial progress. But tension along the 4,500-mile Sino-Soviet border had been considerably relaxed, and the propaganda war between Moscow and Peking was muted for the first time since 1966.

As the crisis in the Far East abated, Soviet decision makers faced westward again, this time to complete unfinished diplomatic business with the United States. In 1968, Moscow and Washington had virtually reached agreement on opening Strategic Arms Limitation Talks (SALT) when the invasion of Czechoslovakia caused the United States to back off in protest. During the early months of 1969, Moscow waited for the new Nixon administration to make up its mind about the SALT talks, while Washington held back, waiting for signs of Soviet cooperation in arranging negotiated settlements in Vietnam and the Middle East. But whatever urgency Soviet leaders may once have felt about promoting a negotiated end to the Vietnam war was largely dissipated by 1969, as the United States began to withdraw its combat forces from South Vietnam and the danger of an American re-escalation that might imperil the communist regime in the North grew increasingly remote. On the continuing

Middle East crisis, the Soviet Union and the United States did open discussions in both a four-power and two-power context in the spring, but they were soon stalemated as the U.S.S.R. proved unwilling to advance or accept any proposals that were not approved by its Arab clients.

In June, when the United States decided it was prepared to open SALT talks without insisting on "linkages," Soviet and American policies were again out of phase. Moscow, preoccupied with the Chinese border crisis, seemed to be having second thoughts. Only after China agreed to resume border talks with the U.S.S.R., in October, did the Soviet Government finally announce that it would send representatives to Helsinki on Nov. 17 to open "preliminary discussions" with the United States on curbing the strategic-arms race.

Moscow's four-month delay in responding to President Nixon's bid to open the SALT talks was believed to reflect not only Soviet uncertainties connected with the China crisis but also division among the leaders over basic questions of nuclear strategy and arms control. One result of the delay—a major reason for it, according to some Western military observers— was that in the interim the Soviet Union essentially closed the nuclear strategic gap between the two superpowers. Before the end of the year, the Soviet Union was expected to have some 1,105 land-based ICBM's deployed, approximately 50 more than the United States. America, however, was credited with a substantial lead in submarine-launched ballistic missiles and intercontinental bombers. At a minimum, the Soviet Union was believed to be seeking through the SALT talks formal recognition that it had achieved strategic parity with the United States. By entering negotiations the Soviet leaders may also have wished to

UPI

Traveling with "Education USA" exhibit touring the U.S.S.R., Russian-speaking guide Irene Murray, of Gulfport, Miss., demonstrates a television teaching aid.

discourage the United States from moving ahead with new strategic programs that were emerging from the research-and-development stage (MIRV and ABM). At year's end the "preliminary discussions" were brought to a successful conclusion with an agreement to begin substantive negotiations in Vienna in the spring.

In the same month that Peking agreed to negotiate the border dispute with Moscow and the U.S.S.R. announced its readiness to open SALT talks with the United States, the election of Willy Brandt as the first Social Democratic chancellor of the Federal Republic of Germany prepared the way for the third major Soviet diplomatic breakthrough of the year. After Brezhnev and other Soviet leaders made notably conciliatory replies to Brandt's bid for improved relations, the Soviet Government informed Bonn on Dec. 7 that it was accepting the long-standing FRG proposal, renewed by the Brandt Government, to open talks in Moscow the following day on a mutual renunciation-of-force agreement between the two countries.

The Soviet move seemed intended as a gesture of favor to Brandt for agreeing to sign the nuclear-nonproliferation treaty and for offering to extend what amounted to *de facto* recognition to the German Democratic Republic (East Germany). With its own economic development stalled, Moscow may also have been responding to the lure of West German credits. As negotiations opened in Moscow between Soviet Foreign Minister Andrei Gromyko and FRG Ambassador Helmut Allardt, it was disclosed that a West German bank consortium had raised a $327,000,000 credit for the U.S.S.R. to finance purchase of giant natural-gas pipes in Germany, the loan to be insured by the FRG Government. Finally by opening negotiations with Bonn, the U.S.S.R. evidently hoped to create a favorable atmosphere in Western Europe for the Warsaw Pact states' proposal to hold an all-European security conference during the first half of 1970.

ARNOLD L. HORELICK
Senior Research Staff, Social Science Department
The RAND Corporation

In September, Soviet Foreign Minister Andrei Gromyko (l) confers with U.S. Secretary of State William Rogers in New York. Meeting presumably helped to open Strategic Arms Limitation Talks (SALT) in November.

UPI

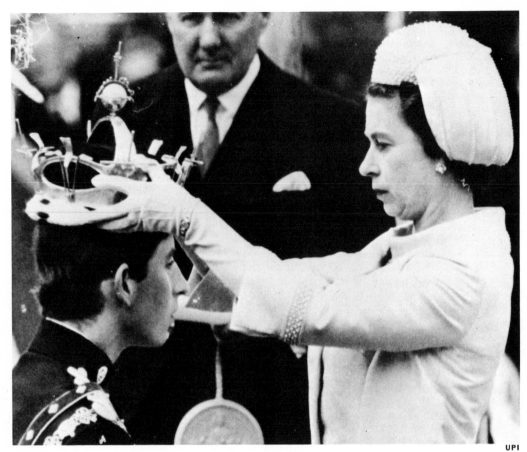

UPI

In a sixty-minute, bilingual ceremony at Caernarvon Castle (Wales) on July 1, Queen Elizabeth II crowns her son, Prince Charles, Prince of Wales.

united kingdom

It was in 1969 that Great Britain lost a role but found a surplus.

The year opened with a conference of 28 heads of state, or of government, of countries of the Commonwealth that has evolved out of the British Empire. It was probably the largest meeting of heads of government since the UN Charter was signed. It achieved almost nothing, only an agreement to continue to cooperate in a close and friendly manner in spite of widespread disagreement. Britain's role as leader—formally preserved by the acknowledgment of Queen Elizabeth II as Head of the Commonwealth—seemed finally to have lost any meaning.

The year ended, however, with a surplus not only in the British balance of payments but even in the balance of trade. While it has had frequent surpluses in its balance of payments, Britain in the past fifty years has rarely achieved an actual trade surplus. The significance of this fact is that with a surplus of private "invisible" trade (banking, shipping, insurance, tourism, oil and the like) of more than £1,000,000,000 ($2,400,000,000), a visible trade balance will give the British Government more room to maneuver than it has had at any time since World War I.

The Government's own current account for overseas transactions is, of course, heavily in the red. However, at the end of 1969, there was a 12-month surplus of some £300,000,000 ($720,000,000), an end-of-year surplus at an annual rate of £500,000,000 ($1,200,000,-000), and a forecast by the National Institute of Economic and Social Research of a 1970 payments surplus of £850,000,000 ($2,040,-000,000) if no major policy changes were made. Such a situation would be almost without parallel in living memory.

One immediate result was a decision to increase Britain's official overseas aid from 0.4 per cent of gross national product to 0.7 per cent in the mid-1970's. Together with private investment in developing countries, Britain's aid program will then reach 1.0 per cent of the GNP, 0.3 per cent above the level urged in the World Bank's Pearson Report.

Most of the rest of the British surplus will be needed to repay the $7,000,000,000 of new international debt incurred in 1966–69. But with foreign money again flowing into London it seems likely that repayment could be accompanied by a strengthening of Britain's reserves.

A slow thaw in the wage-and-credit freeze was starting as 1969 ended. The Bank of England's main discount rate has been as high as 8 per cent. House mortgages have been difficult to obtain even at 10 per cent. There was no increase in the money supply in 1969. Productive investment was very sluggish. The surplus has thus been purchased at a very high cost.

The Political Scene. Dominant factors in the political scene have been the things undone rather than those accomplished.

Two major bills were withdrawn when halfway through the process of being turned into law. One concerned reform of the House of Lords. It was destroyed by an unusual coalition between Labor and Tory backbenchers. The other, the Industrial Relations Bill, would for the first time have provided for sanctions against wildcat strikers.

UPI

Several hundred hippies take over 144 Piccadilly, a 100-room mansion formerly owned by King George VI.

In theory, Prime Minister Harold Wilson withdrew the Lords Reform Bill to make room and time for the Industrial Relations Bill. He declared that the passage of the latter was "essential for the continuance of this government in office." He then withdrew it, handing responsibility for industrial peace over to the Trades Union Congress.

Whether as an effect of this display of political flexibility, or by coincidence, or because the trade figures were coming right, the net result was a sharp reduction in the Government's unpopularity. There had been a 20 per cent gap between Labor and Tory parties in the spring, with the Tories leaping ever further ahead. By fall, the gap was reduced to between 5 and 10 per cent.

The Government's rating may also have been improved by the reduction of the legal age of majority from 21 to 18 years, a pledge to legalize equal pay for women within 5 years, a major reform of the divorce laws, and the

---

UNITED KINGDOM

Area: 94,000 sq. mi.
Population: 55,700,000
Capital: London (pop., 8,000,000)
Government: Elizabeth II, queen—1952; Harold Wilson, prime minister—1964
Gross national product: $88,046,000,000
Monetary unit: pound (1 pound = U.S. $2.40)
Chief products: coal, iron and steel, chemicals, electronics, motor vehicles, textiles, clothing
Foreign trade: exports, $14,812,000,000; imports, $18,520,000,000
Communications: 12,099,000 telephones, 17,-500,000 radios, 16,500,000 TV sets
Transportation: roads, 202,060 mi.; 11,071,000 passenger cars; railroads, 13,500
Education: 8,954,252 elementary and secondary students, 45 universities
Armed forces: 405,000

See map on page 185

UPI

In the fall, 17 of London's 32 boroughs were hit by a series of strikes by sanitation workers.

announcement of a substantially more generous earnings-related state-pensions scheme for the 1980's.

In October, Wilson reconstructed his Government. Anthony Wedgwood Benn, 44, minister of technology, took over the Ministry of Power as well. He became an industrial overlord, with responsibility for most industries, both public and private. At the same time, Anthony Crosland, 51, left the Board of Trade to become secretary of state for local government and regional planning. His new department took over road and rail transportation, docks and waterways, housing and all questions relating to environment. George Thomson, 48, stepped from being minister without portfolio to become deputy foreign secretary and chancellor of the Duchy of Lancaster. As such, Thomson acquired special responsibility for any negotiations about joining the European Common Market.

Northern Ireland. The most important development in home affairs, however, was the recurrence of serious trouble in the partly self-governing province of Northern Ireland. British troops had to be withdrawn from NATO duty for police duties in Ulster, the old name for the six counties of Northern Ireland.

The trouble was sparked by Roman Catholic claims of discrimination against them in the local government franchise, in the allocation of housing and in the provision of jobs by the aggressively Protestant majority in the province. A civil-rights movement formed. It was joined by a politically revolutionary People's Democracy party. Both groups took part in protest marches in, on and around Londonderry, where a substantial Catholic population lives. These led to clashes with Protestants. During March and April a power station near Belfast, the provincial capital, was destroyed, pipelines supplying water were blown up, and several buildings were bombed or burned.

Prime Minister Terence O'Neill resigned in April and was succeeded by Major James Chichester-Clark. Both are members of the Unionist Party. It is predominantly Protestant and supports continuance of the union with Great Britain, which is attacked by both Catholics and Irish Republicans.

In August, serious rioting again broke out in Belfast, and the violence spread to Londonderry. On the request of the Ulster government the British Government intervened. It sent troops to keep public order, and to protect the border with the Republic of Ireland, under the command of Lt. Gen. Sir Ian Freeland.

A commission under Lord Cameron set out a basic program of reform. Another committee, under Lord Hunt (leader of the first expedition to conquer Mt. Everest), recommended the reform of the Royal Ulster Constabulary and

UPI

Teachers march from Regent's Park to Department of Education on Curzon Street, demanding higher salaries.

the Ulster Special Constabulary to remove them both from the arena of controversy. The RUC and the Specials are being relieved of paramilitary duties and will become police forces of the same kind and with the same range of duties as any other United Kingdom police. For emergency duty an Ulster Defense Regiment is to be formed on a part-time or reserve basis. It was hoped that personnel would be recruited from both Protestant and Catholic communities.

Under a reform program the allocation of housing is being taken from local authorities (town governments) and given to an impartial Housing Board. Local government boundaries are being redrawn. One man-one vote became the law for local elections, as it already is for provincial. A Community Relations Board was appointed, as well as an ombudsman with authority to investigate citizens' complaints against government departments.

Foreign Affairs. Prime Minister Harold Wilson visited Bonn in February. His main hope was to obtain a commitment from the West German Government to support Britain's application for entry into the Common Market. This he received. At the same time, he himself pledged Britain to continue to defend the freedom of the city of West Berlin.

By the end of the year the Common Market picture had changed somewhat. Wilson had

In May, United Nurses Association, under the leadership of Patricia Veal, stages protest against low wages.

Wide World

which all market members must introduce, and added that Europe now needs Britain as much as Britain needs Europe. Thus, as the market's own summit meeting was taking place in December, he gave the impression that Britain would take a tougher negotiating line than before.

Wilson flew to Nigeria in March in the hope of using Britain's influence to improve the flow of relief supplies to those in danger of starvation in the battle areas in the war with secessionist Biafra and possibly to bring a settlement of the conflict. The war ended in January 1970. Britain's position as a main arms supplier to the Federal Nigerian Government and as the originator and protector of the Commonwealth of which Federal Nigeria is a member gave Wilson fresh leverage in the area.

On May 30 a new constitution for Gibraltar was promulgated. A guarantee was given that no act would be passed relinquishing sovereignty to Spain without the express consent of the population. The Spanish Government was given to understand that Britain was willing in principle to cede the fortress at some future date, but only if the population gave its freely expressed consent.

Soviet spies Peter and Helen Kroger were exchanged for British teacher Gerald Brooke, a courier for anticommunist groups who was arrested, jailed and ill-treated in the Soviet Union. The Krogers flew to Poland on Oct. 24. Reuters journalist Anthony Grey, under house arrest in Peking following the imprisonment of Communist Chinese journalists in Hong Kong, was released after spending over 26 months in a room 12 by 10 feet.

Other Events. An effort to unite the Church of England and the Methodist Church failed in July when the Anglican Convocations of York and Canterbury failed to produce the required majority. The Methodist Conference voted in favor by 77 per cent.

The Anglo-French supersonic Concorde jet airliner flew for the first time. The French prototype flew in March, the British in April.

In October the Ministry of Technology received five competing designs for a prototype vertical takeoff and landing airliner, suitable for city-center to city-center commercial routes.

In December, Parliament approved a government measure abolishing capital punishment.

Royal Family. In a colorful ceremony at Caernarvon Castle, July 1, Prince Charles, the heir to the throne, was formally invested by the Queen as Prince of Wales. Attaining his majority and also now entitled to the revenues of the Duchy of Cornwall, Prince Charles

UPI

Peter and Helen Kroger, who were convicted in 1961 and sentenced to 20 years in prison for selling submarine secrets to Russia, were exchanged for Gerald Brooke, a teacher jailed by the Russians in 1965.

put in hand a new study of what joining might cost the British balance of payments. Estimates have varied unofficially from a minimum of $600,000,000 to $2,500,000,000 a year. The main costs would accrue from supporting the Common Agricultural Policy. It is not only that this has produced vast unsalable surpluses of dairy products. It requires a switch from Britain's system of deficiency payments to one of levies on food imports. The proceeds of these levies would not be paid to the national treasuries but to the European Economic Community, a fact of overwhelming importance to the world's largest food importer, as Britain is.

Wilson assured Britons that there is no question of joining a federal Europe. He also spoke disrespectfully of the value-added tax,

announced that he would return half of this fortune (£ 220,000—$528,000—a year in total) to the nation.

Considerable controversy blew up later in the year, following remarks made on American television by the Queen's husband, Prince Philip, Duke of Edinburgh, over the question of the royal family's official income.

The privy purse voted by Parliament of £ 475,000 ($1,140,000) a year plus £ 40,000 ($96,000) to Prince Philip has remained unchanged since 1952. Now it is said to be insufficient to allow the Queen and her family to maintain themselves and the ceremonial of royalty in the style to which the nation has become accustomed. The Queen, a rich woman in her own right, has been subsidizing the monarchy. A parliamentary committee is investigating.

The Queen broke with tradition by deciding against a Christmas broadcast and telecast to Britain and the countries of the Commonwealth. An hour-long television movie of the royal family was shown throughout the world during 1969. With this and the investiture, seen by 500,000,000, the Queen felt there might be a danger of overexposure for the British monarchy.

JOHN ALLAN MAY
Chief, London Bureau
The Christian Science Monitor

British Petroleum Co., Ltd.

A self-service gas station begins operation in Essex.

Laborites Tom Dreiberg and Alice Bacon listen as Prime Minister Wilson addresses party conference in Brighton.

Central Press, Pictorial Parade

UNITED NATIONS

"In my view," Secretary General Thant said at the end of the 1969 General Assembly session, "the General Assembly is truly reflective of the international climate. We are now witnessing in many parts of the world the revolt of the young, the weak and the poor. The 24th session of the Assembly has been an expression of this trend.

"This has been an Assembly of the poor against the rich—the weak against the strong—and the young against the old.

"I am not saying that this is a trend in the right direction, or in the wrong direction. It is simply my appraisal of the mood of the Assembly."

It was a fair appraisal of the mood of the world parliament, whatever assessment might be made of the results of the session, diplomatic observers agreed. The poor, the weak and the young powers had spoken up against the rich, strong and old—the Establishment.

Despite blunt warnings from both the United States and the Soviet Union that it must take no action that could upset proceedings at the newly started Strategic Arms Limitation Talks (SALT) at Helsinki, the Assembly voted 82 to 0, with 37 abstentions, to call on the two superpowers to agree "as an urgent preliminary measure, on a moratorium on further testing and deployment of new offensive and strategic nuclear-weapon systems."

And although President Nixon's renunciation of chemical and bacteriological (biological) weapons exempted the use of tear gas and defoliants, small-power pressure brought an 80 to 3 Assembly vote, with 36 abstentions, declaring that both agents are included in the provisions of the 1925 Geneva Protocol on the prohibition of the use in war of asphyxiating, poisonous or other gases.

The effect on the big powers, however, was neither visible nor measurable immediately.

U.S. Ambassador Charles W. Yost was asked: "If you were to single out one item, what seems to you one of the most important achievements of the 24th session?"

"The preparations for the 25th," he said.

Lord Caradon, British minister of state and London's UN ambassador, said a major factor in the session was the importance the delegates attached to 1970, which they hoped would show outstanding progress and be a banner jubilee year for the United Nations.

The Assembly did approve plans for a commemorative 25th anniversary session to be

U.S. delegates to the United Nations include (l-r): Rep. Dante B. Fascell (D-Fla.), Mrs. Shirley Temple Black, Charles W. Yost, Rep. J. Irving Whalley (R-Pa.) and William B. Buffum.

"The New York Times"

UPI

UN Secretary-General U Thant discusses Middle East crisis with newsmen. Undersecretary for Public Information Agha Abdul Hamid (next to Thant) and Undersecretary-General Ralph Bunche (third from r) listen attentively.

attended by as many heads of state as possible and to culminate on Oct. 24, 1970—United Nations Day—with a World Youth Assembly. A committee of 25 was approved to make final plans for a gala celebration. There was no disagreement on this, but the "revolt" against the big powers brought these remarks from Yost:

"The Assembly is a place where 126 nations have a voice, where they can get up and criticize the big powers for acting or failing to act in the ways that they think they should.

". . . The actions of the General Assembly are not binding. They are recommendations which we endeavor to take account of. But we feel free to disagree with them in some cases and this is part of the business of parliamentary democracy. . . . It has never been intended as a world government which legislates for the world. Maybe we will come to that some day. But the actions of the Assembly are recommendations and there isn't any member that doesn't disagree with some actions of the Assembly and doesn't refuse to carry out in some cases actions of the Assembly.

"It is an expression of world opinion; in some cases almost unanimous world opinion, in other cases only marginally majority opinion. So I don't think the fact that we don't agree with and accept every resolution of the Assembly or even some resolutions of the Security Council which are not binding in any way indicates that we are not very firm and strong in our support of the United Nations itself."

A State Department spokesman later supported Yost by declaring that the Assembly's inclusion of tear gas and herbicides under the Geneva prohibitions could not be regarded as an "international consensus."

Actually, the 24th Assembly was remarkable for little other than the diplomatic muscle-flexing of the smaller powers. It did, however, manage to cut down to a small extent on its speechmaking and adjourned an unaccustomed eight days before Christmas and only one day beyond the target date the Assembly had set when it opened in September.

At its outset, Angie Elizabeth Brooks, 41, of Liberia, the second woman and the second black African to be elected Assembly president, told the delegates: "Our weakness seems to lie in the fact that we all too often view world affairs somewhat parochially, as if they were being played out at the headquarters on the East River of New York. We have sometimes failed to realize that neither oratory, nor agreements between delegations, nor even resolutions or recommendations have had much impact on the world at large.

"The sense of satisfaction upon adoption of a resolution pleasing the purposes of one delegation or a homogeneous group of delegations has helped perpetuate the mythology of achievement, so that many of us tend to go happily from one agenda item to the next without seriously considering the possibility or even probability that the resolution adopted will not be implemented. We have lacked, and do lack, in this respect, a sense of reality. . . . Whoever is at fault, the sad fact is that with governments sometimes pursuing one policy for national use and seemingly another for use in the United Nations, we have not achieved the

In native dress, delegates from Swaziland attend opening session of 24th General Assembly.

strength with which the Charter in its totality has endowed us."

In her closing speech on Dec. 17, Miss Brooks appealed for cease-fires and political settlements in the Nigerian civil war, in Vietnam and in the Middle East. That was as close as the General Assembly got to discussing the world's war spots.

But the UN ambassadors of the United States, the Soviet Union, Britain and France, at the behest of the French, started a series of private meetings in April, seeking agreement on principles for a peace settlement that could be given to Ambassador Gunnar V. Jarring of Sweden, UN special Mideast peace envoy, for negotiation with Israel and the Arabs.

They suspended their meetings in July while the United States held bilateral talks with the Soviet Union. When Moscow was slow to answer U.S. proposals for an Egyptian-Israeli settlement—it finally rejected the ideas—the big-four UN ambassadors resumed their secret meetings in December. Although the United States submitted a new plan for a Jordanian-Israeli settlement, there was no sign that the big-four talks were succeeding.

Vietnam did not appear on the Assembly agenda in any guise, although most delegates alluded to it in policy speeches. Thant, having seen the first of his two prescribed conditions for peace—cessation of the bombing of North Vietnam and talks among all parties to the fighting—complied with, made a new pronouncement at the end of the year.

"The first priority for peace should be the emergence of a broad-based national government in South Vietnam which has the confidence and trust and allegiance of most, if not all factions in South Vietnam," Thant said. "Of course, I cannot say that of any other government, but, because of the peculiar situation of South Vietnam and because of the very important repercussions generated by the Vietnamese war on the international scene, I believe that I am quite justified in coming out publicly with this priority item number one."

The Assembly, in its major actions:

For the 20th year refused to evict Nationalist China and seat the Chinese Communists. The vote was 56 to 48 with 21 abstentions.

Approved a number of recommendations on disarmament, including the call to the Soviet Union and the United States for a moratorium, and sent them for more detailed discussion in Geneva where the 18-nation Disarmament Committee had been expanded into the 26-nation Conference of the Committee on Disarmament.

Failed to approve a draft of a treaty prepared by the Soviet Union and the United States on peaceful uses of the seabed and the ocean floor and sent it to Geneva with recommendations for revision.

The Security Council's year was occupied chiefly by complaints by Arab countries against Israel with resolutions of condemnation or censure being passed four times against the Israelis. Portugal came under fire twice in the Security Council on complaints of African countries against its operations from its territories of Angola and Mozambique which the Portuguese hold are integral parts of their country.

BRUCE W. MUNN
Chief UN Correspondent
United Press International

UNITED NATIONS MEMBERSHIP

SECURITY COUNCIL MEMBERS AND TERMS

ALGERIA	until Dec. 31, 1969	HUNGARY	until Dec. 31, 1969	SPAIN		until Dec. 31, 1970
CHINA	permanent	NEPAL	until Dec. 31, 1970	U.S.S.R.		permanent
COLOMBIA	until Dec. 31, 1970	PAKISTAN	until Dec. 31, 1969	UNITED KINGDOM		permanent
FINLAND	until Dec. 31, 1970	PARAGUAY	until Dec. 31, 1969	UNITED STATES		permanent
FRANCE	permanent	SENEGAL	until Dec. 31, 1969	ZAMBIA		until Dec. 31, 1970

MEMBER NATIONS AND CHIEF REPRESENTATIVES

AFGHANISTAN	Abdul Rahman Pazhwak	LAOS	Khamking Souvanlasy
ALBANIA	Halim Budo	LEBANON	Edouard A. Ghorra
ALGERIA	Hadj B. Azzout	LESOTHO	M. T. Mashologu
ARGENTINA	Jose Maria Ruda	LIBERIA	Nathan Barnes
AUSTRALIA	Patrick Shaw	LIBYA	Wahbi El-Bouri
AUSTRIA	Heinrich Haymerle	LUXEMBOURG	Andre Philippe
BARBADOS	Oliver H. Jackman	MALAGASY REPUBLIC	Blaise Rabetafika
BELGIUM	C. Schuurmans	MALAWI	Nyemba W. Mbekeani
BOLIVIA	Walter Guevara Arze	MALAYSIA	Tengku N. Mohamed
BOTSWANA	T. J. Molefhe	MALDIVE ISLANDS	Abdul Sattar
BRAZIL	Joao Augusto de Araujo Castro	MALI	Mamadou Moctar Thiam
BULGARIA	Milko Tarabanov	MALTA	Arvid Pardo
BURMA	U Soe Tin	MAURITANIA	Abdallahi Ould Daddah
BURUNDI	Terence Nsanze	MAURITIUS	Radha Krishna Ramphul
BYELORUSSIAN S.S.R.	Vitaly S. Smirnov	MEXICO	Francisco Cuevas Cancino
CAMBODIA	Huot Sambath	MONGOLIA	Mangalyn Dugersuren
CAMEROUN	Michel Njine	MOROCCO	Ahmed Taibi Benhima
CANADA	Yvon Beaulne	NEPAL	Padma B. Khatri
CENTRAL AFRICAN REP.	Michel Gallin-Douathe	NETHERLANDS	Duco G. E. Middelburg
CEYLON	Hamilton S. Amerasinghe	NEW ZEALAND	John Vivian Scott
CHAD	Bruno Bohiadi	NICARAGUA	Guillermo Sevilla-Sacasa
CHILE	Jose Pinera	NIGER	Adamou Mayaki
CHINA	Liu Chieh	NIGERIA	E. O. Ogbu
COLOMBIA	Jose Maria Morales-Suarez	NORWAY	Edvard Hambro
CONGO (BRAZZAVILLE)	Adrien Bakala	PAKISTAN	Agha Shahi
CONGO (KINSHASA)	Theodore Idzumbuir	PANAMA	Aquilino Boyd
COSTA RICA	Luis Dobles Sanchez	PARAGUAY	Miguel Solano Lopez
CUBA	Ricardo Alarcon de Quesada	PERU	Manuel F. Maurtua
CYPRUS	Zenon Rossides	PHILIPPINES	Privado G. Jimenez
CZECHOSLOVAKIA	Zdenek Cernik	POLAND	Eugeniusz Kulaga
DAHOMEY	Maxime-Leopold Zollner	PORTUGAL	Duarte Vaz Pinto
DENMARK	Otto R. Borch	RUMANIA	Gheorghe Diaconescu
DOMINICAN REPUBLIC	Horacio J. Ornes Coiscou	RWANDA	Fidele Nkundabagenzi
ECUADOR	Leopoldo Benites	SAUDI ARABIA	Jamil M. Baroody
EL SALVADOR	Reynaldo Galindo Pohl	SENEGAL	Ibrahima Boye
EQUATORIAL GUINEA	Gustavo B. Envela-Makongo	SIERRA LEONE	Davidson S. H. W. Nicol
ETHIOPIA	Kifle Wodajo	SINGAPORE	T. T. B. Koh
FINLAND	Max Jakobson	SOMALIA	Abdulrahim A. Farah
FRANCE	Armand Berard	SOUTH AFRICA	Matthys I. Botha
GABON	Jean Davin	SOUTHERN YEMEN	Ismail Saeed Noaman
GAMBIA	vacant	SPAIN	Jaime de Pinies
GHANA	Richard M. Akwei	SUDAN	Fakhreddine Mohamed
GREECE	Dimitri S. Bitsios	SWAZILAND	S. T. Msindazwe Sukati
GUATEMALA	Maximiliano Kestler	SWEDEN	Sverker C. Astrom
GUINEA	El Hadj Abdoulaye Toure	SYRIAN ARAB REP.	George J. Tomeh
GUYANA	P. A. Thompson	TANZANIA	Stephen Mhando
HAITI	Marcel Antoine	THAILAND	Anand Panyarachun
HONDURAS	Salomon Jimenez Munguia	TOGO	Alexandre J. Ohin
HUNGARY	Karoly Csatorday	TRINIDAD-TOBAGO	P. V. J. Solomon
ICELAND	Hannes Kjartansson	TUNISIA	Slaheddine El Goulli
INDIA	Samar Sen	TURKEY	Umit H. Bayulken
INDONESIA	Hadji Roeslan Abdulgani	UGANDA	E. Otema Allimadi
IRAN	Mehdi Vakil	UKRAINIAN S.S.R.	M. D. Polyanichko
IRAQ	Adnan Raouf	U.S.S.R.	Y. A. Malik
IRELAND	Cornelius C. Cremin	UNITED ARAB REPUBLIC	Mohamed A. El Kony
ISRAEL	Yosef Tekoah	UNITED KINGDOM	Lord Caradon
ITALY	Piero Vinci	UNITED STATES	Charles W. Yost
IVORY COAST	Simeon Ake	UPPER VOLTA	Tensore Paul Rouamba
JAMAICA	Keith Johnson	URUGUAY	Augusto Legnani
JAPAN	Senjin Tsuruoka	VENEZUELA	Andres A. Mawdsley
JORDAN	Muhammad H. El-Farra	YEMEN	Mohamed S. Al-Attar
KENYA	A. E. Osanya-Nyyneque	YUGOSLAVIA	Lazar Mojsov
KUWAIT	Muhalhel M. Al-Mudhaf	ZAMBIA	V. J. Mwaanga

President Nixon enjoys one of the pleasures of his high office, a stroll to view the magnificent display of flowering plants on the White House grounds.

united states

The 37th president of the United States, Richard Milhous Nixon, was at his desk at 7:30 A.M., Jan. 21, to begin the first full day of his four-year term. That simple act bespoke the air of expectancy with which he and the nation greeted the advent of 1969. A new President was in charge, giving hope that a new set of solutions would emerge for dealing with the problems, especially Vietnam and the overheated economy, that beset the country at home and abroad.

The presidency had changed hands the day before in traditional inaugural ceremonies at the U.S. Capitol. Democrat Lyndon B. Johnson, grayer and heavier than when he took office in 1963, departed quickly for his beloved Texas ranch. "It hurts good," he had said in laying down the burdens of the White House.

President Nixon, a vice-president throughout most of the 1950's and the first truly partisan Republican to take over in forty years, entered office in a cautious yet confident manner. He had no ambition to bedazzle the nation with innovative, costly schemes but to impress it with businesslike resolution of issues at hand. He began by asking Americans to "lower our voices" and to "go forward together."

Nobody had to guess what he was talking about: the long war in Vietnam, crime in U.S. cities, unrest on the campuses and in the black ghettos, and an inflated economy hurting wage earners as much as wealthy corporations. The divisiveness of these issues, together with the natural discord of the 1968 presidential campaign, had produced an ugly, angry atmosphere that seemed at times to threaten the very future of the Republic.

The President took one hard look at the priority issues—and headed for Europe in February for an eight-day tour of allied capitals. He was not, however, running away. He was out to shore up one of the most neglected alliances during the Johnson years, the North Atlantic Treaty Organization (NATO), upon which America's international security depended most. He called it a "working trip," not a goodwill tour, designed to reassure the country's European allies that the new administration recognized their importance and their interdependence.

Taking off from Washington on Feb. 23, Nixon opened his visit at NATO headquarters in Brussels, then proceeded in turn to London, Bonn, Berlin, Rome, Paris and the Vatican before returning to the White House in the late hours of Mar. 2.

The trip was hailed on both sides of the Atlantic as a success, not because of new treaties or pacts but because Nixon had done what he had set out to do: "to listen" to allied governments that had begun to feel neglected in Washington during the Johnson preoccupation with Vietnam and Asia. His most notable success, perhaps, was in restoring good relations between the United States and France. Imperious French President Charles de Gaulle was not destined to survive politically in 1969, but the "joy" he found in the Nixon visit continued unalloyed in Paris and in Europe throughout the year.

The seeming respite from Vietnam, however, was a mirage. Nixon had been working on the war privately and publicly ever since his first day in office. Henry Cabot Lodge, former ambassador to Saigon and the Nixon running mate in 1960, was named chief U.S. negotiator at the Paris peace talks, succeeding Democrat W. Averell Harriman. Still early in the year, Defense Secretary Melvin R. Laird made his first inspection trip of the Vietnam battle zones. On May 14, in a televised address from the White House, the President set forth a detailed "plan" for negotiating an end to the war. Perhaps more significantly, he signaled for the first time that American troops could be withdrawn as South Vietnamese forces improved.

He called the process "Vietnamization." Its firstfruits were born at his meeting with South Vietnam President Nguyen Van Thieu on Midway Island, June 8. On this Navy refueling station in the mid-Pacific, in the presence of Midway's famed "gooney birds" and American correspondents, Nixon and Thieu jointly announced the withdrawal of 25,000 GI's by Aug. 31. It was the first specific brake on the escalation of U.S. forces in Vietnam that had begun in 1965 and had reached the 540,000 mark by the time Nixon took office in January.

At a Washington press conference in mid-June, the President declared that he hoped to "beat" former Defense Secretary Clark M. Clifford's projected timetable for a withdrawal of all combat forces by the end of 1970. That would still leave more than 200,000 U.S. support troops in Vietnam, but at least, it was said, the actual fighting would have been turned over to the Army of South Vietnam.

The Nixon shift on Vietnam, while greeted with quiet satisfaction in most of the world's capitals, nonetheless sent diplomatic tremors through many nations along the rim of the Pacific, from Japan to India and south to Australia and New Zealand, a vast area of the earth that regarded America as its bulwark against outside aggression. Would the U.S. deescalation in Vietnam mean also a lessening of American interest in Asia and the Pacific?

It was to reassure U.S. allies there that Nixon embarked in late July on a whirlwind round-the-world trip after welcoming back the Apollo 11 astronauts on their mid-Pacific splashdown from man's first lunar landing. That tremendous scientific feat served to help the President impress upon his Asian hosts the power and might of the United States in spite of its problems in Vietnam.

The President set the tone of his Asian trip by enunciating on Guam, that symbolic Pacific bastion, a new American role in Asia. Summarized, it was a reaffirmation of U.S. intentions to remain a "pacific power" even as it sought to lower its military profile. There would be "no more Vietnams" but quite likely more dollars and trade.

The President vowed that the United States would honor its legal treaty commitments in defense of countries, such as South Korea, if they are clearly attacked across national boundaries by a communist nation. The United States also would take a role in defending nonaligned nations, such as Indonesia and Malaysia, against invasion or nuclear blackmail. But U.S. troops will not be used to put down domestic insurgency or rebellion within such countries. The best defense, according to the Nixon doctrine, would be political, economic and social reform by the governments of the countries involved. Perhaps the most significant aspect of the Nixon policy was the President's espousal of the view that not every worrisome military move in the Pacific would be regarded by the United States as a communist design for world expansion.

The President explained his new Asian scheme to leaders in the Philippines, Indonesia, Thailand, India and Pakistan as he winged his way from country to country. The trip was notable also on two other counts.

In Thailand, July 30, Nixon interrupted his stay at Bangkok to make a 5½-hour visit to South Vietnam, specifically Saigon.

It was the first time a U.S. president, and his wife, had visited Saigon in peace or war. Its purpose was to show the rest of the world that security was not so bad as many believed. After conferring with President Thieu at the guarded downtown palace, the President visited Dian, a U.S. combat base 12 miles north. There he told American GI's that the U.S. stand in "this dreary difficult war" would one day be regarded as "one of America's finest hours." Mrs.

Nixon went to an orphanage and field hospital about 15 miles from Saigon, becoming the first president's wife since Eleanor Roosevelt to visit a war zone.

The other notable departure from custom for such tours was the Nixon's weekend stopover, Aug. 2–3, in communist Rumania. Ironically, the President, long a political crusader against communism, got perhaps the biggest welcome of his tour when he arrived in Bucharest. An estimated 500,000 Rumanians lined the 12-mile route of the motorcade from the airport to the city. They cheered the American President, the first ever to visit a communist capital, waved flags, threw flowers and shouted "Nix-on" and "Hoo-rah."

His visit demonstrated Nixon's new conviction that the decade of the 1970's required "negotiation, not confrontation" between capitalist and communist lands. He told Rumanian President Nicolae Ceausescu: "Nations can have widely different internal orders and live in peace."

There was, however, little joy in Paris at the Vietnam peace table in 1969. Despite Nixon's moves and considerable political concessions from his Saigon ally, North Vietnam refused to begin serious bargaining. The President had declared that "progress" in Paris was an essential ingredient for further American withdrawals.

By year's end, with the enemy still intransigent, Lodge had resigned as chief Paris bargainer. Nixon seemed in no rush to fill his post. While career diplomat Philip Habib filled in as "acting" U.S. chief of mission, Nixon unveiled on Dec. 8 what appeared to be the essential American criterion. He told White House reporters that Vietnamization was continuing fast enough to permit continued U.S. troop replacement. Besides a second withdrawal of an additional 40,500 troops by Dec. 15, there would be another troop cutback of 50,000 before Apr. 15, 1970. In other words, the Nixon administration could boast that it was reducing American troops in Vietnam by at least 115,500.

Presidential actions on Vietnam were not taken in a vacuum, however. No sooner had college classes resumed in September than nationwide antiwar demonstrations in cities all across the land were scheduled for mid-October by the Vietnam Moratorium Committee. Nixon said he would not be influenced by the demand for an immediate end to U.S. participation in the war. American policy, he wrote a Georgetown University student, could not be decided by street mobs.

Before the candlelight parades were held, however, the President announced that he was

While dates are drawn from receptacle (on display empty, l) in draft lottery on Dec. 1, a group of college students listens to broadcast of lottery anxiously.

Returning from Vietnam, some marines arrive in San Diego, Calif., making peace signs with their fingers. A handmade peace symbol is draped over the side of the ship.

Members of a prowar group, Americans for Peace—Not Surrender, are permitted to cross through the throng of peace marchers in Washington, D.C., on Nov. 15.

Photos UPI

UPI

Astronaut Aldrin addresses joint session of Congress; Vice-President Agnew and Speaker McCormack preside.

protect higher-ups. Defense Secretary Melvin R. Laird ordered a top-level investigation to determine whether, as some Republican lawmakers contended, the affair had been hushed up at the time by Army brass in Vietnam. President Nixon told a news conference in early December that there "apparently" had been a mass killing at Mylai. He declared all those responsible would be charged with the crime. He resisted appointment of a presidential commission to look into the case, however, saying it could best be handled by existing military and civilian courts.

If Vietnam was the country's overriding emotional hang-up of 1969, the other great headache of Nixon's first year was economic: how to keep wages and prices and supply and demand for goods in some kind of reasonable balance.

Except for economists, bankers and specialists in finance, the nation's economy is the least understood of all its continuing concerns. A housewife looks at her food budget and a schoolboy looks at his allowance with the same objective: how to increase the amount of money available to buy desired and needed items. But a president and his advisers must also worry about the other end of the transaction: how to keep prices within reach of the money available to the average citizen. Unless money and what it buys remain more or less in stable balance, a nation finds itself headed for serious trouble. If the prices of goods and services rise too swiftly and for too long, inflation results. If they drop too sharply, depression results. Either way, the stability of the economy is lost. And when stability vanishes, hard times soon emerge, not only for the housewife and schoolboy but also for business and government.

One major way in which economic instability can be blunted is through government taxing-and-spending policies. Nixon lost no time in 1969 in moving on both fronts. He asked for a continuation of the income-tax surcharge at a 5 per cent rate (instead of the previous 10 per cent) for the first half of 1970 and for a repeal of the 7 per cent investment-tax credit for business. At the same time, he vowed to trim government spending all across the board. Both moves were calculated to dampen the inflationary fire in the nation's economy.

Taxing and spending, however, are sensitive issues in a country like America where government leaders are elected by the people. Thus the two major parties were soon joined in combat on the issues. The Republicans, from President Nixon down, were calling for "fiscal responsibility" from a Congress still controlled

replacing Selective Service Director Lewis B. Hershey, long a target of antiwar students. He also canceled November and December draft calls totaling 50,000 youths. Moreover, he renewed a demand that Congress enact a more equitable system for selecting draftees—a lottery—which it eventually did, subject to complete draft-law revision in 1970.

The peace movement kept the heat on the White House by staging a massive march on Washington in mid-November. More than 300,000 people, mostly young and white, gathered for three days of parades, speeches and a gigantic rally at the Washington Monument. Several thousand radicals fought briefly with police outside the Justice Department and near the South Vietnam Embassy, but the demonstration was on the whole overwhelmingly peaceful. It was also the largest political gathering ever held in the nation's history.

What was quickly to overshadow the November demonstration, however, was the shocking report of a "massacre" of Vietnamese civilians by a group of American soldiers in Mylai 4, a small hamlet, in March 1968. Hawks and doves alike reacted with incredulity to the accounts of soldiers and former servicemen that more than one hundred men, women and children had been ruthlessly murdered. The Army charged a First Lieutenant, William L. Calley, Jr., on six counts of murder. Others contended that the young officer was being pilloried to

UPI

During the violent racial clashes in the predominantly black North End of Hartford, Conn., early in September, police clear littered Main Street. (However, most U.S. cities were relatively quiet in 1969.)

by Democrats. And Democrats, in turn, were demanding "equity" in taxpaying by middle- and low-income citizens. The result was a great battle over the 1969 tax bill between the administration and Congress.

The upshot was a legislative package that cuts everybody's taxes, increases social-security payments to the elderly and retired, and narrows some of the tax loopholes that have favored certain industries like oil for many years.

The 15 per cent hike in social-security benefits, the largest in history, made the bill politically impossible for Nixon to veto. So did the increase in income-tax personal exemptions from $600 to $650 by July 1970 and to $750 in 1973. But Congress also gave Nixon what he wanted in income-surcharge extension and investment-tax-credit repeal. The bill reduced taxes by $9,100,000,000, the second biggest tax cut in history for the American people. But it was more in cuts than the administration had wanted. To compensate, Nixon would have to pare Federal spending during 1970 by a like amount, or face the problem that bothered former President Johnson, going into the red again.

If politics and the upcoming 1970 Congressional elections seemed to dominate Congress' mood in 1969, it was not difficult to understand. For the first time since Zachary Taylor, in 1849, a new president faced a Congress con-

trolled by the Opposition. Without partisan responsibility to the man in the White House, the Democratic-run House and Senate took the bit in their teeth. The hallmark of their independence was a concentration on domestic needs of the country rather than international affairs.

The President indeed had proposed some significant legislation of his own: a postal-system overhaul; revolutionary welfare reform that featured an income floor for the needy; and

UNITED STATES

Area: 3,615,211 sq. mi.
Population: 203,100,000
Capital: Washington (pop., 815,000)
Government: Richard M. Nixon, president— 1969
Gross national product: $943,000,000,000
Monetary unit: dollar
Chief products: corn, wheat, other grains, cotton, vegetables, fruits, coal, iron ore, oil, natural gas, machinery, motor vehicles, electronics
Foreign trade: exports, $38,240,000,000; imports, $36,928,000,000
Communications: 103,752,000 telephones, 250,000,000 radios, 80,900,000 TV sets, 1,768 daily newspapers
Transportation: roads, 3,697,950 mi.; 80,414,- 180 passenger cars; railroads, 224,083 mi.
Education: 51,500,000 elementary and secondary students, 7,100,000 university students
Armed forces: 3,454,000

THE UNITED STATES GOVERNMENT

EXECUTIVE BRANCH

President: Richard M. Nixon
Vice-President: Spiro T. Agnew

Executive Office of the President

White House Office

Counsellors to the President: Bryce N. Harlow; Daniel P. Moynihan
Assistants to the President: Peter M. Flanigan; H. R. Haldeman; Edwin L. Harper; Tom Cole
Assistant to the President for Domestic Affairs: John D. Ehrlichman
Assistant to the President for National Security Affairs: Henry A. Kissinger
Director of Communications for the Executive Branch: Herbert G. Klein
Assistant to the President for Urban Affairs: John R. Price, Jr.
Special Consultants to the President: Leonard Garment; Charles B. Wilkinson
Special Consultant for Systems Analysis: Martin Anderson
Press Secretary: Ronald L. Ziegler
Science Adviser to the President: Lee A. DuBridge
Special Assistant to the President for Consumer Affairs: Mrs. Virginia H. Knauer
Personal Secretary to the President: Rose Mary Woods
Bureau of the Budget: Robert P. Mayo, director
Council of Economic Advisers: Paul W. McCracken, chairman
Central Intelligence Agency: Richard Helms, director
National Aeronautics and Space Council: William A. Anders, executive secretary
Office of Economic Opportunity: Donald Rumsfeld, director
Office of Emergency Preparedness: George A. Lincoln, director
Office of Science and Technology: Lee A. DuBridge, director
Special Representative for Trade Negotiations: Carl J. Gilbert
National Council on Marine Resources and Engineering Development: Edward Wenk, Jr., executive secretary
Council for Urban Affairs: John R. Price, Jr., executive secretary
Office of Intergovernmental Relations: Nils A. Boe, director

Executive Departments

Department of State

Secretary: William P. Rogers
Undersecretary of State: Elliot L. Richardson
Chief of Protocol: Emil Mosbacher, Jr.
Undersecretary for Political Affairs: U. Alexis Johnson
Representative to the Council of the Organization of American States: Joseph J. Jova
Agency for International Development Administrator: John A. Hannah
Peace Corps Director: Joseph H. Blatchford
United Nations Representative: Charles W. Yost

Department of the Treasury

Secretary: David M. Kennedy
Undersecretary: Charles E. Walker
Undersecretary for Monetary Affairs: Paul A. Volcker
Bureau of Engraving and Printing Director: James A. Conlon
Bureau of the Mint Director: Eva Adams
Bureau of Public Debt Commissioner: Donald Merritt

Internal Revenue Service Director: Randolph W. Thrower
Comptroller of the Currency: William B. Camp
Treasurer: Mrs. Dorothy A. Elston
Secret Service Director: James J. Rowley

Department of Defense

Secretary: Melvin R. Laird
Deputy Secretary: David Packard
Director of Defense Research and Engineering: John S. Foster, Jr.
Joint Chiefs of Staff Chairman: Gen. Earle G. Wheeler
Secretary of the Army: Stanley R. Resor
Secretary of the Navy: John H. Chafee
Commandant of the Marine Corps: Gen. L. F. Chapman, Jr.
Secretary of the Air Force: Robert C. Seamans, Jr.

Department of Justice

Attorney General: John N. Mitchell
Deputy Attorney General: Richard G. Kleindienst
Solicitor General: Erwin N. Griswold
Federal Bureau of Investigation Director: J. Edgar Hoover
Immigration and Naturalization Service Commissioner: Raymond F. Farrell
Bureau of Prisons Director: Myrl E. Alexander
Bureau of Narcotics and Dangerous Drugs Director: John E. Ingersoll

Post Office Department

Postmaster General: Winton M. Blount
Deputy Postmaster General: E. T. Klassen
Chief Postal Inspector: William J. Cotter

Department of the Interior

Secretary: Walter J. Hickel
Undersecretary: Russell E. Train
Solicitor: Mitchell Melich

Department of Agriculture

Secretary: Clifford M. Hardin
Undersecretary: J. Phil Campbell

Department of Commerce

Secretary: Maurice H. Stans
Undersecretary: Rocco C. Siciliano
Bureau of the Census Director: A. Ross Eckler
Environmental Science Services Administrator: Robert M. White
National Bureau of Standards Director: Allen V. Astin
Commissioner of Patents: William E. Schuyler, Jr.
U.S. Travel Service Director: C. Langhorne Washburn

Department of Labor

Secretary: George P. Shultz
Undersecretary: James D. Hodgson
Commissioner of Labor Statistics: Geoffrey H. Moore

Department of Health, Education, and Welfare

Secretary: Robert H. Finch
Undersecretary: John G. Veneman
Office for Civil Rights Director: Leon E. Panetta
Consumer Protection and Environmental Health Service Administrator: Charles C. Johnson, Jr.
National Institutes of Health Director: Robert Q. Marston
Commissioner of Education: James E. Allen, Jr.
Commissioner of Social Security: Robert M. Ball

Department of Housing and Urban Development

Secretary: George W. Romney
Undersecretary: Richard C. Van Dusen

Department of Transportation

Secretary: John A. Volpe
Undersecretary: James M. Beggs
Coast Guard Commandant: Adm. Willard J. Smith

Pictorial Parade

Cabinet: front—Kennedy, Treasury; Laird, Defense; Vice-President Agnew; President Nixon; Volpe, Transportation; Mayo, budget director; Finch, HEW; rear—Rogers, State; Blount, Post Office; Mitchell, Justice; Stans, Commerce; Romney, HUD; Hardin, Agriculture; Shultz, Labor; and Hickel, Interior.

Federal Aviation Administration: John H. Shaffer, administrator

Federal Highway Administration: F. C. Turner, administrator

Federal Railroad Administration: Reginald N. Whitman, administrator

Urban Mass Transportation Administration: C. C. Villarreal, administrator

Independent Agencies

Atomic Energy Commission: Glenn T. Seaborg, chairman

Civil Aeronautics Board: Secor D. Browne, chairman of the board

District of Columbia: Walter E. Washington, commissioner

Equal Employment Opportunity: William H. Brown III, commissioner

Export-Import Bank: Henry Kearns, president and chairman

Federal Communications Commission: Dean Burch, chairman

Federal Deposit Insurance Corporation: K. A. Randall, board of directors chairman

Federal Maritime Commission: Helen D. Bentley, chairman

Federal Power Commission: John Nassikas, chairman of the commission

Federal Reserve System: Arthur F. Burns, chairman

Federal Trade Commission: Caspar W. Weinberger, chairman

Foreign Claims Settlement Commission: Leonard v. B. Sutton, chairman

General Services Administration: Robert L. Kunzig, administrator

Indian Claims Commission: Jerome K. Kuykendall, chairman

Interstate Commerce Commission: Virginia Mae Brown, chairman

National Aeronautics and Space Administration: Thomas O. Paine, administrator

National Labor Relations Board: Frank W. McCulloch, chairman

National Science Foundation: William D. McElroy, director

Securities and Exchange Commission: Hamer H. Budge, chairman

Selective Service System: vacant

Small Business Administration: Hilary Sandoval, Jr., administrator

Subversive Activities Control Board: John W. Mahan, chairman

Tennessee Valley Authority: Aubrey J. Wagner, chairman

U.S. Arms Control and Disarmament Agency: Gerard Smith, director

U.S. Civil Service Commission: Robert E. Hampton, chairman

U.S. Information Agency: Frank Shakespeare, director

U.S. Tariff Commission: Glenn W. Sutton, chairman

Veterans Administration: Donald E. Johnson, administrator

arming the attorney general with broad anti-crime powers, including wiretapping authority. Decisions on these were delayed until the 1970 session. The only major Nixon reform to gain approval was the draft-lottery law.

And although he finally came around to it, the House went beyond Nixon's original proposal in voting to abolish the electoral college which has picked presidents since the origin of the Republic. The Senate may act on the proposed constitutional amendment in 1970, although that probably would not be in time for the 1972 presidential election, since the states would also have to ratify it.

Congressional Democrats did not block Mr. Nixon's money needs in Vietnam—about $2,000,000,000 a month—but they fought him down to the wire on his proposal for deployment of the Safeguard anti-ballistic missile (ABM) system. He finally succeeded when the ABM bill passed by one vote in the Senate, the narrowest margin on a national-security issue since the World War II draft-law fight of 1941.

The Senate brought Nixon up short again when it voted down his choice of South Carolina Judge Clement F. Haynsworth for a vacancy on the Supreme Court.

Republican defections, more than Democratic opposition, were responsible for the stinging defeat. None of the Senate's four leaders voted for Haynsworth, whose private-business dealings and judicial rulings on labor and civil-rights cases had earned him the opposition of most Northern, big-state lawmakers.

Many Capitol Hill veterans felt the runaway Congress was due to the absence of strong leadership on the Democratic side. Aging House Speaker John McCormack of Massachusetts appeared to have minimum influence on the floor. Montana's Sen. Mike Mansfield, the majority leader, never did subscribe to the tight-rein theory of previous Democratic floor chieftains.

Congressional leadership also was dealt a serious blow in September with the death of Senate Republican leader Everett McKinley Dirksen. The 73-year-old Illinois lawmaker, famed for his Shakespearean prose and presence, had also been a potent organizer of Republicans and conservative causes in Congress. President Nixon said he would be "remembered as a giant" on Capitol Hill, "a legislator of matchless skills."

In the GOP tussle over a successor, Pennsylvania's 68-year-old Hugh Scott, a Senate liberal, defeated the more conservative Sen. Howard Baker of Tennessee, Dirksen's 43-year-old son-in-law. To succeed Scott as minority whip, the Republicans chose Michigan's 45-year-old Robert P. Griffin, a fast-rising newcomer. The changeover, however, served only to exacerbate Congress' maverick nature in 1969.

On many occasions, Congress' actions were contrapuntal. While it inveighed against inflation, its first act was to raise the president's salary by 100 per cent (to $200,000 a year) and that of members of Congress by 41 per cent (to $42,500 a year). And it repeatedly voted more money for domestic programs than the Nixon administration sought.

In the civil-rights field, the House first approved and later retreated from an amendment to ban school bussing to achieve racial integration.

The Senate first opposed and then accepted the administration's controversial "Philadelphia plan" requiring Federal construction contractors to meet goals in the hiring of Negro workers. The House went along with an administration substitute for a five-year-old voting-rights law, an action that civil-rights groups said would seriously hamper Negro-voter registrations in the Deep South.

On Vietnam, Congressional doves were decidedly more muted in 1969 than during the previous year, under President Johnson. The House, with heavy Democratic support, passed a resolution endorsing Nixon's "plan for peace" in Vietnam. A majority of the senators wrote letters signifying the same. On the Senate side, Chairman J. William Fulbright of Arkansas postponed plans for major hearings by his Foreign Relations Committee into Nixon's Vietnam policy.

A major factor in these moves was the emergence of Vice-President Spiro T. Agnew as a public defender for the administration against antiwar forces and what he termed were the "biased" views of television network commentators and some liberal publications, notably *The New York Times* and *The Washington Post*. Agnew drew massive support from the so-called silent majority of Americans for his attacks on both groups.

In selected speeches around the country, Agnew labeled antiwar leaders as "impudent intellectuals" and "effete snobs." He lambasted the TV commentators for unduly criticizing Nixon's moves on Vietnam. The networks immediately responded with worried assertions that the Government was threatening a form of censorship through its licensing power over broadcasting stations. Nixon, in a press conference, praised Agnew's performance, but said also that he personally felt the news media had been fair to him and his administration. Never-

A beaming Mayor Carl B. Stokes relaxes in his office. After a stiff fight he was reelected by Cleveland voters.

In New Jersey contest for governor, Republican William T. Cahill (r) won over former Gov. Robert B. Meyner.

Sen. Hugh Scott (Pa.), moderate Republican, succeeded the late conservative Sen. Everett Dirksen (Ill.) as GOP leader.

Photos UPI

Upsetting a political pattern, Linwood Holton was the first Republican elected Virginia's governor in nearly a century.

Ralph Smith became new senator from Illinois; he was formerly the state House Speaker.

theless, Agnew speeches, plus Nixon's own appeal for Vietnam support, produced hundreds of thousands of favorable letters from persons all over the country.

On the political-party front, 1969 proved to be a better year for Republicans and conservatives than for Democrats and liberals. The GOP achieved notable successes in the only governorship races of the year. In New Jersey, Rep. William Cahill became the first Republican to be elected governor there in 16 years. In Virginia, Linwood Holton became the first Republican to be elected governor since Reconstruction days, after the Civil War. President Nixon campaigned in both states for his party candidates. The results gave the Republicans 32 of the 50 governorships.

While Republicans waxed jubiliant over their successes in preparing for the crucial 1970 Congressional elections, the Democrats were not to be overlooked totally, however. Of seven special elections to fill Congressional vacancies in 1969, the Democrats won five. Three were seats formerly held by Republican representatives in Wisconsin, Montana and Massachusetts. The GOP managed to retain a seat in California and one in Illinois.

The Democratic National Committee underwent a year of internal party reorganization as the result of the schisms at the 1968 Chicago national convention and the loss of the presidential election. The proposed reforms are designed to "democratize" the selection of national-convention delegates and the procedures of the 1972 presidential convention.

The Democrats' concern over such technical, albeit important, matters reflected the party's disenchantment with itself in 1969. Its most grievous blow, perhaps, was the political setback of its most illustrious prospect for the White House race in 1972: Sen. Edward M. (Ted) Kennedy of Massachusetts.

The youngest and last of the famed Kennedy brothers, 37-year-old Ted Kennedy loomed as the one glamorous figure around whom the Democrats might rally in 1972. At the beginning of the 1969 session of Congress, Kennedy captured the majority whip's post in the Senate, beating veteran Sen. Russell B. Long of Louisiana. The move made Kennedy a key member of the Senate leadership, an ideal springboard from which to launch a presidential adventure. But political and personal tragedy struck on the night of July 18 near

Results of underground nuclear test in New Mexico, Dec. 4: top, at detonation, tower on tracks is sent to safety from ground zero (r); center, dust rises as ground collapses; bottom, crater is formed.

Photos UPI

UPI

Partly masked, the NR-1, a top-secret nuclear-powered research submarine, is launched at Groton, Conn., in January. The 140-foot Navy vessel carries a crew of seven; cost was estimated at $99,200,000.

Water starts to trickle down the American side of Niagara Falls after it is turned on again. As the rock has continued to crumble, water was turned off to allow study of how cascade could be preserved.

UPI

Massachusetts' Martha's Vineyard. Kennedy's car plunged off a narrow bridge into Chappaquiddick Creek, following a party for Kennedy campaign workers. The Senator escaped, but a secretary, Mary Jo Kopechne, died in the accident. His subsequent explanations of what happened were treated with skepticism in many political and public quarters. He pleaded guilty to a charge of leaving the scene of a fatal accident and was given a two-month suspended sentence. The State Supreme Court ordered a closed-door inquest into the case at Kennedy's request. The Senator's political future would hinge in 1970 upon the outcome of that hearing and upon his chances of reelection to another six-year term in the Senate.

Kennedy announced publicly that he would not be a contender for the presidential nomination in 1972, but the declaration served only to spotlight the Democratic Party's shortage of potential candidates to contest President Nixon. Sen. Eugene McCarthy, the Minnesotan who had magnetized the peace movement in 1968, seemed more interested in writing poetry than questing for the White House again. Former Vice-President Hubert H. Humphrey, the 1968 presidential nominee, was back in Minnesota as a college professor and making plans to run for the Senate there.

By default, Maine's Sen. Edmund S. Muskie, who had been Humphrey's popular running mate in 1968, seemed to be the most promising Democratic hopeful for 1972's race. Yet during 1969, Muskie lacked the political muscle and money to mount an organized campaign for the prize three years thence.

The nation and the Republican Party mourned the death on Mar. 28 of Dwight David Eisenhower, 34th president of the United States and famous General of the Army during World War II. The soldier-statesman died quietly at Walter Reed Hospital, following a stroke. He was 78. Presidents and kings from all over the globe joined thousands of ordinary folk from all walks of life in paying final respects before his body, which lay in state in the Capitol Rotunda. President Nixon, who had been Eisenhower's vice-president all during his eight years in the White House, led the mourners in eulogizing "Ike," as he was best known to millions throughout the world. After memorial services at Washington's National (Episcopal)

Scientists from Ohio State University, the first all-female team to work in Antarctica, arrive at McMurdo Station in November. They were scheduled to do research in the nearby ice-free valleys for three months.

UPI

Tearing down the indoor swimming pool at the White House, for expanded press facilities, workmen expose two underground rooms believed to date from the Jefferson era, containing some objects from Lincoln's time.

Cathedral, Eisenhower's body was borne by funeral train to his boyhood home, Abilene, Kansas, for burial there.

As it neared the end of the 1960's, the United States was given a diagnosis of its internal ailments and a prescription for their cure. The assessment came from the blue-ribbon National Commission on the Causes and Prevention of Violence, appointed in June 1968, following the assassinations of Sen. Robert F Kennedy and Dr. Martin Luther King, Jr. Its Chairman was Dr. Milton S. Eisenhower, brother of the former President.

The commission, after 18 months of hearings, concluded that the country was in turmoil because of excessive concentration in recent years on foreign problems, and the neglect of crises at home.

Its 338-page report to President Nixon said it was imperative that the nation switch from a war-defense-space economy to one emphasizing social needs within the United States.

"As the gross national product and tax revenues continue to rise, we should strive to keep military expenditures level, while general welfare expenditures should continue to increase until essential social goals are achieved," the commission said. "While serious external dangers remain, the graver threats today are internal: haphazard urbanization, racial discrimination, disfiguring of the environment, unprecedented interdependence, the dislocation of human identity and motivation created by an affluent society—all resulting in a rising tide of individual and group violence."

As a catch-up device, the commission recommended that the Federal Government spend at least $20,000,000,000 a year on solving domestic problems in the cities of America which, it said, have "been dividing into armed camps," rich against poor, black against white.

President Nixon packed the report in his briefcase for detailed reading at his San Clemente home in California over the New Year holidays. During 1969 he had successfully neutralized the Vietnam war as a major political issue between the two parties. His problem, as he headed into the 1970's, was whether he could end the war and reallocate the money, the so-called "peace dividend," for a concerted attack on the country's internal problems. This would be the acid test of his ability to govern the nation.

J. F. terHorst
Washington Bureau Chief
The Detroit News

UTAH

After 8 days of being entombed, more than half that time without water, in a lead and zinc mine near Lark, miner William V. Jones, 60 years old and the father of 11 children, was rescued on Mar. 9. He had been trapped when a slide tumbled tons of earth and rock around him but apparently suffered little harm. □ Just before leaving office in January, President Johnson signed a proclamation enlarging the Arches National Monument and the Capitol Reef Monument. □ During its 38th session, the state legislature created a new state board of higher education. The new board took authority on July 1.

VERMONT

In St. Albans City the opening of school was postponed from Sept. 2 to Sept. 10 for lack of money. In what some observers called a "tax rebellion," the city voters had three times rejected an increase in school taxes, as they did again on Sept. 9. □ In a referendum in June, voters rejected a proposal to convene a constitutional convention. It would have been the first such convention in Vermont in one hundred years. □ In December a special gubernatorial committee on administrative coordination urged that a new cabinet system of government be established in Vermont. □ Gov. Deane C. Davis proposed the largest state budget in Vermont's history. □ A late December snowstorm provided excellent skiing in Vermont for the holidays.

VETERANS

In June, President Nixon named Donald E. Johnson, of West Branch, Ia., head of the U.S. Veterans Administration. Johnson, who served as national commander of the American Legion in 1964–65, was confirmed unanimously by the Senate on June 19.

Some members of Congress had fought to retain William J. Driver, a career VA employee, as administrator of the agency he had headed since 1965. However, the late Senate Republican Leader Everett M. Dirksen (Ill.) and other GOP members of Congress insisted that a Republican be named to the top veterans-affairs post.

Johnson said that one of his first moves would be a study of ways to improve benefits for returning Vietnam veterans. He said he was particularly interested in finding out why such a small number of these veterans were taking advantage of the college-study payments available to them.

The major veterans organizations made no progress during the year in their fight to have a separate Senate veterans committee created comparable with the one in the House of Representatives. However, the Senate Finance Committee, which has part of the Senate jurisdiction over veterans matters, created a new veterans subcommittee in February 1969 for the first time in 25 years; Sen. Herman E. Talmadge (D-Ga.) was appointed chairman.

The Finance Committee approved in August and the Senate passed in September a package of five bills increasing compensation for widows and children of veterans and expanding government-insurance coverage of veterans. One of the bills increased from $10,000 to $15,000 the group life insurance now available to all 3,500,000 servicemen. It provided that servicemen assigned to a combat area such as Vietnam or to other very hazardous duty could get $30,000 coverage. Another measure would set up a new Vietnam-era veterans life-insurance program under which all veterans who have served since 1964 could get up to $30,000 of permanent-plan insurance. The dependency and indemnity compensation bill was enacted into law in October, but the insurance bills were left over until 1970. As finally enacted, the increase in compensation amounted to $61,600,-000 a year; it would give a 34 per cent increase to widows of deceased servicemen at the lowest rank, and smaller increases in higher ranks. Both branches also voted for an increase in educational and training allowances of veterans extending back to 1955, but final action was left over until 1970. The House voted in August to raise the basic $130-a-month college-education benefit to $165; the Senate voted in October for $190.

The American Legion, at its 51st national convention (Aug. 22-28) in Atlanta, Ga., elected J. Milton Patrick, 54, of Skiatook, Okla., national commander. The Legion declared its total support of the U.S. effort in Vietnam, called on the Nixon administration to set an early deadline for conclusion of negotiations for an honorable peace, and said that if negotiations failed a maximum military effort should be made for total victory.

The Veterans of Foreign Wars, at their 70th national convention (Aug. 15-22) in Philadelphia, Pa., elected Raymond A. Gallagher, Redfield, S.D., commander in chief. The VFW endorsed all necessary steps to ensure victory in Vietnam and opposed strongly any coalition Government in that country.

JOSEPH W. HALL, JR.
Senate Staff, Washington Bureau
The Associated Press

vietnam

The Vietnam war entered a crucial period and passed a significant turning point in 1969. As the year closed, hope was rising that a way out of the morass was taking form.

No one in an official position was being that optimistic publicly, partly as a result of what has come to be known in Saigon as the "Westmoreland complex": the fear of being caught out on a limb as Gen. William Westmoreland was with his overly positive prognosis almost on the eve of the Tet (lunar New Year) offensive in 1968 when the enemy launched its most spectacular, if not militarily significant, attacks.

A companion reason for hedging on predictions that the Vietnam imbroglio might finally be nearing solution was that the intentions of the North Vietnamese were still ominously unclear.

No matter what the future held, 1969 was a crucial, turning-point year, especially on two counts. First, after long haggling over minor details, such as the shape of the table, the four essential parties to the conflict finally sat down in Paris in late January to begin negotiations. The four participants were the United States, North Vietnam, South Vietnam and the Vietcong's National Liberation Front (NLF). Though a year later the talks still had produced no results, this could not detract from the fact that a framework had been established for final settlement.

Second, as Richard M. Nixon succeeded Lyndon B. Johnson in the White House, he made a basic decision pointing the way to American disengagement. In effect, Nixon said that in the final analysis the Vietnamese must decide among themselves on their future government without external pressure, and that the United States would cut its force of more than 500,000 men in South Vietnam. Nixon thus reversed the trend that had started as long before as the Eisenhower administration.

In mid-December, Nixon announced that a total of 110,000 U.S. troops would be out of Vietnam by mid-April 1970, leaving behind about 430,000, with the prospect of possibly another 100,000 home by the end of 1970.

Nixon said he would be guided by three criteria in his troop cutbacks: progress in the Paris peace talks; the level of enemy activity; and progress toward modernization of the South Vietnamese military, thus permitting South Vietnamese troops to take over more of the fighting job from the Americans.

UPI

South Vietnam paratroopers make a spectacular jump after completing airborne training, part of the program for replacing U.S. soldiers with South Vietnam troops.

Women do much of the clearing and rebuilding of Hanoi, North Vietnam, since bombing of North has stopped.

Nixon admitted freely that there had been no progress in the peace conference. The level of enemy activity was down as reflected in lessening U.S. casualties, which were running at an average of about 99 dead a week at the end of 1969. South Vietnamese casualties were several times that number, as greater numbers of their troops were meeting the enemy. "Vietnamization" of the war—that is, replacing U.S. troops with South Vietnamese soldiers—apparently was quickening.

Vietnamization was, in fact, the key word in Washington and Saigon, although in Saigon each U.S. troop-cutback announcement was met with a little louder whistling in the dark.

True, as 1969 ended, ARVN (the Army of the Republic of Vietnam) had not suffered any stunning military setback as the ranks of American support thinned. In fact, several incidents indicated a new fighting spirit among Saigon's forces. They had kept the enemy from overrunning such fire bases as Buprang and Duclap, near the Cambodian border, and the lonely outpost of Tuyenbinh, in the Mekong Delta. Local militia forces, an adjunct of ARVN, repulsed a North Vietnamese battalion as it streaked out of its Cambodian hideaway. About 165 of the enemy were killed as they attempted to storm the Government's mud-and-barbed-wire fort. Elsewhere, particularly in the northern First Corps area abutting on the demilitarized zone (DMZ), ARVN forces were turning in praiseworthy performances.

In spite of such reasons for optimism, the disquieting feeling remained that the Vietcong and the North Vietnamese might be holding

back deliberately, allowing overconfidence to build up in Saigon, and the release of American forces in significant numbers. Then the Vietcong and North Vietnamese might strike suddenly, hoping for a quick kill or at least a Tet-like spectacular success, followed by a political take-over.

To U.S. military analysts, the threat seemed only too real. Regiment after regiment of North Vietnamese forces were positioning themselves above the DMZ. Others were moving with increased boldness into Laos and down the Ho Chi Minh trail. Still others—a total of 35,000 to 40,000—were occupying the eastern and southern provinces of Cambodia, where their presence was no longer denied by Prince Norodom Sihanouk. (Sihanouk's fears of a de facto occupation by the North Vietnamese led in part to his renewal of diplomatic relations with the United States in mid-1969, a significant swing toward the West.)

Coupled with the North Vietnamese buildup behind the porous frontiers of Laos and Cambodia came intelligence reports of thousands of Soviet-made trucks lugging heavy supplies south from Haiphong and Hanoi to sites along infiltration routes into South Vietnam. Pipeline complexes were also in evidence just north of the DMZ.

Officials in Washington and Saigon played the numbers game with infiltration rates, and it was never clear whether the trend was up or down. What seemed more important was that, despite the gigantic South Vietnamese-U.S. military effort, large numbers of North Vietnamese regulars were still infiltrating.

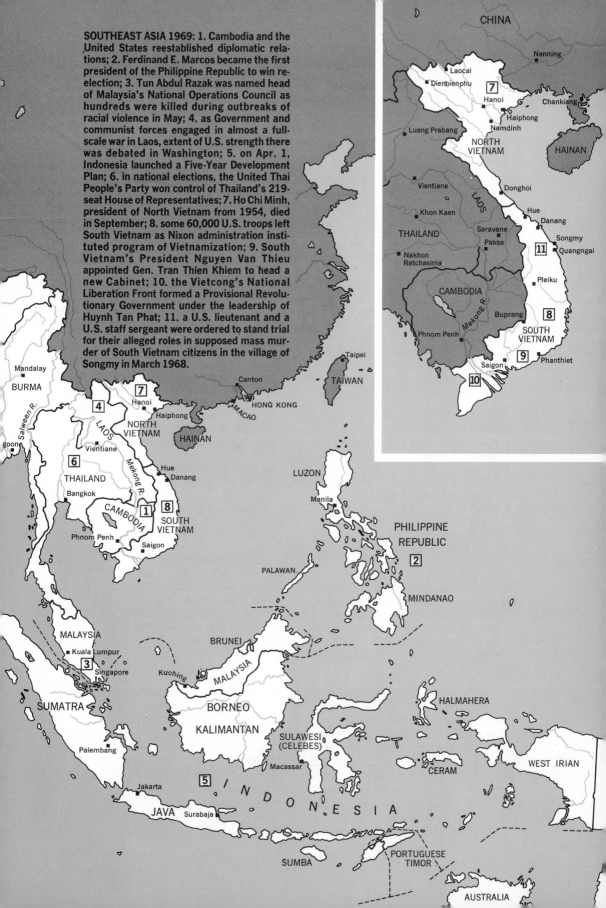

SOUTHEAST ASIA 1969: 1. Cambodia and the United States reestablished diplomatic relations; 2. Ferdinand E. Marcos became the first president of the Philippine Republic to win reelection; 3. Tun Abdul Razak was named head of Malaysia's National Operations Council as hundreds were killed during outbreaks of racial violence in May; 4. as Government and communist forces engaged in almost a full-scale war in Laos, extent of U.S. strength there was debated in Washington; 5. on Apr. 1, Indonesia launched a Five-Year Development Plan; 6. in national elections, the United Thai People's Party won control of Thailand's 219-seat House of Representatives; 7. Ho Chi Minh, president of North Vietnam from 1954, died in September; 8. some 60,000 U.S. troops left South Vietnam as Nixon administration instituted program of Vietnamization; 9. South Vietnam's President Nguyen Van Thieu appointed Gen. Tran Thien Khiem to head a new Cabinet; 10. the Vietcong's National Liberation Front formed a Provisional Revolutionary Government under the leadership of Huynh Tan Phat; 11. a U.S. lieutenant and a U.S. staff sergeant were ordered to stand trial for their alleged roles in supposed mass murder of South Vietnam citizens in the village of Songmy in March 1968.

This was particularly significant in the face of what many seasoned observers concluded as 1969 drew to a close: that hard-core Vietcong guerrilla forces had in fact suffered severe setbacks, and that the enemy's only real hope for a communist military victory in South Vietnam lay mainly with the North Vietnamese.

Such a state of affairs was particularly evident in the vast Mekong Delta, the rice basket of the nation. Even after the U.S. Ninth Division was pulled out in late summer, the Vietcong could make no significant inroads against ARVN regular and militia forces. The North Vietnamese there had made a major decision to infiltrate large numbers of their regular forces into the Delta, or else see it slip to the side of the South Vietnam Government for good. These forces—perhaps three regiments —were positioning themselves in the bleak U Minh Forest and Seven Mountains area of the western and southern Delta, there to wait for an appropriate moment to tangle with the ARVN. If this moment comes it will be a rigorous test of Vietnamization.

As 1969 ended, the number of American dead in the Vietnam war, counted from Jan. 1, 1961, rose above the 40,000 mark, the wounded reaching more than 260,000—during the longest war in the nation's history, though World Wars I and II and the Civil War were still more costly in casualties. Altogether, officials estimated at the end of the year that 1,196,000 American, South Vietnamese and enemy troops had been killed or wounded in nine years of fighting. Enemy forces killed in action topped 582,000 according to Allied estimates, with Saigon forces losing about 98,000.

American losses dropped steadily during the latter half of 1969, as enemy activity decreased and South Vietnamese activity increased. In addition, American tactics had changed. Instead of the gigantic, multibattalion sweep-and-clear operations, notably in the northern First Corps area, there were more small-unit actions and fewer attempts to meet enemy forces unless they posed an immediate threat to a population center or other strategic site.

Thus the Battle of Hamburger Hill, or Dong Apbia, in May was probably the last of its kind. This was a much-criticized effort to gain the top of a forested hill in northern South Vietnam, simply because there were North Vietnamese troops atop it and not because the hill had any long-range strategic importance. American forces were bloodied in repeated attempts to take the hill, with losses reaching about sixty dead before it was conquered. Then eight days later the hill was abandoned, and its scars were soon covered by jungle growth.

Another frequent deathtrap for American forces, the Ashau Valley infiltration route, was swept again in March. It was evacuated, to be patrolled occasionally by reduced forces later in the year.

U.S. forces were spending more time working with ARVN units on small patrols and in ambushes, and in conducting "pacification" programs. The U.S. soldier's regular duty was broadened to include civil affairs, helping the South Vietnamese village or hamlet dweller to dig wells, build roads and schools and to establish self-defense forces. The effort, together with the South Vietnamese Revolutionary Development program, brought what the Government and U.S. officials said was more than 90 per cent "relative security" to the country in the closing months of the year.

It meant that more than 16,000,000 of South Vietnam's 18,000,000 people were relatively safe from communist attack. However, the figures were based on the controversial Hamlet Evaluation System (HES), a determination by American advisers in the field of the status of the hamlets in their areas. The system was open to subjective considerations by advisers, which sometimes did not reflect the true situation. Though admitting this, officials claimed that the system provided reliable trends. The trend was clearly up at the year's end.

During the year two stark stories of massacre came out, both dating from 1968. Late in March 1969, an ARVN soldier tripped on a wire while on a sand-flats patrol ten miles southeast of the old imperial capital of Hue. He tugged at the wire and found it was attached to a pair of skeletal hands. Subsequent digging turned up the bodies of 134 residents of Hue who had been missing since the three-week occupation of the city by the Communists during the Tet offensive of 1968. As the year wore on, a total of some 2,900 bodies were uncovered in the Hue area, accounting for most of the missing. They attested to communist tactics when confronted with ideological opposition. Most of the victims had been beaten to death or buried alive in shallow graves.

The South Vietnamese Government and the United States were just picking up the propaganda value of the Hue massacre when an alleged incident at the hamlet of Mylai (in the village of Songmy), also in the northern part of the country, came to light and sent a shock wave over the United States. According to official Army charges, a company of American soldiers, sweeping an area near Quangngai, were supposed to have killed more than 100 civilians, many of them women and children.

In the Capitol, Washington, D.C., slides are shown of the slaughter of South Vietnamese civilians in Hue under the communist occupation of the city during the Tet offensive of 1968. Here bodies are being buried.

UPI

The Mylai residents had been Vietcong or Vietcong sympathizers, and the hamlet had been attacked by artillery and planes, military authorities said. According to other allegations, some were dead because of the "facts of war" but others had been wantonly killed. The alleged massacre occurred in mid-March 1968 and apparently had been lost sight of in the aftermath of the Tet offensive. Though an investigation had begun at the time, seemingly it was not followed up until tales of the incident reached Washington and became public late in 1969.

As U.S. authorities prepared to prosecute the case, the South Vietnamese Government conducted its own investigation and declared that there had been no massacre. Some twenty persons had died, the report said, but only because they were caught by shells and bombs and not small-arms fire. Vice-President Nguyen Cao Ky called for another, more thorough investigation, but President Nguyen Van Thieu would not agree. Sen. Tran Van Don, a politically ambitious former general, did some probing of his own but came up with only murky conclusions.

As a national leader, Thieu grew slightly in prestige. Nevertheless, his regime's main support still came from his Army and the U.S. establishment, and he continued to lack a solid political base. In early 1969, Thieu had tried to form a six-party coalition: the National Social Democratic Front. He deplored the splintering tactics and the obduracy of South Vietnam's nationalistic politicians, faced with the stringent and effective discipline of the Communists. He called for new responsibility and unity of purpose from the noncommunist majority in the nation, and said this was vital for the coming political confrontation with the Communists.

Launched with fanfare in late May, Thieu's front soon began to break up, losing two of its six parties. Its voice was too weak to be heard on the national scene.

Meanwhile, Senator Don, one of the heroes of the coup that overthrew President Ngo Dinh Diem in 1963, began promoting a "third force" to stand between the Thieu regime and the Communists and lead the nation out of its troubles. Don was in league with retired Gen. Duong Van (Big) Minh, who was chief of state briefly after the coup. Minh advocated a national referendum or similar device to learn the "real" sentiments of the people, which he implied were neither pro-Thieu nor procommunist. Thieu quickly brushed off the idea and indicated that he intended to remain as president for the rest of his term, until 1971. Toward the end of the year, little was heard from either Don or Minh as Thieu sought to strengthen his political position and to undercut any so-called neutralist or procommunist sentiment in the country. Thieu made sweeping criticisms of intellectuals and parliamentarians who criticized his regime, and leveled a direct attack on three deputies who he claimed had communist connections.

In December he sent dossiers on them to the National Assembly and asked that the three deputies be shorn of their parliamentary immunity and prosecuted. When there seemed little likelihood that the Assembly would comply, the Government began organizing demonstrations demanding immediate action. One crowd of about 300 demonstrators crashed into the Lower House, as police stood by. The demonstrators broke windows and shouted at the startled deputies, demanding immediate moves against the three "Communists." The following day about 5,000 people, mostly militant Catholic refugees from the North, demonstrated at Bienhoa, just outside Saigon, and burned the deputies in effigy. It was still not clear at the end of 1969 what, if any, action the badly split parliament would take.

The other significant political development during the year was the replacement of aging Premier Tran Van Huong with Gen. Tran Thien Khiem as the head of a 31-member Cabinet. Huong, in ill health, had been unable to cope with the haggling parliament and had never been accepted by the military establishment, the Government's main support at home.

Apparently Thieu had hoped to replace Huong, a respected Southern-born civilian, with another well-known civilian, but none seemed available. Thus he turned to Deputy Premier Khiem, the top-ranking active military man in the nation who also held the important Interior Ministry. Khiem, a brilliant administrator with little political background, took over the job without fanfare and soon slipped into the background. The choice of Khiem, which technically put a military triumvirate at the head of the South Vietnam Government, was criticized by Americans who had hoped to pump more civilian blood into the Government.

Thieu, a Catholic, had his troubles with the Buddhists, the main religious group, during the year. However, their lack of solidarity kept them from effective opposition. In March a military tribunal sentenced Thich (Venerable) Thien Minh to ten years for allegedly harboring Communists and draft dodgers in his Buddhist youth center. The An Quang, or militant branch of the church, protested. Finally, in October, Minh was pardoned. About a month later, monks of Cambodian ethnic origin staged a sit-down strike near Thieu's Independence Palace, demanding restoration of minority rights. Not long before, the some 2,000,000 Vietnamese of Cambodian origin had been removed from the minorities statute, which, among other things, made them eligible for the draft. The 200 protesting monks sat on the pavement for five days, then were removed by police and taken to their pagoda on the edge of the city. Sporadically they attempted to demonstrate again, and several were injured in clashes with the police.

In early June, Thieu met with Nixon on Midway Island. They announced the first withdrawal of American troops: 25,000 by the end of August. At the end of July, Nixon called at Saigon, remaining for five hours, long enough to give Thieu a resounding word of support.

Within a few days after the Midway meeting, the Vietcong's National Liberation Front announced the formation of a Provisional Revolutionary Government, headed by Huynh Tan Phat. A month later, Thieu invited the Vietcong to participate in elections, to help end the war, but the offer apparently fell on deaf ears.

On Sept. 3, President Ho Chi Minh of North Vietnam died, and his testament, which became required reading for his followers, vowed a fight to the finish to "free" South Vietnam and reunify North and South. At the end of 1969, there was nothing to show that Ho's death had significantly altered the determination of the communist political and military forces.

DAVID M. MASON
Chief Correspondent, South Vietnam
The Associated Press

VIRGINIA

By early 1969 almost all the public schools were integrated; and for the first time since Reconstruction days a Negro, Hilary H. Jones, Jr., a Norfolk lawyer, was appointed to the state Board of Education. □ On Aug. 20, flash floods in the wake of hurricane Camille, especially severe in the western foothills and in the James River valley around Richmond, left at least 74 persons dead, 109 missing, and damage of more than $132,400,000. □ By an annexation-court ruling, Richmond, on Jan. 1, 1970, increased by 44,000 people and 23 square miles, acquired from adjacent Chesterfield County, which was scheduled to receive $27,000,000. □ In the November elections, Linwood Holton (R) was voted governor.

WASHINGTON

The Seattle-First National Bank installed some $500,000 worth of paintings, sculpture and graphics, one of the most valuable private collections on the West Coast. □ Lake Washington, the 35-square-mile eastern border of Seattle, was almost completely restored, with plentiful fish and clear waters. It was the result of a metropolitan-area effort begun in 1961, costing $130,000,000, which included new sewage-treatment plants.

UPI

A protest against proposed cuts in state welfare payments is staged on the steps of the New York State Capitol, in Albany. Growing awareness of their legal rights is leading welfare recipients to action.

WELFARE

Welfare, in its broadest sense, encompasses almost all private and government (public) spending for domestic purposes: programs for social insurance, health and medical care, education, housing, public assistance, veterans' benefits. In a more narrow and acceptable sense, welfare is limited to government programs based on the need of recipients: public assistance, medical and hospital care for the poor and aged, vocational rehabilitation, child welfare, school meals, aid to the blind and the elderly, and relatively new "antipoverty" projects of the Federal Government. But in the most popular sense, welfare is considered public assistance to the poor.

In whatever sense, the concept of welfare has been long ingrained in American society. The U.S. Department of Health, Education, and Welfare, in its publication *Social Security Programs in the United States,* summarizes: "From the earliest Colonial times, local villages and towns recognized an obligation to aid the needy when family effort and mutual assistance provided by neighbors and friends were not sufficient to meet economic adversity. This aid, carried out through the poor-relief system and almshouses, was often given grudgingly. Gradually, measures were adopted to provide aid on a more

organized basis. . . . In the mid-1920's, a few states began to experiment with old-age assistance and aid to the blind."

Social insurance first began with workmen's compensation (that is, industrial-accident insurance). By 1929, workmen's-compensation laws were in effect in all but four states. Retirement programs for certain government employees date back to the nineteenth century. Programs to help military veterans blossomed after World War I. In general, however, public-assistance programs lagged behind these other welfare efforts, and behind public-assistance programs in most other industrialized countries. The groundwork for administering such projects was laid down in Britain almost 150 years ago. One of the original organizers was the Rev. Thomas Chalmers of Glasgow, who created a policy of "cash and care" in helping the poor in his parish. "Welfare state" assistance came full circle in Britain after World War II. In France, family welfare and assistance allowances not too infrequently constitute a substantial share of family income. Scandinavia has long practiced extensive public assistance.

One reason for the lag in adopting social assistance in the United States was the "American Frontier." In a sense, it provided "social security" for the people. Charles I. Schottland, commissioner of social security in the Eisenhower administration, observed: "Prior to 1930, the pressure to insure against the risks of unemployment, old age and sickness was not so great in the United States as in European countries. . . . Land was given to settlers by the Government either free or for a nominal charge. The frontier was opulent with rich forests, minerals and agricultural lands. . . ." It was in this era that a "Puritan ethic" developed, which contends a man should—and can—make it by the sweat of his brow and not the largess of government.

But the severe depression of the 1930's, and the change from a rural to urban society, dramatized the fact that the American worker and his family were becoming greatly dependent on factors beyond their control for their economic well-being and security. Sentiment grew in the direction of providing Federal action and support to supplement or replace local community resources and privately organized charities. Beginning in 1932, Washington made loans, and then grants, to states to pay for direct relief and work relief. Then direct Federal emergency relief and public works were started, and on Aug. 14, 1935, the Social Security Act was signed into law by President Franklin Delano Roosevelt. It was a turning point in welfare.

The act created social-insurance programs to help meet the risks of old age and unemployment. It also provided for Federal grants-in-aid to the states to help meet the cost of assistance to the needy aged and blind, and to needy children who had been deprived of support or care by a parent's death, incapacity or absence from home. Thus a Federal-state system evolved, in keeping with the national philosophy of states' rights. Apart from the Federally imposed social-security payments to the retired elderly, the exact level of payments under these assistance programs was determined by the states and not by Washington.

In the last 35 years, most sections of the milestone 1935 measure, and its subsequent revisions and enlargements, have come to be taken for granted. There is little or no controversy over assistance to the blind and disabled, over vocational rehabilitation and assistance to the elderly, either through retirement benefits or public aid. What remains in controversy is public assistance to families with dependent children (AFDC)—public aid, in other words, to the poor. In many minds, this is what "welfare" is all about in the United States today. Giving taxpayer money to the unfortunate to some extent still rubs against the Puritan ethic. But even more relevant to the controversy is the sharp

increase in both the number of recipients and expenditures under the AFDC program. These two tabulations, compiled from Federal data, illustrate the situation:

SOCIAL-WELFARE OUTLAYS UNDER PUBLIC "NEED" PROGRAMS
(in millions of dollars)

	1950	1960	1968
Total	$3,860	$7,348	$17,858
Public aid	2,496	4,101	11,135
(Includes public assistance and medical vendor payments under Medicare and Medicaid)			
Other health and medical programs	916	2,114	2,901
Other social welfare	448	1,133	3,822
Includes:			
Vocational rehabilitation	30	90	451
School meals	160	399	715
Child welfare	105	212	507

PUBLIC ASSISTANCE BY PROGRAMS

Year	Total	Old Age	AFDC	Disabled	Blind	General Assistance
number of recipients (in thousands)						
1950	6,056	2,789	2,234	69	98	866
1960	7,138	2,332	3,080	374	108	1,244
1965	7,931	2,127	4,457	575	95	677
1968	9,272	2,022	5,707	680	81	782
payments (in millions of dollars)						
1950	$2,395	$1,470	$ 554	$ 8	$ 53	$ 295
1960	3,282	1,632	1,000	238	86	322
1965	4,027	1,601	1,695	439	75	310
1968	5,046	1,393	2,570	561	77	445

It can be easily seen that AFDC is responsible for the bulk of the increase in both expenditures and recipients. Moreover, these increases have occurred in a time of unprecedented national prosperity, when the jobless rolls were at record lows, and when many jobs went begging. As the Tax Foundation Inc. noted:

"The decade of the 1960's brought unparalleled economic development and income expansion. From 1960 to 1968, gross national product increased from $504,000,000,000 to $861,000,000,000. During the same period, per capita income increased from $2,215 to $3,412, despite a population growth of 20,000,000 (11 per cent). The percentage of the population classified as living in poverty declined from 22 per cent in 1960 to 14 per cent in 1968. The overall growth of income, however, by no means solved the problem of public dependence, particularly as related to dependent children."

Former Health, Education, and Welfare Secretary Wilbur J. Cohen noted that "everybody agrees that our welfare system is unsatisfactory: the clients who get the assistance; the people who administer it; the legislators who put up the money; and the social workers who have a role to play."

Before pinpointing the case against the welfare system, consider why AFDC rolls have expanded so greatly in the last few years. One major cause is accelerated migration of rural families to urban areas, where fathers or mothers, or both, are unable to find jobs because of lack of opportunities, lack of skills or racial prejudice. When without job and income, these families much more often than not "go on the dole." In New York City, for example, the number of relief recipients increased from 700,000 on June 30, 1967, to about 1,110,000 on June 30, 1969. The cost of Federal-city relief soared from $454,000,000 to $835,000,000 during this two-year period.

The biggest increases in AFDC rolls have occurred in the 10 states with the highest welfare benefits; the rise averaged 149 per cent in the 1959–67 period. Conversely, the 10 states with the lowest benefits had an average growth of only 11 per cent. The national growth in that period was 75 per cent. Such statistics have led to the charge that families deliberately move from low-paying welfare states (most of which are in the South) to the highest-paying states (most of which are in the Northeast and Midwest). However, some sociologists and welfare experts dispute this; they argue that the sharp job reduction and dislocation have forced families in the rural South to move north. They relocate in hopes of finding good-paying jobs, and take to welfare only when these jobs do not materialize, this line of thought goes.

Be that as it may, it is a fact that welfare rolls also have been increasing because of black militancy and because a new breed of lawyers, social workers and civil-rights leaders has been awakening the poor to their legal rights under AFDC. These efforts are an adjunct to the national "war on poverty." In 1966, Dr. George Wiley pulled together scattered welfare groups to create the National Welfare Rights Organization. It has branches in over 100 cities in 45 states and a long record of activist demands that welfare mothers get all benefits due under law. To this end, the poor have staged sit-down strikes, have marched on city halls and on Congress—all the while demanding that they get not only "adequate income, dignity and justice" but legal extras like telephones, kitchen appliances and a variety of furnishings. Such agitation has added considerable heat to the debate over AFDC. Here it must be recorded that racial prejudice plays a part. Negroes make up about 11 per cent of the total population yet they constitute almost half of the recipients of AFDC.

Ironically, AFDC was originally the least controversial public-assistance program enacted

Harry Schlack, Monkmeyer Press

In a dangerous condition of disrepair, the hallway of an old tenement is inspected by a welfare investigator. Squalid housing is the usual lot of the city poor.

by Congress. It was designed to help widows and their children. In 1935, 90 per cent of all mothers in fatherless homes were widows; the figure is only 8 per cent today. The source of dependency today is not so much the death or incapacitation of fathers, but rather the absence of fathers because of divorce, desertion, imprisonment or lack of a legal father.

The case against the AFDC program, or the "welfare program," is at least fourfold:

1. It offers no help at all to many of the nation's poor. About 12,500,000 Americans hold jobs whose incomes are so small that their households remain below the "poverty level." The Federal Government pegs this level at $3,500 a year for a family of four. But, in general, AFDC rules say that if a family has any private income it is not eligible for welfare. This rule leads to a disputed charge that some poor persons deliberately shun work in order to get on welfare—thus enjoying a better income than if they held a very low-paying job.

2. It offers no one enough aid to raise him above the poverty-income levels. AFDC pay-

Sheets of food stamps are checked for imperfections at the Bureau of Engraving in Washington. The stamps allow poor families to buy more food for the same amount of money—provided they can first afford to buy stamps.

Wide World

ments vary widely among the states: $229 monthly average for families in New Jersey, $241 in New York and $53 in Alabama. But in no case are payments high enough to bring a family of four, for example, up to the $3,500-a-year poverty minimum level.

3. It is surrounded by red tape and humiliating administrative practices. Civil-rights organizations have campaigned to end what they contend is "humiliating treatment" by social caseworkers who "spy" on families at night, pry into intimate affairs, and act more like detectives than social workers when checking on eligibility of welfare recipients. Most welfare administrators concede some merit in such complaints, and agree that resentment against the welfare system has played a role in the tinderbox situation within big-city ghettos.

4. It contributes to family breakdown and moral decay. In most states, AFDC rules preclude giving aid to families that include a man, be he employed or not. The result, a majority of observers argue, is to encourage fathers to desert their families (thus making them eligible for welfare) and to discourage mothers who have been deserted, divorced or widowed from remarrying. Almost one million of today's AFDC households involve father desertions or family estrangements. In a sample of welfare mothers in New York City, almost 60 per cent of those who were separated or divorced were separated or divorced after they went on welfare. The system also reportedly brings on an increase in illegitimate births. Nationally they have risen from 141,600 in 1950 to 320,000 in 1968. Of the 4,200,000 children on AFDC rolls, one fourth are illegitimate.

Economist F. O. Jacobs has written: "Thus a new social pattern begins to form among the poor: The more common it becomes, the more acceptable and normal. Ultimately, marriage and self-support begin to look like luxuries or an expression of impractical idealism to those whose earning power is near the welfare margin. The normal course (for a poor mother) increasingly becomes to adapt one's way of life so as to obtain AFDC plus a share in the earned income of male friends."

In recent years, a broad line of proposed reform has included suggestions to raise the level of payments by imposing a Federal minimum to raise recipients out of the poverty class; to couple higher welfare payments with a requirement that heads of AFDC households accept suitable employment if available; and to eliminate present rules that cut off payments when AFDC household heads do find jobs—even if their income is meager and below poverty levels. A start toward revision was made under a 1967 amendment to the Social Security Act. It requires that welfare recipients take available jobs or lose their payments (in the case of mothers with small children their job availability would depend on availability of child day-care centers), and it put a ceiling on the number of children who can get AFDC payments. The latter provision continues to be extremely controversial and under debate in Congress. Yet even critics admitted this was only a start toward needed revision, and it was not until August 1969 that a national political administration proposed radical and far-reaching welfare changes.

President Richard M. Nixon then outlined a package of welfare reforms that he said would be "a way of independence through the dignity of work." He called the present welfare system "a colossal failure" and proposed to scrap the AFDC program in favor of a "Family Assistance System." The key precedent in Mr.

Nixon's proposals is an understanding that no American family of four be required to live on income smaller than $1,600 a year. This would be the minimum-income standard set up by the Federal Government, the amount that Washington would guarantee every family of four. While the President insisted this would not be a "guaranteed income"—since he linked such contributions with a requirement that all who can learn a skill must accept available employment—nonetheless, liberals were inclined to say this was the first time an administration had virtually agreed to assure a floor under personal and family income. The Government's $1,600 national standard payment for a family of 4 would be assured to all households, including the "working poor" now excluded from welfare assistance. Mr. Nixon's proposals also included a "work incentive" idea: low-income families could continue to get Federal assistance even if they had private income, with the Government funds diminishing up to a point in relationship with outside income.

There were two key parts of the President's welfare program:

1. The Government would set a national standard payment of $1,600 a year to every unemployed family of four. States would be expected to continue supplementing this payment, adding onto it at least 50 per cent but no more than 90 per cent of what the states contribute now. In Mississippi, monthly payments could rise from $38 to as much as $139.63. But monthly payments in New York would remain about the same, leading to objections from New York and other industrialized states that Mr. Nixon's program primarily benefits the South.

2. Working-poor families also would be guaranteed a basic annual income of $1,600. They could earn up to $720 a year in outside income and still get the $1,600. For every dollar earned above $720 a year, the $1,600 Federal grant would be reduced by 50 cents. A family earning $2,000, for example, still would receive $960 in Federal payments. A family of four with $3,920 a year in outside income would no longer be eligible for Federal assistance.

Mr. Nixon also suggested a minimum national standard of $65 a month for the aged, blind and disabled in all states. The Government would contribute the first $50 and half of the other $15. It also would contribute one fourth of any dollar amount over $65.

While Mr. Nixon's program was criticized on several points, most notably that the minimums suggested were too low and that mothers of young children should not be forced to put their youngsters in day-care centers against their will in order to take available employment, the general reaction was that Congress would enact the proposals into law after some changes. The outlook was for action in 1970, which was agreeable to the Nixon administration.

ROBERT W. DIETSCH
Business-Economics Editor,
Scripps-Howard Newspapers

Adapted from "U.S. News and World Report"

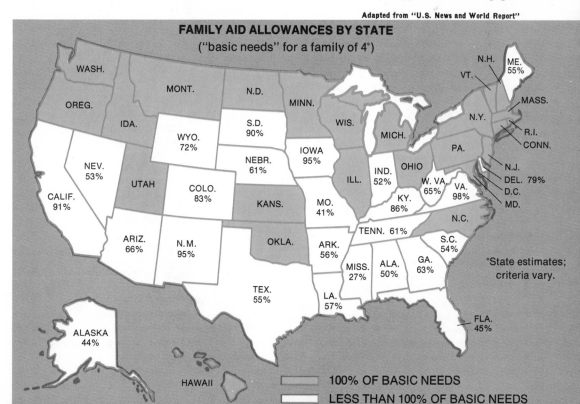

FAMILY AID ALLOWANCES BY STATE
("basic needs" for a family of 4*)

WEST VIRGINIA

Striking coal miners returned to work after Gov. Arch Moore, Jr., signed a bill that recognizes pneumoconiosis (black lung) as a disability-compensation disease. ☐ Another strike, launched on Mar. 3 by the state's highway-maintenance workers, was prolonged as a result of their refusal to answer an emergency call to help dig the state out of a heavy snowfall.

WISCONSIN

On Feb. 19 a predawn fire, of unknown origin, raged through the Afro-American and Race Relations Center at the University of Wisconsin, in Madison. It followed on several days of disorder by about 3,000 of the university's 34,000 enrolled students. ☐ David R. Obey, a Democrat, was elected on Apr. 1 to the House of Representatives seat held by Melvin R. Laird (new secretary of defense), Republican, for 16 years. ☐ In November the legislature rejected resolutions calling for a national convention to rewrite the U.S. Constitution.

WYOMING

Mining continued to be the chief industrial activity—of sand and gravel, bituminous coal, iron ore, clays—though the production of oil and natural gas was becoming increasingly automated. ☐ The once-polluted North Platte River, which winds through east-central Wyoming, was a clear stream again, thanks to the efforts of an oil company, which bore the whole cost. ☐ Drawn to Yellowstone and Grand Teton national parks, tourists made a substantial contribution to the state's income.

YAHYA KHAN, AGHA MOHAMMAD

Pakistan's President and Chief Martial Law Administrator, Gen. Agha Mohammad Yahya Khan, is one of those individuals who early in his career stands out from others. At the age of 34 he became Pakistan's youngest brigadier. At 40 he was his nation's youngest major general. Thus it was not too surprising that on Mar. 25, 1969, at age 52, he became his country's president and third military ruler since the Islamic Republic was founded in 1956.

Born in 1917, a member of the old and distinguished Qizilbash family of Peshawar, he attended Punjab University and the Indian Military Academy. On entering the academy, he was chosen a King's Cadet, a considerable honor. In 1939 he was commissioned and attached to the Second Battalion, Worcester Regiment. Shortly after, he was engaged in operations in the Northwest Frontier region of what was then British-ruled India. After one year with the Worcester Regiment, he was posted to the Third Battalion, Baluch Regiment.

During World War II, Yahya Khan spent five years overseas, seeing action in Egypt, Sudan, Libya, Cyprus, Iraq and Italy. After he came home, he attended the General Staff College at Quetta, from which he graduated in 1946. At the time Pakistan was created and given independent status, Yahya was the only Muslim instructor at the Quetta Staff College. Later he was responsible for starting the first Pakistan Staff College.

Following the partition of India and Pakistan in 1947, Yahya Khan was promoted to lieutenant colonel and in 1951 to brigadier. He commanded an infantry brigade for a while, and later was brigadier of the general staff at Corps Headquarters. He was promoted to major general in 1957 and appointed chief of the general staff (GOC). In 1962 Yahya Khan was appointed GOC of East Pakistan, and he then commanded various active military groups.

General Yahya was closely associated with the reorganization of the Army during his tenure as chief of the general staff. He helped introduce new weapons systems and new tactical concepts, which greatly improved the professional quality and efficiency of the Pakistan Army. Also as chief of the general staff he had the additional responsibility of chairing the Federal Capital Commission; its duty was to select a suitable site for the Federal capital and formulate a master plan for it. When the Capital Development Authority was instituted in 1960, General Yahya became chairman.

During the Pakistan-India conflict in September 1965, Gen. Yahya Khan commanded an infantry division in the Cham-Jaurian Valley. He was awarded the Hilal-i-Jurat, the highest military honor, for his leadership. (His other awards include the Hilal-i-Pakistan and Sitara-i-Pakistan.) In March 1966 he was promoted to lieutenant general and appointed deputy commander in chief. He succeeded Gen. Mohammad Musa as commander in chief, Pakistan Army, in September 1966. As the president and chief martial-law administrator, he is now commander in chief of the entire armed forces and also holds the portfolios for the ministries of defense, foreign affairs and economic affairs.

See Pakistan.

ARTHUR C. MILLER
Senior Editor, *The Asia Letter*

YUGOSLAVIA

As a communist country that has taken an independent path for many years, Yugoslavia is of special interest.

Foreign Affairs. The shadow of the occupation of Czechoslovakia by armed forces of the Warsaw Pact, sharpened by the "Brezhnev doctrine" justifying such intervention whenever the Russians consider socialism to be "endangered" in any communist-ruled state, continued to dominate Yugoslav foreign relations in 1969. During the first half of the year, relations with the countries that participated in the occupation were strained and there was mutual public and official criticism of domestic institutions as well as foreign policies.

The Yugoslavs continued to express strong disapproval of the invasion, anxiety concerning Soviet intentions toward Yugoslavia itself, and determination to offer armed resistance to "aggression" from any quarter. A new, "all-national" defense law, foreseeing and organizing for guerrilla-type irregular warfare as the official defense strategy of the country, was adopted early in 1969. Its stated purpose is to warn the Soviet Union or any other potential aggressor of the regime's serious intent to turn Yugoslavia into "another Vietnam" if necessary. Although Yugoslavia boycotted the world Communist Party conference, held in Moscow in June, relations with the Soviet Union seemed to improve slowly on Soviet initiative later in the year. Soviet Foreign Minister Andrei Gromyko visited Belgrade in September and Yugoslav President (Josip Broz) Tito later declared that they had agreed "that it is best to forget the past and cooperate on those things that are of common interest." The "case of Czechoslovakia" was "finished." Yugoslav officials pointed out privately that theirs was in fact the last concerned country to agree to "forget" Czechoslovakia.

A preliminary conference of ambassadors of nonaligned states, meeting in Belgrade, apparently made little progress toward the calling of a third nonaligned summit meeting, its stated purpose. Yugoslav officials expressed understanding in public and bitterness in private over the failure of other nonaligned leaders to offer diplomatic or moral support when Soviet pressure on Yugoslavia was intense. Attitudes toward the United States and NATO displayed a mixture of worried suspicion that Washington and Moscow had tacitly agreed to recognize one another's "spheres of influence," leaving all of Eastern Europe to the latter, combined with a conviction that the West would "have to" support Yugoslavia in the event of serious Soviet pressures or attack. Relations with neighbor-

Eastfoto

A temporary dam (new lock in background) blocks the Danube River's Iron Gate, a gorge, where Yugoslavia and Rumania are cooperating on the building of a huge power and navigation project.

ing states ranged from excellent with Italy and Rumania to very bad with Albania and Bulgaria, where continuing official insistence that Yugoslav Macedonians are really Bulgarians was viewed as Soviet-inspired.

Domestic Affairs. Fears of Soviet pressure or invasion after the occupation of Czechoslovakia tended, and were deliberately exploited by the regime, to silence dissent at home and reunify a divided political community. The fact that disagreements and friction among Yugoslavia's ethnic groups appeared to be growing was variously interpreted as either a fundamentally healthy concomitant of the further democratization of public life or as a dangerous revival of the ethnic divisiveness that had disastrously strained pre-war Yugoslavia.

On Nov. 27, 1968, serious demonstrations, which resulted in a number of injured and arrested, occurred in the Kosovo Autonomous Province (formerly the Kosovo-Metohija Autonomous Region). There Yugoslavia's Albanian minority constitutes a local majority, and they demanded genuine equality and elevation of the province into a seventh republic in the federation. Less dramatic incidents occurred during 1969, accompanied by the departure from Kosovo of a number of Serbs and Montenegrins, who alleged discrimination and sometimes terrorization by their Albanian fellow-citizens.

YUGOSLAVIA

Area: 98,740 sq. mi.
Population: 20,400,000
Capital: Belgrade (pop., 850,000)
Government: Josip Broz Tito, president—1953; Mitja Ribicic, prime minister—1969
Gross National Product: $9,600,000,000
Monetary unit: dinar (12.5 dinars = U.S. $1.00)
Chief products: wheat, maize, sugar beet, potatoes, wine, livestock, coal, lignite, iron ore, crude petroleum
Foreign trade: exports, $1,264,000,000; imports, $1,797,000,000
Communications: 506,039 telephones, 3,111,000 radios, 1,281,313 TV sets
Transportation: roads, 36,575 mi.; 335,254 passenger cars; railroads, 7,038 mi.
Education: 3,101,910 elementary and secondary students, 195,454 university students
Armed forces: 218,000

See map on page 185

Renewed disputes about the effective equality of Yugoslavia's four official languages and about economic issues—where there should be new investments or modernization, what group is being taxed or is underdeveloped for the benefit of whom, relative priorities of different strategies for economic development, and the like—also still divided Yugoslavs along ethnic lines, amid mutual accusations of cultural or economic "chauvinism." Official speeches reflected concern that unfriendly foreign powers might exploit an alleged "political underground" coalition of dissident Serbian and other nationalists, alienated students, former Stalinists and "centralists." On the other hand, nearly 100,000 young people joined the League of Communists, reversing a 15-year trend toward a rapidly aging party, after that body strongly condemned the occupation of Czechoslovakia.

The League of Communists celebrated its fiftieth birthday by holding its ninth congress in March. Of other ruling communist parties, only the Rumanians sent a guest delegation. Tito, aged 76, was again reelected president of the party. Debate in commissions and plenary sessions was livelier than ever before, a trend welcomed as reflecting the success of post-1966 reforms in "democratizing" the party and encouraging a "free struggle of ideas" concerning "socialist alternatives."

On the closing day of the congress, President Tito announced an unanticipated major organizational change designed to restore some degree of central control over an increasingly centrifugal party: a new 15-member Executive Bureau above and responsible to the Federal Presidium and Conference (the traditional Central Committee has been eliminated by new party statutes). The members, two from each republic and one from each autonomous province plus Tito, are to reside in Belgrade. Since they specifically include the republican party presidents, the change is also designed to weaken the ethnic-based regional party organizations while assuring equal republican representation at the strengthened "collective" center.

General elections for Yugoslavia's unique five-chamber federal parliament and bicameral republican, provincial and communal assemblies were held in April and May. More seats at all levels were contested than ever before in the postwar period, but changes in the complicated nomination procedure were designed to control candidacies more strictly. Some candidates disapproved by local party organizations nevertheless got on the ballot and were elected over party-supported opponents. Reflecting the regime's concern with youth, after widespread student strikes in June 1968, an effort was made to secure the nomination of more young candidates though it was resisted by local party apparatuses and voters. The new parliaments continued a post-1963 trend toward an increasingly effective and independent decision-making role for these bodies in amending, rejecting or initiating legislation and criticizing ministers. The new federal prime minister is for the first time a Slovene, Mitja Ribicic.

Economic Developments. Widespread unemployment, declining growth rates, insolvency in many enterprises, and growing disparities in personal and regional income levels had become serious political as well as economic problems by 1968, although they were among the anticipated short-run consequences of the liberalizing economic reforms launched in 1965. They had successfully stabilized prices and the exchange value of the currency and induced a restructuring of industry and commerce along more efficient, competitive lines. In 1968 the regime responded to pressures from sectors injured by austerity with a series of classic measures that quickly converted recession into boom and stability into inflation. By mid-1969, growth rates were again satisfactory, unemployment was slowly declining (with over 400,000 Yugoslavs working in Western Europe), prices and the foreign-trade deficit were rising rapidly, and the stability of the dinar was again endangered. Inflation largely replaced unemployment as the principal target of press and public criticism of the Government's economic policies.

DENNISON RUSINOW
American Universities Field Staff

ZOOLOGY: ETHOLOGY

Comparative ethology, a relative newcomer among scientific disciplines, is in its broadest sense the observation, recording and comparison of animal behavior, both innate and learned. Ethologists place special emphasis on what animals and birds do in groups, the sociology of wildlife. Whenever possible, work is done under field rather than laboratory conditions. Emphasis is on field observation, since animals in captivity, above all zoo animals, markedly alter their behavior in response to the constraints of captivity. In zoos, many animal inmates abandon the whole important panoply of courtship and breeding; others become lazy when they no longer have to contend in the pecking order for food.

The steadily increasing general interest in the work of the ethologists is no doubt, in part, the natural attraction of its fresh-air-and-field aspects. They seem similar to the working conditions of the great nineteenth-century naturalists from Charles Darwin to Audubon and Fabre. A second popular attraction, again akin to the romance of science in the nineteenth century, is many a layman-reader's desire, whenever possible, to read human traits into animals: anthropomorphism. In the 1960's several best-selling books, written more by popularizers than by disciplined scientists, have turned to ethology in search of grand and sweeping clues to human behavior, as distinct from animal behavior proper. Such clues are definitely implicit in the field of ethology, but are valid only as working hypotheses which most trained scientists handle with discretion. To describe *homo sapiens* as a "naked ape" is at best a catchy metaphor, and not much of an improvement over the Greek stoic Zeno's ancient description of man as "a featherless biped."

The new discipline of comparative ethology first emerged in the 1930's, although it had perhaps been anticipated in such earlier classics as Darwin's own *The Expression of the Emotions in Man and Animals,* and C. Wright Morgan's *Habit and Instinct* (1896). It was in the 1930's that the Austrian Dr. Konrad Lorenz, today acknowledged as the dean of ethologists, first published trail-blazing papers of his own experiments with jackdaws, crows, graylag geese and cichlid fish. These were soon followed by similar, confirmatory experiments by Oxford professor Nikolaas Tinbergen, on the life habits of the herring gull, and Cambridge University's William H. Thorpe, on instinctive behavior. Much of the work of these founding fathers was interrupted by World War II.

Thomas McAvoy, "Life" Magazine © Time Inc.

Trailing Dr. Konrad Lorenz across the grass, the goslings illustrate "imprinting": an urge to follow, induced shortly after hatching, the source of food.

Professor Lorenz himself, drafted into the *Wehrmacht* as a medico, did not return from captivity in Russia until late in 1948. With the help of a kindly grant from the British novelist J. B. Priestley (who released his Austrian royalties) Konrad Lorenz wrote *King Solomon's Ring,* a popular book describing his experiments in the 1930's. It was first published in 1952. Lorenz had studied at Columbia University in the early 1920's (under C. Wright Morgan). He revealed in his first book not only his remarkable way with ani-

Carrying her pup to safety, a red-fox vixen holds the pup's neck in her mouth without harm. Such behavior is usually attributed to maternal instinct, which ethologists consider an inborn pattern released by environment.

Wilford L. Miller from National Audubon Society

mals but a lucid and captivating prose style, in English as well as in his native German.

The fascinating personality of Lorenz and the lifetime devotion he has expended in the patient observation of birds and other animals, help explain his high standing even among the second, younger generation of ethologists who have begun to modify, refine and sometimes question his basic field techniques. While Lorenz's first book won almost universal acclaim, his most recent major work, *On Aggression* (1966), has sparked lively controversy: "Peking man, the Prometheus who learned to preserve fire, used it to roast his brothers: beside the first traces of the regular use of fire lie the mutilated and roasted bones of *Sinanthropus pekinesis* himself." Several social scientists have attacked this as an appeal to some kind of neosocial Darwinism; a close reading of the text, however, shows clearly that this is what Lorenz is warning against.

As a very young man, Konrad Lorenz was uniquely prepared for what was to become his lifetime vocation. His father was a famous Viennese surgeon, Dr. Adolf Lorenz, the orthopedist who founded the school of bloodless surgery. At the University of Vienna, Konrad Lorenz took the premedical and medical course, acquiring a thorough grounding in anatomy, biology, zoology and psychology—classic disciplines that reinforced his naturalist bent. Lorenz grew up at the family home in Altenberg, a natural paradise on a wide bend in the Danube. At four he was captivated by a pet owl, but lost interest when he discovered the owl could not swim. At five the youth switched his interest to ducks, wading through marshy backwaters to gather duckweed-feed

on his legs. By the time he had reached his carefree teens, Konrad Lorenz had made serious studies of the habits and activities of a wide variety of animals and birds.

In his university medical studies, Lorenz noted that most of the textbook wisdom on bird and animal behavior had not made much progress since the days of Aristotle and Pliny. Moreover, much of it was demonstrably untrue, as he already knew from his own long hours of casual but intensive observation. The field was further bedeviled by the controversy between mechanists and vitalists. The study of what birds and animals actually do in the natural state—their behavior patterns—had been woefully neglected. Behavior fell between the two academic laboratory disciplines, biology and physiology.

During his student work on anatomy, Lorenz was already convinced that behavior patterns are not something that animals may or may not do, or do in different ways. Rather, they are definitely something animals of a given species have just as they have claws or teeth. Behavior indeed was as sure a key to the study of an animal's physiology as bone structure to the study of its anatomy.

Lorenz also began to question the word "instinct." This was the breakthrough that established ethology as a discipline in its own right. He felt that instinct had become an umbrella word covering too many distinct phenomena. To say that birds migrate by instinct is somehow to beg the question, as the medieval nominalists did by attributing to water "the quality of wetness" and to birds "the quality of flight." Moreover, modern ornithological research has shown that many birds do

A Laysan albatross yaps to its single egg, deposited on the bare ground. The bird has no nest-building behavior, probably as a result of adaptation to its environment—barren ocean islands without any nest material.

Karl W. Kenyon from National Audubon Society

not migrate. With some of the larger birds, such as storks and cranes, the route is definitely learned; in others, however, such as warblers and nightingales, knowledge of the ancestral route is inborn. Bird migration is one of the obvious major fields of ethological research. It attracts not only the keen interest of the world's growing cult of amateur bird watchers, but also of scientific workers in the closely related field of ecology.

As redefined by Lorenz, instinct is an inherited, specific, stereotyped pattern of behavior. It is different from other kinds of stereotyped inborn behavior in that it is released completely by, rather than guided by, the environment, and by the tendency to accumulate reaction-specific energy. This shows itself in a lowering of the threshold for release, and in a tendency to vacuum activity.

It was again Lorenz who gave the first adequate scientific explanation of the curious process known as "imprinting." Naturalists had long noticed that most young birds that are self-locomotive shortly after birth have a strong following-urge. In nature, this leads the infant duckling, partridge or gosling to follow the mother, the apparent source of food. In experiments conducted with incubator, handraised ducklings, Lorenz showed that the motherless brood can be induced to follow a false foster-parent, e.g., a human being (as a superduck), a mature bird of quite another species, or even a rolling basketball. Moreover, this imprinting phenomenon, when deeply induced, is clearly connected with the imprinted bird's later choice of a mate. Experiment has shown that there is a critical early age (even one hour) in which the imprinting is strongest.

The significance? Ethologists believe that imprinting is originally nature's method of species-identity, and of keeping the species-identity, and of keeping the species separate; i.e., of teaching a young goose that it really is a goose. Other recent experiments have shown that imprinting is also the way certain birds of prey, e.g., peregrine falcons, learn precisely which color field mouse is the proper diet. (The image is imprinted by the feeding parents on the rim of the nest.)

A quite possible interdisciplinary link between animal imprinting and the human case studies of Freud, Jung and Adler may exist. Naturalists have noted that homosexuality is by no means rare in the animal and bird world. The ethologists have now shown that this occurs whenever the normal imprinting process —or the equally important and elaborate mating ceremonies—go mechanically awry. In the many species of birds where the plumage is similar, a false "indicator" (e.g., neck-dipping in geese) can trigger a courtship between two males (or two females). When young male mallards, for the first 75 days of their existence, are kept in purely male groups of some 20 odd (with no sight or contact with females of the species) all become lifelong "male mates," raising families from other's eggs. The phenomenon is also noted in the behavior of male doves.

The implications go far beyond the bird world. A recent newspaper story described the abortive attempt of British zoologists to mate their female panda, Chi-Chi, with the male panda, An-An, in the Moscow Zoo. This was sentimentally presented as an amusing contretemps in the attempt to reach détente in the cold war. Chi-Chi emphatically rejected her prospective husband, but displayed intense affection for the Soviet zoo-keeper. To ethologists, the explanation was obvious. All pandas, or honey bears, are natives of interior China. The Moscow panda An-An, born in China, is a normal male panda. But Chi-Chi, zoo-born in London, had been imprinted by her keeper at an early, formative age. Imprinting again helps explain most of the legends and folk stories of intimate friendships between humans and animals. Mary *imprinted* her little lamb.

From the beginning, what the ethologists have been searching for are not human traits in animals, but for valid evidence of the reverse. Whether, and how, young humans may imprint intensely interests biologists, anthropologists, psychologists—above all the broad hint in the fact that many males, in choosing their mates, follow the you-remind-me-of-my-mother syndrome.

As Konrad Lorenz put it in the 1950's:

"In humans, such a simple thing as a yawn is socially infectious. The same holds true for most of the instinctive activities in social animals. Whenever I imitate the sound and movement of wild graylag geese, I gain considerable influence over their behavior, inducing fly-ups, alarm reactions or greeting ceremonies. I am regarded as a resident supergoose, much as a dog regards its master as a super pack-leader of its own species."

When they gabble, geese are not really talking to each other. They have some 14 exclamations, but these are mere interjections. Their real language consists of "social releasers": visual gestures and movements, some of them very hard for the human eye to catch, and these releasers set up responses, or "releaser mechanisms," in other members of the species.

This writer interviewed Professor Lorenz shortly after he became director of the Max Planck Institute for Behavior Studies at Seewiesen, south of Munich in upper Bavarian lake country. There he is presently engaged in a 15-year project to establish a migrating-goose colony. Observing a battle of ganders out on the lake, he remarked:

"In our own species, this aggressive drive is something that goes very far back into our prehuman past. Any skillful manipulator of mass emotions, by dummying up the right scapegoat, can induce alarm, hysteria, and war in man, the political animal. It is sad but true that hitherto demagogues seem to have had the best working knowledge of this. Bad behaviorists themselves, they stumbled upon the deep, nonrational urges in the human animal.

Latent in all mankind are the terrible drives of a very irascible ape, and they can get out of control. The more we discover about these things, the more we learn about why animals act the way they do, the more we know about ourselves."

One such discovery, which keeps ethologists from being complete pessimists about the future of the human race, is that in most of the higher social animals the aggressive urge is tempered by a powerful inhibition against killing a "conspecific," i.e., a fellow member of the same species. Moreover, this block is strongest when the defeated combatant makes the instinctive gesture of submission, or says "uncle." A vanquished timber wolf bares its throat as a suppliant, and its male wolf rival cannot strike home. A trounced dog will roll over on its back, a helpless position, but it saves him. Thus the Biblical advice about "turning the other cheek" is sound ethology. But only in social animals—in wolves for example, but not in doves. Among mammals, only rats and humans fail to display this inhibition.

As comparative ethology today moves into its second generation, there is basic acceptance of most of the major findings of Lorenz, Tinbergen and Thorpe, above all in their redefinition of instinct. Other, earlier concepts have been modified. More attention is being paid today to new definitions of drives, and many students feel that the "learning process" in animals should be incorporated into "appetitive behavior."

In September 1969, in Stockholm, the Nobel Prize Committee sponsored a symposium consisting of some 36 ethologists and their critics from other disciplines, including the social sciences. The symposium was entitled "The Future of Mankind." Professor Lorenz sounded once again his grim warning that weapons-carrying man still had the "drives of an androgynous ape" built into his nervous system, and that these drives must be redirected rather than denied or ignored. The writer Arthur Koestler countered with what has become to many the major debating point likely to enliven the 1970's:

"Speaking in all humility, it seems to me of doubtful value to attempt a diagnosis of man entirely based on analogies with animal behavior, either Pavlov's dogs, Skinner's rats, Lorenz's graylag geese, or Morris' naked apes. Such analogies are valid and useful. But they are not the whole story." To which most ethologists would themselves agree.

JAMES P. O'DONNELL
European Correspondent and Free-Lance Writer

Index

A

Abernathy, Ralph D., U.S. civ.-rights leader 25
ABM (antiballistic missile) system 19, 161, 303, 324, 472, ill. 162
Aborigines, Australia 101
Abortion law, N.M. 321
Abstract expressionism, in art, with ill. 336
Abu Dhabi, capital, Fed. of Gulf Emirates 301
Accidents 68–69
Ada, Nabokov novel 268
Advertising, with ill. 70
  cigarette 372, 431
Afghanistan 71, 295, ill. 71
Africa, with ill. and map 72–81, 361
  heads of government 79
  highways 213
  literature 275
  nutrition 330, 331
  parks, national 344, ill. 343
  refugees 48
  tourism 444
Africa, South see South Africa
Aga Khan IV, Karim, Muslim leader, ill. 349
Age of Aquarius, song 315
Aggression, in lower animals 494, 496
Agnelli, Giovanni, Ital. auto mfgr. 239
Agnew, Spiro T., U.S. vice-pres. 15, 82, 142, 429, 472, ill. 82, 468, 471
Agriculture, with ill. 83–84, 330
  Alabama, black co-op in 85
  brown-coal fertilizer 358
  Canada 122, ill. 123
  corporate farming, Okla. 335
  Common Market problem 182, 457
  grape pickers' strike 248
  Japan, ill. 242
  Korea 245
  Pakistan 341
  Soviet Union 447
  Tunisia 72
Ahsan, S. M., W. Pak. states. 340
Airbus, shuttle service, ill. 107
Air Force, U.S.
  missiles 303, 304, 305
Airport-departure tax 321
Alabama 27, 85
Alaska 85, 226
  oil 172, 196, ill. 196, 197
  wildlife threatened 143
Albania 85
Alberta, Canada, with ill. 124
Alberta Resources Railway 124
Alcatraz Island, Calif.
  Indians occupy, ill. 222
Aldrin, Edwin E., J., U.S. astronaut 27, 40, 41, 45, 392, ill. 26, 39, 40, 42, 44, 468

Al-Fatah, Arab guerrilla orgn. 299, 300, ill. 298
Algeria 74
  gas, natural 198
Alice's Restaurant, movie, with ill. 307
Allen, James E., Jr., U.S. educator, ill. 175
Allergoids, protein allergens 357
Alliance for Labor Action (ALA) 248
Alliance for Progress 335
Alligators, Fla. 144
Alliluyeva, Svetlana, Stalin's daughter 274
Aluminum industry 228
  Iceland 218
Ambassadors, to and from U.S. 86
Amchitka, Alas., nuclear testing 119
American Ballet Company 154
American Football League 407
American League baseball 401
American Legion 478
American Library Association (ALA) 267
American Museum of Natural History, with ill. 87
Amino acids, in gamma-globulin molecule 357
Amistad Dam, U.S.-Mexico 181, 292, ill. 180
Andean Common Market 252
Andretti, Mario, auto racer 400
Angola, Port. Africa 80, 361
Anguilla, Carib. isl. 19, 132, ill. 131
Animals see Zoology
Antarctica, U.S. female research team, ill. 476
Anthropology, divisions 88–89
Antibiotics research 357
Anti-Semitism 383
Aphrodite, temple of, Cnidus, Turkey, ill. 90
Apollo 9, space project 19, 394
Apollo 10, space project 23, 394
Apollo 11, space project, with ill. 26, 38–45, 215, 370, 392, 427
Apollo 12, space project with ill. 392–93
Arab-Israeli conflict 17, 27, 294, 296, ill. 295, 298, 300
Arab summit conferences 72, 74, ill. 73
Arafat, Yasir, Al-Fatah chief 300, ill. 298
Archeology, with ill. 88–91
  Mexico City 293
  Roman hypocaust, Paris, ill. 195
Archery 420
Arches National Monument, Utah 478
Architecture, with ill. 92–95, 234, 267
  prizes and awards 363
  state capital, Hawaii 210
Argentina 23, 24, 249, 252, 380, ill. 252
Arizona 96, ill. 98
Arkansas 96

Armed forces, U.S. 29, 161
  Vietnam, in 481, 478
Armstrong, Neil, U.S. astronaut 39, 40, 41, 45, 392, ill. 40, 44
Army, U.S.
  Green Beret case, with ill. 150
Artificial hearts 283
Arts, African, ill. 76, 77
  Australia 101
  Canada, with ill. 127–30
  painting, with ill. 336–38
  photography, with ill. 352, 353, 354
  prizes and awards 363
  sculpture 293, with ill. 385–87
Arts and Letters, race horse 412, ill. 413
Asia, highways 212
  nationalism 319
  refugees 48
  See also names of countries
Association of Student Government 178
Astarte, ballet, ill. 60
Astronomy, with ill. 96–98
  orbiting observatories 396
  space 356, 357
Atherosclerosis 282
Atlantis, mythical continent 203
Auckland Harbor Bridge, N.Z., ill. 323
Austria 102
Australia, with ill. 99–101
  man, early traces, ill. 91
  New Zealand, relations with 323
  weather balloons 289
Automation, radio programing 374
Automobiles, with ill. 103–05, 171
  bounty for junked cars 281
  Fiat, Italy 239
  insurance, with ill. 229
  model cars 214
  pollution source 52, 54, ill. 53
  racing 398, 400, ill. 400
  repair costs 104
Aviation 29, with ill. 106–08
  pollution source 52
  reconnaissance planes 231, ill. 233
  skyjacking 34, 209, 239, 299
  United Kingdom 458
  U.S. military planes 162, 164
  weather reports for 289
Awards see Prizes and awards
Ayub Khan, Mohammad, Pak. states. 339
Aztec artifacts unearthed 293

B

Baath Party, Iraq 296
Badminton 420
Balanchine, George, Russ.-U.S. choreo. 153
Ballet see Dance
Baltimore, Md.
  housing 92, 94, ill. 94
Barnard, Christiaan, S. Af. surgeon 282, 391

Money (cont'd)
France 191, 193, 194, 361
German mark, revaluation 204, ill. 205
gold, So. Africa 391
mint, Philadelphia, Pa. 345
tight-money policies, U.S. 169
See also Economy
Montana 305
Montherlant, Henry de, Fr. writer 271
Montreal, Canada 117, 120, 248, ill. 117
Moon, study of rocks 201, ill. 202
Moon landings see Apollo entries
Moonquake sensor 45, ill. 39
Moorer, Thomas H., U.S. admiral, ill. 327
Morante, Elsa, Ital. writer 272
Moratorium, Vietnam 175, 466
Morocco 74
Morse, David A., U.S. labor leader, with ill. 326
Morton, Rogers, U.S. cong. 17
Mosaic hybrids, in genetics 111
Motion pictures, with ill. 306–10
Canada 130
dance films 155
Italy 239
prizes and awards 364
sex in 61, ill. 62
Moynahan, Julian, U.S. writer 268
Moynihan, Daniel P., U.S. offi. 92, 140
Mozambique 80, 180, 361
Murchison Falls, Uganda, ill. 343
Music, Canada 127, 130
classical, with ill. 311–14
popular, with ill. 315–17
prizes and awards 363
radio programing 374
recordings, with list 377
Musical films 309
Musical plays, with ill. 433
Hair, with ill. 315
Muskie, Edmund, U.S. sen. 476, ill. 50
Mylai, Vietnam, alleged massacre 468, 482

N

Nabokov, Vladimir, Russ. writer 268, ill. 269
Nagashima Tropical Garden, Japan, with ill. 95
Nasser, Gamal Abdel, U.A.R. pres., ill. 73
National Arts Centre, Canada 127, ill. 128–29
National Association of Black Students 177
National Committee of Black Churchmen 381
National Football League 407
National Guard
legality of service abroad 244
Nationalism, with ill. 318–19
Anguilla 132
Canada 117, 121, 445
Japan 242
Nationalist China see Taiwan
National League baseball 401

National Library Commission Act of 1969 266
National parks see Parks, national
NATO see North Atlantic Treaty Organization
Natural gas see Gas, natural
Navy, United States
missiles 303, 305
task force in Pacific 21
Nebraska 320
Negro Americans
Alabama, elected in 85
architects 93
black capitalism 139
black manifesto 381
Canada, student protest 120
children's books about 276
employment 248
Evers, Charles 305
hospital strike, S.C. 391
housing 142
models, advertising, ill. 70
North Carolina 329
Oklahoma economic aid 335
Peterson, Harry, Neb. official 320
school desegregation and discrimination 263
student protest 175, 177
theater, in 433, 438, ill. 435
TV programs starring 430, ill. 427
Virginia 484
Negro Ensemble Company 438
Netherlands 320–21
literature 272
Rotterdam Cathedral 380
Neutrinos, solar 97
Neutron stars 96
Nevada 222, 321
Newark, New Jersey
Federal charges against officials 37
Public Library 266
Newbery Medal 277
New Brunswick, Canada 124
Newfoundland, Canada 123, 125
New Hampshire 321
Ne Win, Burmese leader 115
New Jersey 37, 321
New Mexico 321
nuclear testing, ill. 474
New Orleans, La.
Pirate's Alley, ill. 140
Newport Bridge, R.I. 179, 383
News, diary of events, with ill. 14–37
radio programing 374
Newspaper Preservation Act 372
Newspaper publishing 371, ill. 370
New York City
American Museum of Natural History, with ill. 87
City Opera 312
Cultural Center 353
election 321
Grand Central Terminal 94
Metropolitan Opera strike, with ill. 311
Philharmonic Orchestra 312
Public Library 266
Verrazano-Narrows Bridge 179
welfare protest, ill. 485

New York State 321
water tunnel, Westchester 181
New York Times, The, book on 270
New Zealand, with ill. 322–23
parks, national 344, ill. 342
Niagara Falls, ill. 475
Nicaragua 256
Nickel production 228
Nigeria 28, 77–79, ill. 77
Biafra 319
Canada, relations with 120
United Kingdom, relations 458
Nimbus satellites 289
Nixon, Patricia, U.S. First Lady, ill. 15, 383
Nixon, Richard M., U.S. pres. 15, 28, 29, 82, 246, 324–25, 465, 466, 468, 477, ill. 14, 28, 66, 121, 324, 365, 383, 464, 471
anticrime program 148
Belgium, visit to 109
biological and chemical warfare, on 166
business-merger guidelines 57
cities, aid to 140
D.C., proposals for 168
Eisenhower, Dwight, on 156
foreign aid 189, 190
Indonesia, visit to 225
Latin American policy 251
military intelligence 232, 233
Organization of American States 335
postal reforms proposed 362
refugee problem, on 47
St. Lawrence Seaway 25
shipbuilding subsidies 388
talk with astronauts 45, ill. 44
Vietnam war, on 23, 479, 484
welfare reforms 488
Nobel Prizes 271, 326
ethology symposium 496
Noland, Kenneth, U.S. art. 336
Nonferrous-metal production 228
Nonproliferation treaty, nuclear (NPT) 99, 166
U.S. Senate ratifies 19
Noor Khan, Malik, Pak. states. 340
No Place to Be Somebody, play 438, ill. 435
Nordek, proposed Scandinavian customs union 165, 184, 188
North Africa, with ill. 72–75
North Atlantic Treaty Organization (NATO), with ill. and chart 327–28
Canadian forces 21, with ill. 119
United States 465
North Carolina 329
North Dakota 329
Northern Ireland see Ireland, Northern
North Korea see Korea
North Sea, oil in 165
Northumberland Strait ferry, P.E.I. 126
North Vietnam see Vietnam
Northwest Passage, navigation route, 196, 389, ill. 389